THE ILLUSTRATED ENCYCLOPEDIA OF
ANCIENT GREECE

THE ILLUSTRATED ENCYCLOPEDIA OF
ANCIENT GREECE

A COMPREHENSIVE HISTORY WITH 1000 PHOTOGRAPHS

NIGEL RODGERS

LORENZ BOOKS

CONTENTS

THE GLORY THAT WAS GREECE

Our world began with Greece – the world, that is, of Western civilization. The ancient Greeks were the first in so many things that we reveal our debt to them almost every time we open our mouths. Anarchy, astronomy, athletics, ballet, biography, biology, comedy, democracy, diplomacy, drama, ecology, economics, eroticism, history, marathon, maths, music, oligarchy, philosophy, physics, poetry, strategy tactics, technology, theatre, tragedy, tyranny, zoology – all are Greek words. They describe concepts or activities that, while they were not always invented by Greeks, were developed by them into forms we now recognize. Without the ancient Greeks, our modern world would not exist.

Greek civilization reached its zenith in classical Athens, a very small city by modern standards. It did so quickly – in less than 200 years (c.500–300BC) – but the impact has lasted millennia. Nothing like this intensity of experimentation had ever been seen before. Arguably, nothing that the world has seen since has wholly matched it either.

The Greeks were not, of course, the first civilization. They borrowed from many older, more sophisticated peoples around them. They took their alphabet from the Phoenicians (in modern Lebanon), and were influenced by Egyptian sculpture and architecture.

But the Greeks used their alphabet to write poetry, plays, history and philosophy, which the Phoenicians had never attempted. Greeks breathed life into the imposing but static statues of Egypt to create the first wholly naturalistic, lifelike sculptures. These images still form our ideals of the perfect body. Anyone today who works out in a gym (which comes from *gymnasion*, another Greek word) is paying unconscious homage to the Greek ideal of bodily beauty.

The Greeks were the first to think about and question almost everything: politics, religion, the physical world and the moral one. They used Babylonian star books to speculate and calculate daringly (and often accurately) about the universe: one Greek, Aristarchus of Samos, even suggesting that the Earth went around the Sun – a shocking idea at that time and for the next 2,000 years.

Discarding religious or political authority, they were perhaps the most dauntless innovators in human history. Ancient Greece can often seem startlingly modern when compared both to rival cultures and to many later civilizations. This resemblance is not superficial. In some ways, they *were* modern.

From the Greeks' adventurous questioning arose modern science and democracy. These formidable twins now shape the world. Anyone concerned with

Above: Standing high above the sea, the temple to Poseidon at Sunium, built c.440BC, signalled to ships that they were nearing Athens, the Greek city where democracy and classical art both reached their zenith.

Left: The theatre was among the most typical Greek buildings. The theatre at Epidaurus, dating from the 4th century BC, is remarkably well preserved with still marvellous acoustics.

the way in which the *contemporary* world runs needs to know something about the ancient Greeks.

The dilemmas that the ancient Greeks were the first to discuss and confront 2,500 years ago – Is democracy always best? Should every citizen's voice be counted equally? – concern us still.

THE EXPANSION OF GREECE

Today the Greeks are confined to Greece proper and Cyprus. But in antiquity they spread – first all around the Mediterranean as far as Marseilles, and then across western and central Asia. This second expansion occurred under Alexander the Great (336–323BC). A supreme military genius, Alexander overthrew the Persian Empire and founded many cities that helped to Hellenize (the Greeks called themselves Hellenes) western Asia.

This expanded Greek world fell in the end mostly to Rome, which by 30BC had conquered the Greeks, often with a greedy brutality. But the Romans, if lacking Greek brilliance, became superb preservers and transmitters of Greek culture (though not Greek democracy)

across Western Europe. The resulting Graeco-Roman civilization is the bedrock of the modern world. The Greeks are not just ancient history buried in museums: their ideas, arguments, ambitions and culture have helped shape Western history since the Renaissance and still underly much of the modern world. To understand ourselves today, we need to look back to the Greeks.

Below: Delphi was the holiest Greek shrine, considered the centre of the world and sacred to the god Apollo. Its oracle, always deliberately enigmatic, was revered by all Greeks.

PART ONE

THE RISE AND FALL OF ANCIENT GREECE

The story of ancient Greece forms the bedrock of Western civilization. From the legends of the Trojan War, through the history of the Golden Age of Athens and the military regime of Sparta to the campaigns of Alexander the Great, the ancient Greeks have shaped our world. This is an authoritative and highly dramatic account of the birth of the city-states and the civil wars that tore ancient Greece apart. All major conflicts are covered – the Persian Wars, the Peloponnesian War – plus an in-depth focus on the life and conquests of the heroic figure of Alexander. Discover the tactics of great land and sea battles, including Marathon, Salamis and Gaugamela, and ancient Greek military techniques, strategies, operations and training.

Above: The Parthenon, Athens.
Left: Shrine of the priest of Poseidon on the Greek island of Delos.

INTRODUCTION

The Greeks created the world's first democracies, now the officially preferred form of government the world over. Democracy meant rule by all the people, a genuine revolution in human history. There was little in the world of the Mediterranean and Middle East *c.*600BC, where absolute monarchies and priestly hierarchies were the norm, to suggest that this was about to happen.

But in Greece, hereditary monarchy was dying out or had already been replaced by aristocracies or tyrants (meaning unconstitutional rulers with broad popular support, not necessarily dictators), while there was never a separate priesthood. Even more crucial perhaps, in the Classical Age (*c.*500–*c.*300BC) Greece was never unified into a large centrally controlled state. Instead, it remained divided into scores of fiercely independent city-states (as we translate the world *polis*, although 'citizen-state' might be more accurate).

This was partly due to geography. Lacking large river valleys or plains, Greece is divided by mountains into small valleys, which inherently encouraged such individualism. But the results made Greek civilization, as it developed focused on each *polis*, crucially different from all earlier civilizations. No one had really done politics (our word comes from *polis*) before the Greeks took to arguing and experimenting, at times violently, about the best forms of government.

POLITICS FOR THE PEOPLE

To ancient Greeks, modern democracies, where every few years we elect MPs or congressmen to a distant capital, would not seem truly democratic at all. At best Greeks would call them elected oligarchies. A Greek democracy demanded much more from its citizens: fighting as soldiers or sailors; serving on the huge

Below: The Charioteer of Delphi, *dating from* c.470BC, *superbly exemplifies early classical sculpture. One of the very few bronze statues to survive, it was originally painted with lifelike colours.*

Above: Far from being always made of cold white marble, most Greek statues glowed with vivid colour, as shown in this kore, *a statue of a young girl of the 6th century* BC.

juries or councils or as annual officials, often chosen by lot. Every citizen could vote and speak in the Assembly. This directly proposed policies and elected generals, punishing the latter if they failed. This was democracy in its most direct and most radical form.

Pericles, the supreme democratic statesman of Athens, declared in his funeral oration in 431BC: "Everyone is interested not only in their own affairs but in public affairs too, and is well informed about politics. We think that the man who minds only his own business has no business in the city. We Athenians personally decide or discuss policies." (The Greek word *idiot* meant someone who chose a private life – an idiotic choice for Greeks.)

The Victorian philosopher J.S. Mill declared that the Battle of Marathon in 490BC – when Athens first defeated Persia – was of greater importance in *British* history than the Battle of Hastings. Without that victory, Athenian democracy might not have survived. And without democracy, Athens' open society could not have prospered, encouraging theatre, philosophy, science, history, architecture, art and drama.

Greek democracy had, however, definite limits: women were excluded from public life – as in almost all cultures and countries before the 20th century – and slavery was an essential part of Greek life. But almost every civilization, at the time, and for long after, relied on slaves, and slavery in Athens remained mostly domestic and small-scale.

A worse criticism of the Greeks would be their endless wars. Just enough city-states united to repel the Persian invasions of 490–478BC, but that unity proved unique. The Greeks reverted to fighting each other, often calling in outside powers – even Persia – to help. Such disunity led to their conquest, first by the Macedonians, then by the Romans. It was the dark side of the Greeks' pursuit of individual excellence or perfection.

THE PURSUIT OF PERFECTION
The Greeks were intensely competitive as individuals, striving 'always to be best'. (These words of Homer, the greatest Greek poet, about his hero Achilles, inspired Alexander the Great when conquering the Persian Empire.) Greeks were driven by two concepts: love of honour (*philotimaea*) and desire for *areté* (excellence, goodness, perfection, a term applicable to anything from athletics to philosophy). But the pursuit of excellence was not restricted to individuals.

It was the Athenian people, the *demos*, who supported the building of the great temples of the Acropolis – they voted on it in 447BC after impassioned debate. The Athenian people attended the plays of the great dramatists Aeschylus, Sophocles and Euripides. The Athenian experience of the 5th century BC shows that democracy does not have to mean dumbing down to the lowest intellectual level: it can mean

raising up a whole city to unprecedented cultural and political heights. *Areté* was not detached from life but was pursued in the dusty clamour of the streets, even by philosophers such as Socrates.

VIBRANT CLASSICISM
For many people ancient Greece can seem a cold, remote world of smooth marble statues and pristine white temples, lacking human interest. Such images mislead. Far from being cold and passionless, the Greeks burned and quivered with passions and desires – personal, political and intellectual – that often led to disaster, not perfection. Greek statues were once brilliantly painted with vivid colours, eyes and hair giving a startlingly lifelike appearance. Buildings, too, were painted in ways that might seem garish today. Time has stripped the paint and gilding off Greek remains, leaving them more sober-looking than their creators intended.

Few original Greek statues survive – a few in marble, even fewer bronzes. Too often we have only some mediocre copies of the great originals, made for the Romans. We have lost even more Greek painting. What has survived, however, reveals that the Greeks again pioneered a naturalistic art. The far more numerous extant vases, often magnificent artworks, tell us much about Greek daily life.

Above: The influence of Greek art has persisted down the centuries. The front of the British Museum, London, built by Robert Smirke in 1823–46, consciously echoes Greek models.

Below: Among the most famous of Greeks, Alexander the Great of Macedonia (reigned 336–323BC) overthrew the Greeks' old enemy, the immense Persian empire, but also restricted their cities' cherished independence.

TIMELINE

Above: The Parthenon, the supreme Greek temple, still rises above Athens despite the vicissitudes of 2,500 years.

Greece has one of the longest histories in the world. The origins of Classical Greece, that supremely accomplished civilization of the 5th and 4th centuries BC, lie in misty prehistory. Archaeology and legend are at first our sole guides, for history proper begins only c.550BC. (All dates before 550BC are approximate.) Around 2000BC, as Europe's first civilization emerged on Crete, ancestors of the Greeks appeared in the Greek peninsula and archipelago. By 1200BC they had created the Mycenaean civilization, a dynamic, resplendent culture that later generations peopled with heroes, unaware that a Dark Age, illiterate and impoverished, lay between them. The Greek age proper began with the first Olympic Games, traditionally held in 776BC. From then on Greek life accelerated, reaching its undoubted climax between 500 and 300BC, the age of the Persian Wars, Pericles, Socrates, the great dramatists and generals. But Greek history continued to develop long after Alexander the Great's death in 323BC, becoming linked with that of Rome, its political conqueror but cultural captive. Even the fall of Rome in AD476 merely eclipsed Greek brilliance, which re-emerged in the 15th century to bedazzle the Renaissance.

3000–700BC

3000BC Beginnings of Minoan civilization.
2000BC Building of first palaces in Crete; destruction of Bronze Age Lerna.
1700BC Destruction of first palaces in Crete; start of Second Palatial Period.
1600BC Beginnings of Mycenaean civilization in mainland Greece.
1570BC Palaces in Crete rebuilt after earthquake; Minoan culture at its zenith.
1550BC First shaft-graves at Mycenae.
1500–1470BC Volcanic eruption on Thira devastates Minoan civilization.
1450BC Mycenaeans occupy Knossos.
1380BC Final destruction of Knossos; Mycenaean trade and influence spread.
1300–1250BC Building of Treasury of Atreus, Lion Gate at Mycenae.
1287BC Battle of Cadesh between Egypt and Hittites.
1200BC Destruction of palace at Pylos.
1190BC Traditional date of Trojan War; Egypt repels the Sea Peoples.
1150BC Final collapse of Mycenaean civilization; start of Greek Dark Ages.
1050BC Dorian migrations into Greece; Ionian migration to Asia Minor.
900–800BC Rise of aristocracies in Greece.
776BC First Olympiad (Olympic Games).
760–730BC Homer composes *The Iliad* and *The Odyssey*; adaptation of Phoenician alphabet by Greeks.
753BC Founding of city of Rome.
750BC Foundation of Cumae in Italy, first Greek colony in west.
735BC Foundation of the first Greek colonies in Sicily at Naxos (Catania) and Syracuse.
730–710BC Sparta's first conquest of Messenia.
700BC Hesiod writes *Work and Days* and *Theognis*; according to tradition Deioces founds Median kingdom; introduction of hoplite-style fighting.

699–500BC

682BC List of annual *archons* at Athens begins; Gyges seizes Lydian throne.
669BC Sparta defeated by Argos under King Pheidion.
660BC Lycurgan reforms in Sparta; it crushes Messenian revolt.
c.650BC Rise of tyrants across Greece.
632BC Cylon tries to seize power in Athens; first colony in Libya at Cyrene.
620BC Dracon's Law Code published in Athens; foundation of Byzantium on Bosphorus, Naucratis in Egypt.
612BC Fall of Nineveh, Assyrian capital; first Black Sea colonies (Istrus, Olbia, etc).
c.600BC Thrasybulus tyrant of Miletus; Ionian Enlightenment; first triremes; Sappho, Pittacus and Alcaeus in Lesbos.
594BC Legislation of Solon in Athens.
589BC Foundation of Acragas in Sicily.
585BC Eclipse of sun, predicted by Thales, halts battle between Media and Lydia.
561BC Pisistratus seizes power in Athens; Croesus becomes king of Lydia.
550BC Achaemenid Empire of Persia founded by Cyrus the Great; Sparta forms the Peloponnesian League.
546BC Cyrus conquers Lydia; Sparta defeats Argos, annexes Thyreatis.
538BC Cyrus captures Babylon; he liberates the Jews.
527BC Pisistratus dies; succeeded by sons Hippias and Hipparchus.
514BC Harmodius and Aristogeiton kill Hipparchus; Persian expedition crosses the Danube.
510BC Hippias expelled from Athens with Spartan help.
508BC Cleisthenes' reforms in Athens.
507BC The Spartan invasion under Cleomones is repelled; Athens defeats Boeotians and Chalcidians, and gains Chalcidian territory.

499–450BC

499BC Outbreak of Ionian Revolt.

494BC Defeat of Ionians at Lade by Persia; fall of Miletus; Sparta defeats Argos.

490BC Athenians defeat Persian invasion at Marathon.

487BC First recorded use of ostracism at Athens; *archons* appointed by lot.

486BC Death of Darius the Great of Persia: accession of Xerxes.

483BC New silver lode found at Laurium: Themistocles wins debate on building fleet; Persians dig canal through Mt Athos.

481BC League of Corinth formed to resist Persia under Spartan leadership.

480BC Second Persian invasion under command of Xerxes; August battles of Thermopylae and Artemisium; Athens occupied by the Persians; September Battle of Salamis: Persian fleet destroyed; Carthaginian attack defeated at Himera.

479BC Persians under Mardonius defeated at Plataea by Spartan-led army; Persian fleet defeated at Mycale; revolt of Ionia.

478BC Sparta withdraws from Greek alliance; formation of the League of Delos.

474BC Greeks defeat Etruscans at Cumae.

470BC Birth of Socrates.

467BC Battle of Eurymedon: last Persian fleet destroyed by Athens.

464BC Earthquake at Sparta; *helot* revolt.

463BC Cimon leads Athenian force to help suppress Messenians.

462BC Democratic reforms of Ephialtes.

460BC Outbreak of war between Sparta and Athens; pay for jurors introduced.

459BC Athens sends fleet to help Egyptian revolt against Persia.

458BC *Zeugitae* admitted to *archonship*; building of Long Walls of Athens.

457BC Athens conquers Boeotia.

454BC Loss of Egyptian expedition; Confederacy Treasury moved to Athens.

449–415BC

449BC Peace of Callias with Persia; Athens invites the Greeks to restore her temples.

447BC Parthenon begun; Athens loses Boeotia.

446BC 30 Years' Peace with Sparta (actually to 431BC).

443BC Ostracism of Thucydides, son of Melesias, confirms Pericles' supremacy.

438BC Gold and ivory giant statue of Athena set up in Parthenon.

436BC Foundation of Amphipolis by Athens.

432BC Defensive alliance of Athens with Corcyra; Megarian Decree passed.

431BC Outbreak of Peloponnesian War; invasion of Attica by Peloponnesian army.

430BC Outbreak of plague devastates Athens; Pericles tried and fined.

429BC Pericles reinstated and dies; birth of Plato.

427BC Revolt of Lesbos crushed: debate on how to treat prisoners in Athens.

425BC Athenians occupy Pylos and capture Spartans on Sphacteria: Sparta sues unsuccessfully for peace.

424BC Battle of Delium: Athenians defeated in Boeotia; loss of Amphipolis to Spartan general Brasidas leads to banishment of Thucydides; Congress of Gela in Sicily: Hermocrates propounds 'Monroe Doctrine' for Sicily.

422BC Battle of Amphipolis: deaths of Cleon and Brasidas.

421BC Peace of Nicias.

420BC Alcibiades dominates Assembly.

418BC Battle of Mantinea: Athens and Argos defeated by Sparta.

416BC Athens captures and sacks Melos: 'Melian Debate'.

415BC Mutilation of Herms: Syracusan expedition sails; Alcibiades, recalled to face trial, escapes to Sparta.

414–390BC

414BC Sparta reopens war with Athens; sends Gylippus to help Syracusans.

413BC Spartans occupy fort of Deceleia; Demosthenes sent to Syracuse with reinforcements; great battle in Syracuse harbour; disastrous loss of expedition.

412BC Revolt of Athenian allies; Treaty of Miletus between Sparta and Persia.

411BC Oligarchic revolution at Athens; moderate oligarchy proposed.

410BC Battle of Cyzicus leads to restoration of full democracy in Athens.

409BC Carthage invades Greek Sicily.

408BC Athenians under Alcibiades recapture Byzantium and Chalcedon.

407BC Alcibiades returns to Athens; Prince Cyrus comes down to the Aegean.

406BC Alcibiades leaves Athens after defeat at Notion; Battle of Arginusae; Acragas besieged by Carthaginians; death of playwright Euripides.

405BC Lysander, Spartan *navarch*, defeats Athenian fleet at Aegospotami; end of Athenian power, and blockade of Athens; Dionysius I becomes tyrant of Syracuse.

404BC Surrender of Athens; Long Walls pulled down; dictatorship of the 30.

403BC Spartan garrison on Acropolis; Thrasybulus seizes Piraeus; restoration of democracy, and general amnesty.

401BC 'March of the 10,000' behind Cyrus into Persian Empire; Cyrus killed at Cunaxa; Xenophon leads Greeks home.

399BC Trial and execution of Socrates.

397BC Dionysius I captures Motya in Sicily; Sparta makes truce with Persia.

395BC Athens rebuilding Long Walls.

394BC Thebes, Corinth and Athens Army beaten by Spartans at Battle of Corinth.

393BC Athens completes her Long Walls.

390BC Iphicrates defeats Spartans with light-armed *peltasts*.

389–340BC

386BC The King's Peace: Sparta abandons Ionians in return for Persian support.

382BC Spartans seize Cadmaea (citadel) of Thebes and install pro-Spartan oligarchy.

379BC Spartans expelled from Cadmaea; revolution in Thebes led by Epaminondas.

378BC Athens forms 2nd Confederacy.

376BC Timotheus defeats Spartan fleet at Naxos; Mausolus *satrap* of Caria; Jason of Pherae establishes rule in Thessaly.

371BC Thebes routs Spartans at Leuctra but is checked by Jason.

370BC Assassination of Jason of Pherae; Epaminondas marches into Peloponnese.

369BC Foundation of Messene and liberation of *helots* by Thebans.

367BC Death of Dionysius I of Syracuse, succeeded by Dionysius II.

362BC Epaminondas killed at Mantinea; 'Revolt of the Satraps' against Persian king.

359BC Accession of Philip II of Macedon; defeats invading tribes; accession of Artaxerxes III, dynamic Persian king.

357BC Philip captures Amphipolis and marries Olympias; Dion returns to Sicily and 'liberates' Syracuse; start of the Athens' War of the Allies.

356BC Philomelus of Phocis seizes Delphi, starting Sacred War; Philip captures Potidaea; birth of Alexander.

354BC Murder of Dion in Syracuse; Athens makes peace with allies. Onomarchus of Phocis defeats Philip;

353BC Philip captures Methone; death of Mausolus of Halicarnassus.

352BC Philip defeats Phocians and becomes *tagus* (ruler) of Thessaly.

347BC Death of Plato.

346BC Peace of Philocrates ends Sacred War: Philip as protector of Delphi.

340BC Philip attacks Byzantium; Alexander left as regent of Macedonia.

339–327BC

338BC Battle of Chaeronea: Theban and Athenian armies defeated by Philip; death of Isocrates, Athenian orator; murder of Artaxerxes III by Bagoas, his Vizier.

337BC Council of Corinth elects Philip General of the Greeks for anti-Persian crusade; death of Timoleon in Sicily.

336BC Macedonian advance guard sent to Asia; Philip II murdered; accession of Alexander III; swift descent on Greece, where he is proclaimed General; accession of Darius III in Persia.

335BC Alexander campaigns in Thrace; Alexander's destruction of Thebes; Aristotle begins teaching at Athens.

334BC Alexander crosses into Asia; defeats Persians at Battle of Granicus; liberates Ionia; sieges of Miletus and Halicarnassus.

333BC Alexander cuts Gordian Knot; death of Greek mercenary general Memnon; change in Persian tactics; Battle of Issus (November): Alexander routs Persians; Darius flees east.

332BC Siege of Tyre (January–July); siege of Gaza; Alexander enters Egypt.

331BC Foundation of city of Alexandria; trip to consult oracle at Siwah; Alexander routs Persians at Gaugamela; enters Babylon and Susa; Sparta defeated by Macedonia.

330BC Alexander burns Persepolis; Darius murdered by Bessus; Alexander executes Philotas and Parmenion.

329BC Alexander crosses Hindu Kush to Bactria; crosses River Oxus; founds Alexandria Eschate; winters in Bactria.

328BC Campaign against Spitamenes; Alexander quarrels with and kills Cleitus.

327BC Capture of Sogdian Rock; Alexander marries Roxane; tries to introduce Persian *proskynesis*; Pages' Conspiracy – Callisthenes executed; enters India at the end of the year.

326–278BC

326BC Alexander defeats Porus at Hydaspes; conquers Punjab; advance to River Beas, where troops mutiny; forced to turn back.

325BC Conquest of the Malli: Alexander almost fatally wounded; he sails down Indus to Ocean; marches through Gedrosian Desert with many fatalities; voyage of Nearchus along coast.

324BC Execution of corrupt *satraps*; Susa weddings of Persians and Macedonians; mutiny of discharged veterans at Opis; Exiles Decree at Olympia; death of Hephaistion (October).

323BC Alexander enters Babylon; Greek cities hail him as a god; Alexander dies on 10 June; wars of the Diadochi (successors) and Lamian War of the Greeks against Macedonia; revolt of colonists in Bactria.

322BC Ptolemy gains control of Egypt: Lamian War ends in Greek defeat by Antipater; deaths of Demosthenes and Aristotle; Athenian democracy curtailed.

312BC Seleucus I takes over eastern *satrapies*; founds Seleucia-on-the-Tigris.

303BC Seleucus cedes Indian territories in return for 500 elephants.

301BC Battle of Ipsus: death of Antigonus I and division of world into four kingdoms.

300BC Zeno sets up Stoic School in Athens; Seleucus founds Antioch in Syria.

297BC Pyrrhus I king of Epirus (to 272BC).

295BC Library at Alexandria founded.

283BC Death of Ptolemy I, founder of Ptolemaic dynasty, in Egypt.

280BC Seleucus I defeats and kills Lysimachus, ending his kingdom, then murdered himself; Antiochus I succeeds him (to 261).

280–275BC Pyrrhus fights Romans in Italy without success; foundation of Achaean League in southern Greece.

279BC Building of Pharos at Alexandria.

274–200BC

274–232BC Reign of Ashoka, first Buddhist emperor, in India.

270BC Hieron emerges as saviour of Syracuse, assuming crown as Hieron II.

263–41BC Eumenes I of Pergamum starts to assert independence from Seleucids.

264BC First Punic War between Carthage and Rome starts.

c.255BC Bactria breaks away from Seleucid control, followed by Parthia.

245–213BC Aratus dominates Achaean League, seizes Corinth (243BC).

244BC Agis IV (to 241) tries to introduce radical reforms at Sparta and is killed.

241BC End of First Punic War: Rome takes over most of Sicily.

235BC Cleomenes III King of Sparta (to 222BC) introduces radical reforms before being defeated; Euthydemnus I seizes power in Bactria and expands kingdom.

230BC Attalus I defeats Gauls.

229BC Athens 'buys out' Macedonian garrison, in effect becoming neutral.

228BC Rome makes Illyria protectorate.

223BC Antiochus III the Great succeeds to Seleucid throne (to 187BC).

221BC Philip V succeeds to Macedonian throne (to 179BC); Ptolemy IV defeats Antiochus III at Raphia 218.

218–202BC Second Punic War.

217BC Peace Conference at Naupactus: warning of the 'shadow of Rome'.

216BC Romans defeated at Cannae.

215BC Alliance of Philip and Carthage leads to First Macedonian War (to 205BC); Syracuse switches support to Hannibal.

212BC Antiochus starts eastern campaigns; fall of Syracuse to Romans: Archimedes killed in the fighting.

202BC Hannibal finally defeated at Zama.

200BC Egypt defeated by Antiochus III at Ionion, loses southern Syria/Palestine.

199–70BC

197BC Macedonia defeated at Battle of Cynoscephalae.

196BC Flaminius declares 'Liberty for Greeks' at Corinth.

192BC Start of 'First Syrian' War of Rome against Antiochus III.

190BC Antiochus defeated at Magnesia.

188BC Treaty of Apamea: Antiochus loses all land west of Taurus mountains.

171–138BC Mithradates I of Parthia expands kingdom at Seleucid expense.

171–168BC Third Macedonian War.

170BC Eucratides I rules united Indo-Greek kingdom (to 155BC).

168BC Perseus of Macedonia defeated at Pydna; Antiochus IV forced to abandon conquest of Egypt; his intervention in Jerusalem sparks Maccabee revolt.

166BC Romans enslave 150,000 Epirotes, make Delos a free port; slave trade booms.

155–130BC Menander, king of huge Indo-Greek kingdom reaching the Ganges, possibly converts to Buddhism.

146BC Romans sack Corinth; make Achaea and Macedonia Roman provinces.

133BC Attalus III of Pergamum dies leaving kingdom to Rome.

130BC Romans crush Aristonicus' Utopian revolt and make Asia Minor a Roman province; Parthians capture Babylonia.

122BC Gauis Gracchus gives tax-farming rights for Asia and Greece to his allies in Rome, leading to ruinous extortion.

120BC Mithradates VI king of Pontus.

88BC Mithradates VI overruns Rome's eastern provinces offering 'liberty' to the Greeks; massacre of 80,000 Italians on Delos and other islands.

86–85BC Sulla sacks Athens.

73BC Lucullus defeats Mithradates and drives him out of Pontus to Crimea, where he commits suicide.

69BC–AD1462

66–63BC Pompey reorganizes the east: Syria and Bithynia-Pontus become provinces, Judaea and others client states.

51BC Parthians invade Syria; Cleopatra becomes co-monarch of Egypt.

48BC Battle of Pharsalus: Pompey flees to Egypt and is killed; Caesar, following, meets Cleopatra and has affair.

47BC Caesar leaves Egypt; Cleopatra later follows him to Rome; Cicero in retirement summarizes Greek philosophy.

44BC Caesar assassinated.

42BC Battle of Philippi: Cassius and Brutus defeated by Antony and Octavian; Antony takes eastern empire; winters in Athens.

41BC Antony meets Cleopatra at Tarsus.

36BC Antony invades Parthia but is forced to retreat.

31BC Battle of Actium: Octavian's forces defeat Antony and Cleopatra.

30BC Antony and Cleopatra commit suicide: Egypt annexed to Roman Empire by Octavian; Kushans (Scythians) over-run last Indo-Greek kingdom.

AD14 Death of Augustus (Octavian), first Roman emperor; succeeded by Tiberius.

AD66 Nero visits Greece, wins all prizes at the Olympics and declares 'liberty' for Greek cities.

AD124 Hadrian visits Athens and makes it head of Panhellenic League; completes Temple of Olympian Zeus.

AD393 Last Olympic Games held.

AD397–8 Visigoths ravage Greece.

AD529 Justinian closes Academy and other philosophy schools in Athens.

1438 Council of Florence; Bessarion stays on in Italy, rekindling knowledge of Greek.

1453 Fall of Constantinople to Ottoman Turks; some Greek scholars flee to Italy.

1462 Platonist Academy founded in Florence to study Greek philosophy.

Pages 14–17: The coins of ancient Greece were some of the very first ever to be minted. They were often brilliantly decorative, and they remain among the most beautiful and well designed that the world has seen.

CLASSICAL GREECE

The Parthenon, most famous of all Greek temples, rises supremely above the city of Athens. Epitomizing classical Greece, it was built by the world's first true democracy. Greek democracy had emerged only around 500BC and reached its final form just before the Parthenon was built. This is no coincidence: the Greeks passionately sought perfection in their politics *and* in their art. Their achievements in both mark the start of Western history. To this day, men and women fight and die for democracy (a Greek word). The history of classical Greece is, to a large extent, the history of the first democracies.

Democracy was not attained or defended just with words or ideas, much though Greeks loved both. Greeks had to fight for their freedom against internal and external enemies. The greatest external enemy was the Persian Empire. Its rise and fall roughly coincided with Athens' democracy. In the great conflict of the Persian Wars (499–478BC), the fragmented Greek states (around 1,000 scattered from Spain to Cyprus) united to repel the Persian superpower. The major battles of those wars – Marathon, Thermopylae, Salamis and Plataea – are among the pivotal contests in human history.

But the Greeks never united again. Instead, they fought each other unceasingly, until finally they fell to other powers: first Macedonia, then Rome. But in their centuries of independence, the Greeks experimented constantly, trying out every form of government: democracy, monarchy, dictatorship, oligarchy, even communism (on the Aeolian Islands, near Sicily). In doing so, they invented philosophy and history besides politics. Reading Greek history entails far more than reading about ancient ruins: it means rediscovering our political and intellectual origins.

Left: The buildings on the Athenian Acropolis, such as the Erechtheum, still proclaim the achievements of classical Greece at its democratic zenith.

CHAPTER I

THE GREEK AWAKENING

c.2000–500BC

Greek history starts far earlier than the Greeks themselves suspected (or anyone else before recent archaeological discoveries). People who were possibly the Greeks' ancestors appeared in the peninsula around 2000BC. At about the same time, and perhaps not by coincidence, the sophisticated Minoan civilization arose in Crete and the Cyclades. While the Minoans were almost certainly not Greek, the Mycenaeans, who took over Crete and were influenced by its culture, definitely were.

Heroic myths cluster around the Mycenaean palaces of the late Bronze Age (1600–1200BC). This suggests that there is a kernel of truth to most Greek legends, although they should not be regarded as history. Greeks of the historical period proper (from *c.*550BC) mostly believed their legends, especially when related by Homer, but they had only the haziest ideas of their actual pre-history. In particular, they were unaware that between them and their legendary ancestors lay the chasm of the Greek Dark Ages. When Greek life revived after 800BC, it took very different forms from Mycenaean Greece.

One factor remained constant, however: the mountainous landscape, with valleys often isolated from each other, meant that Greece remained divided politically into many small, even tiny states. This helped to give Greek life its passionate intensity centred on the *polis*, the citizen-state.

Left: The huge grave shafts of Mycenae – "rich in gold" according to Homer – are the first Greek buildings, dating to c.1550BC.

MINOAN CRETE
THE FIRST CIVILIZATION 2000–1100BC

Above: This vivid fresco of children boxing was found on Thira, the Aegean island devastated by the volcanic eruption in c.1500BC that is thought to have half-wrecked Minoan civilization.

Below: The grand staircase at Cnossus Palace, the largest of the Cretan palaces, reveals the surprisingly modern-looking ingenuity of Minoan architects.

Europe's first civilization arose in Crete and the Aegean islands during the Bronze Age. It is called Minoan after its legendary king Minos. According to the Athenian historian Thucydides, Minos was the first to rule the seas and islands. Thucydides was long thought to be just repeating myths about the king of Cnossus, who reputedly exacted tribute from Athens: 14 girls and boys to be fed to the Minotaur, the bull-headed monstrous offspring of Minos' wife, Queen Pasiphae, and a bull. But, since Arthur Evans began excavations at Cnossus in 1900, controversially restoring many of the ruins, Thucydides has been proved partly right: there was a great civilization in Crete with outposts across the Aegean.

Cretan civilization started modestly in the 3rd millennium. Around 2000BC the first palaces – multi-storeyed buildings centred on courtyards – were built at Cnossus, Phaestos and Mallia. They were influenced by Egyptian and Near Eastern models, for the Cretans were by then sailing south and east, bringing home ivory and other luxury products in return for jewellery, wine, textiles and olive oil. Egyptian records of the 2nd millennium BC often mention Cretans (as tribute-bearers, although Crete was never a tributary to Egypt), but Minoan civilization soon developed its own highly distinctive characteristics.

A PEACEFUL SOCIETY

Notable among Minoan society's characteristics were its peaceful nature and the prominent role seemingly played by women. However, the Cretans were never total pacifists – they presumably relied mostly on their navy for defence – and ideas of a matriarchy, with women ruling the realm, are probably misplaced. Around 1700BC all the palaces were destroyed by earthquakes.

Above: This figurine, bare-breasted in the courtly Minoan fashion, represents the earth-goddess or possibly one of her priestesses.

But, with Minoan culture vigorously resurgent, they were soon rebuilt as larger, even more elegant complexes.

Below: The Minoan Palace at Cnossus with its characteristic dark-red columns.

Cretans of the period *c*.1700–1500BC (called Late Minoan by Evans, Later Palatial by others) produced pottery, jewellery and other vivid artworks that can still delight. The palaces, especially the largest at Cnossus, had bathrooms with running water and light-wells. Their buildings had dark red columns tapering downwards and rose four or even five storeys high. On their walls, frescoes depicted a graceful, idyllic life, with bare-breasted women in long flounced dresses and with elaborate hairstyles, and clean-shaven men in kilts, surrounded by flowers, birds and dolphins. A cult of the bull was clearly central to Cretan religion, demonstrated by the many images of bulls and by the bull-dance, a game or rite common on murals. (This may underlie the Minotaur legend.) The axe was also a common motif. Paved roads connected palaces with outlying villages and villas around the island. The population of Cnossus town reached *c*.30,000 by 1500BC, making it the largest Mediterranean city of the age.

Minoan culture was not confined to Crete, however, but also flourished in the Cyclades and some other Aegean islands. Most prosperous was Thira (Santorini), which was probably independent. Murals excavated there show a fleet attacking a walled town and reveal Thira's links with north Africa. But the predominant note, as in Crete, was peaceful. After 1600BC, Minoan culture spread to the mainland, with such strong Minoan influence

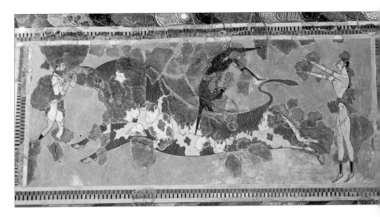

evident in mainland sites that Evans talked of a Minoan Empire. But certainly here the rulers, Mycenaean Greeks, were independent, merely employing Minoan craftsmen to make them precious objects.

THE THIRA ERUPTION

This cheerful civilization was in its prime when an immense volcanic explosion tore Thira apart. It also devastated other islands, including Crete, while preserving part of Thira town under lava like a Bronze Age Pompeii. The date of the eruption remains debated, ranging from 1600BC, the geologists' preferred date, to 1460BC, which suits archaeologists better. Indisputably, when Cnossus Palace was rebuilt *c*.1450BC, it was occupied by Greek-speakers, for clay Linear B tablets written in early Greek have been found there. Although a warlike note emerges in the tablets, Cnossus, 'house of the double axe' (*labyrinth*), remained unwalled.

Then one day *c*.1380BC a fire, caused by accident, earthquake or human attack, gutted the palace once more and it was never rebuilt. Minoan culture now entered its less glorious 'post-palatial' phase. This may not have been totally impoverished – Homer ranked Crete as second only to Mycenae in his 'Catalogue of Ships'. But *c*.1100BC Dorian Greek invaders, who had attacked the Peloponnese already, invaded Crete, finally wrecking the Minoan world.

Above: The cult of the bull was central to Minoan religious life. Bull-leaping, as this fresco reveals, was dangerous. It probably had religious connotations but was conducted insouciantly.

Below: This languid youth is called the Lily Prince. Like most Cretan young men, he wore only a kilt, but he also has an elaborate head-dress.

LINEAR B

Linear B was the third form of writing developed in Crete. The first was a pictographic script, the second was a syllabic system, Linear A, while Linear B was similar but in Greek. Linear B tablets record flocks of sheep, oil jars, horses, spears and chariots, not royal edicts, history or poetry, yet they shed invaluable light on this highly civilized society now ruled by Greek incomers.

MYCENAEAN SOCIETY
THE FIRST GREEKS, 1600–1200BC

Above: The Lion Gate, erected c.1300BC, still guards the entrance to Mycenae. Its massive walls so impressed later Greeks that they assumed they had been built by Cyclops, one-eyed giants.

Below: The Mycenaeans were impressively skilled architects, building corbelled vaults. The 'Treasury of Atreus', which dates from c.1300BC, is not really a treasury but a tomb.

In the 3rd millennium BC a prosperous Bronze Age culture developed in the Greek peninsula in small unwalled towns such as Lerna in the Peloponnese. Around 2000BC these were destroyed by invaders, probably from the north, and for a time urban life totally disappeared. Then *c.*1600 BC a new civilization emerged that built amazing tombs at Mycenae in the north-west Peloponnese filled with so many gold artefacts that Homer's epithet "Mycenae, rich in gold" is justified. This was probably due to the rise of powerful new kings, not fresh invasions, but nothing is known about them.

In Greek legend, including Homer's great poems *The Iliad* and *The Odyssey* written in the 8th century BC, Mycenae was the paramount kingdom, so this first Greek civilization has been called Mycenaean. But Achaean, the term used by both Homer and by contemporary Hittite kings in Anatolia who had diplomatic dealings with them, is more apposite. Nothing suggests that Bronze Age Greece was politically united under Mycenae, although it probably controlled the Argolid plain beneath its citadel, from which paved roads radiated.

MYCENAEAN CULTURE EMERGES

In the 16th century BC the cultural influence of Minoan Crete, then far more sophisticated, was overwhelming on the Mycenaeans. Superb gold cups found near Sparta, showing bulls being tethered by long-haired youths, reveal this. But already distinctive themes favoured by Mycenaeans, such as hunting and warfare, were emerging. The early (*c.*1600BC) gold mask from Grave A at Mycenae shows a fierce bearded warrior most unlike clean-shaven Minoans. After 1460BC Greek warriors, possibly from Mycenae, occupied the palace at Cnossus after the Thira eruption.

Among cultural imports from Crete was writing in Linear B, subsequently adopted in Mycenaean centres. These include nearby Tiryns, Thebes and Orchomenus in central Greece, Athens (although it remained of secondary importance) and Pylos in the south-west Peloponnese. Excavations at Pylos have unearthed a complete Mycenaean palace, with elegant tapering columns and murals depicting hippogriffs and other mythical figures. Uniquely, Pylos was unwalled. Linear B tablets found there reveal a bureaucracy trying to control almost every aspect of daily life. Mycenaean culture spread north into Thessaly, across the Aegean to Miletus on the Asian shore and east to Cyprus. There was probably a palace near Sparta in the fertile Eurotas valley, but none has been found.

PROTECTING MYCENAE

Mycenaean wealth grew throughout the 14th century BC. It probably came from both trading and raiding – piracy, Thucydides noted, was socially perfectly acceptable in legendary times. Greek artefacts, mainly pottery, have been found as far west as Sicily and as far east as Syria. Mycenaean outposts replaced Minoans

SCHLIEMANN AND TROY

In the 19th century, scholars dismissed Homer's epic and other Greek myths as just that: pure invention, with no historical foundation. Ancient Greeks, who had treated such legends as fact, were considered to have been childishly naïve. Considered equally naïve, therefore, was German businessman Heinrich Schliemann (1822–90), who had been fascinated by Greek legends since childhood. Convinced that Homer had not invented the Trojan wars, Schliemann began excavating the site in north-west Turkey reputed to be Troy. He discovered nine superimposed cities, and in 1873 found a treasure that he declared was the Trojan king Priam's. In fact, it was much older. In 1876 he turned to Mycenae and soon struck gold there too – literally, for he found himself looking at the gold death mask of a Bronze Age king. "I have looked on the face of Agamemnon," he declared. Again, he was out by centuries, but he had convinced the world that legendary Greece had existed in some form.

after 1400BC, but the Mycenaeans soon ventured further north than Cretans had ever sailed.

To protect Mycenae against threats from abroad or at home, massive new walls were built around its citadel, incorporating the earlier grave circles. The towering Lion Gate, with two lions flanking a pillar, dominated the new approach. Below, houses belonging to nobles, craftsmen and traders made up a little city. Most palaces had a pillared *megaron* (throne-room), but few reveal much evidence of planning.

THE ENIGMA OF TROY

Up by the Hellespont (Dardanelles) the Mycenaeans found the ancient trading city of Troy, controlling trade routes from the Black Sea, a good enough cause for war. The Trojan War, that epic ten-year siege variously estimated to have occurred between 1250 and 1190BC, remains one of archaeology's enigmas. There *was* a city destroyed around there and then, Troy VIIA, and recent excavations have shown that this was larger than once thought, with impressive palaces. Perhaps a Greek army led by Agamemnon, king of Mycenae, did besiege Troy to retrieve Helen, the Spartan king's beautiful wife abducted by the Trojan prince Paris, as recounted in Homer's *Iliad*. Or perhaps it did not. But the 13th century certainly ended in general wars. Mycenaean civilization, top-heavy, collapsed soon after.

Above: The gold mask that Heinrich Schliemann, the enthusiastic rediscoverer of Troy and Mycenae, called the Mask of Agamemnon is in fact far earlier than the Trojan Wars, dating from the 16th century BC. Its still half-barbaric splendour indicates that the lords of Mycenae had already grown rich, whether this wealth was from trading, raiding or fighting as mercenaries.

Left: The Minoans' cultural influence on the mainland Greeks was for a time overwhelming. This gold cup, found at Vaphio, near Sparta, and dating from the 16th century BC, is Minoan both in its naturalistic style and its bull-taming theme.

THE DARK AGES
1200–800BC

Above: Ephesus was among the greatest of the Ionian cities of Asia Minor, traditionally founded by the Ionians fleeing from the Doric invasions around 1000BC.

Around the year 1200BC almost all the major Mycenaean centres were destroyed by unknown attackers despite their strengthened fortifications. Some sites, such as Pylos, were abandoned, fires baking their Linear B tablets enduringly hard for posterity. Only Athens, secure on its rock thanks to a covered passage running down to a secret well, survived intact. (In legend this survival was due to the self-sacrifice of Codrus, its last king, who thus fulfilled a prophecy that the city would be saved if its king were killed. After such a heroic death, Athens becamean aristocratic republic.) But its status as the one unsacked city reinforced subsequent Athenian beliefs that they alone were autochthonic (sprung from the land), unlike the Dorian newcomers.

Later Greeks remembered the upheavals at the end of the Mycenaean age as the 'return of the Heraclids' (sons of Heracles or Hercules – a Mycenaean prince) to reclaim their inheritance two generations after the Trojan War.

They failed to realize that there had been a complete break between the elaborate, literate world of the Bronze Age palaces and much simpler later societies. The break was not sudden – Mycenae itself was briefly reoccupied and there were actually some new settlements along the east coast of Attica. But what followed was a true Dark Age: illiterate, isolated and impoverished.

MYCENEAN REFUGEES

According to legend, Dorian tribes entered Greece from the north-west, a region untouched by Mycenaean culture, and moved down into the Peloponnese, destroying as they went. Refugees from the kingdom of Pylos sailed first to impregnable Athens and then across the seas to found new cities on the Asian coast such as Smyrna and Ephesus, soon called Ionian. Some Mycenaeans sailed further east to untouched Cyprus, where they maintained a fading Bronze Age lifestyle, complete with chariots and a

Right: By 800BC Greece had become linguistically divided into groups, whose culture as well as dialect were distinctive. Foremost among these groups were Ionian, spoken in Athens, the islands and Ionia, and Doric, spoken in Sparta, Crete and Rhodes.

simplified syllabic alphabet, down to the time of the Persian Wars (499–478BC). Others retreated into Arcadia, the mountainous heart of the Peloponnese, where they preserved their own independence, dialect and customs, albeit in rustic form.

Another explanation for the collapse of Mycenaean civilization is climate change – perhaps a prolonged drought – but there certainly were large migrations and invasions in the years after 1200.

THE DIALECTS OF GREECE

The main reason for accepting in outline the tradition of northern invaders is linguistic. While all Mycenaean Greeks seem to have spoken much the same language (judging by Linear B tablets), in historic Greece there were several major linguistic divisions. In much of the Peloponnese, including the Corinthian Isthmus (though not inland Arcadia), in Crete, Rhodes and some southern Cyclades, the Dorian dialect became the norm. Dorian Greek was in some ways old-fashioned – the *a* in *phrater* (brother) remained long, for example, while it became short in other dialects. In Attica, including Athens, the island of Euboea, many of the Cyclades, most east Aegean islands and many cities on the east coast, people spoke Ionic Greek. This became the language (in grandly poetic form) of Homer, greatest of all Greek poets, in the 8th century BC.

In central Greece – Boeotia and Thessaly, on the large island of Lesbos and the adjacent northern Asian coastline, all colonized from central Greece, Aeolic, a form of Greek closer to Ionian than Dorian emerged, which influenced the language of Hesiod, the second great Greek poet. Another dialect, now called North-western Greek, was spoken appropriately in north-western Greece, while modern scholars, recognizing the similarity between the Greek of the Arcadians and that of the Cypriots, have identified a separate Arcado-Cypriot dialect. This was not, however, recognized at the time. Although there were definite cultural as well as linguistic differences between the

dialect-speakers, all could understand each other well enough – when they wanted to.

FRESH BEGINNINGS

Clues to new developments in this illiterate society come mostly from pottery, whose shards have survived. At first potters continued to produce feebler versions of the ornate Mycenaean 'palace' styles, but c.1050BC a wholly new style emerged in Athens called Protogeometric. Radically simple, content with almost abstract designs and not concerned to fill every empty space, it ranks as perhaps the first truly Hellenic art. (The Greeks now began calling themselves Hellenes: 'Greek' is a Roman word.) Over the next three centuries Geometric art, using stark zigzags and triangles, developed more elaborate shapes but remained stylized. Clothing, too, changed around 1100BC, with simple Dorian cloaks replacing elaborate Mycenaean-style clothes. Almost all buildings were now made of timber, with small thatched cottages serving as temples, befitting a society hardly above subsistence level, ruled by local lords hardly richer than the peasants working for them. Few men looked far afield.

Above: In tradition and probably in reality, Athens was the 'unsacked city' that alone survived the Dorian invasions, perpetuating Mycenaean traditions.

Below: The far simpler way of life that emerged in Greece's Dark Ages (1200–800BC) resulted in a new, simpler style of pottery: Protogeometric and then, as in this 8th-century BC amphora, Geometric.

THE GREEK RENAISSANCE
800–700BC

Above: The stories of Odysseus' wanderings, so magnificently related by Homer, gave generations of potters themes. Here Odysseus is bound to the mast of his ship to resist the fatally alluring song of the Sirens.

Below: Mt Olympus, the highest mountain in Greece and often cloud-capped, was the mythical home of the 12 Olympian gods. It also marked the northern frontier of Greece proper.

Around 800BC this enclosed, static society began to change. The spur was increasing population, growing (if still modest) prosperity at home and renewed contacts with traders from the Levant. The traders were Phoenicians, a Semitic people from the coasts of modern Lebanon who founded Carthage near modern Tunis in 814BC. The use of iron also spread, giving Greek farmers metal axes, ploughs and other useful implements. But Greek society remained essentially aristocratic, meaning ruled by *aristoi* (the best), as hereditary nobles modestly called themselves.

THE GREEK ALPHABET
Eastern influences first appear in art, depicting human beings and animals, often mythical such as sphinxes, in freer if not yet realistic ways. But the greatest single change was the revival of literacy. Around 770BC some Greeks, probably poets, adopted the Phoenician alphabet,

Above: Olympia in the Peloponnese emerged as one of the holiest sites in the Greek world in the 8th century BC, famed for its quadrennial games, the greatest in the Greek calendar, and later for its temple housing an enormous statue of Zeus.

adding the vowels needed for Greek to make 24 letters and adjusting the symbols. Semitic *aleph* became Greek *alpha*, the first letter. More flexible and easier to learn than the 300-character Mycenaean system, the new alphabet spread around the Greek world. Our own Roman alphabet derives directly from it. One of the first uses of literacy was to record the works of Homer, the greatest Greek poet.

HOMER'S *ILIAD* AND *ODYSSEY*
There are no reliable details about Homer's life. He probably lived *c.*750BC on the island of Chios or the adjacent Ionian mainland, and traditionally was blind. Whether the two great Homeric poems, *The Iliad* and *The Odyssey*, were written by the same man remains debated. Homer's theme in *The Iliad* is the wrath of Prince Achilles and its disastrous effects on the last stages of the ten-year Trojan War, of which, however, he gives only fleeting glimpses. In this grand tragedy he lauded heroic values such as *philotimon* (love of honour), *areté*

(meaning variously courage, excellence, perfection), endurance and a fiercely competitive individualism.

By contrast, in *The Odyssey*, his adventure-story-cum-comedy, Odysseus triumphs chiefly by craftiness. Homer's description of an aristocratic society led by kings, with the voices of common people such as Thersites firmly ignored, inadvertently mingles current Iron Age customs with those of the Bronze Age. His heroes ride into battle in Mycenaean chariots and carry Bronze Age giant shields, but they are cremated, not buried as Mycenaeans were. Although they live in palaces, these are simply large houses, lacking the bureaucracies and splendours of real Mycenae or Pylos. Queen Penelope, wife of wandering Odysseus, spins her own wool.

Homer's influence on later Greeks has been compared to that of the Bible and Shakespeare combined – or to Hollywood *plus* television today. All Greeks with any education could quote Homer, and he

inspired men as diverse as the philosopher Socrates and Alexander the Great. In portraying the Twelve Olympians (the chief gods on Mt Olympus) light-heartedly as super-sized humans, Homer's writing had a beneficial side effect. If even Zeus, king of the gods, could be portrayed as hen-pecked by his wife Hera, there was small danger of Greeks being totally over-awed by their gods' majesty. (The Greeks never had a special priestly caste or clergy. This helped philosophy– that quest for truth by non-religious means – to spring up in Ionia two centuries later.)

THE WORK OF HESIOD

Balancing the exuberant aristocratic splendour of Homer's world are the *Theognis* and *Works and Days* of Hesiod, a poet who lived slightly later (*c*.700BC) in rural Boeotia, an area noted for its dullness. An independent small farmer, Hesiod grumbles at the rich and at the weather, but provides useful advice to his feckless brother on when to sow and plough. He has a strong distrust of seafaring and a peasant's attitude to accruing more land. In his *Theognis* he gave a systematic genealogy for the gods and an account of divine myths, darker in tone than Homer's, that also proved very influential on later generations.

Above: This vase, dating from 490BC, illustrates a typically combative scene between Achilles and Memnon from Homer's first great poem, The Iliad, *about the Trojan Wars. Homer's poetry swiftly became the basis of Greek culture.*

Below: Almost nothing definite is known about the life of Homer, the supreme Greek poet, but he was reputedly blind. He certainly was an Ionian Greek, for he wrote in the Ionian dialect.

THE FIRST OLYMPICS

Another vital aspect of Greek life emerged in the 8th century BC: the Olympic Games, traditionally first held at Olympia in west Greece in 776BC. At first just a Peloponnesian event, it soon attracted Greek athletes from all over Greece and overseas to its contest held once every four years. For this, the greatest athletic event in the Hellenic world, the forever-warring Greeks observed a rare truce. After an athlete's loincloth fell off, it was decided that all contestants should compete naked, like the gods. The (usually aristocratic) victor at a major contest such as chariot races was hailed as a semi-divine hero by his native city, often having a statue erected to him. At Olympia were created some of the finest temples and statues. Pheidias, the supreme Classical Athenian sculptor, made a huge statue of Zeus there.

THE EXPANSION OF GREECE
750–580BC

Above: The island of Ortygia off the south-eastern Sicilian coast became the kernel of Syracuse, founded in 734BC, ultimately the greatest and most powerful Greek city in the west. These columns of the Temple to Apollo date from the 6th century BC.

Below: Electrum and silver coins of Phocaea (Ionia) in western Anatolia.

Right: Although only founded in c.580BC, Acragas became the richest of Greek Sicilian cities, thanks to its wool trade. Its 'Vale of Temples' included this Temple to Concordia from the prosperous 5th century BC.

By 550BC Greek 'colonies' – that is, autonomous city-states, not dependent territories – stretched across the Mediterranean from southern Gaul (France) to Egypt, with many more around the Black Sea. Southern Italy was so densely settled with Greek cities that the Romans called it *magna Graecia* (greater Greece). This remarkable expansion, which occurred within about two centuries, was driven chiefly by growing land hunger.

The mountainous nature of much of the country meant that the amount of fertile land in Greece was limited. To make matters worse, the Greek custom of dividing inherited land equally between all surviving sons meant that farms often became too small to be viable. (Most Greeks were, of course, farmers.) When the population began to expand in the 8th century BC, the pressure on the available land grew.

THE FIRST COLONIES

In almost every Greek city there were persistent – if unfounded – traditions that in the legendary past a wise ruler had divided up all land equally, and so subsequent inequalities, which benefited aristocrats, were unjust. A redistribution of land was a recurring wish of ordinary people and the nightmare of ruling aristocracies. To avert revolution, cities

Above: Settlers from Megara founded Acragas (modern Agrigento), once Sicily's wealthiest city,

turned to founding colonies overseas, some of which proved very popular, some less so. The colonists sent out c.630BC from the small island of Thira to Cyrene in Libya, for example, were forbidden to return within six years no matter what happened. (In fact, Cyrene boomed thanks to its wheat and wool.)

The first colonies were founded c.750BC at Cyme and the island of Ischia, near Naples, to obtain the metals Greece lacked. These colonists were soon followed by those from other cities seeking good farmland: Chalcis, from Euboea, founded Naxos, Catania and Rhegium, now Reggio, on the Straits of Messina. Corinth founded Corcyra (Corfu) and in 734BC Syracuse, which was to become the greatest city in the west. The Achaeans of the north Peloponnese founded Sybaris, Croton and Metapontion in southern Italy, all built on prime agricultural land, where they soon grew rich. Even Sparta joined in, founding Taras (Taranto) c.700BC.

After a pause, colonies also began founding their own colonies. Megara, a Sicilian offshoot of the Megara that lies north-east of Corinth, sent settlers west to Selinus (Selinunte) c.630BC and to Acragas

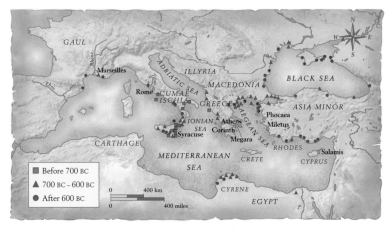

Left: Starting with colonies at Ischia and Cumae around the Bay of Naples in c.750BC, the Greeks founded cities all around the Mediterranean, from the south of France (Marseilles, Antibes and Nice) to Naucratis in the Egyptian Delta, to solve problems of over-population at home.

(Agrigento), later Sicily's wealthiest city, c.580BC. Phocaea, in north Ionia, colonized southern Gaul: Nice, Antibes, Monaco and Marseilles are all in origin Greek. The westernmost Greek city was Emporiae in north-east Spain, a trade centre (as its name suggests). Trade across the whole Greek world grew thanks to such colonization.

New settlers went out not as individuals but in planned groups, at times led by an aristocrat's younger son, sometimes not

THE CITIZEN-STATE
The *polis*, city-state, was the main political unit of Greece. It is more accurate to call it 'citizen-state', for it meant the body of all politically active men, not its buildings. (Women, slaves and resident foreigners were inhabitants but not active citizens of a *polis*.) A *polis* often had citizens living outside its walls, in villages or small towns, who walked into the city centre. When Athens itself was occupied by invading Persians in 480BC, Themistocles, its leader, was taunted with being cityless. He pointed out that Athens consisted of its assembled citizens, who would sail off and found a new city if the united Greek fleet did not stand and fight. A *polis* was always fiercely autonomous.

taking wives with them. Instead, they married local women, often those of native inhabitants they had dispossessed. Not all colonists necessarily came from one city. Small places such as Phocaea recruited landless men from other cities. While most colonies retained strong sentimental ties with their mother city, all were fully independent from the start.

THE BLACK SEA
There was wealth to be had in the north-east around the Black Sea, although attempts to establish colonies in the crowded Levant failed, except briefly at Al-Mina in Syria. The three-pronged peninsula of the Chalcidice was first colonized by Chalcis, and then by Megara. Megara went on to found Byzantium (Istanbul) at a superb site on the Bosphorus in 629BC. Beyond lay the wide cold waters of the Black Sea.

Here another host of colonies sprang up: Sinope, Amisus and Trebizond on the south coast, and Olbia, Panticapaeum and Tyrus around the north, in a chilly region the Greeks found strange. The Scythian hinterland (Ukraine) exported grain, gold, timber and slaves in return for Greek oil, wine and artefacts. Wheat from the Black Sea became increasingly important to Greece, especially to Athens. Ultimately, whoever controlled the Black Sea grain supply could throttle Athens.

Below: The Greeks also settled thickly around the shores of the Black Sea, to them a very alien area. They traded olive oil, artefacts and wine for wheat with the Scythian princes who ruled the steppes and were buried with resplendent grave goods such as this gold comb. Greek influence is evident in the naturalistic style.

HOPLITES AND TYRANTS
700–550BC

Above: This 'Corinthian style' helmet, inscribed with the name Dendas, dates from c.500BC. Such helmets gave hoplites good head protection but limited visibility.

Below: The Chigi Vase (made in Corinth but found in central Italy, hence its name) is the earliest extant depiction of hoplites marching and fighting in formation. It dates from the 7th century BC, by which time the 'Hoplite Revolution' was well under way.

Although Homer's heroes had ridden to war in chariots for individual combat, in the post-Mycenaean age chariots were replaced by horsemen. As only rich aristocrats could afford armour and a horse, warfare remained dominated by noblemen. But by the 7th century BC growing wealth, in part fuelled by trade that provided cheaper metal, meant that more farmers of the middle class (in Athens called *zeugitae*, meaning owning a yoke of oxen) could afford armour and arms. This led to radical changes in warfare and in society.

THE HOPLITES' IMPORTANCE
The main battles of ancient Greece were decided by hoplites, heavy-armoured infantrymen. Fighting in close formation, with their long spears bristling in front of them, hoplites could outface cavalry and dominated warfare in Greece for almost 500 years. The oldest set of hoplite armour, unearthed near Argos, dates from *c.*700BC. It has a plumed helmet covering the head (helmets often covered the whole face, leaving mere slits for the eyes) and heavy metal cuirass covering the body. Most hoplites had metal grieves on their legs and all carried a large (about 1m/3ft in diameter) round shield on their left arm. In their right hand they carried a 3.5m/12ft spear. Each depended for protection on his open right flank on his neighbour. If one hoplite broke ranks and fled, the entire formation could be imperilled. To keep formation required practice. It also implied a novel equality between fighters: now the most blue-blooded aristocrat was equal on the battlefield to an unwashed farmer.

Hoplites made up about one-third of a typical Greek city's adult citizen population. (The majority of Greeks, who could not afford such full armour, were enrolled as light-armed troops, long considered of minor importance on or off the battlefield.) Marching and fighting together bred a new sense of camaraderie among

the hoplite class that had political and social effects. If fighting was no longer the preserve of nobles, soon politics too was seen as concerning far more of the people. As economic growth changed the Greek world, it increased the gap between the rich – who could import new luxuries – and the rest. Discontent with aristocratic rule, long taken for granted, increased. The nobles still monopolized power, but often treated politics as a frivolous if risky game between rival families, like the athletic contests they still dominated. But most Greeks wanted *eunomia* (good government), not *stasis* (the chaotic strife of aristocratic factions).

TYRANTS: NEW-STYLE RULERS

Quick to exploit such feelings were the men, often themselves rogue aristocrats, who seized power in many states as tyrants. (Greek *tyrannos* meant at first just unconstitutional ruler, boss or chief, not dictator in a modern sense.) From the mid-7th century BC tyrants appeared in cities that were often among the most dynamic in the Greek world. Typical was Corinth, a major trading city due to its position on the Isthmus, which produced fine pottery. Cypselus threw out its ruling Bacchiad family in 657BC, expelling other aristocrats and confiscating their property. Once in power, his regime proved so efficient and popular that he dispensed with a bodyguard. After he died in power in 625BC he was succeeded by his son Periander, who ruled for another 40 years.

Cypselus' example was soon followed in other cities such as nearby Megara and Sicyon. In neighbouring Argos the hereditary king Pheidon seems to have *become* a tyrant *c*.675BC, rebasing his rule on popular support. He reorganized the army as a hoplite force to crush the invading Spartans at Hysaia in 668BC. Tyrants, besides providing stable government, enriched their cities with temples and monuments. In Corinth, a dry shipway was built by Periander across the Isthmus, forerunner of the Corinth Canal.

Tyrannies spread across the Greek world from Sicily to Ionia. An unusually benevolent tyrant was Pittacus in Mytilene on the island of Lesbos, who resigned after ten years to general astonishment, the one tyrant to do so.

Among the Greek cities in Asia, tyranny was taken as the Greek norm by their Lydian and later by their Persian conquerors, who granted subject cities internal autonomy.

The last independent tyrant in eastern Greece was Polycrates of Samos, who built a famous temple, befriended the poet Anacreon and was *thalassocrat* (ruler of the seas) for a few years before being betrayed to the Persians and killed in 523BC. Few tyrant dynasties lasted long. At Corinth the tyranny collapsed soon after Periander's death. Tyranny was therefore a transitional phase for most Greek cities, with only unstable Sicilian cities reverting to tyranny in later years. And one supremely important state never experienced tyranny: Sparta.

Left: This vase from c.500BC shows hoplite warriors engaged in single combat. More typically, however, they fought in the disciplined ranks of the phalanx.

Below: A bronze helmet and cuirass, found near Argos and dating from the 7th century BC, are among the finest armour retrieved from the ancient world. Most hoplites would not have been able to afford anything so elaborate, instead having cuirasses of toughened linen.

THE IONIAN ENLIGHTENMENT
650–520BC

Above: Sappho and Alcaeus were two of the greatest poets of the Lyric Age, writing intensely personal poems of love, death and loss as well as more convivial drinking songs and marriage epithalamia.

For the eastern Greeks of Ionia and the adjacent islands the period *c.*650–500BC saw an accelerating widening of horizons that was mental as much as physical. Their merchants, colonists and mercenaries explored the world from the Black Sea down to Egypt and as far east as Babylon (in modern Iraq), bringing home new ideas. This generated a novel vivacity that was different from the heroic age before and from the serious high Classical Age (480–322BC) that followed. Women at this time in Ionia probably enjoyed greater freedom than they did later (although this does not mean that they were remotely equal), while poets wrote more personally about life, love and death. The graceful Ionic column was developed at about this time, while Western philosophy and science were born together in the cities of Ionia. This time is called the Ionian Enlightenment.

THE EGYPTIAN CONNECTION

Ionian nobles, including Alcaeus, were not above contacts with foreigners. Richest and strangest of foreign kingdoms was Egypt, from which came gold, ivory, wheat and papyrus, the best writing material. To preserve Egypt's independence, only recently regained from Assyrian domination, the pharaohs began hiring Greek hoplite mercenaries, already regarded as the world's best infantry. Some of these, employed in the far south of the country, left graffiti on the colossal statues of Abu Simbel that are still legible today. Greek merchants who penetrated into this enclosed, priest-ruled land were ultimately confined to one city, Naucratis in the Delta. Here Greeks from many different cities settled and traded, maintaining Hellenic customs in a very different world.

LYDIAN RULERS

Contacts with sophisticated peoples to the east first stimulated the Greeks, but the influence did not long remain one-way. In Anatolia the rich kingdom of Phrygia (its legendary king Midas' 'golden touch' suggests his immense wealth) was taken over by its neighbour Lydia in western Asia Minor *c.*680BC. Lydia's capital at Sardis was within easy reach of the coast, and Greek cities soon felt Lydian power encroaching on their cherished autonomy. Only Miletus, the largest and richest of the

Left: The expansion of Greek trade – north to the Black Sea, west to Italy and south to Egypt – opened Greek minds to richer, more sophisticated civilizations. It also made some Greeks much richer. Commerce was not at the time regarded as socially demeaning.

Right: Graffiti carved by Greek mercenaries in Egyptian service on the stones of Abu Simbel Temple in Upper Egypt indicate the fruitful interchange between Egyptian pharaohs and the Greeks in the 6th century BC. This special relationship ended with the Persian conquest of Egypt in 525BC.

Ionian cities, remained fully independent behind formidable walls. But the Lydian kings were generally benevolent rulers. They themselves came under such strong Greek influence that they were seen as philhellenes (supporters or admirers of things Greek).

Croesus, Lydia's most famous king, who came to the throne in 560BC, enriched the sanctuary at Delphi, holiest in the Greek world, employed Greek artists and helped to finance the vast Greek temple to Artemis (Diana) at Ephesus, later one of the Seven Wonders of the Ancient World. The Lydians traditionally introduced the first minted coins to the Greeks, who soon produced coins of great beauty themselves. Coinage further encouraged commerce, if widening the gap between rich and poor. Debts could now be computed, and wealth amassed, more easily. Above all, Lydia helped to shield the eastern Greeks from invading barbarians such as the Cimmerians, who ravaged Asia Minor in the 7th century, and from empires further east such as the Medes in Iran. At a battle in 585BC between Lydia and Media, an eclipse of the sun stopped the fighting. Both sides, awe-struck, agreed on the River Halys as a boundary.

PHILOSOPHY AND POETRY

This eclipse had been predicted by Thales, the first known Greek philosopher, who was also a scientist and was therefore interested in, rather than awed by, natural phenomena. A native of Miletus, he thought long and hard about what constituted ultimate reality. A school of philosophers followed him, called Milesian after Miletus. Thales' pupil Anaximander, who lived to *c*.536BC, made the first map of the known world, realizing that the Earth hung unsupported in space though not that it was spherical. To show that philosophers could be practical, Thales reputedly diverted the River Halys to let King Croesus cross it.

The period also saw a flowering of a new form of poetry, not long heroic epics but short, personal lyric verses, often of poignant beauty. (*Lyric* meant 'sung to music of the lyre', a harp-like instrument.) The most famous are the love poems of Sappho of Lesbos *c*.600BC, many addressed to the girls whom she reputedly taught. Only fragments of her bitter-sweet poetry survive. More typical were the witty lyrics of Alcaeus, Anacreon and Archilochus. Archilochus wrote: "Some lucky Thracian has my fine shield, I had to run and dropped it in a wood. But I got clean away, thank God! So damn the shield, I'll get another just as good."

Society, while still aristocratic, grew more pleasure-loving and relaxed. *Symposia* (leisurely drinking parties with conversation and entertainment) became popular among the wealthier.

Below: The Tholos or Sanctuary of Athena Pronaia at Delphi was once the holiest sanctuary in the Greek world.

SPARTA: THE UNIQUE STATE
700–500BC

Above: Spartans attributed their unique constitution to Lycurgus, a semi-mythical figure who reputedly created Sparta's almost totalitarian regime after the city had suffered a major defeat.

Below: The Eurotas valley, in which Sparta sits, is the most fertile in southern Greece, giving Sparta rural wealth.

Sheltered by mountains, the valley of the Eurotas in Laconia in the south-east corner of the Peloponnese was half-isolated. The Spartans, a Dorian people who settled there *c.*1000BC, retained ancient Dorian customs, such as common messes for all male citizens and tribal education for children, that had been abandoned by other Dorians except those in even more remote Crete. But Spartans felt themselves to be different from other Greeks. They were surrounded by non-Dorian (but Greek) peoples in Laconia, whom they reduced to serfdom as *helots* (land-bound slaves who provided food and produce for the ruling class, the *homoioi*), thereby gaining a valuable, if potentially dangerous, servile workforce.

By 700BC warfare had added the large, fertile territory of Messenia to the west, which was "good for ploughing and growing fruit", as the Spartan poet Tyrtaeus wrote. Despite being fellow Dorians, the Messenians were also enslaved. This conquest made Sparta the most powerful state in Greece. But it caused problems at home.

A RADICAL NEW CONSTITUTION

The wars had been won by Spartan hoplites, not aristocratic cavalry, but wealth was increasingly concentrated in the hands of a few. This caused discontent among ordinary Spartans struggling to maintain hoplites status. The resulting military weakness was shown up in defeat by Argos in 668BC and a revolt in Messenia. With Spartan power in danger of collapse, radical changes were needed.

Later, all reforms came to be attributed to Lycurgus, a semi-mythical figure, but the Delphic oracle, which Sparta regularly consulted, possibly played a part. Probably several individuals, including King Polydorus, were involved in helping to refound the state in the mid-7th century BC, giving it a constitution that was unusually complete and rigid. It was admired but not copied by other Greeks.

In theory, land was divided into equal lots owned inalienably by 9,000 *homoioi* (the elite ruling class, also known as 'Equals' and 'Spartiates'). They never worked their land but lived off the labour of the *helots*. The broad expanses of Messenia, reconquered by 640BC, gave Spartiates the landed wealth and leisure to train full time as soldiers. The Spartan army, distinguished by its scarlet cloaks and unbreakable discipline, became the one professional force in Greece, acknowledged as the best. In return for economic security, Spartiates surrendered their whole lives to the state.

DORIC DISCIPLINE

Every Spartan baby was examined by officials for deformities. Those considered unfit were exposed on a mountain. (Infanticide was practised in other Greek cities too but never so systematically.) At the age of seven, a boy was taken from his mother to begin his *agoge* (special training in a barracks). Wearing only a

thin tunic and no shoes, even in winter, he never had enough to eat, being expected to steal more food yet whipped if caught. At every stage he faced ferocious competition and punishments. Such training produced tough, obedient soldiers, taciturn – hence our word laconic (from Laconian) – dour and unimaginative.

At the age of 20 Spartiates had to win election to a mess, where they ate repellent meals, mostly 'Spartan black broth' (reputedly made from pork, blood, salt and vinegar). Homosexual affairs between prefects and younger boys were common. But Spartiates also had to produce children for the state after a strange marriage ceremony in which the bride's hair was shorn and she was dressed as a boy. Girls, too, exercised nearly naked, which shocked other Greeks.

Spartans were intensely pious, revering the gods, but they built few temples – Thucydides said that no one later seeing Sparta's sparse monuments would ever guess its power. Commerce was banned and there was no coinage, iron bars remaining the currency. Only *perioeci* ('dwellers around' in small towns who had to serve in the Lacadaemonian army), led normal lives. Every year 'war' was declared on the *helots*, during which potential rebels were secretly killed. Spartan art and poetry soon atrophied.

THE SPARTAN SYSTEM

Sparta strangely mixed oligarchy, democracy and monarchy. There were two kings – from the dynasties of the Agiads and

Above: From the age of seven Spartan boys faced endless military-style drill. Toughness, conformity and unflinching obedience to orders were the aim, all individualism being stamped out.

Below: In its earlier days, before the grim regimentation of the Lycurgic system, Spartan potters produced fine vases such as this of Prometheus.

THE SPARTANS AND ALCOHOL
Despite worshipping many gods, the Spartans never worshipped Dionysus, the wine god. Also no *symposia*, the convivial drinking parties, were held in Spartan high society. Instead, young Spartiates were warned of the evils of alcohol by having *helots* paraded grotesquely drunk before them, to demonstrate the effects of inebriation.

Eurypontids, both claiming descent from Hercules – who alone escaped the *agoge*. Only when leading the army abroad did they have real power. At home, they were constantly checked by the *ephors* (five officials chosen annually who wielded huge, if shadowy, power in this police state). The assembly consisted of all Spartans over the age of 30, who voted only on proposals put to it, one side shouting down the other – a method that Aristotle called childish but Jean-Jacques Rousseau later admired. There was also the *gerousia*, or senate, of men aged over 60 chosen for life.

Such a system was meant to defy all change, but some Spartiates finally became more equal than others. In the 4th century BC, as wealth from its newly gained empire flooded in, Lycurgus' system broke down. But by 550BC Sparta had forged a league of most states in the Peloponnese who were happy to follow it now that it seemed invincible.

ATHENS: REFORMERS AND TYRANTS 620–514BC

Above: Olives, which grow extremely well in Greece, became the main crop of Attic agriculture after Solon prohibited the export of wheat.

Right: The olive, mythical gift of the goddess Athena to her favoured city, is normally harvested in late winter or early spring. The trees take about 15–20 years to start bearing fruit and far longer to reach their prime. The olive-harvest was a popular topic for vase-painters, many of whose products were used to export the oil around the Mediterranean.

In the 7th century BC Athens was a relative backwater. Although Attica, long united under Athens, was one of Greece's largest states, it lacked wide fertile valleys. It was still ruled by a clique of Eupatrid (hereditary noble) families, who controlled the Areopagus, the supreme council. But Athens was not immune to wider economic and social changes. In 632BC Cylon, an aristocratic Olympic victor, seized the Acropolis, aiming to establish a tyranny. The *archon* (head official) Megacles – of the Eupatrid Alcmaeonid family, the most famous in Athenian history – tricked Cylon and his supporters out of the Acropolis and killed them. But the problems remained. Many poorer Athenians were *hektemoroi* (small farmers who owed their noble overlords a sixth of their produce). Falling into debt, they and their families might be enslaved and sold abroad, a fate that was even worse than a *helot*'s in Sparta.

In 625BC the Eupatrid law giver Dracon drew up and published the first written law code. Athenians could now see how severe their laws actually were: someone could supposedly be executed for stealing a cabbage. (These laws were later called 'draconian'.) Popular discontent with the status quo grew until in 594BC Solon, a Eupatrid but a noted critic of the rich, was given special powers. With them he launched a reform programme designed to avert tyranny by satisfying both the people and the rich.

"FREEING THE BLACK EARTH"

Solon's first measure was a "shaking off of debts". He stopped debt being secured on a person's liberty and freed all those already enslaved – he even tried to buy back Athenians sold abroad. He ordered the pulling up of stones that marked off land for aristocrats' tithes, "freeing the black earth" as he put it, and forbade the export of wheat from Attica to keep it cheap. Instead, he encouraged the export of olive oil; olive trees grow well in Attica, although they need 30 years to mature. Solon reformed the constitution, allowing all free citizens to attend the Assembly, which elected the *archons*. He established the Council of the 400, drawn by lot from the Assembly, as a preliminary debating body to balance the Areopagus. But he made both Eupatrids and rich commoners eligible for *archonship*

Right: The rapid growth of Athenian wealth and population under the Pisistratid 'tyrants' (meaning extra-constitutional rulers, not necessarily despots) in the 6th century BC led to a massive building programme. The huge Temple of Olympian Zeus proved too much even for the Pisitratid regime, however, and remained uncompleted for six centuries.

and so of the Areopagus, the highest court. Social divisions were now based on wealth not birth, allowing greater mobility. But Solon did not redistribute land as hoped or feared, for he was no revolutionary. "I gave the people such recognition as they deserved," he wrote, and went off on his travels. He left Athens more equitable if not democratic, for it was still led by aristocrats.

This was the problem. There were fierce divisions between the 'Coast' party of commercial interests and the 'Plain' of landowners, both led by irresponsible aristocrats. Years of bloody 'anarchy' – without elected *archons* – in the 580s saw war against next-door Megara go badly. Pisistratus, a noble who as *polemarch* (commander) had conquered Salamis island in 565BC, finally made himself tyrant in 561BC with other nobles' backing. They soon fell out and he was exiled. But he then made not one but two comebacks, the second time permanently in 546BC, supported by a third party of poorer farmers.

THE PISISTRATID REGIME
Once finally in power, Pisistratus surprised everyone by his moderation. Although some political rivals went into exile, there were no purges. Pisistratus helped Solon's reforms to take root by shielding the state from aristocratic faction. Unbullied by the rich, ordinary Athenians learnt to play a part in running their city. Pisistratus raised a tax of 10 per cent on farm produce, made loans on easy terms to help small farmers and started an economic boom, underpinned by stable government. To export Attic olive oil, superb new-style red figure vases

(on a black ground) were produced from 520BC onwards. Now Athenians became the finest of all Greek ceramicists. Athens also gained outposts on the Hellespont (Dardanelles), essential for protecting grain imports from the Black Sea. It still had only a tiny navy, however.

Athenian culture was not neglected either. Reputedly the first definitive edition of Homer's poems was compiled under Pisistratus' patronage, with ceremonial readings. He also inaugurated the Festival of the Great Dionysia, whose contests between different choruses later gave birth to Athenian tragedy and comedy. Among other monuments, he started a gigantic temple to Zeus, king of the gods, not completed for six centuries. When Pisistratus' sons Hippias and Hipparchus jointly succeeded their father at his death in 527BC and continued his policies, theirs must have seemed the most stable regime after Sparta's in Greece. But it was not to last.

Below: One of the 'Seven Sages of Greece', Solon, reformed the Athenian constitution, trying to avert social revolution or tyranny – unsuccessfully with regard to the latter.

ATHENS: THE DEMOCRATIC REVOLUTION 514–490BC

Above: The bright colours and alert energy of this koure *(young girl) embody Athens' optimistic energy at the dawn of democracy in the late 6th century* BC.

The trigger for the downfall of the Pisistratids was a quarrel over a boy's affections (very Greek, some might think), but the real causes went much deeper. By 514BC many states considered tyrants to be oppressive and turned for help to Sparta, which generally disliked tyrants as upstarts. When Harmodius and Aristogeiton, who were later hailed as liberators and had fine statues erected in their memory, killed Hipparchus for personal reasons in 514BC, the surviving Pisistratid, Hippias, became paranoid. Retreating to the Acropolis, he started a truly tyrannical reign of terror that brought about his own downfall.

THE ROLE OF CLEISTHENES

Cleisthenes, head of the Athenian Alcmaeonid family but currently in exile, had been wooing the Delphic oracle with gifts. Whenever Sparta consulted the oracle, it now replied: "Free Athens!" Finally, in 510BC a Spartan army under King Cleomones marched into Attica, and Hippias, with his supporters, fled to the Persians. Cleomones, like most Athenian nobles, then expected a return to the good old days of noble-led factions with the people merely acting as supporters. But Athens had changed. It was the genius of Cleisthenes to realize and take advantage of this.

After losing the election for the *archonship* in 508BC to Isagoras, who had Cleomones' backing, in 507BC Cleisthenes proposed a radical reordering of the whole state. In future the Assembly of all citizens voting together would be completely sovereign, and a new Council of 500, chosen by lot from all citizens irrespective of wealth, would act as a *probouletic* (preliminary debating) body. Cleisthenes abolished the old Ionic 'tribes' and replaced them with ten new ones, all artificial despite being named after ancient heroes. Each new tribe had three electoral wards called *trittyes* (thirds).

Right: The 'Treasury of the Athenians' at Delphi, lavishly built all in marble, was probably erected in the 490s BC by the young democracy in gratitude to Apollo's oracle, whose utterances "Free Athens!" had so aided the city.

These 30 *trittyes* contained *demes* from all three old rival factions: the city and its environs, the coastal lands and the uplands. Every citizen had to register afresh in a *deme*, which was administered by a locally elected *demarch*, and was then allocated to a *trittyes* and so to a tribe. This vastly reduced the influence of local squires on elections.

Unsurprisingly, Isagoras and his aristocratic supporters were horrified. They called on Cleomones, who had no time at all for such dangerous democratic ideas and marched straight back to Athens. There he exiled 700 Alcmaeonid supporters – Cleisthenes had already wisely withdrawn – re-established the old regime and then retired with Isagoras to the Acropolis for a celebratory dinner. But while they were celebrating, the noise of a popular rising in the streets below first amazed and then alarmed them. Although lacking any proper nobles to lead them, the people of Athens had risen in revolt on their own – an unprecedented event. Soon, surrounded and without provisions, the Spartans and Isagoras had to surrender ignominiously and leave Athens.

Cleisthenes now returned in triumph, and his reforms were implemented. He probably at this time added some immigrants from Ionia, long resident in the city,

to the citizen list. As a safety valve, to stop any individual growing too powerful, he also introduced a novel scheme: ostracism. Every year there would be a vote on whether to hold an ostracism. If 6,000 citizens wanted to, they would inscribe names of men to be ostracized on bits of pottery (*ostrakia*). The man most frequently named had to go into exile for ten years but did not lose his citizenship or property. Cleisthenes, whether or not he had intended to, had created the first full democracy in Greece, probably in the whole world.

DEMOCRACY TRIUMPHANT
The new democracy in Athens was soon to be put to the test. Cleomones, burning for revenge, summoned the armies of Sparta and her Peloponnesian allies, much the most formidable force in Greece, to invade Attica, while the Thebans and Chalcians, Athens' old enemies, attacked from the north-east. The Athenians were undaunted and marched out to Eleusis to meet the Spartan-led army – which promptly turned back. The Corinthians, a major contingent of the army, had changed their minds, while the other Spartan king, Demaratus, for reasons unknown, also went home, forcing Cleomones to follow suit. The Athenians then swung east to defeat the Thebans before crossing to Euboea, where they routed the Chalcians. They subsequently settled 4,000 colonists on Chalcian land.

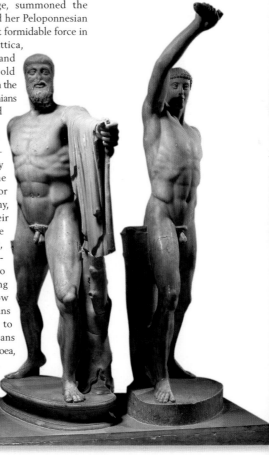

Below: Harmodius and Aristogeiton are shown here as the heroic liberators who killed the tyrant Hipparchus in 514BC. Although only a Roman copy of the second pair of original Greek bronzes – which were made in the 470s BC, the first pair having been carried off by the Persians in 480BC – the original group's dynamic strength shines through. It typified Athenian democracy's abounding new self-confidence.

CHAPTER II

THE PERSIAN WARS

499–478 BC

The great war between the Greeks and Persians was the pivotal event in Greek – and ultimately European – history. If the Greek cities had been defeated and become subjects of the Persian Empire, Greek brilliance could have been dimmed. The emergence of full democracy might have been stunted, even aborted. Defeating the Persians gave the Athenians the confidence to experiment further with radical democracy at home. But the Persians, although defeated, were never despicable foes. Although the Greeks liked to mock their enemies' 'Asiatic luxury', the Persians proved both formidable fighters and wise rulers.

In a few decades Persia had created the world's first global empire, stretching from the southern Balkans to the fringes of India. It governed its subjects with enlightened imperialism, tolerating different customs and gods. Life for the conquered had advantages, which some Greeks appreciated, but it lacked the one element that Greeks prized above all: total freedom. The Persian invasion of Greece achieved what nothing else did: it united enough of the feuding Greek states to defeat the invaders. Even Spartans and Athenians fought side by side. But the final glory must go to Athens, whose citizens were prepared to see their temples and homes burnt twice by the Persians rather than surrender. Greek victory over Persia made classical Athens, and so Western civilization, possible.

Left: The grand staircase of the palace of Darius I at Persepolis, ceremonial capital of the immense Persian Empire.

THE RISE OF PERSIA
550–494BC

Far to the east of the Greek cities, in mountainous southern Iran, lived a people whom the Greeks called Persians. Unsophisticated but indomitable, fine archers and horsemen, they long paid tribute to their cousins the Medes, whose empire rivalled Lydia's and Babylon's.

CYRUS, KING OF KINGS

In 550BC Cyrus of Persia unexpectedly overthrew the king of Media, becoming ruler of a united Achaemenid empire (named after Cyrus' ancestor). He enrolled the Medes as such almost-equal partners that Greeks later called collaborators or supporters of Persia 'medizers'.

Such distant events meant little to most Greeks. They seldom ventured far into Asia, although some knew of Babylon, the greatest city on Earth. But in 546BC Croesus of Lydia, an Asian monarch the Greeks knew well, attacked this new empire. He had been encouraged by the Delphic oracle's typically ambiguous pronouncement: "If you cross the River Halys [the frontier] you will destroy a mighty empire."

The first battle proved inconclusive, so Croesus withdrew west to his capital at Sardis, considering the fighting over as winter approached. He was wrong: Cyrus followed him and outside Sardis defeated Lydia's fine cavalry by sending ahead a line of camels, whose smell panics untrained horses. Sardis, with its treasures, fell to Cyrus.

Harpagus – Cyrus' best general and a Mede – then moved along the coast with a huge army, with most cities submitting to the new superpower. Some, however, preferred flight to surrender: the whole population of Phocaea sailed off. But life

for the conquered was tolerable. Persia usually reappointed existing tyrants, democracy being still almost unknown, although the tribute paid – 400 talents of silver– was siphoned to the distant Persian capital at Susa, not spent locally. Susa was linked to Sardis by the Royal Road of 2,400km/1,500 miles, down which messengers galloped bearing royal edicts. Some Persian nobles soon acquired estates in Asia Minor.

In 539BC Cyrus took Babylon 'the mighty city', liberating the captive Jews, most of whom returned to Jerusalem to rebuild their Temple. Persian rulers, though Zoroastrians (precursors of

Above: The Persian kings acquired unprecedented wealth as well as power. But they only minted coins, such as these gold and silver pieces, for use in cities in their western provinces.

Right: Croesus' notoriously rich kingdom of Lydia (in Asia Minor) was the first to fall to the Persian advance. Defeated by Cyrus the Great of Persia in 546BC, Croesus was, according to Herodotus, put on a pyre to be burnt, a scene shown on this vase of c.480BC.

the Parsees), were religiously tolerant. Cyrus' conquest of the Fertile Crescent made him the mightiest monarch yet, aptly hailed as Great King or King of Kings. Cambyses, succeeding his father in 530BC, annexed Egypt, but when he died mysteriously in 522BC the empire was shaken by rebellions. Darius, an Achaemenid relative, had to crush numerous rivals after proclaiming himself Great King.

DEMOCRACY AND REVOLT

Once secure on the throne, Darius determined to march into Europe. In 512BC he had pontoon bridges (mostly of Ionian ships) built for his army to cross the Bosphorus and River Danube. He vanished into the Scythian steppes for so long that some Greeks suggested destroying the Danube bridge – an idea wisely rejected, for Darius finally reappeared. Despite failure in Scythia, Persian power advanced along the north Aegean coast until even Macedonia acknowledged it. In 500BC Aristagoras, tyrant of powerful Miletus, suggested to Artaphernes, the Persian satrap (governor), a joint attack on Naxos, a Cycladic island. Artaphernes agreed, but it proved a fiasco. Aristagoras, fearing for his power if not his life, now jumped from being a pro-Persian tyrant to an anti-Persian democrat.

It was a popular move. The democratic revolt he started spread fast across an Ionia tired of foreign kings and domestic tyrants and inspired by Athens' new democracy. The geographer Hecataeus suggested seizing temple treasures to finance the revolt – in vain, but a Pan-Ionian Council was called, a common currency adopted and appeals sent to Greece for help. The Spartans, typically parochial, ignored them, but Athens and Eretria sent ships. In 498BC allied forces marched inland to capture and burn Sardis. Returning, they were caught in open country by Persia's superb cavalry and routed. While the Athenians returned home chastened, other Greeks from Byzantium to Cyprus now joined the revolt.

THE FALL OF MILETUS

Fierce fighting in Cyprus in 497BC, with the Greeks victorious at sea but defeated on land, led to the island's reconquest. Soon Persia subdued the northern states too. Yet the Ionian fleet, 350 ships strong, remained intact at Lade off Miletus, itself now besieged. On the fleet hung the fate of the revolt, but Ionian sailors chafed at the discipline needed to maintain battle-readiness while Persian gold won over many doubters.

When battle finally came in 494BC, the powerful Samian and Lesbian sections deserted and the other Ionians were defeated. The fall of Miletus followed and Persian revenge was brutal: most Milesians were killed or enslaved, their boys castrated, their daughters sold into harems, their city repopulated with others. The revolt was over. But, in a statesman-like act, Persia allowed some Ionian cities to remain as democracies.

Above: The tomb of Cyrus the Great at Pasargadae in the Iranian mountains. Cyrus (reigned c.560–530BC) was the founder of the Persian Empire, defeating the Medes, Lydians and Babylonians and annexing their kingdoms.

Right: Under Darius I, king 522–486BC, Persia's empire reached its greatest extent, stretching from the Danube to the Aral Sea. In the west, Darius' armies clashed with the mainland Greeks. He ordered the building of the first palaces at Persepolis, whose impressive ruins survive.

THE BATTLE OF MARATHON
490BC

Above: The tumulus at Marathon, raised over the bodies of Athenian soldiers killed in 490BC, commemorates the first real Greek victory over the Persians.

With the Ionian revolt crushed, the Great King Darius turned to the Greek cities that had helped the rebels burn down Sardis, his western capital: Eretria on the island of Euboea and Athens. Envoys went around Greece demanding earth and water as tokens of submission. Many states, overawed by Persian power, complied. But at Sparta the envoys were thrown down a well and told to find earth and water there, which enraged Darius.

Athens responded no better, trying and executing his envoys. However, Cleomenes, that unusually dynamic Spartan king, was deposed around then, having gone mad – or so it was said officially. He was probably killed in secret.

In spring 490BC a Persian fleet commanded by Datis sailed into the Aegean carrying an army around 25,000 strong, including the cavalry victorious earlier in Ionia. Crossing the Aegean, the Persians took and sacked Naxos, enslaving its citizens. However, Datis offered incense at Apollo's shrine on nearby Delos, prudently honouring the Greek god. As the armada sailed on, island after island submitted, giving hostages. In July the Persians reached Euboea, where Datis landed his army. After five days of fighting, Eretria was betrayed by some nobles who preferred Persian rule to local democracy. The city was burnt to the ground in awful warning. Then the fleet turned south-east for Attica.

On board was Hippias, the now aged ex-tyrant of Athens, who hoped that the Persians would restore him to power and still had some contacts in the city. He told the Persians the best spot to land: the open beach at Marathon 40km/25 miles north of Athens, which made perfect cavalry country.

MILTIADES' STRATEGY

Miltiades, who was an Athenian but also the tyrant of the Chersonese with a fine military reputation, had persuaded the Athenians that the army should go out to meet the Persians when they landed, rather than skulk behind Athens' walls. So almost the whole hoplite force, c.10,000 men, marched north in time to

Left: The Persians relied mainly on skilled archers and fine cavalry, for their infantry was generally inferior to the Greeks'.

THE FIRST MARATHON

The race against time back to Athens by the hoplites involved marching "as fast as their legs could carry them". They covered 40km/25 miles in six hours – the very first 'marathon'.

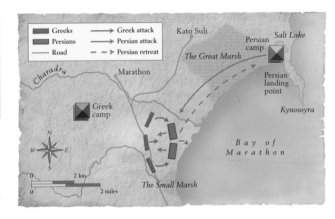

stop the Persians break out of their beach-head. The *polemarch* (commander) was Callimarchus, but Miltiades, though only a divisional general, actually decided the tactics. A messenger, Philippides, was sent running the 225km/140 miles to beg the Spartans for help.

The Spartans, although pledged to assist, were celebrating their festival of Carnea and would not move before the full moon of 12 August. Their religious scruples were probably genuine; so was their reluctance to leave the Peloponnese. Philippides was returning disappointed when, in the blinding midday heat, he encountered the god Pan – an encouraging meeting, for Pan announced that the Athenians would triumph.

Dug in above the plain of Marathon, the Athenians watched and waited for the enemy to make the next move. So, looking up from their camp by the marshes or beached ships, did the Persians. The Athenians were encouraged by the arrival of 800 hoplites from their ally Plataea, the little city's whole army. But, still outnumbered, the Athenians were really awaiting the Spartans, due to march within a week. The Persians, who had spies everywhere, knew this too. Finally, Datis secretly re-embarked his cavalry at night to take Athens by surprise. But an Ionian, slipping across the lines, warned the Athenians: "The horsemen have left!" After persuading his co-generals, Miltiades ordered a general attack.

NOVEL BATTLE TACTICS

Even without cavalry, the Persians outnumbered the Greeks, so Miltiades decided on a novel tactic: the Greek centre would thin out to match the

length of the Persian line. As the sun rose, the Athenian citizen-army began its descent to the plain, a mass of armour bristling with spears. In its centre Themistocles and Aristides, political opponents reconciled, commanded their respective tribes. As the Greeks closed to within 160m/175yd of the Persians – within bowshot – they broke into a run to crash into the lighter-armed enemy.

Soon their wings had driven back the Persians but their centre, facing the best Persian troops, was itself repelled. With remarkable discipline for amateur soldiers, the Greek wings swung to close in on the Persian centre. After fierce fighting, the battle turned, Persians fleeing in panic towards their ships or into the marshes, pursued by the Athenians. At the battle's end, reputedly only 192 Greeks had been killed for 6,400 Persians.

But Miltiades knew that the Persian fleet was still sailing for an unprotected Athens. Covered in dust and blood, the weary hoplites raced back to the south coast, arriving just in time. The Persians, seeing the armoured ranks drawn up again above the beach, abandoned their attempted landing and sailed off. Athenian hoplites had beaten the hitherto invincible Persian army in open battle. The Spartans, arriving belatedly, could only applaud, visit the battlefield and then go home quietly impressed.

Above: After the Persians had landed and made camp by the Bay of Marathon, the Athenian army occupied the hills above – an ideal spot for keeping watch, and for launching a charge downhill.

Below: The stele (funerary carving) on the tumulus at Marathon portrays an Athenian citizen-soldier, one of the hoplites who routed the Persians.

COUNTDOWN TO WAR
488–481BC

Above: View of Mount Athos in northern Greece, off whose rocky shore Mardonius was once shipwrecked in a storm.

Below: Persia's lengthy preparations for the grand invasion of 480BC included cutting a canal through the flat peninsula north of Mt Athos shown below. This was intended both to protect the invasion fleet from storms that had wrecked earlier ships and to overawe the Greeks.

For ordinary Athenians victory at Marathon appeared to lift the threat of Persian invasion for good. But they were wrong. The Great King was only marginally harmed by what was to him a peripheral battle. It needed to be avenged, of course, but the Persian Empire was still expanding and the conquest of Greece – an invitingly divided if troublesome land – remained on the agenda. This time, however, the Achaemenid Empire would act like the superpower it was. Overwhelming force on land and sea would be gathered to shock and awe Greece into submission.

PREPARATIONS FOR WAR

Mardonius, a noted young Persian general, had earlier been shipwrecked in a storm off Mt Athos in northern Greece, so it was decided to dig a canal through the Athos peninsula's neck to avoid this recurring. Thousands of conscripted workers took three years to dig a canal deep enough for galleys, while a pontoon bridge was built over the Hellespont (Dardanelles) to let the invading army cross speedily. Destroyed by storms, it was hastily rebuilt. Supplies were stockpiled in forts along the Aegean north coast and the River Strymon in Macedonia bridged. The death of Darius in late 486BC interrupted preparations only briefly. The throne passed smoothly to Xerxes his son (and Cyrus' grandson) and a revolt in Egypt was suppressed. Finally, in April 481BC, the Great King left Susa – a date marked by a solar eclipse – and slowly marched west with imposing majesty.

Forces had been levied from across his huge empire, from Africa to India. Some were not experienced fighters but many, such as the Persian cavalry, Saka mounted archers, fishmail-armoured Medes and the 10,000 Immortals (royal guards), were. The fleet, too, was mostly professional, its 300 Phoenician galleys being thought the best afloat. Herodotus, seldom reliable on figures, totals the Persian forces at 1.7 million – an absurd figure, such a horde being impossible to feed. Modern estimates suggest *c*.250,000 soldiers, supported by a fleet of *c*.600 warships.

To deny Greece help from its Western compatriots, Carthage was urged to attack Greek Sicily. Meanwhile, Persian gold subverted north Greece. Macedonia was already a client state; Thessaly, due south, seemed ready to 'medize', its nobility favouring Persia. Beyond, central Greece looked open to pressure, while many Aegean islands were Persian-controlled. The stage was set.

THE GROWTH OF DEMOCRACY

Back in Athens, at first it was politics as usual. Celebrated for his Marathon victory, Miltiades led an attack on Paros

Left: The trireme, with 170 rowers (all free citizens) and 30 marines, was the backbone of the Athenian fleet by 480BC. Although such ships certainly had three tiers of oars, how they really worked has never been established. The Olympias, a recreation launched in 1987, moved only slowly, soon exhausting even its youthful crew.

Above: The years leading up to the Persian invasion of 480BC saw the emergence of full democracy in Athens and, not by coincidence, of classical naturalism in the arts, exemplified by the 'Critias Boy' of c.482BC.

in 489BC. He failed abysmally, was prosecuted, heavily fined and died in debt. After 487BC election to the *archonship* was replaced by sortition (lottery). This reduced the powers of the *polemarch* (military *archon*), for a randomly chosen leader might lack military experience. Instead, the ten *strategoi* (generals) elected from each tribe became the real commanders. This marked a further advance in democracy: anyone, not just the rich, could be elected *strategos*. Ostracism was now used, probably for the first time. Among those ostracized were Pisistratids and Alcmaeonid aristocrats. The young democracy was flexing its muscles.

THE BIRTH OF ATHENS' NAVY

Athens remained mainly a land power, proud of its hoplites' victory at Marathon. One man, however, saw danger in this. Themistocles, a stocky, energetic man, brilliant at courting the people, was a radical democrat though aristocratic himself, at least on his father's side. Elected *archon* in 493BC, he began in the 480s to press for a huge expansion of the navy. This was unpopular with the rich, who would have to pay for it, while small farmers saw no need for it. When in

483BC a huge new lode of silver was found at the mines of Laurium, a great debate began in Athens about how to spend it. Aristides, now the conservative leader (nicknamed 'the Just' because he famously took no bribes), suggested distributing the windfall among the citizens, an idea with obvious appeal.

But Themistocles urged that it all be spent on a massive new navy of triremes, the triple-tiered galleys that now dominated sea war. As a Persian threat still seemed remote, Themistocles pointed instead to the island of Aegina visible across the water, whose ships raided Attic coasts with impunity. His eloquence finally carried the day.

A crash programme was begun that within three years gave Athens the largest navy in Greece: 200 triremes, each requiring a crew of 170 citizen rowers and 30 sailors and marines. This vast new force – which committed ordinary Athenians to learn to fight at sea, sweating at their oars rather than parading proudly on land – was built and trained within three years. Just in time, it turned out. Meanwhile Aristides was ostracized, Athenians sickening of hearing him forever called 'the Just'.

THERMOPYLAE: LEONIDAS AND 'THE 300' 480BC

Above: In Persia's grand army of c.250,000 men – the largest force yet assembled – were tens of thousands of archers. They fired so many arrows at the Spartans at Thermopylae that the Greeks joked at being able to fight in the shade.

In late 481BC news of the huge army being assembled at Sardis reached the Greeks, its numbers amplified by the Persians, masters of psychological warfare. Persian envoys again went around Greece demanding submission. Most cities prevaricated. Athens and Sparta called a Panhellenic League at the Corinth Isthmus, to which 40 states sent envoys. Many did not. Swallowing its pride, Athens accepted Spartan leadership on land *and* sea, despite providing most of the fleet. The League warned possible 'medizers' that their lands would be 'tithed to Apollo', i.e. taken from them, if they collaborated.

THE ORACLE'S PROPHECY

But Greeks were hardly encouraged to resist by the Delphic oracle's doom-laden prophecies. "Fly far, far away; Leave home, town and castle and do not stay," it told the Athenians. When they asked again, they were told to trust in the "wooden walls" but warned: "Divine Salamis will destroy the children of women." This perplexed the Athenian Assembly, some taking "wooden walls" to mean those once surrounding the Acropolis, others their new fleet. Themistocles, now Athens' effective leader, favoured the latter, and his advice was accepted: if necessary, the Athenians would evacuate their entire city and take to the sea. Their decision saved Greece.

DEFENCE POSITIONS

In June, when some Thessalians suggested holding the pass at Tempe beneath Mt Olympus, 10,000 hoplites went north. They had to return hastily, for Persian forces found other undefended passes. The next possible line was in central Greece, where the mountains almost touched the sea at Thermopylae. A fleet based at Artemisium in west Euboea could support an army there. King Leonidas, with an elite of 300 older Spartiates ("all with living sons") set out, collecting allied troops en route until 7,000 hoplites manned an old wall at Thermopylae. Meanwhile, 200 triremes sailed north to Artemisium. There they awaited the Persian colossus.

This took its time, advancing in slow splendour, "drinking rivers dry" as June passed into July. From Delphi came a cryptic last message: "Pray to the winds!" Greeks knew that, as summer advanced,

Left: As news of Persian invasion plans reached the Greeks in late 481BC, a pan-hellenic Congress was called at Corinth, the wealthy city controlling the Isthmus. There 40 cities agreed plans that gave the Spartans overall command at land and sea and threatened retribution for any state that 'medized' (collaborated with the Persians).

sudden storms could arise in the Aegean, knowledge the Persians lacked. Leonidas was not on a suicide mission, although the Delphic oracle had prophesied Sparta's fall unless one of its kings died. He hoped to hold the Persians long enough for the main Spartan army, due to celebrate the Carnaean and Olympic festivals in August, to march north. Thermopylae was a splendid position provided it was not outflanked by sea or by land. But there were paths over the mountains, known to locals.

In August, the ground shaking beneath their feet, the Persians finally arrived. So did the winds, gales scattering both Greek and Persian fleets. Xerxes, who could not let his huge army stand still for long or it would starve, ordered a direct assault on the Greeks by heavy infantry – Medes used to mountain warfare. They were not, however, used to Spartiates in their killing prime and made no progress against the hoplite wall. Then the elite Immortals joined the battle, to be repelled also.

THE BATTLE OF THERMOPYLAE
At sea things were more equal, both fleets reassembling, only battered. But a Persian force, sent to outflank the Greeks

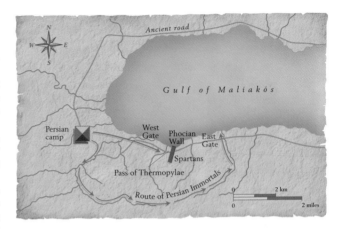

Above: The narrow pass at Thermopylae, where the mountains then nearly touched the sea, provided the best defensive position in Greece. Sparta's king Leonidas, with an advance army of 7,000 men (including 300 Spartiates) marched north to hold it. But a mountain path allowed the Persians finally to circumvent the Greeks.

Below: This statue of a Spartan warrior – possibly even a portrait of King Leonidas himself – reveals the disciplined determination that made Spartans the best soldiers in Greece.

DELPHI'S AMBIGUOUS ROLE
The Delphic oracle, sacred to Apollo, was the most revered in Greece. Its site, stunningly beautiful, was called *omphalos* (navel of the world). There the Greeks dedicated many of their finest shrines and offerings. Its Pythean priestess gave famously obscure replies to questions, so preserving its reputation for infallibility. But Delphi's role in the great Persian wars was so inglorious that it could be suspected almost of 'medizing'. In 480BC Persian power appeared overwhelming to the shrewd priests, and Greece's chance of victory looked poor. The Delphic priests were realists: better to maintain a diplomatic neutrality than openly support either side.

by sailing down Euboea's east coast, was wrecked, removing a major threat. The running naval battle that followed in the straits off Artemisium saw the Greeks, though outnumbered, undefeated. Then catastrophic news from Thermopylae changed everything.

Persian gold had found a local traitor, Ephialtes, to guide them over a mountain path to behind the wall. The Immortals followed him on a night march up to a pass where some Phocians, stationed as guards, panicked, withdrawing to let the Persians descend.

Leonidas had just enough warning to send off most troops before being surrounded. Then, with his Spartiates, some unwilling Thebans and dogged Thespians, probably about 1,500 men in all, he took his last stand. This was bloody and desperate, the Spartans fighting with bare hands after their swords and spears had splintered, until finally all lay dead around the corpse of their king. The road to Athens lay open.

SALAMIS: VICTORY AT SEA
480BC

Above: The island of Aegina, with its fine temple to Apheia, sheltered many Athenian refugees forced to evacuate their city.

Below: Themistocles, the Athenian leader, realizing that the Greek fleet lacked the skill and numbers to win a battle in open waters, tricked the Persians into sending their fleet into the narrows between Salamis island and the mainland. There the Greeks' heavier but inexperienced galleys crowded the Persians together so that they could not move, and so won decisively.

Days after Thermopylae, Themistocles reached Piraeus with the battle-scarred Greek fleet. It had slipped away by night after hearing of Leonidas' end. He now oversaw the evacuation of Athens. Women and children trundled possessions down to embark for Aegina, Troezen (which offered to educate all Athens' children) and Salamis. This small island became the Panhellenic League's headquarters and the tented city of Athens-in-exile. Not everything could be taken – one dog swum loyally after his master's boat, dying as he reached land. Nor would every Athenian leave. Some diehards retreated to the Acropolis behind wooden barricades. After firing the barricades, the Persians captured the citadel. They killed everyone there, including priests and priestesses, burning the temples – an act of sacrilegious terror never forgotten. They looted the main city while the Great King deliberated.

A NAVAL WAITING GAME
At Salamis there was disagreement among the Greeks. Some Peloponnesians, alarmed as the Persian fleet neared

Salamis, wanted to retreat to the Isthmus, where a wall had been built. This option, which abandoned all hope of regaining Athens quickly, was rejected by Themistocles. He also realized that the Greek fleet, outnumbered and less skilled than the Persian, must not fight in open waters. Battle at Artemisium had shown that only at close quarters could Greeks hope to defeat Persians. It was necessary to be bottled up at Salamis, as the other Greek leaders finally accepted. A waiting game followed, but neither side could afford to wait for too long.

Persia had problems too. It had lost so many ships – through storms and enemy action – that it no longer had overwhelming naval superiority. The Greeks had about 300 seaworthy triremes by this time, the Persians probably only around 100 more. Persia could not afford to divide its fleet again, as it had before Artemisium, to threaten the Peloponnese simultaneously. Also, it was already mid-September. The campaigning season would not last much longer before autumnal storms began.

GREEK TRICKERY
Xerxes was therefore delighted when a secret messenger arrived from Themistocles, claiming his master was really the king's friend. The Greeks, he announced, were divided – the Persians must have found this credible – with many planning to flee. All the Persians had to do was to send ships to the straits' exits to catch the Greek triremes sailing off at dawn. (Sails were stowed away while fighting.) Xerxes gave his orders: Egyptian galleys would guard the western exit while the main fleet, of Phoenicians, Ionians and Carians, would enter the eastern straits to seize the fleeing Greeks. He himself would oversee his forces from a throne on the shore.

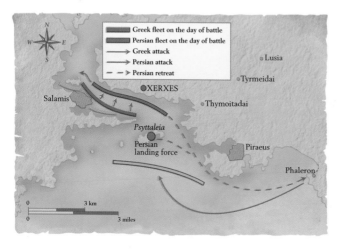

Greek fleet on the day of battle
Persian fleet on the day of battle
Greek attack
Persian attack
Persian retreat

Lusia
Tyrmeidai
XERXES
Salamis
Thymoitadai
Psyttaleia
Persian landing force
Piraeus
Phaleron

0   3 km
0   3 miles

That fateful night, probably the 19/20 September, Persia's ships sailed to their appointed stations.

THE BATTLE OF SALAMIS

However, Themistocles' message was a hoax designed to lure the Persians into the Salamis straits, less than 1.6km/1 mile wide. According to Herodotus, only Themistocles knew of this. But the overall plan must have been widely discussed and agreed earlier, for the Greeks reacted swiftly to news of the Persian advance brought by Aristides. (All Athenian exiles had been recalled.)

As the sun rose over Salamis, the Persian ships nosed forward under their royal master's eye: Phoenicians on the right closest to the mainland, Carians and Cilicians in the centre, Ionians on the left. Facing them were Athenian ships on the Greek left, seemingly recoiling in fear, Peloponnesians in the centre and Aeginetans on the right. Xerxes saw far-off Corinthian ships hoisting sail and appearing to flee westward, as he had been told. All seemed to be going to plan.

Suddenly the Athenians stopped backing to surge forward, singing a *paean* (hymn). The Phoenician flagship, commanded by a brother of Xerxes, was attacked first, its royal admiral killed as he boarded an Athenian trireme. Soon the heavier Greek galleys were smashing into Persians ships too tight-packed to manoeuvre or even row properly. Some of the Persian fleet beached their crippled ships on the mainland. Several Phoenician

captains were summarily executed by Xerxes for cowardice. Queen Artemisia of Halicarnassus, a Persian vassal, won his praise for apparently sinking a Greek ship, but this was actually a Persian galley blocking her escape. The Corinthians now returned to join the battle while the Egyptian squadron still waited idly.

By the afternoon the Greeks had won a crushing victory: only 40 of their own ships sunk for 200 of the Persians, the Phoenicians suffering especially. Persian power had experienced its first momentous defeat. King Xerxes returned ignominiously but safely by the same road to Asia. He left behind his unbeaten and large professional army, and much of Greece still in Persian hands.

Above: A 19th-century artist's colourful vision of the Greek fleet re-entering the Piraeus, the port of Athens, in triumph after the Battle of Salamis.

Below: King Xerxes ordered the building of a pontoon bridge over the Hellespont (Dardanelles) to allow the immense Persian army to cross from Asia to Europe early in 480BC. Jean Adrien Guignet's 19th-century painting shows Xerxes at the Hellespont.

PLATAEA: VICTORY ON LAND
479BC

The Athens to which its citizens returned that autumn was a gutted, half-ruined city. There was little comfort there. Nor were the Persians safely distant. The Persian general Mardonius, allowed to cherry pick an army for his command in Greece, had chosen the best – Persian and Median heavy cavalry, Sakae mounted archers – before settling in Thessaly for the winter. There began a war of words and nerves. Paradoxically, the Athenians, whose navy had effectively won the war at sea, now needed the Peloponnesians to fight a land battle in Boeotia to prevent Persia re-invading Attica.

AN OFFER OF PEACE...
The Spartans, with the immediate threat to the Peloponnese removed, were again loath to commit themselves, being worried about Argos, their old enemy close to home. Further arguments at League headquarters in Corinth produced no agreement, although when Themistocles visited Sparta he was fêted as a hero. This did him little good in Athens, where his

Above: A statuette from the 6th century BC showing a typically tough Spartan hoplite soldier, the victor of Plataea.

opponents, the formerly ostracized Aristides and Xanthippus, were elected *strategoi* (generals) for 479BC. To Athens that spring came Alexander I of Macedonia, a wily monarch who had involuntarily entertained the Great King earlier. The offer he brought to the Athenians amid the rubble of their wrecked Agora sounded tempting: the Great King would, if Athens changed sides, not only forgive all of Athens' past acts against him but grant it special self-governing status, like Tyre or Sidon, money to restore her temples and support against her enemies. "Why be so mad as to resist the King?" asked Alexander. "You can never beat him and cannot hold out forever."

... REJECTED
The Athenians responded magnificently: "We know well enough that Persian power is many times greater than ours... But we want above all to be free, so we will never surrender... Tell Mardonius that the Athenians say: 'While the sun takes his normal path, we will make no agreement with Xerxes, but will defend ourselves, trusting in the gods and heroes who fight for us and whose temples he has burnt'." With this Alexander was dismissed. In June, Mardonius swept south again into Attica, and Athenians evacuated their city for the second time in ten months. Their envoys in Sparta warned that they might be forced to accept Mardonius' peace offers after all.

Left: After their victories, the Greeks liked to portray their opponents as unmanly cowards. This vase shows a Persian almost running away. In fact Persians were fine soldiers, despite defeats on land and sea in 480/79BC, but Greek hoplites made far better infantry than their Persian counterparts, as Plataea showed.

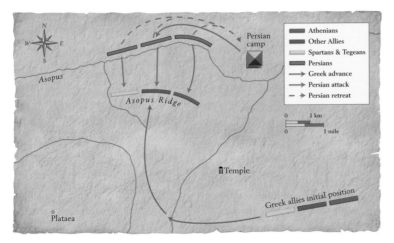

Left: The Persian army under Mardonius met the massed Greek hoplite forces in 479BC in a plain near Plataea in central Greece for the deciding land battle. When the Greeks began moving from their hilltop positions, Mardonius attacked their exposed flanks. But the disciplined Spartan phalanx routed the Persians.

Suddenly, Sparta's *ephors* announced that their army was already on the march with its allies. Mardonius, on hearing the news, torched all Athens before withdrawing to Boeotia, good country for horsemen.

PLATAEA: THE SPARTAN VICTORY
Mardonius' army numbered 60–70,000, judging by the size of the fortified camp he built near Thebes. In contrast, Aristides led 8,000 Athenian hoplites to join the League forces at Eleusis under the command of the Spartan regent Pausanias. (One Spartan king was still a boy, the other was Leotychides, commanding the fleet.) There they swore the Oath of Plataea, which began: "I will fight to the death and will not count my life more precious than freedom." It marked the high point of Greek unity. Then the hoplite army of *c.*40,000 men, the largest yet assembled, crossed into Boeotia. It took up a position on the slopes of Mt Cithaeron above the River Asopus.

There both sides waited, for Pausanias would not descend into a plain favourable to cavalry, while Mardonius would not attack uphill against hoplites. Mardonius finally sent mounted archers under Masistius, a famed nobleman, to make the Greek hoplites break rank. But Masistius was himself killed, his death grieving the Persians. The Greeks were less well supplied with food and water than the Persians, however, especially after their main spring had been destroyed, and so Pausanias decided to move the Greek army east toward Plataea, on to the low Asopus ridge, to improve water supplies. They began moving by night – a difficult manoeuvre that found many not in their new posts at dawn.

Mardonius, seeing the Greeks in such confusion, ordered an attack on the Spartans and their Tegean allies: *c.*11,000 men cut off from the main army. While Theban hoplites attacked the separated Athenians, Persian archers hailed arrows at the Spartans, killing many men. Yet Pausanias would not give the order to charge until the omens from sacrifices predicted victory. When they finally did, the Spartans rolled forwards, their disciplined phalanx carving a way through the Persians. After Mardonius, conspicuous on his white horse, was killed, his troops broke and fled toward their fort. But this proved to be no refuge, as the Athenians stormed it, killing all inside.

This battle marked the end of the Persian invasion. On the same day traditionally, the Greek fleet across the Aegean defeated the Persian fleet at Mycale (a naval battle fought on land), to which the Persians had retreated. This completed the Greeks' triumph.

Below: Spartan hoplites such as this soldier proved superior to the Persians at Plataea, the greatest land battle yet fought in Greece.

VICTORY IN THE WEST
480–474 BC

Above: Coins such as this, showing a triumphant charioteer and a winged nike (victory), were struck to celebrate victories such as Gelon's defeat of Carthage at Himera in 480BC.

Above: The Greeks produced the world's first really beautiful coins, often to celebrate victories. This fine piece commemorates the Syracusan victory over the Carthaginians in 480BC.

Right: Greek colonies spread throughout all Sicily except the north-west, where the Carthaginians maintained some fortified trading posts. The island's fertile interior remained inhabited mostly by native Sicels, who only slowly became Hellenized.

Before 500BC, Carthaginian and west Greek colonies had only occasionally fought each other. The Carthaginians, who were primarily merchants, established what were really large fortified trading posts, while the Greek colonies often became rich trading and farming cities. Carthage had prevented Greek colonization of southern Spain, Corsica and Sardinia, but in Sicily it had only three small cities in the north-west around Palermo. By contrast, Greek cities lined Sicily's south, east and north-east coasts.

Tyrants were a common form of government in western Greek cities around 500BC, gaining power easily amid the recurrent political crises. Gelon, already tyrant of Gela, seized Syracuse in 485BC and made it capital of what became Sicily's most powerful state. He forcibly moved to Syracuse the luckless populations of Gela and other nearby cities. Linked by marriage to Theron, tyrant of Acragas (Agrigento), the second largest Greek city in Sicily, Gelon treated his poorer citizens badly, enfranchizing only the rich. His power lay in his many mercenaries, whom he made citizens of

Syracuse. But his fleet of 200 triremes and army of 20,000 hoplites made him formidable, and in 481BC the Panhellenic League begged for his assistance against Persia. In return, he demanded leadership of the League either by land or sea, both unacceptable to Sparta. As it turned out, Gelon had pressing problems close to home and gave no help to the League.

CARTHAGINIAN EXPANSION
The Persians, probably using the Phoenicians as intermediaries, had urged Carthage to distract the western Greeks.

IN PRAISE OF TYRANNY
Pindar and Bacchylides, among the greatest poets of the 5th century BC, hymned the achievements of the tyrants Gelon and Hieron, their poems dwelling on the luxurious splendours of both their courts. Hieron also made lavish offerings to the Greek shrines at Olympia and Delphi, the most famous probably being the superb bronze charioteer of c.470BC.

Divisions among the Greeks now gave Carthage, already larger and richer than any other city in the Mediterranean, an opportunity to gain control of all Sicily. Theron of Acragas had just expelled Terillus, ruler of Himera, a Greek city on the north coast. Terillus appealed to the Greek tyrant of Rhegium (Reggio), who in turn asked Carthage for help. With this excuse, an armada that must have been long prepared sailed from Carthage. It was reportedly 300,000 strong, with Carthaginian infantry plus Libyan, Iberian, Sardinian and Ligurian mercenaries, transported in 3,000 ships and guarded by 200 galleys. Only the last figure seems credible, but it was certainly a huge force meant, like its Persian equivalent, to overawe the Greeks.

THE SIEGE OF HIMERA

Hamilcar, the Carthaginian *shophet* (commander), embarked this army and sailed for Palermo, where he landed only after losing most of his horse-transports in storms – a loss that was to prove crucial. He then marched on Himera and besieged it, building a fortified camp by the sea and another one inland for his vast army. Theron, reaching Himera just ahead of the Carthaginians, ordered its gates to be walled up (to prevent surrender as well as to keep out the enemy) and sent urgent messages to Syracuse. Gelon, who had been waiting, marched with 50,000 men to join forces with the Himerans, who reopened their gates.

Both sides then waited – showing that the Carthaginians lacked overwhelming superiority – until Gelon had a stroke of luck. Hamilcar had asked Selinus, a half-Greek Sicilian ally, to send him some cavalry. Their reply fell into Gelon's hands, and Syracusan cavalry entered the Carthaginian camp disguised as Selinans. Then they attacked the Carthaginians from the rear.

The battle that followed was confused and bloody. The Syracusan infiltrators killed Hamilcar as he was sacrificing to the gods (in one story he immolated

himself on a pyre), but the battle was nearly lost when many Greeks stopped to plunder the Carthaginian camp. Final victory was total, however, with few Carthaginians returning home. Instead, many mercenaries ended their lives as slaves, building grand temples for the Greek cities, especially in Acragas' Vale of Temples. But the Carthaginian colonies in north-west Sicily were left alone.

A TIME OF PEACE AND PLENTY

The following decades were prosperous ones for Greek Sicily. Hieron peacefully succeeded his brother Gelon as ruler of Syracuse in 478BC. He won a great naval victory four years later when the Etruscans, still expanding their power in central Italy, were defeated at Cumae (Cyme) in 474BC. This marked the end of Etruscan expansion as definitively as Himera and the east Greek victories had checked Carthaginian and Persian power.

After 460BC democracy replaced tyranny in most major Sicilian cities. They then enjoyed a long period of unusual domestic accord and foreign peace in what came to be seen as Sicily's golden age, marked by splendid temple-building at Acragas and other cities.

Above: The Valley of the Temples at Agrigento in Sicily is one of the world's most important archaeological sites.

Below: Syracuse became the richest and most powerful Greek city in Sicily, spreading up the hills from the original island colony of Ortygia. The fortifications at Euryalus high above were to prove crucial to its defence.

CHAPTER III

ATHENS AT ITS ZENITH

478–431BC

Between its triumph in the Persian Wars in 479BC and the Peloponnesian War that began in 431BC, Athens enjoyed a golden half-century, becoming the greatest of all Greek cities. Although the era ended in political and military disasters, these do not diminish Athens' achievements, as classical culture and full democracy came of age. When Pericles, the democratic statesman, claimed that Athens was 'the educator of Greece', he was not bragging. Athens demonstrated that democracy, in its deepest (if not widest) sense, could encourage intellectual and cultural excellence: not dumbing down but climbing up. In drama, art, philosophy, architecture and politics it was a brilliant age.

Classical Athens had its downsides. Its brilliance came partly from ruling and taxing its supposed allies; full enjoyment of democracy was denied to women, foreign residents and slaves; and Athens could behave brutally toward its enemies. Athenians, intoxicated by their city's primacy, often displayed an arrogance that finally united many other Greeks against them. Despite such faults, Athens incarnated so much of what is noblest about ancient Greece that we still see it mainly through Athenian eyes. Even other Greeks acknowledged this quality. Pindar of Thebes, a city often hostile to Athens, wrote: "O shining city, violet-crowned and famous in song/Bastion of Hellas, glorious Athens, city of godlike men".

Left: The Parthenon, built between 447BC and 432BC, embodies Athenian genius at its most radiant.

SPARTAN FAILINGS, ATHENIAN INITIATIVE 479–478BC

Above: The Parthenon in Athens, set high on the Acropolis. Without its city walls, Athens was very vulnerable to attack.

Below: Under the guidance of Themistocles, one of Athens' greatest democratic statesmen, the city hastily rewalled itself after the wars, now incorporating the Diplyon and Kerameikos areas.

After the defeats of the Persian army at Plataea and the Persian fleet at Mycale in Ionia in 479BC, many Greek islands and cities in Asia happily threw off their Persian allegiance. This meant that the Panhellenic League had to decide how to defend the eastern Greeks against Persia. The Spartans suggested moving their populations to Greece proper, where they could have the territory of cities that had 'medized' (collaborated with Persia). After this impractical plan was vetoed, the League decided to continue the war against Persia, which still controlled many strongholds in the north and east Aegean.

The League's fleet sailed north to the Hellespont in the summer of 479BC, where they found that Xerxes' grandiose pontoon bridge linking Europe and Asia had been demolished. The Peloponnesians, reassured that the Persians could not easily reinvade, now sailed home. But Xanthippus, the Athenian *strategos*, led the Athenian and Ionian ships to attack Sestos on the Hellespont. This was no easy task, as it turned out, for

its Persian governor held on for months. But by winter Sestos fell and Xanthippus could return triumphant to Athens.

REFORTIFYING ATHENS
Back in Attica, the Athenians had returned for the second time to their city, most of which had been systematically destroyed by the Persians in their brief reoccupation that June. Only a few fine houses, where Persian grandees had stayed, were left intact. The city resounded to the noise of frantic rebuilding as Athenians tried to get roofs over their heads before the autumn rains.

Booty from Plataea may have helped some hoplite heroes, but for most citizens it was a very hard time. This did not mean that they could afford to neglect politics, however.

In its unwalled state, Athens was acutely vulnerable to any enemy. Sparta, which famously had no walls but relied on its armies, suggested that a rewalled Athens might become a base for the Persians if they returned. Instead, they suggested that Athens use the Peloponnese as its natural fortress. This argument convinced no one in Athens. But to keep the Spartans away while the Athenians were re-fortifying their city, Themistocles returned to Sparta, where he convinced the Spartans that the Athenians were only rebuilding their homes, not their walls, inviting them to send envoys to see for themselves. The envoys were promptly seized as hostages until the walls were finished.

The crash rebuilding of Athens' walls (only around the inland city itself at this stage) produced walls 8m/25ft high and 2.5m/8ft thick, enough to deter any Greek army at the time. The Spartans, grudgingly accepting this fait accompli, agreed to continue the war against Persia in 478BC.

DISGRACE OF PAUSANIAS

The League's forces were still nominally commanded by Pausanias, the Spartan victor at Plataea. His fleet of 20 triremes joined a much larger Athenian and Ionian force, and they sailed to Cyprus, conquering part of it. They then moved north to Byzantium on the Bosphorus and ejected the Persian garrison from that strategically important city. Meanwhile King Leotychidas of Sparta and Themistocles led a joint land campaign to reconquer northern Greece. Spartan proposals to punish 'medizing' states were blocked by Themistocles, however, who realized that this could boost Sparta's own power.

During 478BC it became apparent that Pausanias, like many Spartans away from domestic austerity, was highly corruptible. At Byzantium he began behaving in ways that were not only autocratic, offending the allies, but also non-Greek. He adopted Persian clothes (wearing purple trousers) and other luxuries and began corresponding secretly with Persian satraps. The Spartan *ephors* finally recalled him, but it was too late for Sparta's prestige. Pausanias' subsequent career ended with his deposition and death by starvation, again revealing Sparta's systemic short-comings. Meanwhile, the Ionian Greeks had turned to Athens for leadership in the continuing war against Persia.

Above: The Hellespontine region (Dardanelles) became a crucial campaigning area after the Persian Wars. Wheat supplies for Athens from the Black Sea had to pass through its straits.

Right: The victorious commander at Plataea, Pausanias, later fell out with other Greeks and his own government. Recalled to Sparta and accused of treason, he was starved to death in a temple where he had sought sanctuary.

THE CONFEDERACY OF DELOS
478–460BC

Above: This serpentine column (now in Istanbul) was set up at Delphi to celebrate Greek victories. Initially it had Pausanias' name on it but this was soon removed.

Below: The new anti-Persian confederacy, formed in 477BC and led by Athens, chose the small Cycladic island of Delos, sacred to the god Apollo, for its headquarters and treasury. The alliance was known as the League or Confederacy of Delos.

In the winter of 478–477BC the Confederacy of Delos was established under Athenian leadership. Its aim was to continue the war against Persia. Despite the great victories of the previous two years, there was reason to fear a resurgence of Persian power. The Ionians, repelled by Pausanias' arrogant behaviour, had realized Sparta's inadequacy as a leader in overseas warfare, hence the setting up of the Confederacy. Sparta faced serious problems with Argos and the *helots* (Sparta's slave class) that preoccupied it over the next 20 years.

The Confederacy's headquarters was the small island of Delos in the Cyclades, sacred to Apollo. In its Council, every member from the smallest to the largest (Athens) had one vote. All swore to have "the same friends and enemies", a standard Greek oath, and to continue the alliance "until iron should float" (i.e. forever). This clause later created problems because it offered members no way out.

PAYMENT OF PHOROS
Every city – which from the start included most Ionian and Aeolian cities in Asia Minor, the adjacent islands, most

Above: The Athenian Aristides, nicknamed 'the Just' for his honesty, became the Delian League's first treasurer, impartially assessing the contributions due from each state.

of the Cyclades and all the Euboean cities except Carystus – made contributions in kind (ships) or in cash. Aristides, renowned for his honesty, became the first treasurer and assessed every *phoros* (contribution). The total revenue from 200 cities came to 460 talents, enough to maintain 100 Confederate galleys. Athens' own fleet had 200 triremes. Revenue was counted by ten Athenian officials called *hellenotamiae* (treasurers of the Greeks). Smaller members found it easier to pay in cash than to equip a trireme. Gradually, more and more members, and especially any who rebelled, moved from being independent contributors of ships to mere *phoros*-payers – a demotion that often caused resentment.

THE LEAGUE
Athens generally favoured democracy in League members, but seldom imposed it without invitation by an internal faction.

Democracy alienated some states' richer citizens, who faced higher taxes under such regimes. Athens later began interfering in tributary members' legal affairs, transferring disputes between members to Athenian law courts. This had advantages – distant Athenian juries were often impartial – but further infringed cities' cherished independence.

THE RISE AND FALL OF CIMON

The Confederacy's early years were glorious. Cimon, son of Miltiades, the victor of Marathon, was Aristides' protégé. As an Athenian *strategos* and leader of the Confederate fleet, he ousted Pausanias from Byzantium, which was enrolled in the Confederacy. In 476BC he attacked the Persian fort of Eion on the River Strymon. Its commander, Boges, held out for a long time, finally immolating himself, his wives and children on a pyre rather than surrender. Cimon failed to take Persianheld Doriscus east along the coast, but in 474BC captured the island of Scyros, a pirate stronghold. The bones of Theseus, the legendary Athenian king, were found there and brought back in triumph. Athens settled *cleruchs* (colonists) on Scyros, the first of many such colonies. Carystus to the south was compelled to join the alliance, and Naxos, when it tried to secede in 469BC, was forcibly prevented – justifiably perhaps, as the war against Persia was continuing.

A convivial, conservative nobleman, Cimon dominated Athenian politics alongside Aristides after Themistocles was ostracized in 471BC. (The great radical had made many enemies, and Athenian politics were volatile.) In 467BC Cimon sailed east and destroyed a new Persian armada of 200 galleys and the accompanying army on the River Eurymedon in southern Asia Minor, ending Persia's hopes of revenge. The cities of Pamphylia and Lycia were then enrolled in the Confederacy. Spoils from the allied victory were used partly to rebuild the Athenian's Acropolis walls – a contentious use. Possibly this provoked

Thasos, a rich island controlling gold mines in Thrace, to revolt in 465BC. It took two years' hard fighting before Cimon could suppress it. Meanwhile, Athenian squadrons, fully professional after years of campaigning, sailed across the eastern Mediterranean unchallenged.

EARTHQUAKE IN SPARTA

When an earthquake in Lacademonia in 464BC triggered a *helot* revolt that the Spartans could not repress, Cimon argued that Athens should help Sparta, still her ally. He led 4,000 Athenian hoplites, noted for their siege skills, to help take Mt Ithome, the *helots'* walled refuge. But the Spartans soon grew alarmed at having democrats inside their country, while Athenians were dismayed to discover the true nature of *helot* serfdom. Humiliatingly, Sparta told the Athenians to leave, but retained its other allies.

This rebuff led to Cimon's ostracism on his return in 461BC, for Ephialtes, a new radical, had emerged to dominate Athenian politics. Soon after, a war broke out that came to divide much of Greece into two hostile camps: Athenian and Spartan. But Athenian power was still expanding. When a fleet campaigning in Cyprus was asked to assist an Egyptian revolt against Persia, it sailed south.

Above: Cimon, son of Miltiades and ally of Aristides, emerged as the chief Athenian strategos *after 478BC. He led the League of Delos in a triumphant series of campaigns, driving the Persians from the Aegean. At home Cimon kept open house, entertaining lavishly like the old-style aristocrat he was.*

Below: The Portara Gateway, Naxos. In 469BC Naxos tried to quit the League. This attempt was suppressed by Athens, which argued that the war against Persia required all members to keep fighting.

DEMOCRACY'S COMPLETION
462–458BC

Above: An ostrakon, a small potsherd used in the yearly poll to decide who should be ostracized (sent into temporary exile), one of the 'safety valves' of democracy devised by Cleisthenes. Many popular leaders, including Themistocles, were ostracized.

Below: Naval power in the ancient Mediterranean depended on galleys crewed mainly by citizens. Athens' trireme fleets, which ruled the Aegean for much of the 5th century BC, gave seasonal employment to c.30,000 citizen-rowers, forging a link between democracy at home and an aggressive anti-Persian policy abroad that soon became imperialist.

Little is known about Ephialtes, the radical democrat who in 462BC clipped the powers of the Areopagus, the ancient court, and so helped to finalize democracy. His person or policies evidently roused violent passions, however, for he was assassinated soon afterwards – something rare even in Athens' often turbulent democracy.

But Ephialtes' legacy lived on in the career of Pericles, the Alcmaeonid aristocrat who became the greatest democratic statesman in ancient history. Pericles was to guide Athens through nearly 30 years of unparalleled brilliance.

CURBING THE AREOPAGUS
The Council of the Areopagus (named after the Hill of Ares, or Mars, where it sat) retained some powers as well as immense prestige in 462BC. Composed of ex-*archons* after their year in office (all chosen by lot since 487BC), it heard charges against elected officials after their year in power. It also probably supervised the whole body of the law, with wide if undefined powers as the main court of appeal. All this made it a force to be reckoned with, and, with its members still recruited from only the two upper classes, it tended to be conservative.

Ephialtes had paved the way for the reduction of its old powers by accusing several Areopagites of corruption. With Cimon out of sight in Sparta and then ostracized, Ephialtes was able to persuade the Assembly to transfer almost all the Areopagus' powers to itself, either in the form of the Council of Five Hundred or, when constituted as a *heliaea*, as a jury court. (The council and juries were chosen by lot so that they accurately represented the *demos*, the people.) All that was left to the Areopagus was its jurisdiction in murder and arson cases and care of the sacred olive trees. *Archons*, however, still gave a preliminary hearing to lawsuits.

DRAMA AS PROPAGANDA
Powerful propaganda in defence of this democratizing reform came in the form of Aeschylus' last, perhaps greatest, dramatic trilogy, the *Oresteia*, first produced c.458BC. The final play in the trilogy, *Eumenides* (The Kindly Ones), focuses on the plight of Orestes. Guilty of the hideous crime of matricide, Orestes flees from Delphi to Athens pursued by the Furies. On the hill of the Areopagus, Athena, patron goddess of the city, appears, rescues him and founds the Areopagus as a court specifically to deal with such cases. The Furies are then tamed and become the Kindly Ones.

Since Aeschylus, the first of the three great Athenian dramatists, came from the hoplite class (his proudest boast on his tombstone was that he had fought at the Battle of Marathon), his views probably voiced those of many ordinary Athenians.

Ephialtes and Pericles were therefore not considered to be dangerous extremists, but were merely completing the constitutional reforms begun by Cleisthenes 50 years earlier.

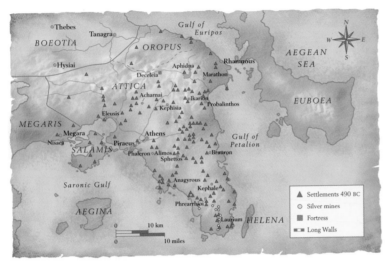

Left: Attica in c.450BC *showing the demes (the basic unit of Athenian political and social life after Cleisthenes' democratic reforms of 508BC, on membership of which citizenship depended), the Long Walls and the silver mines at Laurium. Even at its greatest extent, Attica was always hemmed in by potential enemies.*

SPREADING POWER

Around the same time, Pericles introduced pay for jurors, probably at a rate of one obol a day, later raised to two. As this was less than the average daily wage, it was not an inducement to idleness (as Aristophanes, the comic playwright, suggested in his play *The Wasps* of 426BC), but it did mean that poverty would not prevent poorer citizens from acting as jurors. In 458BC the *archon*ship also became a paid office to which the *zeugitae* (the middle or hoplite class) now became eligible, so robbing this ancient office, descended from the royal council, of its last aristocratic distinction. There were by this time ten *archons* (literally rulers) of whom three went back to Athens' legendary past: the *basileos*, or king *archon*, with a priestly role; the *polemarch*, originally the military commander; and the eponymous *archon*, who gave his name to the year of his election. Athens dated events by referring to the 'year so-and-so was *archon*'. Later, dating from the first Olympiad (776BC) was adopted.

THE LOTTERY IN ATHENS

Athenians made extensive use of sortition (lotteries) to choose men for many important public posts. In Athens *archons* were chosen by lot after 487BC, as were jurors and other officials. Such a way of choosing officials seems odd today, but there were sound reasons behind it: it reduced the chances of undue influence being brought to bear on anyone; it spread the benefits and the burdens of active citizenship widely; and it was regarded as incorruptible. Elaborate mechanisms for rattling the tokens with the citizens' names on them have been recovered.

Below: The approach to the Acropolis, with the ruins of the temple of Athena Nike (Athena the Victor) standing out to remind citizens of the glories of their city, as it approached its zenith.

THE FIRST PELOPONNESIAN WAR 460–446BC

Cimon's humiliation broke Athens' last ties with Sparta, though in truth they had long been fraying. While Sparta's growing jealousy of Athens was held in check by *helot* revolts, Athenian power had yet to acknowledge its limits. For a short but intoxicating time, it seemed that Athens would replace Sparta as *hegemon* (leader) of mainland Greece as well as of the Delos Confederacy, while gaining a major role in Egypt. Although such hopes were shattered, Athens emerged undefeated from this First Peloponnesian War, though strained by her experiences.

In 459BC Athens allied with Argos, Sparta's traditional enemy, and settled some Messenians (rebel *helots* whom the Spartans had allowed to leave Mt Ithome) at Naupactus on the Gulf of Corinth. Both were hostile acts. War finally broke out in 459BC when Megara, Athens' small neighbour, quarrelled with Corinth and left the Spartan Alliance, allying instead with Athens. An Athenian expedition helped Megara to build long walls down to its port at Nisaea, so cutting the Isthmus road. Aegina, Athens' old naval rival, was invaded

Above: An Athenian citizen-soldier bidding farewell to his family, a typical scene from the First Peloponnesian War.

Left: A relief of Athena mourning by a grave stone. Nobly restrained in her grief, the goddess epitomizes the heroism of Athens at the time, when many citizens died fighting for their city as far away as Egypt.

> ### DIFFERING ALLIANCES: SPARTA VERSUS ATHENS
>
> The Confederacy of Delos, which by 450BC had become an Athenian empire, had started with a formal council. Always dominated by Athens as the strongest member, this disappeared by *c*.450BC. What we term the Peloponnesian League, but which was at the time called 'Sparta and her allies', seems to have had no official organization. Sparta proudly used to point out that – unlike the Athenian Empire, where finally only the two large islands of Lesbos and Chios kept their own fleets – all Sparta's allies maintained their fleets and/or armies, central to their independence. But it would have been awkward for Sparta to levy financial contributions, for most Peloponnesian states supplied armies, not fleets. Sparta could in practice be just as bullyingly exploitative toward her allies as Athens was to hers.

in 458BC and, after a year-long siege, capitulated, being forced into the Confederacy. A diversionary attack by Corinth on Megara was meanwhile repelled by a scratch Athenian force of old men and youngsters.

At around the same time Athens built her own double Long Walls. These linked the city to the booming port of Piraeus, making her almost impregnable to direct land attack, something that Themistocles had long ago wanted. In late 457BC a land battle at Oenophyta saw Boeotia come under Athenian control also – an unusual situation that continued for ten years. Athens then won over Phocis and Locris, small states to the west of Boeotia, parts of Thessaly and the city of Troezen in the Peloponnese.

She seemed set to become the hegemon, the dominant Greek power, on land as well as at sea.

DISASTER IN EGYPT

What offered Athens even greater prospects of power in the 450s BC was Egypt. Immensely rich, Egypt was never happy under Persian rule. Its Persian satrap was killed in an uprising in 459BC led by Inarus, a Libyan who appealed to the Confederate fleet then in Cyprus. The Athenians dispatched a fleet of 200 ships to expel the Persians from Egypt. In return, shiploads of wheat went north to Athens. But in 456BC a Persian army drove the Athenians from Memphis (Cairo), blockading them on an island in the Nile Delta for 18 months. The whole expedition was lost, few of its 40,000 men escaping to distant Cyrene.

CIMON'S RETURN TO VICTORY

Alarmed at this disaster, and fearing a Persian fleet might enter the Aegean, the Athenians transferred the Confederate Treasury to Athens. (Once there, even after the panic ended, it was run conveniently in Athens' interest, one sixtieth of the total revenue being deducted annually as administrative costs.) Cimon, back from his ten-year ostracism, helped to arrange a truce with Sparta and was elected *strategos* to lead another fleet east. This, again 200 ships strong, sailed to Cyprus in 450BC, with 60 ships going to help another revolt in Egypt. They returned for a last victory at Cypriot Salamis, won by Cimon on his deathbed. In 449BC the Peace of Callias was signed between Athens and Persia. By it Athens gave up southern Asia Minor and Cyprus but the Great King agreed to keep Persian troops 80km/50 miles away from the west and north-west coasts, acknowledged as being in the Athenian sphere.

THE 30 YEARS' PEACE

Most of Athens' gains in central Greece soon unravelled: defeats in Boeotia led to its loss, and Phocis and Locris broke away

about then, as did Megara and Euboea. (Oligarchs in these states were generally anti-Athenian).

Only Euboea was finally reconquered after hard campaigning by Pericles. Athens had to abandon all its conquests except Aegina in the 30 Years' Peace of 446BC. This was signed between the Athenian Empire, as it had now become, and the Peloponnesian League.

Above: The Lions at Delos, where the Confederate Treasury was first kept.

Below: Control of the grain routes from the Black Sea remained vital to Athens' survival. Among Greek colonies in the area was Istrus near the Danube Delta.

TOTAL DEMOCRACY
ATHENIAN DEMOCRACY IN ACTION

Below: Athena, maiden goddess of wisdom and the crafts, was very aptly the special deity of Athens, a city Aristotle later called "the city hall of wisdom". Hailed as promachos, *defender or champion, she was often shown with helmet and spear. Her eponymous city repeatedly fought for its existence and glory.*

Democracy (*democratia*) means the rule of the *demos* (the people) – literally so in Athens and other Greek cities that followed her pattern of total democracy. The twin aims of Athenian democracy were to give power to the whole populace and to avoid any individual or group gaining undue power by holding office repeatedly. In practice, this meant elevating amateurism to unprecedented

heights – with results that were far less disastrous than might have been expected. Socrates the philosopher was only one of many critics of such amateurism, however. The great exceptions to this avoidance of experts were the ten annually elected *strategoi* (generals) – posts therefore sought by ambitious men, whether or not they had military talent. Pericles was re-elected as a *strategos* repeatedly (14 times after 443BC), but his power still rested ultimately on votes in the Assembly, which could censure all officials. Thucydides, a superb historian but indifferent general, was exiled for losing a crucial battle.

THE ROLE OF THE ASSEMBLY

The Assembly of all eligible male citizens (*ecclesia*) was literally the government, not a chamber of elected representatives. It listened to foreign ambassadors and voted for war or peace. Any citizen could speak, voicing his opinions before the massed citizenry. (This put an obvious premium on public speaking, and richer citizens from the mid-5th century BC began paying to acquire the rhetorical skills needed to sway the crowds.) Decrees passed by majority vote at each meeting of the Assembly were prominently displayed on whitened boards in the Agora in central Athens so "that any who wished could read them". (Most male Athenians could read a bit, though fewer could write well.)

The Assembly met in the open, originally in the Agora, the commercial and social centre. After 500BC it moved to the Hill of the Pnyx, west of the Acropolis. Speakers stood on a plinth to address the Assembly below on a platform built *c.*400BC, whose remains can be seen today. The Assembly met every nine days on average, although heralds could summon emergency meetings often initiated by

Right: As Athenian democracy reached its zenith, it celebrated its goddess and itself by building the Parthenon, most sublime of Greek temples. In this painting by the Victorian artist Sir Lawrence Alma-Tadema, Pericles is shown visiting the work in progress, talking to the sculptor Pheidias at work on the great frieze.

a *strategos*. To convene a quorum of 6,000 citizens for it, Scythian policemen would drag a cable covered in red dye through the Agora from the north, thus herding citizens into the Assembly. Any citizen who was found outside the Assembly that day with red dye on his clothes faced possible punishment.

THE DISENFRANCHISED

This quorum number of 6,000 was, however, probably only one tenth of the total citizenry at Athens' zenith. Many citizens lived in distant parts of Attica, too far from the city to attend Assembly frequently, while *cleruchs* (settlers) on the islands would seldom have voted. No provision was made to represent these absent citizens in Athens. (Our best information about Athens' constitution comes from Aristotle, the learned, perceptive, sometimes critical 4th-century BC philosopher.)

Metics (registered foreign residents settled in Athens) had no vote, nor could they own property. *Metics* rarely won citizenship, even for outstanding services to the state. Women, slaves and children never had the vote either. So Athenian democracy had its definite limits, especially after the Citizenship Law of 451BC, which stipulated that both of a citizen's parents had to be Athenian. (This would have excluded Themistocles from citizenship.) The law, proposed by Pericles, met a public desire to limit the benefits of Athenian citizenship and also encouraged *cleruchs* resident overseas to marry Athenian women left at home.

THE COUNCIL AND HELIAEA

Although the Assembly was the sovereign government, the *Boule* (the Council, originally composed of 400 men, though increased to 500 after Cleisthenes' reforms in 507BC) discussed beforehand what matters would (usually) be debated. The Council was in theory a microcosm of the Assembly. Its members were chosen by lot from all citizens aged 30 or more; none could serve in it more than twice and never in consecutive years, so keeping it amateur. The Council was therefore only a filter for the Assembly, although in the 4th century BC it took a more active role in guiding it. This *probouletic* business was time-consuming, and from 460BC councillors received modest pay. Most citizens served as councillors at least once. No one, as Pericles said, was excluded from politics because of poverty.

Many would have served more often in a *heliaea* (jury court). These were large courts (at least 201, sometimes 2,001 men), again chosen by lot to avoid corruption or intimidation. As professional lawyers or judges did not exist, plaintiffs and defendants made their cases in person. The jurors, after deciding the verdict by majority voting, decided the penalty too, although the defendant would suggest his own. Almost all Athenian citizens played a civic or political role at some stage, just as all fought in the army or fleet. This was total democracy in action.

Below: After 500BC the Assembly met at the Hill of the Pnyx, on which stood a plinth. From it speakers addressed the assembled sovereign people.

ATHENS THE EDUCATOR
THE IDEAL CITY

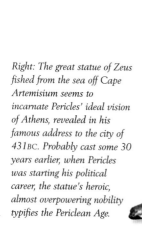

Above: The Parthenon in Athens, erected in the 5th century BC, became the most famous temple in the world.

"Our city is open to the world, we do not at fixed times deport people to prevent them discovering our military secrets. This is because we rely not on hidden weapons but on our courage and loyalty.... We do not let our love of beauty make us extravagant, nor our love of wisdom soften us. We see wealth as something to be used properly, not to boast about. No one needs to be ashamed of being poor: shame lies in doing nothing about it. Everyone is interested not only in their own affairs but in public affairs too, and is well informed about politics. We think that the man who minds only his own business has no business in the city at all. ... Taking everything into account, I declare our city is the educator of Greece."

So spoke Pericles in his funeral oration for Athenian soldiers at the start of the Peloponnesian War in 431BC. He was expressing an ideal of his city, of course (Greeks were given to idealizations), but this vision had found concrete form in the art, drama and architecture of the previous 30 years. This embodiment continued for almost 30 years after his death in 429BC. As Athens flowered, she became the educator of Greece, then later of Rome, and so of the whole Western world. The temples especially, with their statues and other artworks, elevated Athens – celebrating her gods, heroes and herself – to an almost godlike level.

THE TEMPLES' DEBATE

By ending the long war against Persia, the Peace of Callias in 449BC triggered a debate in Athens about the purpose of her empire, especially about the contributions still paid by subordinate member states. A Panhellenic congress proposed at about this came to nothing, as Sparta predictably refused to attend.

Athens had sworn in 479BC not to rebuild the Acropolis temples burnt down by the Persians until revenged. Their smoke-blackened ruins still dominated the city skyline. Pericles proposed that, with victory won, some of the money used for the fleet should go to rebuilding the city's temples. Athens had sacrificed these (and the rest of her city) for the Panhellenic cause in 480–479BC. Now it was payback time.

Not every Athenian – let alone every subject of the empire – agreed. Thucydides, son of Melesias (not the great

Right: The great statue of Zeus fished from the sea off Cape Artemisium seems to incarnate Pericles' ideal vision of Athens, revealed in his famous address to the city of 431BC. Probably cast some 30 years earlier, when Pericles was starting his political career, the statue's heroic, almost overpowering nobility typifies the Periclean Age.

historian but his cousin, also related to Cimon), led the opposition in Athens. Other Greeks would feel insulted, he said, when they saw money scheduled for war being used to "gild and adorn our city like a harlot, with costly statues and 1000-talent temples". But Thucydides lost the argument. Temple-building would give employment in Athens for citizens no longer rowing the fleets. Besides, Athenians felt they deserved their city's restoration and decoration. Thucydides was ostracized.

BUILDING THE PARTHENON

In 447BC work began on what has become the most famous temple in the world: the Parthenon, within which rose the huge *chryselephantine* (gold-and-ivory covered) statue of Athena Parthenos, the virgin warrior goddess renowned for wisdom. The Parthenon, which employed the latest techniques of *entasis* – by which columns curved in to appear regular in size when seen from afar – was mainly designed by Ictinus, and completed in 432BC. The statue of Athena, and the carvings of the frieze depicting the

Pan-Athenaic Procession running around the Parthenon (some of which are now the Elgin Marbles in the British Museum) were the work of Pheidias. Both men were supreme geniuses.

SUPERSTITION TO PHILOSOPHY

Pericles served prominently on the commission overseeing work on the Parthenon. Pheidias was one of his friends. So, more controversially, was Anaxagoras from Clazomenae, a philosopher who taught that the sun was only a vast hot stone – "bigger than the Peloponnese" – and not divine. This struck some people as impious, even tempting fate. Protagoras of Abdera, another philosopher, proclaimed: "Man is the measure of all things!" Pericles, who believed in an exalted equality, shrugged off old superstitions in the bright noon of Athenian democracy, as the city drew the greatest minds of the Greek world to her.

Above: The frieze depicting the grand Pan-Athenaic Procession running around the Parthenon was carved under the direction of Pheidias, one of the greatest sculptors of classical Greece.

Right: Theseus Diadoumenus *is the work of another brilliant but very different sculptor of High Classicism, Polyclitus of Argos, who often worked in Athens. His statue shows the legendary Athenian king as a perfectly proportioned young man. (Polyclitus was obsessed with mathematical proportion.) This is a Roman copy of a Greek original.*

THE RICH PAY FIRST

There was no regular income tax in Athens. Instead, most great festivals, and many of the triremes, were financed by the 1,200 or so richest citizens. These Athenians who chose, or were chosen, to finance a particular event did not simply pay for particular dramas (the *choregeia*) or religious festivals: they had to put them on, recruiting and rehearsing the actors and musicians needed. These demands were called *liturgia* (public burdens). For a *trierarch*, his liturgy meant building, equipping, crewing and commanding a trireme – a great effort. But love of honour and *areté* (excellence) drove wealthy Athenians to compete with each other in such active munificence in the 5th century BC.

CHAPTER IV

WORLD WAR IN MINIATURE

431–404BC

The Peloponnesian War marked a turning point in Greek history. Before it, Athens seemed set on an upward trajectory, which could have led to most of Greece becoming united under its leadership. Afterwards, although Greek civilization continued to develop, any such possibility vanished. The long wars between 431 and 404BC affected almost all the Greek world, half-ruining much of it. We call it the Peloponnesian War, showing our Athenian perspective; for Sparta and its allies, it was the Athenian War. It has been called a world war in miniature, as important as the Persian Wars.

The war divides into two stages. In the first, 431–421BC, the Spartans often tried to attack, although they had only one brilliant general, Brasidas, whose death led to an uneasy peace. This was broken by the Athenian attack on Syracuse in 415BC. Defeat in Sicily imperilled Athens' overseas empire and its democracy at home. Athenian democracy showed itself at its worst in rejecting peace offers until final defeat. Thucydides' superb history covers the war to 411BC. If not impartial, writing with only just controlled passion, he is searchingly intelligent. His words sum up the war: 'The Peloponnesian War not only lasted a long time, but brought with it unprecedented suffering for Hellas. Never before had so many cities been captured and then devastated; never before had so many people been exiled or lost their lives.'

Left: The funerary stele of Chareidemos and Lykeas, two Athenian hoplites among the many killed in the war.

THE PELOPONNESIAN WAR
ORIGINS AND STRATEGIES

Above: Pericles was Athens' master-strategist at the war's inception, but he did not foresee the devastating plague that killed thousands of citizens, including himself.

The 30 Years' Peace between Athens and the Spartan Alliance of 446BC had run only half its course before war broke out again. Both sides could be blamed for particular incidents, but these would not have led to such a prolonged, bitter war without deep underlying rivalry.

EARLY BEGINNINGS
Corcyra (Corfu) was originally a Corinthian colony, and so was expected to show some loyalty to its mother city. It was also a rich mercantile state with a large fleet of 120 triremes. Further, it lay on the important route west to Sicily. When it appealed to Athens in 433BC over a quarrel with Corinth about their joint colony Epidamnus (Durres in Albania), Athens sent ships to assist it.

Below: The immediate cause of war was a clash between Corinth and Corcyra (Corfu) in 434BC. Athenian support for Corcyra, seen below, soon led Corinth to urge Sparta to declare war on Athens.

These had orders not to fight unless necessary but ended up defeating the far larger Corinthian fleet. Suspecting that war was now inevitable, in 432BC the Athenians issued a decree excluding Megarans from Athens and its empire. By threatening Megara with economic ruin, the decree aimed to force the city, controlling the route from the Isthmus, to ally with Athens as before.

Corinth and Megara, enraged, both appealed to Sparta to fulfil its duty as Alliance leader. Sparta, led by its pacific old king Archidamus, prevaricated, calling a congress at Corinth in late 432BC. There, Corinth dramatically described Athens' boundless energy and aggressive intentions, which swayed many Spartans. Futile diplomatic exchanges followed before Sparta finally agreed to war. As Thucydides put it: "It was not so much what their allies said to them but their fear of Athens' power" that decided them. The Spartans often proved surprisingly cautious.

ATHENIAN STRATEGY
In the first years, Athenians broadly kept to the strategy proposed by Pericles: they treated their city as an island within the Long Walls linking it to Piraeus. Abandoning the Attic countryside and small towns to Spartan invasion avoided risking full-scale defeat in the open field. But it meant evacuating the population, who had to camp in unhealthy discomfort where they could between the walls. Raids on the Peloponnese aimed to divert and harry the Spartans, but Athens did little at first to exploit its naval superiority. Pericles aimed to 'win through' – to wear out the other side through greater economic and military strength. Athens had much the better and larger fleet (300 triremes besides those of Corcyra, Lesbos and Chios), while its empire made it far

the wealthiest Greek state, with 6,000 talents in reserves. A fund of 1,000 talents and 100 triremes were set aside for emergencies. Pericles' hopes that the empire's normal *phoros* (taxes) could finance the whole war proved over-optimistic, however.

SPARTAN STRATEGY

The Spartans, with much the best army but no strategic vision, stuck to old ideas of hoplite warfare: march into Attica, defeat Athens' army, make Athens sue for peace within a year. Unfortunately for them, the Athenians refused to give battle. As Peloponnesian forces seldom stayed in Attica for more than a month, they did not even close the vital Laurium silver mines at first. However, they did damage Attic agriculture, cutting down its olive trees. These, replanted after the Persian Wars, had only just reached full maturity. Their loss was a blow even to

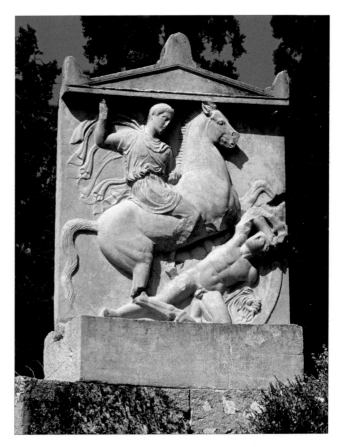

Athenians living inside the city, for many town-dwelling families still owned their ancestral farms.

Sparta claimed to be 'liberating the Greeks' from Athenian rule. Slowly it realized that only with Persian gold could it acquire the large professional fleet needed to beat Athens at sea. This meant abandoning Greek cities in Asia to Persian rule in exchange – not what most of them wanted, and a blot on Panhellenic honour. Caught in this dilemma, Sparta's strategy for a long time was ineffectual, succeeding only when atypically brilliant men guided her policies: Brasidas, a general who had escaped the mental rigidity that Spartan education induced, and Alcibiades, an Athenian traitor.

Above: The tomb of Dexeios, a young cavalryman killed fighting near Corinth, typifies the idealized, heroic but understated attitude of Athenians throughout the classical period in fighting for their city.

AN IDEOLOGICAL STRUGGLE?

The Athenians generally favoured, though did not always enforce, democracy in their subject or allied states. The Spartans preferred narrow oligarchies among their allies and neighbours, to keep the democratic virus away. Oligarchs in Lesbos hoped for Spartan support when they revolted against Athens in 428BC. (It never arrived.) In the singularly bloody civil war that racked Corcyra in 427BC, the Athenians backed the island's democrats partly because the Peloponnesians supported its oligarchs. Brasidas, marching through Thessaly in 424BC, was welcomed by local oligarchs, although – as Thucydides noted – the *demos* (people) remained pro-Athenian. But when in 415BC the Athenians attacked Syracuse, the great Sicilian city, they were fighting other democrats. Generally, disputes about types of government were of secondary importance in the prolonged struggle for hegemony.

SIEGE, PLAGUE AND REBELLION 431–427BC

Below: At the outset of war in 431BC, Athens was at its political and cultural peak, as masterworks such as this Amazon, copy of an original by Pheidias, shows.

In late May 431BC, "when the wheat was ripe", an unstoppable 30,000-strong Spartan-led army rolled into Attica, burning everything in its path. It was trying to provoke the Athenians, crammed behind their walls, to come out and fight. They did not, and after a month Sparta's Peloponnesian allies, who made up most of the army but lacked *helots* (Sparta's slave class) to work their farms, insisted on returning home.

SIEGE OF PLATAEA

Over the border in Boeotia, Plataea, allied to Athens, was besieged by Thebes. Thebes had jumped the gun in March by trying to seize Plataea in a night attack. The coup failed, the Theban infiltrators were killed and Plataea's civilians evacuated to Athens. Then the Theban army arrived to besiege the tiny city. It took four years before it fell. All the surviving garrison was killed and the city razed to the ground – a vicious start to the war. Meanwhile, Athenian ships raided the Peloponnese around Troezen to little effect. However, the speech that Pericles made at the funeral of the Athenian soldiers first exalted democracy to the sublime levels of the Elgin marbles, at least according to Thucydides who heard it. "Individual Athenians adapt to every different sort of action with versatility and grace. We have raised marvellous monuments to our power. Future ages will wonder at us, and we need no Homer and his poems to praise us.

Our courage has blazed paths across every sea and land. This is the city for which these men nobly fought and died."

THE PLAGUE

In 430BC disaster struck Athens in a way that Pericles had not foreseen: plague, reputedly from Egypt, which kept recurring. It was probably smallpox, judging by Thucydides' graphic description. (He had it himself, noted the symptoms with clinical detachment, and recovered.) It hardly affected the land-locked Peloponnese, but it killed nearly one-third of Athens' population of *c.*175,000 crowded together.

PERICLES' FALL AND RETURN

This was the first, and in some ways worst, disaster of the war, and the people turned on Pericles as a scapegoat. An attack he led had failed to capture Epidaurus, its target. He lost office, was

---

INEFFECTUAL SIEGE CRAFT

Despite being supreme on land, like the Spartans, or at sea, like the Athenians, the Greeks before 400BC were oddly inept at siege warfare. Compared to contemporary Persians or to monarchs of the 4th century such as Alexander the Great, they often seemed powerless before any well-built, well-defended wall. If surprise attack or treachery (or the two combined) failed, blockading a city until it starved was the normal way to capture it. Greek armies had battering rams and ladders and might try mining under walls or even primitive flame-throwers, but they lacked other siege engines. Only in the 4th century did Sicilian and Macedonian rulers revolutionize siege warfare with powerful catapults and gigantic siege towers.

Right: War required all citizens of military age (between 18 and 60) to serve in the fleet or army. Here Pericles, rather fancifully, is depicted fighting alongside his friend the sculptor Pheidias. In fact, Pheidias left Athens soon after the war's start and Pericles, as leading strategos, commanded the fleet.

accused of corruption and fined. Pheidias, his friend the great sculptor, was also fined. Another friend, the philosopher Anaxagoras, had to flee the city and return to his native Lampsacus after questioning the gods' existence, an act of dangerous impiety in troubled times. Even Pericles' mistress Aspasia, who had joined their dinner parties (very few women did), was prosecuted.

But Athenian public opinion swung back and Pericles was reinstated as *strategos*. Meanwhile, campaigns in two important areas, the Gulf of Corinth, and around the Chalcidic peninsula in the north, had mixed results. Demosthenes (the 5th-century BC *strategos*, not the 4th century orator) led not unsuccessful operations in the west, although he lost many men in them.

THE REVOLT OF LESBOS

In 428BC the oligarchical government of Mytilene on Lesbos revolted, taking most of the island with it. Lesbos, which was still a free ally of Athens, had no specific complaints, so its revolt was a huge shock. To pay for its suppression, a novel property tax, the *eisphora*, was introduced. Mytilene appealed to Sparta, which sent one adviser. By May 427BC the Lesbian leaders, under pressure from their starving people, finally had to surrender to the Athenian forces.

On the news of their surrender, a great debate arose in the Assembly about how to treat the rebels. Cleon, now the leading radical, urged that all male citizens on Lesbos should be executed. His proposal was carried, and a galley sailed with the grim news. But another politician, Diodotus, persuaded an extraordinary Assembly meeting to be merciful (on the pragmatic grounds that the Lesbian *people* had not revolted) and another galley was sent in hot pursuit. It reached Lesbos just in time and only the ringleaders were executed. But most land on Lesbos was allocated to Athenian *cleruchs*. As absentee landlords, they let it out to locals, who had to pay rent for farms that had previously been their own.

Below: While most Peloponnesian states followed the Spartan-led alliance, most islands and ports were part of Athens' empire, making the war look like one between land and sea. But there were exceptions such as Corinth, a great pro-Spartan port.

SPARTA'S DEFEAT AND PEACE
425–421BC

*Below: This superb
Nike (statue of victory) is
one of the first semi-nude
female statues in classical art.
The marble statue
was made by Paionius
for the Messenians of
Naupactus, celebrating
the part they played in
the Athenian victory over
Sparta in 425BC.*

Athens had seldom contemplated attacking the Peloponnese on its south-west flanks. It had only one ally, Zacynthus, in the area, yet Achaea and Aetolia, south and north of the Corinthian Gulf, were friendly neutrals and at Naupactus near the Gulf's mouth lived *helots* from Messenia, who were fanatically loyal to Athens. A civil war, waged with appalling savagery, led to the Corcyran democrats regaining control of most of the island. An Athenian squadron sailed to Sicily in 428BC in response to Ionian cities' appeal for protection against their Doric neighbours.

SURRENDER AT PYLOS

The Athenian *strategos* Phormion had defeated larger Peloponnesian squadrons in 429BC in the Corinthian Gulf by dazzling seamanship. (On one occasion Athenian galleys forced the enemy fleet to form a defensive circle with bows pointed outward. Around this, Athenian triremes rowed closer and closer, forcing their enemies inward to foul their oars.) After Phormion's death, in 426BC Demosthenes, another adventurous *strategos*, saved the *helots* of Naupactus from a Spartan attack. Next year, although no longer *strategos*, he accompanied a fleet bound for Sicily. This was blown into the Bay of Pylos on Messenia's west coast by a storm. Demosthenes persuaded the sailors to

*Above: The capture of 140 Spartiates (full
Spartans) on the Island of Sphacteria in 425BC
by Athenian general Demosthenes horrified
Sparta and led it to sue for peace – an offer
Athens rejected. The war then resumed.*

build fortifications on the peninsula of Pylos. Then the main fleet sailed on west, leaving Demosthenes with a small force.

Horrified at the presence of Athenians on Spartan soil, Sparta sent a fleet and troops to eject them. Some 420 Spartiates (Sparta's elite ruling class) with *helot* attendants occupied Sphacteria island to the south. But the wooded Pylos peninsula proved very defensible. Demosthenes' men, although outnumbered, repelled Spartan attacks by land and sea. Brasidas was badly wounded while disembarking.

The Athenian fleet, which had turned back on hearing the news, swept into Pylos Bay to defeat the Spartan ships.

Now the Spartans on Sphacteria, themselves besieged, faced starvation. Among them there happened to be some very important Spartiates.

Sparta, panic-stricken, proposed a truce. To ensure that food was supplied to the marooned Spartiates, it handed over 60 ships and sent envoys to Athens, suggesting peace on the status quo ante as in 431BC. Urged by Cleon, the Assembly rejected this proposal, but kept the 60 ships on a technicality. War resumed, with well-bribed *helots* swimming across to Sphacteria by night with food for the besieged Spartiates. But when Cleon arrived with Athenian reinforcements, including light-armed troops, they stormed Sphacteria at night. Athenian archers and javelin throwers harassed the exhausted Spartans until they surrendered. About 140 Spartiates became prisoners.

This unprecedented Spartan surrender, amazing all of Greece, boosted Athenian self-confidence dangerously. They seized Cythera, an island off Sparta's south coast to which some *helots* had managed to escape. (But Athens never attempted to rouse the resentful *helot* serfs inside Lacedaemonia, which might really have crippled Sparta.) Cleon, aggressively imperialistic, produced a new, heavier tribute list for the empire, often doubling subject cities' *phoros* (taxes). But trouble was growing in the north.

THE LOSS OF AMPHIPOLIS

Amphipolis, founded by Athens in 436BC on the River Strymon by the Macedonian border, was a key city for the empire, controlling a bridge, trade routes and gold mines. In 424BC Brasidas marched north, with no Spartiates but only 700 *helots* armed as hoplites (presumably promised their liberty). He gathered other troops en route to a stunning series of victories. These were won by diplomatic as much as military means, Brasidas having great, if menacing, charm. Some Chalcidic cities were disgruntled with Athenian rule and Brasidas initially had the backing

Above: The Temple to Hephaestus, built c.440BC, overlooked the Agora, Athens' social centre.

of the Macedonian king Perdiccas. When Brasidas reached Amphipolis after marching through a winter night, he offered its citizens such easy terms that they surrendered. Thucydides, the *strategos* commanding a squadron at Thasos, hastily sent ships in support, but too late.

Back in Athens, Thucydides was exiled (not ostracized) for the loss. This was perhaps unfair, as he had lacked the forces needed to defend the long north coast against Brasidas, Sparta's best general. Athens, defeated in a hoplite battle by Thebes at Delium in 424BC, had ignored Brasidas' campaign until it was too late. Cleon finally was sent as *strategos* with a decent force – 1,200 Athenian hoplites plus allies – in 422BC to stop Brasidas from winning more cities. In a battle outside Amphipolis, Brasidas and Cleon were both killed, leading to peace in 421BC.

THE PEACE OF NICIAS

Intended to last for 50 years, the Peace of Nicias – named after the conservative Athenian politician – attempted a return to the status quo ante. Athens returned all gains except Nisaea, Megara's port, being promised the return of Amphipolis and other northern cities. (She never got them.) Sparta returned her conquests, but the peace marked a defeat for her. Her allies refused to accept it, accusing Sparta of neglecting the Alliance's interests.

Below: Trapped on the island of Sphacteria, the Spartans effectively became hostages in their own territory thanks to Athenian tactical brilliance.

THE FALSE PEACE
421–415BC

Above: The debauched features of Alcibiades as imagined by an artist of the Roman period. The flamboyant aristocrat of the Alcmaeonid family led Athens into disastrous adventures.

When agreeing to the Peace of Nicias, Sparta was acutely conscious that the 30 Years' Peace with Argos, her old rival in the Peloponnese, was about to end. Argos had recovered from the devastating defeat in 457BC, but needed help to challenge Sparta, still the region's powerful *hegemon*. As Argos was now a democracy, Athens was the obvious choice. Many younger Athenians were bored with a peace that offered no chances of gain or glory.

ALCIBIADES' RISE TO POWER
The young Alcibiades (born *c*.450BC) now emerged as a prominent figure in Athenian public life. An Alcmaeonid and former ward of Pericles, he had been wounded while fighting bravely at the Battle of Potidaea in 430BC. His life had been saved by Socrates, a fellow hoplite

who became a friend. In alliance with the radical Hyperbolus, Alcibiades, handsome, rich and flamboyant, began to dominate the Assembly. Elected *strategos* in 420BC, he persuaded Athens to ally with Argos and other states in the Peloponnese against Sparta. But the Assembly did not choose Alcibiades as *strategos* for the army sent to Argos in 419BC, which proved a mistake. After numerous manoeuvres, King Agis of Sparta defeated the joint Athenian-Argive army at Mantinea in 418BC, which, as Thucydides said, "wiped out the disgrace of Pylos". It also triggered regime change back in Argos. Under a new oligarchy, it allied with Sparta, which recovered its own self-confidence.

In Athens, Alcibiades also switched sides, forming an alliance with the conservative Nicias. Their supporters combined to ostracize Hyperbolus in 418BC, leaving Alcibiades undisputed leader of the radical democrats, who were also the keenest imperialists. This was no paradox: the prospect of employment as rowers in the fleet or of becoming *cleruchs* (colonists) made imperialism especially attractive to the *thetes* (the poorest class). Nicias, never a good general, led an unsuccessful expedition to regain Amphipolis, but Alcibiades was really looking elsewhere.

THE CAPTURE OF MELOS
Melos was a small Cycladic island that had managed to stay out of the Athenian Empire. Neither wealthy nor of much strategic value, it refused to submit to Athens, which accordingly sent a fleet and army to take it in 416BC. Athens must

Left: The Erechtheum, a temple rivalling the Parthenon in ingenuity and elegance if not size, was started in 421BC after the Peace of Nicias. It was only completed in 405BC, the year of Athens' final disastrous defeat.

have expected an easy victory, but the Melians, though vastly outnumbered, fought back. It took a long siege and Athenian reinforcements before Melos was captured. As was the custom, all Melian men of military age were killed, their women and children enslaved and their land given to 500 Athenian *cleruchs*.

The most interesting aspect of this small campaign was the debate beforehand between the Athenian envoys and Melian magistrates, to which Thucydides devoted nearly a whole chapter. In it, the Athenian envoys propounded a nakedly self-interested imperialism that the historian deplored and few Greeks at the time would have defended so openly.

THE LURE OF SICILY
Sicily has been called the Greek America. It was a land of huge potential wealth and power and a major grain exporter, chiefly to the Peloponnese. But its cities were very Greek in their constant wars. This gave an expansionist Athens opportunities. It had sent small fleets west in the 420s BC to assist Ionian cities against Doric neighbours, and to keep Sicilians too

Right: Nike Unlacing Her Sandal: *this superb statue of victory came originally from the Temple of Athena Nike on the Acropolis. It was begun in c.428BC and finished during the brief peace, when Athens indeed seemed victorious.*

preoccupied to help Sparta. But at a congress at Gela in 424BC, Hermocrates, the democratic leader of Syracuse, persuaded the Sicilians not to let outsiders such as Athens meddle in their affairs. Faced with this 'Monroe Doctrine' (excluding old Greece from western Greek affairs), the Athenian fleet returned home.

By the year 415BC, however, much had changed. Egesta, a city in Sicily's extreme west, appealed for help against its neighbour Selinus, an ally of Syracuse. Athenian envoys sent to investigate returned with tales of Egesta's fabulous wealth. These stirred dreams of easy riches in the Assembly and, swayed by Alcibiades, it voted to help Egesta. Nicias warned against so risky a project, but this only led to the force being doubled and he himself was appointed a *strategos*, with Alcibiades and Lamachus. Alcibiades sailed in June 415BC as one of the three *strategoi* commanding the armada. It had 134 triremes and transport ships with 30,000 infantry but almost no cavalry.

Right: The Valley of the Temples in Sicily. The island became a land of huge potential wealth and power and a major exporter of grain, chiefly to the Peloponnese.

DISASTER IN SICILY
415–413 BC

Above: Procles Saying Farewell to his Father, *a scene typical of Athens in wartime when every citizen did his military service, and many did not return.*

Below: Crucial to besieging Syracuse were the heights of Epipolae above the city, where the fortress of Euryalus stood. Failing to hold this point, the Athenians were doomed.

Arriving in the west, the Athenians found a cool reception at Rhegium (Reggio), on the Strait of Messina. They also discovered that Egesta had deceived them about its wealth: it was not rich at all. But, as there could be no ignominious speedy return, a council of war debated the likely options. Nicias suggested arbitrating between Egesta and Selinus, then sailing around the island before returning; Alcibiades wanted a diplomatic initiative to win allies; Lamachus, the one soldier among the *strategoi*, urged an immediate knockout blow at Syracuse, the real enemy. He failed to convince the others, however, and the Athenian fleet cruised down the coast past Syracuse, capturing one Syracusan trireme.

Athenian troops finally landed late in the season in Syracuse's Great Harbour. Here they had a success, their seasoned hoplites defeating the Syracusan army despite the latter's superior cavalry. But Nicias, senior *strategos*, then sailed the army back to Catania for the winter, which was spent trying to find allies rather than preparing for war.

ALCIBIADES' ESCAPE

While the Athenian fleet cruised past Syracuse, a state galley arrived for Alcibiades. He was being recalled to Athens, accused of profaning the Eleusinian Mysteries, the holiest and most revered of all ritual celebrations in Athens. Eluding his captors, he disappeared, to be next heard of in Sparta. His recall was the work of enemies in Athens, where he was soon tried and condemned in absentia.

WALLS AND COUNTER WALLS

In spring 414 BC the Athenians returned suddenly, caught the Syracusans off guard and seized part of Epipolae, the plateau to the west. Control of this large plateau now became central to the siege, for through it ran all roads going north. As the Athenian fleet was still superior at sea, cutting these roads would isolate Syracuse. To achieve this, the Athenians began building a double wall with a circular fort at its centre.

Syracuse was led by Hermocrates, a democratic leader comparable to Pericles, but his position remained precariously dependent on success. For the moment it looked as if the Syracusans faced defeat. Although they started to build cross walls to cut off the Athenians in turn, they were slower builders. (How much of the mainland city, as opposed to Ortygia, the citadel, was walled remains uncertain.)

Lamachus was killed during fighting around the walls, leaving the indecisive Nicias as the sole *strategos*. However, Nicias had important contacts inside Syracuse who could, he hoped, deliver the city peacefully to him. In fact, the Syracusan Assembly was about to consider peace negotiations when a Spartan force slipped past the Athenians into the city, commanded by a Spartiate of unusual energy: Gylippus.

Gylippus breathed new heart into the defence. The strong point at Labdalum was captured, an Athenian trireme taken in the Great Harbour and a new cross wall started on the northern plateau. Remarkably complacent, Nicias ignored this and instead built a fort at Plemmyrium, south of the Great Harbour, to facilitate supplies. But the Athenians were losing the cross-wall race. In a battle on Epipolae Heights, Gylippus worsted the Athenians and completed the third cross wall past the Athenians, cutting them off from land routes. Encouraged, the Syracusans began training their own large fleet, which until then had hidden from the Athenians. As fighting would be in the confined waters of the Great Harbour, the Syracusans strengthened their triremes' prows.

REINFORCEMENTS ARRIVE

Nicias wrote home despairingly in late 414BC, calling for reinforcements or recall. The Assembly, loath to abandon its Sicilian dreams, voted to send a second force of 73 ships and 15,000 men under Demosthenes. Before it arrived, the Syracusan fleet sallied forth and, in a series of engagements, damaged many Athenian ships crammed tightly together, as well as Athenian morale. This was already low because their camp on the beach near the marshes was in an unhealthy malarial spot. But the arrival of Demosthenes in 413BC with his large force alarmed the Syracusans.

RETREAT AND DISASTER

Demosthenes realized that only swift action could save the Athenians. He launched a night attack on the cross walls, which, after initial success, ended in chaotic disaster. As reinforcements could now enter Syracuse freely, Demosthenes urged immediate withdrawal by sea. Nicias hesitated until two naval defeats by the Syracusans – who closed off the Great Harbour – forced him to agree to a retreat, though by land. But an eclipse of the moon caused the superstitious Nicias to delay this plan for a month.

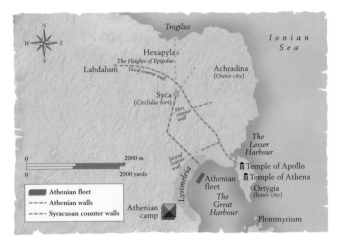

When the Athenians at last began their retreat, with only c.20,000 men left, the Syracusans harassed them continuously. Athenian discipline finally broke as they scrambled down to a river desperate for water, and their army surrendered.

Nicias and Demosthenes were killed, most of the rest becoming slaves in the mines. There many died in appalling conditions, although some reputedly won freedom by reciting lines from Euripides, the Athenian playwright already known in Sicily. Athens' western venture had ended in disaster with the loss of 40,000 men and 200 ships.

Above: Syracuse, on its island citadel, was hard to besiege. The Athenians tried to cut the city off by building a wall, but Syracusans under the dynamic Spartan Gyllipus built a cross wall that cut them off instead.

Below: Oarsmen in a Greek trireme. Control of the seas was always vital to Athenian power. When all the Athenians' ships were destroyed at Syracuse, they were effectively doomed.

AFTER SYRACUSE
REACTION AND REVIVAL, 413–408BC

Above: From Sardis, Persia's regional capital, Tissaphernes the Persian satrap watched the Greek world, aiming to exploit Greek divisions to regain long-lost territories.

Below: The Council of 400 that replaced democracy did little except build a fort at Piraeus, whose ruins are depicted here by J.R. Herbert, a 19th-century artist. The Council soon gave way to a revived democracy.

Events in Syracuse were to have huge repercussions back in Greece. In Sparta, Alcibiades, who had evaded his Athenian captors, impressed his dour hosts, eating Sparta's revolting black broth with gusto and saying that all Athenian aristocrats considered democracy an 'acknowledged folly'. He gave the Spartans dangerously good advice: they should send an adviser to Syracuse as requested. And they should reinvade Attica, not returning home after a month's ravaging, but instead occupying the fort of Deceleia all year round.

Deceleia was 16km/10 miles north of Athens, well placed to menace the city. Its permanent Spartan garrison prevented Athenian farmers from returning to cultivate their land, as in the war's first part, and it cut the overland road to Euboea. (Some Athenian farmers had moved livestock to that island.) Worse, Deceleia attracted *c.*20,000 runaway slaves over the next decade, often skilled workers vital to the Athenian economy, as a result of which the Laurium silver mines, dependent on slaves, were abandoned.

> ### OLIGARCHIC IDEAS
> Aristocratic opposition to democracy went underground during Pericles' ascendancy. Aristocrats benefited from the empire as victorious generals or from overseas properties. But long wars led to higher taxes, such as the *eisphora* (property tax), which hit the richest. Disgusted by the rise of common (if wealthy) men such as Cleon, some aristocrats longed for the 'good old days' before democracy. One anonymous aristocrat, called The Old Oligarch although he was probably young, wrote a pamphlet, *Athenian Constitution*, *c.*424BC. Its importance lies less in sneers against democracy ("the common people dress as badly as slaves") than in showing how strong oligarchical sentiment always remained.

In Athens there was a revulsion against all regarded as responsible for the disaster, be they radical democrats or fortune-tellers – in fact almost anyone

except the ordinary Athenians who had really voted for the expedition, as Thucydides noted dryly. The emergency reserve of 1,000 talents and 100 triremes was broached, and a Board of Ten older men, including the octogenarian playwright Sophocles, supplemented the long-established Council of 500.

GROWING REVOLTS

The Athenian defeat at Syracuse roused the hopes of many people who were discontented with Athenian power. In Lesbos, oligarchs planning to revolt appealed to Sparta and this time got a response: King Agis, realizing Lesbos's proximity to the vital grain trade route, sent a fleet of 100 ships to the eastern Aegean in 412BC. Its arrival triggered revolts in Chios and Ionian cities. In addition, Sparta – again on Alcibiades' advice – had approached Tissaphernes, satrap of Sardis. Persia had adhered to the Peace of Callias, keeping away from the Aegean coast, but Athens had rashly annoyed the Great King by supporting a rebel, and Persia still wanted its former territories back. By the Treaty of Miletus in 412BC, Sparta apparently agreed to Persian claims over all Greek states ever under its rule, in return for money.

Alcibiades arrived that winter in Sardis. His seduction of King Agis' wife meant he was no longer welcome in Sparta, but he charmed Tissaphernes. Alcibiades suggested that regime change in Athens might work to Persia's advantage and he was the man to effect it. He made contacts with the Athenian fleet at Samos. This was manned chiefly by *thetes*, the poorest Athenians, but even they, disillusioned by defeat, now listened briefly to talk of oligarchy, which might win Athens vital Persian gold.

Many middle-of-the-road Athenians, led by Theramenes, felt a change in the constitution was needed, although Athens had responded vigorously to recent revolts, recruiting and dispatching a new fleet. Aristophanes' comic play *Lysistrate*, produced in spring 411BC, depicting Athens' women refusing sex to their husbands unless they made peace, voiced general

war-weariness. After some democratic radicals were murdered amid growing terror, it was proposed that the franchise be restricted to the 5,000 richest citizens. Meanwhile, a Council of 400 would rule, the Assembly being abolished. "It was no small thing to destroy the Athenian people's freedom after 100 years of democracy," commented Thucydides, but the 400's rule, from June to September 411BC, revealed their shortcomings. They built a fort at Piraeus and made unsuccessful peace overtures to Sparta. Meanwhile, Alcibiades, crossing to Samos, won over the Athenian fleet. This declared itself the true Assembly and went on the offensive, led by Thrasyllus and Thrasybulus.

DEMOCRACY RESTORED

Two naval victories led to the restoration of democracy in Athens. The first at Cynossema in late 411BC restored Athenian morale; the more decisive one at Cyzicus (in the sea of Marmara) in the spring of 410BC annihilated the Peloponnesian fleet, despite Persian support. Sparta now offered peace on the basis of the status quo – an offer rejected by the Assembly, now again sovereign in Athens, as the 400 had been overthrown.

Above: A hoplite in an elaborate helmet. All major land battles were decided by these heavy-armed infantry.

Below: The dangerous charm and charisma of Alcibiades, who long bedazzled Athens, comes over well in this Roman copy of a Greek original.

THE FALL OF THE ATHENIAN EMPIRE 408–404BC

Above: The Piraeus was Athens' great port and its lifeline, for the city was crucially dependent on wheat, which was imported from the Black Sea through the Hellespont.

Alcibiades had overstated his influence with Tissaphernes to the Athenians. That devious Persian satrap, wanting to keep Sparta and Athens involved in mutually exhausting wars, dangled the prospects of Persian alliance – and gold – before both.

ALCIBIADES' RETURN TO ATHENS

Despite gaining no Persian alliance, Alcibiades retained immense appeal for the Athenians. He seemed to be the one man who might still win them the war. Gaining command of the main Athenian fleet, now in the north, he retook Chrysopolis and Chalcedon on the Bosphorus. Then in 408BC he recaptured Byzantium, usually thought impregnable on its peninsula. This ensured safe passage for ships carrying vital wheat from the Black Sea through the Bosphorus to Athens. It was time for his triumphant return to Athens.

Alcibiades reached Athens in June 407BC. His popularity surged yet higher when he gave a ceremonial military escort to the religious procession down the Sacred Way to Eleusis. (For years the Athenians had been going by ship to avoid the Spartans.) Alcibiades was now elected *strategos autocrator* (supreme commander), a role denied even Pericles. Returning to take control of the fleet, however, he made a disastrous mistake. Going off possibly to raise revenue – Athens was desperately short of cash – he left the rest of the fleet under the command of Antiochus, an experienced sailor but a drunk. Antiochus provoked and lost an unnecessary battle to the Spartans at Notion in spring 406BC. With his reputation now shattered, Alcibiades thought it wiser to retire to his castle on the Hellespont.

THE COSTLY VICTORY

The Spartan fleet was now commanded by a new *navarch* (admiral), Lysander, an unusually formidable Spartan. Lysander befriended the youthful Prince Cyrus, known as Cyrus the Younger, who had far-ranging powers. Cyrus soon committed Persia to Sparta, which in turn agreed to Persian demands. With Persian gold, Lysander could hire rowers at better rates than Athens, soon building up a large professional fleet.

But Athens was not defeated yet. Lysander was replaced as *navarch* by the less competent Callicratidas. At Arginusae, south of Lesbos, in late 406BC, the Athenians defeated the Spartan fleet again in a hard-fought battle. But in a storm at the battle's end, many Athenian sailors whose triremes had been sunk

Left: In 405–404BC, during the last winter of the war, the Spartans blockaded a starving Athens until finally the city surrendered.

were left to drown. When the news reached Athens, the Assembly, dominated by Cleophon, another demagogue, became hysterical. (Many had lost friends or relatives in this disaster.) The Assembly tried six *strategoi* for incompetence for not rescuing the drowning men. Among those found guilty and executed were Thrasyllus, Athens' best general at the time, and Pericles the Younger. Such collective trials were almost certainly illegal, but only Socrates the philosopher was brave enough to protest, nearly being lynched in the process.

Athens had now exiled or killed its last good leaders. Cleophon also persuaded the Assembly to reject further Spartan peace offers. Reportedly, he was drunk at the time.

ENDGAME AT GOAT'S RIVERS

Lysander, resuming command of the Spartan fleet in 405BC, took a 200-strong Peloponnesian fleet up to the Hellespont and captured Lampsacus on the south of the Straits, where he stationed his fleet in August. The Athenians, gathering all their ships, pulled up their fleet opposite him on the exposed beach of Aegospotami, Goat's Rivers. It was not a good spot, as supplies had to be brought every day from Sestos, 4.5km/3 miles away. Every day the Athenians rowed out to try to force a battle, but the Spartans refused. Alcibiades rode down from his castle to warn the Athenians to move, but they ignored him.

After four days, the Athenians had returned to cook lunch on the beach when Lysander's fleet sailed over. He caught the Athenians defenceless, taking their ships almost without a fight. About 4,000 Athenian sailors were summarily killed. So complete was the Spartan victory (only 20 ships under Conon escaped) that treachery was suspected. It meant the final end of Athenian seapower, and doomed the city.

The news reached Athens at nightfall, a night 'on which no man slept'. Lysander took his time, sweeping around the

Right: Athena, patron goddess of Athens, thanking Hera, patron goddess of Samos. The carving of 402BC celebrates the fact that Samos was one of the few cities that remained loyal to Athens until the war's bitter end.

Aegean and sending in all Athenian *cleruchs* to swell the numbers of starving citizens. Cleophon again vetoed the first peace proposals. Then the Assembly turned on him and had him executed for evading military service.

As the Spartan blockade tightened, a conference was called among the victors to decide on Athens' fate. Thebes and Corinth wanted the city destroyed, but the Spartans, thinking back to the Persian Wars, would not agree. Instead, Athens had to pull down the Long Walls to Piraeus, give up all overseas possessions, accept the return of all exiles, surrender all but 12 ships and accept a Spartan garrison.

In April 404BC Athens capitulated and Lysander entered the city in triumph. The long war was over.

Below: The theatre of Dionysus, where Athens, despite the disasters – political, social, economic – of a war being lost, continued to produce some of the world's greatest tragedies.

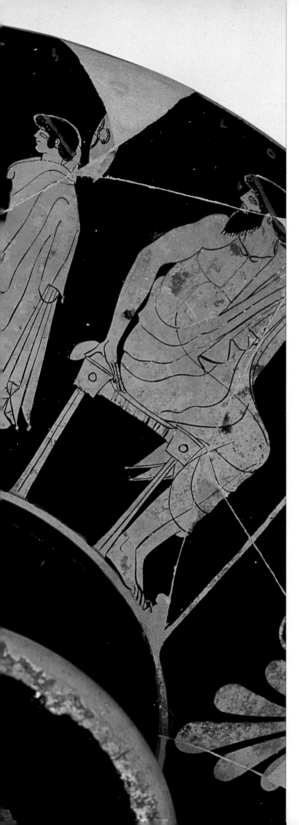

CHAPTER V

THE GREEKS:
THE FIRST INDIVIDUALS
c.650BC–AD147

The Greeks were among the first people about whose lives, loves and luck we can still read with interest and sympathy. This is partly due to the histories and biographies that survive (many have not). But it is also because the Greek *polis* gave some men, if few women, far more scope to be individuals than earlier absolutist monarchies had. Only in Sparta, that dour militaristic state, were there few individuals. Among the Macedonian monarchs, ruling huge empires after Alexander's conquest of Asia, glamorous personalities emerged, although none competes with Alexander himself.

The Greeks tended to hero-worship great generals, athletes, artists and poets. This tendency led, from the 4th century BC, to proclaiming victorious generals or monarchs as gods. This seductive flattery continued into the Roman Empire. Average Athenians must have looked very different from the godlike beings, with perfectly proportioned bodies and features, depicted in the friezes on the Acropolis, but Greeks revered those more blessed than themselves. A Greek *polis* was composed of gods and semi-divine heroes as well as living men.

Counterbalancing such hero-worship was the strong Greek love of gossip and scandal. The Greeks loved to talk and exchange rumours in the *agora* (market place) in every *polis* and at leisurely *symposia* (dinner parties). At times they wrote down this gossip. This helps make the Greeks among the first true individuals in human history.

Left: Greek vases often depict aspects of everyday life, as in this scene of masters and pupils writing or playing the flute.

SOLON: THE GREAT REFORMER
C.640–558BC

Above: Olive trees were important because olive oil became Attica's chief cash crop after Solon's reforms.

Below: This cup by the potter Exekias, showing the wine-god Dionysus in a vine-festooned ship, illustrates the age's general conviviality, when symposia (dinner parties) became widely established.

The first Greek individuals emerge around 600BC, when myth begins to give way to more solid, if not always reliable, fact. Lycurgus, for example, legendary founder of Sparta's unique constitution, remains just that: an undatable legend. But with Greeks who lived possibly only a generation or two later, we know enough to gain a general picture. Solon of Athens was the most revered of the Seven Sages of Greece and Athens' first great statesman. He is also the first Greek about whom we can form an (almost) valid biographical picture.

Solon was a Eupatrid, from an old aristocratic family that traced its line back to the (legendary) kings of Athens.

SOLON'S SOCIAL LEGISLATION
Solon allowed childless men to leave their property to whomever they liked, and legislated about the size of dowries to be given in marriage and about divorce. He introduced state-controlled brothels, whose transactions were taxed, while imposing restrictions on the public movement of free Athenian women. This cannot have helped their already low status.

But he was not born to riches: his father, Exestecides, had spent much of his modest wealth on charitable works, according to the biographer Plutarch. Solon started life writing poetry – this was the Lyric Age of Greece, when people naturally wrote in verse – without overt political intentions, often on religious or philosophical matters. But he was soon caught up in public life amid increasing political crises. The old aristocracy still monopolized and often abused its almost feudal powers, causing tensions with other Athenians, be they the new rich or the newly pauperized.

The problem only worsened when Dracon made Athens' laws public in 622BC, for now all could see their full severity. Solon emphasized that his sympathies lay with the poor. "Often the wicked prosper while the righteous starve; Yet I would never swap my state for theirs, Or my virtue for their gold. For mine endures, while riches change everyday," he wrote. But he restored the family fortunes by trading as a merchant, then a perfectly respectable occupation, even for an aristocrat. (Early Greece was a land of inspired polymaths and amateurs.)

SOLON'S GROWING REPUTATION

Solon first won fame for the conquest of Salamis, the island off the Attic coastline. He seems to have captured it from Megara more by guile than force, but the conquest was not permanent. His reputation grew further when he helped to unite Panhellenic opinion, represented by the 12 states in the Amphictyonic Council, against impious Crisa, which had tried to seize Delphi, seat of Apollo's oracle *c.*596BC. In 594BC the Athenians turned to Solon in desperation, for he alone might have the impartial wisdom to solve the problems of indebtedness and factionalism that threatened Athens with *stasis*, the civil strife that was the feared opposite of *eunomia* (social harmony).

REFORM, NOT REVOLUTION

Solon was no revolutionary, and he did not redistribute land as some expected. But nor did he make himself tyrant, as his friends had expected. Instead, his reforms aimed to avert tyranny, then common in Greece. He abolished enslavement for debt and the old aristocratic custom of taking one-sixth of every farmer's produce, and he freed Athenians sold into slavery abroad. He divided Athenian society into four classes based on wealth, not birth. The top two classes alone remained eligible for public office and membership of the Areopagus, the highest council and court, but everyone could attend and vote in the Assembly or the *Heliaea*, the jury court now supplementing the Areopagus. This last privilege, Plutarch noted, was "at first worth very little but later became extremely important".

Right: After inaugurating his reforms, Solon went travelling for 10 years to allow his changes to settle down. Visiting Egypt, immemorially ancient to Greeks, he conversed with priests at Sais, learning the tale of the end of Atlantis. The philosopher Plato, Solon's descendant, later wrote down this story in Timaeus.

TRAVELS AND OLD AGE

Aware that he had annoyed almost as as many people of every sort as he had pleased, Solon ordained that his new laws, exhibited on revolving wooden blocks for all to see, should remain in force for a century. He then set off on his travels for ten years, hoping that in his absence Athens would settle down and his reforms take root.

In Egypt Solon debated with the priests of Sais and recorded their legend (or history) of Atlantis, the drowned superpower. Two centuries later Plato, one of his descendants, publicized the Atlantis story in his *Timaeus*.

According to tradition, Solon also visited King Croesus of Lydia but was totally unimpressed by the fabulous royal wealth he was shown (although this story seems implausible on grounds of chronology). Returning home, Solon warned against the tyrannical intentions of Pisistratus – in vain, for Pisistratus seized power in 561BC. The new tyrant must have retained some affection for the man who had reputedly once been his lover, however, as Solon was never arrested, dying at a ripe old age.

Above: No original portraits of Solon survive, but this fine copy of the Roman period suggests his mixture of shrewdness, farsightedness and nobility.

BENEFICIAL TYRANTS
PITTACUS, PISISTRATUS & POLYCRATES

'Tyrant' to Greeks in *c*.600BC was no more abusive than 'chief' is to us. The men who won and exercised extraordinary power could even sometimes be called 'beneficial tyrants'.

PITTACUS OF LESBOS, *c*.650–570BC
Pittacus was born in Mytilene on the island of Lesbos, then growing fast both economically and culturally. He may have been an impoverished aristocrat, although

Above: Sometimes called 'the philosopher-tyrant' because of his self-restraint and tact, Pittacus ruled Mytiline sagely for 10 years, before retiring not a penny richer.

Below: The magnificent Ionic columns of the Temple of Olympian Zeus in Athens date from the 2nd century AD, but the temple's immense ground plan was laid out in the 6th century BC by the Pisistratids, who built on a newly magnificent scale.

enemies later sneered that he was a commoner. As was so often the case, the nobility was oppressing the people economically while their dynastic feuding shook the city. Pittacus led Mytiline's forces to a great victory over the Athenians at Sigeum *c*.600BC.

Around 590BC Pittacus was chosen by the people as *aesymnetes* (supreme ruler), but only for ten years. Pittacus used his powers wisely, granting a general amnesty and ruling with moderation, if firmness, and encouraging trade. One of his most notable laws doubled the punishment for crimes committed when drunk. He was not, however, draconian. Although he had to banish both Alcaeus and Sappho, the greatest poets of the age, for their intrigues, they later returned. ("Forgiveness is better than repentance," was a saying attributed to him.) Like Solon, he wrote in rather good verse. After ten years, he resigned all power and retired to private life no richer, to general surprise. He was considered one of the Seven Sages of Greece.

PISISTRATUS OF ATHENS, *c*.600–527BC
Pisistratus, descended from the legendary kings of Pylos, won fame as *polemarch* (war leader) for capturing the island of Salamis from Megara *c*.565BC. He was so popular that he started a new party called the Hill (there were already Plain and Coast parties). After appearing one day in the Assembly, apparently wounded by enemies, he was voted a bodyguard of 50 men – armed with clubs, not spears. With it, he seized the Acropolis as tyrant in 560BC. According to Herodotus, he "governed the country in an excellent way", but opponents drove him out in 556BC.

By allying with Megacles, head of the Alcmaeonids, he staged a comeback by an absurd ruse: he persuaded a tall young woman to dress up as Pallas Athene, the city's goddess, complete with spear and helmet, and enter Athens in a chariot acclaiming Pisistratus. ("The silliest trick in history", wrote Herodotus witheringly.) Pisistratus quarrelled with the Alcmaeonids too, going back into exile. He then established a base on the Strymon in north Greece and allied with Thebes and Argos. With their backing, he finally returned to power in 546BC.

Once established, Pisistratus, far from acting despotically, mellowed. He even dispensed with his bodyguard, walking around like any citizen. He could do this because life in Athens during the next 30 years improved all around. Solon's agrarian reforms, especially those encouraging the export of olive oil, were bearing fruit. Both farmers, and the craftsmen who made the increasingly splendid vases for the oil, benefited. Pisistratus also encouraged Solon's constitution, tactfully manipulating it to ease supporters into major posts while the Assembly slowly gained confidence.

If Pisistratus had the common touch, chatting easily with farmers, he also rebuilt links with some nobles, including Miltiades, head of the Philiads, who went off to establish a fort on the distant Hellespont (Dardanelles). This helped to safeguard grain imports. His sons Hippias and Hipparchus succeeded after his peaceful death in 527BC. They continued his policies until 514BC, when the assassination of Hipparchus induced paranoia in Hippias.

POLYCRATES OF SAMOS, REIGNED 540–523BC

Polycrates seized control of the island of Samos c.540BC, aided by his two brothers. Unfraternally, he killed or exiled them to rule alone, but he proved a popular ruler thanks to his massive public works. He built a huge aqueduct, tunnelled through rock for over 1.6km/1 mile; a grand temple to the goddess Hera, stupendous fortifications and a vast harbour mole. Aristotle, exaggerating for once, compared his projects to the pyramids.

Polycrates patronized poets such as Anacreon, while ruling the seas with a fleet of 100 galleys. He paid for this splendour partly by piracy – his ships raided friends and enemies alike, but he reputedly returned goods to the former – but chiefly through an alliance with Amasis, Pharaoh of Egypt. Amasis hired the Samian fleet to defend Egypt against Persia. But when Persia was about to attack Egypt, Polycrates changed sides, sending ships to help the Persians.

This did him little good, for he was tricked out of his island fortress by an invitation to Sardis. There the Persian satrap had him crucified – a form of execution the Persians had pioneered but that was later adopted by other peoples.

Above: A 16th-century painting by Giovanni Fedini shows Polycrates of Samos. Growing alarmed that his good luck tempted fate, Polycrates threw his best ring into the sea to appease the gods. But a fisherman, catching an unusually fine fish, offered it to the tyrant. Inside it was the ring. Polycrates realized he was doomed.

Left: Noblest of the many grand projects that Polycrates, the tyrant of Samos, undertook was the Heraion, the vast new temple to Hera, Samos' patron goddess.

DEMOCRACY'S CHAMPIONS
CLEISTHENES AND THEMISTOCLES

Cleisthenes was, according to Herodotus, the founder of "democracy for the Athenians", while Themistocles saved Athens from Persian conquest. These two statesmen played a major part in the development of Athens.

CLEISTHENES: FATHER OF DEMOCRACY, c.570–500BC

Cleisthenes' career started in typically aristocratic factionalism, for he was an Alcmaeonid. But it ended most atypically in democratic revolution. He became chief *archon* in 525BC, when the tyrants Hippias and Hipparchus were letting other aristocrats share office. Later, he quarrelled with the Pisistratids and went into exile. He used his wealth for an abortive invasion of Attica and, more fruitfully, to win over the Delphic Oracle. This persuaded Sparta, once friendly to the Pisistratids, to expel Hippias in 510BC.

King Cleomenes and his Athenian ally Isagoras expected a return to old-style aristocratic politics, and Isagoras was elected *archon* in 508BC. At this stage

Above: The determination and ambition of Themistocles, the radical democrat and saviour of Athens in the Persian Wars, is evident in this bust.

Below: Politics in Athens was still largely a competitive sport between rival aristocrats, who might meet at friendly symposia, until Cleisthenes changed the rules of the game.

Cleisthenes, refusing to play the old game, "added the *demos* (people) to his faction", in Aristotle's words. This means that he got them on his side, but his real intentions remain debated. His radical constitutional reforms created ten entirely new *phylae* (tribes), each with a *trittyes* (third) representing all three parties: Coast, Hill and City [Plain earlier]. This almost eliminated local aristocrats' hold on politics. Other reforms to the Council, and the introduction of ostracism (to banish uppity politicians), confirmed the new democracy. Athenians clearly liked it. When Isagoras returned to Athens with Spartan support and banished 700 opponents, they felt confident enough to rise against him, restoring their democracy, of which Cleisthenes was the perhaps unwitting father.

THEMISTOCLES: SAVIOUR OF ATHENS, c.525–459BC

Themistocles was an outsider in Athenian politics, having a non-Athenian mother and a father "of no particular mark" (in Plutarch's words). But, since he saved Athens from Persian conquest, he ranks with the very greatest Greek statesmen and generals.

Themistocles was intensely ambitious, although his father tried to warn him off politics. (Pointing to some rotting hulks on the beach, he said that *that* was how Athens treated discarded politicians.) Themistocles had no support from aristocratic networks (he did not even belong to a smart gymnasium), but in 494BC he was elected *archon*. He had chosen to live in the rundown Ceramicus (potters') area, where he got the ears and votes of poorer citizens. As news of Persia's suppression of the Ionian revolt crossed the Aegean, filling Athens with dread – it had helped Ionia burn

down Sardis in 498BC – Themistocles urged the fortification of Piraeus. Until then the beach of Phalerum had been Athens' port, but it was perilously exposed. By contrast, Piraeus was on a rocky peninsula with three natural harbours. Work started on its walls and docks but, while Themistocles saw Athens' future as a seapower, few Athenians yet agreed.

In 490BC Themistocles was one of the *strategoi* (generals) at the Battle of Marathon, but Miltiades masterminded that hoplite victory. After Miltiades' death, Themistocles emerged as leader of the anti-Persian radicals. The Assembly began flexing its democratic muscles, using Cleisthenes' novelty: ostracism. Meanwhile, war with Aegina, the powerful nearby island, revealed Athenian weakness at sea. As his noble opponents were ostracized, Themistocles faced one last formidable rival: Aristides the Just. Aristides was a conservative famed for exceptional honesty, but it was Themistocles who saw the growing danger from Persia. When in 483BC a new vein of silver was found at the Laurium mines, Themistocles proposed to use the wealth from this to build a fleet of 200 triremes, not distribute it as a windfall. Aristides, losing this argument, was ostracized in 482BC. But by 481BC all Greece was alarmed at the Persian threat.

SPINNING THE PROPHECIES
At the last debate in the Assembly before war in 480BC, Themistocles spun Delphi's gloomy prophecies to show that Athenians should use the fleet to win at Salamis, not flee to the west or retreat to the Acropolis. In the long negotiations with the Peloponnesians, Themistocles often swallowed his pride. He even accepted Spartan command of the allied fleet, although Athens contributed most ships. Finally, with the Greek fleet stationed at Salamis, Persian armies thronging the shore and Persian ships approaching the island, Themistocles' trick of a secret message to the Great

King persuaded Xerxes to dispatch his fleet. Once lured inside the Salamis straits, it was crushed.

Themistocles showed the same cunning when, after Persia's defeat, Sparta protested at Athens rebuilding its city walls. Going to Sparta, he prevaricated masterfully, persuading Sparta to send envoys to Athens, who then became hostages until the walls were completed. Despite this, Themistocles was ostracized in 470BC, partly because of his boastfulness. Fleeing Greece, where he had many enemies, he became governor of Magnesia, a Greek city *inside* the Persian Empire. But he reputedly killed himself rather than obey Persian orders to fight Athens, for he was no traitor. Thucydides, no admirer of radicals, summed up Themistocles: "He showed indisputable, quite exceptional natural genius... he was unrivalled at doing exactly the right thing at exactly the right moment."

Above: A griffin from Susa, the administrative capital of the Persian Empire, whose growing power overshadowed Greek life for decades until countered at Salamis and Plataea.

PERICLES: THE SUPREME DEMOCRAT c.495–429BC

Above: Aspasia, Pericles' mistress for many years, attended symposia and talked to philosophers, which was most unusual for any woman in Athens. Highly intelligent, she bore Pericles a son who after Pericles' death was legitimized as an Athenian citizen, also a rare honour.

Few elected politicians give their name to an age. None can match Pericles, whose name is synonymous with Athens' most brilliant decades. An Alcmaeonid by birth (he was Cleisthenes' great-nephew), Pericles was a visionary democrat by conviction, dominating Athenian politics for 30 years (460–429BC). Abraham Lincoln modelled his Gettysburg address on Pericles' funeral oration of 431BC.

Pericles entered public life by sponsoring Aeschylus' *The Persians* in 472BC. Unusually, this play dealt with recent events, praising Athenian democracy and its role in the Persian Wars. Both were policies of Themistocles, who was ostracized soon after. Pericles then joined forces with Ephialtes, a noted radical. In 462BC they persuaded the Assembly to transfer most remaining powers from the Areopagus to the Assembly or *Heliaea* (jury court). This marked Athens' transition to full democracy. After Ephialtes'

ANAXAGORAS

Pericles spoke only rarely in public so that people did not grow tired of his voice. But when he did, he was the greatest orator of his day, with a "nobility in his speech utterly free of vulgar mob-oratory", according to Plutarch. Pericles had learned his skills partly from Anaxagoras of Clazomenae. This philosopher so impressed contemporaries that he was nicknamed 'Brain Personified'. Anaxagoras questioned conventional wisdoms. Solar eclipses, for example, were natural phenomena, not signs from the gods. This was intellectually too daring even for Athens, however, and Anaxagoras had to flee the city in 428BC, accused of impiety.

murder by enraged opponents, Pericles became the radicals' leader, though still only in his thirties.

Pericles introduced modest payment for jurors and Council members – just enough to ensure that poverty stopped no Athenian from attending them. During subsequent wars he proved a competent *strategos*. After the Peace of Callias in 449BC ended the Persian Wars, Pericles urged that surplus public money be used to rebuild the temples on the Acropolis, whose blackened ruins had been left as sharp reminders of the Persian occupation. But this was a controversial use of tribute from allied states, and some Athenians, led by Thucydides son of Melesias, attacked him for it. Pericles, who exalted Athens' role as the educator of Greece,

Left: The Temple of Athena Nike (Victorious), although finished in 425BC after Pericles' death, derived from his vision of Athens as the 'school of Hellas', a beacon of democracy.

won the argument, and Thucydides was later ostracized. Athens under Pericles was, Thucydides the historian wrote, "ostensibly a democracy but actually ruled by one man". But, despite his "high note of aristocratic, even regal leadership" in Plutarch's words, Pericles remained accountable to the Assembly.

ARCHITECTURAL PATRON

Pericles' role in the building of the Parthenon, one of the world's most sublime buildings, alone would ensure his fame. He arranged for Ictinus and Callicrates to design the temple and Pheidias its superb frieze. He saw the project through to swift completion, gaining a name for financial probity, then rare. He also oversaw the building of the Odeon, a covered theatre where plays were previewed, and encouraged Herodotus to read aloud from his *Histories*, the world's very first.

WAR AIMS

Pericles was an imperialist, crushing the revolt of Samos in 440–439BC, for example. He was elected *strategos* every year from 443 to 430BC, heading the Board of Generals with increasingly professional ease. Pericles probably felt that the Athenian Empire benefited all Greece, sheltering it from Persian power, encouraging democracy and, by keeping down piracy, boosting trade. Certainly Athens thrived, with Piraeus becoming the eastern Mediterranean's greatest port. But such open imperialism created many enemies. In 433BC Pericles claimed that he could see war "bearing down from the Peloponnese". How far his policies provoked that war remains debatable.

In the Peloponnesian War that started in 431BC, Pericles' overall strategy – retreat behind the Long Walls, let the Spartans ravage Attica, but maintain naval superiority – was approved by the Assembly. When plague hit the city in 430BC, however, the people turned on him and falsely fined him for speculation. He was reinstated only just before his death from after-effects of the plague in autumn 429BC.

Pericles married and divorced when young. Divorce was common in Athens, but it was customary to marry again. Pericles did not, pre-ferring the company of his mistress Aspasia; he was exclu-sively heterosexual, unlike many Greeks. He cultivated a lofty dignity in both public and private life, restricting his social life as he grew busier. The poet Ion of Chios found him "insolent and conceited", but perhaps caught him on a bad day. He is always portrayed with a helmet because, his enemies said, he wanted to hide his odd-shaped head. He seems to have had no other obvi-ous vices. His deathbed statement that "no Athenian ever put on mourning because of me" (i.e. his policies produced no needless casualties) may be ques-tionable, but his place as Athens' greatest leader is not.

Left: Pericles' vision of a democracy that raises its citizens up, rather than dumbs them down, inspired later democrats such as American President Abraham Lincoln, who modelled his Gettysburg Address on Pericles' famous Funeral Oration of 431BC.

Below: The archetypal picture of Pericles in his helmet, which he would have worn as strategos (elected general). He often wore it on other occasions too – to hide the odd shape of his head, according to his enemies.

DEMOCRATS IN DEFEAT
ALCIBIADES AND DEMOSTHENES

Below: Demosthenes, orator, politician and attempted saviour of Athenian independence from Macedonia's rising power, is shown here with a scroll.

Although no two men were less alike than Alcibiades and Demosthenes, both ended their lives in exile and failure after early successes.

ALCIBIADES, *c.*450–404BC

The last Alcmaeonid to lead Athens, and almost the last aristocrat in politics, Alcibiades had a dangerous Byronic glamour. Related to Pericles, whose ward he became on his father's death in 447BC, he was notably handsome and self-willed. As a boy, when defeated in a wrestling match, he sank his teeth into his opponent's arm. Accused of fighting like a girl, he replied that he was biting like a lion. Throughout his life, he ignored all the rules.

COMMAND AND DESERTION

Alcibiades met Socrates when they were fellow soldiers at Potidaea in 430BC. The philosopher saved Alcibiades' life – a favour Alcibiades returned six years later at Delium – and tried to guide the gifted young man towards philosophical virtue. This was in vain, for Alcibiades, while flattered by Socrates' attentions (in Plato's *Symposium* he is shown trying to seduce the older man), was interested in fame and power. He cut off the tail of his dog so that everyone would comment on its state, and trailed a long purple cloak around the Agora. But when his chariot won first prize in the Olympic Games, and two others belonging to him came second *and* fourth, he could claim a truly Homeric victory. Athens loved him for it.

Standing for election as *strategos* in 420BC, Alcibiades faced little competition from Nicias, the timid conservative leader, or Hyperbolus, a radical and noted windbag. As *strategos*, Alcibiades created an anti-Spartan alliance in the Peloponnese. Not re-elected – which helped to lead to allied defeat at Mantinea – he looked elsewhere for glory, notably to Sicily,

Below: Alcibiades enjoyed a strange second career as an adviser in Sparta after being exiled. Sparta, although notoriously austere and lacking appeal for a sybaritic nobleman, boasted some fine temples, as these ruins reveal.

which was alluringly rich. Alcibiades urged an expedition there, finally with success. But he had made enemies by his arrogance and his scandalous friends who mocked the city's gods. When the herms (good-luck statues set around Athens) were found mutilated, he was accused of sacrilege. Denied a chance to clear his name, he sailed with the Syracusan expedition in 415BC but was recalled to face fresh charges. Escaping his captors, he reached Sparta. There he charmed his hosts and gave them excellent advice: invade Attica again and occupy the fort of Deceleia permanently. This devastated Athenian farming and mining.

Alcibiades' lack of patriotism was common among Greeks. But when he seduced the wife of King Agis, he had to leave Sparta fast. He crossed to Asia and persuaded Tissaphernes, a Persian satrap, that he could make Athens Persia's ally. The Athenians now wanted him back. As Aristophanes wrote, "they long for him, hate him and cannot do without him". Elected *strategos* by the fleet at Samos, he recaptured important cities on the Bosphorus in 408BC. He returned to Athens in seeming triumph in 407BC, but, when his helmsman Antiochus lost a pointless battle, he slipped away to his Hellespontine fort in disgrace. From it he rode out to warn the Athenian fleet about its dangerous position at Aegospotami – in vain. He was killed by assassins in Persian pay, who surprised him in bed with his last mistress, Timandra. She buried her lover, the last Alcmaeonid, in a foreign field.

DEMOSTHENES, 384–322BC

The finest of all Greek orators, Demosthenes was the last great Athenian democrat, who battled to save his city from foreign domination. Although he ultimately failed, his was a noble failure.

Orphaned when young, Demosthenes saw his guardians steal his inheritance and had to fight to regain it. A bookish, unathletic boy, he cured a stammer to become a superb professional speech-writer, the equivalent today of a barrister. Athens remained the foremost Greek

naval state, with interests around the Aegean. This led her to clash with Macedonia, rising fast under its ambitious new king Philip II. Demosthenes, realizing that Athens' independence could not survive Macedonian hegemony, became leader of the anti-appeasement party in Athens. To rouse his countrymen, who preferred to employ mercenaries rather than fight themselves, he made four fiery speeches: the *Philippics* ('against Philip'). In these, he urged resistance to Philip's promises and threats.

Demosthenes' great political achieve-ment was the alliance with Thebes, Athens' old rival, against Macedonia in 338BC. He fought as a citizen-hoplite in the Battle of Chaeronea, but this proved Philip's greatest victory. Philip, who wanted Athens' fleet for his planned war on Persia, dealt with Athens gently. Later, while Alexander was conquering Asia, Demosthenes defeated Aeschines, his main Athenian enemy in a brilliant speech, *De Corona* (On the Crown), defending his right to honours for services to his city. After Athenian democracy was finally crushed by Macedonia in 322BC, Demosthenes killed himself rather than fall into Macedonian hands.

Above: Alcibiades counted among his friends the penniless philosopher Socrates, who had saved his life in battle in 430BC. Socrates discerned signs of greatness in the self-indulgent aristocrat, but Alcibiades disappointed his teacher by preferring worldly fame to areté *(virtue, excellence).*

Below: Demosthenes was a superbly rousing orator, but his words proved useless against Macedonian revolt.

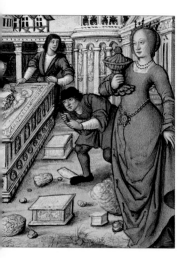

Above: A fanciful medieval portrayal of Artemisia, the fighting queen of Halicarnassus.

EXCEPTIONAL GREEK WOMEN
ARTEMISIA, OLYMPIAS AND ASPASIA

Women in classical Greece proper played no role in public life. But in Ionia and Macedonia, where they had more freedom than in Athens, some remarkable women emerged.

ARTEMISIA OF HALICARNASSUS, ACTIVE *c.*480BC

Artemisia, queen of Halicarnassus (today Bodrum) in Caria, was an exceptional queen. She took part in Xerxes' invasion of Greece, giving him unusually forthright advice. Her father, King Lygdamis, was Carian, but her mother was a Cretan aristocrat. Widowed young, Artemisia stepped into her unknown husband's royal shoes and ruled the city even after her son grew up.

She supplied five galleys to the Persian fleet in 480BC – Herodotus thought them the best ships after Sidon's – commanding them in battles off Euboea. When Xerxes held a council of war before the battle of Salamis, she alone advised against attacking the Greek fleet, saying that the Greeks could not stay long on the small, crowded island. Her advice was not taken and the Persians advanced to their defeat. In their rout, Artemisia's galley, chased by an Athenian trireme, rammed a Calyndian ship that was on her side but in her way. The Athenian trireme, thinking that Artemisia's ship was an ally, abandoned its pursuit. Artemisia saved her life by this quick thinking and gained kudos with Xerxes, watching from his shoreside throne. Thinking she had actually rammed a Greek ship, the King exclaimed: "My men are fighting like women and my women like men!"

ASPASIA, MISTRESS OF PERICLES

Aspasia came from Miletus, the most sophisticated city in the Greek world until its sack by the Persians in 493BC.

Like many adventurous Ionians after 480BC, she migrated west to Athens in search of her fortune. She became Pericles' mistress at about the time he became Athens' effective leader *c.*450BC, their relationship lasting until his death in 429BC.

She must have been highly intelligent as well as attractive, for Pericles' circle included the greatest minds of the age. Reputedly, she joined in discussions with the philosophers Protagoras and Anaxagoras, unlike a normal Athenian wife. (Significantly, we do not even know the name of Pericles' wife, whom he divorced.)

Aspasia's son Pericles, unlike Pericles' legitimate sons, inherited some of his father's talents as well as his name. Aspasia must also have helped to bring up Alcibiades, Pericles' brilliant but troublesome ward.

Right: This Roman-era portrait bust of Aspasia, Pericles' mistress, captures the intelligence, independence and noble beauty of the great statesman's lover.

Her relationship with Pericles fed slanderous gossip. He was depicted on stage as being in her power, although this was clearly not true. She was, however, caught up in the attacks on Pericles after plague broke out in 430BC and accused of impiety, according to Plutarch. After Pericles' death, however, her son Pericles was legitimized and granted Athenian citizenship, which was a rare honour. Aspasia then married Lysicles, a wealthy politician. She may have had the luck to die before 406BC, when her son was one of the six *strategoi* unjustly condemned to death for abandoning drowning sailors after the Battle of Arginusae.

OLYMPIAS, MOTHER OF ALEXANDER, *c.*364–316BC

Even wilder than Macedonia, Epirus, on the north-western edge of Greece, was ruled by kings who claimed descent from Achilles, greatest of Homeric heroes. Olympias, daughter of King Neoptolemus, reputedly met Philip of Macedonia at the mysteries (initiation into the religious ceremonies) on the island of Samothrace and fell in love. More probably their marriage in 357BC was arranged for political motives, as Philip covered his back (literally) with marital ties.

The birth of Alexander a year later produced the essential male heir, but the marriage was unhappy. Olympias was a tempestuous character, whose wrath could rival that of Achilles. Often ignored by Philip – who had mistresses, boyfriends and six other wives – Olympias turned to religion. She took part in the Bacchic mysteries, kept a sacred snake in her bed and sacrificed thousands of animals. She helped to choose her son's first two tutors and probably encouraged his belief that a god, not Philip, was his real father. Alexander inherited her fiery temper and supported her when she left Macedonia, enraged by Philip's last marriage to Eurydice. But he was reconciled with Philip, while she was divorced by him, returning only after Philip's murder in 336BC.

Olympias honoured the corpse of the assassin Pausanias, which suggests complicity in the murder, and had Eurydice killed. Alexander left her as queen in Macedonia when he crossed to Asia, but she quarrelled repeatedly with Antipater, his general. Hearing this, Alexander exclaimed that his mother charged him dearly for nine-months' lodging in her womb. In the long wars after Alexander's death, she retreated to Epirus, then returned to kill the half-witted King Philip III in 317BC. Besieged in Pydna herself a year later, she was starved into surrender. Macedonian soldiers sent to execute her refused "out of respect for her royal rank", so relatives of her victims finally killed her.

Left: Olympias, wife of Philip II of Macedonia and mother of Alexander the Great, was a passionate, fiery woman who frequently quarrelled with her husband. After her son's death she played a major role in Macedonian dynastic politics.

Below: Although classical Athens was an intensely masculine society, the city revered a female deity, Athena Parthenos, the warrior-goddess whose cult image was carried aloft in every Panathenaic Festival. This statue is a copy of Pheidias' lost masterpiece.

EXTRAORDINARY SPARTANS
CLEOMONES AND BRASIDAS

Above: The agora of the ancient city of Sparta, home of one of the most absolute military regimes the world has ever known.

Below: David's famous depiction in 1814 of Leonidas, who with his Spartans fought the Persians to the last man at Thermopylae in 480BC, typifying Spartan bravery and military competence. But a more imaginative general such as Cleomones or Brasidas with 7,000 allied troops might have held the pass indefinitely.

Although the Spartan system discouraged individuality, some kings or generals escaped the general levelling, if at considerable personal risk.

CLEOMONES I: SPARTA'S DYNAMIC KING, REIGNED c.520–c.490BC

Even Cleomones' birth was controversial. His father, King Anaxandridas, had taken a second wife after his first failed to have children, but he kept her too. His second wife duly gave birth to Cleomones, but other boys were born soon after to the king's first wife.

Cleomones, succeeding to the throne c.520BC, soon showed unSpartan cunning. The tiny city of Plataea in 519BC asked for Sparta's protection against her powerful neighbour Thebes. Cleomones suggested that Athens, much closer, would be a better ally, thus embroiling Athens, still friendly to Sparta, with Thebes. The two cities' resulting enmity suited Sparta. In 510BC Cleomones led a Spartan army to expel Hippias from Athens, for the Delphic Oracle had urged the Spartans to free the city. Cleomones probably knew that Cleisthenes, the Alcmaeonid, had bribed the Oracle, but he did not expect the subsequent democratic revolution. Marching back to Athens to support his aristocratic friend Isagoras, Cleomones was besieged on the Acropolis and had to bargain with the Athenian *demos* for his freedom – a humiliation for a Spartan king, which deepened when his avenging invasion of Attica collapsed in 506BC due to divisions in the army.

Cleomones' position after such a defeat may have been shaky in Sparta – he had envious half-brothers – but he ignored Ionian appeals for help against Persia in order to concentrate on Sparta's real enemy: Argos.

In a brilliant ruse in 494BC, Cleomones attacked the Argives during lunch, when they were not expecting it. After the defeated Argives took shelter in a sacred wood, he had it burnt down, killing 6,000 and crippling Argos for a generation. Cleomones may not have helped Ionia, but he still pursued a vigorous anti-Persian policy. The Athenian defeat of Persia at Marathon was partly due to his pressure on Athens' enemy Aegina to stop it 'medizing' (collaborating with Persia).

Cleomones fell from power c.490BC in mysterious circumstances after his part in bribing the Delphic Oracle to help depose Demaratus, his fellow-king, had been exposed. This encouraged his radical ideas about becoming sole king of a broader-based state than Sparta. For support he appealed to the Arcadians, Spartan allies in the Peloponnese. His scheme failed, he was deposed and declared mad. Locked up, he was said to have committed suicide, but was almost certainly killed. Sparta thus lost an unusually dynamic king.

BRASIDAS: A SPARTAN
BY MISTAKE, DIED 422BC

Brasidas had so many non-Spartan qualities – flexibility, diplomacy, eloquence – that he should really be considered a Spartan by mistake. An officer's son, he grew up brave and tough but also able to think for himself, lacking the characteristic Spartan arrogance. Brasidas came to prominence in 431BC when he rescued Methone in the Peloponnese from an Athenian sea-borne attack with only 100 hoplites. He received an official award for this. He was less successful in 429BC in western Greece, for the Athenian fleet was vastly superior to the Peloponnesian.

But he shone again at the Spartan attack on Pylos in 425BC, when he urged on hesitant Spartans landing on the rocky shore. Badly wounded disembarking, he took no further part in what became Sparta's most shameful defeat.

His real opportunity came in 424BC, when Perdiccas of Macedonia and some northern cities appealed to Sparta for aid against Athens, wanting Brasidas as the general. Sparta would not risk Spartiates (soldiers from the ruling class) so far north but let Brasidas recruit 700 *helots* (slaves), whom he armed as hoplites. Picking up 1,000 allied mercenaries as he went, he saved Megara from Athenian attack. Marching swiftly through a hostile Thessaly, he reached Acanthus in the Chalcidice. This, like many Greek cities, was divided. Most Acanthians were content as Athens' allies, but they let Brasidas talk to them. He was so persuasive, promising to respect their liberties, that they went over to Sparta's side. Thucydides noted they were also worried about their grape harvest, with Brasidas' troops camped in their vineyards. Two other cities, Stagira and Argilus, joined on similar terms.

Then Brasidas had his greatest success, marching through the winter night to capture the unguarded bridge over the River Strymon. Beyond it lay Amphipolis, hugely important to Athens. Here again Brasidas triumphed by his oratory, offering such easy terms that the city

surrendered, unaware that Athenian *strategos* Thucydides was belatedly hurrying to their rescue. History's gain was Athens' loss, for she never recaptured Amphipolis. Brasidas had further successes through combined diplomacy and generalship, skilfully keeping his mixed army of mercenaries and ex-*helots* in fighting form. He was killed in battle at Amphipolis in 422BC leading a charge against Athenians attacking the city. With him died Sparta's most remarkable general.

Above: These hoplites and chariot from Laconia, c.500BC, show characteristic Spartan toughness. Such an upbringing created brave foot soldiers, not adventurous generals, who remained a rarity.

Below: Sparta occupied the fertile Eurotas Valley beneath Mt Taygetus, some of the richest farmland in Greece.

CONTRASTING GENERALS
CIMON AND EPAMINONDAS

Above: Miltiades, who
masterminded Athenian
victory at Marathon over
Persia in 490BC, was the
father of Cimon, another
great general.

While Cimon of Athens was a bluff aristocrat but an excellent soldier, Epaminondas
of Thebes was a general of genius who
briefly made his city hegemon of Greece.

CIMON OF ATHENS, c.508–449BC
Cimon was the son of Miltiades, architect
of the victory at Marathon in 490BC, but
his mother was descended from Thracian
kings. Cimon lacked "any spark of Attic
cleverness and eloquence" said Plutarch,
yet gave "an impression of great nobility
and candour". Miltiades had died in
disgrace and debt, so Cimon's youth was
impoverished. He long lived with his sister
Elpinice, which fed malicious rumours of
incest, until the rich Callias married her
for love and paid off their debts. Cimon
himself often fell in love with aristocratic

women, including Isodice from the rival
Alcmaeonids. He was also fond of drink
and kept open house on his estate, where
all were welcome.

In 480BC, as Persian forces approached
Athens, Cimon led the young knights up
the Acropolis to dedicate their bridles to
Athena before taking up spears and
shields to serve as marines, a timely
gesture. He fought bravely at Salamis and
with Aristides commanded the Athenian
fleet in 478BC against the Persians. The
allied commander was the Spartan
Pausanias, but he behaved so outrageously
– raping freeborn girls, dressing in Persian
robes – that the Greeks turned to Athens
for leadership. Cimon became commander
of the Delian League fleet, often
re-elected *strategos* and capturing Persian
strongholds. He also retrieved the
supposed bones of Theseus, Athens'
legendary king, from Scyros. His finest
triumph came in 467BC, when he led a
fleet to defeat the Persians at the River
Eurymedon, destroying 200 ships and
its army. By then, with Themistocles
ostracized, Cimon appeared supreme in
Athens, but city politics was fickle.

In 464BC an earthquake hit Sparta,
triggering a *helot* rising. In despair, Sparta
appealed to Athens, still an ally, for help.
Cimon led 4,000 hoplites into Messenia,
but they were rudely dismissed by the
Spartans, who distrusted democrats. Back
in Athens, radicals exploited Cimon's
absence to introduce political reforms. For
opposing these, he was ostracized. When
war broke out between Athens and the
Peloponnesians, Cimon volunteered to
fight as an ordinary hoplite at Tanagra in
457BC – in vain. After his ostracism ended
in 451BC, however, he commanded the

Left: A 19th-century recreation of the sea
Battle of Salamis in 480BC, in which
Cimon took part.

fleet that sailed against Cyprus. There he died, but his body was brought back in honour to Athens.

EPAMINONDAS OF THEBES
c.418–362BC

Epaminondas was Thebes' greatest general and statesman, who raised it briefly to hegemony in Greece and freed the *helots* of Messenia from Spartan oppression. The son of an impoverished noble, he studied under Lysis, the last Pythagorean philosopher. Epaminondas always led a life of almost ascetic poverty, refusing all gifts and bribes.

Thebes had been Sparta's keen ally against Athens in the Peloponnesian War but Spartan postwar arrogance drove it to ally with Athens in 395BC. In 382BC a Spartan coup installed a corrupt junta backed by a Spartan garrison in the Cadmaea, Thebes' citadel. Anti-Spartan feeling in the city grew until in 378BC a group of exiles returned. Disguised as prostitutes, they assassinated the junta's leaders and declared a democracy. Epaminondas and his friend Pelopidas now radically reorganized the Theban army. Instead of the usual eight-deep line of hoplites in the phalanx, with the best soldiers on the right, they raised the number to 50 deep on the left wing and trained it to attack at an angle. The core of this new army was the crack Sacred Band, 150 pairs of homosexual lovers bound by love and honour. Even Sparta's militarized pederasty had not produced this, but Epaminondas himself was unusual in never marrying and having only male lovers.

The new-model army proved its worth by crushing the Spartans at the Battle of Leuctra in 371BC, killing 400 Spartiates, a feat that astonished Greece. Soon the Thebans invaded the Peloponnese, liberating the Messenians from centuries of slavery. Epaminondas now revealed political as well as military genius. Messene was refounded as the *polis* of free Messenia, with imposing fortifications, and Megalopolis (big city) was founded

as a new capital for Arcadia, blocking Sparta's easiest egress north. Both cities were moderate democracies heading federations, like Thebes. Deprived of its *helot* serfs, Sparta sank forever to second-rank status. But Epamonindas could not establish a lasting peace. Athens, alarmed at Thebes' new power, allied with Sparta, and war continued. Epamonindas died in 362BC at the Battle of Mantinea fought against a mixed alliance. Thebes' brief hegemony was ended, but he deserved the inscription on his statue that, through his efforts and vision, "Greece was free" at least in part.

Above: The Apadana Staircase in Persepolis, capital of the giant empire that Cimon grew up trained to fight. Temperamentally pro-Spartan, he thought Athens should solely attack Persia.

Below: Thebes' heart was the Cadmaea, a citadel dating back to the Bronze Age, in which these remants of Mycenaean walls survive.

THE FIRST HISTORIANS
HERODOTUS AND THUCYDIDES

Below: Thucydides took as his theme the long war between Athens and the Peloponnesians. Hoplites such as these bore the brunt of the land fighting.

Although there had long been royal and religious chroniclers, analytical history starts with the Greeks. The term *historia* (inquiry or research) was actually first used by Herodotus.

HERODOTUS, 'FATHER OF HISTORY', *c.*490–425BC

Herodotus came from Halicarnassus (today Bodrum), an Ionian city with a strong Carian element. It supplied ships for the Persian fleet in 480BC but later joined the League of Delos, so it stood midway between Asia and Greece culturally and politically. This was apposite, for Herodotus, almost alone among Greek writers, viewed non-Greeks with an inquisitive, sympathetic eye, free of racial prejudice. Probably due to political troubles, he moved to Athens *c.*446BC, where he recited part of his *Histories* in public, then a common practice. He was paid 10 talents at Pericles' instigation for this, a large sum. He probably ended his days in Thurii in southern Italy.

Little else is known of him, but, through his writings, the reader gets to know a genial, intelligent, often discursive but never boring man. For Herodotus was not only 'the father of history' but an insatiably curious polymath. His researches led him to visit Egypt, Babylonia, the Black Sea and other areas, collating tales, legends and often surprisingly accurate facts, geographical, cultural and historical, about the ancient world. These make up the long preamble to his grand theme: the Great War between the Greeks and Persians of 499–478BC.

Herodotus was often, in the best sense, non-judgemental. He records different versions of an event, leaving the reader to decide between them. He can be over-credulous, as when describing the gold-digging ants of India, but he can also be sceptical – sometimes unduly so, for he dismissed the reports of Phoenician sailors circumnavigating Africa from east to west that the sun shone on them from *the north*. He was unfair to some individuals such as Themistocles, who appears only late in his account of the

Above: The probing intelligence of Thucydides, greatest of Greek historians, emerges in this Roman copy of an original Greek bust.

Persian invasion of 480BC. This probably reflects the bias of his sources, which he may not have fully realized. Herodotus knew little about military matters, never having been a soldier. He also had no idea of numbers, giving the total figure for Xerxes' invasion force as 1,700,000 men – absurdly large. But he wrote in clear Ionic Greek, being one of the first great prose writers.

THUCYDIDES, *c.*457–400BC

Little more than a generation younger than Herodotus, Thucydides was very different as a man and as a writer. While the supernatural still figures in Herodotus' picturesque accounts, Thucydides ignores dreams and omens. He may have read or heard Herodotus' work but probably regarded it as more of a muddle than a model. His great theme was the calamitous war between the Peloponnesians and Athens, which he was uniquely qualified to record. "I made it a principle not to write down the first story I heard, nor even to accept my own overall impressions. Either I myself witnessed the events described or I heard them from eye-witnesses whose reports I checked as

carefully as possible," he wrote. He has been called the 'historian's historian' because his analytical approach and sparse prose can often seem dry compared to other writers, but underneath boil surprising passions.

Thucydides was an aristocrat, related to Cimon and to the Thucydides who was ostracized for opposing spending tribute money on the temples. He grew up a conservative democrat but keenly admired Pericles, whose radical days were over by then. Thucydides was elected *strategos* in 424BC, but his command proved disastrous: he failed to save Amphipolis, that jewel in the Athenian Empire's crown, arriving too late with reinforcements, although he held the small port of Eion. Court-martialled, he was exiled, but being defeated by a general such as Brasidas was no disgrace, many felt. In exile, Thucydides devoted himself to his *History*, a rigorous analysis of the causes as well as course of the Peloponnesian War. After 404BC and Athens' final defeat, he returned to his city and probably died suddenly, for his history breaks off abruptly in late 411BC.

Thucydides thought that Athenian politics degenerated after Pericles' death, as demagogues such as Cleon (as he saw the man who had pressed for his banishment) came to dominate the Assembly. But although he treated the ineffectual Nicias kindly because he was a rich conservative, he also discerned the visionary statesman in Themistocles, an earlier radical. He perhaps overstated the defensiveness of Pericles' strategy, but his military judgement is sound. He also had a marked philosophical streak, shown in his account of the debate over the attack on Melos in 416BC, where the Athenians argue that 'might is right'. He was an inspiration to later historians, but none matched his intellectual rigour or brilliance.

Above: Herodotus was born in Halicarnassus (Bodrum), a city on the Greek world's edge, which helped make him unusually broad-minded.

Below: Often known as the 'father of history', Herodotus's historiae (inquiries) are the first true histories.

LATER GREEK HISTORIANS
XENOPHON, POLYBIUS & PLUTARCH

Above: The philhellenic Roman emperor Hadrian (ruled AD117–138) favoured Plutarch and Arrian, giving both imperial office.

Below: In this medieval picture, the translated works of Xenophon are presented to the French king Louis XII (reigned 1498–1515), showing the lasting fame of the ancient historian.

Later Greek historians, writing of people long dead, often had no first-hand accounts but relied on earlier histories that have vanished. But Xenophon did experience the later Peloponnesian War and his Anabasis himself.

XENOPHON OF ATHENS, c.430–354BC

The historian Xenophon was evidently always attracted to strong characters: first to Socrates, then the Persian prince Cyrus, and lastly Sparta's King Agesilaus. Born in Athens, Xenophon joined Socrates' circle, but it is doubtful how much of his philosophy he understood. His *Apology* defends Socrates so successfully that it seems bizarre that the philosopher was ever prosecuted for 'impiety'.

Xenophon left Athens soon after its defeat to make his fortune as a mercenary. He joined 'The 10,000' Greek hoplites whom Cyrus recruited to overthrow his brother Artaxerxes, the Great King. Xenophon immortalized their adventures in *Anabasis*, a gripping tale of the 'march upcountry' towards Babylon and their retreat under his leadership in 399BC after Cyrus' death. Xenophon reveals his generalship but conceals his enrichment from the campaign.

Returning to Greece, he settled in Sparta on a large estate given him by Agesilaus – a revealing choice. His most important historical work is his *Hellenica*, which continues Thucydides' account, starting "The next day..." and running to 362BC. Xenophon's account, while valuable, does not compare with Thucydides', especially in its later parts. In *Cyropaedia* (Boyhood of Cyrus) he gave a fictionalized account of the youth of Cyrus the Great, and also wrote on topics from horsemanship to housekeeping.

POLYBIUS, c.200–120BC

In the 2nd century BC Rome slowly, often brutally, took over the Greek world. By good fortune, the process found a perceptive, sympathetic historian in Polybius of Megalopolis in Arcadia. A general in the Achaean League, he was taken as a hostage to Rome in 167BC. There he met Scipio Aemilianus, one of Rome's great generals, becoming his friend and adviser on Greek affairs. He learnt Latin and came to admire Rome, seemingly still in its Republican prime. Permitted to travel, he visited Spain, Gaul and Africa. Allowed to return home in 150BC, he kept up links with Scipio, accompanying him to Carthage in the Third Punic War (149–146BC).

Polybius wrote the definitive history of Rome's rise to world power during 220–145BC in 40 books. He attempted to explain why this happened and to reconcile Greeks to Rome's new dominance by showing the excellence of its balanced

Above: Plutarch's Parallel Lives *(this is an edition of 1657) coupled 25 famous Romans with 25 famous Greeks, to demonstrate that there had once been Greek men of action and there were also Roman thinkers.*

constitution (in fact, already under growing strain). Although his style is turgid, his approach, as a former general and politician, is practical and intelligent, free of national prejudice. Most of his work survives only in paraphrases by later writers, but he deeply influenced Livy, the great Roman historian.

PLUTARCH, *c.*AD46–*c.*125

Born at Chaeronea in Boeotia, Plutarch is famous for his *Parallel Lives*, 50 biographies of paired-off famous Greeks and Romans. In them he aimed to show Greeks that Rome had produced more than just soldiers and to remind Romans that there had once been great Greek generals and statesmen. In his *Lives*, Plutarch too often accepted unreliable secondary sources as true, but his great gifts as a story-teller later influenced Renaissance writers such as Shakespeare.

Plutarch was more than just a biographer, however, being also a philosopher and a priest at Delphi and an active public citizen in Chaeronea. He was educated chiefly in Athens, where he became an adherent of Platonism. He also visited Rome several times, becoming a friend of the consul Sosius Senecio and ultimately of the philhellenic emperor Hadrian (AD117–138). The emperor made him governor of Achaea (south Greece) and gave him consular honours, but Plutarch remained devoted to his small home *polis*. Sadly aware that Greece's great days were past, one of his chief concerns was to restore the shrine at Delphi. Among his other works are a diatribe against Herodotus and his *Moralia*, essays attacking Stoicism and Epicureanism.

ARRIAN (FLAVIUS ARRIANUS), *c.*AD87–*c.*147

Arrian was an upper-class Greek, from Nicomedia in Bithynia (north-west Turkey), who lived at the zenith of the Roman Empire. His greatest achievement was to write a history of Alexander the Great that made intelligent use of primary sources such as Ptolemy and Aristobulus – officers who had served under Alexander but whose accounts have been lost. Arrian's eight-volume *Anabasis* (March Upcountry) survives, as does his *Indica*, a book about India based on accounts by Megasthenes of *c.*300BC and on the voyage made by Alexander's admiral Nearchus from the Indus. From Arrian we derive most of our knowledge of Alexander's life and character.

Arrian had a glittering career himself. His father was a Roman citizen, and he studied under Epictetus, the Stoic philosopher. Arrian rose to the highest office in the Roman state, becoming consul in AD129 (still an unusual honour for a Greek) under the emperor Hadrian, whose friend he was. He later was governor of Cappadocia (eastern Anatolia), commanding two legions with which he repelled an invasion by the Alans, a nomadic tribe from Central Asia.

Above: Plutarch, most prolific of ancient biographers, wrote 200 books in total. He was also a philosopher and priest.

Below: Sides of a gold coin of Alexander the Great, the subject of Arrian's great history, the book that gives us our definitive view of the world-conqueror.

PHILOSOPHERS IN POLITICS
THALES, EMPEDOCLES & DEMETRIUS

Early Greek philosophers were often closely involved in politics, for philosophy, a Greek invention, grew up in the streets and agoras of the *polis*, not in academic seclusion. This interaction had fruitful, sometimes surprising, results.

THALES, *c*.624–547BC

Greek philosophy was born in the Ionian port of Miletus, the largest and richest Greek city before 500BC, with Thales of Miletus, the very first philosopher. For Thales, philosophy meant *thinking* about every aspect of life, not quietly accepting old myths and legends. Speculating about the nature of the universe, he decided

Below: A view of the Sicilian volcano Mt Etna erupting. Into its fiery heart Empedocles, the democratic statesman and mystical philosopher, threw himself, according to legend. More probably, he died peacefully in Olympia.

that water was the basic principle of everything, which was not so absurd for Greeks living by the sea. He learned enough about astronomy, possibly in part from Babylonia, to predict the eclipse of the sun in 585BC.

One day, he was walking along so lost in thought that he fell into a well and had to be rescued. Annoyed at becoming a laughing stock, Thales decided to get his own back. Shrewdly noting early indications that there would be a bumper olive harvest, he bought all the oil presses nearby and later charged his fellow Milesians extra to rent them, showing that philosophers could be practical too. Even shrewder was his suggestion that the Ionian cities, already threatened by powerful Asian monarchies, should form a league with its centre at Teos, a small, centrally sited city. Unfortunately, his advice was not taken and Ionia was conquered by Persia in 545BC.

EMPEDOCLES, *c*.495–*c*.432BC

Empedocles of Acragas was remarkably multi-talented. Not only philosopher and poet, he was also scientist, doctor and social reformer, a man of such visionary enthusiasm that some thought him a charlatan, others an almost divine hero. Both Aristotle and the Roman philosopher-poet Lucretius admired him, and it is only through their paraphrases of him that fragments of his work have survived.

In the 5th century BC Acragas (today Agrigento) was the richest city in Greek Sicily, as its splendid Doric temples show. Though born into its aristocracy, Empedocles was a radical democrat. He played a key role in overthrowing the tyrant Thrasydaeus in 471BC and establishing democracy in Acragas, which lasted until the Carthaginian attack in 406BC. He guided the city through its greatest period in a way comparable to that of Pericles in Athens. He then retired in 445BC to travel. According to legend, he began proclaiming himself a god and committed suicide by throwing himself into the volcano of Mt Etna. More probably he died of natural causes in the Peloponnese, where his poems were recited at the Olympiad of 440BC.

As a philosopher Empedocles was among the most important pre-Socratic thinkers. He wrote a long poem, *On Nature*, of some 6,000 lines (only 350 of which survive) in which he propounded his general theory of the universe. He postulated four elements – earth, air, fire, water – governed by two opposed forces: Love, which attracts and unites, and Strife, which repels and divides. He realized that air was solid and suggested that light from the Sun must take some time to reach the Earth. This remarkably anticipates modern physics. All his science was tinged with mysticism, however, following the pattern set by Pythagoras, the pioneer of mystical mathematics.

DEMETRIUS, *c.*350–283BC
Plato had dreamt of a 'philosopher-king' ruling with supreme wisdom, but in the ten-year rule of Demetrius of Phalerum, Athens experienced almost the opposite. Demetrius might be called a rogue-philosopher, for he behaved outrageously, unlike any normal 'lover of wisdom' (which is what philosopher means).

A student of Aristotle but an Athenian citizen, Demetrius was installed in 317BC as a quisling ruler by Cassander, the Macedonian general ruling Greece. Demetrius' books on philosophy have

been lost, only those on cooking, hairdressing and fashion surviving. This seems apposite for his strange regime. He reputedly organized processions led by a mechanical snail that spat saliva and accepted absurdly flattering epithets such as *lampito* (brilliant). Although it was a time of economic hardship, he gave wild parties and ordered 1,500 bronze statues raised in his honour. He was not brutal, but power lay with his Macedonian masters. When Cassander lost power and Demetrius was overthrown, the Athenians melted his statues down into chamber pots, now they were at last free to express their true feelings about him.

Above: The growing wealth of the Greek world, revealed in grand temples such as those at Acragas in Sicily, encouraged the development of philosophy.

Below: The temple of Hercules at Acragas, one of the many fine temples erected in the 5th century BC, when Acragas was a flourishing democracy under the enlightened guidance of the polymathic Empedocles.

DEMETRIUS THE LIBRARIAN
Demetrius went on to advise Ptolemy I of Egypt about establishing the Library at Alexandria. With a reputed 500,000 volumes, it became the greatest library in the Ancient World. This suggests that Demetrius made a better librarian than philosopher-king.

CHAPTER VI

THE STRUGGLE FOR SUPREMACY

404–322 BC

With the end of the Peloponnesian War in 404 BC, an era of liberty seemed at hand. But this illusion was soon shattered. Sparta showed itself unfit to lead Greece, favouring corrupt despotisms. Spartan arrogance united former enemies, Athens allying with Corinth and Thebes and even Persia. The collapse of Spartan power after 371 BC saw Thebes as hegemon of Greece, but its achievements – spreading democracy, new forms of federalism – only worsened general instability. Men left home to fight as mercenaries while wars exhausted their own cities, leaving them prey to outside powers.

The first such power was Dionysius I, who created a vast Sicilian empire. Greece looked west in alarm, but Dionysius hardly interfered in its affairs and his empire soon collapsed. Jason of Pherae and Mausolus of Halicarnassus proved even more transitory as hegemons. Then a truly formidable power emerged: Macedonia. Philip II exploited Macedonian strength and Greek weakness to create a solidly based hegemony. At Corinth in 337 BC he declared a war of Panhellenic revenge against Persia. Alexander, his brilliant son, far exceeded his plans, so ending the Classical Age of Greece.

Left: The Temple of Apollo, Delphi, Greece's spiritual heart. Macedonia won Delphi, confirming its status as hegemon.

SPARTAN SUPREMACY
POWER AND CORRUPTION, 404–377 BC

On Athens' surrender in April 404 BC, Thebes and Corinth pressed for its total destruction. The Spartan commander Lysander refused, however, remembering Athens' glorious stand against Persia and aware that Athens, broken but still the largest Greek city, was a potential ally. At Athens Lysander installed an oligarchy, 'The Thirty Tyrants', backed by a Spartan garrison under a *harmost* (governor). The city, disarmed, became an ally of Sparta, as did most cities in its former empire, although the Thirty did not last long.

For smaller states, Lysander favoured *decarchies*: cliques of ten reactionaries eagerly wielding power long denied them. As Plutarch wrote: "In appointing these officials, Lysander simply handed out power to his cronies, giving them absolute powers of life and death." Backing each *decarchy* was a *harmost* and garrison. The tribute that had flowed into Athens was diverted to Sparta, but Sparta's former allies Thebes and Corinth gained nothing. This alienated them.

Below: The walls of Athens are pulled down to the sound of flutes after its final defeat in 404 BC. This left the city nakedly vulnerable but, thanks to Lysander's intercession, Athens itself was spared destruction.

THE MARCH OF THE '10,000'

After the Peloponnesian Wars many Greeks, who knew only soldiering, were idle amid economic depression. In 404 BC Cyrus, governor of western Asia, in rebellion against his brother Artaxerxes II, the new Persian king, required mercenaries. He hired *c.*10,000 Greek *hoplites*, who were seen as the world's best infantry, to boost his army. Well aware that Greeks would not march far from the sea, he claimed, on starting out in 401 BC, to be fighting only Pisidian bandits inland.

Among the Greek officers was a bright young Athenian Xenophon. Marching ever further east, the Greeks grew restive when they realized that they had been misled. But they were induced by extra pay to keep going until they entered Babylonia (Iraq), then a fertile, exotic land.

At Cunaxa, Artaxerxes' army finally met his brother's. In the ensuing battle the Greeks were victorious but Cyrus was killed, leaving the Greeks lost in an alien empire. After the Persians murdered their generals in negotiations, the '10,000' chose as a new leader the persuasive Xenophon, who promised to lead them home. He kept his promise. They marched up through the unknown mountains of Kurdistan and Armenia, finally reaching the Black Sea at Trapezus, a Greek city (modern Trabizond), before turning for home.

Xenophon, a good writer as well as general, vividly recorded his adventure in *Anabasis* (March Upcountry). The Persian Empire's apparent vulnerability led many Greeks to dream of expansion east, with momentous later consequences.

TROUBLE AT HOME AND ABROAD

Although Sparta could now afford to maintain a fleet, the overall results were disastrous. On leaving their austere homeland, Spartans often became totally corrupt, and Spartan *harmosts* also became infamous for predatory sexual behaviour in Greek cities under their rule. Back home, Sparta's unique egalitarian system was undermined by its new wealth, since rich Spartans got richer, buying up land from poorer ones, who no longer qualified for Spartiate status. Sparta soon faced a shortage of Spartiates, the basis of its power, worsened by the relative freedom of its women, who preferred to marry richer Spartans. As a result, Sparta's birth-rate began to fall.

Sparta had supported Prince Cyrus' rebellion against his brother, King Artaxerxes II of Persia, but Cyrus was killed fighting at Cunaxa in 401BC. The Greek cities of Ionia, now free once more, appealed to Sparta for help against Persia, leading it into war with its former ally. The Spartan king Agesilaus, Lysander's protégé, led an army to Asia to attack Persia, gaining early successes. But, thanks to Persian gold, Athens began to revive, rebuilding its fleet. Lysander himself was killed in 395BC fighting at Thebes, which, like Corinth, had allied with Athens in the 'Corinthian War'. Documents found after Lysander's death revealed that he wanted to make Sparta's monarchy elective but more powerful, suiting Sparta's new imperial role.

In 394BC an Athenian fleet in Persian pay defeated the Spartans off Cnidus. This victory was countered by a bloody battle at Corinth when Spartan discipline crushed the armies of Thebes, Corinth and Athens. But when Athens rashly sent fleets to support anti-Persian rebels in Cyprus and Egypt, Sparta restored its ties with Persia, the new arbiter of Greece.

THE KING'S PEACE

Under the Persian King's Peace of 386BC, Sparta abandoned Cyprus and Ionia to Persia. The Peace theoretically guaranteed all European Greek cities' autonomy and forbade all confederations except Sparta's, considered a free alliance. This let Sparta destroy the Arcadian city of Mantinea, claiming that its existence violated the Peace, and move against a newly formed Chalcidic Confederacy.

En route north in 382BC, a Spartan army helped a pro-Spartan coup in Thebes. This action, actually breaking the Peace, marked the apogee of Spartan power. Three years later, a counter-coup led by Epaminondas ejected this regime, and Thebes allied with Athens. Spartan power was again threatened. Seven years later it would be crushed at Leuctra.

Above: Funerary stele of Democlides, an Athenian soldier killed at the Battle of Corinth in 394BC, when Spartan discipline managed to defeat the combined armies of Athens, Thebes and Corinth.

Below: The '10,000', the mercenary force led by Xenophon the Athenian, finally reach the Black Sea after a gruelling march through the Asian interior. They were jubilant at being back on the coast, so central to Greek life.

ATHENS: CRISIS AND RECOVERY 399-357 BC

Above: The 4th century BC
*saw artists turn away from
the severe heroism of the
5th century. Their new
appreciation of female
beauty is epitomized by the
Aphrodite of Cnidus, one
of Praxiteles' masterpieces.*

Few cities appeared more defeated than Athens in 404BC, deprived of its empire, fleet, walls and democracy. But within a decade it had recovered, becoming once more a great naval power, albeit one chronically short of money. Even more swiftly, it regained its democracy, which worked smoothly until extinguished by Macedonian generals in 322BC.

'THE THIRTY TYRANTS'

Athens' defeat was welcomed by its oligarchs. Under Lysander's menacing eye, in July 404BC the Assembly voted power to 'The Thirty Tyrants'. The two leaders were the extremist Critias, one of Socrates' former students, and Theramenes, a moderate. They set up a body of the Eleven, ruthless special police. Only 3,000 citizens had civil rights; the rest were powerless. Leading democrats were killed in a reign of terror, as were moderates such as Niceratus, Nicias' son, and rich *metics* (foreign residents) such as Polemarchus. Athenians were ordered to arrest their fellow citizens, so implicating themselves in the regime's crimes. Most complied, but Socrates refused – and uniquely went unpunished.

Democrats fled to nearby states, whose feelings towards Sparta were changing fast. In December 404BC Thrasybulus, Anytus and 70 other exiles seized the fort of Phyle near the border. The junta's attempt to eject them failed due to a snowstorm, and they gained support. Alarmed, the oligarchs quarrelled, with Theramenes being killed as Critias took control. He appealed for Spartan help, and a garrison of 700 occupied the Acropolis. After another attempt in May 403BC to dislodge the democrats failed, Thrasybulus captured Piraeus. Critias, trying to retake it, was killed in the fighting.

Again the oligarchs appealed to Lysander, but King Pausanias, his bitter enemy, now intervened, changing Spartan policy. Pausanias let the oligarchs withdraw to Eleusis while Athens worked out a new settlement. By late 403BC, democracy had been restored with a general amnesty. Athens was free again.

*Right: The stele of Dexileos, who
was killed in 393BC, during the
war against the Corinthians,
and buried at the Kerameikos,
a quarter built up in the age
of Themistocles.*

THE TRIAL OF SOCRATES

In 399BC Meletus, supported by Anytus, accused Socrates of "not believing in the city's gods, of introducing new gods … and corrupting the young". No court records exist of this most famous trial, but Socrates' followers Plato and Xenophon gave vivid descriptions, although neither was present. Meletus is unknown but Anytus was a democratic hero of Phyle. Socrates had fought bravely too, but was better known as an incessant questioner of customs: religious, social and political. Among his ex-students were Alcibiades, the traitor, and Critias, leader of 'The Thirty Tyrants' – odious connections. But, due to the amnesty, Socrates could not be attacked on political grounds.

A charge of impiety, however, was different. Religion in ancient Greece was a public affair: offend the gods and you risked your city suffering. The 501 jurors – chosen by lot to represent public opinion – must have seen Socrates arguing in the streets. Back in 423BC he had been caricatured in Aristophanes' play *The Clouds* as a Sophist smart alec, who taught the young about new, amoral gods. This made audiences laugh, but by 399BC

many felt that Socrates' constant questioning was no laughing matter. Even so, the majority finding him guilty – 280 to 221 – was small. When he mockingly proposed public dinners as his punishment, the majority for the death penalty was larger, but he was expected to escape. Instead, he chose death. Martyr of philosophy or teacher of tyrants? Both are valid viewpoints, but Socrates was the *only* man executed for his beliefs in classical Athens.

Above: The trial of Socrates in 399BC was a seminal, still contentious event in Western intellectual history. In this 17th-century painting the philosopher, accused of corrupting the young and introducing new gods, kills himself by drinking hemlock, still debating with his followers.

THE SECOND CONFEDERACY

Although free, Athens was hardly prosperous, but it could draw on the gold of Persia, then hostile to Sparta. Athens was soon fighting Sparta, in 394BC allying with Corinth and Thebes. In 390BC Iphicrates, an innovatory *strategos*, defeated a Spartan force outside Corinth using *peltasts* (light-armed troops). With Persian money Athens had rebuilt its Long Walls by 393BC.

Refortified, Athens began trying to regain its empire, rashly helping Evagoras of Cyprus in revolt against Persia. This led to Spartan–Persian rapprochement in the 'King's Peace' of 386BC, reaffirming Spartan hegemony in Greece. Sparta's actions over the next years united Greece against it, however. After an attempted

Spartan raid on Piraeus in 378BC, Athens allied with Thebes and formed a totally new naval confederacy of its own.

Aimed against Sparta, this tried to avoid the mistakes of the first confederacy by having a separate council for the allies that Athens could not dominate and forbidding *cleruchies* (settlements). Initially popular, with 70 states joining, its fleet defeated the Spartans at Naxos in 376BC. The *strategos* Timotheus sailed victoriously round the Peloponnese in 376BC, defeating the Spartans at Alyzia in 375BC. With further operations hampered by lack of money, however, the war dragged on.

Right: The new, almost languid sensuality of 4th-century art is apparent in Praxiteles' Hermes and the Infant Dionysus.

THEBES: A BRIEF HEGEMONY 377–362 BC

Above: The sphinx, the mythical creature connected through the Oedipus legend with Thebes. Its enigma in a way illustrates the Theban dilemma: freeing the Peloponnese from Spartan tyranny brought chaos, not democratic order.

Below: Epaminondas' novel tactic at Leuctra, when Sparta was for the first time defeated in open battle, was to increase the weight of his left wing, massing Theban hoplites 50 deep so that they punched through the weaker lines of their opponents.

In the winter of 379–378 BC the Spartan-backed junta in Thebes was overthrown in a dramatic coup. The plotters, led by Pelopidas, entered the junta's symposium one evening in drag as courtesans and killed them all. They then instituted a new democracy, which joined the second Athenian Confederacy. While Thebes repaired its defences against inevitable Spartan counter-attacks, Epaminondas and Pelopidas, both *polemarchs* (commanders), reorganized the Theban army, making it far more professional. They founded, or refounded, a crack corps, the Sacred Band: 150 pairs of lovers, mature men bound to each other by the strongest ties possible. Over the next 40 years they proved to be the best hoplites in Greece.

In 371 BC Athens and Sparta, tired of inconclusive warfare and worried about the rise of Thebes, signed the Peace of Callias. This reaffirmed the principle of each city's autonomy, as in the 'King's Peace' 15 years earlier, but the Spartan and Athenian leagues were specifically excluded. Theban control over Boeotia was not, however, for it was contentious.

(Thebes had recaptured Plataea to the east, whose citizens fled to Athens, while to the west Phocis, another old Athenian ally, was attacked. Thebes was therefore excluded from the peace.) Just weeks later, in July 371 BC, Sparta sent a Peloponnesian army under King Cleombrotus against Thebes, which had only one ally: Jason of Pherae in Thessaly.

BATTLE OF LEUCTRA

Cleombrotus, approaching Thebes from the south, found the Theban army drawn up at Leuctra. The Spartans, like everyone in Greece, expected to win, as they had won every set battle for 200 years. They probably had *c.*11,000 men, mostly allies, against *c.*7,000 Thebans. Cleombrotus with his crack troops was on the Spartan right, as usual. But Epaminondas put his best troops on his *left*, deepening the Theban phalanx from the usual 8–12 men to 50 – a vast increase in striking power. Although Sparta's slingers defeated the Thebans, the Theban cavalry worsted the Spartans. Then the Theban hoplite wedge crashed into the Spartan right, breaking it. Cleombrotus was killed, his army collapsing like dominoes. About 400 full Spartiates were killed – a huge loss – and Sparta's legendary invincibility was over.

The immediate consequences of the victory were muffled by Jason of Pherae, who rapidly marched south to Leuctra to impose a truce. The Spartans were allowed to evacuate Boeotia. But when Jason's power ended soon after with his assassination, Thebes became Greece's new hegemon. This alarmed Athens almost as much as Sparta.

THE PELOPONNESE SET FREE

As news of Sparta's unprecedented defeat – by *inferior numbers* – spread around Greece, states long subject to its heavy

Map showing battle positions with legend:

0 — 1 km
0 — 1 mile

Epaminondas elite troops

- Spartans
- Thebans
→ Theban attack
→ Spartan attack

Left: When Epaminondas led the Theban army into the Peloponnese in the winter of 370BC, he founded a huge new federal capital, Megalopolis, to which smaller settlements nearby, such as Bassae with its renowned temple, sent delegates.

rule began to revolt. Its loathed *harmosts* (governors) were thrown out, replaced by democracies. Among the first to revolt were the Mantineans of Arcadia, long denied a proper *polis* by Sparta. While their old city was rebuilt and rewalled, Mantinea helped form a Pan-Arcadian Federation with a new capital, Megalopolis (great city). Defended by double walls, it had a grand theatre, *agora*, temples and a federal army of 5,000 men.

Arcadia was a federal democracy, with most of its citizens having a vote. In 370BC revolution at Tegea led it to join Arcadia, but Tegea's exiled oligarchs appealed to Sparta. Arcadia in turn appealed to Athens, but, as Athens proved non-committal, it turned to Thebes. This was Epaminondas' chance.

FOUNDING MESSENE

In late 370BC a Theban army invaded the Peloponnese. Almost unopposed, it ravaged the long-inviolate territory around Sparta itself; the unwalled city seemed set to fall. But winter floods swelled the River Eurotas and the only bridge was strongly defended, so Epaminondas withdrew. This was a huge blow to Spartan pride, but worse followed. Epaminondas led his army into Messenia, whose long-enslaved *helots* rose en masse. A new city of Messene was founded in 369BC on Mt Ithome, with splendid new walls 8km/ 5 miles long. Messenian exiles flocked back to their new *polis*, whose very existence doomed Spartan power. There were only 1,500 full Spartiates left anyway.

Athens, meanwhile, allied with Sparta. This was not so odd, for in the subsequent confused years states constantly changed sides. The Arcadians themselves did not want to swap Theban hegemony for Sparta's.

Pelopidas then led expeditions to Macedonia, trying to extend Thebes' influence north, while Dionysius (tyrant of Syracuse) and Persia intervened in Greek affairs, neither to much effect.

Epaminondas made four invasions of the Peloponnese, the last ending in his fatal victory at Mantinea in 362BC – fatal both to him, for he died of his wounds, and to Theban hopes of supremacy. With Pelopidas also dead, Thebes lacked great leaders. While it had finally ended centuries of Spartan supremacy and helped to free the Peloponnesians, Thebes' hegemony left Greece more exhausted and divided than ever.

Below: The massive walls of the Arcadian Gate in Messene, a city beneath Mount Ithome that Epaminondas founded in 369BC as a secure polis for Messenians who had been long enslaved by Sparta.

THE SYRACUSAN EMPIRE
411–337 BC

Above: The ruins of Motya, the Carthaginian stronghold in western Sicily that Dionysius I besieged.

Below: The ruins of Carthage near modern Tunis. The perennial threat of this great enemy of the Greeks in Sicily was invoked by Dionysius I to justify his prolonged tyranny.

When Syracuse defeated the Athenian invasion in 411BC, it was a democracy like Athens, as Thucydides noted, but a very unstable one. Hermocrates, leader of the defence, took 25 ships east to help Sparta, but radicals in the city then banished him. They also embroiled Syracuse in a war with Carthage, which had colonies in western Sicily. Called in by half-Greek Segesta against its rival Selinus, the Carthaginians landed with a huge army in 409BC. This captured Selinus and took Himera, another Greek city. Reputedly 3,000 Greek captives were sacrificed to Carthage's gods afterwards.

DIONYSIUS' GROWING POWER
Hermocrates was killed soon after while trying to re-enter Syracuse. Carthage then attacked Acragas, Sicily's richest city. Acragas' notoriously soft inhabitants – guards on night duty were limited to one mattress, two pillows and a quilt each – fled in panic in 406BC after a relief effort failed. As the Carthaginians besieged

Gela, the next city along, panic grew in Syracuse too. Dionysius, one of Hermocrates' officers, accused the generals of treachery, becoming a *strategos* himself. In 405BC Syracusans voted him sole powers as *strategos autokrator* (supreme general) and a bodyguard of 1,000. With it, he made himself tyrant. His rule, a demagogic dictatorship but with rich backers, lasted until his death.

Dionysius' first campaign to save Gela in 405BC failed, and he had to abandon half of Greek Sicily to Carthage. Refugees streamed into Syracuse, swelling its population, as did deportees from Naxos (Taormina) and Catania – Greek cities that he had attacked without provocation. Dionysius made Ortygia, the old island core of the city, into his citadel, expelling from it all but 10,000 trusted mercenaries. Inside its turreted walls he survived a serious revolt in 403BC. Around Syracuse city he built the strongest walls yet seen, enclosing *c.*1,200ha/3,000 acres.

Meanwhile, he was planning revenge on Carthage, the excuse for his tyranny. Over the next years Syracuse rang to the sound of hammers and anvils. An army 80,000 strong, and a navy of 300 galleys – including the first quadriremes and quinqueremes, larger and more powerful than triremes – were assembled. Dionysius also developed the first siege engines to hurl heavy stones 300m/325 yards. Most Syracusans, whatever they felt about his tyranny, supported this armaments programme.

THE SIEGE OF MOTYA
With his base assured, in 397BC Dionysius renewed the war with Carthage. Marching to the far end of the island, he besieged the city of Motya. This was thought impregnable on its island, but Syracusan engineers built a causeway

across the bay to let their siege-engines attack it. The battle was long and bitter. Even after their walls were breached, the Motyans fought back street by street, until a night attack finally crushed them. For the first time since 480BC, Greeks had captured a Carthaginian city. The resulting slaughter was terrible until Dionysius, mindful of the slave market, halted it.

COUNTER-ATTACK AND FURTHER CONQUESTS

Next year Himilco of Carthage, landing with an army, recaptured but did not rebuild ruined Motya, instead founding Lilybaeum nearby. Marching east, he founded on the site of Naxos a new city for the native Sicels, Taormina, later to be a Greek city. Himilco defeated the Syracusan fleet, but his attack on Syracuse itself met with disaster, thanks to its strong walls, an outbreak of plague in his army and a brilliant counter-attack by Dionysius. Dionysius let Himilco himself escape, but he had won the war. The peace treaty he made in 392BC was Machiavellian: the Carthaginians were restricted to the north-west of the island but not ejected, remaining a potential threat to justify his continued tyranny.

Master of Greek Sicily, Dionysius now turned to Italy. He had asked for a bride from Rhegium (Reggio) on the Straits of Messina, but was offered only their hangman's daughter, an unforgivable insult. In 391BC he duly attacked Rhegium. Initially defeated at sea, he waged war on the mainland with great success. He finally captured Rhegium after a long siege in 387BC, enslaving its citizens. He now controlled both sides of the Straits and much of southern Italy, the powerful city of Taras (Taranto) being his ally. Dionysius founded colonies up the Adriatic as far north as Hadria on the River Po, with trade flourishing in this new empire. After another war with Carthage, he had to cede Sicily west of the River Halcyus in 383BC. This still left him with most of the island, the greatest power in the Greek world, both feared and courted.

TYRANNY AND CULTURE

Dionysius liked to claim that he was not a tyrant, simply a *strategos* with exceptional powers. The Assembly continued to re-elect him – it had no option – and the city prospered as an imperial capital. But Syracusans were heavily taxed, under military rule and surrounded by barbarous newcomers. Dionysius himself, like many dictators, suffered from paranoia. He had visitors to his court strip-searched for weapons and allowed no one to shave him except his daughters.

Above: The Temple of Hercules in Acragas, the famously rich Greek city in western Sicily that fell without a fight to the Carthaginian advance in 406BC.

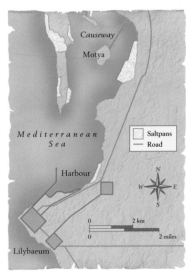

Left: Motya on its island was long considered impregnable. But Dionysius' engineers built a causeway out to it on which they brought up siege engines to take it in 397BC.

Above: The nymph Arethusa on a coin designed by Euanitos in the 4th century BC. Syracuse produced some of the most beautiful Greek coins that have ever been minted.

Below: Façade of the Temple of Concord at Acragas (Agrigento), Sicily.

He did not even trust his wives – he had several simultaneously, for political reasons – but made them await him lying naked on a bare bed surrounded by water, so that he could see they had no daggers under the sheets. According to Plutarch, the tyrant hired prostitutes to spy on the citizens, executing 10,000 Syracusans as alleged traitors.

Dionysius harmed rather than helped Hellenism overall. He destroyed old Greek cities that opposed him, replacing their citizens with non-Greeks so that they no longer counted as true Hellenic *poleis*. But he admired Greek culture, inviting the hedonistic philosopher Aristippus, once a student of Socrates, to stay at his luxurious court. (The two men got on surprisingly well.) And Dionysius had literary ambitions himself, entering several contests.

In 367BC Athens, trying to woo him as an ally, awarded his *Ransom of Hector* first prize at the Lenaean festival. Overjoyed, Dionysius drank so much that he died. The Roman historian Cornelius Nepos acquitted Dionysius of a tyrant's three typical failings – lust, avarice and greed – but his empire rested wholly on force.

DION AND DIONYSIUS II

Dionysius I claimed to have left an "empire bound with steel", but the 29-year-old heir Dionysius II lacked his father's ruthlessness. He ended a war with Carthage, but a peaceful warlord risked seeming redundant, especially as he did not concentrate on ruling the empire. Instead, he swung between debauchery – he was excessively fond of wine and women – and philosophy, to which his relative Dion introduced him. Dion, an aristocrat who had married into the tyrant's family, meanwhile continued as chief minister.

Dion had once studied under Plato, the Athenian philosopher, and he persuaded the amenable young ruler to invite Plato to his court. Plato, already in his sixties, reluctantly agreed and made two visits to Syracuse, both of which turned out badly since Dionysius proved as idle a philosophy student as he was a ruler. Philistus, head of a rival faction, turned Dionysius against Dion, who went into exile in Athens.

Below: Part of the walls around Syracuse that Dionysius extended and strengthened to cover 1,200ha/3,000 acres, making his capital much the largest Greek city.

PLATO AND THE PHILOSOPHER-KING

Although born into its ruling class, Plato turned his back on Athens' democratic politics after Socrates, his revered master, was put to death in 399BC. He spent years abroad, in Italy meeting Archytas, the Pythagorean philosopher-ruler of Taras. Visiting Sicily in 388BC, he fell foul of Dionysius I's paranoia. Arrested and deported, he was reputedly sold as a slave. Although soon rescued, it left him thinking tyranny even worse than democracy.

Plato now founded his Academy, the world's first university, outside Athens. In it a select few, including Dion, could study undisturbed. There Plato wrote *The Republic*, his blueprint for the ideal society ruled by an intellectual elite, but he did not envisage its realization on Earth. Yet when Dion begged to him to come and teach the young Dionysius II, he could hardly refuse. It was an unparalleled chance to educate this powerful ruler as a 'philosopher-king' guided by selfless wisdom of the truest kind.

Dionysius greeted Plato's arrival with delight. He dismissed his call-girls and fellow-boozers and began to study maths, which Plato thought essential for philosophy. But the young tyrant soon grew bored and, although he refused to let Plato leave, slipped back to his old ways. Finally allowed home, Plato returned to philosophy with relief. But in 357BC he was again invited, this time by Dionysius himself, who claimed to be studying philosophy seriously. Wearily, Plato again made the long voyage, only to find that the tyrant considered himself his equal as a philosopher. Plato was imprisoned and only freed because Archytas of Taras intervened. Back in Athens, he wrote *Laws*, his last and grimmest work on politics, effectively taking Sparta as his model.

Above: Plato the Athenian philosopher made three visits to Syracuse, the last two in the hope of turning its young ruler Dionysius II into a 'philosopher-king'. All ended in failure.

He returned to Sicily in 357BC with a tiny force, landing at Heraclea in the west. Marching on Syracuse, he was welcomed and seized the outer city, proclaiming the restoration of democracy. Dionysius, away in Italy, returned in time to save Ortygia. Murderous civil strife followed, Dionysius' Italian mercenaries slaughtering the citizens when they voted out Dion. Dion returned to save the city but ended becoming a tyrant himself, assassinated in 354BC.

TIMOLEON'S RESTORATION
A decade of civil war ravaged Sicily, numerous tyrants emerging only to be quickly murdered. Finally in 345BC Corinth, Syracuse's mother-city, sent out Timoleon, a man of exceptional integrity and ability. He drove out the tyrants and in 339BC defeated the Carthaginians, who had again attacked. Timoleon restored a limited democracy, re-peopling Syracuse with 60,000 new immigrants from old Greece. He retired universally honoured, dying in 337BC, but his settlement unravelled within a few years.

Right: Ortygia, the island core of Syracuse that Dionysius I made into his own citadel, expelling all citizens living there.

ABORTIVE EMPIRES
JASON AND MAUSOLUS, 375–353BC

Above: The fertile plains of Thessaly, here seen from the rocks of Meteora, provided good pasture for Jason's excellent cavalry.

Below: The island, now peninsula, in Halicarnassus (modern Bodrum) on which Mausolus built his citadel with a double harbour for his growing fleet in c.360BC.

In 362BC Theban victory at the Battle of Mantinea reconfirmed that Sparta could never regain her old position but left everything else more unsettled than before. Epaminondas' death at Mantinea had ended Thebes' brief hegemony, never fully accepted by most of Greece. By then, all the traditional main powers faced varying degrees of financial and political exhaustion. The resulting vacuum in Greek affairs began to pull in more powerful rulers from the Greek fringes. Two new powers emerged that seemed poised to dominate Greek politics, but both rapidly faded after their ruler's death.

JASON OF PHERAE
REIGNED 380–370BC

Thessaly, the northernmost part of Greece proper, was unusually large and fertile – promising territory for any would-be dynast or ruler. With better-watered pastures than southern Greece, it supported superb cavalry on a scale unthinkable further south. But it had long remained divided between feuding aristocratic clans – all claiming descent from Hercules, like the kings of Sparta, the most notable being the Aleuads. Its coastal cities were intermittently independent. This disunity made Thessaly a pawn in the hands of outside powers, Persian, Athenian or Spartan. Xerxes had recruited its cavalry for his great invasion of 480BC, but their 'medizing' did not undermine Thessaly's status as fully Greek. Although by the 4th century BC life based on the *polis* was spreading throughout Thessaly, it needed a leader of genius to unite it. In Jason, Thessaly briefly found one.

The ancient title *tagus* (lord) of Thessaly had long been awarded to a ruler who could unite the land. By 380BC Jason, tyrant of Pherae in south-central Thessaly, was powerful enough to be hailed as *tagus* by other clans and cities. He began organizing a Thessalian army on a federal basis. By then he had also intervened in Euboea, if ineffectually, for Sparta opposed him. The Spartan outpost at Heraclea near Thermopylae blocked his way south into central Greece.

The news of Sparta's shocking defeat at Leuctra by Thebes in July 371BC gave Jason his opening. He raced south with his cavalry, moving so fast through hostile Phocis that it could not stop him, and reached Boeotia in time to act as armed arbitrator. The Thebans had to let the Spartans, still numerically the larger army, return to the Peloponnese. Jason did not want an over-mighty Thebes. On his way home he demolished the fortress of Heraclea, opening the way into Greece.

Jason's army, composed of Thessalian cavalry and mercenary infantry, was now the strongest in Greece, and he began building a navy. He seemed the new Greek hegemon and talked of a Panhellenic war against Persia. He aimed to dominate the next Pythian festival at

Delphi, one of the greatest in the calendar, and to become President of the Amphictyonic Council controlling Delphi. But one day, late in 370BC, as he was reviewing his cavalry he was assassinated by some Thessalian nobles for personal reasons. His son Alexander succeeded him as *tagus* but lacked his ability. Alexander was defeated by Thebes in 364BC, although that victory cost the Theban general Pelopidas his life. Alexander lived on until 358BC, his powers much reduced.

MAUSOLUS OF CARIA
RULED 377–353BC

In the 4th century BC the Persian Empire's westernmost satraps in Asia Minor gained increasing powers that made them, if not independent, in practice far more powerful, even able to pass on their titles to their heirs. Several joined the 'Revolt of the Satraps' in the 360s BC, which shook the empire. Of these dynasts, Mausolus, who succeeded his father as satrap of Caria in south-west Asia Minor in 377BC, was the most powerful. He moved his capital from inland Mylasa

down to Halicarnassus, where he ruled with half-Hellenic, half-Carian splendour. He built himself a castle on the island (now peninsula) outside Halicarnassus and a double harbour for the city.

Now established, he began to expand his power: south-east toward Lycia, north toward Miletus and, most significantly, west over the islands. This meant a clash with Athens. The Second Confederacy in Athens was proving increasingly unpopular, as she reneged on initial promises not to exploit her allies, planting *cleruchs* (colonists) in Samos again, for example. In 357BC, when Chios, Cos and Rhodes revolted in the so-called 'Social War', they looked to Mausolus for support. He shrewdly let these Greek cities govern themselves, providing only small garrisons. But his mini-empire came to nothing, for he died suddenly in 353BC, after which his widow Artemisia ruled.

To commemorate her husband, she built his tomb, the Mausoleum, at Halicarnassus, which became one of the Seven Wonders of the World. Its magnificence displayed the dynasty's wealth and gave us the word 'mausoleum'.

THE 'SACRED WAR'
357–346BC

Above: Delphi was sacred to Apollo, here seen in relaxed mode playing with a lizard, in a sculpture by Praxiteles.

Delphi was the holiest place in the Greek world, sacred to the god Apollo. For centuries cities across the Greek world, besides non-Greek kingdoms such as Lydia, had enriched the shrine with temples and statues. Set in a cleft in the mountains, Delphi itself was a tiny, powerless *polis*. Its accumulated wealth relied for protection less on awe of the god, real though that was, than on the Amphictyonic Council, backed by general Greek support. 'Sacred Wars' arose when states contested control of the shrine. The most significant resulted from Thebes' renewed attempts to dominate her immediate neighbours. It paved the way for Macedonia's domination.

PHOCIS SEIZES DELPHI

In 357BC the Theban-dominated Amphictyonic Council fined the little state of Phocis for "cultivating sacred ground", which was an excuse for letting Thebes attack. As expected, Phocis would (or could) not pay the massive fine. Unexpectedly, their leader Philomelus seized Delphi early in 356BC and 'borrowed' Delphic gold to hire a mercenary army of 5,000 men. He won Spartan and even Athenian tacit approval if not active support, but killed himself after having been defeated by the Thebans in 354BC.

Thebes, thinking the war over, hired out many of its best troops to a Persian satrap, but Onomarchus (Philomelus' successor) took over the tattered Phocian army. He helped himself to more of Apollo's money, made alliances, with Pherae among other places, and recruited fresh troops. With these he won a series of startling victories, defeating Philip II of Macedonia in Thessaly in 353BC.

At this stage Phocis ruled most of central Greece, but Philip, returning with a larger army, drove the Phocians from Thessaly in 352BC. When Athens sent a force to hold Thermopylae, however, Philip prudently retreated to Thessaly, for the moment not wishing to offend Athens, still the greatest Greek city.

MACEDONIA'S VICTORY

The power of Phocis relied totally on Delphic money to pay its mercenaries. As this ran out, its fortunes began to decline, hastened by internal divisions. Onomarchus, killed in battle, was replaced by Phalaecus, who was soon dismissed (in theory, though in practice he still held Thermopylae, the gates of Greece). Both Athens and Sparta were

Left: The Tholos of the temple to Athena Pronoia built in Delphi, c.390BC. Delphi was filled with sacred treasures. Melted down, these paid for a large mercenary army, so briefly making tiny Phocis hegemon of Greece.

Right: Consulting the Delphic Oracle. The god spoke to supplicants through his priestess the Pythia, who sat, probably drugged, on a stool over a chasm. Delphi's utterances were notoriously ambiguous.

preoccupied with events elsewhere when Thebes appealed to Philip for help against Phocian troops ravaging its borders. Philip moved swiftly south, Phalaecus surrendering Thermopylae to him by secret agreement. Philip now crushed Phocis, broke it up into small villages and took its seats on the Amphictyonic Council.

Most Greek states, Sparta excepted, then signed the Peace of Philocrates of 346BC, which recognized Philip's actions. The Sacred War was finally over. The real victor was neither Thebes nor Phocis but Macedonia, rising fast under its dynamic and cunning king to become the new hegemon of Greece.

MERCENARIES

The word 'mercenary' is pejorative today, but the Greeks called such soldiers either *xenoi* (foreigners) or, more politely, *epikuroi* (helpers). The profession, if scarcely glamorous, was not shameful. Greek mercenaries had fought in Egypt in the 6th century BC, and in the 5th century mercenary *peltasts* (light troops) were used at times. But only in the aftermath of the long Peloponnesian War (431–404BC) did mercenaries become important. Greeks who knew no other trade than soldiering now sought employment as mercenaries. Arcadia, the impoverished heart of the Peloponnese, was a major source of such soldiers, but they came from other cities facing hard times too. Probably the most famous was Xenophon. An Athenian ill at ease with his city's restored democracy, Xenophon, joined the army of the rebel Prince Cyrus in 401BC. He ended leading the '10,000', the Greek hoplites forming the army's core, back to the Greek world. He was not the only such mercenary, however.

Conon, the one Athenian *strategos* to escape the disaster at Aegospotamae in 405BC, hired himself out to the Persians over the next years, fighting Sparta at sea. Other 4th-century Athenian generals at times fought as mercenaries when they could not pay their armies, among them Iphicrates and Timotheus, two of Athens' best generals. More remarkably, King Agesilaus of Sparta (ruled 399–360BC) in his last years took service in Egypt, in revolt against Persia, to earn money for his now desperately strained city. This did attract criticism, however, since Spartan kings were descendants of the divine hero Hercules, not just ordinary generals.

Demosthenes, Athens' great 4th-century orator, often chided his fellow citizens for relying on mercenaries rather than fighting themselves. But in real emergencies Athenian citizens would still fight, as they did at Chaeronea in 338BC (if unsuccessfully). Since many wars in the 4th century hardly seemed worth fighting, hiring skilled mercenaries often seemed preferable.

Above: The tomb of Dioscorides, a mercenary. Mercenaries became common in Greek armies from the 4th century BC onwards, as ordinary citizens grew less inclined to fight.

MACEDONIA'S RISE TO POWER
359–336BC

Above: The lion commemorating the Sacred Band, the elite corps of 300 Thebans killed at the Battle of Chaeronea in 338BC.

Below: At Chaeronea, Philip on the right feigned retreat, drawing on the Athenians, who exposed their flank to a cavalry charge by Alexander.

North of Mt Olympus, mythical home of the gods, lay Macedonia – to other Greeks a huge, strange, half-barbaric country. It had played an often ambiguous role in Greek affairs since the reign of Alexander I, king during the Persian invasion of 480BC. Although Macedonia had had ambitious monarchs, its frequent relapses into chaos meant that it was never more than a local power. All this changed with astonishing swiftness, however, when Philip II came to the throne in 359BC.

PHILIP'S POLICY OF EXPANSION

Philip had spent his youth as a hostage in Thebes, where he admired the military skills that gave Thebes its brief hegemony. Inheriting the Macedonian throne after his brother Perdiccas III was killed fighting Illyrian tribes, he defeated the invaders decisively in 358BC, pushing inland as far as Lake Ochrid. In 357BC Philip married the Epirote princess Olympias, who bore him a son, Alexander, in 356BC. That same year he seized Amphipolis, the key city founded by Athens but lost in 424BC, which

Above: Philip II, the ruler who transformed Macedonia from chaotic backwater to Greek superpower, was only 24 when he came to the throne in 359BC.

controlled the crossing of the River Strymon. Philip conned the Athenians into thinking that he was taking it for them, but kept it himself. With Amphipolis came the gold mines of Mt Pangaeus. Philip exploited these far more energetically, its gold underpinning his growing strength. He reorganized the Macedonian army, no longer basing regiments on clans or families. He created the Macedonian phalanx, a porcupine of pikesmen, and formed the Companions, a royal guard of elite cavalry. With this new,

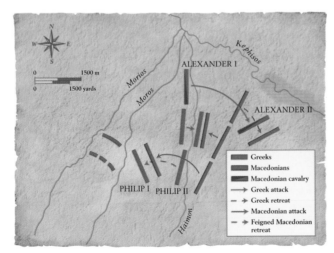

ALEXANDER I

ALEXANDER II

PHILIP I   PHILIP II

	Greeks
	Macedonians
	Macedonian cavalry
→	Greek attack
⇢	Greek retreat
→	Macedonian attack
⇢	Feigned Macedonian retreat

increasingly professional army under his excellent general Parmenion, he began his policy of relentless expansion.

In 356BC Philip took Pydna and Potidaea, cities on Macedonia's own coast, and captured Crenides inland on the Thracian border. Defeated in Thessaly by Phocis' superior numbers in 353BC, he took revenge soon after at the Battle of the Crocus Field, routing the Phocians with his cavalry. This victory made Philip *tagus* of Thessaly, controlling the port of Pagasae, and he added Thessaly's superb cavalry to his army.

A THREAT TO ATHENS

Although Philip was checked at Thermopylae in 352BC by Athens, he had transformed Macedonia's position. He could do this because the southern Greeks were distracted by other events: Thebes by the Sacred War; Athens by the revolt of its allies and Mausolus of Caria; and Sparta by problems close to home. In 349BC Philip besieged Olynthus, the main Chalcidic city. The Athenians, despite an alliance with it, did nothing to help and

Below: Demosthenes, Athens' last great democrat and a renowned orator, whose Philippics (speeches against Philip) led his city finally to fight Macedonia.

Philip captured it in 348BC, razing it to the ground. In 347BC Philip turned east to conquer the area around the River Hebrus in Thrace. His growing power now started to threaten Athens' vital grain supplies through the Hellespont.

When Thebes asked Philip for help against Phocis in 346BC, he marched south, finding Thermopylae unguarded. He trounced the Phocians, whom he denounced for stealing Apollo's gold, taking their seats on the Amphictyonic Council (a great coup, for it meant Macedonia's recognition as fully Greek), and presided over the Pythian games. The war-weary Greeks accepted his new status in the Peace of Philocrates. But he had grander plans: to be hegemon of Greece.

BATTLE OF CHAERONEA

In 342BC Philip marched north-east into wild Thrace. Despite falling gravely ill, he made all Thrace acknowledge his suzerainty. Alarmed at developments, which further threatened Athens' Black Sea grain, Demosthenes persuaded Perinthus and Byzantium to turn against Philip. In 339BC, when Philip besieged Byzantium, Athens declared war and sent a fleet, forcing him to withdraw. Philip, seizing 200 grain ships meant for Athens, marched into Phocis.

Demosthenes now persuaded Athens to offer an alliance to Thebes, its old rival. A tense debate in Thebes led to acceptance. The two great powers of old Greece (Sparta being now insignificant) mobilized. The two armies met at Chaeronea in August 338BC. Philip's right wing, facing the inexperienced Athenians, feigned a retreat. As the Athenians advanced, they opened a gap between themselves and the Thebans into which Prince Alexander charged with the Macedonian cavalry. Then Philip's disciplined troops turned to counter-attack. The Athenians fled. Only the Theban Sacred Band stood its ground to the last man. The Battle of Chaeronea had proved fatal to Greek liberty.

Above: A coin showing Dionysus, god of wine and ecstasy, widely worshipped in Macedonia and Thrace.

Below: This fine bronze statue of a youth, made c.340BC and found in the sea, suggests that by the mid-4th century BC Greeks lacked their earlier heroic determination.

THE END OF CLASSICAL GREECE 337–322BC

Above: Lycurgus of Athens, in control of the city's finances for 12 years, oversaw the construction of new shipyards and the rebuilding of the Theatre of Dionysus.

Below: In 338BC Philip called a Panhellenic Congress at Corinth, chosen because it had been the seat of resistance during the Persian Wars.

Philip used his crushing victory at Chaeronea wisely, as might be expected from such an astutely diplomatic leader. He treated Thebes, which had broken its treaty with Macedonia, more severely than Athens, placing a Macedonian garrison in the Cadmaea (the citadel of Thebes) but giving Athens the border town of Oropus. Philip himself returned 2,000 Athenian captives, but retained the Chersonese peninsula so that he could cut Athens' grain supplies at will. Philip then invaded the Peloponnese. Meeting no resistance, he ravaged Spartan territory, leaving it yet more isolated and powerless but still feared by its neighbours.

In 338–337BC Philip established the League of Corinth to promulgate his grand design: a Panhellenic war against Persia to avenge its attack on Greece nearly 150 years earlier. For this he ideally wanted Athenian naval help and certainly a quiescent Greece behind him. To ensure the latter, he planted Macedonian garrisons at Ambracia in the west, Chalcis on Euboea and Corinth. The Greeks voted him Captain General of the Greeks and he sent an advance force into Asia. But he himself never followed it. Returning to Macedonia, he celebrated the marriage of his daughter with her uncle Alexander of Cleopatra (he had already divorced Olympias, Alexander's mother). When in 336BC Philip was assassinated, seemingly for personal reasons, many in Greece must have expected Macedonia to relapse into its customary chaos. They were to be devastatingly disappointed.

ALEXANDER AND GREECE
Rapidly establishing himself as Philip's heir, the 20-year-old Alexander raced down into Greece – cutting steps in the sides of Mt Ossa when the Thessalians demurred at letting him pass – to squash potential revolts. Thessaly accepted him as its leader and the League at Corinth elected him General. Returning north, he swept through Thrace, crossing the Danube – the first Greek soldier to do so – before turning west to defeat the Illyrians. There he heard that the Thebans, believing a rumour of his death, had risen and massacred some Macedonian officers, besieging the rest of the garrison in the citadel. Returning south at lightning speed, he stormed Thebes in September 335BC, razing the ancient city to the ground and enslaving its inhabitants.

After this act of exemplary terror, Greece was cowed. Alexander took only 20 ships from Athens when he crossed into Asia in 334BC, mainly as hostages. He left Antipater, one of his best generals, with an army in Macedonia to control Greece. Many Greeks secretly hoped for

ATHENS REBUILDS ITSELF

During the peaceful if drought-stricken years of Alexander's conquest of Asia, Athens enjoyed an autumnal calm. She rebuilt her dockyards, increasing her fleet to 400 galleys. Lycurgus, effectively Finance Minister for 12 years from 338BC, reconstructed the city's theatre of Dionysus, built the Panathenaic Stadium and rebuilt the Lyceum. There the philosopher Aristotle used to take his walks, teaching as he went, giving the name 'Peripatetic' (from *peripatetikos*, to pace to and fro) to his school. The Laurium silver mines were reopened, and the military training of *ephebi* (young citizens aged 18–20) was reorganized.

Alexander's defeat and death. In 331BC, Agis III of Sparta, a young monarch with more ambition than sense but financed by Persian gold, rose against the Macedonians. His army was routed at Megalopolis by Antipater and he was killed. Greece lapsed into acquiescence.

THE EXILES' DECREE

In 324BC Alexander issued an edict ordering every Greek city to take back its exiles. This caused problems for some cities, especially Athens. Its *cleruchs* had colonized Samos, so Samian exiles wanted their land back. Athens sent envoys to remonstrate with Alexander. (His other demand – that he be worshipped as a god – caused relatively few problems, for some Greeks had already been given divine honours.) Meanwhile Harpalus, a corrupt Macedonian high official, appeared at Athens with quantities of gold, some of which Demosthenes allegedly took. Then came the long-awaited news: Alexander was dead.

THE LAMIAN WAR

At first few could believe it. "If he were dead, the whole world would stink of his corpse!" declared Demades, an orator.

But as the Greeks realized that it was true, many joined Athens' revolt against the Macedonians. (Aristotle, tainted by his associations – he had been Alexander's tutor – fled from Athens to avoid it "repeating its mistake with Socrates".)

The Athenians seized Thermopylae and kept Antipater and his army beseiged in the city of Lamia through the winter of 323–322BC. But despite this initial success, the Lamian War went badly for the allied Greeks: they often did not agree on their actions, their best general, Leosthenes, was killed in the siege and Athens could not afford to man more than half of its new fleet.

After reinforcements reached Antipater from Asia, he broke out. At the Battle of Crannon in August 322BC the combined Macedonians defeated the Greeks decisively. This time peace was truly dictated. Athens' democracy became an oligarchy, with a Macedonian garrison in the Piraeus. The democratic leaders fled into exile, Demosthenes taking poison rather than face capture. With him died classical Greece.

Above: Philip in later life, arbiter of Greece, supremely experienced both as a general and a diplomat.

Below: The plains of Boeotia, called the 'dance floor of Ares (Mars)' because many battles were fought there. Alexander, by destroying Thebes in 335BC, shocked Greece into accepting his power.

ALEXANDER THE GREAT AND HIS HEIRS

Alexander the Great remains one of the most dramatic figures in world history. He was indisputably a military genius, overthrowing the vast Persian Empire, but views about him remain divided. The Victorian historian Thomas Carlyle called him "Macedonia's madman". More recently he has been damned as a paranoid alcoholic, murdering all in his way, perhaps before being finally murdered himself. To many at the time – be they democrats such as Demosthenes, or inhabitants of cities that he erased, such as Thebes, Tyre or Persepolis – Alexander was purely destructive. But others have seen him as transcending Greek chauvinism, trying to create a global empire that united conquered and conquerors. To romantics he has always appealed. Alexander saw himself as a reincarnation of Achilles, the Homeric hero who preferred a glorious early death to long but obscure life. In this at least he succeeded: his name has passed into legend across Asia as well as Europe.

Alexander's dazzling successes were possible only because of the achievements of his father Philip, who created the best army yet seen. If a lesser general than his son, Philip was a better politician. Alexander's successors extended Greek power and culture across Asia, creating the civilization known as Hellenistic. Although endless wars wrecked many kingdoms, Greek culture continued to spread, finally influencing art in countries as distant as India and China. The last Hellenistic monarch to resist the rise of Rome was Cleopatra VII of Egypt, a queen of legendary glamour. But Alexander's final heir proved to be Rome itself.

Left: The Alexander Mosaic from Pompeii, showing Alexander charging towards a terrified King Darius in his chariot, probably at the Battle of Issus.

CHAPTER VII

THE RISE OF MACEDONIA

359–336BC

Alexander's achievement appears so dazzling that his career has often eclipsed that of his father, Philip II. But without the patient state building of Philip, who started his reign in most unpromising circumstances and ended it as Greece's acknowledged leader, Macedonia would never have become the military powerhouse that it was by 336BC. In that year Alexander succeeded to the throne over his murdered father's body – a typical Macedonian scenario, some may have thought.

Several earlier monarchs had tried to unify this kingdom – which remained closer to the heroically chaotic world of Homer than a Greek *polis* – but their attempts had died with them, and their deaths had seldom been from natural causes. Although invaders and feuding nobles constantly threatened it, Macedonia was the largest, potentially wealthiest of Greek states. Endowed with fertile plains and wide pastures, it was occupied by a warlike people usually loyal to the throne if not always to the person occupying it. Yet Macedonia remained on the fringe of the Greek world until its meteoric rise under Philip II in the 350s BC. One of the most Machiavellian as well as energetic of rulers, Philip used bribes and promises as well as force to divide and conquer at home and abroad. After Philip's reign, Macedonia remained a major power in the Mediterranean world until the advent of Rome overwhelmed all the Greek states.

Left: Macedonia's new wealth and old martial energy are shown in this gold quiver from the royal tombs at Vergina.

EARLY OBSCURITY
c.480–359BC

Above: Mt Olympus, the highest peak in Greece and mythical home of the gods, lay within the Macedonian kingdom. Greek-style games were held at Dion on its slopes.

North of Mt Olympus, the greatest mountain known to the Greeks, stretched a realm that few southern Greeks knew at all and one about which even fewer normally cared, even though Macedonia had long protected Greece proper from barbarians to the north.

It was a land-bound kingdom, the coastal cities such as Olynthus being mostly colonies of southern cities. Aegae, Macedonia's ancient inland capital, overlooked the rich Emathian plain near the sea. Macedonia itself could be roughly divided into two zones: the lowland area, where royal authority ran, and the highland zone to the north and west, which was mountainous and thickly forested. Here, in walled, isolated villages, Macedonians still lived lives that Homer might have recognized but that would have struck classical Greeks as uncouth. Often herdsmen or subsistence farmers, these 'Upper Macedonians', such as the Lyncestids, acknowledged only clan chieftains. Beyond these tribal communities lived real barbarians: Illyrians and Celts to the north and north-west and Thracians to the north-east,

waiting their chance to descend on the rich lowlands. Their invasions mattered much more to clans such as the Lyncestids or Orestids than to any distant king down on the coast, who could give them little protection against such attackers.

MACEDONIAN KINGS

The first notable Macedonian monarch was Alexander I (reigned 498–454BC). His reign coincided with the great Persian invasion of 480BC, in which he played an ambivalent role. He first accepted Persian overlordship in 491BC, when the Persian general Mardonius led an army west along the Aegean's north coast. In 480BC he involuntarily entertained King Xerxes himself – an expensive guest with his huge court and army – before accompanying the Persians south. But Alexander also sent ambiguously worded warnings to the Greeks. In spring 479BC he acted as the Persian's go-between, trying to persuade Athens to change sides. This was an ignominious role, but other more typical Greek states, most notably Thebes, also 'medized' (supported Persia).

Despite this, Alexander I was called the 'Philhellene' and was credited with expanding the kingdom, his reign later being remembered as a golden age. He was succeeded by his son Perdiccas II (reigned 453–413BC), who steered a delicately neutral path between the great powers of his age, Athens and Sparta. Brasidas, Sparta's greatest general in the Peloponnesian War, was invited north in 424BC by Perdiccas (among other states) to counter Athenian power. However, king and Spartan soon quarrelled as their aims diverged.

Left: Pella was Macedonia's new capital, chosen by king Archelaus in 413BC. In it the young Alexander III later was born and grew up, while Philip extended his power.

A NEW CAPITAL

Under Archelaus (413–399BC), the capital was moved down to Pella near the coast, leaving Aegae as the ceremonial centre. A determined policy of modernization ensued. Archelaus half-tamed the warlords of upper Macedonia, uniting the two halves of his realm. The army was reorganized on professional lines and straight roads linking new forts were built, as Thucydides noted. The Athenian poet Agathon and playwright Euripides were welcomed to Pella – Euripides wrote his last tragedy *The Bacchae* there – while Zeuxis, the famous painter, lavishly decorated its new palace. Socrates, offered refuge in Macedonia when facing trial in Athens, quipped that none would go to Macedonia to see its king but all wanted to see his new palace. So Archelaus and his court were not barbarous. But after his death Macedonia entered a confused decade, with four kings in quick succession. Stability was restored by Amyntas III (393–369BC), father of Philip II and grandfather of Alexander, but Macedonia remained marginal to Greek politics.

Above: Euripides, the Athenian playwright, was among the writers and artists invited to Macedonia by King Archelaus trying to Hellenize his rough kingdom.

Below: This stele of the young Xantos, from Pella, Macedonia's capital, was made c.400BC and is classically Hellenic in style.

MACEDONIANS: GREEKS OR BARBARIANS?

Alexander I was proud to be called *philhellene*, lover of things Greek, but this title was normally awarded to rulers who were definitely *not* Greek. Croesus of Lydia, the monarch overthrown by Persia in 546BC, was termed philhellene, as were some Asian rulers after Alexander. Many Greeks of the Classical Age thought that the Macedonians were barbarians, but the Boeotian poet Hesiod, writing *c.*700BC, considered them to be Greeks, speaking the same Aeolic dialect as the Boeotians. Two centuries later the Persians, encountering the Macedonians after conquering the Ionians, classed them as Greeks, albeit of a distinct hat-wearing type.

Certainly Macedonians were not savage like the Thracians and Illyrians further north. They may have had odd northern accents (they pronounced Philip

as Bilip, for example) and no real *polis* or citizen-state, but the same was true of Aetolians in north-west Greece, and nobody disputed their right to attend the games reserved for Greeks. The Macedonian kings, the Temenids, claimed descent from the ubiquitous sons of Hercules, who, according to legend, had left Argos *c.*650BC to settle in Macedonia.

It helped Macedonia that Olympus, home of the gods, was within its boundaries and that the games held at Dion on its slopes were clearly Greek. Generally, southern Greeks accepted Macedonia's kings as true Hellenes but disdained their rough subjects, who still had to kill a wild boar or lion to be thought a proper man. After Alexander the Great, as Macedonia grew increasingly rich and sophisticated, such distinctions vanished.

PHILIP II: THE RISE TO POWER
359–334 BC

Above: A silver tetradrachm (4-drachmae coin) of 354BC, when Philip II was starting to turn Macedonia into a great military power.

Below: The Roman-era amphitheatre at Philippi, the former city of Crenides refounded by Philip II as a military colony in 357BC to guard his eastern frontier.

In 359BC Perdiccas III of Macedonia, elder son of Amyntas III, was defeated and killed fighting Illyrian invaders on his western frontiers. At the same time savage Paeonians invaded from the north. These disasters eclipsed the modest yet real achievement of Perdiccas' reign: he had thwarted renewed Athenian attempts to regain Amphipolis (the crucial city on the River Strymon), briefly installing a Macedonian garrison there. Perdiccas left a son, Amyntas, aged two, but he also had a younger brother, Philip, aged only 24.

Philip had earlier been a hostage for three years in Thebes, where he had seen the training that at the time made Theban hoplites the best in the world. He reputedly also had an affair with Pelopidas, the much older general. On his brother's death, Philip took over the government, at first as regent for his infant nephew but soon becoming king himself. (Amyntas seems to have grown up weak-willed if not feeble-minded.)

Philip bought off the Paeonians – he knew the power of money – while defeating a pretender backed by the Athenians. Philip then released all the Athenian prisoners without ransom and openly renounced claims to Amphipolis, while secretly offering to swap it for Pydna, a free city in the Athenian Confederacy, so gaining Athens' support. He spent his first winter recruiting and training a new army. Early in 358BC, with 10,000 infantry and 600 cavalry, he routed the Illyrians, killing 7,000 of them.

AN EXPANDING EMPIRE

In 357BC Philip turned east and attacked Amphipolis, which appealed to Athens for help – in vain. Once Philip had captured Amphipolis, he kept it, outwitting the Athenians, who were preoccupied with revolts in their Confederacy and in Euboea. He also seized Crenides inland. He renamed it Philippi, making it a Macedonian military colony, the first of many. These moves secured his hold on Mt Pangaeus and its gold and silver mines.

He soon had the mines worked far more intensively than before to yield 1,000 talents a year – as much revenue as the Athenian Empire had enjoyed in its prime. "Money", Philip observed, "is the sinews of war". Soon after, he took Pydna and Potidaea, giving the latter to Olynthus. This, the most powerful Chalcidic city, had earlier sought Athenian support but now became his well-bribed ally, at least for a time. During his siege in 354BC of Methone, another Athenian ally, Philip lost one eye, marring his good looks.

AN ASTUTE MARRIAGE

Angered by Philip's actions, Athens encouraged his northern neighbours (Thracians, Illyrians and Paeonians) to attack Macedonia, but he beat or bought

Above: Olympia, site of the quadrennial Panhellenic games where Philip's horses won a prize in 356BC, usefully boosting his Hellenic credentials.

them off, using his trusted general Parmenion. Philip also employed non-military means to secure his position. In 357BC he married Olympias, niece of the king of Epirus to his west. Whether romance or *realpolitik* guided his choice (the two reputedly caught each other's eye at a midnight mystery rite on Samothrace), it was an astute move, and Olympias quickly bore him a son, Alexander, in 356BC. News of the birth reached him at the same time as that of a victory for his horses in the Olympic Games, making him a happy king. But events at another site sacred to all Greece were to give him his biggest chance yet.

THESSALY, EPIRUS, THRACE
Since seizing Delphi and its treasuries in 356BC, tiny Phocis had become the most powerful state in Greece, its mercenary forces defeating all armies sent against it. These included Thebes' and, in 353BC, Philip's, but his troops in Thessaly were outnumbered. While Phocian power was built on a dwindling supply of stolen gold, Philip's was based on the rising power of Greece's largest state. Returning to Thessaly in 352BC with a larger army, Philip routed the Phocians at the Battle

of the Crocus Field. He was then acclaimed *tagus* (ruler) of Thessaly, displacing the tyrants of Pherae. This gave him Thessaly's superb cavalry and brought him to the borders of central Greece itself.

Here, however, he was thwarted. Eubolus, then dominating the Athenian Assembly, sent a force to hold the crucial pass at Thermopylae. Not wishing to fight what was still Greece's greatest city just yet, Philip retreated and turned his attentions north. In 351BC he expelled King Arybbas, his wife's uncle, from Epirus, establishing her suitably grateful brother in his place. He brought further western tribes into Macedonia, extending his power to the Adriatic.

On his other flank lay Thrace, mountainous and wild. Profiting from divisions between its quarrelling princes, Philip pushed into its interior, founding Philippopolis, his second city, on the River Hebrus. His power now touched the Chersonese – that peninsula on the Dardanelles controlling Athens' essential grain supplies.

Above: A tetradrachm showing Philip on horseback wearing a kausia, *the traditional Macedonian broad-brimmed hat.*

Below: This mural depicts the Rape of Persephone. From a royal tomb at Vergina (ancient Aegae), it shows the latest Greek artistic styles being adopted in Macedonia.

A NEW ARMY AND A NEW STATE: THE RULE OF PHILIP II

Above: The young Philip II, a fine Roman copy of an original Greek statue.

Below: Macedonia, lying outside Greece proper, was far bigger than any normal Greek state but dangerously exposed to northern invaders. Once united, with its frontiers secured and its potential exploited, it became the greatest power in the Greek world.

Philip created the most formidable army Greece had yet seen, able to defeat Greece and (under his son) conquer Asia. It outclassed Sparta's professional armies, invincible until defeated by Thebes in 371BC. Macedonia's army was huge (by Greek standards), highly professional and increasingly filled with national pride. Philip had inherited a kingdom that was oddly archaic if vigorous, looking back to the Homeric age. He left it the indisputable Greek superpower.

The Macedonian state consisted of two parts: the king himself, who was war leader, supreme judge, high priest and government; and the Assembly of adult male Macedonians, who also constituted the army and acted as a crude court. There were no elected magistrates or Council as in a Greek *polis*. Nor was there a dangerously powerful old hereditary aristocracy, in lower Macedonia at least, although family background still mattered greatly. Philip promoted many new men, whether they came from old Macedonia or elsewhere.

Above: This vase from the 4th century BC depicts a rather fanciful battle scene. While Philip's victories were still won by his footsoldiers, cavalry was becoming increasingly important.

MACEDONIA'S MONARCHY

Unlike Persia, Macedonia was not an absolute monarchy. Macedonians bared their heads but did not bow before their king, whom they addressed by name, not as 'Majesty'. Any Macedonian could appeal to Philip for judgement. Kings ruled by hereditary right as members of the Temenid dynasty. If there was more than one claimant to the throne, who succeeded depended on their luck and skill in winning over generals and courtiers. Their choice was then put to

TOUGHENED PROFESSIONALS

Demosthenes complained that Macedonian armies campaigned throughout winter, unlike those of Athens or Thebes, whose citizens had to return to their farms every autumn. Only the Spartans had done this in the past. Macedonians managed this because Philip, doubling his country's size, gave newly conquered lands as estates to his followers, with slaves to work them. This enabled many Macedonians to become full-time soldiers.

The slave-worked mines of Mt Pangaeus remained the basis of Philip's revenues, allowing him to mint gold coins, the first Greek to do so. Only Persia's Great King was richer. Yet Macedonia's army was even tougher than Sparta's. While most Greek armies allowed one servant per hoplite, Philip allowed only one attendant per ten hoplites and banned carriages for his officers. He forced his men to march 48km/30 miles or more a day, summer or winter, over rough tracks. They often had to carry 30 days of supplies on their backs, to keep baggage trains as small as possible.

Philip once reproved a soldier for washing with hot water, saying that only women who had given birth should be allowed such luxury. Women were anyway banned from camp. All this was highly effective, not least because Philip himself endured every hardship and danger, being repeatedly wounded. He had emulated Spartan discipline and toughness on a larger scale.

Above: Although horsemen in the ancient world had no stirrups to hold them in place, they could still fight effectively with both lance and sword, as this coin from Taranto of c.300BC shows.

the Assembly, who voiced approval by clashing their spears, not voting. So the monarchy had a broad popular base.

Once accepted, a strong king in practice had almost boundless power, while a weak one soon lost his throne and his life. A king had, above all, to lead the army. The core of this in 359BC was the Companions (*Hetairoi*), originally 600 upper-class Macedonian horsemen. Philip increased their numbers steadily until by 338BC this royal cavalry numbered 4,000. Philip invented the title 'Foot Companions' for six battalions comprising 9,000 heavy infantry and created the Shield Bearers, 3,000 crack foot guards who, on the battlefield, linked the cavalry and infantry. He reorganized the army by forming battalions more on a territorial or tribal basis than a clan one. By 338BC he could field about 30,000 infantry and 5,000 cavalry, besides garrisoning numerous forts across his empire. This was unprecedented power.

USE OF THE PHALANX

Philip's chief military development was the much-improved phalanx, now a bristling porcupine of spear-men. They carried longer spears than ordinary hoplites: sarissas up to 5m/15ft long. No one could hold such a spears in one hand, so shields became smaller, being slung on the left arm. The phalanx was often massed up to 60 men deep (Philip remembered Theban examples) and was geared for attack, its flanks being covered by other troops. Discipline was vital to maintain formation, but with experienced Macedonian pike-men the phalanx could deliver an unstoppable punch. Philip also hired archers from Crete and engineers such as Polyeidus of Thessaly, who developed siege engines and catapults.

CREATING A UNITED KINGDOM

To unite his kingdom, Philip transplanted populations, settling highlanders in his new cities such as Philippi. He forced upland barons to send their sons to become royal pages at Pella, where they learned soldiering, royal service and some Hellenic culture – and acted as hostages. Philip cemented his power by seven marriages, including one to an Illyrian princess and two to Thessalians. But his prime marriage long remained that to Olympias of Epirus, Alexander's mother.

Below: A view of Pella, the thriving Macedonian capital under Philip II and his successors, where Alexander grew up, with a fine mosaic pavement in the foreground.

CONQUEROR OF GREECE
349–336 BC

Above: Philip II was notably handsome until he lost an eye at Methone in 354 BC.

Below: Philip's greatest victory came in 338 BC at Chaeronea, when he gained control of Greece. This lion, erected later over the mass grave, honours the Theban dead.

In 349 BC Philip attacked Olynthus, his former ally and leader of the Chalcidic League. He had an excuse – Olynthus had aided a Macedonian rebel – but Philip had long had his eye on this, the richest city in north Greece. Roused by Demosthenes' impassioned oratory, Athens finally sent the city help in the form of 2,000 men, but they were too few and too late: Philip captured Olynthus in 348 BC, destroying it and enslaving its inhabitants. He then annexed the other Chalcidic cities, whose leaders he had often bribed beforehand (he was as good at bribery as he was at strategy). Stagira, which resisted, was destroyed. With his power further boosted, Philip turned south. Athens, exhausted by minor wars around the Aegean and recurrent problems in Euboea, badly needed peace, but she was to get it on unfavourable terms.

AMPHICTYONIC COUNCIL LEADER

In 347 BC the Thebans, unable to repulse the Phocians still ravaging western Boeotia, appealed to Philip to become leader of the Amphictyonic Council theoretically controlling Delphi. This was the opening he had long wanted. Sending friendly letters to potential supporters in Athens, Philip invited Greek envoys to Pella, kept them waiting while he conquered more Thracian forts and then proposed peace on the terms of the status quo. During the extended diplomatic exchanges, he suddenly marched south, passing Thermopylae, where the Phocian commander Phalaecus surrendered in exchange for his liberty.

Philip then invited the Athenians to send envoys to another conference to deal with Phocian sacrilege, but Demosthenes persuaded them to ignore his offer. Philip, dominating the Amphictyonic Council, dealt with the Phocians quite lightly, fining them and breaking them up into villages, taking Phocis' seat on the Amphyctionic Council for Macedonia. That year he presided over the Pythian Games held at Delphi. He could now pass as a true Hellene; he also seemed a lesser evil to many small states than Sparta, still feared for its past misrule. At the Peace of Philocrates in 346 BC Athens had to accept terms that gave her nothing important while Thebes, Philip's new ally, regained its hegemony over Boeotia. This rankled with the Athenians. For Philip, the peace brought vital recognition of his position in central Greece.

OPEN WAR

Philip did not sit on his laurels. He led his army north-west into wildest Illyria, reaching the Adriatic probably near modern Dubrovnik. Then he turned north-east to annex Thrace. During this campaign, in which he reached the Danube, he fell seriously ill and was also wounded again. Demosthenes, in his 'Philippics' speeches, mocked the "limping one-eyed monster so fond of danger that to increase his empire he has been wounded in every part of his body". But Philip's campaigns had a purpose. With troops on the Black Sea and Sea of Marmara, he could now threaten Athens' crucial grain supplies from the region. Meanwhile, his envoys poured gold into the pockets of potential friends across Greece. These included Aeschines, Demosthenes' chief opponent in Athens.

In 340 BC Philip, returning from the Danube, attacked Selymbria and then Byzantium on the Bosphorus. He captured neither, mainly because he lacked ships to counter Persian and Athenian naval support, but late in 340 BC he seized

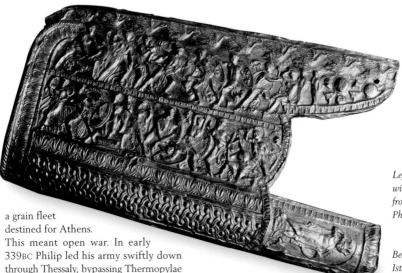

Left: Gold quiver decorated with scenes of soldiers fighting, from the probable tomb of Philip at Vergina.

Below: Byzantium (today Istanbul) shown in a 16th-century Ottoman map. Philip suffered one of his rare defeats when he besieged this city, vital to controlling grain supplies through the Bosphorus, in 340BC. But he still managed to seize a grain fleet destined for Athens.

a grain fleet destined for Athens.

This meant open war. In early 339BC Philip led his army swiftly down through Thessaly, bypassing Thermopylae into Phocis, where he seized the town of Elataea. His excuse was that further problems over Delphi required his assistance. In reality, Macedonia's main army now directly threatened Athens.

Demosthenes' finest hour had arrived. He had sensibly prepared for it by naval reforms, making the trierarchy, by which the richest citizens paid for triremes, more equitable. But Philip was a threat *on land*. Demosthenes now persuaded Athens to offer Thebes, its disliked neighbour but one with a powerful army, full alliance. Athenian concessions won Thebes over and Philip finally faced the two greatest powers in old Greece united. On 2 August 338BC the armies, which were roughly equal in size if not skills, met at Chaeronea.

BATTLE OF CHAERONEA

Philip placed the 18-year-old Prince Alexander on his left commanding the crack Companion cavalry opposite experienced Theban hoplites. He himself led the Footguards facing the Athenians. Philip advanced, attacked and suddenly seemed to flee. The Athenians pursued him recklessly, opening a great gap behind them. Through it charged Alexander to surround the Thebans. Philip then

counter-attacked, soon routing Athens' citizen-soldiers. But the crack Theban Sacred Band, 150 pairs of homosexual lovers, fought to the last man. Athens lost over 1,000 dead with 2,000 taken prisoner. Chaeronea, a resounding triumph for Philip, was a disaster for Greek freedom.

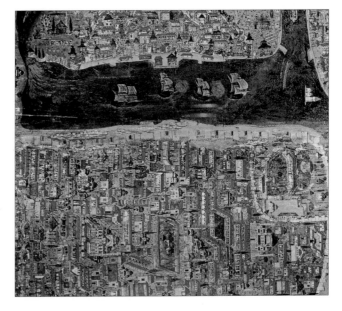

PHILIP: TRIUMPH AND DEATH
338–336BC

As undisputed victor, Philip could dictate the peace terms. Athens had to surrender the Chersonese (Dardanelles peninsula), becoming dependent on Macedonia's goodwill for the safety of its grain fleet. But in other ways, as even Demosthenes admitted, the peace was generous to her. She regained Oropus, long disputed with Thebes, and paid no indemnity. She also got back her prisoners without ransom, while young Prince Alexander ceremoniously returned the ashes of her dead soldiers. In return, the Athenians erected a statue to the Macedonian king. Philip's leniency to Athens was based on realism: Athens still had her long walls and large fleet, which would have made a direct attack very difficult. He also wanted her naval support for his anti-Persian crusade, while attacking Athens would harm his image as a true Hellene.

To Thebes, his former ally, Philip showed no such generosity. He broke up the Boeotian federation, long dominated by Thebes, restored the destroyed cities of Plataea and Orchomenus and put a Macedonian garrison in Thebes' citadel, the Cadmaea, to support a narrow pro-Macedonian oligarchy.

MERCY TO SPARTA

To that other once great city, Sparta, Philip behaved differently. When the Spartans refused to send envoys to the Council of Corinth, saying they were accustomed to lead other Greeks, not follow them, Philip invaded Laconia. He seemed about to take Sparta – this would not have been difficult, as Sparta's army was tiny – but desisted.

He knew that Sparta still appeared to menace her smaller neighbours, making them pro-Macedonian. He simply ravaged Sparta's lands and reduced her territory still further, giving the Dentheliatis border area to Messenia, Sparta's

Below: Found in the royal tombs at Vergina (ancient Aegae, the old capital), this silver vase reveals the wealth and sophistication Macedonia attained under Philip II.

Above: Philip was the first Greek ruler to mint coins in gold, such as this stater showing the god Apollo. He could do so thanks to his acquisition of the gold mines of Mt Pangaeus.

worst enemy. Then he called a Panhellenic Council at Corinth in the winter of 338–337BC.

Philip chose Corinth partly because of its central position and wealth but mainly because of its associations. It had been the seat of the Panhellenic League in the Persian Wars almost 150 years earlier, when many Greek states had for once united against Persia. Isocrates (436–338BC), the Athenian writer, had long urged the Greeks to stop fighting each other and turn against Persia, inside whose supposedly decaying empire they could easily win booty and new lands. He now hailed Philip as fulfilling his idea of a Panhellenic crusade.

A COMMON PEACE

Philip, happy to accept the aged orator's praise, had his own reasons for a Persian campaign, but first he had to settle affairs in Greece. Elected Captain-General of all the Greeks, a novel post, he announced a Common Peace. Superficially, this promised an end to Greece's incessant feuds by guaranteeing existing constitutions and banning any redistribution of land. Actually, as pro-Macedonian oligarchs had taken over in many places, it meant that he controlled much of Greece. To reinforce his hold, Philip stationed garrisons in Corinth, Ambracia and Chalcis (in Euboea), besides Thebes. Philip then announced a Panhellenic war of revenge, sent Parmenion ahead with 10,000 troops into Asia and returned north. Before he conquered Asia, there were domestic affairs to deal with.

ASSASSINATION

"Wounded is the bull; the end is near; the sacrificer is at hand." So spoke the Delphic oracle, ambiguous as ever, in response to Philip's enquiries. Flushed with success, Philip assumed the bull to be the Persian Empire. In the summer of 336BC at Aegae he celebrated the marriage of his young daughter Cleopatra to her uncle Alexander of Epirus. Such close ties were acceptable among royalty, for it was certainly no love match. In 338BC Philip himself, however, had fallen in love with and married 17-year-old Eurydice, niece of his general Attalus. She produced a daughter and then, in 336BC, a son. Philip promptly divorced Olympias, whose Epirote connections were no longer needed, making Alexander deeply worried about his future.

That wedding day, however, when Philip watched the procession of the Twelve Olympian gods at Aegae, followed by his own image in Olympian size, he was flanked by both Alexanders: his son and his new son-in-law. Suddenly a young guard called Pausanias rushed up and stabbed Philip, who died instantly. Pausanias, caught as he tried to escape, was summarily executed.

The true motive behind the murder died with him – conveniently for many people, perhaps. The story went that Pausanias, once Philip's lover, had been raped by

Left: Isocrates (436–338BC) was an Athenian orator who had long called for Greece to unite against Persia. In his last years he hailed Philip as the ideal leader for such a Panhellenic crusade.

servants of Attalus, whom he had slandered. Why Pausanias should then want to murder the king is unclear. What is clear is who benefited: Alexander, Philip's son by Olympias, due to be left behind in the coming war on Persia, and Olympias, Philip's ex-wife in bitter exile. Politics in Macedonia seemed to be reverting to their chaotic norm. But Philip, although cheated of winning an Asian empire, had built his kingdom so solidly that it did not fall apart. This was his real achievement.

Below: This elaborately decorated gold lamax or coffin found in the royal tombs at Vergina (ancient Aegae) contains what may be Philip II's bones. Such flamboyant riches recalled the splendours of Mycenaean Greece, the age of heroes, not of the cash-strapped democracies then the norm in Greece proper.

CHAPTER VIII

THE YOUNG ALEXANDER

356–336BC

Alexander was a phenomenon from birth – or so it was later told. The stories of his early years are so colourful that they approach the legendary. But there is no doubt that he was an infant and then adolescent prodigy. Remarkably precocious, he tamed a savage stallion at the age of 12 and was left as regent of the kingdom in his father Philip II's absence when only 16, repelling an invasion and founding his first city. When just 18 he led the decisive cavalry charge at the Battle of Chaeronea and then a delicate diplomatic mission to Athens.

Life in the Macedonian court – stimulating, exhilarating, never easy – encouraged rapid developers, but only a year later Alexander's position as heir apparent seemed endangered by Philip's last marriage. A year after that, he found himself king at the age of 20, ascending the throne over his father's corpse. What involvement if any he had in Philip's murder is unknown, but his succession was far from inevitable. Yet southern Greeks who confidently expected Macedonia to collapse into its traditional feuding after the death of Philip were soon disappointed. Within weeks Alexander was master of his own kingdom; within months he had made a lightning descent through Greece, claiming Philip's powers and titles. The Balkan campaign that followed, and the blitzkrieg return that destroyed Thebes, showed the Greeks that he was already even more dangerous than Philip.

Left: Lion hunt mosaic of c.310BC from Pella showing the young Alexander hunting lions.

BIRTH AND CHILDHOOD
356–347BC

The baby who became Alexander III, Alexander the Great, was born in July 356BC to Olympias, daughter of the royal house of Epirus, and Philip II of Macedonia. According to Plutarch, before his birth Olympias dreamt that lightning struck her womb, while Philip dreamt that her womb showed a lion's seal. Philip received the news of the birth of his first (legitimate) son on the same day his horses won at the Olympic Games and his troops took Potidaea. Philip's Temenid family claimed descent via Hercules

Left: Two scenes from The Romance of Alexander, *a fantastical history written about Alexander long after his death. Here it shows Alexander consulting the Delphic Oracle (above), which is a fiction, and with his horse Bucephalus (below), who existed.*

from Zeus, whose mountain home rose abruptly on their kingdom's southern flanks. Olympias' family traced its descent from Achilles, Homer's heroic prince. So Alexander had the most illustrious forebears imaginable. This helped shape his exalted view of his destiny.

Little is known of Alexander's childhood. The young prince could not have seen much of his father, who was away on his wars. His mother chose his first two tutors. One of them was her cousin Leonidas, who emulated his Spartan namesake, hero of Thermopylae, in toughness and austerity, confiscating anything exotic or luxurious in Alexander's belongings. When Alexander later conquered the Lebanon, he sent wagonloads of incense to Leonidas, telling him not to be mean to the gods. By contrast, kind old Lysimachus became so attached to Alexander that he followed him to Asia.

Such sober male influences countered the erratic behaviour of Alexander's mother. Olympias reputedly kept sacred snakes in her bed and worshipped Dionysus, god of wine and orgies, and the sinister Hecate, goddess of suicide and the underworld. "While others sacrifice tens and hundreds of animals, Olympias sacrifices them by the thousand and tens of thousand," wrote a student of Aristotle, the philosopher who came to know the intrigues and personalities at the court at Pella well.

NEW ARRIVALS AT PELLA
Pella was growing fast at this time, as Philip's conquests attracted diplomats, courtiers, artists, merchants and exiles. Among the last was the Persian Artabazus,

Left: The birth of Alexander in 356BC, shown in this mosaic of c.310BC from Phoenicia, was preceded by portents of greatness, according to later legends. Phoenicia was a part of Asia that became Hellenized after his conquest.

a former satrap of Phrygia. He brought with him Barsine, his beautiful young daughter, ten years older than Alexander. Alexander talked to Persians with friendly curiosity, discovering the virtues of this civilized people. Years later, when they met again in Asia, Alexander reappointed Artabazus as satrap, while Barsine became one of his mistresses. Many newcomers to Pella were southern Greeks: Nearchus the sailor from Crete, Demaratus the soldier from Corinth. All became Alexander's lifelong friends, although most Macedonians looked down on Greek hirelings.

THE PEACE CONFERENCE

In 346BC Philip's combination of guile, cash and force led to his triumph. Macedonian armies entered central Greece ostensibly to 'punish' Phocian sacrilege. For the resulting peace conference at Pella emissaries came from all over Greece, including two from Athens: Demosthenes and his opponent Aeschines, probably in Philip's pay.

By then Alexander was ten, old enough to appear and "play the lyre and recite and debate with another boy", according to Aeschines. A year later a row blew up in Athens amid accusations that one or other of the politicians had flirted with the already handsome young prince and been unduly influenced by him.

Whatever the truth, it suggests that Alexander was already politically alert and also reveals the prevalence of homosexuality in Greek public life.

Above: A view of Mt Olympus, the mountain home of the Olympian gods. Alexander came to believe that he was indeed the son of Zeus, king of the gods.

BUCEPHALUS: ALEXANDER'S HORSE

When Alexander was twelve, he began one of the greatest relationships in his life – with a horse. His friend Demaratus had offered Philip a huge black stallion costing 13 talents, more than three times anything paid for a horse before. Philip ordered the horse to be led out but it bucked and reared, refusing all orders. Philip was about to reject it when Alexander offered to tame him. Taking the horse by his halter, Alexander patted and quieted him. Then he mounted and galloped around to universal applause, Philip exclaiming proudly that Macedonia would never contain such a boy. Or so the story goes. Alexander had noticed that the horse was shying at its own shadow. By turning its head to the sun, he overcame its fears.

Alexander called his horse Bucephalus, 'Ox-head', because of a white mark on his black head. Bucephalus became

devoted to his royal master, following him literally to the ends of the Earth. Alexander rode him in his greatest battles and taught him to kneel fully armoured before him. When hill tribes near the Caspian Sea kidnapped the horse, Alexander's anger was so terrible that they returned him at once.

Alexander last rode Bucephalus into battle against the Indian rajah Porus in 326BC. Soon after, Bucephalus died of old age, being perhaps 30. (The Greeks did not know how to tell a horse's age by its teeth, the standard method.) Alexander commemorated his beloved stallion by founding and naming a city after him in what is now northern Pakistan.

Below: Alexander astride Bucephalus, the black stallion he rode to the ends of the Earth. Alexander was above all a cavalry commander.

EDUCATION AND YOUTH
346–340BC

Above: Aristotle, once Plato's most brilliant student in the Academy in Athens, was chosen by Philip to tutor the young prince. If unheroic in appearance, Aristotle had much the greatest mind of his generation, widening Alexander's mental horizons.

Below: A medieval painting of Aristotle's school for Alexander and his companions at Mieza, where he taught the boys subjects from zoology to drama.

Alexander had only one full sibling, his young sister Cleopatra, of whom he was very fond. But Macedonian girls played little part in public life, although they were not as secluded as those in Athens. To prepare his precocious, intelligent but emotionally volatile son for public affairs, Philip encouraged noblemen's sons to join what became the select group of Alexander's close companions. Foremost among these was Hephaistion, son of Amyntor, a Macedonian aristocrat.

HEPHAISTION

Alexander, who had learned to read when very young, was obsessed throughout his life by Homer's great poems, especially *The Iliad*, which related the exploits of his irascible supposed ancestor Achilles. In *The Iliad* Achilles is passionately devoted to his friend Patroclus, a devotion that by the 4th century BC was widely seen as erotic, although this is not how Homer shows it. Almost certainly Alexander and Hephaistion were lovers,

then and for years after, although Alexander always said that only sex and sleep reminded him that he was mortal. A homosexual relationship between the two boys would have been thought acceptable, even laudable, in Macedonia's militaristic society.

The one surviving portrait of Hephaistion does not suggest great beauty, and records indicate an utterly loyal, if rather dull, subordinate, who ended his career as Alexander's Grand Vizier. Dull but devoted loyalty was what Alexander needed at this stage, however, for his parents were constantly quarrelling. Philip was taking other, younger wives, often for reasons of state, making Olympias ragingly jealous. Alexander must have been the unhappy recipient of her hysterical rants.

Olympias reputedly also introduced a Thessalian prostitute into Alexander's bedroom to test his virility. Understandably, he rejected her – all his life Alexander hated prostitution or rape.

Other boys from the Macedonian nobility, including two sons of Antipater (one of Philip's best generals) and some from Upper Macedonian clans, notably Harpalus, joined the magic circle, soon guided by the age's greatest mind. For Philip wanted the best tutor money could buy for his adolescent son. In 342BC he chose another north Greek: Aristotle.

THE PHILOSOPHER-TUTOR
Born in 384BC in Stagira, a small city in the Chalcidice recently deleted by Macedonia, Aristotle had been the most brilliant student at Plato's Academy in Athens. He had left Athens on Plato's death in 347BC, probably disappointed at not being chosen as the next head of the Academy. Going north to the Troad (Dardanelles), he joined a community of philosophers and soon married the daughter of Hermias, a local ruler, at whose court he then lived. He later joined the polymath Theophrastus on Lesbos, where he carried out zoological investigations. So he was no reclusive academic (if unheroically "thin-legged and small-eyed") when he landed in Macedonia in 342BC to teach the 14-year-old prince. He stayed for four years based at Mieza, a small coastal town.

"[Aristotle] taught him writing, Greek, Hebrew, Babylonian and Latin. He taught him the nature of the winds and sea; he explained the stars' courses, the revolutions of the heaven…. He showed him justice and rhetoric and warned him against the looser sort of women." This comes from *The Romance of Alexander*, a most unreliable biography. Neither Aristotle nor Alexander learned Hebrew, Babylonian or even Latin (Rome was still struggling for survival in central Italy, although Aristotle, hearing of it, noted that it had the institutions of a *polis*). But Aristotle did teach Alexander a huge amount about the natural world.

Bertrand Russell, the 20th-century philosopher, thought that Alexander must have been "bored by the prosy old pedant". However, Aristotle had courtly

Right: A giant bronze head of Hephaistion, Alexander's first friend and very probably first lover. Hephaistion became Alexander's trusted second-in-command, his death causing the king huge grief.

manners – his father Nicomachus had been physician to Amyntas III, Philip's predecessor – and at only 42 was not old. Alexander's interests in botany, zoology, geography and biology were fired by Aristotle, and he later sent specimens from Asia back to his old tutor. Aristotle also deepened his knowledge of Greek literature, especially of the great Athenian playwrights, Euripides becoming one of Alexander's favourite authors. But the boy grew into a man of action, not thought, probably never much interested in Aristotle's ethics or metaphysics.

GREEKS AND BARBARIANS
On one point they differed profoundly. Aristotle had the typical Greek prejudices about 'barbarians', meaning all non-Greeks, including Persians. He considered them inherently inferior, to be treated as slaves. Quite early in his career, Alexander began thinking and behaving differently. This led him ultimately to clash with his own soldiers – and with Callisthenes, Aristotle's relative who was appointed as Alexander's official historian. Yet Aristotle must have widened and enriched Alexander's view of the world. Aristotle was enriched in the worldly sense by his stay in Macedonia. When Aristotle died in 322BC, he had 18 slaves – the sign of a rich man and unusual for a philosopher.

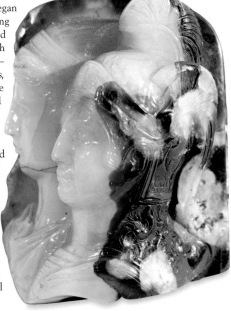

Below: Olympias, shown here in a cameo portrait with her son Alexander, was a stormy character, frequently clashing with her unfaithful husband and trying to turn her son against the king. Alexander inherited much of her fiery temperament and mysticism.

FIRST COMMANDS AND FAMILY QUARRELS 340–336BC

Above: Epirus on the north-western fringes of Greece was even wilder than Macedonia. It was the home of Olympias, to which she retreated after being divorced by Philip. Alexander, who had quarrelled with his father, accompanied her but soon returned.

Below: Alexander and a friend, perhaps Craterus, hunting lions, in a mosaic from Pella of c.310BC. Alexander loved hunting almost as much as war, although he did neither naked.

Far more central to Alexander's upbringing than studying botany or even Homer was his military training. All Macedonian boys learned the basics of arms drill and riding while young. By his teens Alexander was as good at riding and using arms as could be hoped. He was also a passionate hunter, pursuing the bears, lions and boars found in Macedonia's forests – a traditional royal pastime. What could not be known in advance, and could hardly be taught, was the knack of leadership, vital in the informal but absolute monarchy of Macedonia.

THE DEFEAT OF THE MAEDI

While Philip was away campaigning in Thrace and then engaged in the long, ultimately fruitless sieges of Perinthus and Byzantium in 340BC, Alexander was left as regent. This reveals Philip's confidence in a son still only aged 16, although his experienced general Antipater was on hand to give advice if needed. Alexander's military skill was tested almost at once, for an invasion by a Thracian people called the Maedi (who may have heard of the king's absence) threatened Macedonia's eastern borders. Gathering the reserves, Alexander marched forth and defeated the Maedi, pursuing them back into Thrace. To commemorate his victory, he founded a city he called Alexandropolis, the first city of many to bear his name.

BATTLE OF CHAERONEA

What Philip, who had founded only two cities himself, thought of this is not recorded, but he was clearly impressed enough by his son's military skill to give Alexander command of the cavalry on the left wing of the Macedonian army at the Battle of Chaeronea in 338BC. This was a battle mostly fought between, and decided by, hoplites. Alexander's well-timed charge cut off the amateur Athenian infantry from their Theban allies. He then turned on the more experienced Thebans, keeping them surrounded until the Macedonian infantry caught up with and destroyed them. (Greek cavalry was generally ineffectual against well-trained hoplite infantry.) Alexander had shown that he could lead horsemen in a dashing charge *and* control them.

Shortly afterwards Philip appointed Alexander to lead the guard of honour that ceremoniously returned the ashes of Athens' dead soldiers to the city – something essential to Greek burial rites. As a special guest, Alexander was shown around Greece's greatest city. He reputedly turned down the offer of a young boy as company for his bed, again showing his dislike of prostitution. What he thought of Athens itself, which even Plato, who had very mixed feelings about his native city, had called "the city hall of Greek wisdom", is unknown.

QUARRELS AND EXILE

This harmony between father and son did not last. Back in Macedonia, Philip married for the seventh time, his bride

this time being the 17-year-old Eurydice, great niece of Attalus, one of his leading marshals. Unlike many of Philip's politically motivated earlier marriages, this time he was in love. Worryingly for Alexander, Eurydice's children would be full Macedonians, not half-Epirote like himself. One drunken night Attalus invited the company to pray for "a true Macedonian heir". Alexander, enraged and flushed with drink, caused a row. His father, also drunk, staggered up drawing his sword but stumbled and fell. "Here is the man who would cross to Asia but falls between the couches!" jeered Alexander. Taking his mother and close companions, he went into exile in Epirus.

Olympias remained in exile until Philip's death. But Philip still needed an adult heir, while Alexander soon grew bored in provincial Epirus and wanted to return home. Accordingly, within months things were patched up between father and son, the reconciliation helped by Eurydice's first child being a girl. Alexander remained nervous about his position, however, as was demonstrated by the Carian marriage fiasco.

Above: In this excellent copy of a bust by Lysippus, one of the age's finest sculptors, the visionary dynamism and ruthlessness of the young conqueror are apparent.

THE CARIAN MARRIAGE FIASCO

Arrhidaeus was Philip's half-witted son by a dancing-girl. Such a minor royal was good enough to offer as a husband for the daughter of the Carian satrap, who wanted to ally himself with Philip, thus usefully extending Philip's influence into Asia. However, Alexander, hearing of this, secretly proposed himself as a husband instead, fearing that Philip was preparing to give his kingdom to Arrhidaeus. The delighted Carians accepted the prospect of the much more impressive Alexander until Philip vetoed the plan, exiling many of Alexander's friends who had convinced him to take this action. Taking fright, the Carians then sought a match with a Persian satrap, so wrecking Philip's carefully laid plans.

THE DEATH OF PHILIP

In 336BC Eurydice gave birth to a boy, a rival to Alexander. That same summer Philip announced the marriage of Cleopatra, his daughter by Olympias, to Alexander of Epirus, her uncle. This marriage meant that Philip no longer needed a marriage tie with Olympias, whom he promptly divorced. Alexander again felt insecure, especially as he would be left behind as regent when Philip invaded Asia. But he accompanied his father that fateful morning in August 336BC into the theatre at Aegae to watch the procession of the Olympian gods. Within minutes Philip was dead, assassinated for unknown reasons by Pausanias, a bodyguard. Alexander was the obvious heir. But his succession was by no means automatic.

SECURING THE THRONE AND GREECE 336–335 BC

Above: The wealth of Macedonia is revealed by this gold-decorated breastplate found in the royal tombs at Vergina (ancient Aegae), dating from Philip II's reign.

Below: The fine Ionic columns of the royal palace at Pella, the capital where Alexander spent his last winter in Macedonia in 335–334 BC.

Although he was the obvious heir, Alexander's succession was not assured. His cousin Amyntas, shouldered aside 20 years before, had a claim to the throne, as had Eurydice's infant son. But Alexander was known to the army and nobility. When Alexander of Lyncestis stepped forward to hail Alexander as king, things moved his way. The assassin Pausanias, caught as he fled to a waiting horse, was speedily executed. So too were Amyntas, Eurydice's son and two Lyncestid brothers whose loyalty was suspect. Such precautionary ferocity became a hallmark of his reign. Alexander announced a timely tax cut and organized funeral games for his father. Philip was buried in royal splendour in tombs that have only recently been discovered.

At first Alexander could count on the firm support of only one of Philip's three marshals, Antipater. Of the two others, he had Attalus, his enemy, who was commanding the advance guard in Asia, quietly murdered. This was done with the consent of Parmenion, the last of the three. (Parmenion's sons were serving with Alexander, making them useful hostages.) With the throne secure, he led the army between the two halves of a dissected dog – an old Macedonian rite – and then turned south in October.

Greece was in ferment. News of Philip's murder had raised anti-Macedonians' hopes everywhere, and Alexander had to quash them quickly. As Thessaly refused to let him pass through the Vale of Tempe, he cut steps in the side of Mt Ossa to bypass it, being duly elected leader by the astonished Thessalians, henceforth faithful allies. Bursting into Greece at the head of his army, he deflated opposition, being elected head of the League of Corinth in succession to Philip. Then he turned north. Before he left for Asia, there were Balkan tribes to be pacified.

THE BALKANS – AND THEBES

His first target in 335 BC was the Triballians, a Thracian people who had ambushed Philip three years before. Finding the crucial Shipka Pass defended by Triballians holding carts poised to roll down on his army, he ordered his men to lie flat on the ground with their shields over them. The carts rumbled past harmlessly above and Alexander resumed the attack, using slingers and archers to lure the Triballians into the open, where his infantry crushed them. The Triballians then retreated to the River Danube's far banks. Alexander lacked ships to ferry his whole army across, so the Macedonians filled their leather tents with straw and crossed the river on these impromptu rafts, protected by catapult fire. Forming up on the other side, they routed the amazed Triballians, some of whom joined this increasingly polyglot army. Alexander was the first Greek commander to cross the Danube.

Alexander next moved against the Illyrians on the north-west frontier. Getting trapped in a narrow wooded valley, he formed a phalanx 120 deep. With its massed sarissas making a terrible swishing sound and its shields clashing, he routed the Illyrians by fear rather than arms. A later night attack had completed their defeat when news from the south required his rapid return: Thebes had revolted on

DIOGENES AND ALEXANDER
Diogenes of Sinope (404–325BC) was a most original philosopher. Despising worldly goods, he slept in a tub and performed all bodily functions in public. He believed that only one thing mattered: distinguishing between virtue and vice. His scorn for convention won him the nickname *cynos* (dog), and his followers were known as Cynics. Reputedly, when visiting Corinth in 336BC, he met Alexander. Was there, the king asked, anything he could do for him? Yes, said Diogenes, get out of my sunlight. Impressed, Alexander said that if he had not been Alexander, he would have chosen to be Diogenes. Certainly both men pursued their aims with single-minded extremism.

Below: At Corinth, busy organizing the Panhellenic League against Persia, Alexander encountered the ascetic Cynic philosopher Diogenes living in a tub.

rumours that Alexander was dead, killing some Macedonian officers and restoring its democracy.

In two weeks Alexander marched his army 800km/500 miles south – an unbelievably fast pace. The Thebans at first could not believe it, but when they did, they were defiant,. However, no help came from any other Greeks. In the resulting battle outside the city the Macedonians were hard-pressed at first, but the Thebans left a side gate open behind them. The Macedonians pushed through it and Thebes fell to them. All its 35,000 inhabitants were killed or enslaved and all its buildings, except the temples and the house of Pindar, its famous poet, destroyed. One of Greece's most ancient cities was no more.

After this act of calculated terror, which the League of Corinth rubber-stamped, Alexander had no further problems with the Greeks. He demanded but did not get Demosthenes from Athens, instead taking 20 Athenian triremes as hostages. Then he returned home to prepare for invasion by a winter of feasting and planning.

Above: A romantic depiction of Alexander's triumphs by the 19th-century artist Gustave Moreau. Alexander's lightning conquests soon passed into legend.

AIMS AND STRENGTHS
334BC

Above: This elaborate krater *(drinking vessel) of gilded bronze from Macedonia illustrates the kingdom's recently acquired wealth.*

Below: Alexander, here shown on the Sidon Sarcophagus *carved soon after his death, always led his armies from the front in battle.*

Alexander was not the first Greek ruler to conceive of attacking the Persian Empire. Jason of Pherae and Philip, his father, had both had invasion plans, aborted only by their murders, and the idea had been suggested by Isocrates among others for decades. The 'March of the 10,000' – the Greek mercenaries who had penetrated the Persian Empire and returned almost unharmed in 401BC – appeared to show up the vulnerability of Persia. Persia had regularly hired Greek hoplites ever since, who continued to dominate warfare around the Mediterranean and in Egypt. But the unsuccessful campaigns of the Spartan king Agesilaus in Asia Minor in the 390s BC indicated that conquering Asia needed more than just a decent general and hoplites. (Problems back in Greece had called Agesilaus home anyway.) If Persia lacked heavy infantry to match Greek hoplites, it had fine cavalry in abundance.

AN UNKNOWN EMPIRE

Few Greeks had any idea of what an eastern campaign might entail. While some had visited Susa, the administrative capital (in south-western Iran) as envoys, mercenaries, captives or craftsmen, none realized the empire's true immensity. Even Aristotle, who probably knew more geography than any other Greek, vastly underestimated the distance between the Aegean and Susa. And the Iranian heartland of the empire stretched east of Susa. To traverse the broad plateaux and mountain ranges of Asia and so conquer Persia, cavalry was needed in force, backed by an army that was professional in every department.

STRONG ARMY, WEAK NAVY

Alexander had such an army, thanks to Philip, for the first time in Greek history, based on the infantry grouped into massive phalanxes that were invincible in the right conditions. He also had the commando-style Shield Bearers, siege engines and catapults, Cretan archers and Thracian and Illyrian irregulars as slingers and javelin-throwers. Above all he had excellent cavalry, including some Thessalians, who had taught the Macedonians their highly effective wedge-attack formations.

In 334BC, after Alexander had crossed into Asia, he fielded about 43,000 infantry and 6,000 cavalry – by Greek standards a huge army, though modest by Persian. Alexander left Antipater in Macedonia with another force of 12,000 infantry and 1,500 cavalry, plus garrison troops across Greece and the Macedonian Empire. The gold and silver from Mt Pangaeus, coupled with the lands newly conquered by Philip and worked by slave labour, helped to pay for all this. Even so, he started his campaign in May 334BC 600 talents in debt.

The one major Macedonian weakness was its lack of a decent navy: it had only 160 triremes, including its unwilling allies. Athens had 400 triremes, although it lacked the needed sailors. This was the biggest Greek fleet, but Athens was ambivalently neutral. The 20 Athenian ships Alexander took acted chiefly as hostages in the fleet, most of which he dismissed anyway in 334BC.

Ultimately, Alexander's greatest asset was his own genius and luck, in which he believed from the start and which his men soon came to accept. Good generals and the best army in the world were his tangible strengths.

AN EVOLVING PLAN

What exact aim Alexander had in mind when he began his attack in spring 334BC remains debatable. The historian William Tarn wrote: "The primary reason Alexander invaded Persia was that he never thought

of *not* doing so. It was his inheritance."
Alexander's declared purpose in 334BC
was to exact revenge on Persia for its
invasion of 480–479BC. Most Greeks,
however, did not see this as his real reason.
Probably, like some of his officers, they
expected Alexander simply to conquer
Asia Minor, raid the Persian heartland
and return with loot. Rivalry with his
dead father – a semi-conscious desire to
conquer more rapidly and completely than
Philip had – may have spurred Alexander
on at first, but his *pothos* (longing) and an
increasingly imperial vision led him ever
further east.

ALEXANDER THE ASIAN EMPEROR

On landing in Asia, Alexander threw
a spear on to the shore, symbolically
claiming the empire by right of conquest.
He then appointed a Macedonian as
satrap of coastal Phrygia, the first province
conquered, seeming to continue the Persian
imperial system. Soon after, however, he
posed as liberator of the Greek cities in
Asia Minor, and later sent back to Athens
from Susa the statues of Harmodius and
Aristogeiton, the Athenian tyrannicides,
carried off in 480BC. But he began
reappointing Persians as satraps to rule
their provinces after Gaugamela in
331BC, his greatest victory. By then he was
seeing himself as heir to the
Achaemenids, the rulers of Asia. As such,
he had to impress his Asian subjects,

Above: Alexander at the charge. He loved warfare more than anything else, having a truly Homeric delight in battle.

and he began wearing elements of
Persian royal dress and adopting Persian
court customs such as *proskynesis*,
bowing to the throne. Such innovations
proved very unpopular with his
Macedonians. Alexander, who had started
the war as a Greek avenger, ended it as a
Greek-speaking Asian emperor.

Left: The phalanx remained a vital part of Alexander's army, although in battle he usually relied on cavalry to deliver the knockout blow.

PERSIA: AN EMPIRE IN DECLINE? 404–336BC

The Achaemenid Empire created by Cyrus the Great and Darius I (556–486BC) was the greatest power on Earth, ruling all lands between the Indus and Macedonia. The Greeks in the Persian Wars (490–478BC) had managed to defeat Persia only by an unusual display of unity. It then took the fleet of Athens and her allies in the Delian Confederacy years of hard fighting to clear the Aegean islands and coasts of Persian bases. When Athens tried to interfere in Cyprus and Egypt, she was crushingly defeated.

The Peace of Callias of 449BC had definitively confirmed that the Aegean islands and cities would be Athenian, while the rest of Asia, including half-Greek Cyprus, would be Persian, as would Egypt, the second richest satrapy in the empire. Athens in truth had stripped Persia of only a few coastal cities.

> ### TREACHERY AT COURT
> Persian power depended finally on the Great King, who in turn depended on his courtiers. Artaxerxes III had made Bagoas, a eunuch, his Grand Vizier (first minister) – eunuchs were often employed at court because they were thought to present no threat. Bagoas had ideas of his own, however, and in 338BC he poisoned his royal master, as he did the next king. Bagoas then chose Darius Codomanus, a nobleman with only a distant claim to the throne, as the next ruler. In 336BC he became king as Darius III, the last Achaemenid. Darius promptly had the treacherous eunuch killed; but he was to prove no match for Alexander, who became king that same year.

EGYPTIAN INDEPENDENCE

Egypt, however, proudly conscious of its ancient civilization, was never happy under Persian rule. Its *fellahin* (peasants) were swayed by its powerful priests, who were angered by obvious Persian contempt for their religion. As a result, Egypt revolted frequently. It rebelled three times in the 5th century BC and after 405BC was independent for 60 years, relying on Greek hoplites to repel the Persians. These included King Agesilaus of Sparta in his cash-strapped old age.

Egyptian independence was a humiliation as well as a financial loss for the Great King, but not a serious threat to the Persian Empire in the way that the revolt of Prince Cyrus in 401BC was. Jealous of his older brother Artaxerxes, who had just succeeded to the throne, Cyrus had had unusually wide powers in Asia Minor. He used them to recruit a rebel army, whose core consisted of 'The 10,000' Greek hoplites, and 'marched

Below: The Apadana Staircase at Persepolis, built under Darius I (521–486BC), showing the 10,000 Immortals, the elite royal Foot Guards so-called because when one died, he was immediately replaced.

upcountry' (as recorded in soldier-turned-historian Xenophon's work *Anabasis*). Persian imperial forces did not try to check his passage until he reached Cunaxa, just north of Babylon. The rebels won the ensuing battle, thanks mainly to the Greeks. But Cyrus, who had personally tried to kill his detested brother, was killed. The subsequent return home of the Greeks under Xenophon's command made a colourful tale, and it taught the Persians the need to hire Greek hoplites. This was easy for the wealthy empire. The real problem was the satraps.

THE REVOLT OF THE SATRAPS

The Persian system of government gave satraps remarkably wide powers, both financial and military, over their often large provinces. The size and diversity of the Persian Empire and the slowness of communications perhaps made such devolution inevitable, and the 'King's Ears', as the royal agents were known, acted as a check. But in the distant reaches of the empire (western Asia Minor was a full three months' march from Susa even on the Royal Road) satraps tended to establish hereditary dynasties. These semi-ducal rulers developed local ties, ambitions and rivalries that could undermine loyalty to the crown in distant Susa.

In the 360s BC many satrapies in western Asia rose in what has been called the 'Revolt of the Satraps'. Even Cappadocia in the Anatolian interior rebelled, as did Cyprus (again) and Sidon in Phoenicia. In Caria the dynast Mausolus began to extend his power, while Egypt remained independent. Since coins, essential to pay mercenaries, were minted only in western satrapies, this loss threatened the Persians' recruitment of essential Greek mercenaries and of its fleet, mostly supplied by Phoenicia, Cyprus and Caria. The whole empire west of the Euphrates appeared lost.

In 358BC Artaxerxes II, an incompetent drunk, was succeeded by Artaxerxes III Ochus, a far better ruler. Like Philip II,

Above: Two of the 10,000 Immortals, Persian noblemen who formed the Foot Guards. They were, however, the only heavy infantry the Great King had at his disposal.

Below: A gold winged-lion rhyton (drinking vessel) of the 6th century BC, emblematic of the splendour and wealth of the Persian empire.

his contemporary, Artaxerxes played off his enemies against each other, while mustering immense forces from the Persian heartlands. With them he crushed Artabazus, satrap of coastal Phrygia (north-western Asia Minor) and began regaining the whole peninsula, helped by the death of Mausolus in 353BC. In 344BC Persia recaptured Sidon after a long siege and went on to regain Egypt, although brutal reprisals there made its rule hated. By 340BC Persian power in the west had been fully restored, it seemed, and Artaxerxes could help the cities of Perinthus and Byzantium when Philip besieged them.

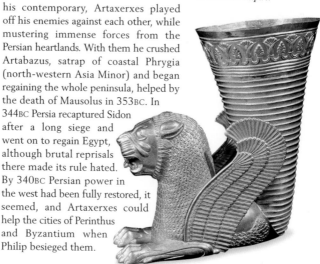

Above: By the 330s BC, the Persian empire had amassed 230,000 talents in its royal treasuries at Susa and Persepolis. Only a tiny fraction of the gold mountain was made into fine gold rhytons such as this.

PERSIA: STRENGTHS AND STRATEGY 335–333BC

The Greeks in the 4th century BC generally underestimated Persian power, their views shaped not just by the March of 'The 10,000' but by broader Greek prejudices about 'barbarians' as inherently inferior beings. But Persia remained the superpower of its age, though perhaps one with clay feet. From only a day's march inland (*c.*48km/30 miles) from the Aegean coast eastward, the Great King's power remained substantially intact. Along the Royal Road that ran nearly 2,400km/1,500 miles from Sardis to Susa

messengers still galloped, bearing satraps' reports to the empire's capitals and returning with royal edicts. Babylonia, the empire's richest province and home to the earliest civilization, lay sheltered in its arc, supplying the food and other raw materials vital to the empire. The Phoenician cities, which provided professional fleets of 300 or more galleys, likewise remained under Persian suzerainty. Egypt had recently been regained and Caria and Cyprus were once more under control. None of these cities or peoples was pro-Persian but, with the exception of Egypt, none was strongly anti-Persian either. Imperial rule was usually sufficiently flexible and tolerant not to alienate its subjects.

MILITARY STRENGTHS ...

But the core of the empire remained the Iranian peoples: the Medes and the Persians, devoted to the throne and the empire, if not always to the king himself. They were united also by their common Zoroastrian religion. The Great King was not regarded as a god by the quasi-monotheistic Persians, but his role and power were seen as divinely sanctioned, under the special protection of Ahura Mazda, the Wise Lord.

Persian boys were traditionally taught to ride, shoot straight and never tell a lie. The result was very capable, tough horsemen and excellent archers. Persian archers' composite bow could fire arrows 183 metres/200 yards, and the home province of Persis (Fars) alone potentially provided 30,000 archers. On the lush pastures of Media around Ecbatana 200,000 heavy Nisaean horses grazed,

Left: A Lydian leading horses, from a relief in Darius I's palace in Persepolis. The peoples of all western Asia contributed to Persia's massive military strength.

Above: Persian power finally depended on the Great King and the last Achaemenid ruler. Darius III, pictured in his chariot, proved to be no general or even warrior when he faced Alexander.

ready to supply mounts for the 120,00 or so cavalry that the Great King could almost immediately call upon.

... AND WEAKNESSES
Only in infantry were the Persians at a disadvantage. They had 'The 10,000' foot guards, called 'Immortals' because (reputedly) the moment one died he was replaced by another. But for their other heavy infantry they had long turned to Greece. There were said, with only small exaggeration, to be 50,000 Greek mercenaries fighting on the Persian side in the two main battles, more than all the troops in Alexander's army. They proved generally loyal to their paymasters.

DISTANT THREATS
East of Media, across the high plateaux of eastern Iran and Central Asia, ran the Khorasan Highway, not a paved military road but a time-honoured route for merchants as well as armies, stretching to Bactria and Sogdiana (today Uzbekistan) in Central Asia. North of these satrapies lay arid empty steppes from which savage nomads could suddenly emerge.

These had long posed a far greater threat to the Persian heartland than Greek sailors scudding around the Aegean like pirates.

NO FIXED STRATEGY
Gold and silver tribute, from Egypt to Sogdiana, had flowed for two centuries into the royal treasuries at Susa and Persepolis, the grand ceremonial centre, creating a gigantic reserve of 230,000 talents – riches beyond the dreams of any Greek power. But all still depended vitally on the king. Darius III, although he had killed a man in single combat and was imposingly handsome, proved neither a good strategist nor a competent field commander. Twice at vital moments in battle he was to panic and flee, giving Alexander victory. Such physical cowardice or loss of nerve would have mattered less if he had remained behind the front. But Persian kings were generally expected to lead their armies

Faced with an aggressive invader, Persia could have tried to stop Alexander's army from crossing the Hellespont in 334BC, but the inferior Macedonian fleet was unopposed. They were then faced with a choice: confront Alexander head on in battle or wear him out by a scorched-earth policy, retreating east into Asia while trying to raise revolts at his rear to cut him off. Greece was full of men unhappy with Macedonian hegemony, and Persia had the money to finance revolts. This was the strategy advocated by Memnon, the mercenary from Rhodes who had risen high in Persian service, marrying a Persian wife and being granted estates in Asia Minor. His advice was at first ignored, leading to defeat at Granicus in 334BC, and then followed only half-heartedly by local satraps reluctant to devastate their provinces to deny the Macedonians food. The long defence of Halicarnassus and successful counter-attacks in the eastern Aegean were part of Memnon's policy. But Memnon died in June 333BC, and his death led to a complete change in Persian strategy that soon proved disastrous.

Above: The Cyrus Cylinder, possibly from the reign of Persia's first monarch, was found at Babylon. It proclaims Persian ideals at their highest: "I will respect the traditions, customs and religions of the nations of my empire and never let my governors and subordinates look down on or insult them as long as I shall live." Such tolerance underlay Persian imperial success.

Below: The Palace of 100 Columns, one of the palaces in Persepolis in which court conspiracies arose to hamper Persian efforts to resist the Macedonian invasion.

CROSSING TO ASIA
334BC

Above: The ruins of Troy, which Alexander visited in 334BC and refounded as Alexandria-Troas. The city thrived for centuries afterward as a polis. It was also an early tourist site.

Early in May 334BC Alexander said goodbye to his mother, who reputedly told him the 'secret' of his birth. They never met again. Then he turned his back on his homeland and marched his army through Thrace to the Hellespont. There the remnants of Parmenion's advance force were waiting – they had been driven out of Asia – and the 160 ships mostly supplied by reluctant allies.

The Straits, only 4.5km/3 miles wide, had nasty currents, but the Macedonians were more worried about the threat of a Persian fleet, superior in size and skill. None appeared, however, either because a short-lived revolt in Egypt two years before still required its

presence or, more probably, due to general indecisiveness and lack of preparation on the Persian side.

SACRIFICE AND LIBATIONS

Taking the helm of the royal trireme himself, Alexander led 60 ships across the Straits, the remainder taking a different route with Parmenion. Halfway across, he sacrificed a bull to Poseidon the sea god and poured out libations to the Nereids, sea nymphs. Alexander was always meticulous about observing such rites. He then changed into full armour. As the galley grounded on the Asian shore, he hurled his spear into Persian soil, symbolically claiming it as his, and leapt ashore, the first of the Macedonians. The landing, like the crossing, went unopposed, indeed probably unremarked, by the Persians, who were slowly assembling an army inland at Dascylium.

THE TOMB OF ACHILLES

The landscape around the Macedonian army was redolent with legend and myths. It was here, according to Homer, that the Achaeans had landed almost 1,000 years before to start their ten-year siege of Troy to win back Helen, the abducted queen of Sparta. Alexander felt he was literally treading in the steps of his hero Achilles. Now was the time and place to honour him

The splendid Troy of the 'topless towers' had long decayed to a mere village when Alexander approached it. His helmsman Menoitus crowned him with a golden laurel as he entered. Then, stripping

Left: Alexander shown between Hercules (on the right), a semi-divine hero with whom he was increasingly to identify, and Poseidon, the god of the sea, whom he was always careful to propitiate with due sacrifice.

THE PROBLEM OF SOURCES

Alexander used to lament that there was no Homer then living to immortalize him like Achilles in *The Iliad*. But he took with him an official historian: Callisthenes, a relative of Aristotle. Callisthenes boasted that he would make Alexander immortal, and at first depicted him sycophantically. But Callisthenes was executed in 327BC for conspiring against the king and his history has not survived. Nor has that of three other eye-witnesses: Ptolemy, Nearchus and Onesicritus.

Ptolemy, a boyhood friend of Alexander, became one of his generals and later founded the Ptolemaic kingdom of Egypt. He wrote knowledgeably but portrayed himself favourably while depicting rivals such as Perdiccas negatively. Nearchus, another boyhood friend, who commanded a fleet, lost all influence after Alexander's death. He wrote mostly on India and his voyages. Onesicritus was a philosopher who rather magnificently

tried to portray Alexander as a philosopher in arms. This required radical factual distortion. All three men's histories are lost. So too is that of Aristobulus, another eye-witness. An architect to Alexander, he compiled his history only when he was in his eighties.

Many later historians wrote about Alexander, one of the best being Quintus Curtius Rufus, a Roman of the 1st century AD. Plutarch and Arrian both wrote in the 2nd century AD under the Romans, and their biographies survive. Plutarch coupled Alexander with Julius Caesar in his *Parallel Lives*, which slanted his whole account. Arrian, who had been both a consul in Rome and a general, based his often excellent history, the best ancient account available, on Ptolemy and Nearchus. He presented a generally favourable yet not rose-tinted view of Alexander, but he was writing more than 400 years later.

Above: A coin of 323BC showing the goddess Athena from Sicyon, a Greek city in the League of Corinth, the last year of Alexander's reign.

Below: Achilles bandaging a wounded Patroclus, a scene inspired by (but not actually in) The Iliad. Alexander saw himself as a reincarnation of Achilles, the supreme hero, casting Hephaistion as a second Patroclus.

naked, he raced with his companions to the tomb of Achilles, placing a garland on it. Hephaistion ran similarly to the tomb of Patroclus. This was a very public declaration of their relationship.

At the altar of Zeus, Alexander prayed to Priam, legendary king of Troy, not to be angry with him as a descendant of Achilles, the Greek who had slain his son. Then he sacrificed at the temple of Athena, dedicating his suit of armour to the goddess. In return, he took from the temple a shield and weapons reputedly dating from the Trojan War. This set would accompany him across Asia as far as India. (Alexander, who always slept with a copy of *The Iliad* under his pillow, would face far greater challenges than his hero Achilles, however.) He granted Troy a new democratic constitution, renaming it Alexandria-Troas, under which name it flourished in subsequent centuries. Alexander then turned inland to meet and fight for the first time Persian forces.

CHAPTER IX

THE GREAT VICTORIES

334–330BC

Alexander first faced the Persian army at the Granicus in May 334BC as an unknown young general confronting a mighty empire. Three and a half years later, after he had routed the grand Persian army on open plains in the empire's heart, he was being hailed as the new lord of Asia. Alexander had won three of the most important battles in history, two of them against far larger armies. In between he had captured the island city of Tyre, long thought invincible, after one of the hardest sieges ever undertaken. All these events show his strategic vision and tactical genius. Many Persian satraps and generals now began going over to his side, accepting the new reality of power, just as he began accepting Persian noblemen as administrators of his new-gained empire.

In between these battles came one of the most mysterious episodes in the life of any world conqueror: Alexander's pilgrimage to the shrine of the Egyptian god Ammon deep in the Libyan desert. What he learned there, in the sanctuary of the deity whom the Greeks identified with Zeus, remains unknown, but it seems to have spurred him to yet further efforts. In Egypt he also founded the city of Alexandria at the mouth of the Nile, an action that in itself would have made his name immortal. If he was indeed the son of a god, as he now began proclaiming on his coins and in his speeches, then literally nothing was impossible for him.

Left: The Battle of Gaugamela, Alexander's crowning victory, depicted by the Renaissance artist Albrecht Altdorfer.

VICTORY AT GRANICUS
334 BC

Above: Alexander, filled with battle lust, leading his cavalry at Granicus, a sculpture attributed to Lysippus.

Below: The Persians had taken up a defensive position above the steep slopes of the river Granicus, for some reason placing their own cavalry in front of their Greek mercenary infantry. Alexander led his right wing further out before crossing the river to attack the Persian cavalry's flank, leaving his infantry to wade across the river downstream.

The Persians had failed to prevent the Macedonian army from crossing into Asia, probably because their fleet sent to repress an Egyptian rising a year earlier had not yet returned. However, they knew of the long-planned invasion, and the slowness of their reactions came from divisions in the regional high command.

MILITARY DIVISIONS

The generals in charge of the Persian army included Memnon, a Greek general from Rhodes, and Arsites, satrap of coastal Phrygia. While Memnon was no casual *condottiere* (leader of mercenaries) – he had been 15 years in Persian service, married a Persian wife and driven the Macedonians out of Asia the year before – he was no Persian aristocrat either, unlike the other generals. Many Persians had owned large estates in the area for generations. Perhaps for this reason his advice that they should retreat, laying waste the land and luring Alexander deep into Asia Minor while threatening his communications, was rejected by the other generals. Besides, Alexander, despite recent victories in the Balkans and at

Thebes, was still little known as a commander. There was no reason as yet to think him invincible.

PREPARING FOR ATTACK

So, gathering their forces, the Persian commanders decided to confront the invaders. Their troops were mostly local levies, although they included heavy armoured cavalry from Cappadocia in central Anatolia, making some 15,000 horsemen in all, plus c.20,000 Greek infantry. The Persians, who were not crack troops, were for once outnumbered by the Macedonians, whose forces totalled c.50,000. The Persians therefore needed a good position to offer a fight. They found one on the River Granicus, a small but swift river with steep banks.

Alexander's army encountered the Persians one May afternoon, unusually late in the day to start a battle. Parmenion, Philip's old general, reputedly advised waiting until dawn to attack, but Alexander replied that he would be ashamed if, after crossing the Hellespont, he let a mere stream delay him. He decided to launch a sudden attack before the Persians were fully prepared. (Or so wrote Arrian, our most reliable source.) Whatever the timing, Parmenion commanded the left wing while Alexander took the right, leading the Companion cavalry, his best troops.

ALEXANDER'S TACTIC

Plunging into the Granicus with his squadrons further upstream than expected, Alexander led his troops across obliquely, forcing the Persians to make a rapid adjustment. In Plutarch's words, Alexander "advanced through a hail of missiles towards a steep, well-defended bank, fighting the current that swept his men off their feet. His leadership seemed rash but he persisted... and reached the

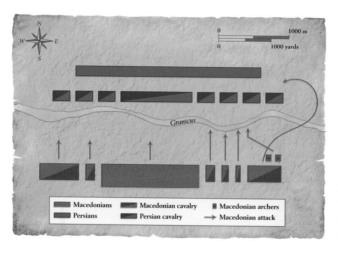

Granicus

Macedonians	Macedonian cavalry	Macedonian archers
Persians	Persian cavalry	→ Macedonian attack

Left: Alexander's conquests took him from central Greece right across Asia to northern India, regions earlier known to Greeks only through legends and hearsay. As he marched east, he founded numerous cities to safeguard his conquests. Many have since prospered.

wet, muddy opposite bank, where he was forced to fight at once, man to man, before his supporting troops could get into formation... The Persians charged with a roar... closing in on Alexander whose shield and white-plumed helmet they recognized... the Persian generals Rhoseaces and Spithridates attacked him together." Alexander, almost killed when Spithridates split his helmet with an axe, was saved only by Cleitus 'the Black', who speared the Persian. On such timely intervention hung the whole fate of Asia.

The Macedonian cavalry, their long cornel-wood spears outreaching their opponents' lances, soon worsted the Persian cavalry. Seeing their generals killed, they turned and fled, leaving c.1,000 dead. The Greek mercenaries, who had been kept uselessly in the rear, now tried to make a stand. But, outnumbered and surrounded, they soon surrendered, although they managed to wound Alexander's horse.

AFTER THE BATTLE

"[Given by] Alexander, son of Philip, and the Greeks except for the Spartans, [taken] from the barbarians who live in Asia." With these words Alexander dedicated 300 suits of Persian armour taken from the defeated Persians to the goddess Athena on the Athenian Acropolis – significantly, the same number as the 300 Spartans who had fallen gallantly fighting Persia at Thermopylae in 480BC. This was brilliant propaganda. It ignored the fact that Granicus was overwhelmingly a *Macedonian* victory, stressing the tiny part played by Greeks on Alexander's side. Equally brilliant was the emphasis on the Spartans, who alone among the Greeks were not enrolled as Panhellenic allies (however reluctant) in the League of Corinth. Less clever was Alexander's treatment of the captured Greek mercenaries. He treated them all as traitors to the Panhellenic cause, killing many and sending 2,000 back to labour as slaves in Macedonia. This helped Macedonia's economy but, when other Greek mercenaries heard of it, they naturally chose to fight on rather than surrender.

Alexander visited the wounded Macedonians, recognizing many by name and praising their deeds. For the 25 Companions killed fighting, he decreed a hero's reward: Lysippus, the court sculptor, made statues of each and their families were exempted from taxation.

Below: Alexander crossing the Granicus as seen by the 17th-century artist Charles Lebrun. He was nearly killed in this, his first battle against Persia.

LIBERATING IONIA
334–333BC

Above: Miletus, one of the most defensible and important Ionian cities, was surrendered to Alexander by its garrison after only a short fight.

Below: Sardis, Persia's regional capital, was handed over to Alexander by its Persian governor without a blow but with its treasury. This combination earned the adaptable Persian a post on Alexander's staff.

After Granicus, Alexander forbade his men to plunder and marched upcountry to Sardis, the Lydian capital. The Persian commander surrendered, handing over its treasure and gaining a place on the Macedonian staff. Alexander promised to restore Lydia's old customs but made a brother of Parmenion its governor. His real concern was with the coastal Greek cities, whose liberation was among his avowed objectives.

THE RETURN OF DEMOCRACY
The cities of Ionia, some of the proudest in the Greek world, had been under Persian rule directly or indirectly since the King's Peace of 386BC. Persia had normally favoured oligarchies, finding them easier to deal with than democracies, but the result was growing political tensions between rich and poor inside these cities. This discontent erupted on the news of Alexander's victory. At Ephesus, one of the largest cities, a pro-Persian junta was expelled. Alexander restored the exiled democrats, who began taking bloody revenge until he forbade it. Other cities now welcomed him, as he "broke up oligarchies everywhere, men being given their own laws and exempted from the tribute they had paid the barbarians [Persians]". Instead Alexander, with forceful tact, asked for *syntaxeis* (contributions) to his war chest.

While Alexander favoured democracy in Ionia for essentially pragmatic reasons, elsewhere preferring other forms of government, his actions marked a true liberation, long remembered with gratitude by the cities concerned. Fifty years later, a decree from the little city of Priene, rebuilt on his orders, proclaimed: "There is no greater blessing for Greeks than freedom." Whether Greek cities on the Asian mainland were incorporated into the League of Corinth remains debatable. The non-Hellenic countryside around certainly remained unfree, with Macedonia simply replacing Persia as its feudal overlord.

SURRENDER AT MILETUS
At Miletus, strongly defended on its headland, the garrison resisted, encouraged by the large Persian fleet now nearby. Refusing to fight at sea, Alexander moved rapidly to the assault, battering his way into the city with his siege engines. The garrison, who had swum out to a tiny island, happily accepted Alexander's offer of clemency, 300 enlisting in his army.

Alexander then unexpectedly disbanded his fleet, saying he would conquer the sea by land, in other words capture the Persians' bases in Asia. In truth, he could not afford to pay 160 triremes' inactive crews of 32,000 men. He kept only 20 Athenian ships, whose crews served as hostages for their city.

SIEGE OF HALICARNASSUS

On the southern edge of Ionia lay Halicarnassus, a half-Greek, half-Carian city, its massive walls rising in a semicircle with a sea-girt citadel. Memnon, now commander of lower Asia and the whole fleet, was there with many Greek mercenaries. Alexander, marching toward it through the forests inland, was approached by Ada, widowed queen of Caria, into whose family he had tried to marry three years before. No longer a nervous adolescent but an assured king, he welcomed her surrender, reappointing her as queen with a Macedonian commander. He then became her adopted son, so winning over the Carians. (What Olympias back home thought of this is unrecorded.) But to take Halicarnassus required force.

After early skirmishing and an unsuccessful attempt to take a nearby port by surprise, the Macedonians filled in many of the city's ditches. They now turned their catapults against its walls, knocking them down in parts. But the garrison, sallying out at night, torched many of these wooden engines. Some Macedonian soldiers, getting drunk, then launched an impromptu attack on the city that ended disastrously. Memnon personally led the defenders out to repulse them. Another sortie three days later panicked the Macedonians until Alexander himself led a counter-charge, driving the defenders back. The city, shutting its gates prematurely, lost many troops and Memnon ordered a retreat to the castle. He soon sailed away, although the castle held out for a year. The two-month siege had been won more by force than great generalship.

CUTTING THE GORDIAN KNOT

It was now autumn, normally a time for rest and recuperation, but these were not concepts that Alexander recognized. Giving all recently married troops winter leave (a popular measure that also boosted the birth-rate), he entered Lycia and Pamphylia, whose steep coastlines were dotted with small Greek cities.

Capturing these in his role of Panhellenic liberator – Aspendos, one of the chief cities, betrayed him and was severely fined – he turned north. Uniting with the troops back from Macedonia, he entered central Anatolia.

At Gordium he saw the Gordian Knot in the old palace of golden King Midas. Whoever untied it, said the legend, would control Asia. After fiddling fruitlessly, Alexander drew his sword and cut through it, in a way fulfilling the prophecy. But as he marched east that summer of 333BC, he left Memnon with a large fleet still threatening his rear.

Above: The lion of Didyma, one of the many Ionian cities that flourished again after Alexander's conquest, which was for them a true liberation.

Below: The Temple of Athena Polias at Priene, an Ionian city rebuilt with Alexander's help to become almost the perfect polis. Alexander's restoration of Priene as a democracy was long remembered with gratitude.

AN UNEXPECTED BATTLE: ISSUS 333BC

Above: Darius III, the last Achaemenid king, in growing terror as he spots Alexander hurtling towards him.

Below: At Issus, Persian numerical superiority was annulled by the narrowness of the site. Alexander thinned his centre and led his cavalry on the right in an oblique attack that crumpled up the Persian centre where Darius was.

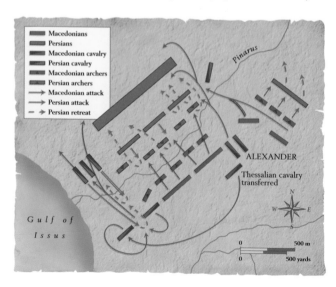

As Alexander approached the Cilician Gates, an easily defended pass through the Taurus Mountains, the Persians abandoned it. They had burnt their fields, either following Memnon's scorched-earth policy or just panicking, so the Macedonians entered Cilicia unopposed. There Alexander fell gravely ill after bathing in a river. Warned by letter that his Greek physician Philip was trying to poison him, Alexander showed Philip the letter, took his medicine – and recovered. But he had lost two months lying ill.

DARIUS'S NEW STRATEGY

The general situation, meanwhile, had changed completely. Memnon, the Persians' general, died in June 333BC on campaign in the Aegean. This bad news led Darius to rethink his strategy. Deciding to go to war in person, he began massing armies, moving to Babylon. Persia had abundant cavalry even without horsemen from its further satrapies, but lacked heavy infantry apart from the 10,000 Immortals and some youthful trainees. So Darius recalled the 15,000 Greek hoplites fighting under Memnon's successors. When Persian forces left Babylon in September, they totalled *c*.150,000, far more than the Macedonians. But most had little or no military experience.

By late September, Alexander had recovered. Unaware of recent events, he decided to continue capturing Persia's naval supply ports. Parmenion went ahead to seize the Syrian Gates, the pass through the Amanus mountains, while Alexander hunted and waited on events in the Aegean. Then came startling news: the main Persian army was camped beyond the Amanus range. Alexander raced east with his army.

Leaving the sick at Issus in the corner of the gulf, he continued south down the coast, hoping to catch the Persians in the rear. But Darius, growing anxious, decided to seek out Alexander. He moved north behind the Amanus while Alexander, unaware, marched south on the coast. When the Persians crossed the Amanus, they had cut Alexander off. The Persians mutilated the Macedonian invalids they found at Issus, although some escaped to warn Alexander. He seemed trapped with no escape route.

BATTLE BY THE SHORE

Alexander, swinging around, marched his weary men back through the night until the two armies faced each other between the sea and mountains. As usual, he commanded the Companion cavalry on the right, Parmenion taking the left. Darius sent light troops up into the mountains. Alexander countered by sending archers to drive them back. He then reinforced his left wing by the coast but thinned his centre. Darius was in the Persian centre with his Greek mercenaries. Between them lay the stream of the Pinarus, swollen by autumn floods. At noon on 1 November 333BC, Alexander gave the signal to attack.

The Macedonian cavalry surged forward, crossing the river. The infantry followed more slowly, raising their fearful war cry "ALALALAI!" The two armies met head on. Macedonian cavalry at once broke through the Persian line. Then Alexander wheeled his horsemen obliquely in toward the centre, rolling up the Persian riders on their flanks in a brilliant manoeuvre. He was heading for Darius, very visible in his chariot. Parmenion repulsed the Persian cavalry but in the centre Persia's Greek mercenaries threatened the exposed phalanx until Alexander's advance forced them to retreat. Darius, seeing Alexander cutting relentlessly toward him, turned his chariot and fled. Swapping his chariot for a horse, he abandoned even his royal cloak. Alexander pursued him until night fell, then turned back. Victory was his, won by audacious cavalry tactics.

AFTER THE BATTLE

The Persians had suffered heavily, although the traditionally cited figure of 110,000 dead is incredible. The Macedonians had 4,500 wounded and many hundreds dead. Hearing women crying nearby, Alexander discovered they were Darius' womenfolk, mourning a king they believed dead. He sent reassurances,

ordering that they should be treated as royalty. Next day at their meeting, the Persian queen mother did obeisance to the taller Hephaistion. Realizing her error, she was mortified until Alexander said: "You make no mistake, madame, he too is Alexander."

He also met Barsine again, whom he had known long ago in Pella. She now became his mistress and bore him a son, forming a useful link between east and west. He then visited the wounded Macedonians, congratulating each man he had seen in battle and arranging a magnificent funeral for the dead. On the battle site he founded a city: Alexandria, today Alexandretta.

Above: After the battle, Alexander went with Hephaistion to comfort Darius' women, mourning a king they assumed dead. The queen mother saluted Hephaistion as Alexander, a mistake Alexander courteously shrugged off. This is the Renaissance artist Veronese's grand depiction of the scene.

Below: The Battle of Issus was primarily a cavalry action, which is how Jan Brueghel painted it in this dramatic canvas of 1602.

THE SPOILS OF VICTORY

Alexander was astonished by the luxury of the Persian royal tents. Even on campaign, Darius travelled in style: "When he [Alexander] saw the gold bowls, pitchers and tubs, exquisitely worked and set in a chamber fragrant with incense and spices, when he entered a tent of remarkable size and height, set with sofas and tables for his dinner, he looked at his Companions and remarked: 'This, it seems, is what it is to be king.'"

THE SIEGE OF TYRE
332BC

Above: The siege of Tyre in 332BC, as imagined in a medieval miniature.

Below: A battle scene between Macedonians and Persians from the Sidon Sarcophagus. *Sidon, Tyre's neighbour and rival, supported Alexander.*

Dispatching Parmenion to Damascus to seize the Persian war chest of 2,600 talents there, Alexander turned south to the cities of Phoenicia. Along with Cyprus, Phoenicia supplied the Persians with their fleet, although it had little love for the empire. Sidon, where a revolt had been brutally suppressed 12 years before, welcomed Alexander, as did Byblos. Tyre, the most powerful Phoenician city, invited Alexander to sacrifice to Hercules, its patron god, in old Tyre on the mainland, but refused to let Macedonians – or Persians – into the island city. Alexander, who could not leave a great naval power neutral behind him (as he told his army) decided to capture it. This was easier proclaimed than done.

CONSTRUCTING A MOLE
Tyre, a walled island 4.8km/3 miles in circumference, was reputedly impregnable, having once withstood a siege by a Babylonian king for 13 years. It lay 800m/880 yards from the mainland in sea that was 180m/600ft deep. On the land side its thick walls rose to 45m/150ft and it had a powerful fleet. Alexander had no fleet at all and his torsion catapults had a maximum range of only 270m/300 yards. Yet in January 332BC he began to build a mole, or causeway, out of the ruins of old Tyre to let his catapults and siege towers reach the city. So started the seven-month siege, the greatest in antiquity.

At first all went well, but as the mole entered deeper waters, it came within range of Tyrian catapults, while triremes sallied from the city's twin harbours to rain arrows on the workers. Alexander ordered in siege towers as protection. In response, the Tyrians secretly built a vast fireship. When a favourable wind blew, they sailed this floating bomb across the waters. On impact, it was ignited, torching the mole's towers and catapults. Undaunted, Alexander ordered the mole rebuilt, only this time wider to take more

engines and towers. Then he went north to friendly Sidon, where he had some very good news.

The fleets of Sidon and neighbouring cities had returned, deserting the Persian side. With their 100 ships, plus 120 from Cyprus and 9 from Rhodes, Alexander now had supremacy at sea. Attempts to lure Tyre's fleet out failed, however, for the Tyrians blocked their harbours. Instead, the other Phoenicians built floating battering rams protected by roofs of fireproof hide. They rowed these around to attack Tyre's weaker seaward walls.

Meanwhile, Alexander's engineers rebuilt the mole wider and at an angle to the prevailing wind. On to it rolled the tallest siege towers yet seen: 20 storeys high with battering rams and catapults on their upper decks. Soon Tyre was besieged on all sides.

LONG RESISTANCE OF TYRE

But the Tyrians were not defeated yet. Hanging leather skins stuffed with seaweed from their battlements, they cushioned their walls against missiles. They dropped rocks on to siege ships and sent underwater divers to cut the Macedonian vessels' moorage cables, after which the Macedonians switched to solid chain. Then the Tyrians used sharp poles to slice through the ropes holding the battering rams and poured red-hot sand on to the besiegers below, penetrating the attackers' armour and causing them agony. By late June, as stalemate threatened, some advised a truce; Tyre was no longer so vital since other fleets had become allies. A letter came from Darius, offering all land west of the Euphrates, his daughter in marriage and 10,000 talents. Reputedly, Parmenion urged acceptance but Alexander refused. He wanted the whole empire – and he would not leave Tyre untaken.

THE FINAL ONSLAUGHT

One hot July noon, when the besiegers were lunching or snoozing, Tyre's best ships slipped out and attacked the Cypriot fleet, sinking five galleys. Alexander broke off his lunch to lead the counter-attack, sinking all the Tyrians. By now Tyre was both starving and without allies. Alexander began an all-out attack on every side of the city at once. The fleets attacked the seaward walls and both harbours while siege towers and catapults assaulted the land side from the mole. Overwhelmed, the Tyrian defences collapsed and the Macedonians poured into the city early in August. Alexander had conquered the sea from the land.

Alexander killed 8,000 Tyrians, crucifying 2,000. The rest were sold into slavery, the customary fate. Tyre gained a Greek name and constitution but never regained its primacy. As Alexander advanced toward Egypt, only Gaza, the old Philistine stronghold, refused to surrender. Its siege took two long months, during which Alexander was twice wounded. When Gaza finally fell, Alexander dragged its commander, Batis, around the walls behind his chariot – an excruciating death. (Achilles in *The Iliad* had similarly dragged Hector around Troy, but the Trojan prince was already dead. This was gratuitous cruelty.)

Above: Totally destroying the old Phoenician city of Tyre, Alexander refounded it as a Greek city. It thrived under the Roman empire, as Roman-era ruins attest.

Below: Tyre, on its massively fortified island, was thought impregnable. Alexander proved otherwise, but it took him seven months and tested his military genius to its limits.

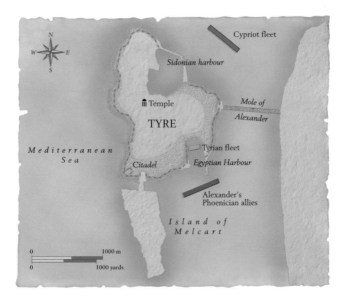

EGYPT: THE FOUNDING OF ALEXANDRIA 332–331BC

Above: Alexander, crowned as Pharaoh by Egyptian priests, was depicted on temple carvings as being greeted by Ammon Ra, greatest god of the Egyptian pantheon.

Below: A 19th-century view of the great harbour at Alexandria showing all that remains of the lighthouse, once one of the Seven Wonders of the World. For 1,000 years after its foundation in 331BC, Alexandria was one of the greatest cities on earth.

Egypt had known, and generally accepted, the Greeks as traders, mercenaries and colonists (at Naucratis in the Delta) for more than two centuries. It had even seen some of the very first tourists, such as Herodotus, that insatiably curious historian-traveller of the 5th century BC.

PERSIAN MISRULE

The country had been in intermittent revolt against Persia for 130 years, remaining independent for more than 60 years of the 4th century BC. (Its customs and religion, which intrigued the Greeks, seem to have annoyed the Zoroastrian Persians, who were essentially monotheistic.) Persian behaviour had been at best insensitive, at worst deliberately offensive, to Egypt's powerful priesthood and the devout *fellahin* (peasantry), who made up the bulk of this strongly hierarchical society.

"In Egypt," Plato had observed, "it is impossible for a king to rule without the priests." Persian soldiers had reputedly roasted and eaten the sacred bull Apis, replacing it with a donkey – an animal the Egyptians loathed. But despite this, many Egyptian temples had retained their estates under Persian rule.

When Alexander crossed the desert in late 332BC, the Persian governor of the frontier fort of Pelusium opened its gates to him. Alexander then sailed up the Nile to Memphis unopposed. In the ancient capital he was enthusiastically welcomed by the people and priests and lodged in the old palace of the pharaohs. Alexander sacrificed to the Egyptian gods, especially Apis, and was crowned Pharaoh, as inscriptions in the temples attest. As Pharaoh, he was the son of Horus, the divine son of the sun god Ra, and also beloved son of Ammon, creator of the Universe. These titles impressed him far more deeply than his Companions probably at first suspected.

CHOOSING THE SITE

Alexander held athletic games "to which the most famous performers came from all over Greece", according to Arrian, then sailed down the west branch of the Nile and around Lake Mareotis to the sea. Here he was struck by "the excellence of the site, convinced that if a city were built upon it, it would prosper. Filled with enthusiasm, he himself oversaw the layout of the new city, indicating the site for the

THE ROSETTA STONE

Much of what we know about ancient Egypt under the ancient Pharaohs and the Ptolemies derives from the Rosetta Stone, a trilingual slab dating from 196BC. In that year Ptolemy V (descended from Alexander's general Ptolemy I) set up the stone bearing a declaration in three languages: Greek (the language spoken in Alexandria and in government); demotic Egyptian (spoken by native Egyptians); and hieroglyphs (the ancient sign-writing read only by priests). Ptolemy V's government, facing problems after military defeats and peasant revolts, put up trilingual stones proclaiming that Ptolemy was the truly anointed Pharaoh. This stone was found in the city of Rosetta – hence its name – during the French occupation of Egypt under Napoleon in 1799. It was taken to London after the British expelled the French. The French had made copies of the writing and after 1815 a race developed between the two countries to decipher the stone first. The brilliant French Egyptologist François Champollion finally cracked the hieroglyphs in 1822–4.

Right: The stone found at Rosetta contained trilingual inscriptions that enabled the Egyptologist Champollion finally to decipher it in 1824.

market square and the temples, Greek gods being chosen along with the Egyptian Isis, and the exact limits of its walls." (Arrian again.) Alexander sprinkled barley meal taken from his soldiers' rucksacks to mark out the city's walls – an omen that Aristander, his prophet, interpreted to mean that the city would enjoy the fruits of the earth.

GREATEST MEDITERRANEAN CITY

There had long been a trading post on the offshore island of Pharos, on which, according to a legend, the lovers Helen and Paris of Troy had hidden after fleeing Sparta. Sheltering the harbour from the prevailing north winds that kept the site cool in summer, Pharos became famous for the giant lighthouse on it. Alexandria itself soon became the greatest city in the Mediterranean, a trading metropolis renowned for luxury and culture, with the biggest library in the world.

Alexander could not have foreseen all this, but he certainly envisaged the city as Egypt's new capital, well sited to receive the grain and other products flowing down the Nile, while looking out toward Greece. Alexander settled Macedonian veterans, Greeks, prisoners and some Jews in his new city. Later, under the Ptolemies and Romans, Alexandria seems to have lacked a council and assembly, but its founder may have originally granted it these vital aspects of a Greek *polis*. Alexandria-in-Egypt, despite many vicissitudes, would flourish until the Arab conquest nearly a thousand years later.

Below: Sailing unopposed up the Nile to the ancient capital Memphis, Alexander was welcomed by the Egyptians, who had come to loathe the Persians.

EGYPT: THE PILGRIMAGE TO SIWAH 331BC

Above: The Temple of Horus at Edfu was built under the Ptolemies, the Hellenistic kings who succeeded Alexander. It is the best preserved of all Egyptian temples.

Below: The Temple of Ammon at Siwah, the mysterious oasis-shrine that Alexander visited in 331BC.

The most mysterious episode in Alexander's life may have originated in a simple desire to explore the vague western frontier of Egypt, his newest conquest. Early in 331BC he led a small group west along the coast from the Nile. Then he turned due south into the desert, heading for Siwah, an oasis 320km/200 miles inland with a famous shrine. Siwah had long been revered by the citizens of Cyrene, the greatest Greek city in Libya. Cyrenians worshipped its ram-headed god Ammon/Amun as Zeus. (The Greeks, being tolerant polytheists, often identified other people's deities with their own.) Through Cyrene's influence, Siwah's fame had spread to Greece proper, where it was seen as an African version of the Delphic oracle. But Siwah itself, although visited by a few Greeks remained mysterious.

UNKNOWN MOTIVES

Alexander's true motives for this long diversion, while Darius was slowly assembling Persia's Grand Army beyond the Euphrates, remain disputed. For some people his desert pilgrimage reveals his mystical belief in his destiny; others view it as an attempt to bolster his position with his new subjects, Egyptian and others. Callisthenes, the official historian, said that it was due to Alexander's "thirst for glory and because he heard Hercules and Perseus had gone there before him". These were heroes Alexander always strove to rival.

HOLY GUIDES

Riding camels, the party left the coast at Paraetonium, entering a sand desert. After four days' wandering, they had almost run out of water when a rainstorm enabled them to refill their water bottles.

From then on they travelled by night to avoid the heat through a landscape later described by the Victorian traveller Bayle St John: "A gorge black as Erebus lies across the path and on the right stands a huge pile of rocks, looking like the ruins of some vast fabulous city.... There were yawning gateways flanked by bastions of immense altitude; there were towers and pyramids and crescents and domes and dizzy pinnacles and majestic crenellated heights, all invested with unearthly grandeur by the magic light of the moon."

Unsurprisingly, Alexander's party became lost, until (according to Ptolemy) two holy serpents appeared to guide them through the Pass of the Crow and down to the first oasis. Beyond a glittering white salt desert lay Siwah itself, green and lush with palm and fruit trees.

THE ORACLE'S ANSWER

The chief priest emerged from the temple to invite Alexander into the sanctuary, not requiring him to change his travel-stained clothes, like most supplicants. The other Macedonians, left in an outer courtyard,

can have heard little of what went on in the temple's dim recesses, but Callisthenes recorded it as if he had: "The oracles were not given in spoken words as at Delphi or Miletus, but mostly given in nods and signs, just as in Homer '[Zeus] spoke and nodded assent with his dark brows.' The prophet answered for Zeus, telling the king directly that he was the son of Zeus." All Alexander would say afterwards was that he was pleased with the result.

Returning without trouble to Memphis, he divided Egypt's government between civilian and soldiers, a sensible arrangement he later repeated elsewhere. Then he moved north, gathering his armies at Tyre for the decisive encounter with Darius' Grand Army.

Above: At the remote but famous sanctuary of Ammon, whom the Greeks identified with Zeus, Alexander was reputedly told that he was the son of Zeus, an answer that fully "satisfied him".

ALEXANDER THE GOD

"Zeus is the father of all men but makes the best especially his own," Alexander once said. For Greeks, there was no sharp division between gods and men, the world being filled with gods. The kings of both Sparta and Macedonia claimed descent from Hercules, the mythical hero who became a god. Lysander, the Spartan general who defeated Athens in 404BC, was hailed as a god by grateful oligarchs. Philip II was later portrayed like an Olympian deity on some coins and statues. After his Siwah pilgrimage, Alexander began invoking Zeus as his father, implying his own divinity. (He regarded Ammon as a form of universal Zeus, not a local deity.) This later caused problems. When Alexander first tried to get Macedonians to offer him *proskynesis* – the homage Persians paid their Great King, although monotheistic Persians never *worshipped* their monarch – he had to back down.

Finally, in 324BC Alexander, at the height of his powers, ordained his deification, which produced varying reactions. The Ionian cities, already worshipping Alexander, complied happily; the Spartans replied laconically: "Alexander can call himself a god if he wishes"; and Demosthenes probably spoke for most Athenians when he said, "Alexander can be the son of Zeus – and of Poseidon also if he wants." After his death, Alexander was often depicted as divine with the horns of Ammon, and many of his successors claimed godlike attributes.

Right: Alexander with the horns of Ammon, the Egyptian deity he claimed as his father, on a coin issued by Ptolemy I (ruled Egypt 323–284BC).

THE GREAT VICTORY: GAUGAMELA 331 BC

Above: Indo-Greek tetradrachms and staters struck by the kings of Bactria.

Below: The Azara Herm, a copy of an original by Lysippus, showing the dynamic conqueror in distinctly tough-looking mode. Alexander was always keenly aware of the propaganda value of his image.

Alexander waited in Tyre through the early summer until he heard that Darius had mustered the Persian Grand Army in Babylonia. He did not want another inconclusive battle like Issus but needed to defeat the Persians totally and openly. However, Darius was based in Babylon 1,120km/700 miles from the Mediterranean, far beyond Alexander's knowledge. In July, Hephaistion went north to the River Euphrates with an advance guard. He found himself facing Mazaeus, a Persian satrap of Syria, with 3,000 troops, mostly Greek mercenaries. For some weeks the two forces faced each other, perhaps exchanging secret messages. Then, as Alexander approached with his 47,000-strong army, Mazaeus retreated, burning the fertile Euphrates valley. Alexander took the northern unburnt route towards the Tigris – a fast-flowing river hard to cross if defended.

THE SITE OF THE BATTLE

Curiously, his army was unopposed as it crossed the river, the cavalry wading in upstream to shelter the infantry. The land around was invitingly unravaged. Darius probably was luring the Macedonians on to a spacious battlefield (the plain of Gaugamela) of his choosing. On 20 September the Moon eclipsed. Alexander sacrificed to the Sun, Moon and Earth, revealing astronomical knowledge learned from Aristotle and also Greek piety. Aristander, his prophet, interpreted the ominous event favourably. Then Alexander heard that Darius was camped nearby with a "force much larger than at Issus". Ignoring advice to try a night attack

Above: The archetypal image of Alexander at the charge, huge-eyed and with wind-swept hair.

(always risky), Alexander rested his army while he reconnoitred. What he saw was awesomely impressive.

Darius had mustered the largest army that he could feed, perhaps 250,000 men. He meant to win by sheer numbers. Crucially, he had c.40,000 cavalry, while Alexander had only 7,000. Only in heavy infantry were the Persians weaker, deprived of Greek recruits. To let their chariots charge smoothly, the Persians had cleared the ground while fixing stakes to protect their flanks. Having seen the Persian set-up, Alexander planned at leisure, keeping the Persians waiting for two nights. At noon on 1 October 331 BC the battle for Asia began.

THE OPPOSING ARMIES

On the Persian left was the formidable Bactrian and Scythian cavalry commanded by their satrap Bessus. Mazaeus commanded the cavalry on the right. In the centre was Darius, protected by 15 Indian elephants (whose smell panics horses that are unused to them), 6,000 Greek hoplites, the Persian infantry and

200 scythed chariots. The Persians could potentially outflank the Macedonians on both sides.

Alexander slanted his whole army obliquely, with 10,000 sarissa-wielding heavy infantry in the centre. Their right flank was protected by 3,000 mobile Shield Bearers, linked to the Companion cavalry on the right led by Alexander himself. Ahead of them ran 2,000 archers, slingers and javelin throwers. On the left wing, under Parmenion, were the Thessalian horsemen and remaining Macedonian cavalry, forming the anchor of the slanting line. Alexander's wing actually found itself opposite Darius' centre. To counter flank attacks, Alexander ordered the infantry to face about if needed to form a square – a manoeuvre requiring perfect discipline. At the tip of each cavalry wing, infantry units of veteran mercenaries were concealed, a tactic first recommended by Xenophon.

Alexander began battle by leading his wing to the right while holding back Parmenion's troops. This drew the Persian left flank out, away from their elephants and defences. The Bactrians charged, trying to outflank the Macedonians, but the latter's cavalry wedges turned to face them, foot soldiers emerging to drive back the disconcerted Bactrians. In the centre the chariots were countered by archers. Any surviving chariots rattled harmlessly through infantry ranks that opened up.

THE FLIGHT OF THE KING

As Alexander intended, a gap appeared to the left of Darius' centre. Into it he led his Companion cavalry in a wedge-shaped attack heading for the Great King. The Shield Bearers followed on foot. Darius, again seeing nemesis on a black horse bearing down, again turned and fled – Alexander reputedly got close enough to kill the royal charioteer. Meanwhile, the Persian cavalry under Mazaeus on the right beat back Parmenion's wing, pushing past into the Macedonian camp. There they discovered the Persian Queen Mother, who looked at them in stony,

immobile silence until they withdrew. Other gaps appeared in the central Macedonian line but the troops turned to form oblongs. Then news of the Great King's flight demoralized the Persian army. Mazaeus, recalling his unbeaten cavalry, rode hard for Babylon.

The battle had been won by just 3,000 cavalry Companions supported by 8,000 Shield Bearers under Alexander's visionary leadership. He tried to pursue Darius, but swirling masses of retreating troops, thick clouds of dust and then nightfall hampered him. Darius swapped his chariot for a horse and rode into the mountains of Media. On the battlefield Alexander was hailed as lord of Asia.

Above: The Battle of Gaugamela, *as painted by the French 17th-century artist Lebrun. Macedonian victory at this huge battle determined the fate of half Asia.*

Below: Heavily outnumbered at Gaugamela, Alexander slanted his army obliquely so that the right wing, under his command, attacked the Persian centre. Alexander's wedge-shaped cavalry formations cut through the Persian ranks and Darius fled in contagious panic.

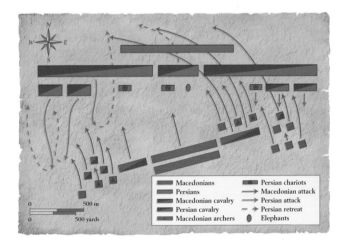

Macedonians	Persian chariots
Persians	Macedonian attack
Macedonian cavalry	Persian attack
Persian cavalry	Persian retreat
Macedonian archers	Elephants

0   500 m
0   500 yards

IN BABYLON
331BC

Above: The Babylonians offering Alexander the city's keys, from a French medieval painting.

Below: Alexander entered Babylon in triumph, its citizens welcoming him as a liberator from Persian misrule, depicted in an 18th-century painting by Gasparo Diziano.

When Alexander reached Arbela 112km/70 miles away, he realized that Darius had vanished into the mountains of Media (Kurdistan), at which point he abandoned the pursuit. After burying his dead (Persian casualties far outnumbered Macedonian, but even they had suffered heavily, Hephaistion being among the wounded), he quit the battlefield.

South lay Babylon, the greatest metropolis of Asia, "surpassing in splendour any city in the known world", as Herodotus had written 150 years earlier. Still a great trading city, Babylon was also an important religious centre. Its Chaldean priests were famed as mathematicians, astronomers and astrologers. Babylon's defences of brick-built walls were 60m/200ft high and wide enough for chariots to drive around two abreast, according to Herodotus. Surrounded by deep moats, they rivalled Tyre's.

ALEXANDER WELCOMED
But there was to be no siege of Babylon. As the Macedonians warily approached the city, its gates opened and the Persian general Mazaeus rode out with his sons to greet Alexander. Behind him came Babylonian priests chanting and dancing, with city magistrates bearing gifts to indicate their surrender. Alexander mounted a special chariot to ride in triumph up the dead straight avenues toward the royal palace, a complex with 600 rooms. This welcome from Babylon's elite was both politic and heart-felt.

PERSIAN MISRULE
Like Egypt, Babylon and Babylonia had often been maltreated by the Persians. While Cyrus, its first Persian ruler, had meticulously respected Babylon's customs and deities, later kings such as Xerxes had abused the city, demoting it from being the satrapy capital after a revolt and expropriating its temple treasures. Persian rule had drained Babylonia of wealth and even population (it had to send 500 eunuchs and 1,000 talents of silver to the Persian court each year). Many farms had been given to Persian nobles as estates, while the irrigation channels on which Babylonia's fertility relied were neglected.

THE HANGING GARDENS OF BABYLON

One of the Seven Wonders of the Ancient World, the Hanging Gardens of Babylon displayed Babylonian wealth and ingenuity. Traditionally they were built *c.*600BC for Amytis, the Median-born wife of King Nebuchadnezar II, homesick for her green native mountains. Babylon had many massive ziggurat temples and other buildings, often with walls 25m/80ft thick, mostly dating from that period.

Archaeologists have not yet decided which ruins in Babylon are the Gardens described by Greek writers such as Strabo and Diodorus Siculus in the 1st century BC. Diodorus wrote: "The approach to the Garden sloped like a steep hill and the several parts of the structure rose from one another tier on tier. On all this earth had been piled and was thickly planted with trees of every kind that, by their size and beauty, delighted beholders... Water machines raised abundant supplies of water from the river,

Left: The Hanging Gardens of Babylon, one of the Seven Wonders of the Ancient World, as imagined in a a 19th-century illustration.

though hidden from view." Clearly the Babylonians had pumps to raise water from the Euphrates, and they waterproofed their brickwork. Confusion comes from a translation error: the Greek word *kremastos* means *overhanging*, not hanging. Creepers and branches overhung the walls of this sky-garden.

Above: The Ishtar Gate, Babylon's grandest ceremonial gate, for which the city was renowned, was dedicated to Ishtar, the goddess of sacred prostitution.

TEMPLES AND BROTHELS

Concerned as ever to give the local gods their due, Alexander sacrificed in the temple of Bel-Marduk, Babylon's patron deity. He then clasped the hand of the golden statue to show that, like the old Babylonian kings, he received his power direct from the god. He took the old title King of the Lands and ordained the rebuilding of E-sagila, the great ziggurat-temple 60m/200ft high, damaged by Xerxes. He also ordered that Greek plants be added to the varieties growing luxuriantly in Babylon's famous Hanging Gardens, although few probably survived Babylon's heat. But he reappointed the Persian Mazaeus as satrap, with Apollodorus as Macedonian military governor – a wise balance repeated elsewhere later. Persians who knew the locality were obviously useful.

While Alexander was restoring the temples, his men were enjoying the city's equally famous brothels, helped by a generous pay bonus. Quantities of gold, in ingots rather than coin, had been found in the city, which were minted into coins to pay the army. (Herodotus had noted the strange Babylonian custom that required *all* women to ritually prostitute themselves in temples before marriage.)

After a month's rest and recreation, the army marched out south-east towards Susa and Persepolis, the Persian capitals.

Below: Babylon's walls gleamed with enamelled bricks depicting animals such as this lion.

THE DESTRUCTION OF PERSEPOLIS 331–330BC

Susa, the eastern terminus of the Royal Road that ran west to Sardis, lay in the Elamite plain, not Persia proper. Although reputedly even hotter than Babylon, Darius I (522–486BC), the greatest Achaemenid king, had made it his growing empire's administrative capital. From Susa's huge palace, orders, threats and bribes had gone out to Greece for nearly 200 years, so its name sounded sinister to Greek or Macedonian ears. However, the army entered Susa unopposed.

WEALTH OF SUSA AND PERSEPOLIS
The Macedonians were stunned by the accumulated wealth of the Persian kings – 50,000 talents of silver, according to Arrian, plus rich carpets and furnishings. Among the treasures were the bronze statues of Harmodius and Aristogeiton, the Athenian tyrannicides carried off by Xerxes when he sacked Athens in 480BC. Alexander sent them home, reaffirming his Panhellenic credentials. Another incident pointed to new dilemmas for Alexander. Sitting on the Great King's throne, his feet did not reach the royal footstool (Persian kings were generally tall), so a table was fetched. The sight made Alexander's old friend Demaratus cry with joy but caused a Persian court eunuch to burst into tears. To reconcile such disparate groups would prove very difficult, but at present Alexander was still Panhellenic leader. Even more treasure was stored at Persepolis, the

ceremonial capital in Persia's mountainous heart. Sending Parmenion with the baggage by the slower road, in December Alexander took the direct route with the Companion cavalry and best troops. En route he crushed some tribesmen, accustomed to demanding tribute from passing Persians, by a dawn raid that shocked them into surrender and paying *him* tribute of 30,000 sheep a year. (They were shepherds, not farmers.) Finally he entered Iranian territory, unknown to the Greeks, and approached the Persian Gates.

THE PERSIAN GATES
The Gates were a formidable natural barrier of rock strengthened by walls, blocking a 2,150m/7,000ft high pass. Lining them were 40,000 troops, whose catapults showered boulders and arrows on the Macedonians. Mauled, the latter hastily retreated. For a moment Alexander seemed baffled. Then a shepherd told him of a rough path that ran high up behind the pass. Leaving some men with orders to attack when they heard trumpets, he took the others on a night march of 17km/11 miles through snow-covered forests. Dividing his forces at the summit, he sent heavier troops down to the River Araxes to cut off the retreat. Then the rest sprinted 9.6km/6 miles uphill to surprise the Persian outposts in the dark. They fled without giving the alarm. At daybreak Alexander attacked the unsuspecting Persians from the rear while Craterus launched a frontal assault. Bewildered, the Persians scattered, jumping from cliffs or being killed trying to flee. The road to Persepolis lay open.

THE WEALTH OF PERSEPOLIS
The palaces of Persia stood on an artificial mound 18m/60ft high in the valley of Mervdasht, then fertile but now arid.

Above: Two bull-headed columns among the ruins of the huge palace of Darius I in Persepolis, which Alexander burnt one drunken evening.

Left: A gold rhyton (animal-shaped drinking vessel), part of the immense treasures stored at Susa and especially at Persepolis, then considered the "richest city on earth."

Approached by magnificent staircases were the audience halls of Darius and Xerxes, with the palaces around them. Their brick walls, 20m/65ft high, were covered in gold and glazed tiles, while huge columns with bull-head capitals supported high roofs. Alexander's men had never seen anything like this "richest city under the sun". The Persian governor showed Alexander around the palaces, including the royal treasury, containing 120,000 talents of gold and silver.

Alexander ordered 10,000 pack animals to carry the treasure to Susa for safekeeping and reinstated the Persian governor. Only then did he let his men loot the palaces, producing an orgy of destruction that wrecked many great artworks. Guards and inhabitants were killed indiscriminately until the king ended it. Seeing a statue of Xerxes shattered on the ground, Alexander began to have doubts about how far he could continue a war of revenge. But the greatest destruction was still to come.

BURNING THE PALACES

Among the intrepid women who had accompanied the army from Europe was Thais, the beautiful Athenian mistress of Ptolemy, the general and historian. Ptolemy never mentioned her role in the drunken night that saw the burning of the palaces, but others did. At a banquet

Above: Darius made Persepolis the ceremonial capital of his immense empire in the 6th century BC, building palaces intended to overawe his subjects with magnificent staircases such as this.

where music played and women such as Thais were present, Alexander and his companions drank heavily. Thais teasingly said it was up to the women to punish the Persians finally for their attack on Greece and burn the palaces. The Companions guffawed approval and Thais, seizing a torch, led a wild procession up the great staircases. First Alexander, then Thais, threw a flaming torch on to the floor of Xerxes' Hundred-Columned Hall. Its cedar-wood columns quickly caught light, as did the other palaces. Soon all were ablaze, as archaeology has confirmed. The Panhellenic crusade had achieved its declared goal.

Below: Another view of the palace of Darius I at Persepolis, whose high walls were once covered with glazed and gold tiles.

CHAPTER X

THE LORD OF ASIA

330–323BC

The capture of Persepolis, followed by the murder of Darius, changed Alexander's policies and attitudes. He no longer saw himself as a Panhellenic leader but as king of Asia, if not exactly Great King. Increasingly, Iranian nobles accepted him as such, but this did not mean an end to his wars.

Persia had left many tribes in remoter eastern provinces unsubjugated – not something Alexander was prepared to do. To be true ruler of all the satrapies, he had to fight guerrilla wars in areas unknown to Greeks. His military genius always won through, but he faced growing problems with his own soldiers. As lord of Asia he had to appear suitably regal, adopting at least some oriental customs. These proved anathema to Macedonian veterans, still the core of his army. In an increasingly tense atmosphere, plots were discovered – or fabricated – that led to old comrades being killed. When Alexander marched yet further east into India, his men finally rebelled.

Robbed of his desire to reach the world's limits (as he understood them), Alexander returned to Babylon, where he died aged not yet 33. Unusually open-minded, he had tried to unite the Persian and Macedonian nobility to create a new ruling class. Although this new elite would speak Greek, the plan led the Macedonians to outright mutiny. Alexander, suppressing this, continued with ever more grandiose plans. These died with him, however, as did all hopes of a united empire.

Left: The pass into Kafiristan among the Hindu Kush mountains, north-western Pakistan.

FROM PERSEPOLIS TO HERAT
330–329BC

Above: Alexander's pothos (longing) for the distant horizon shines through this bust. Wanderlust may explain part of his endless journeying.

Below: A fertile valley in the Elburz Mountains in northern Iran, which the Macedonians crossed in 330BC. The area makes an exception to the aridity of much of the Iranian plateau.

Alexander headed north to Ecbatana (Hamadan) in May 330BC. With a 60,000-strong army, he expected to fight another battle. But although Darius had his eastern satraps' troops and a few Greek mercenaries, he again turned and ran. This time, his irresolution proved fatal. Bessus, a distant relation, seized and deposed him, determined to retreat east to Bactria, his far-off satrapy. In early June, Alexander reached Ecbatana, where he paid off his Greek allies and Thessalian cavalry, officially ending the Panhellenic crusade. Some chose to re-enlist at increased rates; the rest returned home.

DARIUS' DEATH
The moment he heard of Darius' capture, Alexander took 500 horsemen in hot pursuit east beyond Ragae (Tehran). But they caught up with the Persian rebels too late. Bessus, seeing him approach, had murdered Darius, abandoning his baggage to flee east. The body of the last Achaemenid was found in a wagon by a Macedonian, bound in gold chains. When Alexander saw his enemy's corpse, he wrapped it in his own cloak and sent it to Persepolis for royal burial – actions that reveal that he saw himself as Darius' heir.

ALEXANDER HEADS EAST
So, increasingly, did the Persian nobility. As Alexander's army passed through the wooded Elburz Mountains and down to Zadracarta on the Caspian Sea, Persian nobles, including the Grand Vizier implicated in Darius' murder, appeared. Alexander pardoned him and many others. Obviously he needed experienced Persian-speakers (few Macedonians ever spoke much Persian) to run the complex imperial administration.

Artabazus, whom Alexander had met long ago at Pella and whose daughter Barsine had been his mistress, arrived with his seven sons, some of them former satraps. Alexander welcomed them all warmly. Darius' 1,500 Greek hoplites were pardoned and enlisted in the army

– but at the old, lower rate. At Zadracarta Alexander held games by the seaside. His men, relaxing for two weeks, admired this strange sea, which hardly tasted of salt but teemed with fish. Most Greeks thought that the Caspian opened north on to the Ocean, which they regarded as encircling the world. (Unknown to them, the Caspian's north coasts had been discovered under Darius I nearly 200 years before.) The prospect of being so near the world's edge must have aroused Alexander's *pothos* (longing) again. But his route lay south-east into the heartland of old Iran.

A KING TO THE PERSIANS

As the army marched south-east from Meshed into Areia (west Afghanistan), news came that Bessus was "wearing his diadem erect", in other words had proclaimed himself Great King.

Partly in response to this, Alexander now began adopting some aspects of Persian court etiquette to impress his new subjects. These included elements of Persian dress, a sensitive subject to Macedonians, who thought trousers laughably effeminate. Alexander avoided trousers but began wearing a diadem (cloth band) and Persian robes such as a purple-striped tunic. He also introduced Persian court ceremonial, with cup bearers, eunuchs and (reputedly) 365 concubines. Ushers and chamberlains now controlled access to the king, who sat enthroned in splendour. All this differed sharply from the informal Macedonian court, so at first Alexander ran parallel courts, one for Persians, another for Macedonians.

In Ariana, Alexander founded another city, now Herat, and reappointed its satrap Satibarzanes. There were dangers in employing Persians, however, for Satibarzanes at once revolted. Alexander, turning back, defeated his army but Satibarzanes himself escaped with some men.

PHILOTAS AND PARMENION

In September 330BC, Alexander faced trouble closer to home. A plot was uncovered to kill him in which Philotas, son of the veteran general Parmenion and a boyhood friend, was allegedly involved. Found guilty by the Macedonian army, recovering for a moment its old judicial role, Philotas was stoned to death.

Secret orders sent by special couriers then ensured the killing of Parmenion, who was commanding the reserve forces in distant Ecbatana, a position of great power on the route back home. But while Philotas had a trial and execution, if one based on doubtful charges, Parmenion's death has been considered by some historians as tantamount to murder. The elderly general, Philip's old friend, was simply stabbed to death.

Below: A winged gold ibex of the Achaemenid period. Ibex were common in the remote mountains of Central Asia, the home of independent Iranian barons, whom Alexander had to fight or charm into accepting his rule.

THE ROAD THROUGH OXIANA 329–328 BC

Above: Double bull-headed pillars, typical of Persian architecture's majestic elegance, which Alexander came to appreciate.

The campaigns of the next two years reveal Alexander's unbeatable determination, as he pushed deeper into central Asia. In October 329 BC he entered Drangiana (Halmand), there founding another Alexandria: Kandahar. He decided to approach Bactria, Bessus' huge central Asian satrapy, from the south-east. As always, he chose the hardest route.

As winter deepened, he led 40,000 men up the south flanks of the Hindu Kush, known to Greeks as the Indian Caucasus. Men and horses suffered terribly on the snow-covered slopes of the highest mountains they had yet seen, afflicted by altitude sickness. But, encouraged by their king, who personally helped the stragglers, they marched on. By moving in mid-winter, they surprised hibernating tribesmen who might have harried them – and wrong-footed Bessus. Alexander founded another city, Alexandria-in-the-Caucasus, near Kabul, resting his army before continuing north in early May. A gruelling climb over another spur of mountains brought the army down into Bactria and its chief city of Bactra (Balkh).

DEATH OF BESSUS

Bessus, panicking at Alexander's sudden appearance, fled north to Sogdiana, so losing almost all support. Alexander, cheered by hearing that the treacherous satrap Satibarzanes had been killed, crossed the desert to the Oxus, the huge river dissecting the land. Here he faced a problem: there were no bridges and no timber with which to build any. So he ordered his men to stuff their leather bags with hay and swim across on these. Startled, the Sogdians offered to surrender Bessus, thinking this would end the pursuit. Ptolemy, one of Alexander's chief generals, rode out to collect the captive traitor. Bessus was then displayed naked by the roadside, and repeatedly whipped as the army passed by. Later in Ecbatana he was mutilated and impaled – a punishment Arrian, the philosophically minded historian, damned as barbarous, but which the Persians expected.

DEATH IN SAMARKAND

The Sogdians had expected Alexander to turn back after Bessus' capture, but he marched on towards the River Jaxartes,

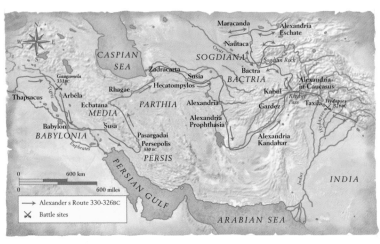

Right: Alexander's route east only occasionally followed the obvious roads, as he zigzagged north and south in pursuit of enemies, sometimes retracing his steps. He was always master of the unexpected approach.

THE CITY-FOUNDER

Alexander is credited with founding at least 18 cities, often replacing older settlements, which may make him the greatest city-founder ever. Some have thrived, others have vanished, and many survive under new names (Kabul, Khojend). Alexandria-in-Egypt, which was new, rapidly became one of the world's greatest cities. The colonists Alexander planted across Asia were mostly soldiers who, because of illness, age or wounds, could not keep up with his unending blitzkriegs. Supplementing this Greek-Macedonian core were varied locals and captives.

After Alexander's death some colonists, who had seldom been volunteers, tried to return home but were forced back to their new cities by Alexander's successors. Whatever Alexander's motives were for these foundations (some people have seen them simply as military bases to control his empire), they helped to spread Hellenism widely, if thinly, across Asia. As the ruins of Ai Khanum in Afghanistan (another Alexandria) show, such cities could boast fine theatres, gymnasia and temples – all considered essential for a Greek *polis*.

Above: Herat in western Afghanistan is one of the 18 cities Alexander founded (or refounded) as military colonies, most of which have since flourished. The cities were planned as typical Greek poleis, each with a theatre, agora, gymnasium, temples and a council.

Below: Often campaigning in mid-winter across high mountains to catch enemies unawares, Alexander and his army had to cross snowed-up passes. Innate Macedonian toughness and Alexander's example kept the army going.

taking Samarkand (Miracanda) en route. The river marked the outer limits of the Persian Empire. Here Alexander founded another city, Alexandria-Eschate (the Furthest), today Khojend. Then rebellion in the rear led by Spitamenes, one of Bessus' associates, forced him to send 2,000 troops to relieve Samarkand.

He himself crossed the Jaxartes to defeat Scythian horsemen on the river's far side, who were hindering his operations. These nomads, cousins of those north of the Black Sea, were duly defeated, but in the desert Alexander contracted dysentery from bad water. In other fights he was wounded twice, once severely. Then came news that Spitamenes had defeated the Samarkand relief force, and Alexander had to gallop madly with some cavalry to save Samarkand. Spitamenes simply vanished into the mountains, involving the Macedonians in protracted guerrilla warfare. When the army returned to Samarkand in late summer 328BC, tempers were frayed, despite the welcome arrival of 21,000 reinforcements (mostly Greek), led by Nearchus, an old friend.

To relax, they drank to excess even by Macedonian standards. (Water in Samarkand was notoriously brackish.) In their drunkenness they quarrelled, resentments at Alexander's orientalizing

policies resurfacing. Cleitus the Black, a *hipparch* (cavalry general) who had saved Alexander's life at Granicus, taunted the king, saying that he owed his success to his soldiers and Philip. Enraged, Alexander seized a spear and ran Cleitus through. Then, overcome by remorse at murdering an old friend at dinner, he withdrew to his tent and lay for three days without eating or drinking. Finally his soldiers decided that the anger of Dionysus, the wine god whose festival they had overlooked, lay behind it. This incident reveals Alexander's touchy pride and sometimes homicidal rage.

Above: As Alexander marched ever further east, he encountered and conquered ever higher mountains, such as the Kohi-i-Baba range. On one of them he found true love in Roxane.

Below: The wedding of Alexander to Roxane, here painted by the 18th-century Italian artist Marianno Rossi, took place high up on the Sogdian Rock. There were no offspring until a son was born after Alexander's death.

MARRIAGE ON THE ROCK
327BC

In late 328BC, Alexander's fortunes changed for the better. In November, Spitamenes, whose guerrilla raids had been growing desperate, was killed by his own troops; his severed head was thrown into Alexander's camp. Early in 327BC, Alexander renewed his campaign in eastern Sogdiana, ignoring snow blizzards that claimed the lives of 2,000 men, determined to quash the last opposition.

Near modern Hissar on the Koh-in-Noor mountains, rebels had found refuge in a local baron's castle on the Sogdian Rock, reputedly 3,600m/12,000ft high. When Alexander demanded their surrender, he was told to grow wings and fly. Angered, he chose 300 volunteers to climb by night up the sheer icy rock face. On the climb 30 men died. But, when morning broke, the Sogdians looked up to see what they thought was an army high above them. Overwhelmed, they at once surrendered.

LOVE AT FIRST SIGHT
Among the captives was the stunningly beautiful daughter of Oxyartes (another Sogdian baron), Roxane, whose name meant 'little star'. Alexander fell in love with her at first sight. As she was a captive, he refused to force marriage on her despite the obvious political advantages that would accrue. Luckily, politics and passion coincided, for Roxane accepted him and a sky-high wedding was celebrated on the Rock. The castle held enough supplies to feed an army for two years – a most useful dowry. The newly weds together cut a loaf of bread with Alexander's sword, each then eating one half (an old Persian custom).

Alexander took his army and bride back to Bactra, which he replanned as a splendid Greek city. He also ordered that 30,000 upper-class Persian boys be enrolled for training as soldiers. Their weapons were to be Macedonian and their language Greek. Their families

were given no choice about this conscription, the first of many measures intended to create a united Perso-Macedonian ruling class. The next measure was even more contentious.

THE PAGES' PLOT

The Persians used to offer *proskynesis* (obeisance) to superiors, especially to the Great King, in differing ways according to their own class. This did not entail Persian nobles grovelling on the ground, as later historians supposed, although common people did kowtow, as would special suppliants. Instead, Persian noblemen would bow and, extending their hands, blow a kiss. Their superior would respond by embracing them in ways varying according to rank. All Persians paid *proskynesis* to the Great King, but this implied no worship of the Persian monarch, who was no god. However, *proskynesis* was how the Greeks honoured their gods, not their monarchs, and its prevalence among Persians soon led to serious misunderstandings.

Callisthenes, the campaign's official historian and cousin of Aristotle, used to boast that Alexander would be famous only due to his history. (Ironically, it has since been lost.) In it he had often praised the king as godlike. Among other things he tutored the royal pages, Macedonian boys in their teens, in the same way that

Aristotle had taught Alexander. Most Greek rulers regarded a tame philosopher as essential to court life, and Alexander kept on good terms with Aristotle for a long time. Callisthenes, however, while indisputably learned, was also silly.

Alexander realized that it was galling to Persian nobles to see the Macedonians approach him, their king, with rough informality while they had to make formal obeisance. With some close friends such as Hephaistion he conceived a way to get Macedonians to pay him *proskynesis* too. One night at dinner in Bactra a gold cup filled with wine went around the tables. Each guest, forewarned, stood up, drank a toast and did *proskynesis*, bowing slightly, before going up to receive a kiss on the cheek from Alexander. All went smoothly until the cup reached Callisthenes. He drank, did *not* bow but still expected a kiss, which Alexander refused. "So, I go the poorer by a kiss", Callisthenes said.

Nothing more happened that night. But soon after, when the army was on the move again, a serious conspiracy was discovered among the pages. One boy, Antipater, humiliated by a flogging he had received for killing a boar before Alexander (a major breach of etiquette), formed a plot with friends to kill the king while he slept.

As it happened, Alexander stayed up drinking until dawn so the plot misfired. But, unable to keep quiet, the pages talked about it until it reached the ears of Ptolemy. Arrests, interrogations and torture followed. The pages asserted that Callisthenes had urged them on. He was arrested, tortured and hanged. Whether he was behind the plot remains unknown, but he articulated the anti-Persian attitudes of Greeks and Macedonians, who, feeling they were the victorious master-race, refused to adopt oriental customs.

Plans to introduce *proskynesis* were probably shelved for the time being, as the army turned east towards India, Alexander's next and most adventurous goal.

Left: North of Sogdiana lay steppes inhabited by Scythian and other nomads, whose realm spread across Eurasia to the Black Sea. This gold vase, if Scythian in style and content, may have been made by Greek craftsmen.

Below: Aristotle, Alexander's old tutor, had suggested his relation Callisthenes as the campaign's historian and tutor to the royal pages. But Callisthenes filled the young pages' heads with lofty theories that led them to plot against Alexander and so to their arrest and execution. Callisthenes had already angered the king by refusing to salute him in the Persian manner.

INDIA: THE WORLD'S END
327–326 BC

Above: Alexander attacking Porus, the Indian rajah on an elephant, from a coin struck to celebrate the victory.

The Persian Empire had once stretched to the River Indus, but its Indian satrapies (now north-west Pakistan) had long been lost by Alexander's time. India was known to Greeks as a wildly exotic land – filled with gold-hunting ants among other wonders, according to Herodotus – and fabulously rich. Its kingdoms were powerful but divided.

For Alexander, to have refused such a challenge was unthinkable, although he had no idea how huge and varied India really was. There was almost no contact at the time between Greece and India. One problem he did recognize was that of India's elephants, whose smell terrified horses that were unused to them.

The army Alexander led into India in late 327 BC was now half-Asian. He had left many older soldiers in Bactria as settlers or garrisons, recruiting instead 30,000 Bactrian and Sogdian horsemen. While most of the Macedonian infantry had abandoned its long sarissas in favour of shorter, more manageable spears and there had been changes in the army's structure, its core and senior officers remained solidly Macedonian.

Below: If less famous than his battles with the Persians, Hydaspes was perhaps Alexander's finest victory. Facing a superior enemy with elephants across a monsoon-swollen river, Alexander deceived Porus by dividing his forces and taking half of them upstream to cross secretly. His other troops then crossed in direct attack. The resulting battle was hard fought but Porus became a loyal ally.

STAND-OFF AT THE HYDASPES

The direct route into India lay through the Khyber Pass. But Alexander, wanting to secure his lines of communication, turned left for an arduous campaign against mountain tribes in the wild Chitral and Swat regions.

The climax came early in 326 BC with the capture of the rock-fortress of Aornus on the summit of Pirsar 1,500m/5,000ft above the Indus. Misunderstanding local legends, the Greeks identified a local god as Dionysus, the wine god who had visited India. This misread myth further fuelled Alexander's dreams of conquest.

When the army descended to the Indus, it was welcomed by the ruler of Taxila. This made an enemy in Porus, rajah of Pauravas just to the east. Porus gathered a large army, including 85 elephants, on the east bank of the River Hydaspes (now the Jhelum), which the Macedonians reached in May.

The stand-off resembled that at the River Granicus eight years earlier, but this time Alexander was heavily outnumbered and also faced the challenge of many elephants. The Hydaspes, swollen by recent rains, was also a far more formidable river than the Granicus, being at least 0.8km/½ mile wide.

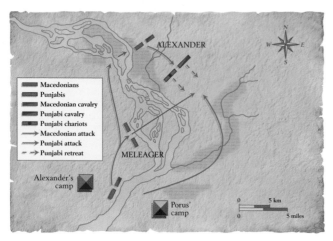

Macedonians
Punjabis
Macedonian cavalry
Punjabi cavalry
Punjabi chariots
→ Macedonian attack
→ Punjabi attack
- → Punjabi retreat

ALEXANDER

MELEAGER

Alexander's camp

Porus' camp

0   5 km
0   5 miles

VICTORY OVER PORUS

Alexander reacted with typical ingenuity. First, he gave the impression that he was making a permanent camp. From it he launched boats on the river every night to exhaust the Indians by constant false alarms. Then, his moves disguised by rain, he secretly divided his forces, leaving Craterus with half the army. He covertly marched his force of 11,000 infantry and 5,000 cavalry 24km/15 miles upriver. Here a wooded island enabled his men to cross by night, the infantry in specially built boats, the horsemen wading through water that rose to their horses' necks. They reformed on the far bank to meet Porus' advance guard coming toward them.

Other Macedonians under Meleager now crossed halfway up the river to catch the Indians on their flank. Alexander deployed his normal oblique attack to devastating effect, his light infantry dispersing to counter the elephants while the cavalry again delivered the knockout blow. After long, hard fighting, Porus' army was routed in perhaps Alexander's most brilliant victory. Alexander, accepting Porus' surrender, restored his old kingdom and generously added to it. In return, Porus became a loyal ally. Alexander struck a series of splendid coins and medals showing elephants and Indian archers. But his appetite for Indian conquests had been sharpened, not sated.

THE ARMY'S REFUSAL

Alexander had heard that east along the Ganges lay the vast but decadent kingdom of Ksandrames, ripe for conquest. East of that must flow the all-encircling Ocean, or so Aristotle had taught. He sacrificed to the Sun and in June began planning the advance from the River Hyphasis (the Beas, east of Amritsar), where his army was encamped. As he did so, the torrential monsoon rains began.

Right: Alexander's army crossing the Indus to fight Porus, an illustration from a medieval French manuscript of Quintus Curtius, one of the ancient histories of Alexander.

The Macedonians had never experienced such deluges. Rivers rose 9m/30ft and burst their banks, and snakes emerged in terrifying numbers. In the wet heat the soldiers' clothes rotted. For men who had marched 19,000km/12,000 miles, it was too much. When Alexander tried to enthuse them about the lands waiting to be conquered, they were silent. Then Coenus, a trusted veteran, voiced the general longing to return home.

Alexander, declaring that he would force no one to follow him but advance alone if needed, retired to his tent – but to no avail. His army was adamant. Finally, reluctantly, furiously, he agreed to return, to his soldiers' tearful joy.

Above: The river Indus rises in the mountains to the north, becoming vast as it enters the plains of Porus' kingdom.

Below: Alexander crowned with victory, a contemporary coin.

THE LONG RETURN
326–325 BC

Above: Although severely wounded at the siege of Multan in 325 BC, Alexander still led his men from the front.

Below: The upper reaches of the Indus, the great river down which Alexander and his fleet of 800 ships sailed to the Indian Ocean.

Returning to the River Hydaspes, Alexander found the fleet that Craterus had prepared, made from timber cut in the Himalayas. Alexander had decided to return not by the same land route but by sailing down the rivers to the Ocean. He left behind two new cities – Nicaea (Victoryville) and Bucephela, commemorating his victory and his beloved horse.

In November 326 BC the army, *c.*120,000 strong, embarked in a fleet of 800 ships. Alexander "stood in the bows of his ship and poured a libation [offering] into the water from a golden bowl, solemnly invoking the river… After a libation to Hercules his ancestor, Ammon and the other customary gods, he ordered the trumpets to sound and the whole fleet began to move downriver." Hephaistion marched on the left bank and Craterus on the right as flank guards.

A BRUSH WITH DEATH

At first, the voyage seemed an exploratory cruise. Local tribes, overawed by the armada, submitted peacefully,

although rapids caused problems for the amateur fleet. (Several galleys, including Alexander's own, were sunk, the king having to swim for his life, but the fleet was reassembled.)

Ahead, the warlike Mallians refused to submit – to Alexander's joy. He surprised them by a cross-desert march, besieging their capital Multan in early 325 BC. The outer city was soon captured but, attacking the citadel, ladders broke, leaving Alexander with three companions on top of the wall. When Alexander jumped down to fight *inside* the walls, an arrow pierced his lung. Peucestas shielded him – with the sacred shield from Troy – until other Macedonians burst in, slaughtering everyone in the city in furious grief that their king had been killed.

In fact, Alexander survived, for his doctor removed the arrowhead. But rumours of his death persisted, so a mere week later he was taken by boat to the camp. To convince his men that he was alive, he not only got up but mounted his horse, "at which the entire army applauded wildly over and over again… pressing against him, touching his hands, knees or clothes". His lung wound proved so bad that he never again walked, let alone fought, without pain. His officers berated him for recklessly endangering his life, and the army's safety, but, as Arrian said, "in truth he was fighting mad… for him the sheer joy of battle was irresistible".

THROUGH THE DESERT

Alexander reached the Indian Ocean in July. Here the fleet was almost wrecked by gigantic storms and surprised by the tides, both unknown in the Mediterranean. He founded another Alexandria as a port, with an eye to India's potential for trade. He sent his new elephant corps and 10,000 veterans back by an easy northerly route, but had

different plans for himself. He intended to march his army through the Gedrosian (Mekran) desert, something never done before even in legend. Meanwhile, Nearchus was to sail the fleet along the coast to the Euphrates, keeping in touch with the army. Like all Greek fleets, Nearchus' ships could not stay long at sea.

At first the army's journey was pleasant: myrrh trees grew so abundantly that the soldiers crushed the precious herb beneath their feet. But soon supplies, especially of water, ran short, and although they often marched by night rather than by day, the heat was overpowering. The men slaughtered and ate their animals, including horses – a lack of discipline that Alexander ignored.

At one stage in the endless desert even their guides got lost and Alexander had to lead the army back down to the coast to find the trail.

Although Alexander now always rode, he shared the hardships in other ways, especially thirst. On one occasion some soldiers, finding a trickle of water, filled a helmet and took it to Alexander, who, wrote Arrian, "with a word of thanks took the helmet and poured the water on the ground in full view of the army. The effect of this action was extraordinary, as if every man in the army had had a good drink... proof not only of his powers of endurance but of his genius in leadership." But this genius did not save thousands from dying. Only about a quarter of the original 40,000-strong army survived – the one true defeat in Alexander's career.

REUNITED WITH NEARCHUS

Reaching the desert's edge after 60 days' march, he sent camels racing ahead to order supplies. Alexander's progress then became a glorious Bacchanalian revel as the army unwound after its ordeal.

Reunited in December 326BC, Alexander wept with joy at seeing his old friend Nearchus again, thanking Zeus and Ammon, saying this reunion gave him more joy than all his conquests. Nearchus, too, had had a hard journey. His sailors had suffered from heat, thirst, hunger and alarming encounters with whales – never seen by Greeks before – and coastal tribes when the sailors had landed looking for water and food. But Nearchus had lost only one ship.

Above: A trireme, the archetypal Greek triple-tiered galley that Alexander's men built even on the shores of the Indus for his fleet that sailed down river to the Indian Ocean.

Below: Alexander decided to return to Persia marching through the centre of the vast Gedrosian (Mekran) desert shown here, an unprecedented venture. He himself survived, but three quarters of his army died in what was his worst, if scarcely known, defeat.

THE WRATH OF THE KING
324BC

Few of the governors appointed by Alexander, Persian or Macedonian, had ever expected to see him alive again. Fourteen of the empire's 23 satrapies were showing signs of revolt. Rumours of Alexander's near-fatal wounding at Multan, then his disappearance into the desert, had encouraged even an old friend such as Harpalus, imperial treasurer, to act independently – he had begun minting his own coins in Babylon. Alexander, as the news reached him, reacted by launching a reign of terror. In it many governors, soldiers and officials were executed for corruption or disloyalty, including 600 Thracian mercenaries who had abused their power in Media. Harpalus fled to Athens, taking his two mistresses and 6,000 talents with him, money later used to finance the anti-Macedonian cause.

Above: The Heraion, the main temple on Samos. Alexander's decree that all Greek exiles should return caused huge problems for Athens, which had settled many colonists on the island.

Below: On his return to Persia Alexander found that the tomb at Pasargadae of Cyrus the Great, founder of the Persian Empire, had been desecrated. He had the tomb's priestly guardians executed, commissioning the architect Aristobolus to restore it.

PASAGARDAE AND PERSEPOLIS
Dismissing Nearchus, who sailed on to the Euphrates, Alexander continued into Persia proper. Revisiting Pasargadae, the capital of Cyrus the Great, which he had

seen briefly in 330BC, he was horrified to discover that Cyrus' tomb had been desecrated, allegedly by its priestly guardians. Alexander had these Magi tortured but learnt nothing. He ordered Aristobulus, an architect-biographer, to restore the tomb completely. The task took Aristobulus many years, but the restored tomb still stands. Moving on to Persepolis early in 324BC, Alexander gazed at the blackened ruins of the palaces, perhaps now regretting that drunken night's destruction six years before.

ADOPTING PERSIAN CUSTOMS
Now he was concerned to gain the loyalty of the Persian nobility, crucial to running the empire. Personal feelings were not wholly absent, however. Bagoas, his Persian lover, for some reason hated Orsines, the aristocratic Persian governor of Persis. So Alexander had Orsines stripped of his rank and crucified without trial, his place being taken by Peucestas.

Peucestas, who had saved Alexander's life at Multan, was unusual among Macedonians in having learned Persian. He followed his king in adopting modified Persian court dress. This was what Alexander wanted all his officers to do, although most grumbled about copying slavish barbarian habits. The king had his eyes on the future, however. Reunited with Nearchus and other companions in April 324BC at Susa – whose Persian governor he imprisoned for corruption – he announced perhaps his most ambitious plan, concerning love more than war.

THE MARRIAGES OF SUSA
Alexander took two new wives – the daughters respectively of Darius and of Artaxerxes III, an earlier Great King. Persia's kings traditionally were even more polygamous than Macedonia's. Hephaistion married another princess,

THE PYRE OF CALANUS

Alexander was no "stranger to the loftier flights of philosophy, though the slave of his own ambition" in Arrian's words. Intrigued in 326BC at Taxila by *gymnosophists* (ascetics who had renounced wordly ambition), he asked some to accompany his army. Only one did, Calanus, becoming Alexander's close friend. When the army reached Persepolis in 324BC, Calanus, "who had never been sick in all his life", fell seriously ill. He decided to end his life despite Alexander's entreaties. Ptolemy was told to prepare a pyre and Calanus was "escorted to it by a solemn procession of horses, men, soldiers ... bearing cups of gold and silver and royal robes." As the flames mounted, Alexander, who "felt there was something indecent in witnessing such a friend's ordeal" ordered trumpets to sound and men to raise the battle-cry. Even the elephants joined in a noisy farewell to the man whose ideals were so very different from a world-conqueror's.

Left: Calanus, the Indian gymnosophist (fakir), who had followed Alexander, decided to die on a pyre when the army reached Persepolis in 324BC.

Above: Alexander dressed as Ares, the god of war, in a fresco from Pompeii – copying a Hellenistic original – showing his marriage to Statira, daughter of Darius III, in 324BC.

while 80 of the most senior officers also took high-ranking Persian wives. Alexander then gave official blessing to about 10,000 of his men's unions with Asian women, with sizeable gifts. Children of these mixed marriages would be Macedonian, the nucleus of a Perso-Macedonian ruling class.

RESTRUCTURING THE ARMY

He took his army north to Opis on the Euphrates in June. There he greeted as 'successors' the 30,000 Persian youths trained as Macedonian soldiers so that they could integrate seamlessly with the rest of the infantry. Noble Iranians such as Roxane's brother were enrolled in the crack Companion Cavalry, while 10,000 older Macedonians were to be honourably discharged and sent home.

These moves caused widespread mutiny. "Go and conquer with your daddy Ammon," some soldiers jeered, deeply affronting Alexander. Ordering the arrest and execution of 13 of the ringleaders, he declared they would still be "poor beggars in animal skins" without his father's and especially his leadership. Then he dismissed the whole army, appointing Persians to every post.

Stunned, the soldiers begged his forgiveness. There followed a tearful reconciliation, a banquet at which Alexander prayed for *omonia* (harmony) between Persians and Macedonians – and the veterans went off after all. Exactly as Alexander wanted.

Right: Back in Persia, Alexander adopted many luxurious Persian customs to impress his Asian subjects. The Persian crown had become hugely wealthy, as this gold rhyton indicates.

THE FINAL YEAR
323 BC

Above: Alexander wearing a lion-head helmet, one of the many heroic images made after his death.

Below: A bull from the Gate of Ishtar in Babylon, the city to which Alexander returned in 323 BC and where he died.

In August 324 BC Alexander issued an edict ordering Greek cities to take back all their exiles. This decree, announced at the Olympic Games, was applauded but caused turmoil in Greece. Many exiles had been wandering the world for years, often as mercenaries. There was often no room for them at home, especially in Athens. The city faced the prospect of thousands of *cleruchs* who had settled in Samos returning if Samian exiles regained their lands. Athens sent several embassies to the king to remonstrate. But Alexander was now little concerned with the plight of distant Greek cities, as he moved among the great capitals of his empire.

More Persians than Macedonians now held prominent posts at court and in the army, both of which looked ever more oriental. Alexander sat on a golden throne wielding a golden sceptre; his royal tent was supported by golden pillars; 500 Persian Immortals matched the 500 Macedonian Companions; and bilingual ushers, staff bearers and concubines thronged the court. Balancing such oriental splendours, many Greeks –

Above: The great stone lion outside Ecbatana (Hamadan) where Hephaistion, Alexander's oldest friend, died in 324 BC. It was possibly erected to honour Hephaistion.

actors, poets, secretaries, philosophers, engineers, doctors – found employment at the new king of Asia's court.

THE LOSS OF HEPHAISTION

By October the court was in Ecbatana, the old Median capital. Here Hephaistion, Alexander's vizier, or second in command, fell ill and died, probably of typhoid. No matter that their passions had cooled since boyhood love and that Bagoas was a younger, presumably more attractive rival: Alexander plunged into an orgy of grief.

He crucified Hephaistion's unfortunate physician – Hephaistion, apparently recovering, had ignored the doctor's veto on drinking wine – and threw himself on to the corpse. He shaved his head and had the manes and tails of his horses clipped. (Achilles, his hero, had similarly mourned his lover Patroclus.) He sent messengers to Siwah, sanctuary of Zeus-Ammon his father, to ask how he should honour his dead friend. The answer came back: "as a semi-divine hero". A pyre costing an

unprecedented 10,000 talents was prepared in Babylon and funeral games involving 3,000 contestants were staged. A great stone lion which is still standing was probably erected outside Ecbatana in Hephaistion's memory. Then Alexander sought consolation in his favourite activity: war. A winter campaign against the Cosseans, a primitive mountain tribe, provided his last triumph.

PLANNING THE NEXT CAMPAIGN

were from Carthage – a city ... bly intended to conquer – but there were also Scythians, Etruscans, Celts, Ethiopians, Libyans and Iberians. (Rome, however, was probably still too small to be involved.) But he ignored Chaldean priests, who warned him against entering Babylon, saying the omens were bad. He knew these priests had embezzled money that he had earmarked for rebuilding their great temples.

Alexander also proclaimed his own deification, perhaps encouraged by delegates from the Ionian Greek cities. This was unusual but not unprecedented. Lysander the Spartan general had earlier been hailed as a god, as had Dion the Sicilian politician, and Alexander had far

exceeded their achievements. At dinner parties he now began wearing divine robes, which shocked some people but again was not totally unprecedented.

DEATH IN BABYLON

But real gods are immortal. Alexander reputedly attended several hard-drinking parties in May that took him 36 hours to sleep off. At the end of the month Medius, a Thessalian noble, gave a particularly riotous party. Afterwards, Alexander took to his bed with a fever that steadily worsened. The troops, alarmed at his absence, insisted on being admitted to his bedroom. He acknowledged each with a movement of the eyes. Three days later, on 10 June 323BC, Alexander died, aged not yet 33, after a reign of 12 years and 9 months.

Rumours soon circulated that he had been poisoned, possibly with strychnine, by Macedonians alarmed at his orientalizing of the monarchy. Far more probably he died of a marsh fever hitting a constitution already much weakened by wars, numerous wounds and excessive drinking. He left behind a stunned world and no obvious heir to his huge empire. When asked who should succeed him, he had mouthed only the reply: "the strongest".

Above: Alexander's grand entry into Babylon, the destined capital of his empire, as envisaged by the French painter Charles Lebrun.

Below: Mourning for Alexander was widespread. He was long remembered as a semi-legendary figure across half Asia, as this Bukhara miniature from 1533 shows.

ALEXANDER'S LEGACY
A MILITARY GENIUS

Above: Of all the cities founded by Alexander, none surpassed Alexandria-in-Egypt, soon one of the richest and most sophisticated cities on earth. Its greatest building was the huge pharos (lighthouse), whose light could be seen 50km/31 miles away.

Below: Alexander was portrayed in many different guises, even rather improbably here as the rustic god Pan.

Few individuals have had as great an impact on world history as Alexander; fewer still have generated so much controversy, arousing reactions ranging from adulatory enthusiasm to stark disgust. For some 20th-century historians he was a Greek precursor of tyrants such as Hitler, Mao or Stalin. Ernst Badian, voicing such views, described Alexander at his life's end thus: "After fighting, scheming and murdering in pursuit of... power, Alexander found himself at last on a lonely pinnacle over an abyss with no use for his power and security unattainable." For other, more romantic, historians, Alexander was a chivalrous superman, spreading Hellenic civilization but free of Greek racism. With such divergent views, it can be hard to discern the man from the myth.

Above: Alexander as Helios Cosmocrator, omnipotent sun god, in this 1st century BC medallion. He became the archetypal god-king, aped but never equalled by Hellenistic and Roman successors.

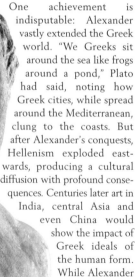

THE SPREAD OF HELLENISM
One achievement is indisputable: Alexander vastly extended the Greek world. "We Greeks sit around the sea like frogs around a pond," Plato had said, noting how Greek cities, while spread around the Mediterranean, clung to the coasts. But after Alexander's conquests, Hellenism exploded eastwards, producing a cultural diffusion with profound consequences. Centuries later art in India, central Asia and even China would show the impact of Greek ideals of the human form. While Alexander did not plan this, it was the result of his conquests.

If politically Alexander wanted a Perso-Macedonian fusion – an enlightened policy abandoned by his successors – he remained Hellenic in culture. He might wear half-Persian clothes and employ Persian nobles, but he hardly (if at all) spoke Persian. In religion also he remained Greek, as in his attitude to cities and trade. The Persians had founded only a few cities as military bases, distrusting merchants. But most of Alexander's cities were founded as true *poleis*. Trade often concerned Alexander, for he founded Alexandria-in-Egypt and another city at the mouth of the Euphrates. As Greek colonists transformed the cities of western Asia, Greek became the common tongue from the Aegean to central Asia.

The immediate results of Alexander's conquest were power and riches on an intoxicating scale for his successors. He had spent 10,000 talents (ten times the annual revenue of classical Athens at its height) just on Hephaistion's funeral – a sign of the rich new world he had opened up. The scale of his achievement long remained unrivalled.

ALEXANDER'S EXTREMISM

Personally Alexander was a man of extremes in almost everything – fighting, feasting, drinking, weeping – except sex. Probably bisexual like many Greeks, he had at least two mistresses, three wives and two male lovers, but was always keener on war than love. He was a fighter before all else.

His ambition, his *pothos* (longing) for conquest, led to the deaths of hundreds of thousands of people. If he had lived, he was not intending to rule his empire in peace. "He would not have stopped conquering even if he had added Europe to Asia and the British Isles to Europe," wrote Arrian. "On the contrary, he would have sought unknown lands beyond them, for it was always his nature… to strive for the best."

Such Homeric striving was heroic but hardly statesmanlike. His chosen role models – Achilles the pugnacious prince, the muscle-bound demigod Hercules, Dionysus the god of wine – suggest he was starting to believe in his own myths.

In the real world, Alexander can be blamed for not leaving an heir – preferably fathered in Macedonia before he even set out for Asia. He must partly be blamed for the chaos that shattered his empire after his death, which might have come far sooner. From the Battle of Granicus to the siege of Multan, Alexander recklessly endangered his life. He was lucky to have lived so long.

Above: Alexander's most notable achievement was his overthrow of the Persian Empire, epitomized in these fallen bull-head capitals. But his visionary plan to unite the Persian and Macedonian nobility in a new ruling class died with him.

THE LEGEND OF ALEXANDER

The myth of the undefeated super-hero soon eclipsed any personal failings. His successors, mostly Macedonian generals, obviously looked back to him, repeating his gestures if not his brilliance. Ptolemy I of Egypt, for example, minted magnificent coins showing Alexander as Ammon. The Romans also became obsessed by Alexander's legend.

Julius Caesar wept when he saw a statue of Alexander and realized that, at the age the young conqueror was already dead, he had achieved nothing memorable. Pompey, Caesar's rival, also imitated Alexander both in his rather absurd bouffant hairstyle and in calling himself Magnus (the Great).

The less flamboyant first emperor Augustus, after defeating Cleopatra VII, last of Alexander's successors, laid a wreath on Alexander's tomb in Alexandria in 30BC in homage. In AD216 the manic emperor Caracalla, opening the same tomb, seized Alexander's armour, which he wore for his own projected attack on the east. (Caracalla was murdered soon after.) Centuries later the first Holy Roman Emperor Charlemagne (reigned 768–814) consciously copied Alexander. A thousand years after that, Napoleon I always travelled with a portrait of Alexander. He is still widely admired for his undoubted military genius, the greatest in antiquity.

Above: Posthumous coin struck for Alexander the Great after his death in 323BC.

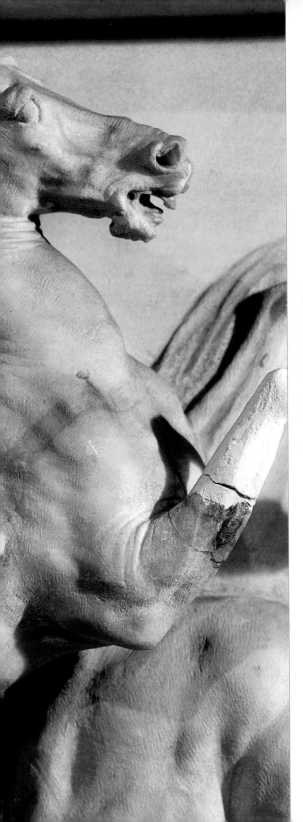

CHAPTER XI

ARMS
AND
ARMOUR

*c.*2000BC–AD138

Although the classical Greeks were often at war, and almost every citizen served at times as a soldier, they long remained mostly amateur fighters. War between each Greek *polis* (citizen-state) involved citizens directly, at least until mercenaries became common. So when citizens voted for a war, they were putting their own and their families' lives at risk. Even Sparta, that militaristic state, seldom started wars enthusiastically.

Greek warfare centred on set battles between hoplites, heavy infantrymen fighting in line. Hoplites were enrolled from citizen-farmers able to afford their own armour. Cavalry, recruited from the rich, was relatively unimportant. The many poorer citizens provided irregular troops and, in Athens, the crucial rowers for triremes, the triple-tiered galleys. (Slaves were seldom used for these, as they required feeding all year.) Hoplites and triremes proved a winning combination. They repelled the Persian invasions and the Carthaginians in the west. But they were later outclassed by the large professional armies of Macedonia and later monarchies, who deployed cavalry on a regal scale, elephants as tanks and more powerful catapults. They also built far bigger galleys. But ultimately even they could not counter the rising power of Rome.

Left: Alexander, shown on the Sidon Sarcophagus, *loved battles. He was primarily a cavalry commander.*

THE HOPLITE
THE ARCHETYPAL GREEK SOLDIER

Above: An Athenian ephebe *(young man) pouring a libation. Military training in Athens was standardized only in the mid-4th century* BC. *Earlier the Athenian army, if at times successful, was amateur compared to its fleet or to Sparta's army.*

Below: The superb discipline of Spartan hoplites repels a charge by Thessalian horsemen. Constantly drilled, Spartans for centuries made the best hoplites in Greece, distinguished by their scarlet tunics and the Lambda (L) on their shields (for Lacedaemonia, the name of the Spartan state).

Although Homer's legendary heroes had ridden out to individual combat in chariots, chariot warfare probably never developed in Bronze Age Greece because of its mountainous terrain and small plains. Even Homer's heroes in *The Iliad* had to dismount to fight on foot. But light-armed guerilla-style troops were seldom very important either.

For the central centuries of Greek history, wars were decided by heavy infantry in set battles. These gave the victor control of the fertile farmland around each *polis*, which was absolutely vital to a city's existence.

The key Greek foot soldier throughout Greek history was the hoplite (from *hoplos*, shield or armour). These heavily armoured spear men, fighting in close formation, dominated Greek warfare from *c.*700BC until Rome's final conquest of Greece in the 2nd century BC. Hoplites, emerging as the archetypal Greek soldier by *c.*700BC, were recruited from middle-class farmers who owned 2–4ha/5–10 acres of land. Typically, these made up about 35 per cent of the *polis'* population.

ARMOUR

What hoplites wore in battle became almost a uniform. However, as each man supplied his own armour, there were considerable variations, depending on the citizen's wealth. Equipment, a major expense, was handed down from father to son if in good repair. The earliest, and among the most complete, surviving suit of hoplite armour is that of the Panoply Grave at Argos in the Peloponnese from *c.*720BC. The solid bronze cuirass (body armour) has a front and back plate, with the front plate fitting over the back plate's edges. The breastplate attempts to follow the contours of the body beneath, but a lining of some sort was presumably worn. Later, reinforced linen cuirasses became common, which were cheaper and lighter than metal cuirasses. Great men such as King Philip II had iron cuirasses decorated with gold.

Greaves (leg-guards made of bronze or iron and padded with leather) protected legs up to the knees. Helmets gradually evolved into the standard 'Corinthian type', which covered all the face, leaving mere slits for the eyes and mouth. It gave excellent protection for the head but made it hard for the wearer to hear orders. A new type of helmet, the 'Chalcidian', was therefore developed, which left openings around the ears. All helmets had crests of horsehair to make hoplites look taller and more imposing.

The hoplite carried a large shield, about 1m/3ft across and weighing at least 9kg/20lb. Made of wood but edged and faced in bronze, this was held with a single handgrip. Carried on the left arm, it defended the fighter's left side well but his right not at all. This made every hoplite dependent on his right-hand companion not breaking rank in the battle line. Training was needed to keep *en taxei* (in line – modern Greek for 'okay').

his *Anabasis*. The phalanx, the standard formation for hoplites, changed only slowly over the years. In later versions, which were pioneered by Epaminondas of Thebes in the 370s BC and developed by Philip II of Macedonia (359–336BC), hoplites were massed up to 50 men deep, hugely increasing their impact in full frontal charge. The length of their spears also increased – finally up to 6m/20ft – while shields shrank to about 60cm/3ft and were slung from the neck. In the Macedonian phalanx, both hands were needed to hold a sarissa, but only the first five or six ranks' spears projected. The rest remained upright, helping to shield against arrows. When sarissas were swayed en masse, they made a threatening swooshing sound. But a deep phalanx was unwieldy on uneven battlefields This led to defeats by Rome's more versatile legions at Cynoscephalae in 197BC, Magnesia in 190BC and Pydna in 168BC – battles that marked the end of hoplite warfare.

Left: A Greek hoplite and a cowering Persian archer who has lost his bow. The Greeks' recent defeat of the Persians at Plataea had boosted their military pride, but the Persians were never negligible foes.

The result was a much more disciplined if less glamorous form of fighting than that of *The Iliad*.

WEAPONS
The hoplite's key weapon was his thrusting spear, called a sarissa, originally about 2.7m/9ft long. He also carried a sword about 60cm/2ft long as a cutting weapon for close fighting. Hoplites, massed eight and sometimes 16 men deep, relied on the initial shock of their charge to break the enemy line. If this failed, they turned to shoving and jostling, poking their spears either down at the neck of their opponents or up under their cuirasses.

LORDS OF THE BATTLEFIELD
πExperienced hoplites were seen as lords of the battlefield, and not just in Greece. The defeat of larger Persian armies – at Marathon (490BC) and Plataea (479BC) – by Greek hoplites revealed their supremacy over Persian infantry and cavalry. Greek hoplites were employed as mercenaries by the Egyptian pharaohs in the 6th century BC and by the Persian kings after 401BC, when the rebel Prince Cyrus 'marched upcountry' with the 10,000 mercenaries, as related by Xenophon in

Below: Hoplites fighting in formation, from a Corinthian vase of c.600BC. The 'hoplite revolution' had recently made these heavy infantrymen central to Greek warfare, but most armies remained glorified militias. Sparta was the outstanding exception.

CAVALRY AND IRREGULARS
HORSEMEN, SLINGERS AND ARCHERS

Aristotle thought that cavalry had once formed the Greeks' main fighting force, but he was probably mistaken. The *hippeis* (knights) retained their upper-class status in Athens, but lack of decent pasture always prevented cavalry from dominating warfare in Greece proper. Horses remained a luxurious status symbol. The Spartans, egalitarian in their militaristic way, used horses only to carry hoplites into battle. Cavalry was at times employed for scouting and to harry or pursue defeated infantry, but its total numbers remained small.

Plataea, the great land victory in 479BC over the Persians, was won despite the Greeks' lack of cavalry versus mounted Persian troops. This reinforced Greek views that cavalry hardly mattered. Even at Chaeronea in 338BC, when Philip II crushed the armies of Athens and Thebes, the main fighting was done by hoplites, despite Alexander's dashing cavalry charge. In the open spaces of Sicily, however, cavalry could prove useful: at the siege of Syracuse (415–413BC) the Athenians suffered from lack of horsemen to counter harrying Sicilian cavalry.

In Thessaly and Macedonia, lands of relatively spacious plains, cavalry always counted for far more. Significantly, these were lands where aristocracy and monarchy long survived. Alexander employed cavalry as his main aggressive arm (his 'hammer') in his Asiatic campaigns, but the infantry phalanx remained the 'anvil' needed to finish off the Persians.

LACK OF STIRRUPS
There was a technical reason why cavalry was less important in the ancient world: stirrups had not been invented. This made charging with a lance tricky, for the shock of impact threatened to unseat the rider. However, Thessalian and Macedonian horsemen used long spears, also called sarissas, with cornel-wood hearts. Such cavalry were used as his shock troops by Alexander, charging the enemy ranks directly – but Alexander's main victories were against Asian cavalry, not Greek hoplites. Highly experienced riders simply learned to grip harder with their legs to stay on. Philip II increased the number of elite Companion cavalry from only 600 at the start of his reign in 359BC to *c.*4,000 by the end, financed by his remarkable conquests.

THE COMPANION CAVALRY
Alexander's Companion cavalry was divided into eight squadrons (*ilai*) of 200 men commanded by an *ilarch*. The royal *ila* commanded by Alexander was larger at *c.*300 men. Their novel wedge-shaped formations had two advantages: they could break

Below: Alexander personally commanded his cavalry, his royal ila (squadron) of c.300 horsemen, often spearheading the attack in battle. This triumphant statue is by the 17th-century French sculptor Pierre Puget, hence the anachronistic stirrups.

through the enemy ranks and they could deploy laterally, greatly increasing their effective power.

Besides Macedonian and Thessalian horsemen, 900 light Thracian and Paeonian mounted scouts accompanied Alexander into Asia in 334BC.

CAVALRY ARMOUR

According to Xenophon, writing *c*.380BC, a cavalryman wore a cuirass with protection for the thighs, a guard for the left, unshielded, arm and a 'Boeotian' helmet giving good all-round vision. (He advocated riders slinging javelins rather than using lances.) Horses themselves were normally unarmoured. Possibly some Persian cavalry ranked as cataphracts (heavy armoured horsemen), such as the units from Bactria under Bessus at the battle of Gaugamela in 331BC, but most horsemen at this time were light cavalry.

PELTASTS, SLINGERS AND ARCHERS

At the other social extreme to the cavalry, and far more numerous, were the citizens who could not afford hoplite armour. Most served as light-armed troops called peltasts, after the pelta, the light wicker-work shield they carried. This was cut out on top to improve visibility. Their minimal armour was based on Thracian originals. In battle they fought as skirmishers, harrying the enemy with javelins before the main hoplite forces met, then falling back, sometimes sheltering behind the hoplites' shields.

Greece's mountainous terrain might have encouraged more frequent use of such mobile irregulars, but in practice they remained marginal. In 426BC the Athenian general Demosthenes saw his hoplites worsted by peltasts in remote Aetolia. He adopted their tactics to devastating effect on the island of Sphacteria in 425BC, where 292 Spartiate hoplites had to surrender to light troops. In 390BC another Athenian general, Iphicrates, defeated a regiment of 600 Spartan hoplites near Corinth by having his peltasts provoke them to break ranks and charge out. But although this won Iphicrates great acclaim, it did not seriously affect Sparta's power.

There were also slingers and archers, considered almost cowardly fighters because they did not close up with the enemy like proper hoplites. By the late 5th century BC Cretan and Scythian archers were being employed as mercenaries, using composite bows of bone, horn, wood and sinew. These had a maximum range of *c*.140m/150 yards. Slingers were also increasingly used, those from Rhodes being considered the best. Later the Balearic Islands provided many slingers. At up to 280m/300 yards, a sling's range was greater than a bow's and it could fire stone, clay or lead shot, of which the last was particularly lethal. Philip and Alexander used numerous Thracian slingers in their armies.

Above: A mounted archer riding bareback, from an Attic red-figure plate, c.520–510BC.

Below: Lighter-armed troops such as peltasts played an increasingly important part if secondary role in battles from the 4th century BC onwards.

AMATEURS AND PROFESSIONALS
TRAINING AND FORMATIONS

Only two Greek armies before the rise of Macedonia could be called professional: the Spartans and later, for a few decades in the 4th century BC, the Thebans. All the rest were citizen-militias of varying degrees of proficiency. Two years' part-time military training on the basis of the tribe was the norm in Athens, and probably elsewhere. But adult citizen-hoplites must have practised the all-important keeping *en taxei*, 'in line', perhaps in their local gymnasium. (In Switzerland, the one modern democracy remotely comparable to ancient Greece, citizen-soldiers still train every year for a few weeks.)

EPHEBES

By the 4th century BC training for young Athenian citizens had become standardized. *Ephebes* (male citizens aged 18–20) were enrolled under ten *sophronistai* (drill masters), one for each tribe. A *kosmetes*

Above: The 'Corinthian'-style hoplite helmet of the classical period gave excellent protection if limited vision.

Below: Hoplites fighting at close quarters. Each large round shield gave good protection to the man to the left but each man's right flank was left exposed. Hence the importance of drilling to keep en taxei, in line, something at which Spartans excelled.

> ### SPARTAN DISCIPLINE
> On land, Spartans were the only professionals before Philip II. Xenophon, the Athenian who settled in Lacedaemonia, gave an enthusiastic account of Spartan *askesis* (discipline). This started in infancy and continued full-time throughout a Spartan's life – something no other city could afford without enslaved *helots* to work their farms. Xenophon praised the way in which Spartan hoplites, if their ranks were broken, could swiftly reform the line, even with Spartans they did not know, and form up from a column on the march to meet sudden frontal or flank attack. Thucydides, less uncritically, admired the efficient Spartan system for passing orders down the line from commander to platoon level.

(marshal) elected by the Assembly supervised them. *Ephebes* did a year's duty in guard-houses in Piraeus and along the borders, where they learned to fire bows and javelins and use rudimentary artillery, and to fight in line. *Ephebes* of each tribe ate together in barrack messes. At the year's end they appeared before the Assembly, where they proudly displayed their new skills.

Athens could field about 30,000 hoplites in the mid-5th century BC, but these were not fully professional, as defeats from Delium in 424BC by the Thebans to Crannon in 322BC, another Macedonian victory, revealed.

NAVAL STRENGTH
Athens' navy was the city's professional force, the one such navy in classical times. Although founded only in 483BC at Themistocles' urging – its half-trained crews repulsed the Persian fleet at Salamis

in 480BC however – it soon became highly professional. By the time of the victory at Eurymedon in 467BC, Athens had gained naval supremacy across the eastern Mediterranean. Each trireme's 170 rowers, recruited from the poorer citizens of Athens and other cities, became skilled, serving under professional *trierarchs* (captains) and helmsmen.

The efficiency of Athens' trireme fleets was stunningly displayed when the *strategos* Phormion defeated a larger Peloponnesian force in 429BC in the Corinthian Gulf. The Athenians drove the enemy ships into a defensive circle with bows pointed outwards. They then rowed closer and closer around until their back-paddling enemies' oars became fatally entangled with each other. Athens' thalassocracy (sea power) was unchallenged until its catastrophic defeat in Sicily in 413BC, when it lost nearly 300 ships with their skilled crews. But triremes, cramped and unseaworthy, could not stay long at sea, and needed to be beached almost every night.

SPARTAN ARMY STRUCTURE

According to Xenophon, every unit in the Spartan army, no matter how small, had its own officer. The basic unit was the *enomotia* of 36 men, four being grouped into a *lochos* (band) of 144 men, commanded by a *lochagos*. Four *lochoi* made up a division, commanded by a *polemarch* (warlord), with six such divisions in the Spartan army proper. There were few full Spartiates by the 4th century BC, however, the core army being supplemented by Peloponnesian allies. On the march, each Spartiate was accompanied by a *helot* carrying his supplies of barley, cheese, onions and salted meat. Greeks, unlike Romans, did not regularly make their camps into one-night forts.

Right: Spartan discipline had its finest hour at Thermopylae in 480BC, when Leonidas and the 300 fought to the last against the Persian hosts, a scene that inspired the French artist Jacques-Louis David 2,400 years later.

THEBES' SACRED BAND

Although little is known of early Thebes, it is clear that it too had well-trained hoplites. At Plataea in 479BC, the Thebans (fighting on Persia's side) resisted the allied Greek army stubbornly, its elite Sacred Band dying to a man.

After Thebes' liberation from Spartan occupation in 378BC, its great general Epaminondas thoroughly reorganized the Theban army, making it into a first-class fighting machine, capitalizing on an upsurge of Theban patriotism. In particular, he increased the depth of the phalanx to 50 on the traditionally weaker left wing – a stroke of genius that defeated the Spartans at Leuctra in 371BC and in several later contests.

He also resuscitated or reorganized the Sacred Band, so that it now consisted of 150 male lovers bound to each other in love and death, making them the best soldiers in Greece. Whether he changed Thebans' actual arms and armaments, perhaps anticipating the smaller Macedonian hoplite shield slung from the neck, remains unknown.

Above: Not all military service was fighting or drilling. These two hoplites are playing keritizein, a hockey-like game, with their spears.

GREEK WARSHIPS
PENTECONTERS AND TRIREMES

Above: Quinqueremes were the largest galleys that were practical, used from the 4th century BC onwards by Macedonian and later by Roman generals until the Battle of Actium in 31BC.

All Greek warships, like those of every other Mediterranean state until AD1600, were galleys. Galleys carried sails for voyages, but the nature of naval warfare meant that warships always needed huge numbers of rowers in battle. Lacking effective artillery, fights consisted of closing with the enemy and ramming or boarding. For this, concentrated bursts of powered speed, which massed rowers alone could provide, were essential. In a trireme (the archetypal Greek galley), 170 of the 200 crew were rowers, about 15 were marines (soldiers) and the remainder sailors.

PENTECONTERS AND BIREMES
Early galleys, copying Phoenician models, were penteconters rowed by 50 men. These were the ships, described by Homer, in which Odysseus sailed – and ended up shipwrecked. Built of pinewood with spruce oars, penteconters had removable masts that slotted into the keel. They were steered by oars at the stern, rudders being unknown, with bronze-clad rams. As rowers' open benches offered no comfort and galleys carried little water, ships were beached at night and during the winter. The Phoenicians added a second row of oars over the first, creating faster biremes.

TRIREMES AND LARGER GALLEYS
In the mid-6th century BC biremes were superseded by triremes with three tiers of oars, the topmost supported on an outrigger. A standard Athenian trireme was *c*.37m/121ft long and *c*.5.5m/18ft wide at outrigger level. Oars were *c*.4.5m/15ft long and almost certainly all the same length. There were 27 rowers on each side on the lowest tier, working their oars through portholes close to the water, and 27 rowers on the middle tier. The top ranks of 31 men rowed through an outrigger. Rowers were close-packed inside the hull, the lower ones having their noses almost in the bottoms of those above and in front. (The smell was noted by Aristophanes, the comedian.) Each galley had two anchors at the bow and two steering oars at the stern.

Triremes dominated Greek naval warfare until the development of quinqueremes in the mid-4th century BC. These either had two extra tiers or two men pulling each oar.

Even larger galleys are recorded, with 10, 12 and even 40 tiers of rowers. But such vessels were increasingly unwieldy. After Rome's victory over Cleopatra and Antony's mostly quinquereme fleet at Actium in 31BC, biremes again became the norm in the Mediterrenean.

Below: Another view of triremes. In battle, a galley's sails were stowed away, as triremes fought mainly by ramming enemy ships.

BATTLE TACTICS

A vital crew member was the flautist, who piped time for the rowers. Keeping time required much practice, but a well-trained trireme crew created a formidable fighting machine. This could reach maximum speeds of 24kph/15mph over short distances, accelerating very fast (for a ship). Cruising speed was only half that, but could be maintained all day. As the galley's main weapon in the classical period was its bronze ram, a favourite Athenian tactic was to shoot alongside an enemy trireme (shipping oars on the exposed side) so that the ram on the Athenian trireme's bow broke off all the enemy's oars, crippling it. Another tactic was to pass the enemy and then execute a rapid turn, ramming the enemy in his vulnerable stern. A development, perfected by the Rhodians, the finest Greek sailors after 322BC, was to dig in the front oars so that their prow dipped and their ram hit the enemy beneath the waterline, his most vulnerable point.

All such tactics required truly professional crews. Only Athens, which had about 350 triremes in its standing fleet by 431BC, could normally maintain these. Later, when Alexander's successors built huge fleets of massive vessels, galleys became primarily floating platforms for catapults and marines.

Above: A dramatic vision of a trireme at full tilt under sail and oars. The oarsmen were tiered above each other.

THE *OLYMPIAS*

In 1987 the first trireme since antiquity was launched in Greece, the *Olympias* (named after Alexander the Great's mother), commissioned into the Greek navy. The successful construction, launch and sailing of this galley answered some of the questions that have plagued historians – for example, all oars *were* the same length. But although rowed by fit young athletes from (mostly British) universities, it has not resolved all problems. It failed to reach the speeds expected, despite heroic efforts by its oarsmen. Major communication problems were solved only by electrically piping orders to the lower tiers. (This being impossible in ancient Greece, there must have been other ways of relaying commands.) Further, the 170 modern rowers could keep time only by singing together, and this is almost certainly *not* how the Greeks kept time. The ship's trierarch

could never have given orders if everyone was singing. Also, the lower tiers of *Olympias'* rowers became so thirsty that they drank all the water on board and more had to be brought in. This suggests that, splendid though the *Olympias* is, it is not the full solution to the trireme question.

Above: The Olympias, *the only recreation of an ancient galley ever built or sailed. How accurate it is remains disputed, for it proved slow and exhaustingly heavy to row for any time.*

FORTIFICATIONS AND SIEGES
DEVELOPMENTS IN DEFENCE

The walls of Bronze Age citadels such as Mycenae and Tiryns still rise impressively over the Greek landscape. Built before 1200BC, these Cyclopean walls (so-called because later Greeks thought that giant Cyclops had built them) remained unsurpassed as defences for 700 years. This was due mainly to the genius of their original creators, and partly to the inadequacy of later Greek builders (and besiegers) before 500BC. When the Greeks started building in stone again after the Dark Ages that followed the collapse of Mycenaean civilization (*c*.1100BC), they looked back to Mycenaean models for inspiration.

EARLY CITADELS
Mycenaean builders had initially built walls with rough-cut polygonal stones, following the contours of the hills their citadels dominated. Later, cut rectangular stones were used at crucial areas, although the interior of the walls was always rubble, as it was in many later walls. The Mycenaeans, like other Bronze Age cultures, were formidable movers of megaliths. The walls of Mycenae itself are on average 5m/16ft thick, built of massive stones some weighing up to 10 tonnes/tons each. The Lion Gate at Mycenae, with its proud emblem of royal lions flanking a sacred pillar above the main gate, embodied the best defensive principles. Attackers approaching the gate would face withering fire from defenders firing through slits in the walls on both sides above.

The fortifications at nearby Tiryns are even more complex, containing galleries with vaulted roofs built into the walls. Mycenaean Athens too had walls, of which fragments remain visible. A covered path leading down the Acropolis' side to a spring helped her remain 'the unsacked city', untaken (at least in legend) by the invading Dorians.

PROJECTING TOWERS
By *c*.600BC Greeks were again building walls in cut stone, not rubble or mud-brick. However, the fortifications of Emporion on the island of Chios, which are among the earliest surviving, are inferior to Bronze Age predecessors. The big innovation over the next 200 years was the projecting tower. By the 5th century BC regularly spaced two-storey towers, placed not just at gateways but along walls, were common, allowing defenders to hail missiles down on attackers with their battering rams.

When, in the winter of 479–478BC, Athens hastily rebuilt its city walls after the Persians had evacuated the burnt-out city, these were *c*.8m/25ft high and 2.5m/8ft thick. After Athens had built the similar Long Walls connecting it to Piraeus *c*.4.8km/3 miles away, it became almost invulnerable to land attack – provided it always retained control of the sea. Athens' walls had towers punctuating them and recessed 'courtyard' gateways, which exposed attackers to flanking fire (useful but minor developments).

Above: Interior of the eastern blockhouse, whose covered passages enabled the garrison to move undetected, of the massive walls of Tiryns.

Below: The Cyclopean Walls of Tiryns, built at the Mycenaean zenith, c.1300BC, long remained the most imposing walls in Greece. Awestruck Greeks later attributed such massive works to giants (Cyclops).

Throughout the Peloponnesian War (431–404BC) the Spartans almost never attempted to attack Athens directly.

Forts, usually on frontiers, also proved hard to capture. A typical fort such as Eleutherae on the south of the pass between Cithaeron and Mount Pastra, built c.400BC to guard the road from Thebes to Athens, had walls c.1.8m/6ft thick and c.4.5m/15ft high, with projecting towers with crenellations.

LINES OF FORTIFICATION
The Spartans acted differently toward the tiny town of Plataea, however, which they began besieging in 429BC. Efforts to use primitive flame-throwers or to build siege mounds for direct attacks came to nothing because the Plataeans raised their own walls. So the Spartans resorted to circumvallation, building a double wall to starve out Plataea's inhabitants. They finally succeeded, unlike the Athenians at Syracuse who spent two fruitless years (415–413BC) trying to cut the city off. Only the Persians, who took Miletus in 494BC with massive assault mounds, could normally capture walled cities.

CATAPULT POWER
Fortifications began to change when in 399BC Dionysius I, tyrant of Syracuse, started assembling forces on an unprecedented scale to attack Carthaginian bases in Sicily. Before launching his attack, he turned Syracuse itself into the best-defended large city in the Mediterranean. He extended its walls to cover the whole plateau of Epipolae, an area of nearly 1,400ha/3,500 acres. Running along the ridges, these culminated in the major fortress of Euryalus.

Its massive catapult battery, which was redesigned by Archimedes 160 years later, was raised on five solid stone pylons 11m/36ft high and carried heavy catapults able to fire down on attackers – the higher the catapult, the greater its range. These walls for long repelled even the Romans in 212BC, who finally had to capture the city by treachery.

The development of powerful catapults in the 4th century BC made platforms for defensive firepower increasingly important. Towers became taller, pierced with loopholes for artillery. The 2nd-century BC walls of Assos, in north-western Asia Minor, have slit windows for bolt-throwing catapults halfway up and broader openings on top of their fine ashlar masonry for stone-slingers. Assos' projecting towers are rounded, making them less vulnerable both to mining and to catapult attacks.

Above: The fort of Euryalus, part of the defences with which Dionysius I made Syracuse almost impregnable to land attack, the first real advance in fortifications.

Below: The development of powerful catapults in the 4th century BC soon affected Greek defences. These rounded towers at Assos could repel enemy catapult bolts.

CATAPULTS AND SIEGE TOWERS
MASSIVE MACHINERY

Above: Demetrius I, king of Macedonia 317–288BC, gained the title Poliorcetes (besieger) for his huge siege towers that rose to seven floors. But even with such giants he proved unable to capture the city of Rhodes, abandoning his towers after a long siege in 304BC.

Below: Soldiers attacking a city. (These scenes comes from the Nereid funerary monument, hence their nakedness. Greek soldiers always wore body armour while fighting.)

Until the discovery of gunpowder in the 14th century AD, catapults were the most powerful weapons any army could field. (Catapult is in origin a Greek word meaning to hurl down.) But as ways of capturing cities they were surpassed by siege towers, which in the 4th century BC, became gigantic, fundamentally altering the relationship between attacker and defender in sieges. From then on, no city could regard itself as impregnable. Although the Assyrians had used catapults in the 7th century BC, their true pioneer was Dionysius I of Syracuse, who established war laboratories for his great attack on the Carthaginians in 397BC.

NON-TORSION CATAPULTS
Two types of catapult were used: non-torsion and torsion. The first was like a far stronger hand-held bow that needed drawing back by muscle power or ratchets. The early ones were just scaled-up crossbows called *gastraphetes* (literally 'stomach bows', as the butt of the bow rested in the stomach), with trigger mechanisms. There were obvious limits as to how far even the strongest men could draw these by muscle power. But, when set on a stand and using a winch to draw the string, huge composite bows (made of horn, wood and sinew) could be very powerful. They could fire bolts – even two simultaneously – for 182m/200 yards, out-ranging normal bows.

Such catapults, mounted on siege towers, would keep defenders cowering behind their walls, as happened at Motya in Sicily. But defenders could also install catapults on walls to shoot down besiegers, as occurred during Alexander's epic siege of Tyre in 332BC. Onomarchus of Phocis had used non-torsion catapults to repulse Philip II in 354BC, an unusual defeat that taught Philip the value of these weapons. Other Macedonian rulers and later the Romans used these giant crossbows widely, the Romans deploying them even in the field. They remained expensive weapons, however. When King Archidamus II of Sparta saw one, he was stunned, exclaiming: "By Hercules, now men's courage is a thing of the past!"

TORSION CATAPULTS
Philip's great engineer Polyeidus of Thessaly developed true torsion catapults, probably only after 340BC when Philip had signally failed to capture the cities of Byzantium and Selymbria. These catapults derived their power from twisted springs (*tonoi*) made of animal sinew, hair or similarly resilient material. Their potential was much greater and they could fire heavier bolts or stones, reputedly weighing up to 82kg/180lb, at least twice as far as non-torsion catapults.

Such weapons could be used to smash down walls and buildings and lob flaming material into cities. Alexander first used them to devastating effect when attacking Halicarnassus in 334BC, and again at Tyre

and at Gaza two years later. But the fall of Tyre, which had long thought itself impregnable behind tall walls and on an offshore island, was due mainly to Alexander's siege towers.

SIEGE TOWERS

Again, Dionysius of Syracuse – whose military resources far outstripped those of any normal Greek *polis* – was the first to deploy great siege towers during his siege of Motya. These were six storeys high and could be moved on wheels. They bristled with catapults and archers on their upper floors, whose fire drove the defenders off their battlements, and with battering rams on their lower floors that smashed down the city's walls.

Alexander built even larger siege towers to capture Tyre in 332BC, reputedly *c.*37m/120ft high, so topping Tyre's walls. They were hung with sheep-skins to ward off enemy missiles, with drawbridges falling from each storey to let men pour out of their many floors, battering rams swinging out at various levels and a borer on a long iron-tipped pole at their base to poke into walls. Such a tower was called, very aptly, a *helepolis* (city-destroyer).

After Alexander's death, his successors ostentatiously tried to exceed him in siege towers as in other things. Demetrius I, king of Macedon, one of Alexander's most flamboyant successors, was among the great innovatory besiegers of history, nicknamed Poliorcetes (The Besieger).

In his (finally unsuccessful) attack on the city of Rhodes in 304BC he used a *helepolis* designed by Epimachus, an Athenian. This was reputed to be *c.*45m/150ft high with a 21m/70ft square base. Its surface was covered with iron plates to protect it from missiles. Inside it had nine storeys and twin staircases, and was crammed with catapults. Its wheels were pivoted, meaning it could move sideways as well as backwards and forwards, and it was apparently propelled by 3,400 men.

Despite such massive dimensions, Demetrius' *helepolis* failed to capture Rhodes, partly because the Rhodians diverted their sewage outlets to it, causing it to sink into the mire. Demetrius abandoned both the siege and his mega-machine. By selling off its remains, the Rhodians managed to build their great statue of Helios, the sun god. Later machines were less massive and unwieldy.

Above: In siege warfare as in other matters the Romans were the direct heirs of the Hellenistic kings, using machines such as this catapult to throw large stones impressive distances.

Below: Mobile siege towers, enabling attackers to top walls, were revived in the Middle Ages in forms that often mirror those of the ancient world. This comes from De Machinis Bellicis (About War Machines) published in 1449.

GREEK WONDER WEAPONS
ELEPHANTS AND ARCHIMEDES

Above: Archimedes' most practical invention was his screw. The Archimedes' screw proved invaluable in irrigation, as this sculpture showing a North African worker using the screw to irrigate his vineyard demonstrates.

Besides conventional or obvious weapons, the Greeks and Macedonians at times resorted to more remarkable, though usually less effective, ways of making war. One was the elephant, a naturally unwarlike giant since dubbed the 'tank of antiquity', although it was much less reliable than most tanks. At the other extreme were the high-tech weapons that Archimedes, one of the greatest Greek scientists, invented for the defence of Syracuse in 212BC. Neither in the end proved very effective.

THE DEPLOYMENT OF ELEPHANTS

Elephants were unknown to the Greeks and Macedonians until Darius III, desperately mobilizing the Persian Empire's resources to repel Alexander, deployed 15 Indian elephants in the centre of the Persian line at Gaugamela in 331BC. The aim was to stampede the Macedonian cavalry (and to alarm the Macedonian infantry), because horses not used to elephants panic at their smell. Alexander, however, avoided them by

his oblique attack. The next time he encountered elephants was more serious. At the battle of the River Hydaspes in 326BC Porus, rajah of Pauravas, had 85 elephants lined up in front of his army, but Alexander's infantry opened their ranks to let them pass harmlessly by. Yet Alexander was impressed enough to form an elephant corps of his own. He sent it back by an easy route to Persia to form part of his increasingly grand and oriental court.

Within a few years of Alexander's death, Indian elephants had become a must-have weapon for any Macedonian dynast. They now had turreted howdahs carrrying archers and often carried bells and armour. In 305BC Seleucus I ceded his Indian provinces to the emperor Chandragupta Maurya in return for (reputedly) 500 elephants. With this huge elephant corps he crushed his chief rival Antigonus I at the Battle of Ipsus in 301BC, confirming both his dynasty's future and, it appeared, the importance of elephants.

The Seleucids established a stud farm for their Indian elephants outside their capital, Antioch in Syria. The Ptolemy rulers of Egypt, their great rivals, countered by capturing and training north African 'forest elephants'. These were relatives of the African elephant proper that have since become extinct. Comparatively small, they were ridden astride like a horse, and were not thought as effective as Indian elephants. (These were the elephants that Hannibal later led over the Alps.)

Left: Archimedes reportedly designed huge mirrors to focus the sun's rays on Roman ships besieging Syracuse in 212BC. Attempts to replicate this secret weapon have had no success, but he certainly designed remarkable cranes and catapults in the defence of his city.

ARCHIMEDES' INVENTIONS

Syracuse, the greatest Greek city in the west, had allied itself with Rome under Hieron II of Syracuse (ruled 265–215BC) and prospered greatly. But his successors unwisely repudiated the alliance after Hannibal's third annihilatory victory at Cannae. The Romans, alarmed, sent an army under Marcellus to capture the city.

Syracuse's formidable walls were backed up by other, more remarkable wonder weapons devised by its most illustrious resident: the mathematician and scientist Archimedes (287–212BC). When Roman quinqueremes tried to attack Syracuse on its seaward side by acting as floating siege towers, some being lashed together, a hail of missiles from catapults firing through slits forced them to retreat. Later, a Roman night attack was countered by giant cranes concealed behind the walls swinging out to drop huge stones on the Roman galleys or to grab them by their prows and so sink them. Marcellus finally had to capture the city by stealth, which was not the preferred Roman way.

Above: A Roman soldier, discovering but not recognizing Archimedes at work during the fall of Syracuse, killed him – against the orders of Marcellus, the Roman commander. Archimedes' innovatory strengthening of Syracuse's defences had made the city almost impregnable.

A DOUBLE-EDGED WEAPON

Elephants were a double-edged weapon. If terrifying charging en masse, they were prone to run amok and do as much damage to their own side as the enemy in battle. Further, ways were soon found to counter them. At the siege of Mantinea in 312BC spikes concealed under the earth by the city's defenders penetrated the beasts' soft feet to devastating effect. In reality, elephants were more prestigious than effective. In the last great battle when they were used, when the Seleucid army faced the Romans at Magnesia in 190BC, they hurt the Romans less than the Macedonians. Soon after, the Romans hamstrung the Seleucid elephants in their stud farm, ending the Seleucids' supply.

Right: After Seleucus I acquired 500 elephants in return for ceding his Indian lands, elephants became seen as super-weapons. In fact, although en masse they were formidable, they were hard to control in battle and could easily turn against friendly troops.

CHAPTER XII

FROM ALEXANDER TO HADRIAN

323BC–AD138

Alexander's sudden death without a proper heir plunged his empire into chaos. It also ended his dream of Perso-Macedonian unity. The large kingdoms that emerged from the Wars of the Diadochi (successors) are called Hellenistic, because they were essentially Hellenic (Greek) in culture and politics. But their rulers were Macedonians. Although few of these kingdoms lasted very long, Greek culture was everywhere triumphant, reaching even into India. Luxury and magnificence, epitomized by the huge statue of the Colossus of Rhodes, marked the age. Trade boomed across this wide new world, while women enjoyed greater freedom. In the end, most of it fell to the relentlessly expanding power of Rome.

One woman embodies the age and its passing: Cleopatra VII, last Hellenistic queen of Egypt. With her death in 30BC the Romans controlled the Greek world, which they had half-wrecked with their wars. The *pax Romana*, the long Roman peace that followed, allowed Greek cities to recover, while the Romans adopted and spread Greek culture. This process reached its climax under the philhellenic Hadrian (AD117–138).

Left: The Colossus of Rhodes, *a huge statue of the sun god which collapsed, painted by Louis de Caulery c.1580-1622.*

THE WARS OF THE SUCCESSORS 323–275BC

Above: Coin showing Ptolemy I, one of Alexander's generals and the first Ptolemaic king of Egypt (322–283BC). He was the ancestor of Cleopatra VII, the last and most famous Ptolemaic queen.

Below: Seleucus I, founder of the Seleucid Empire that at times stretched from the Aegean to the Hindu Kush. Seleucus had an Iranian wife, so all later Seleucid kings had some Persian genes.

Asked on his deathbed in June 323BC who should be his heir, Alexander reputedly said: "the strongest". This proved prophetic, for he had scarcely stopped breathing before his generals began fighting to control the empire. There were, however, two possible heirs of Macedonian royal blood, to whom the army turned: Alexander's idiot half-brother Arrhidaeus (who became Philip III on succeeding to the throne) and Roxane's son, Alexander IV, born in September. If Hephaistion, Grand Vizier and Alexander's oldest friend, had lived, the latter especially might have survived. As it was, the two simply became pawns of the warring generals (the Diadochi).

At first all the contestants paid lip service to the concept of an empire united under the joint kings, who reigned over rather than ruled the empire. Three men initially appeared to dominate the scene: Perdiccas, Alexander's second-in-command; Antipater, the old general left as viceroy of Macedonia, and Craterus, commanding the discharged Macedonian veterans. Perdiccas, acting as regent in Babylon, read out what he claimed was Alexander's will to the army.

This included megalomaniac plans for war against Carthage, gigantic temples and massive transfers of population between Europe and Asia. Proving as unacceptable as intended, it was unanimously rejected.

Ptolemy, one of Alexander's boyhood friends, was made governor of Egypt, to which he added Cyrene (east Libya). Antipater, crushing the Greek states in the Lamian War in 322BC, became guardian of the young kings, establishing a Macedonian power base that he left to his son Cassander on his death. In central Asia a revolt by unhappy colonists who wanted to return home was quelled. Antigonus I, governor of Phrygia (central Asia Minor), now began extending his power south. By 316BC he had emerged as the strongest single ruler with the aid of his son Demetrius. But endless wars prevented him gaining more than western Asia, despite brilliant sieges by Demetrius, who built giant siege towers to attack Cyprus and Rhodes. Meanwhile Lysimachus carved out a kingdom in Thrace and northern Asia Minor.

THE RISE OF SELEUCUS

In 312BC Seleucus, once Alexander's infantry commander, became governor of Babylon and all lands eastward. After one of the joint kings, Alexander IV, the last of Alexander's family, was murdered by Cassander in 311BC, Antigonus took the title of king, later followed by Ptolemy and Seleucus.

In 303BC Seleucus ceded his Indian provinces to King Chandragupta Maurya in return for 500 war elephants, a huge force. Allied with Lysimachus, he used this to defeat and kill Antigonus at the Battle of Ipsus in 301BC (there were 75,000 troops on either side), gaining the title Nicator (victor). In all these conflicts, Macedonian soldiers remained remarkably loyal to their generals, while native populations suffered in silence the passage of the warlords with their armies. Whether their rulers were Macedonian or Persian hardly worried them.

By eliminating the only potential reunifier of Alexander's empire, the Battle of Ipsus led to the emergence of four distinct kingdoms: Ptolemy I firmly controlling Egypt and southern Syria;

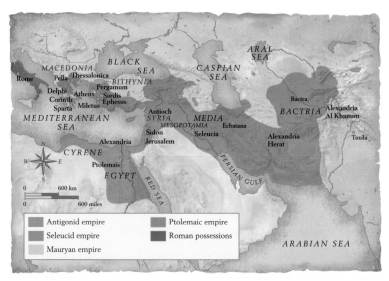

Antigonid empire
Seleucid empire
Mauryan empire
Ptolemaic empire
Roman possessions

Left: Alexander's successors divided up his huge empire into constantly warring kingdoms of markedly unequal size.

Below: The winged Nike (victory) of Samothrace, one of the finest Hellenistic statues, was probably commissioned to celebrate a victory by Antigonus II, king of Macedonia, in c.250BC.

Cassander shakily ruling Macedonia and parts of Greece; Lysimachus expanding his power in Thrace and Asia Minor; and Seleucus with a huge empire stretching from the Aegean to central Asia. Lysimachus' expansionism led to the next war. When in 281BC Lysimachus was defeated and killed by Seleucus, his kingdom collapsed completely. In contrast, after Seleucus' own murder in 280BC, his son Antiochus I succeeded him smoothly, ruling from the new capital of Antioch in north Syria.

Meanwhile the *poleis* (citizen-states) of Greece itself, dominated by Macedonia, periodically regained or lost their freedom. Macedonia installed garrisons at the four 'chains of Greece': Corinth, Piraeus, Chalcis in Euboea and Demetrias in Thessaly. Macedonia normally favoured oligarchies, but the distinction between democracy and oligarchy was growing blurred. All the old citizen-states were hugely outgunned by the new kingdoms.

ARRIVAL OF THE GAULS

No one was prepared for the impact of the Gauls, however. These wild Celtic invaders burst into Greece *c.*280BC, even threatening Delphi, the holiest

shrine in Greece. Antigonus II, king of Macedonia and grandson of both Antipater and Antigonus I, triumphantly repelled them in 278BC, consolidating his position and earning some Greek gratitude.

The Gauls, crossing into Asia, were defeated by the Seleucid Antiochus I in 275BC. They were permitted to settle in central Asia Minor in the land called subsequently Galatia after them.

THE BALANCE OF POWER

These battles confirmed the new balance of power. Much the richest and most stable kingdom was that of the Ptolemies, based in Egypt but extending its power into Syria and the Aegean islands. If much the smallest kingdom, Macedonia, had excellent soldiers and the prestige of the old Macedonian crown, while the huge realm of the Seleucids at times tempted its monarchs with the (unrealizable) prospect of recreating Alexander's whole empire.

War, however, was the norm between the kingdoms and frontiers remained very fluid.

THE GREEK PHARAOHS
PTOLEMAIC EGYPT, 322–200BC

Ptolemy had noticed the potential of Egypt when Alexander annexed it in 332BC. The richest satrapy in Persia's empire after Babylonia, Egypt was unusual in being a distinct nation, defensible behind its deserts. When Ptolemy obtained its governorship in 322BC, he covertly began creating a separate state, annexing Cyrene. Kidnapping Alexander's embalmed corpse when it was en route to Macedonia, Ptolemy finally installed it at the new capital Alexandria in a grand mausoleum that also held the Ptolemies' tombs. He defeated and killed Perdiccas, who had attacked him for this act. (Perdiccas' men were reputedly devoured by Nile crocodiles after the battle.)

Ptolemy founded only one new city, Ptolemais, in the south, for the bulk of the population remained Egyptian *fellahin* (peasants). To them, the Ptolemies were pharaohs, god-kings, hailed by the priesthood, who initially welcomed them after Persian misrule. The Ptolemies tried to

Above: Alexandria's most famous symbol was its pharos (lighthouse), the light of which could be seen 50km/32 miles off, as depicted on a 2nd century AD Roman coin.

Below: The tombs of Anfouchy of the 3rd century BC are among the few structures of the Ptolemaic era to survive. (Most are under water or have been destroyed.) The tombs reveal mixed Greek and Egyptian influence in the burial of the dead.

THE PTOLEMAIA
In the winter of 275–274BC a huge festival, the Ptolemaia, was staged in Alexandria to celebrate both the dynasty and its patron deity Dionysus, god of wine and theatre. Great floats processed along the Canopic Way. They carried wild animals, including a white bear; a huge winepress worked by men dressed as satyrs dispensing 114,000 litres/25,000 gallons of wine; women dressed as maenads, the god's ecstatic followers; a pole 55m/180ft high representing a gigantic phallus; models of the morning and evening star; and, in the rear, 57,000 marching soldiers.

impress their subjects by restoring temples damaged by the Persians and building new ones in the time-hallowed style, such as that at Edfu begun in 237BC. But no Ptolemy before Cleopatra VII (51–30BC) ever learned Egyptian. They relied instead on Greek or Macedonian administrators and *cleruchs* (Macedonian military colonists who received grants of land). When Ptolemy I died – in bed, unlike most Successors – in 283BC, he was succeeded by his son Ptolemy II (283–246BC). This cultured monarch married his sister Arsinoe, reviving the old Egyptian custom. More dynamic than her husband, Arsinoe effectively ruled Egypt until her death in 270BC.

GOLDEN AGE
The 3rd century BC was the Ptolemies' Golden Age. Ptolemy II's chief minister Apollonius perfected the fullest state bureaucracy yet seen, regulating every aspect of life. The marsh of the Fayum was reclaimed and Greek officials introduced new crops, including vines and olives. But Egypt's staple product

Above: Egypt, unlike most Persian satrapies, had had a strong national identity since the time when the first pyramids were built.

powerhouse); a great temple to Sarapis; and an artificial hill dedicated to the god Pan. In the east royal palaces were grouped round parks, with fleets of luxurious royal pleasure barges. Beyond them stood the Hippodrome for chariot races and the Gymnasium, an important institution in Hellenistic life where men met to socialize as much as to exercise.

Alexandria was never regarded as part of Egypt proper. While it had a council of some sort, it was never a *polis* in the full Greek sense either. But Greek was the official language spoken by everyone of importance, although many races at first rubbed shoulders amiably enough.

The splendour of Alexandria depended finally on the overworked *fellahin*, for long ignored except as serfs. But in 217BC Antiochus III invaded from Syria. To repel him, Ptolemy IV conscripted Egyptian peasants en masse into the army. The resulting Egyptian victory at Raphia repelled the Seleucids for a time but revealed the growing weakness of the dynasty. Riots, strikes and rebellions began to appear in the 2nd century BC, as an increasingly corrupt bureaucracy oppressed ordinary Egyptians.

Above: Alexandria, the great port, was Ptolemy's chosen capital, replacing inland cities such as Memphis.

Below: The pylon (gateway) of the Temple of Horus at Edfu. Begun in 237BC, it exactly replicates the styles of earlier temples, for the Ptolemies posed as pharaohs to their Egyptian subjects.

remained grain, grown by serfs tied to the land who owned nothing, not even their seed corn. All products were either heavily taxed or royal monopolies like papyrus, the precursor of paper. The resulting wealth flowed down the Nile into the royal treasury, enabling the Ptolemies to maintain huge fleets and armies. Crete, Cyprus, Samos, Cilicia and southern Syria became part of their empire, although the last was disputed by the Seleucid kings in the Syrian Wars.

ALEXANDRIA THE COSMOPOLIS

The fruits of this systematic tax-gathering were enjoyed in Alexandria, the world's first cosmopolis, welcoming Greek and other immigrants, including many Jews. With its double harbour and *pharos* – the lighthouse rising 90m/300ft, with colossal statues of a Ptolemy and his queen as pharaohs at its base – the city became the greatest in the Mediterranean. Its population probably passed 500,000 by 200BC. Its trade eclipsed that of Athens or Carthage, reaching down the Red Sea to India by 116BC. The Canopic Way, an avenue 45m/150ft wide lined with colonnades, ran west from the Gate of the Sun through the city, intersecting with similarly grand boulevards. In the west stood the Library-cum-Museum (the world's largest such building, with 500,000 scrolls, which became Hellenism's intellectual

Above: A coin of Antiochus III the Great (reigned 223–187BC), who restored Seleucid power across Asia. He took southern Syria from Egypt before finally being defeated by Rome.

Below: Perge was one of the many Greek cities in Asia Minor that frequently accepted Seleucid suzerainty while keeping its internal autonomy.

SARDIS TO SAMARKAND
THE SELEUCID EMPIRE, 312–200BC

More than any other successors, the Seleucids earned the right to call themselves Alexander's heirs, since they were the greatest disseminators of Greek civilization. At its peak in 280BC their empire stretched from the Aegean, where Sardis was the regional capital, to Samarcand in central Asia, an area of 3,885,000 sq km/1,500,000 square miles. It had a population of *c.*30 million – five times more than Egypt's.

To control this huge realm, Seleucus I and his son Antiochus I (281–261BC) continued Alexander's policy of founding cities at strategic points on a grand scale. (Seleucus alone reputedly founded 50). These were settled mostly with retired Macedonian troops who often married local women, their descendants later becoming full citizens. From them the Seleucids could recruit fresh generations of troops.

SELEUCIA DISPLACES BABYLON
Most new cities were called Antioch, Seleucia, Laodicea (after Seleucus I's mother) or Apamea (after Apama, his Persian wife and mother of Antiochus I). Alone of Alexander's successors, Seleucus did not repudiate his Persian wife and employed some Iranians, although the culture and politics of his new empire were Hellenistic. Seleucus I, by 312BC ruling Babylonia and eastern satrapies, founded Seleucia-on-the-Tigris on the site of Opis (now Baghdad), where a canal linked the two rivers and Alexander had once prayed for Perso-Macedonian harmony. It rapidly grew to displace Babylon as the commercial metropolis of western Asia, and Babylon fell into decay.

Seleucia's population – 600,000 in the 1st century BC, according to the geographer Strabo – remained proudly Greek, with a council, elected officials and assembly. It included people of Babylonian ancestry among its citizens.

Nearly every Seleucid foundation resembled a Greek *polis*, at least internally. Like the Romans later, the Seleucids saw their empire as a confederation of cities, to which they granted autonomy and land, sometimes with seed corn and equipment. In return, the cities were generally loyal to the dynasty, often hailing its kings as gods.

ANTIOCH THE CAPITAL
The main Seleucid capital was Antioch-on-the-Orontes in northern Syria, only 24km/15 miles from the Mediterranean, which was important to the sea-loving Greeks. Founded in 300BC, Antioch soon rivalled Alexandria in splendour and sophistication. It became the terminus for caravan routes across Asia, taxes on trade being vital to Seleucid revenues. Antioch was peopled initially with Macedonian and Athenian colonists, but many Jews

settled there later. Near Antioch the Seleucids established a stud farm to breed their renowned Indian war elephants, a pillar of their power. (Another pillar was the standing army, c.70,000 strong, the biggest yet seen.) The kings founded so many cities in northern Syria along the fertile Orontes valley that it resembled a second Macedonia. It was one of the few parts of Asia to be so fully Hellenized, though Phoenicia and parts of Mesopotamia were also lightly settled with Greek cities.

THE LOSS OF THE EAST

Further east, Greek cities were mere outposts of Hellenism amid an unchanged rural population. Few Iranian nobles adopted Greek customs. Generally, Graeco-Macedonian settlers' ingrained contempt for 'barbarians' doomed Seleucid attempts at mass Hellenization.

The Seleucid Empire from the start contained several types of state. Most manageable were city-states the kings themselves had founded – or, in the Aegean and Phoenicia, conquered – whose autonomy they normally respected. Far older were priestly temple-states, whose power and prestige the kings tried to curb while respecting their religious role and immunity from taxation. In Babylonia, the most civilized and richest part of their empire, the Seleucids attempted with some success to win the support of priests and merchants.

However, on the Iranian plateau, heartland of the Achaemenid Empire, they had less impact. The Seleucids had to rely on powerful satraps, or governors, who in turn depended partly on still feudal Persian nobles, who ruled their estates from their castles. The huge distances from the Seleucid heartland of Syria-Babylonia usually prevented effective royal control.

Around 255BC Diodotus, governor of Bactria, revolted against Antiochus II (ruled 261–246BC) and the huge province was lost to the empire, permanently as it turned out. But at least Diodotus was

Right: A bust of an unknown philosopher, one of the many Greeks attracted to the new cities that the Seleucids founded across their huge empire, which had all the trappings of a polis: agora, gymnasium, stoa, theatre.

Macedonian. In 247BC, Arsaces, king of the Parthians, an Iranian people, broke away from Diodotus, and his successors began expanding his kingdom in central Iran. In the 2nd century BC the Parthians over-ran ever more Seleucid territories, finally capturing Babylonia by 130BC.

To restore Seleucid power, Antiochus III made a grand military expedition through the east in 212–206BC. He forced rebel governors to recognize his suzerainty but accepted Bactria's independence, despite defeating it. He began calling himself Great King, like the Persians, but such triumphalism proved premature. Soon after he returned, the remoter satraps reasserted their independence. No later Seleucid ventured so far east. Seleucid power would soon face a new enemy: Rome.

Below: Ephesus, as the Aegean terminus of the transasiatic trade routes, flourished anew under the Seleucids, whose westernmost capital it sometimes was. These houses date from c.300BC.

MACEDONIA AND PERGAMUM
HELLENISTIC POWERS

Above: The fortifications of Acrocorinth high above the port, one of the 'chains of Greece' or garrisoned citadels with which the Macedonian kings controlled Greece.

Below: The dramatically sited theatre at Pergamum (Asia Minor) proclaimed the power and wealth of the Attalid dynasty, at its peak in the 2nd century BC.

0From Macedonia, a country large only by the standards of classical Greece, came the armies that had conquered half of Asia and most of the colonists needed to establish the new Hellenistic cities. But even this combined effort did not exhaust the kingdom. It remained one of the key players in the eastern Mediterranean until Rome finally ended its existence in 168BC. Its army and navy, if relatively small, were very fine, while its much-contested control of Greece gave it both prestige and power. Macedonia itself became increasingly wealthy and fully Hellenized in the 3rd century BC. The *koine*, the common Greek dialect based on Attic (Athenian), replaced the old Macedonian dialect, as it did across the Hellenistic world.

Cassander, son of Alexander the Great's old regent Antipater, killed the boy-king Alexander IV, last of the old royal house, in 311BC. He founded the great city of Thessalonica and ruled Macedonia until his death in 297BC. Demetrius I 'the Besieger' then briefly regained control of Macedonia and Greece, but lost both when Pyrrhus of Epirus invaded from the west and Lysimachus attacked from the east. For a moment Macedonia's very existence seemed threatened until Demetrius' son – and Antipater's grandson, for the successors intermarried – Antigonus II (284–239BC) won the throne.

ANTIGONUS AND HIS SUCCESSORS
Beating the invading Gauls decisively at Lysimachia in 278BC, Antigonus reasserted Macedonia's role as a major power and ensured the future of his dynasty. He defeated the Spartans and Athenians in the Chremonidean War (267–262BC), reasserting Macedonian hegemony over Greece through the four strategic forts called the 'chains'. But he treated the Athenians tactfully. In alliance with the Seleucids, he also repulsed the Egyptian navy off Cos and Andros, checking Ptolemaic expansion in the Aegean. Antigonus encouraged Macedonia's agriculture and trade, drawing most of his revenue from his own estates without taxing his people heavily, despite extensive use of mercenaries. Private houses excavated at Pella and Thessalonica reveal Macedonian wealth and sophistication at this time.

Antigonus' successor, his son Demetrius II, was killed in 229BC fighting northern barbarians – Macedonia long acted as a breakwater against such invaders. He was succeeded in turn by his son Philip V in 221BC after a regency. Philip was handsome, energetic and ambitious. Hailed as a saviour of Greece at the Conference of Naupactus in 217BC, which attempted to find a lasting peace,

two years later he fatally allied himself with Carthage against Rome. Hannibal, its great general, appeared to be winning the Second Punic War (218–202BC). This led to the First Macedonian War. A Roman force landed in north-west Greece, did some desultory fighting and made an alliance with the Aetolian League in central Greece. Peace was made on a return to the *status quo ante* in 205BC, but Rome's suspicious attention had now been turned on Macedonia.

THE RISE OF PERGAMUM

Pergamum, a previously obscure hill town in north-west Asia Minor commanding the fertile Caicus valley, became one of the great Hellenistic powers under its Attalid rulers. Its rise began in 263BC when its governor, Eumenes I, broke away. Although the Seleucids forced him to disgorge most territorial gains, he remained independent. After his successor Attalus I (241–197BC) won a dramatic victory over the Gauls, he assumed a crown and the title *Soter* (saviour) of Hellenism.

Attalus began looking west, cultivating Rome's friendship by reporting the (allegedly) dangerous ambitions of Philip V of Macedonia and the Seleucids. His son Eumenes II (197–160BC) continued this pro-Roman policy. Crucially, Eumenes supported the Romans at the Battle of Magnesia in 190BC.

Gaining a huge slice of territory in Asia Minor in return for this help, Eumenes II made Pergamum one of the architectural and artistic marvels of the Hellenistic world. Its temples and theatres rose dramatically up its hillside, while its library rivalled Alexandria's. The melodramatic splendour of the Pergamum Altar epitomizes the kingdom's flamboyant wealth. To challenge Egypt's monopoly of papyrus, parchment was reputedly invented at Pergamum, from which comes its name. Royal herds of cattle and flocks of sheep produced the hides needed for this tough, enduring writing material. In its autocratic bureaucracy, Pergamum resembled Egypt more closely

than the Seleucid realm, with many peasants working for the crown as serfs. Although the kings treated the old Ionian cities that came under their control after 189BC with diplomatic restraint, most Greeks could never forget that Attalid wealth and power stemmed from craven collaboration with Rome.

Above: The Pergamum Altar, *one of the grandest and most flamboyant in the Greek world, expresses the wealth of the Attalid kingdom of Pergamum at its 2nd-century peak. It is now in Berlin.*

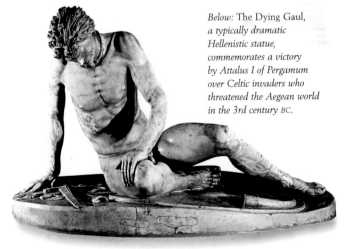

Below: The Dying Gaul, *a typically dramatic Hellenistic statue, commemorates a victory by Attalus I of Pergamum over Celtic invaders who threatened the Aegean world in the 3rd century* BC.

THE GREEKS IN THE EAST
BACTRIA AND INDIA, 350–320 BC

Above: Antimachus I, Hellenistic king of Bactria (Afghanistan), conquered north-western India in c.180BC, minting fine coins such as this.

Below: Eucratides I, king of Bactria c.170–155BC, ruled a huge Indo-Greek kingdom stretching from Merv in Central Asia to Taxila in northern India.

Alexander had founded cities in Bactria (Afghanistan), Sogdiana (Tadzhikstan) and in north-western India (Pakistan) primarily for military purposes. Their often unwillingly retired soldiers would, he intended, safeguard strategically important routes and provide fresh recruits in their sons, whose mothers would be local women. Or at least that was the idea. But 20,000 settlers revolted even before Alexander's death, returning to their colonies only under compulsion from Macedonian generals

The Seleucids continued Alexander's colonization policy but on a wider, and generally much sounder, basis. They re-established some cities and founded many further ones (often named Antioch) but made each a proper Greek *polis* with a proper council, assembly, theatre and gymnasium.

ARTISTIC FUSION

Whether or not Menander converted to Buddhism, the fusion of Greek aesthetic form with Buddhist religious ideas proved hugely influential. Chinese and even Japanese art echoes Hellenic forms, while the huge Buddhas of Bamiyan, dating from c.AD500, showed traces of Greek art. The intellectual impact proved long-lasting, too. The *Gorgi Samhita*, an astronomical work of AD230, states: "Although the Yavanas (Ionians, i.e. Greeks) are barbarians, the science of astronomy originated with them, for which they should be revered like gods."

THE RUINS OF AI KHANUM

These cities retained their Hellenic identity for a remarkably long time, as the ruins of Ai Khanum show. Originally Alexandria-on-the-Oxus in Bactria, perhaps refounded by Seleucus I, it is sited in what was then a fertile area. The ruins include a huge gymnasium, a big terraced theatre near the river, large private houses and a palace with ornate Corinthian columns around a grand courtyard. Around 300BC Clearchus, a pupil of Aristotle, brought from distant Delphi the traditional maxims for the Five Ages of Man (as the Greeks numbered them) to be inscribed in this gymnasium. A papyrus with scraps of Aristotle's philosophy has been unearthed nearby, suggesting that Greek citizens of this central Asian *polis* discussed philosophy after exercising in the gymnasium. The city reached its peak c.200BC.

THE GRAECO-BACTRIAN STATE

In 255BC Diodotus I, the Seleucid governor of Bactria, declared himself independent – perhaps despairing of

Above: Elephants, the 'tanks of ancient warfare', came mostly from India, where Alexander had encountered them in numbers at the Battle of the Hydaspes.

effective help from the Seleucids against nomadic invaders – and founded the Graeco-Bactrian state. His son Diodotus II (248–235BC) took a royal title and negotiated with the Parthians, now also independent, before being overthrown by Euthydemus I (235–200BC). An energetic king, Euthydemus retook Herat from the Parthians in the west, while in the northeast he penetrated into Sinkiang, now in China. Antiochus III defeated him but had to accept him as a subordinate ruler in 210BC. Most of what we know of these monarchs comes from their fine coinage, for there are few written records.

THE INDO-GREEKS

Seleucus I had ceded his eastern provinces to the first Maurya ruler Chandragupta in return for (reputedly) 500 elephants in 303BC. He acknowledged the rise of this new power in India by marrying one of his family to a Maurya. Although this had little political effect, it helped with Greek cultural diffusion, to which India proved very receptive. Chandragupta's grandson Asoka, possibly part-Greek by birth, became the first Buddhist emperor (274–232BC). He had

Buddhist decrees inscribed in Greek on pillars in Kandahar, showing the importance he attached both to his new pacifist religion and to his Greek-speaking subjects. He also employed Greek craftsmen.

DEMETRIUS AND HIS HEIRS

In the early 2nd century BC, with Maurya power declining, the Graeco-Bactrian monarchs began to regain lost territory and move east. Euthydemus' son Demetrius I (200–185BC) retook some Mauryan lands, founding a colony, Demetrias, near Ghazni. His kingdom was divided between three heirs. One, Antimachus I, controlled all of what is now northern Pakistan, minting resplendent coins. His successors ruled from Taxila, minting bilingual coins in Greek and Brahmi, the script of the Ganges valley. Another Indo-Greek monarch Demetrius Aniketos (Unconquered) issued coins in Greek and Prakrit. Increasingly, these coins began to bear Indian emblems, such as Lashkmi, the Hindu goddess, or a sacred tree, among Buddhism's holiest symbols. Some were even square, the preferred shape in Indian bazaars. In India the Greeks proved receptive to local culture, dropping their usual chauvinism.

Eucratides I (*c*.170–155BC), who took the Indian title Maharajasa (great king), ruled a united Indo-Greek kingdom from Merv in central Asia to Taxila. His successor, Menander (155–130BC), extended his power far east down the Ganges valley, his troops reaching Patna. His gold and silver coins have been found over a huge area, although he did not rule it all. He may, however, have converted to Buddhism, for he figures in Buddhist legends as Milinda the Just. Menander was succeeded by further Indo-Greek rulers, among them Queen Agathocleia, who ruled in her own right. But in the 1st century BC Scythian tribes, the Kushans, invaded Bactria and then north-western India, overthrowing the last Indo-Greek kingdom by 30BC.

Below: While all the Indo-Greek kingdoms had vanished by 30BC, Greek artistic influence persisted for centuries. It shaped depictions of the Buddha, as this Bodhisattva of Gandhara of the 4th century AD reveals.

OLD GREECE: THE AETOLIAN AND ACHAEAN LEAGUES, 320–180BC

Although Macedonian kings dominated old Greece after 322BC, garrisoning key points, Greek political – and economic and social – life was not dead. However, many smaller cities, while still cherishing their beloved autonomy, realized that they now had to band together in leagues to survive. In doing so, they showed continued Greek ingenuity and innovation until the steamroller of Roman conquest squashed all independence.

THE AETOLIAN LEAGUE
Isocrates, the 4th-century BC propagandist, had long called for Panhellenic union against 'barbarians'. Around 367BC, in the mountainous backwoods of Aetolia, many villages or cantons actually formed such a defensive league. This developed a remarkably flexible and inventive constitution, with a president and commander-in-chief annually elected who could not be re-elected on successive years. Other officials included a cavalry leader, secretary and seven financial stewards.

Above: Ruins of the Tholos, Sanctuary, Athena Pronala, Delphi, control of which site signified control of old Greece.

The League Assembly held two regular meetings a year, before and after the campaigning season, at the hilltop temple of Apollo at Thermum. Every adult male citizen had a vote and there was a federal *boule* (council) with 1,000 delegates. Each state was represented according to its population while retaining internal autonomy. Much business was later delegated to a committee of 40, for the League became less democratic as it grew. Policy remained in Aetolian hands, although some new states became honorary Aetolians.

The Aetolian League showed its strength after Alexander's death. Although its army was only 12,000 strong, it captured Naupactus on the Gulf of Corinth, repelling attacks by the Diadochi. By *c.*300BC it had gained control of Delphi. Although Delphi was never part of the League, the Aetolians justified their hold on the great shrine by defeating the Gauls in 279BC. In 245BC the Aetolians crushed the Boeotians, extending their power across central Greece. They generally opposed the Macedonians, posing as defenders of Greek liberty, but were also notoriously friendly to pirates.

Allied with Rome, they fought in the Second Macedonian War (200–197BC), their cavalry playing a decisive role in Roman victory at Cynoscephalae. Then, feeling that Rome had ignored them in the subsequent peace, they rashly invited the Seleucid Antiochus III into Greece in 192BC. After his defeat in 189BC, the League was reduced to Aetolia and became dependent on Rome, which later broke it up.

Left: Old pillars of the Temple of Apollo, Corinth, one of the 'fetters of Greece' held by the Macedonians.

Left: This painting by Victorian artist and humourist Edward Lear shows the narrow pass of Thermopylae. This, which always remained key to the control of Greece proper, for the 'Hot Gates' controlled access to central Greece from the north.

Below: This graceful terracotta figure comes from Tanagra in Boeotia, one of the numerous tiny cities that made up the powerful Aetolian League.

THE ACHAEAN LEAGUE

Equally significant was the Achaean League, which emerged *c.*280BC on the Peloponnese's north-west coast. Originally composed of ten coastal cities, by 251BC it included Sicyon near Corinth, which was not actually in Achaea. From Sicyon came Aratus, who for a generation headed the League as president and commander-in-chief, being re-elected every other year. The League's constitution emulated the Aetolians' but with differences. Only citizens over the age of 30 could vote in the *synedos*, or Council, which made it more conservative than the Assembly. Both met four times a year at Aigion on the Gulf, once to elect League officials such as the *hipparchs* (the cavalry commanders). Votes were taken by city, not head, to stop locals swamping the vote, but only richer citizens could afford to travel to Aigion. Each city retained its internal autonomy and coinage but followed League foreign policy.

Aratus, a passionate League patriot if no great general, pursued an anti-Macedonian policy. In 243BC he surprised the Macedonian garrison of Corinth by a night attack, adding that great port to the League. Over the next years, as Macedonia faced northern invasions, the League grew to include Argos, Megalopolis and finally almost all the Peloponnese except Sparta. These new citizens were all willing League members. But the League faced a resurgent Sparta after the reforms of Cleomones III, who captured city after city by appealing to the poor. Aratus was forced to call in the Macedonians to defeat the Spartans at Sellasia in 222BC. Under Philip V, however, the League's relations with Macedonia deteriorated and it turned to Rome. Philopoemon, its next great leader, accepted Roman help only very reluctantly. It was needed to defeat a resurgent Sparta again, which ultimately led to that proud city being enrolled in the League.

After Philopoemon's death from poisoning in Messenia in 182BC (Messenia had become another involuntary member) the Achaean League remained pro-Roman, but this did it no good at all. In 167BC, after the final defeat of Macedonia by Rome, 1,000 chiefly democratic Achaean hostages were taken to Rome, among them Polybius, the future historian. (Only 300 out of the 1,000 lived to return home.) Polybius himself came genuinely to admire Rome's unique constitution and wrote about Rome's rise to power. He also tried hard, if finally in vain, to persuade his country-men to accept increasingly stringent Roman demands.

ATHENS AND RHODES
323–170BC

Two cities dominated the Aegean in the Hellenistic period culturally and commercially: Athens and Rhodes. The former, still the greatest Greek city in 323BC, slowly ceded economic supremacy to Rhodes, the new mercantile power, but retained its cultural primacy. Rhodes became the wealthiest independent *polis* of the age and an unusually fine example of limited democracy. Both cities ultimately fell to Rome's imperialism despite their attempts to placate it.

Above: Athens, liberal and usually peaceful, still attracted the greatest philosophers such as Zeno of Citium, founder of Stoicism.

ATHENS: GREECE'S INTELLECTUAL AND CULTURAL CAPITAL
The Lamian War of 323–322BC, when the Greek alliance was crushed by Macedonia, ended Athenian independence and full democracy. Cassander's protégé Demetrius of Phalerum's bizarre regime in Athens mixed philosophy, authoritarianism and sybaritism. When Demetrius I the Besieger ousted Cassander's men in 307BC, democracy was partly restored, although the Assembly was no longer supreme. Exploiting Macedonian weakness during the Gaulish invasions of 280BC, Athens

Below: The entrance to Rhodes Harbour, where the Colossus *once stood.*

regained full independence but lost it to Antigonus II of Macedonia in 262BC. Antigonus, while installing a garrison in Piraeus, treated Athens tactfully – he saw it as his cultural capital, as did increasingly many Greeks.

The city's economy revived thanks to new veins of silver found at the Laurium mines, and later its control of Delos' free port. In 229BC Athens managed to buy out the Macedonian garrison, becoming effectively neutral. It cultivated Rome's friendship in the 2nd century BC, long escaping the worst wars.

Athens' importance was now overwhelmingly intellectual and cultural. It remained, most of the time, a modified democracy and it became the definitive home of philosophy. Epicurus and Zeno of Citium founded their respective schools – Epicureanism and Stoicism – c.300BC in the city, alongside the existing Platonists and Aristotelians. At the same time, Menander started the New Comedy, the origin of all subsequent 'sit coms'. Non-political in content but psychologically astute, it influenced Roman writers such as Plautus.

Hellenistic kings competed to honour Athens with fine buildings. The Seleucid Antiochus IV in the 170s BC paid for work to be restarted on the gigantic Temple of Zeus abandoned 340 years earlier, although it was not completed until the Emperor Hadrian's reign three centuries later.

On the east of the Agora in 140BC Attalus II of Pergamum built the Stoa, a huge colonnade, the last and largest of many. Beneath such colonnades the philosopher Zeno taught (so his followers were named 'Stoics'). Stoas sheltered shoppers and other citizens too. Athens' Indian summer of prosperity lasted until after 100BC, when it rashly sided with Mithradates of Pontus against Rome.

Right: Many Hellenistic monarchs endowed Athens, still the supreme Hellenic polis, with grand buildings. The Seleucid king Antiochus IV in 174BC paid for work to restart on the vast Temple of Olympian Zeus begun in the 6th century BC, but work had not gone far before Antiochus' murder cut off funds.

RHODES: A MARITIME REPUBLIC

In 406BC Rhodes's three small cities united to form a single democratic *polis*. Ruled by outside powers in the 4th century BC, after Alexander's death Rhodes declared itself free and expelled its Macedonian garrison. When Demetrius I besieged it in 305–304BC with giant siege towers, it repelled him. Rhodes enjoyed a period of great prosperity down to 166BC, displacing Athens as the hub of the Aegean. Its wealth came from its superb position at the centre of trade routes to Sicily, the Black Sea and Egypt. In 170BC its two per cent carrying tariff, primarily on wheat, yielded a million drachmas. As a result, Rhodes became the Hellenistic world's banking centre.

Rhodian democracy was limited but its aristocracy had a strong sense of *noblesse oblige*, richer citizens helping the poorer. Because of this, Rhodes enjoyed unusual social stability. All citizens served in the fleet. This albeit small fleet, comprising about 50 galleys, mostly quinqueremes,

became the best in the Hellenistic world, again paid for by the rich. Rhodes suppressed piracy as Athens had once done, promulgating a maritime code later adopted by imperial Rome. When an earthquake shattered the city in 226BC, other Greek states combined to restore it, so central had Rhodes become to their political and commercial wellbeing.

Rhodes favoured a neutrality that protected its trade, but allied itself with Rome against Philip V and Antiochus III because it feared their ambitions. Its immediate reward was large: Lycia and Caria, former Seleucid territory in Asia Minor. But Rome, growing suspicious of *any* Greek state's true independence, thought it was too neutral in the Third Macedonian War (171–168BC) and made Delos a free port, so ruining Rhodes' trade. Rhodes remained culturally important, attracting poets such as Apollonius Rhodius in the 3rd century BC and philosophers such as Poseidonius (135–50BC). The future emperor Tiberius withdrew there in 6BC, actually in a sulk at being sidelined in the imperial succession but supposedly to study philosophy.

Below: In Athens, the classical tradition in art continued, creating vivid new works such as this Maenad of c.100BC.

THE COLOSSUS OF RHODES

Symbol of Rhodes' maritime wealth and one of the Seven Wonders of the World, the famous *Colossus of Rhodes* according to legend straddled the harbour entrance. In reality it did not but was impressive enough: a bronze statue of the sun god 33m/110ft high. Falling in the earthquake of 226BC, even its mighty remnants long impressed visitors. The much-copied statue of snake-strangled Laocoön and his sons marked the Rhodian school of sculpture's zenith *c.*180BC, but the whole city was adorned with artworks.

REVOLUTION IN SPARTA
244–192BC

Above: The Vix Crater *is an unusually fine example of Laconian craftmanship.*

Below: This scene of martial readiness comes from the Vix Crater, *which was made in* c.500BC *when Sparta was in its austere prime – an age some reformist kings wished to revive.*

Since Sparta's crushing defeat by Thebes in 371BC and subsequent loss of Messenia, it had been of only minor importance, even in Greece. Its falling birth rate, coupled with the concentration of land among ever fewer rich people, meant that there were fewer full Spartiates – only 700 by 300BC – to be the hoplites that still formed the army's core. Discontent among the disenfranchised, who had lost their lands and citizenship, threatened Spartan stability. Despite this, memories of Sparta's former hegemony remained potent among both its neighbours and rulers.

AGIS THE REVOLUTIONARY

In 244BC Agis IV became king, determined on a return to the legendary excellence of the 'Lycurgan' constitution. Agis planned to divide the land into 4,500 equal lots, cancel all mortgages, allow many Spartans to regain their citizenship and enfranchise some *perioeci* (second-class citizens). This horrified conservatives: the magistrates (*ephors*), his co-monarch Leonidas II and rich citizens. Agis drove Leonidas into exile and deposed some *ephors*, but when Leonidas returned in 241BC, Agis was killed.

CLEOMENES' REFORMS

In 235BC Cleomenes III became king. Although he was the son of Leonidas, listening to Agis' widow had made him a revolutionary. He was also inspired by the teachings of the Stoic philosopher Sphaerus. Realizing that force was needed to implement reform, Cleomenes drove through revolutionary changes. He abolished debt; nationalized the land, dividing it into 4,000 lots for Spartiates and 15,000 for *perioeci*; and boosted the number of Spartiates by promoting *perioeci* or even *helots* (serfs). He also sold 1,000 *helots* their freedom, an unheard-of move.

In 229BC Cleomenes marched north and annexed some Peloponnesian cities in the Aetolian League, intending to cement domestic reform by victories abroad. Poor people in many cities flocked to him, hoping that his reforms would be emulated. This initially helped him in his war with the Achaean League. But after winning two minor victories over the Achaeans, Cleomenes returned home to pursue his revolution. He executed four conservative *ephors* and abolished their ancient office. With Sparta's army now hugely increased, he

seemed poised to conquer the whole Peloponnese. In despair, the Achaean League's leader Aratus called in the Macedonians, his bitter enemies, and their combined forces defeated Cleomenes at Sellasia in 222BC. He fled into exile in Egypt, where he committed suicide, while Sparta itself fell to invaders for the first time in its history. But the problems – principally the growing gap between rich and poor – remained, and not just in Sparta.

THE LAST SPARTAN KING

In 207BC Nabis, who was of royal blood, took the throne probably after murdering the young king Pelops. He at once re-enacted Cleomenes' reforms but in an even more drastic manner. Forming a private bodyguard of freed *helots* and mercenaries, he seized land from the rich to pay for the restoration of the common meals so important to Spartan life. Adroitly allying with Rome in the Second Macedonian War (200–197BC), he survived until a disgruntled Aetolian officer assassinated him in 192BC. Sparta was then forcibly enrolled in the Achaean League. When Rome destroyed the

Achaeans in 146BC, Sparta became technically free under Rome's protection, but it was now a museum city. The emperor Augustus restored its port and it long continued its strange customs to entertain Roman tourists.

Above: Young Spartans Exercising, *painted by Edgar Degas in 1860. Among Sparta's unique features had been the way girls also exercised nude, shocking other Greeks. This way of life was in decay by the 3rd century BC, ruining Spartan strength. But some Spartan customs were long maintained to amuse Roman tourists.*

UTOPIAN REVOLUTIONS

Growing social and economic problems in many cities fused with Stoic teachings of the universal brotherhood of men to create an explosive mixture in the 2nd century BC. The founder of Stoicism, Zeno of Citium (333–262BC), had outlined in his *Republic* (now lost) revolutionary proposals for the just society, but his ideas had remained just ideas: Stoic philosophers in Athens were no firebrands. However, Zeno's ideas were elaborated by later thinkers such as Iambulus. He wrote *c.*200BC about a mythical Island of the Sun, a communistic utopia (though that word had not been invented) where all men were equal and worshipped the Sun-god. Slave risings, common at the time and always put down with great brutality, arose out of pure misery.

Especially appealing, therefore, was the utopian state that Aristonicus, the illegitimate half-brother of Eumenes II, the last king of Pergamum, attempted to inaugurate.

Eumenes had left his kingdom, which included Ionia, to the Romans in 133BC, but most Ionian cities had no wish to become subjects of Rome. When Aristonicus proclaimed his utopian City of the Sun at Pergamum, freeing slaves, many Greeks, including the Stoic philosopher Blossius of Cumae, joined him. Their army defeated a consular Roman army. It took Rome three years' hard fighting before its legions could crush the Greek utopians. Rome's revenge, typically bloody, marked the final end of Greek political experimentation.

THE WESTERN GREEKS
320–211BC

Above: Hieron II's long reign in Syracuse (269–215BC) saw unprecedented peace and prosperity. The altar he erected was the longest ever built at c.200m/650ft.

Below: Pyrrhus, king of Epirus (319–272BC), fought as a mercenary general for the Italian Greeks against Rome 280–275BC. His initial victories proved so costly they became known as 'Pyrrhic'.

In the 4th century BC Taranto (Taras) was the wealthiest city in Greek Italy, thriving on its trade, wool production and the purple dye obtained from molluscs in its lagoons. The philosopher Archytas guided its mixed democracy while also remaining on good terms with Dionysius I, tyrant of Syracuse. But after Archytas' death c.340BC, the Tarentines felt threatened by Italian hill tribes, despite having a large fleet. They summoned Alexander of Epirus, brother-in-law of the great Alexander, to help them, but he was murdered in 330BC. Then a far more formidable enemy emerged: Rome, expanding into southern Italy, founded Venosa, a military colony, only 144km/90 miles north of Taranto while extending the Via Appia, its first great military road, south-east towards Brindisi. The Tarentines grew alarmed.

TARANTO AND ROME AT WAR
In 282BC the Greek city of Thurii, Taranto's rival across the Tarantine Gulf, appealed to Rome for help against Lucanian raiders. The Romans reacted by sending a fleet into the Gulf. This broke an earlier agreement with Taranto, which in reprisal sank some Roman ships and then mocked Rome's ambassadors for speaking bad Greek.

War followed in 280BC. Taranto called in King Pyrrhus I of Epirus, the best professional general of the time, to help it. His skilled army, with its elephants and *phalanxes*, was expected to crush the amateur Romans. Pyrrhus indeed won two

---

After Hieron's death in 215BC, his grandson Hieronymus sided with Carthage after Hannibal's seemingly crushing defeat of the Romans at Cannae. This catastrophic mistake led to his murder amid chaos. The Romans rallied and sent Marcellus, one of their best generals, to subdue Syracuse. Despite Archimedes' brilliant weapons (they included catapults and, reportedly, burning mirrors), the Romans finally took the city by surprise assault in 212BC.

Marcellus had ordered Archimedes' life be spared. But in the general slaughter the great scientist was killed by a Roman soldier, who, speaking no Greek, did not recognize him. Archimedes' fate epitomizes his city's, for Syracuse was ruinously sacked by the Romans, with Marcellus carrying off the finest artworks himself. Incorporated into the province of Sicily, of which it became the capital, Syracuse never regained its old importance or vigour.

---

major victories, marching almost up to Rome's walls. But the Romans fought doggedly on, learning to counter the elephants and replacing their own losses. After one victory, Pyrrhus exclaimed that he could not afford another such – hence 'pyrrhic (unaffordable) victory'. But, seeing the Romans methodically pitching camp each night, he admitted that his enemy was "not barbarian".

After Pyrrhus withdrew from Italy in 275BC, the Romans advanced south and Taranto had to accept a Roman alliance. By 272BC all of Magna Graecia ('greater Greece', Italy's Greek cities) was in Roman hands.

THE STRUGGLE FOR SICILY

The order that Timoleon had brought to Sicily, especially Syracuse, did not long survive his death in 334BC. In 317BC Agathocles overthrew Syracuse's government with Carthaginian backing. He made himself dictator and won support from the lower classes by terrorizing the rich. Quarrelling with Carthage, he then boldly invaded Africa itself in 310BC, but had to withdraw in 307BC. But he still made himself ruler of most of Sicily, even capturing Corcrya (Corfu) and taking a royal title. After his death in 289BC his successor, Hicetas, was defeated by the Carthaginians and deposed. In the ensuing chaos, Carthage looked set to conquer the whole island until King Pyrrhus briefly intervened.

After Pyrrhus left Sicily, Hieron, one of his officers, seized power in Syracuse. He was acclaimed king as Hieron II after defeating rampaging Italian mercenaries. Hieron ruled Syracuse remarkably well for 54 years (269–215BC). He revived some of its past glories, helped by his wife Philistis' descent from Dionysius I. Shrewdly switching to support Rome in the First Punic War (264–241BC), Hieron gained most of eastern Sicily as his kingdom. He adorned Syracuse with public buildings, including the world's biggest altar (200 x 22m/650 x 74ft), and employed Archimedes, the great scientist, to fortify it. Hieron also built the largest warship yet seen, the 5,000 tonner *Alexandria*. His tax system, the Lex Hieronica modelled on the Ptolemys', took one tenth of crops grown in the kingdom – a relatively light tax, which the Romans copied. Syracusan prosperity is revealed in the fine private house recently unearthed.

The rest of Sicily was not so fortunate, being long fought over between Carthage and Rome – Acragas (Agrigento), then, Sicily's second richest city, was twice

Right: The Colosseum in Rome, the city whose fast-rising power increasingly dominated Greek politics.

sacked and once burnt. Sicily became after 241BC Rome's first *provincia* (province), ruthlessly exploited for its wheat farms. The slave gangs who worked these huge farms revolted en masse in 135–132 and 104–100BC. Meanwhile, Greek urban life decayed.

Above: Taranto (Taras) was the richest Greek city in Italy, with a fine double harbour and a thriving purple dying industry. Yet, despite hiring the finest general Pyrrhus, it fell to Rome in 272BC.

THE SHADOW OF ROME
220–188 BC

Above: Flaminius, the Roman general who defeated Macedonia at Cynoscephalae in 197BC and then promised Greeks 'freedom' at Corinth.

Below: A relief from the Temple of Neptune of c.100BC in Rome reveals Greece's growing cultural impact on the Romans.

In 217BC a peace conference was held at Naupactus (Lepanto) to try to end Greece's constant wars. Agelaus of Naupactus, welcoming the delegates, pointed to the titanic struggle between Rome and Carthage then racking Italy. Now, he said, was the time when Greeks must join together like men wading through a torrent, "for if the cloud now rising in the west should spread to Greece, I fear we shall be begging the gods to give us back the chance to call even our quarrels our own."

PHILIP VERSUS ROME

His prophetic words were applauded by the delegates. However, Philip V of Macedonia, attending the conference, then made a fatal error. After Hannibal's great victory at Cannae in 216BC he, like most people, thought that Rome was doomed and so allied himself with Hannibal. He had his reasons – Roman power had been pushing down the Illyrian (Dalmatian) coast toward Macedonia. But Philip failed to realize that Rome had vast reserves of manpower and was now also the strongest *naval* power in the Mediterranean since creating its navy in the First Punic War (264–241BC). Macedonia, in contrast, had let its once fine navy decay. (On the only occasion on which a Macedonian fleet entered the Adriatic, trying to carry reinforcements to Hannibal, it fled as soon as it saw Roman ships.)

The First Macedonian War (215–205BC) was rather a non-event. Rome was too busy with events in the western Mediterranean to send large forces to Greece. The treaty of 205BC simply restored the *status quo ante*. But Rome was now increasingly interested in Greek affairs, while some Greeks thought they could call on this new power to help them in their disputes with each other.

In 200BC Rhodes and Pergamum, both of which distrusted the Seleucids and Macedonians, told the Romans that the two kings had made a secret plan agreeing to divide up the Ptolemaic Empire. They had probably not, but that year Antiochus III defeated the Egyptians at Panion, annexing southern Syria and Palestine. Meanwhile Philip seemed to be menacing Rhodes and Pergamum. Convinced, Rome declared war, sending its now battle-hardened legions east. With Aetolian cavalry to help, Philip's army was routed at Cynoscephalae in 197BC, and his power restricted to Macedonia. In particular, he gave up the 'chains of Greece', the forts that had held Greece captive. He was, however, left on the throne of Macedonia

'FREEDOM' FOR GREECE

Greece, declared the victorious Roman general Flaminius to a congress at Corinth, would now be free. Roman troops would be withdrawn shortly. The delighted Greeks applauded so loudly that "birds dropped from the air stunned", and they hailed Flaminius as a god, the first (not the last) Roman so honoured. But what Flaminius meant was that Greek cities could enjoy much the same limited autonomy as cities in Italy did as 'clients' of Rome, not that they would be totally free. From this misunderstanding came much later grief. But Rhodes, Pergamum and the Achaeans at the time happily accepted the peace, with only the Aetolians disgruntled at gaining nothing. In 194BC Roman troops duly left Greece.

THE FIRST SYRIAN WAR

By 200BC Antiochus III the Great seemed on top of the world. He had restored Seleucid suzerainty over the east, at least in theory; beaten the Egyptians and finally won southern Syria, long his dynasty's ambition; and pushed Pergamum back, regaining control over western Asia Minor to the Aegean. He seemed to the suspicious Romans to be about to recreate Alexander's empire. Worse, he welcomed Hannibal, Rome's arch-enemy now in exile, at his court. Antiochus even sent troops across the Hellespont, rejecting Roman protests.

In 192BC the Aetolian League invited Antiochus to intervene in Greece proper. After some hesitation and diplomatic manoeuvres, Antiochus despatched 10,000 men – enough to annoy the Romans, but not enough to impress potential Greek allies. So began what Rome called the First Syrian War. Defeated on land by the Romans at Thermopylae in 191BC (the Aetolians gave no real help), Antiochus' fleet was defeated at Myonessus after a hard battle by a combined Roman and Rhodian fleet. Finally at Magnesia in Asia Minor in 190BC, Antiochus' grand army, 70,000 strong with chariots, elephants and *cataphracts* (armoured cavalry), was routed. Scipio Africanus, who had defeated Hannibal, masterminded the Roman victory, but Pergamum's cavalry

won the day, defeating the Seleucid phalanx, which fought to the bitter end.

Pergamum had its reward two years later in the Treaty of Apamea, which gave it almost all Asia Minor west of the Taurus Mountains. Rhodes made useful gains too. The Seleucid Empire now ended at Cilicia, and it had to pay Rome 15,000 talents in reparations – a cripplingly vast sum, though payment was phased.

Above: Monument to the Battle of Cannae in which Rome suffered seemingly total defeat by Hannibal in 216BC. This led Syracuse and Macedonia to ally with Carthage.

Left: Hannibal, Rome's greatest enemy, was welcomed at court by Antiochus III, a move by the Seleucid king that roused Rome's enmity.

GREECE MADE CAPTIVE
188–146BC

Above: Perseus, last king of Macedonia, was utterly defeated by the Romans at Pydna in 168BC. His kingdom was divided into four client states before being annexed by Rome in 144BC.

Below: The circular Temple of Hercules Victor (once called the Temple of Vesta) in Rome is truly Hellenic in style. It was probably built in c.120BC by Greek craftsmen.

If Rome's policy toward the Greeks in the next decades often seemed brutal and hypocritical (promising freedom at one moment, crushing any sign of independence at the next), this reflected Rome's own ambivalence. Beyond ensuring that no power could challenge Roman hegemony, the Senate was divided. A few senators had little wish for new entanglements in Greek affairs, but other, more ambitious, Roman politicians wanted plunder and glory in the Greek east. There they could depose kings, be hailed as gods and amass unprecedented wealth. Further, Greeks themselves began coming to Rome with their quarrels, making Rome their judge.

Not all Greeks accepted this. Democrats in the cities now looked to Macedonia against Rome – many cities in Greece and Asia were still democracies, although Rome favoured oligarchies. The monarchs also had their discontents – and strengths. Although the Seleucids had lost

their western lands, their empire still stretched east to Persis and south to Egypt's frontier. Macedonia likewise retained its old recruiting grounds. Ptolemaic Egypt, however, was in terminal decay although hugely rich, clinging desperately to its Roman alliance. Only Pergamum, now booming, willingly toed the Roman line.

THIRD MACEDONIAN WAR
In 179BC Perseus succeeded his father Philip V in Macedonia. Although he renewed the treaty with Rome, he forged marriage ties with both the Seleucids and the king of Bithynia (north-west Asia Minor), while overhauling the army. This alarmed Eumenes II of Pergamum, who persuaded Rome that Perseus posed a new threat. The result was the Third Macedonian War (171–168BC) in which Rome mobilized huge forces. Perseus' crushing defeat at Pydna in 168BC, despite the success of his phalanx charge, marked the end of Macedonia. Perseus was taken in chains to Rome, where he died in prison; Macedonia was split into four republics. When these quarrelled, Rome finally made Macedonia a province in 146BC.

ANTIOCHUS' AMBITIONS

In 175BC Antiochus IV seized the Seleucid throne. He was ambitious and talented, if also eccentric – he 'stood for election' like a Roman magistrate, probably mocking the new superpower's constitution if also bewildering his subjects. But he had the old Seleucid ambitions toward Egypt. In 169BC he invaded Egypt, overrunning most of it. Rome sent an envoy, Caius Popilius, who traced a circle in the sand around Antiochus and told him not to step beyond it until he agreed to withdraw. Antiochus, not wishing to challenge Rome, withdrew.

On his way home to Syria, he stopped in Jerusalem, where the Hellenizing faction of the priestly state of Judaea (one of many priestly states in his kingdom) appealed for help. Not realizing that Jews were somehow *different* from his other Semitic subjects, Antiochus despoiled the Temple, installed a Syrian garrison and erected a temple to Olympian Zeus on the site. This was probably just part of his general Hellenizing programme. But the furious revolt that broke out, led by Judas Maccabeus the High Priest, finally drove the Seleucids from Judaea for good. (Rome supported the Maccabees). However, Antiochus' attention was focused on the growing Parthian threat to the east. With his death in 164BC, the great days of the Seleucids were over, although the kingdom survived for another century.

DELOS: SLAVE ISLAND

The Romans, thinking that Rhodes had not supported them wholeheartedly against Perseus, deprived it of the tiny island of Delos in 167BC, which became a free port. It also rapidly became the greatest slave market yet seen, reputedly able to handle 10,000 slaves a day.

Right: The flow of skilled Greek captives into Rome gave rich Romans ample domestic slave labour, such as this maid. From a fresco at Herculaneum.

The slaves were mostly Greek or Hellenized people, victims of Rome's new aggressiveness. In 167BC the whole population of Epirus was enslaved, 150,000 of them glutting the slave markets. Direct taxation was abolished that year in Rome – not a coincidence.

CLASHES BETWEEN ROME AND THE ACHAEANS

In 166BC Rome took 1,000 mainly democratic hostages from the Achaean League, although the League had supported Rome. Among them was Polybius the historian. Polybius had Philopoemon, head of the Achaean League, wonder: "Should we work with our masters and not object, so that soon we get even harsher orders, or should we oppose them as far as we can, so... we can check their impulses?" The Achaeans did both after Philopoemon's death in 182BC, clashing with Rome when it demanded they relinquish not only Sparta, which was reasonable, but also Argos and Corinth both of which had been League cities for generations.

Above: If Rome conquered Greece politically, Greece conquered Rome culturally. Socrates was among the philosophers educated Romans came to revere.

CHAOS IN THE AEGEAN
150–80BC

Above: Sulla, the brutal if highly effective Roman general who sacked many Greek cities in 86BC.

Below: The Temple of Poseidon at Sunium outside Athens. It escaped the fate of the city itself, which was sacked by the Roman Sulla for supporting Mithradates, king of Pontus.

The Romans had mixed, sometimes ignoble, motives behind their actions toward the Greeks – greed and paranoid suspicion must have been the most obvious to the Greeks, if not ones that the Romans would have recognized. However, Rome can hardly have foreseen the disastrous consequences of its actions.

LARGE-SCALE PIRACY
By making Delos a 'super-port', soon very popular with Italian merchants, it wrecked the basis of Rhodes' wealth. This undermined Rhodes' fleet, which had kept down piracy. Piracy now revived on a new and massive scale. (Athens, to which Delos was theoretically restored, now lacked the strength or will to reassert its old thalassocracy, sea-power.)

By 100BC pirates were raiding right across the Mediterranean from strongholds in Crete, Lycia and Cilicia, where they lived beyond any law. Slaving was one of their main activities, and they attacked Roman as well as Greek shipping. At one stage pirates captured the young Julius Caesar. Waiting for his ransom to be paid, Caesar told his captors that he would catch them and have them crucified. They laughed; he kept his word. But although the pirates attacked far up the coasts of Italy, at one point even capturing Roman magistrates off the coast of Latium, the Romans did almost nothing to check this threat until the *Lex Gabinia* of 67BC.

TAX REFORMS AND CORRUPTION
Worse still for Greece, the concessions made by Gaius Gracchus to Roman *publicani* (tax-farmers) in 122BC to win support for his radical reforms at home led to a new venality in Roman provincial administration. The tax rates levied on provinces such as Macedonia and Achaea may have been no higher than earlier, but the *publicani* extorted vastly higher taxes from the hapless provincials for their own profits. It was a disastrous way of raising revenue.

By the 1st century BC Roman government had grown detested as the proconsuls (governors) themselves became openly corrupt, knowing they faced no real danger of prosecution back in Rome. As Cicero, the great Roman writer, said: "No words can say how deeply we are hated by foreigners because of the foul behaviour of the men we have sent out recently to govern them."

Cicero's successful prosecution of Verres, an infamously corrupt governor of Sicily who had plundered the island, was as rare as his own probity while governing Cilicia.

THE RISE OF MITHRADATES
Greek colonies had long been dotted around the Black Sea, but after Alexander's reign Greek culture began to penetrate inland also. Pontus, a fertile, well-wooded region on the south coast with abundant mineral deposits, was

ruled by kings of Iranian descent who became increasingly, if superficially, Hellenized. One of these kings, Pharnaces I (220–185BC), extended his power around much of the Black Sea.

Mithradates V Pontus (*c.*150–120BC) was the most powerful king in Asia Minor after Pergamum's end. His son Mithradates VI Eupator (120–63BC) became one of Rome's greatest adversaries and the last, rather unlikely, champion of Greek freedom. Mithradates V started by extending his power around almost the whole Black Sea, annexing the half-Hellenized kingdom of the Cimmerian (Crimean) Bosphorus in 108BC. This kingdom, which controlled Greece's vital grain supply, was threatened by Scythian tribesmen and so welcomed Mithradates' protection. He had less success with kingdoms in the Anatolian interior such as Cappadocia, but Tigranes of Armenia became his son-in-law, guarding his eastern flank. Meanwhile he built up a formidable army under a Greek general, Archelaus.

THE SACK OF ATHENS
This army was first tested in 88BC, when, reacting to an attack by his neighbour Bithynia, Mithradates swiftly overran western Asia Minor. His proclamation of liberation from the loathed *publicani* delighted the Greeks. When he crossed over to Greece itself, even long-neutral Athens rose in his support. A massacre of 80,000 Roman and Italian *publicani* and other businessmen forced Rome into a vigorous response. Sulla marched east with 100,000 men to defeat Mithradates at Chaeronea and Orchomenus.

Athens, which he besieged through the winter of 87–86BC, surrendered too late: Sulla's army sacked the city, even removing columns from the Temple of Olympian Zeus to Rome. Other Greek cities were similarly devastated and had to pay Rome a massive indemnity. This was collected by *publicani*, who also charged interest of 50 per cent on unpaid taxes. This crippled Greece for decades.

Problems with his rivals in the Popularis party in Rome soon claimed Sulla's attention, however, and he agreed to a peace on a return to the *status quo ante* in 85BC. Mithradates surrendered all his gains and retreated to his Black Sea empire. But his strength had only been tried, not exhausted.

Above: The Agora of the Italians at Delos. After being made a free port by Rome in 166BC, Delos boomed, attracting many Italian businessmen.

Below: Mithradates VI, king of Pontus, Rome's last formidable enemy in the Hellenistic East.

THE POWER OF THE DYNASTS
84–42BC

Above: While the Romans fought each other, Parthia became Persia's successor east of the Euphrates under kings such as Mithradates I. He was still happy to be titled Philhellene, however.

From the sack of Athens in 86–85BC on, the fortunes of the Greek world were inextricably linked with those of Rome's feuding dynasts – heads of the city's noble families whose ambitions tore the Republic and its empire apart.

Sulla returned to Rome to become dictator, purge his enemies in a bloodbath, reorder the constitution on deeply reactionary lines and then suddenly, to general astonishment, retire in 80BC. While his seemingly iron-cast settlement in Rome soon started unravelling, he had also left much unfinished business in the Greek world and a thoroughly unstable situation in Asia. Egypt, although theoretically still independent, now leaned heavily on Roman support. Many Romans became tempted by the idea of annexing this, the Mediterranean's richest kingdom, but, being unable to agree on how to do so, left it shakily independent for the time being. A brief war with Mithradates in 84–83BC came to little, but the king's strength remained undiminished.

HOSTILITIES AND MITHRADATES

In 73BC Rome faced its most serious slave revolt ever when Spartacus raised a force soon amounting to 150,000 men in Campania. The revolt took two years and a major military campaign to suppress. Meanwhile, Mithradates, alarmed at how Rome was handling its new acquisition of neighbouring Bithynia, bequeathed to it in 74BC, renewed hostilities. He invaded Bithynia, again threatening Rome's position in Asia. Lucullus, an associate of Sulla, was sent east with a large army to subdue him but faced problems with a mutinous army and Mithradates' skilful tactics. Gradually, however, he exhausted Mithradates by the usual Roman attributes – tenacity and willingness to endure high casualties. Mithradates finally had to seek refuge with his son-in-law in Armenia. (Tigranes had extended his power south to create a large kingdom.) Before Lucullus could kill either of them, he was recalled in 66BC. His command passed to a far more dashing general.

POMPEY THE GREAT

Pompey was (relatively) young and handsome and had a fine military record when the *lex Gabinia* gave him wide powers to deal with the pirates. Swiftly raising a combined land and sea force of 100,000 men, he rooted out the pirates – more by bribes and threats than military action – in only three months.

In 66BC the triumphant general was given Lucullus' command by an impatient Roman people. Over the next four years Pompey earned the title 'the Great' (which he had assumed already) by a statesmanlike mixture of diplomacy and force. Forcing Mithradates out of Pontus – to which he had returned – he drove him to his last resort: a fortress in the Crimea. There Mithradates committed

Left: Julius Caesar, charming, charismatic and unscrupulous, emerged victorious from Rome's first round of civil wars. His affair with Cleopatra VII probably produced a son and further tied Egypt to Rome.

suicide in 63BC – by the sword, after failing to poison himself. He had reputedly made himself immune to all poisons by taking a daily antidote.

With Mithradates dead, Pompey rearranged the east at leisure. Tigranes' empire was abolished but he was left in Armenia, which became a client state of Rome. So did a string of small kingdoms from the Caucasus down to the Red Sea. Pompey, capturing Jerusalem, entered the Holy of Holies in the Temple, gravely if inadvertently offending the Jews. Judaea also became a client state. The rump of the once great Seleucid Empire became the Roman province of Syria, ultimately the new centre of Roman power in the east. Pompey's settlement was brilliant: it almost doubled Rome's revenues and lasted in essence more than 100 years. Pompey returned to Rome in 62BC to celebrate another triumph.

GREECE THE BATTLEFIELD

In 49BC the first in a new round of civil wars broke out in Italy when Caesar, returning from conquering Gaul, 'crossed the Rubicon' into Italy proper without disbanding his army. (His many enemies had prevented him from standing for consul *in absentia*, and to return to Rome as an ordinary civilian would have been suicidally risky.) Greece found itself the hapless battlefield as Roman dynasts battled for supremacy. Pompey retreated to Greece where, in 48BC, he was defeated at the Battle of Pharsalus in Thessaly, being killed soon after when he landed in Egypt. Caesar, in hot pursuit, had a different encounter, with the young Cleopatra VII, co-monarch with her brother Ptolemy XIII. She had an affair with Caesar and probably a son, Caesarion. Suppressing an uprising, Caesar made her sole ruler.

Right: Pompey entering the Temple in Jerusalem. This unwittingly sacriligious act angered Jewish priests, some of whom were killed by Roman soliders when they rioted. From a medieval manuscript by Jean Fouquet.

Right: Pompey was Caesar's chief rival in the struggle for supremacy in Rome.

After Caesar's assassination in 44BC, another round of Roman civil wars racked the Greek world. The conspirators, or 'liberators' as they styled themselves, Brutus and Cassius, crossed to Greece to raise fresh armies. To pay for them, Cassius exacted yet more money from the exhausted Greek cities. Brutus and Cassius were defeated by Mark Antony at the double Battle of Philippi in November 42BC. The Roman Empire was then provisionally divided, Antony taking control of the east while Octavius Caesar, adopted son of Julius, took control of the west.

CLEOPATRA AND ANTONY
50–30BC

Above: Cleopatra, as this bust suggests, was not stunningly beautiful, but she was witty, charming and very wealthy – qualities Antony appreciated.

Below: The meeting of Antony, victorious Roman overlord of the East, and Cleopatra, last Hellenistic queen of Egypt, was one of unparalleled splendour, here envisaged by the great 18th-century painter Tiepolo.

By 50BC only Egypt, fabulously rich, remained independent of Rome. The Ptolemies relied on Roman support against external aggressors, but internally their rule was insecure. Alexandria was increasingly turbulent, while in Egypt proper the over-taxed *fellahin* and priesthood no longer supported the dynasty. Intermarriage between sister and brother, an Egyptian custom the Ptolemies adopted, may explain the feebleness of later male rulers. Their queens, in contrast, proved ruthless and dynamic. Before the dynasty's end, one great queen tried to restore Ptolemaic glory.

Cleopatra VII was born in 69BC, daughter of Ptolemy XII. From 51BC she was co-ruler with her younger brother and husband Ptolemy XIII. When Pompey, fleeing from Julius Caesar, landed in late 48BC, Ptolemy XIII's agents executed him and presented his severed head to Caesar, expecting him to be delighted. He was

not – Caesar prided himself on his clemency. He was, however, won over by the youthful charms of Cleopatra, smuggled into his chambers in a carpet. Or so legend goes.

CLEOPATRA AND CAESAR
Cleopatra was not, if contemporary portraits are honest, especially beautiful, but she was intelligent, charming and witty. She was ambitious, too, wanting to restore the Ptolemies' former empire. Her affair with Caesar, a womanizer of immense charm, probably produced a son, Caesarion. Caesar supported her against her brother, but the Alexandrian mob took against the Romans. Vicious street fighting led to part of the Library being burnt and almost to Caesar's and Cleopatra's death. They were saved by Jewish guards, which made Caesar pro-Jewish. Cleopatra duly became sole monarch. In spring 47BC, with order restored, Caesar hastened away. Cleopatra later followed him to Rome, there to witness his assassination in 44BC and the recurrence of Roman civil war. Returning to Egypt, she watched and waited on developments.

THE GREAT LOVERS
Mark Antony had been Caesar's trusted lieutenant, giving his funeral oration. Now he had to accept young Octavian, Caesar's great-nephew and adopted son, as an equal partner in the Second Triumvirate (pact) in 43BC. But he was regarded as the better soldier and, by many Romans, as a better man. He also got on well with Greeks.

After his victory at Philippi in 42BC, Antony wintered in Athens, debating and dining, before sailing east to be hailed as the god Dionysus by the Greeks of Asia. But although divine, he was still short of money. When he summoned Cleopatra

Right: Cleopatra (as painted by Cabanel, a 19th-century French artist) was not really Egyptian by culture or descent. But Roman propaganda portrayed her as a decadent oriental femme fatale, *bewitching Antony.*

Right: Cleopatra (as painted by Cabanel, a 19th-century French artist) was not really Egyptian by culture or descent. But Roman propaganda portrayed her as a decadent oriental femme fatale, *bewitching Antony.*

to meet him at Tarsus in Cilicia, he wanted her wealth, not her body. But Cleopatra made a spectacular entry. "The barge she sat in, like a burnished throne/Burned upon the water. The poop was beaten gold:/Purple the sails and so perfumèd that/The Winds were love-sick with them" as Shakespeare, following Plutarch, later put it. Antony fell in love with her – and she probably with him – and they sailed to Alexandria for a winter of amorous luxury. They founded a club, the 'Inimitable Lives', revelling through the night, and cruised up the Nile. When he bet her that she could not eat a dinner worth a million sesterces, she dissolved a vast pearl in wine and drank it. Antony's role as Dionysus was apt, for the wine-god was the Ptolemies' patron deity. Cleopatra herself often appeared as the goddess Isis.

Meanwhile, Octavian faced major problems – revolts in central Italy, attacks on Rome's grain supplies – that forced him to ask Antony for help. This was given. In 36BC Antony's grand attack on Parthia proved a disaster, although he made Armenia a client state in 34BC. At the 'Donations of Alexandria' that year, Antony sat enthroned beside Cleopatra as she was hailed as Queen of Kings. He gave provinces from Rome's empire to their two children and hailed Caesarion, Caesar's son, as King of Kings. Cleopatra's ambitions seemed fulfilled.

DECLINE AND FALL

All this was a marvellous propaganda gift to Octavian. His poets depicted Antony as bewitched by an oriental *femme fatale*. Even so, when war was declared in 32BC, a third of the Senate went east to join Antony, whose forces were still large. But Antony alienated Roman supporters by letting Cleopatra join him in Greece,

and desertions began. The final battle at Actium in 31BC was an anticlimax, Antony and Cleopatra fled south to Alexandria for a last winter of love. Octavian followed the next year. After another defeat, Antony tried to kill himself. Dying, he was reunited with Cleopatra, who had retreated to her mausoleum. There she cheated Octavian of a triumph by poisoning herself with asps. If Antony had won, Egypt would have remained independent for longer and the Greek cities might have enjoyed more independence, but the Roman Empire would not have been radically different.

Right: Antony, dying from stabbing himself, was finally reunited in death with Cleopatra in the mausoleum to which she retreated.

AUGUSTUS AND THE PAX ROMANA 27BC–AD14

Above: The Corinth Canal, the construction of which was started under the philhellenic emperor Nero in AD66.

Below: The theatre at Taormina in Sicily, where a Roman superstructure sits on a Greek base, exemplifies how Greek and Roman cultures intermingled. Taormina was Greek in origin while Sicily itself only became fully Hellenized under Roman rule.

The death of Cleopatra VII marked the end of the Hellenistic age. The whole Greek world west of the Euphrates now lay under Roman control, directly or indirectly. Much of it had been ravaged by Rome's own civil wars: the grandfather of Plutarch the historian had been forced to carry sacks of grain on his back up mountains for Antony's army during the Actium campaign in 31BC; Corinth was a gutted ruin; Athens, though still a revered intellectual centre, was exhausted; so were the once brilliant cities of Ionia.

AUGUSTUS' RULE

Augustus, as Octavius was soon titled, had triumphed as leader of upright Romans against what he had depicted as a decadent Hellenistic world. The Greeks perhaps at first expected little from this Roman emperor (from Latin *imperator*, commander), but they were agreeably surprised. Augustus spent two years in the East, re-establishing it along lines laid out by Antony and Pompey. Herod the Great was confirmed in his Judaean kingdom, as were rulers of petty Hellenistic states fringing Rome's eastern provinces.

Roman frontier provinces such as Syria were governed by legates sent out by the emperor, often commanding legions stationed there. Egypt alone was treated differently, becoming the private fief of Augustus governed by an equestrian (knight) not a senator. This reflected imperial nervousness about giving power to a potential rival from the Senate. The first governor was Gaius Gallus, chosen because, as a poet, he might appeal to Alexandrians. (Unfortunately power went to his head and he was forced to commit suicide.) Augustus wisely refused to attack Parthia. Although he extended Rome's northern frontiers, to the Mediterranean world itself he brought peace, the long-lasting Pax Romana.

LOCAL GOVERNMENT

Most provinces in the Greek world, such as Achaea, Macedonia and Asia (western Anatolia), were governed by proconsuls appointed by the Senate if overseen by the emperor. The letters between the emperor Trajan and Pliny the Younger *c.*AD110 show just how close this supervision could be. Such governors had few troops, for much of the Roman Empire long remained lightly guarded and lightly governed. Most of the governing was done by local citizens themselves.

The empire has been called a 'confederation of cities', although the population remained mainly rural. But the local aristocracies – Rome never favoured democracies even when a republic – administered their own cities, competing to build ever grander temples, baths and theatres. (A few cities such as Tarsus had Roman rights, meaning that citizens such as St Paul were Roman citizens.) Rome's light-touch imperialism stemmed from its own lack of bureaucracy, reflecting Roman preferences. Alexandria was ruled directly, but it had long lost its council.

PROSPERITY REGAINED

Linking the cities of the newly stabilized, extended empire was a remarkable network of roads, ultimately covering 80,000km/50,000 miles. These encouraged trade, but sea routes remained far more important. Here the suppression of piracy, started by Pompey and maintained by Augustus and his successors, was crucially important.

The resulting boom saw Corinth, refounded under Augustus, become a wealthy port again. Old Ionian cities such as Miletus, Ephesus and Smyrna became unprecedentedly rich, with populations passing the 100,000 marks, as did Hellenistic cities such as Alexandria and Antioch. Athens enjoyed renewed if modest prosperity, exporting its fine Pentelic marble – and craftsmen – while educating young Roman aristocrats. Augustus built a grand new agora and *odeion* (roofed theatre) in Athens, and a small temple for the cult of Rome and Augustus on the Acropolis, stressing Roman power at the heart of Greece.

TAX REFORMS

Also of crucial importance were changes in the tax collection. Caesar had wanted to abolish the rapacious and loathed *publicani* (tax-farmers) outright, aware of their ruinous effects. The more cautious

Below: The Temple of Hera at Acragas in Sicily, whose partial recovery under the Pax Romana was typical of many Greek cities.

Augustus gradually replaced them with appointed officials whom he could trust. Taxation for most provinces was relatively small. The sales tax, for example, was only 1 per cent, and customs dues were 5 per cent. Where *publicani* survived or were introduced, their rapacity could engender revolts, as in Britain in AD61 and Judaea in AD66.

TWO CENTURIES OF PEACE

At the end of his life in AD14 the emperor Augustus was moved by a demonstration. The passengers and crew of a ship just arrived from Alexandria, greatest of Hellenistic cities, put on garlands and burnt incense to him, saying that they owed their lives and liberty to sail the seas to him.

This peaceful prosperity continued for another two centuries. The walls of most cities not actually on the frontiers, even of Rome itself, were allowed to decay in a period that was, by historical standards, phenomenally peaceful. No wonder that most Greeks were happy to honour Augustus and his successors as divine – honours that wiser emperors did not boast of in Rome itself.

Above: The Temple of Hadrian at Ephesus, one of many Ionian cities that attained its greatest prosperity in the 2nd century AD under the long Pax Romana. Hadrian was a famously philhellenic emperor.

Below: A cameo of Augustus, the first Roman emperor (27BC–AD14). Augustus admired the High Classicism of Periclean Athens.

GRAECO-ROMAN SYNTHESIS
CICERO TO HADRIAN, 80BC–AD138

Above: Bust of Cicero, the Roman orator, writer and politician who summarized and translated into Latin many works of Greek philosophy, ensuring their survival.

Below: The Maison Carrée in Nimes, a Roman colony in southern France. The temple, built in Augustus' reign, embodies Graeco-Roman synthesis, for its columns are classically Greek but its plan is wholly Roman.

In 80BC Cicero, an intensely ambitious young Roman politician, arrived in Athens to study philosophy. He was among the first in a stream of Romans who, over the next 400 years, would go to Greece to study philosophy and rhetoric. Cicero's stay had a huge impact on philosophy over the next 1,500 years in Western Europe. While his prime interest was politics, he turned to writing philosophy full-time when forced into (temporary) retirement by Caesar's ascendancy in the 40s BC. In a few years he summarized in Latin much of Greek thought, especially Stoicism, in *De Republica* and *De Finibus* ('Concerning the Highest Ends'). In his books, which survive intact unlike most ancient literature, he established Latin equivalents for basic Greek philosophical terms such as morality, quality and happiness.

Cicero's achievement in translating and synthesizing Greek thought typifies the growing Graeco-Roman fusion.

After 200BC Greek culture had flooded into Rome in the form of looted artworks and thousands of slaves, the latter often better educated than their masters. They became secretaries, librarians, doctors and tutors. While Roman nobles tended to regard Greeks politically as irresponsible, deceitful and even decadent, many admired Greek culture almost uncritically for a time.

The temple of Hercules Victor in Rome, built *c.*120BC as a perfect circle with slender marble columns, is almost wholly Greek in form. Equally Greek are the wall paintings – surviving best in Pompeii thanks to Vesuvius – probably made by Greek artists working for Roman masters. By Cicero's time, educated Romans were fluent in Greek. A century later Quintillian, the Roman grammarian who taught the sons of emperors, suggested that boys should learn Greek before they learned Latin, so essential was it to their education.

NERO'S INFLUENCE

"Greece made captive captured her conqueror and introduced the arts into rough Latium," wrote Horace, one of the emperor Augustus' chosen poets. If this Roman cultural inferiority was fading by the early 1st century AD – mainly thanks to Horace and other great Latin poets such as Virgil – Greece was still seen as the exemplar, even by some emperors.

In AD54 the 17-year-old Nero, the last of Augustus' descendants, became emperor. With genuine artistic interests if not talents, he patronized artists and architects – especially those building and adorning his vast new imperial palaces – and composed plays. Seneca, Nero's tutor and first minister, wrote philosophy and tragedies, which, if not publicly staged at the time, survived to influence later playwrights such as

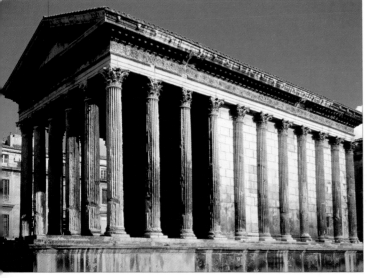

Right: Admetus and Alcestis Listening to the Oracle, *a fresco from the 'House of the Tragic Poet' at Pompeii,, reveals how familiar Romans became with Greek myths and how popular Greek styles were in Italy in the 1st century* AD. *This work copies a Hellenistic original.*

Shakespeare. But Nero performed in public himself – something thought shameful for a noble Roman – at first in Naples, a still Greek city. He also tried to introduce Greek athletic games without success. When Nero entered the Olympic Games, he won *all* the prizes, the first and last time this happened. More positively, he proclaimed 'freedom' for Greek cities and ordered the digging of the Corinth Canal, although his engineers stopped when they hit bedrock. Nero's reign ended in civil war in AD68, however, and there was a brief Roman reaction under his successors.

THE PHILHELLENIC EMPEROR

In AD128 the emperor Hadrian dedicated the Pantheon, temple to all the gods, in Rome. This most famous and best preserved of Roman temples exemplifies Graeco-Roman synthesis. Behind a giant portico essentially Greek in inspiration rises a majestic dome wholly Roman in conception. Hadrian, who commissioned and possibly helped to design it, was the most philhellenic of all great emperors, to the point that his enemies called him Greekling (*graeculus*).

Regarding Athens as his favourite city, he made it head of a new Panhellenic League and built an entire new quarter, besides completing the Temple of Olympian Zeus started 640 years before. He was elected archon (the office still existed), initiated into the Eleusinian Mysteries, the holiest in Greece, and wore a beard like a Greek philosopher.

Equally Greek was his passion for Antinous, a youth of royal descent and so his social equal, to be wooed not raped. Hadrian's grief at Antinous' death struck many as undignified, but in his reign (AD117–138) the Greek-speaking half of

the empire finally recovered its self-confidence and began to supply important officials. Under Hadrian too began the systematic codification of Roman laws, where Greek humanism and idealism lightened Roman pragmatism.

TWO-WAY INFLUENCE

The influence did not run all one way. The Greeks adopted some Roman architectural features, using arches and vaults more often. Gladiatorial games, that most Roman entertainment, were also introduced to the Greek world. Initial revulsion – there was a riot in Antioch at the first – evaporated as Greeks, too, developed a taste for these brutal thrills. More positive and far more significant was the emergence of a new Graeco-Roman ruling class, exemplified by men such as the orator Aelius Aristides or Dio Cassius, a Greek who became a Roman consul and historian. By AD200 a single Graeco-Roman culture had developed across the empire.

*Above: The emperor Hadrian, in whose reign (*AD117–138*) Greeks became almost equal partners with Romans. Hadrian himself was made archon of Athens, a city he loved deeply.*

GREECE REBORN:
RENAISSANCE AND RENASCENCES

Above: Desiderius Erasmus
(1466–1536), the pioneering
Renaissance scholar who
learned Greek to translate the
Bible, so unwittingly paving
the way for the Reformation.

Below: The stadium at
Olympia, site of the ancient
Olympic Games last held
in AD393.

Linked to Rome, ancient Greece declined with it. The last Olympic Games was held in AD393; five years later invading Visigoths ravaged the peninsula, looting the temples. Finally, in AD529 the Academy in Athens was closed on the (east Roman) emperor Justinian's orders. Early Christianity, though Greek-speaking, was almost as hostile to Hellenism as the barbarians were. By AD600 ancient Greece was dead. All knowledge of Greek was lost in Western Europe. "*Graecum est: non legitur*" ("it is Greek, not read") medieval monks wrote besides passages in Greek. Only translations of Aristotle from the Muslim world, which retained some Greek knowledge, revived interest in that philosopher in the 13th century.

THE REVIVAL OF HELLENISM
The ghost of Greece, however, lived on. In 1438 the Council of Florence tried to reconcile differences between the Eastern and Western Churches. It had small success, but among the Eastern bishops was Bessarion, a scholar who stayed in Italy, befriending other Greek fugitives after Constantinople fell to the Turks in 1453. They brought with them manuscripts – principally by Plato, Greece's greatest

philosopher – which Bessarion collected. In Renaissance Florence, Cosimo de' Medici founded a Platonist Academy in 1462 to study Greek and philosophy. Soon Plato's birthday was being celebrated, and Socrates was being hailed as a pagan saint, by cardinals and princes as well as scholars.

ART AND THE SCRIPTURES
The Renaissance engendered a Platonic desire (as *eros* best translates) for spiritual truth incarnate in physical beauty. Newly discovered Roman copies of Greek statues inspired Renaissance artists. Botticelli's *Birth of Venus* illustrates Greek myth in romantic Neoplatonist mode, while Michelangelo created art sublimely Platonist in aspiration. If this artistic and intellectual rebirth hardly affected politics – democracy was unthinkable in Renaissance Europe – it resurrected classical art in the Western world.

THE ENEMIES OF DEMOCRACY
For many scholars Socrates has been seen as a martyr to intellectual freedom, put to death by the rudely ignorant mob. But this veneration can at times lead to ambivalence about democracy itself. Socrates exists for us mainly in the pages of Plato, and Plato was no friend of democracy. In the 20th century, as totalitarian tyrannies on the right and left flourished, the political philosopher Karl Popper attacked Plato as one of the great enemies of the 'open society', inspiring Fascism *and* Communism. Popper's attack (in *The Open Society and its Enemies* 1945) coloured more than one generation's views, although it has since been criticized. The questions and dilemmas first raised by the Greeks remain alive to trouble or inspire us to this day.

A novel use of Greek was for studying the Scriptures, originally written in Greek. Desiderius Erasmus (1466–1536) was amazed to find the Vulgate (Latin Bible) riddled with errors. His translations and biting commentaries caused a furore, paving the way for the Reformation. Erasmus spent years in England teaching Greek at Cambridge University, which became a centre of the New Learning. Queen Elizabeth I herself learned Greek. By 1600 knowing Greek was essential for any self-respecting scholar. But Hellenism's full impact had yet to be felt.

THE SHOCK OF THE OLD

In the late 18th century, travellers returned from Greece with news of a radically simple yet powerful architecture. Finds at Pompeii, that time capsule of Graeco-Roman art buried by Vesuvius, were already leading the arts toward a purer Neoclassical style. But the brutally gigantic Doric columns seen in classical Greek temples amazed Europe and America. Confronted for the first time with true classical Greek architecture, architects reinvented their own art. The British Museum in London, the Brandenburg Gate in Berlin and much of Edinburgh shows how Greek temples could be lovingly recreated in the most unlikely places.

The late 18th century was the age of revolution in America and France. While the American Founding Fathers looked mainly to Republican Rome for models, the Achaean League's federalism also inspired them. Full democracy, not thought practical in America in the 1780s, was embraced in revolutionary France ten years later. Some French Revolutionaries, following the philosopher Jean-Jacques Rousseau's primitivist ideas, looked to Sparta as an ideal state. But the full (male) franchise, fleetingly achieved by the First French Republic for the first time for 2,000 years, was inspired by democratic Athens. Not by coincidence, fashions of the time echoed those of Greece and Rome in architecture, furniture and women's clothes.

Literature reflected the new 'Hellenomania'. Poets in England such as Keats and especially Shelley, who wrote dramatic poems such as *Prometheus Unbound* modelled on Aeschylus, supported radical democratic politics. Shelley's friend Lord Byron gave his life in the cause of resurrecting Greek liberty. Politically, the Greek precedent became ever more inspiring as democracy spread in the 19th and early 20th centuries. Abraham Lincoln deliberately modelled his Gettysburg speech on Pericles' funeral oration. Later generations still feel the lure of Greece, the true birthplace of democracy.

Above: The Pantheon in Rome, Greek in its name (meaning 'for all the gods') and fusing Greek and Roman ideals, is the finest ancient classical building extant. It was an inspiration to Renaissance artists and architects, especially to Raphael (1483–1520), who is buried inside it.

Right: The Laocoön, the remarkable Hellenistic statue whose rediscovery in Rome in 1506 proved a crucial inspiration for Michelangelo, the greatest Renaissance sculptor.

PART TWO

THE ANCIENT GREEK WORLD

The legacy of ancient Greece, the world's first great classical civilization, has shaped the way we live today. Visually, her sculptors and artists and the creation of the classical orders of architecture have influenced the development of art all over the world. Legends of the twelve Olympian gods, the Trojan War and Hercules and other Greek heroes form one of the world's richest mythologies. Intellectually, the work of Socrates, Plato, Aristotle and other Greek philosophers and political thinkers has led to the birth of democracy as the most widely accepted form of good government. Artistically, Greece's great playwrights, Euripides, Sophocles and Aristophanes, brought about the first flowering of the drama as an art form. This absorbing account of Greek society covers every aspect of the life and work of its many peoples.

Above: The ancient Citadel at Mycenae.
Left: The Erechtheum, Athens.

INTRODUCTION

The world we live in today was made by the ancient Greeks. This is no overstatement, although the Greeks had no cars, computers or aircraft and lived very simple lives. The way we perceive both our external and internal worlds springs from the way the Greeks began to think, talk and act, with unprecedented energy, 2,500 years ago. Our architecture, astronomy, technology, medicine, athletics, theatre, maths, drama – history itself – began with the Greeks. The Greek roots of these words reveal how Greeks blazed the way that the Western world has followed since. Without the Greeks, the modern world could not exist today. Insofar as the whole world today follows Western precedents, it ultimately is following the Greeks.

The Greeks did not invent everything, of course. Egyptians and Babylonians had earlier made vital discoveries in architecture and astronomy, and Greek thinking had notable gaps – the Greeks had no concept of zero, for example. But the Greeks enjoyed in their *poleis* (their city-states), a freedom to think and speak that was lacking elsewhere at the time and in most other places for long after. In their open societies they thought and talked freely, forging artistic and intellectual prototypes for millennia to come. This happened despite – or perhaps because of – their relative poverty. Even by the standards of their time, the Greeks were far from rich.

A POWER TO SURPRISE

Greek art still has the power to surprise. People who know only white marble statues of obscure gods or heroes in museum corridors understandably feel that nothing could be more dead and cold than these frigid white males.

Above: The Charioteer of Delphi, *one of the few Greek bronze statues to survive, seems almost hieratically solemn in his long robe. Dating to c.473BC, this was an offering from Hieron, ruler of Syracuse. His eyes still have their original inlay.*

This is the wrong reaction, however. What we usually see today are dull Roman copies, in stone or marble, of lost Greek originals. Those statues, often of bronze and always brilliantly painted, with eyes inlaid with bright stones and hair separately coloured, must have once seemed thrillingly, even alarmingly, alive.

The Riace bronzes are twin statues of athletes (or warriors) fished out of the sea off Italy in 1972. Preserved almost miraculously intact, they give an idea of Greek sculpture at the start of the Classical period. The athletes, made by an unknown but brilliant artist in about 470BC, quiver with muscular energy. With traces of paint still adhering to their lips, teeth and eyes, they look as if they have just stopped exercising in the gymnasium (which is another Greek word for a

Left: The Greeks spread from their cramped peninsula across the whole Mediterranean, founding independent poleis as they went. Some of the cities, such as Marseilles, Naples and Byzantium (today Istanbul), still thrive.

Greek concept). Striding confidently forward, they appear in their nakedness almost dangerously alive and glamorous, not at all like cold statues in museums.

Even less survives of Greek painting, but sketchy if vivid murals from royal tombs in Macedonia of *c.*330BC hint at what has been lost. Later Greek painting styles, often dazzlingly realistic, survive in copies made in Pompeii, buried intact by Vesuvius' eruption in AD79.

Greek temples, their architects' supreme achievement, looked very different from today's austere ruins, being painted and even gilded in ways that might strike modern eyes as shockingly gaudy. (Such decoration served to emphasize, not disguise, their form, however.) When complete, the buildings and statues on Athens' Acropolis glittered in the sunlight, trumpeting the pride – or arrogance – of the world's first democracy.

DEMOCRATIC EXCELLENCE
The Greeks never thought that popularity and artistic excellence were incompatible – that their direct democracy must involve cultural or intellectual dumbing down. Classical Athens at its zenith in the

5th century BC demonstrated the exact opposite. The whole citizen body (not the whole population, but a large section of it) voted for the building of the temples on the Acropolis, still among the most admired buildings in the world. The same ordinary citizens listened to day-long performances of plays by Athenian playwrights and then chose the prize-winners. Posterity has generally agreed with their judgements, which cannot be said of every critic.

Greek theatre, however, was not like the theatre today, but more like a combination of opera, ballet, musical and concert. An event of high culture, it was also a political rite for the whole people. Up to 17,000 spectators could sit in the theatre in Athens, which, like all Greek theatres, was open to the sky. Theatre had strong religious connotations, being sacred to Dionysus, god also of wine and ecstasy. Gods and myths were never far from Greek life.

MYTHIC RESONANCES
Every culture has its myths, sometimes embodying archetypal human truths, but few legends have proved so enduringly

Below: This entrance corridor, dating from the 4th century BC, leads to the Stadium at Olympia. This was one of the holiest of Greek shrines, where the quadrennial Olympic Games were held for almost 1,200 years from 776BC.

Above: Taken from the sea off Euboea, this majestic bronze of Zeus, king of the gods, dates from c.460BC. It is one of the finest original Greek statues to have survived.

Below: The Temple of Aphaia on the island of Aegina has survived unusually intact. Built c.510–490BC and sited on a rocky hilltop, it is one of the most complete and perfect examples of a Doric temple.

inspirational as the Greeks'. We still talk casually of someone's Achilles heel, of Pandora's box or Herculean labours. Greek myth has also provided universal metaphors or analogies for some of the greatest modern artists and scientists.

Freud, father of psychoanalysis, kept a statue of the Sphinx – Egyptian in origin, but absorbed into Greek legend at an early date – in his study in Vienna, along with statues of Eros, god of sexual desire. Working on his theory of the Oedipus Complex, derived from Sophocles' tragedy *Oedipus the King*, he wrote: "Oedipus' fate moves us because it might have been our own", making the doomed king of myth a modern everyman. Picasso, before painting *Guernica*, the 20th century's most famous painting, had returned to the myth of the Minotaur, which had long fascinated him. The Minotaur is one of Picasso's most compelling images because this half-human, half-taurine monster of ancient Crete expresses perfectly the artist's anguish about war.

Many 20th-century poets and playwrights turned to Greek mythical archetypes. W.B. Yeats often used Greek myths in his poems and majestically translated Sophocles' tragedy, *Oedipus at Colonus*. T.S. Eliot tried to revive Greek poetic drama in *Sweeney Agonistes* and *The Family Reunion*. W.H. Auden reworked Greek legends in poems such as *The Shield of Achilles* and *Atlantis* to illustrate the dilemmas facing modern humanity. The playwright Eugene O'Neill adopted the themes of the *Oresteia*, a trilogy of plays by Aeschylus, to describe the impact of the American Civil War, while Tennessee Williams recast the myth of Orpheus, the archetypal poet, for his confessional play *Orpheus Descending*. The grandest Greek legend of all, the Trojan War, fascinates Hollywood still.

THE BIRTH OF REASON

Out of the mythic background there emerged the first scientific and philosophical attempts to understand and explain the world, human and natural. Early philosophers were also scientists and mathematicians, with Thales reputedly being the first to predict a solar eclipse in 585BC. Pythagoras, a figure about whom myths cluster, was a philosopher, mathematician and mystic. He traditionally discovered the theory of the triangle bearing his name and suggested that the Earth floats freely in space. This proved immensely stimulating, for it was soon realized that the Earth must be round.

Working in the Museum/Library of Alexandria, the era's intellectual powerhouse, Eratosthenes calculated the globe's circumference remarkably closely. Aristarchus even suggested that the Earth spins around the Sun – a suggestion too far for the age, but one that later inspired Copernicus in the 16th century. In the 2nd century BC, Euclid laid down the elements of maths in books that remained authoritative until almost 1900. In medicine, Hippocrates originated the clinical analytical approach that still underlies modern doctoring. (Many Greek intellectual achievements were to be preserved in the Islamic world during western Europe's Dark Ages.)

The Greeks invented history and philosophy also. Other cultures had shown historical and philosophical interests, but only the Greeks, uniquely free from priests and kings, could examine the past with critical freedom – *historia* actually means 'inquiry'. Only in free cities like Athens could philosophers debate the aims of human life or the nature of the cosmos. (Socrates, pushing Athenian tolerance beyond its limits, was executed, but his trial was unique in Greek history.) Little wonder that Herodotus is known as 'the father of history' or that later Western philosophy has been called 'footnotes to Plato', Socrates' greatest disciple.

ATHLETES AS HEROES

The Greeks were not just intellectuals: they also pioneered competitive sports, for 'gymnasium', 'athletics' and 'Olympics' are Greek words. The Olympic Games, the first great sporting contest, started in 776BC. It was held every four years for almost 1,200 years at Olympia in southwestern Greece. (The modern games rekindled the Olympic torch 1,500 years later.) Modern concepts of the perfect body derive from Greek ideals. Physical excellence was seen not as a way of keeping fit – although the Greeks were very fit – but as part of a holistic concept of life, uniting body, mind and spirit. Musical and poetry contests were also held at many games.

Victorious athletes, who won only a crown of olive leaves, returned home to be greeted as heroes, touched with divinity. Statue, such as the *Charioteer of Delphi* were raised to their triumphs, and sacrifices were made to them after their deaths. The suppression of the Olympic Games in AD393 symbolized the passing of ancient Greece.

ATHENS, ROME AND JERUSALEM

By the end of the 1st century BC most Greeks were living under Roman control. This loss of liberty, although resented at the time, had its compensations, for the Romans proved willing preservers and

transmitters of Greek culture. Educated Romans such as Cicero studied in Athens, and Cicero later translated much Greek philosophy into Latin.

The same adoption and adaptation shaped Roman literature and religion. Paradoxically, a religion that spoke Greek finally destroyed the world of ancient Greece. Jesus and Pontius Pilate must have talked in Greek, then the common language of every educated man across the Mediterranean world. The New Testament is written in Greek, the word Christ (*Christos*) being Greek for Anointed One.

Without the impact of Hellenism, Christianity might have remained just an obscure heretical Jewish sect – as imperial Rome initially regarded it. As it grew, Christianity was deeply influenced by Plato's philosophy, propagated by two great thinkers: the heretic Origen and the saint Augustine. Rome's political collapse in the west after AD400 hardly interrupted this religious process. Athens, Rome and Jerusalem are still the triple pillars of the Western world. Christian or otherwise, we remain the heirs of Greece.

Above: The Temple of Poseidon at Sunium is superbly sited overlooking the sea. Built around 440BC by an unknown architect, it was a landmark for sailors rounding the cape as they headed for Athens.

Below: The Erechtheum, one of the temples on the Acropolis, was named after the ancestor of Theseus, the legendary king of Athens. It was completed in 405BC.

TIMELINE

Ancient Greek history, both cultural and political, stretches back to the early Bronze Age in the Aegean, a time about which very little is definitely known.

The history of ancient Greece, however, does not really end with the end of antiquity, whenever that is defined. (Some time between the 4th and 7th centuries AD is the general consensus). The story of ancient Greece's cultural and intellectual influence continues long after ancient Greece itself had vanished, for the idea or ideal of Greece resurfaced in the 15th century AD in Renaissance Italy and is still powerful today.

Dates and events cluster most thickly around the great central centuries, from 500 to 300BC. This was the Classical Age in Greek culture and politics, to which later generations looked back in awe and often tried to emulate.

All dates mentioned are BC (BCE) unless otherwise stated. Almost all dates before 500BC, and many dates afterwards relating to cultural events, are conjectured or approximate.

Below: The theatre in the Sanctuary of Apollo at Delphi of the 4th century BC.

Above: The Late Minoan palace at Cnossus, Crete, dating to c.1500BC.

2000–600BC

2000BC Building of first palaces in Crete.
1700BC Building of new Cretan palaces after major earthquake.
1600–1550BC Zenith of Minoan art in Crete and Aegean Islands; *Lily Prince* fresco at Cnossus; first royal grave shafts at Mycenae; murals painted in Thira.
*c.*1500BC Volcanic eruption of Thira ravages central and southern Aegean.
1400BC Destruction of Cnossus palace.
*c.*1300BC Building of Palace of Nestor at Pylos, of citadel at Tiryns and 'Treasury of Atreus' at Mycenae.
1280BC Building of Lion Gate at Mycenae.
1190BC Traditional date of Trojan War.
1100BC Final collapse of Mycenaean civilization; beginning of Dark Ages.
1050BC Dorian migrations into Greece; Ionian migration to western Asia Minor.
800BC Wooden temple to Hera on Samos; start of Middle Geometric Style.
776BC First Olympic Games (traditional).
*c.*750BC Foundation of Cumae in Italy, first Greek colony in west; Homer writes *The Iliad*.
730–710BC Homer writes *The Odyssey;* Sparta's first conquest of Messenia; beginning of hoplite fighting.
700BC Hesiod writes *Theogony* and *Works and Days;* Greek colonization of western Mediterranean intensifies.
*c.*650BC Carving of *Auxere Statuette;* creation of Lion Avenue at Delos.
*c.*630BC Birth of poet Sappho.
*c.*620BC Poet Alcaeus born; *Chigi Vase.*
620BC Dracon's Law Code in Athens.

Above: Terrace of the Lions, Delos, a sacral avenue of the 7th century BC.

600–500BC

600BC Aesop traditionally compiles *Fables;* Polymedes of Argos sculpts *Cleobus* and *Biton*, a pair of *kouroi.*
594BC Legislation of Solon in Athens.
590–580s BC Poets Sappho and Alcaeus flourish in Lesbos; Temple of Artemis in Corfu; Temple of Hera at Olympia.
585BC Thales, the 'first philosopher' of Miletus, predicts solar eclipse.
575BC Birth of poet Anacreon.
570BC Births of philosophers Pythagoras and Xenophones of Colophon.
*c.*560BC *François Vase* made by Cleitias.
550BC Achaemenid Empire of Persia founded by Cyrus the Great; Sparta forms the Peloponnesian League; temples of Zeus and Apollo at Syracuse.
546BC Cyrus conquers Lydia and begins conquest of Ionian Greeks; Pisistratus reaffirms power as *tyrannos* of Athens.
540s BC Temple of Apollo at Corinth begun; temples of Hera at Samos and Artemis at Ephesus built by Theodorus of Samos (died 540BC); Exekias makes *Dionysus in a Ship*, a glazed *kylix* (cup).
525BC Emergence of black figure vases in Athens; birth of playwright Aeschylus; Treasury of Siphnians built at Delphi.
520s BC Pisistratid tyrants start Temple of Olympian Zeus in Athens.
518BC Birth of Theban poet Pindar.
511BC Phrynicus wins prize for his first tragedy.
510BC Temple of Aphaia at Aegina.
508BC Cleisthenes' radical reforms lead to full democracy in Athens.

Above: Athenian Treasury, Delphi, built by the new democracy in 510BC.

Above: The Temple to Poseidon at Sunium built c.440BC.

Above: Caryatids of the Erechtheum on the Acropolis, Athens, 4th century BC.

500–460BC

*c.*500BC Birth of Anaxagoras and Hippodamnus; Heraclitus active.

499BC Outbreak of Ionian Revolt; Athens sends force to help.

496BC Birth of Sophocles.

495BC Birth of Pericles.

494BC Defeat of Ionians by Persia; Phrynicus' play *Fall of Miletus* causes uproar in Athens.

490BC Athenians defeat Persians at Marathon; birth of Pheidias; *Apollo of Piombino* bronze nude cast.

484BC Birth of Euripides.

480BC Battles of Thermopylae and Salamis, Persian fleet destroyed; *Critios Boy* made: first truly classical statue.

479BC Persian army defeated at Battle of Plataea.

477BC Critios and Nesiotes sculpt (2nd) statues of Harmodius and Aristogeiton.

473BC *Charioteer of Delphi* bronze.

472BC Aeschylus's *Persians* staged.

471BC Ostracism of Themistocles.

*c.*470BC Birth of Socrates; death of Phrynicus; Riace bronzes made.

*c.*468BC *Labours of Hercules* frieze carved by 'Master of Olympia'.

467BC Battle of Eurymedon – end of Persian threat to Aegean.

462BC Democratic reforms of Ephialtes and Pericles.

*c.*460BC Outbreak of war between Sparta and Athens; birth of Hippocrates, first great physician; bronze *Zeus* from Sunium cast; *Amazonomachia Vase* made by 'Niobe Master'.

460–430BC

458BC Pericles completes reforms; Aeschylus' *Oresteia;* Long Walls of Athens.

457BC Birth of Thucydides the historian.

456BC Death of Aeschylus; completion of Temple of Zeus at Olympia.

*c.*450BC Birth of Aristophanes; Pheidias completes his first statue of Athena Lemnia; *Apollo* carved for Temple of Zeus at Olympia.

449BC Peace of Callias with Persia; Athens invites Greeks to help her restore her temples.

447BC Parthenon and the Panathenaic frieze (*Elgin Marbles*) begun.

446BC Pindar writes last *Ode;* 30 Years' Peace with Sparta (actually to 431).

443BC Ostracism of Thucydides, son of Melesias, confirms Pericles' supremacy.

440S BC Temples to Hephaestus in Athens and to Poseidon at Sunium.

438BC Gold and ivory giant statue of Athena by Pheidias set up in completed Parthenon; Euripides' *Alcestis* staged; death of Pindar.

437–432BC Propylaea built on Acropolis; Herodotus completes his *History.*

*c.*435BC *Doryphorus* (Spear-carrier) statue by Polyclitus; Anaxagoras and Protagoras teaching in Athens in Pericles' circle.

431BC Outbreak of Peloponnesian War; Pericles' Funeral Oration; Euripides' *Medea;* Pheidias creates gold and ivory statue of Zeus at Olympia.

430BC Plague devastates Athens; Pericles tried and fined; birth of Xenophon; death of Anaxagoras.

429–404BC

*c.*429BC Birth of Plato; Zeuxis, 'master of realism', painting in Athens.

428–425BC Mnesicles builds temple to Athena Nike on Acropolis; Aristophanes' *Acharnanians;* death of Herodotus.

424BC Loss of Amphipolis to Spartans leads to banishment of Thucydides, who starts writing his history of the war.

421BC Peace of Nicias; Paionius sculpts marble *Nike* in Olympia.

415BC Syracusan expedition sails under Nicias and Alcibiades; Alcibiades recalled.

413BC Disastrous loss of Syracusan expedition; Euripides' *Electra;* building of Temple of Apollo at Bassae.

411BC Oligarchic revolution at Athens.

406BC Euripides' *Bacchae* staged in Macedonia; deaths of Euripides and Sophocles.

405BC Athens' defeat at Aegospotamoi.

404BC Surrender of Athens; Long Walls pulled down; dictatorship of The Thirty.

Below: The Parthenon at Athens, the supreme Greek temple, 5th century BC.

Above: Sculpture depicting horse racing, from the Agora, Athens.

Above: Corcyra (Corfu) was one of the most important Corinthian colonies.

Above: Pillars of the Temple of Apollo, Corinth from the 6th century BC.

404–360BC

403BC Restoration of Athenian democracy and general amnesty.

401BC 'March of the 10,000' Greek mercenaries; Xenophon leads them home.

401BC Posthumous production of Sophocles' *Oedipus at Colonnus*.

400BC Death of Thucydides.

399BC Trial and execution of Socrates.

394BC Tombstone of Dexileus at Athens.

393BC Athens completes rebuilding of her Long Walls.

392BC Aristophanes' last play, *Women in Parliament*.

387BC Plato founds his Academy just outside Athens.

386BC The King's Peace: Sparta abandons Ionians in return for Persian support.

384BC Birth of Aristotle; Timotheus builds Temple of Asclepius at Epidaurus.

379BC Anti-Spartan revolution in Thebes led by Epamonindas and Pelopidas.

376BC Athens defeats Spartan fleet at Naxos; Mausolus becomes satrap of Caria; Jason establishes rule in Pherae.

375BC Praxiteles carves *Satyr Pouring Wine* for Athenian Agora.

371BC Peace of Callias between Sparta and Athens; Thebes defeats Spartans at Leuctra, becoming hegemon.

369BC Foundation of Messene and liberation of *helots* by Thebans.

367BC Dionysius I of Syracuse dies, succeeded by Dionysius II; Plato visits Syracuse to teach Dionysius philosophy.

362BC Epamonindas' death at Mantinea ends Thebes' hegemony.

360–330BC

359BC Accession of Philip II of Macedon.

357BC Philip marries Olympias.

356BC Birth of Alexander the Great.

352BC Philip defeats Phocians and becomes *tagus* (ruler) of Thessaly.

350BC Praxiteles sculpts *Aphrodite of Cnidus*; Scopas sculpting Maenads.

354BC Demosthenes' first public speech; murder of Dion in Syracuse.

347BC Death of Plato; Aristotle leaves Athens; building of Mausoleum at Halicarnassus with sculptures by Scopas.

341BC Birth of Epicurus in Samos.

340BC Philip attacks Byzantium; Alexander left as regent of Macedonia; Lysippus sculpts *Apoxymenos*.

338BC Battle of Chaeronaea: Theban and Athenian armies defeated by Philip.

337BC Council of Corinth elects Philip as general to lead anti-Persian crusade.

336BC Philip II murdered; accession of Alexander III.

335BC Alexander destroys Thebes; Aristotle starts teaching at Athens, founds Lyceum; Apelles painting at court of Alexander.

334BC Alexander crosses to Asia; defeats Persians at Granicus; liberates Ionia.

333BC Alexander routs Persians at Issus.

331BC Foundation of Alexandria; trip to consult oracle at Siwah; Alexander routs Persians at Gaugamela; enters Babylon.

330BC Praxiteles carves *Hermes and the Infant Dionysus*; *Abduction of Persephone* murals painted at royal tombs, Vergina; Apelles paints *Battle of Issus* mural.

329–300BC

326BC Alexander reaches northern India, where his troops force him to turn back.

323BC Alexander dies in Babylon; Lamian War, revolt of Greeks against Macedonia.

322BC Ptolemy gains control of Egypt: Greeks defeated by Macedonia; deaths of Demosthenes and Aristotle; Athenian democracy curbed.

*c.***320**BC Ptolemy Leochares sculpts *Apollo Belvedere*; Lysippus sculpts *Hermes*; *Deer Hunt* mosaic from Pella by Gnosis.

317BC Menander's comedy *Dyscolus*.

312BC Seleucus I takes over eastern satrapies; founds Seleucia-on-the-Tigris.

310BC Birth of poet Theocritus and astronomer Aristarchus.

307BC Epicurus settles in Athens and begins teaching philosophy.

*c.***300**BC Zeno of Citium founds Stoic School in Athens.

301BC Battle of Ipsus: division of Hellenistic world into 4 main kingdoms.

Below: The Theseion, Athens, 5th century BC, *one of the city's best preserved temples.*

Above: Greece's mountainous nature meant the country was relatively poor.

Above: The Cycladic island of Delos was sacred to the god Apollo.

Above: Olympia was the site of Greece's greatest athletic festival.

299–200BC

295BC Ptolemy I founds Library at Alexandria; Euclid starts writing his mathematical *Elements*.

287BC Birth of Archimedes in Syracuse.

281BC Seleucus I defeats and kills Lysimachus, then is murdered himself; Antiochus I succeeds him (to 261).

279BC Building of Pharos at Alexandria.

*c.***275BC** Aristarchus of Samos proposes heliocentric theory.

274–232BC Reign of Asoka, first Buddhist emperor in India, of part Greek descent.

270BC Hieron emerges as saviour of Syracuse, assuming crown as Hieron II.

264BC First Punic War between Carthage and Rome starts.

*c.***255BC** Bactria breaks away from Seleucid control, its example followed by Parthia.

250BC *Nike* of Samothrace sculpted.

229BC Athens 'buys out' Macedonian garrison, in effect becoming neutral.

*c.***225BC** Eratosthenes calculates circumference of the Earth.

221BC Philip V succeeds to Macedonian throne (to 179BC); Ptolemy IV defeats Antiochus III at Raphia (218).

218–201BC Second Punic War.

217BC Peace Conference at Naupactus: warning of the 'shadow of Rome'.

216BC Battle of Cannae.

212BC Fall of Syracuse to Romans: Archimedes killed in the fighting.

202BC Hannibal finally defeated at Zama.

200BC Egypt, defeated by Antiochus III at Ionion, loses southern Syria/Palestine.

200BC *Boy Pulling Thorn from Foot* sculpted.

199–1BC

197BC Rome defeats Macedonia at Cynoscephalae in 2nd Macedonian War.

190BC *The Finding of Telephus* mural painted at Pergamum.

188BC Treaty of Apamea: Seleucids, defeated by Rome, lose Asia Minor.

180–160BC Pergamum Altar erected.

168BC Polybius taken to Rome as hostage.

166BC Romans enslave 150,000 Epirotes, make Delos a free port; slave trade booms.

*c.***150BC** Demetrius of Alexandria paints *topographoi* landscapes; First Pompeiian Style of wall painting emerges.

146BC Romans sack Corinth; make Achaea and Macedonia Roman provinces.

120BC Nile Mosaic from Praeneste.

*c.***100BC** Hagesandros sculpts *Venus de Milo*; *Alexander Mosaic* made at Pompeii.

86–85BC Sulla sacks Athens.

*c.***80BC** Second Pompeiian Style.

78BC Cicero studies at the Academy.

66–63BC Pompey reorganizes the east.

50BC *Laocoön* copy made in Rhodes.

*c.***45BC** Cicero writes *Scipio's Dream*.

44BC Caesar assassinated; renewed Roman civil wars.

44–22BC Strabo the geographer active.

42BC Battle of Philippi: Cassius and Brutus defeated by Antony and Octavian; Antony takes eastern empire, winters in Athens.

31BC Battle of Actium: Cleopatra and Antony defeated by Octavian.

30BC Egypt annexed to Roman Empire.

4BC Birth of Seneca, philosopher, and Apollonius of Tyana, mystic; Third Pompeiian Style of wall painting emerges.

AD1–1462

AD14 Augustus, first emperor of Rome, dies.

AD46 Birth of Plutarch, historian.

AD60s Heron active in Alexandria.

AD65 Death of Seneca.

AD87 Birth of Arrian, historian/general.

AD120 Birth of Pausanias, travel writer; building starts on Hadrian's Villa at Tivoli.

AD131 Hadrian completes Temple of Zeus in Athens, becomes *archon* (ruler).

AD140s Ptolemy, astronomer/cartographer, active in Alexandria.

AD160s Galen, physician, active in Rome.

AD169 Emperor Marcus Aurelius starts writing philosophical *Meditations*.

AD204 Birth of Plotinus in Alexandria.

AD250s/60s Plotinus teaching in Rome, Emperor Gallienus among his students.

AD313 Edict of Milan: Emperor Constantine I accepts Christianity.

AD324–30 Constantinople founded as 'New Rome'.

AD361–3 Emperor Julian's *Orations and Letters Against the Christians*.

AD393 Last Olympic Games held.

AD395 Roman Empire finally divided.

AD410 Sack of Rome by Goths.

AD412 St Augustine begins writing *The City of God*.

AD485 Death of Neoplatonist Proclus.

AD529 Justinian I closes Academy and other philosophy schools in Athens.

1438 Gemiston Plethon unveils esoteric Neoplatonism in Italy.

1453 Fall of Constantinople to Turks.

1462 New Platonist Academy founded in Renaissance Florence.

ARCHITECTURE AND ART

Mention 'ancient Greece' and many people will think of temples consisting solely of columns, of blank-eyed white statues of naked men or women without arms. Such 'pure' but boring images are misleading. The temples we see today laid open to the sky are only the sunbleached skeletons of structures once adorned with statues and painted deep crimson, blue and gold. The white marble statues that today seem so chilling are seldom Greek originals (these were usually of bronze and always vividly painted) but dull, semi-competent Roman copies. The art the Greeks themselves created was more intense, astonishing and original than the art now lodged in museums. But it needs a leap of the imagination to realize this, for so much has been lost.

In painting, sculpture and architecture, Greek artists' drive toward ideal form was linked to their increasing skill at realistic depiction. The statues created by Pheidias and Polyclitus in the 5th century BC are both mathematically and anatomically perfect. With them, the human nude became the template for Greek concepts of humanized divinity. Our ideas of the perfect body, along with our ideas of architectural perfection epitomized in the Parthenon, spring from the Greeks. They envisaged the entire world in humanized form, but they also believed that mathematical principles underlie the universe.

The historian Plutarch, describing the temples of the Athenian Acropolis erected 500 years before his lifetime, wrote: "They were created in a short time for all time. Each building in its fitness was even then at once age-old. But in freshness and vigour each seems even now recent and newly made." His words apply equally powerfully to sculpture and to painting.

Left: Part of the Acropolis of Athens in 1857, site of the most famous Greek temples, as seen by the Belgian artist Florent Mols before restoration.

CHAPTER XIII

THE RISE OF GREEK ARCHITECTURE

Greek architecture, at its zenith in 480–320BC, did not have a long history. The Minoans and Mycenaeans had raised sophisticated buildings, but these were forgotten in the Dark Ages after 1200BC. When the Greeks began building again after 700BC, they started from scratch. Within 300 years they moved from timber and mud-brick huts to the symmetrical all-marble Parthenon in Athens. This meteoric rise owed a little to external influences but it soon became an original, self-sustaining achievement. If, after 400BC, Greek architecture changed only slowly, this did not bother the Greeks. They were less interested in ephemeral fashion than in perfection. This explains why they long stuck to *trabeated* architecture, dependent on column and lintel, although they knew of *arcuated* architecture, which involved the use of arches, vaults and domes.

A Greek temple was intended to be viewed from the outside. Today we see Greek temples almost inside out, with their interiors open to the sky, their exteriors stripped of all colouring and adornment. The Greeks never believed decoration was a crime, although they painted buildings to emphasize the forms, not disguise them. The forms themselves were perfection. Greeks also built *stoas* (porticoes), theatres, council halls and fountains.

Left: All Greek temples were brightly decorated. Only marble skeletons remain, their inner sanctuaries now open to the sky.

MINOAN ARCHITECTURE
2000–1400BC

Above: The Grand Staircase of the Palace at Cnossus, with its tapering Minoan columns, dates from c.1550BC.

Below: The Palace at Cnossus was laid out around courts, passages and staircases in a seemingly haphazard way – perhaps the origin of the myth of the Labyrinth.

The first European architecture emerged in Minoan Crete in *c.*2000BC. Minoan culture (named after the mythical King Minos) spread across the Aegean, but its centre was Crete. The Minoans' origins remain uncertain, but they were almost certainly not Greeks. Their buildings, while colourful, comfortable and ingenious, lack the Greeks' passion for symmetry. But the Minoans deeply influenced the Mycenaeans, who *were* Greek.

Cretan architecture focused on palaces, not tombs, temples or citadels. The Minoans built palaces not on a superhuman scale to overawe their subjects, as in Egypt or Babylonia, but as cheerfully decorated rambling homes and administrative centres. All had large storerooms with jars containing olive oil and wine. They were also unfortified. This suggests an unusually peaceful culture, possibly relying on a navy for external defence. (Traditionally, Minos was the first ruler of the seas.) Cnossus and Phaestus are the largest, best-excavated palace sites, but there were several other smaller sites, some termed 'royal villas'.

THE FIRST PALACES

The first palaces arose around 2000BC as increased trading links with Asia and Egypt quickened economic life. Asian and Egyptian models may have first inspired Minoan builders but they soon developed distinctive features. These include light-wells, alabaster veneer over walls made of mud-brick, ashlar or gypsum, columns made of inverted tree trunks tapering downwards, and porched courts. Often fine staircases lead to the *piano nobile* (main floor) with the best rooms upstairs, anticipating a later Mediterranean custom.

The most striking feature of the first palaces is the absence of any real plan. Rooms and courtyards seem to have been added piecemeal as need arose. The perhaps deliberate asymmetry has led to Minoan architecture being called 'accumulative'. The overall effect is pleasingly picturesque rather than grandly imposing.

CNOSSUS: HOUSE OF THE DOUBLE AXE

Around 1700BC a devastating earthquake destroyed most major buildings in Crete – the island is notoriously seismic – and all the palaces were rebuilt. This time there are signs of planning at least at Cnossus, the greatest palace, which was colourfully, if controversially, half-restored by the archaeologist Arthur Evans in the early 20th century. He thought that Cnossus now ruled the whole island.

At Cnossus a grand central court 91.5m (nearly 100 yards) long formed the new palace's core. Aligned nearly north–south, the court was flanked by colonnaded terraces rising three, perhaps four floors above. Opening off it to the west lay the Throne Room, the throne flanked by superb griffin frescoes. To the east rose a Grand Staircase, now reconstructed,

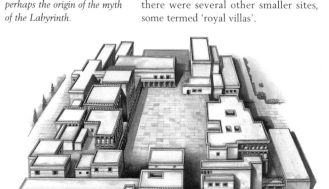

while beneath was the 'Queen's Megaron', decorated with gay frescoes of dolphins. Nearby was a bathroom with running water and flushing toilet, more advanced than anything known much later in classical Greece.

A suite of rooms nearby, the finest on the ground floor, is called the Hall of the Double Axes from the two-bladed axes, religious symbols, carved on its walls. It also served as a throne room. The Hall was open at both ends, with columns separating it from a light well at the west. Beyond a colonnade was another light well. There were no solid internal walls, only wooden partitions fitted with double doors. Open in summer and closed in winter, these kept the apartments comfortable all year. There were similar rooms on the floor above.

West of the courtyard ran a maze of magazines holding vases of oil, connected by dark corridors. These probably inspired the legend of the Labyrinth in which lurked the Minotaur, bull-headed offspring of Queen Pasiphae and a bull, eating Athenian maidens. But the overall

Below: A reconstruction of the Throne Room at Cnossus, where King Minos may once have sat, flanked by painted griffins.

tone of the palace is cheerful. It should really be called the House of the Double Axe, *labrys* meaning 'axe' in Lydian, a language related to old Cretan. Covering 2ha (5 acres), Cnossus was the largest, most sophisticated building in the Mediterranean world. Phaestus and other smaller palaces echoed its splendours, all being brightly painted inside and out, with tapering dark red or blue pillars rising above landscaped gardens. All were destroyed between 1500 and 1400BC.

Above: Phaestus in southern Crete was the site of the second-largest palace, similar in overall design to Cnossus.

Below: Minoan palaces rose to four or even five floors, with light wells flanked by columns.

MYCENAE: A CITADEL-PALACE
1550–1100 BC

Above: The Mycenaeans were brilliant engineers, building huge corbelled domes of great sophistication.

Below: The Lion Gate, the monumental entrance to Mycenae, built c.1280 BC.

Mycenaean buildings were very different from the Minoans'. The Mycenaeans – whom Homer called Achaeans – had overrun the peninsula by 1900 BC. A warlike Greek-speaking people, they came into contact with the Minoans around 1600 BC, growing wealthy through trading, raiding or fighting as mercenaries. After 1450 BC they dominated Crete itself, trading from Sicily to Egypt. They used their wealth to transform their hill forts into elaborate citadels. Inside them the Achaean warrior-kings built palaces that reveal their debt to Minoan culture.

MYCENAE "RICH IN GOLD"

Greatest of their citadel-palaces was Mycenae, "rich in gold" in Homer's words. Mycenae dominated the fertile Argolid plain, controlling the trade routes to the Corinthian Isthmus. In legend, its rulers, the feuding Atreids, were acknowledged as High Kings by other Greeks. Its lords and those of nearby Tiryns have left the most dramatic fortifications in Bronze Age Europe before the Middle Ages.

At the centre of every Mycenaean palace and large house lay a *megaron* (great hall). Square or rectangular, this room had four pillars around an open circular hearth, often under a lantern roof that let smoke out and light in. The megaron served as the main baronial hall and sometimes as the throne room. (At Mycenae there was another throne room.) A *propylaeum* (ceremonial gateway) was common at the megaron's entrance, often with a porched court in front of that.

All were arranged on a clear axis to create an imposing approach. The axial plan of Mycenaean buildings resurfaced in later Greek architecture. Beyond or above the megaron lay private royal apartments, built of timber and mud-brick like most Mycenaean dwellings. These had murals so Minoan in style that Cretan artists might have been employed, but the themes – horses, chariots, warriors – were very different from Crete. Bathrooms similar to those at Cnossus have been found at Tiryns and elsewhere, but much of Mycenae's royal palace has fallen down a ravine.

THE LION GATE

A visitor to Mycenae at its 13th-century peak would have approached up a steep well-paved chariot road to see the Lion Gate towering above him. Built c.1280 BC, it was part of massive fortifications enclosing the whole hill. The Lion Gate consists of three giant slabs of cut ashlar, with the lintel surmounted by two great stone-carved lions, whose now-lost heads once turned to snarl downward. The regal menace of this sculpture derives from Hittite models (in Anatolia), but the lions flank a Minoan-style column, revealing a cultural mixture. Entering, the visitor would pass on the right tomb circles from the 16th century BC (where the archaeologist Heinrich Schliemann later found

what he thought was the mask of Agamemnon.) A chariot ramp zigzagged up to the palace, but those on foot could use a direct staircase.

While the palace itself was small compared to that at Cnossus, let alone those in Egypt – its court measured only 15 by 9m (50 by 30ft) and the megaron was about the same size – it was flanked by sizeable other houses such as the House of Columns. A smaller version of the palace, its colonnaded court anticipates those of wealthy Greek dwellings 1,000 years later. There were no great temples, the Mycenaeans presumably conducting their worship outside.

'TREASURY OF ATREUS'

The most imposing Mycenaean structure is a tomb, the 'Treasury of Atreus', so-called because of a misconception by its discoverers. Lying outside the citadel and dating from *c*.1280BC, it might have been the tomb of Agamemnon, the Achaean leader in the Trojan Wars, and others of the Atreid dynasty. It is a *tholos*, a circular chamber with a dome made of corbelled stone resembling a beehive. It is entered by a 38m (120ft) long *dromos*, a long narrow passageway burrowing into the earth, with walls of cut stone giving a suitably sepulchral approach. The door to the tomb has tapering sides and an inward slant, a style derived from Egypt. Above it is a triangular opening to relieve pressure on the lintel, once richly decorated with Minoan-style spirals.

The tomb's doors, originally of bronze, were flanked by columns of green limestone crowned with mouldings resembling Egyptian water-lily capitals. The tholos chamber, 13m (43ft) high and 14.5m (47ft 6in) in diameter, had a smooth interior surface once covered with gold, silver and bronze decorations. Although a tholos is not a 'true' dome – a corbelled dome relies on corbelled or projecting stones to close the gap – the 'Treasury of Atreus' remained the world's largest masonry dome until the building of the Pantheon in Rome 1,400 years later.

Below: The so-called 'Treasury of Atreus' at Mycenae, actually a vast royal tholos-type tomb, where the kings of Mycenae were buried in splendour with their treasures.

Above: A reconstruction of the citadel at Mycenae protected by its massive walls, for long the greatest in all Greece.

TIRYNS AND PYLOS
CONTRASTING PALACES 1500–1150BC

Two very different palaces in the Peloponnese's far corners reveal the variety of Mycenaean palace architecture.

TIRYNS: THE MIGHTY CITADEL

Tiryns, standing on a ridge a few miles to the south-east, is better preserved than Mycenae, though lacking its dramatic legendary associations. Homer called it "mighty-walled". This is, most unusually for Homer, a poetic understatement, for its walls are truly massive, being 6m (20ft) thick and originally even higher.

The upper citadel was fortified in c.1400BC along the crest of the ridge. Its walls were formed of massive rough-hewn blocks, probably inspired by Hittite examples in Anatolia. (The Mycenaeans and Hittites were in diplomatic and trading contact, so knowledge of the massively fortified Hittite citadel at Hattusa could have reached Greece.) The main Eastern Gate at first opened directly on to the slope but was progressively improved until the gate was approached from the north and then along a passageway between high walls.

Above: A passage within the massive Cyclopean walls of Tiryns, the most complete Mycenaean citadel-palace to have survived.

Below: The megalithic walls at Tiryns, still standing after 3,200 years, which later Greeks thought must be the work of giants.

CYCLOPEAN WALLS

The Greeks who lived after the 12th-century BC collapse of Mycenaean civilization assumed that only the Cyclopes, mythical one-eyed giants of vast strength, if little brain, could have built such massive structures as Mycenae or Tiryns. This was not such an absurd assumption, for the megaliths ('big stones') of the walls of Mycenae, Tiryns and similar palaces are huge stone slabs. On average they weigh 5–7 tons, crudely hammered into place. Some are even larger. The lintel above Mycenae's Lion Gate is estimated to weigh at least 20 tons, being 4.5m (15ft) long by 2m (7ft) wide and 1m (3ft) tall. Mycenae, like most Achaean citadels, stands on top of a steep hill. How builders who had only bronze tools excavated and then transported such huge stones remains unknown. Clearly, the kings of Mycenae could call on massive labour forces, free or servile.

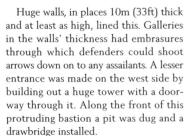

Huge walls, in places 10m (33ft) thick and at least as high, lined this. Galleries in the walls' thickness had embrasures through which defenders could shoot arrows down on to any assailants. A lesser entrance was made on the west side by building out a huge tower with a doorway through it. Along the front of this protruding bastion a pit was dug and a drawbridge installed.

The palace these walls tightly enclosed was, in contrast, very modestly sized. In the 13th century BC it was reconstructed with a Minoan-style outer propylaeum, which measured approximately 13.5 by 13.75m (44 by 46ft) giving on to a smaller propylaeum. Beyond lay the megaron, its plastered floor painted with squares of marine life. Its design perpetuated

Minoan fashions of centuries before. So did the murals of women dressed in fashions seemingly copied from Cnossus. Around the megaron clustered the living apartments, including the bathroom. This had a 20-ton block of limestone as its floor, however, a markedly non-Minoan touch.

THE PALACE OF NESTOR

Safely distant from the Argolid's battle-fields in the south-western Peloponnese are the ruins of the palace called after Nestor, Homer's venerable king. According to legend, Nestor's father came from Thessaly to found a new kingdom in Messenia. Nestor later took 90 ships to fight in the Trojan Wars, forming the second largest Greek contingent. Archaeology seems to confirm legend. An early Mycenaean settlement on a hill overlooking Navarino Bay was replaced about 1300BC by a new palace. This flourished – unwalled, most remarkably for a Mycenaean – for the next 100 years.

The Palace of Nestor is the most complete Mycenaean palace excavated. The new palace was entered from a formal propylaeum through a simple porchway with a single fluted wooden column, with a guard by the door. Across an inner courtyard paved in stucco with great pillars on both sides was a modest megaron and beyond that the Great Megaron, measuring 13 by 11.2m (42 by 37ft). At its centre was a great round hearth with a lantern to let smoke out.

Against the east wall stood the throne, flanked by frescoes of lions, griffins and deer. Here it is easy to imagine that Homeric heroes such as Nestor and Telemachus might have feasted while bards sang of the Trojan War. But Homer is never a wholly reliable guide for archaeologists. Stairs led to domestic rooms above, while to the north-east lay workshops, offices and store-rooms.

The Palace of Nestor at Pylos was, like most Aegean buildings, built of ashlar stone around a timber frame with timber pillars. This made it vulnerable

to fire, and fire destroyed the palace soon after 1200BC. From clay writing tablets baked in that fire we read of preparations to repel the invaders, perhaps northern Dorian tribes. Pylos, last and most graceful of the Mycenaean palaces, was apparently the first to fall. But refugees from Pylos sailed east. Some found shelter in Athens, the 'unsacked city', others sailed on to Ionia in the eastern Aegean.

Above: The magnificently constructed tholos tomb at Pylos, perhaps the royal burial place of the Neleid dynasty mentioned by Homer.

Below: The megaron (reconstructed) of the Palace of Nestor at Pylos, the last-built and most elegant of Mycenaean palaces.

THE DARK AGES
1100–600BC

Above: The huge columns of the Temple of Amon at Karnak were a possible influence on early Greek architecture.

Below: The Temple of Hatshepsut, Egypt, was perhaps an influence on early Greek temples.

Some time after 1200BC the Mycenaean world collapsed. In its place emerged a simpler, poorer world with limited horizons and even more limited architecture. Greeks, as we can now call them (*Greek* is a Roman name, they called themselves Hellenes) forgot the reality of Mycenaean life but hazily remembered its legendary heroes. It is uncertain if Dark Age Greeks remembered actual Mycenaean architecture, although they may have been influenced by grand Egyptian temples they saw. But over the next few centuries there was to be no building in stone at all.

THE FIRST BUILDINGS
The oldest structure unearthed is at Lefkandi on Euboea island, dating from *c.*1000BC. Remarkably large – 45 x 9m (150 by *c.*30ft) – it was perhaps a cross

Above: The Hippostyle Hall at Karnak must have awed Greek traders and mercenaries with its imposing stony grandeur.

between a tomb and temple, with a stone base but mud-brick walls and thatch roof, surrounded by a colonnaded court with timber pillars. More typical are two small temples near Corinth to Hera, the wife of Zeus, considered mother of the gods. These were simple wooden thatched huts with timber porches and rounded ends. Around 800BC a temple to Hera was built on Samos. While still built of wood, it anticipates later temples in its strict rectilinear plan. It was large – 30m (100ft) long – and *peripteral*, i.e. its inner *cella* was surrounded by an external colonnade added *c.*750BC. (It was rebuilt several times over the next centuries, each time progressively more grandly.) All these buildings had pitched roofs, unlike most Bronze Age structures.

The whole tradition of Greek architecture probably originated in the carpentry techniques needed to make these timber buildings. So thought Vitruvius, the influential Roman architect writing in the 1st century BC. In the *entablature* of the Doric

EGYPTIAN INSPIRATION?

While Greece languished in its Dark Age, Egypt recovered from attacks by the 'Peoples of the Sea'. It continued its millennial culture with little perceptible change in its architecture. Greece had strong trading links in the 7th and 6th centuries BC with Egypt, Naucratis being founded as a Greek colony in the Delta. Possibly Greek traders or mercenaries brought home knowledge of the massive, almost Doric-looking columns of the Temple of Amon at Karnak or the Temple of Hatshepshut, Deir El Bahri, the latter dating from c.1470BC. Egyptian influence on contemporary Greek sculpture is indisputable, but remains debatable on the development of Greek temples.

order, the first of the three Greek orders of columns (usually demonstrated in the capitals of the columns), *triglyphs* represent the end of the original wooden crossbeams, *guttae* were the pegs used to fasten them and *metopes* were the spaces between the beams. The Greeks stuck faithfully to these forms, often called 'petrified carpentry', long after they began building in stone.

CLAY TILES, STONE COLUMNS

A key development was the invention of terracotta (fired clay) roof tiles after 700BC. Tiles, being much heavier than timber or thatch – some early examples from the mid-7th century weigh 30kg (66lb) each – led to the need for stone columns and masonry walls to support them. They also produced ridge roofs with a shallower pitch. Among the first stone temples, that of Poseidon, on the Corinthian Isthmus of c.650BC, had walls wholly of cut stone, but its columns were wooden. At the Temple of Apollo at Thermon in north-western Greece of c.630BC, the upper walls were made of mud-brick but its wooden entablature (the superstructure between the capitals

and gutter) had brightly painted terracotta panels showing gorgons and other mythical creatures. Parts of this survive. Its tiled roof was supported by 15 wooden columns on each side and five at each end, a prototypical Doric temple.

By 600BC the Greeks were starting to build temples wholly in stone, with roofs made of terracotta tiles on wooden beams. By then the basic form for later Greek temples was established. Temples, flanked by columns, generally faced east, with their main altars outside. The *procella*, or vestibule, of the east front led directly to the cella, which held the statue of the god or goddess in sacred darkness.

Above: The Temple of Poseidon at Isthmia, dating from c.650BC, was one of the first Greek temples with stone walls. This picture shows it at a much later date when it was far more ornate.

Below: The Beach of Aphrodite in Cyprus, the one part of the Greek world where Mycenaean customs long survived almost unchanged.

THE EMERGENCE OF THE GREEK TEMPLE 600–530BC

In the 6th century BC the tempo of Greek life began to accelerate. This cultural and social quickening reflected the economic recovery that made even archaic Greece wealthier than the Mycenaean world. Wealth was now more equally spread, also. This affected Greek architecture, for money was spent building temples for all the city, not palaces just for kings. A surge of confidence in building techniques led to the construction of early stone temples.

These temples are large, often with crudely massive Doric columns. The columns' gigantic size may reflect early architects' anxiety about supporting the new tiled roofs and masonry entablatures. Equally possibly, they were built so heavily just to impress.

From the start, all temples were designed to be seen mainly from the outside, as were almost all Greek buildings. At first, columns were overwhelmingly of the Doric order, or type. This consisted of a fluted (grooved) column rising directly from the ground like a tree trunk – early columns were often monoliths –

Above: The Temple of Hera at Samos of c.580BC, *whose lower walls still stand, is among the earliest surviving Greek temples. (The columns are of a later date.)*

Below: At Selinus (Selinunte) in Sicily, three temples from the 6th century BC remain, with some massive Doric columns intact.

with a shallow capital supporting an entablature decorated with a triglyph and metope frieze. ('Doric' refers also to one of the two main Greek dialects, the other being Ionian. The Peloponnese, southern Aegean islands and many Sicilian cities were Dorian, but the Doric order was at first the architectural norm even among Ionians. The most perfect Doric temple of all is the Parthenon in Ionian Athens.)

Among the earliest temples with a full Doric order was the Temple of Artemis at Corcyra (Corfu), built c.590BC. Long since demolished, its pediment had sculpted figures – a giant gorgon surrounded by panthers at the front to frighten away evil spirits, with a *gigantomachia* (battle of gods and giants) on the sides. Built c.580BC, the Temple of Hera at Olympia, site of the Olympic Games, has its base walls still standing, although the present three Doric columns are later. Its cella walls were of limestone masonry at the base but the rest of the structure was still mud-brick.

The Temple of Apollo at Corinth from c.540BC has seven giant Doric columns standing. Originally there were six columns at the temple's ends and 15 on each side, each column being a limestone monolith 6.6m (21ft) high covered in stucco. Their bare forms, high above the Gulf Corinth, are still powerfully dramatic. The base under the columns rises in a gentle convex curve, the first example of *entasis*, the device to correct the illusion (if seen from a distance) of drooping in the middle that would arise if the base was really level.

TRIGLYPHS AND METOPES

This temple also shows Greek architects grappling successfully with a fundamental problem of the Doric order: Greek architects insisted on putting a triglyph over each column,

Above: The Temple of Apollo at Corinth dates from c.540BC, where seven giant Doric columns are still standing. The other 35 have long since fallen.

symbolizing the weight carried by the column. But they also wanted to end every frieze with a triglyph, not a less-powerful metope. As corner triglyphs could not be placed centrally over corner columns, end columns were placed closer together than the rest, while end metopes are 5cm (2in) wider than the others. Greek architects soon recognized such subtleties.

FIRST TEMPLES IN THE WEST
Founded in 735BC, Syracuse became one of the richest cities in this booming new world. Two Doric temples were built in Syracuse in the mid-6th century BC: the Temple of Olympian Zeus and that of Apollo. Both had 17 columns on each side and six across the end. In the Temple of Apollo, several survive and have been reinstated. They are monoliths, 8m (26ft) high, tapered and irregular in size. Those at the opposite corners of each end differ by as much as 30cm (1ft) in diameter from those at the other. The height of some columns is only four times their diameter. The effect, bulky rather than accomplished, suggests that this was a

pioneer building. At Selinus, in western Sicily, ruins remain of three huge temples, partly restored, dating also from the 6th century BC. All boast massive columns.

On the Italian mainland at Poseidonia (Paestum), the 'Basilica', actually a temple to Hera of the 6th century, has similar monumental columns with vast capitals. The bare virile power of these early temples much impressed visiting Neoclassical architects in the 18th century, who did not realize that originally all temple columns had been stuccoed.

Above: At the Temple of Apollo at Syracuse, built in the 6th century BC, monolithic Doric columns survive, exuding primitive strength.

Below: At Poseidonia (Paestum) in southern Italy, the 'Basilica', actually a temple to Hera of the 6th century BC, has monumental columns with vast overhanging capitals.

THE DEVELOPMENT OF THE GREEK TEMPLE 530–480BC

Above: The upper colonnade of the Temple of Aphaea, c.500BC, which is most unusually part-intact.

Under the Pisistratids, a dynasty of enlightened tyrants who ruled Athens intermittently from 560 to 510BC, the city became increasingly prosperous. It also emerged as one of Greece's leading cultural centres, and now began building proper Doric temples.

The Temple of Athena Polias, the divine guardian of Athens, was probably the very first temple erected on the Acropolis, being built in about 530BC. It had sculptures on its pediments carved in marble and in the round – a double first. Later, a huge temple to Olympian Zeus was started east of the Acropolis but the Pisistratids lost power in 510BC before it had progressed beyond its base plan. (It was finally completed under the Emperor Hadrian in AD130.)

After Athens' triumphant defeat of the Persians at the battle of Marathon in 490BC, a new temple to the city's goddess was started on the Acropolis and a propylaeum built at the Acropolis entrance with fine Doric columns.

However, all the Acropolis' buildings were torched in the two Persian invasions and sacks of 480–479BC, and any reconstructions remain predominately conjectural. While walls and columns were now of stone, roofs still had wooden beams.

THE TEMPLE OF APHAEA

The great Doric Temple of Aphaea, goddess of sailors and hunters on the island of Aegina south of Athens, survives remarkably well. Built c.510–490BC, the temple is sited on a rocky hilltop with superb views. Most of its columns survive almost up to roof level, allowing the upper colonnade to be seen half-extant for once. The *pteron* had six monolithic columns on the ends and 12 on the sides, sloping inwards to increase the impression of strength. The columns again have entasis (convex swelling) to make the columns appear regular when seen from afar. The *stylobate* has an upward curve.

Built of local limestone, the Temple of Aphaea now gleams serenely pale gold, but originally it was faced with cream-painted marble stucco and had bright-painted ornamental features such as lions' heads. Its triglyphs and guttae were painted dark blue, while other parts of the entablature were deep red – colours that were later used on the Athenian Parthenon. This again reveals how mistaken earlier ideas about Greek 'pure white marble form' were. Greek temples, like the lives of the Greek themselves, blazed with impassioned colour. The older sculptures from the temple's west pediment depict graceful smiling warriors, while figures on the east front, carved 20 years later, are more heroically muscular, indicating the revolution that was starting to transform Greek sculpture.

Left: The 'Temple of Neptune' at Poseidonia (Paestum) of c.510BC is the best-surviving western temple.

GIANT TEMPLES OF THE WEST

Out in the Greek west, temples were built of remarkable size, splendour and quirkiness. Most notable of these is the Temple of Olympian Zeus at Acragas (Agrigento) in south-western Sicily. Although only founded in 580BC, Acragas was among the wealthiest cities in the Greek world. It built the largest Doric temple ever, measuring 110 by 53m (361 by 173ft), with columns originally 20m (65ft) high.

The temple, started c.505BC, was unfinished when Carthaginians sacked the city in 406BC and almost nothing remains. Raised on a platform 4.5m (15ft) high, its huge outer columns, seven at each end and 14 along the side, were engaged (half-sunk) into the walls. This was a novel idea, perhaps designed to help carry the weight of the large entablature. At the temple's corners, however, the columns were necessarily three-quarters round. Further, the entablature, walls and half-columns were not made of solid masonry blocks but built of relatively small stones. As the diameter of each column exceeded 4m (13ft), this must have made them easier and cheaper to build.

The Acragas temple has another peculiarity, which gives it its nickname 'Temple of the Giants'. From masonry fragments since reassembled and from medieval records, made before the temple was destroyed by quarrying, we know that the temple incorporated huge male figures, about 7.6m (25ft) high, the Atlantes. (They are named after the mythical giant who upheld the heavens on his shoulders.) These titans supported the architrave, standing on a ledge, one between each pillar. Remnants of their vast forms have been tentatively reassembled. It is unlikely that the temple's interior was ever roofed over.

THE 'TEMPLE OF NEPTUNE'

North at Poseidonia (Paestum) on the Italian mainland, the so-called 'Temple of Neptune' (really yet another temple of Hera, that most important of goddesses),

was started c.510BC. It has survived better than any other western temple. Its pediment, outer columns and architraves are still almost intact. It is relatively conventional in plan, with a pteron of six by 14 columns, measuring 24 by 59m (79 by 196ft). Here, too, the external columns, 8.9m (29ft) high, taper sharply, giving this temple also an impression of rugged, almost truculent strength. The western Greeks, rich but remote from the accepted conventions on the mainland, were developing an original, albeit quirky, form of architecture.

Above: A typical Doric temple showing the brightly painted and richly carved frieze and pediment, and the marble pillars, with the slight convex curve known as entasis that made them appear straight.

Below: The Temple of Aphaea on Aegina shows the Doric temple approaching perfection. It was built c.510–490BC.

THE IONIC TEMPLE
560–400BC

Above: Ionic columns are chiefly identified by their rolled-up forms resembling cushions or rams' horns, which create their distinctive volutes.

While the Doric order at first dominated the Greek world, it was soon rivalled by the Ionic order, a more slender, graceful style of column and capital (head). The Ionic order first appeared in the sophisticated Ionian cities and the Aegean islands in the 6th century BC, spreading to the mainland. It became seen as the feminine order, in contrast to the more 'virile' Doric order.

Preceding the Ionic order was the Aeolian, a capital common in Aeolis in north-western Asia Minor around 600BC. This had *volutes* (spiral scrolls) growing up and out of the column, supporting a rectangular slab. (It is now thought that there was no direct connection between the Aeolian and the Ionian orders, for the oldest Ionic capitals date only from 560BC, while their volutes, in the form of rams' horns or scrolls, turn downward and inward. Also, Aeolic columns had no bases but Ionic columns stood on elaborate bases.)

THE FIRST IONIC TEMPLES

The first true Ionic columns appeared in two vast temples: the Heraion at Samos and the Artemision at Ephesus. Remarkably similar, they were both built in the mid-6th century BC by Theodorus of Samos (died 540BC). An architect of genius, he wrote the first architectural treatise, now lost. King Croesus of Lydia, wealthy overlord of Ephesus, paid for most of its temple. Both buildings were dipteral, i.e. they had a double *pteron* (colonnade), an imposing feature perhaps inspired by Egyptian examples.

Both temples were later destroyed by fire, although that at Ephesus was rebuilt more grandly to become one of the Seven Wonders of the World in the Hellenistic and Roman ages. Both had two rows of eight columns at the entrance, with the columns' spacing and thickness gradually increasing toward the centre to make them look regular seen from afar, as with most Greek temples. At the Heraion on Samos the two central columns were 8.6m (28ft) apart while the outermost pairs were only 5.9m (17ft) apart. It was about 88.4 by 45.7m (290 by 150ft).

The Temple of Artemis at Ephesus was even larger, measuring 109 by 55m (358 by 171ft). Built of limestone covered in marble, the first temple to be so built, its tall, slender columns had richly moulded bases, each with a horizontally fluted *torus*. Sculptural display was ornamental rather than structural in a way that became typically Ionian.

Left: The Ionic columns of the north porch of the Erechtheum, started in 421BC and completed in 405BC, are among the earliest extant uses of the Ionic order in Athens.

Ionic columns had no triglyphs or metopes. Instead, in Asiatic Ionic temples rows of *dentils* ran below the cornice, while in west Aegean Ionic style there was a band of stone, often richly sculpted.

THE TREASURY OF THE SIPHNIANS

One of the first half-extant Ionic temples, built in 525BC, the Treasury of the Siphnians at Delphi, was also the first marble temple on the mainland. Although its base is limestone, its superstructure uses Siphnian marble for the main wall, Naxian for its outer decorations and Parian for its sculptural adornments. Its porch boasts two large free-standing *caryatids* (female statues) similar to those later erected at the Erechtheum on the Athenian Acropolis. The caryatids wear tall hats carved with figures of men and lions. The frieze and even the pediment have sculpted figures carved in high relief, all once brightly painted in red, blue and green. Unpainted, fresh-cut marble must have gleamed blindingly white in strong Greek sunlight.

BUILDING IN MARBLE

Although Greece was blessed with abundant limestone, Greek architects around 500BC began to realize that building completely in marble made it possible to produce far clearer, crisper outlines for both orders of columns. However, marble was very expensive except near quarries. The first major use of marble in temple-building at the Artemision of Ephesus was made possible by King Croesus, a famously rich ruler. Pisistratus reputedly used marble roof tiles for his Temple of Athena Polias in the 530s BC, but he had connections with Paros. Even for the Siphnians, it must have been costly to haul the marble for their small treasury up the mountains to Delphi.

Once they had done so, however, others felt the urge to compete. Cleisthenes, the wealthy Athenian radical aristocrat, probably sponsored the building of the Treasury of the Athenians c.500BC. This, also resembling a mini-temple, is the first

Doric all-marble building. In Athens itself marble remained forbiddingly expensive until a quarry was opened on nearby Mt Pentelicus soon after 500BC. When Athens finally began rebuilding after the end of the Persian wars, it found marble of the highest quality on its doorstep. New claw chisels were needed to work this harder, more brittle material, but the remarkable results on the Acropolis astound us still.

Above: The Treasury of the Athenians at Delphi built soon after 500BC, resembling a mini-temple, is the first Greek all-marble structure, and still Doric in style.

THE PARTHENON
A PERFECT TEMPLE

Above: The Parthenon, perhaps the most famous temple in the world, was built by Ictinus and Callicrates from 447BC. It brought the Doric temple to perfection.

Below: The Parthenon on the Acropolis as it may have looked in its prime, lavishly decorated and colourfully painted. Built as a gleaming statement of Athenian national pride, it housed the great cult statue of Athena, tutelary goddess of the city.

When the Athenians returned to their burnt-out city in 479BC after the Persians had been defeated, they ignored the blackened stumps of their temples on the Acropolis. In the Oath of Plataea that year they had sworn not to rebuild the temples as a reminder of Persian sacrilege in burning them. For decades anyway, they were occupied in fighting Persia. But in 449BC the Persian wars ended with the Peace of Callias. The Athenians then debated what to do with the tribute money still flowing in from their allied (or, increasingly, their subject) states in the Delian League.

Pericles – the radical aristocrat who so dominated the age that he has given his name to it – urged the money be used to rebuild the city's temples. His proposal triggered a violent debate. Some Athenians agreed with Thucydides, son of Melesias, cousin of the historian, that this would be a misuse of the funds. But Pericles won the argument.

Work began in 447BC on what many consider the world's most perfect building: the Parthenon, temple of Athena, virgin (*parthenos*) goddess of the city. Within 15 years the Parthenon had been completed. It has become the archetypal image of ancient Greece.

Above: The frieze running around the Parthenon showing horsemen in the Panathenaic Procession, carved to the general designs of Pheidias.

Pheidias, the great sculptor, had overall charge of the project, but the joint architects were Callicrates and Ictinus. The latter wrote a book about the Parthenon's construction, which, like much Greek literature, has been lost. But the temple itself embodies the key principles of Greek classicism so closely that it has been read almost like a book by successive archaeologists.

FOR THE GODS' EYES ONLY?
A strange aspect of the Parthenon is the position of the frieze, 161m (534ft) long, running high up around the cella's exterior. Meticulously carved, this must have been almost impossible for contemporary observers to see fully, being overshadowed by the architrave above when the temple was intact. The outer columns would have half-obscured it if seen from far-off. To look at the frieze standing close up on the stylobate must have required painful neck-craning. Possibly it was designed only for the all-seeing eyes of the gods. In this it anticipates Gothic cathedral carvings.

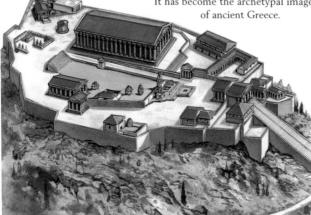

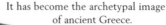

MARBLE COLUMNS AND GILDED STATUES

The building of such a huge marble structure in less than ten years – the sculpting took a further five years to complete – was an unprecedented feat. About 22,000 tons of marble were needed for the Parthenon and the Propylaea, the ceremonial gateway. Fortunately, Mt Pentelicum's quarries were only 13km (8 miles) away. Marble column drums surviving from the burnt earlier temple to Athena were incorporated into the new building, which rested partly on its predecessor's base.

The pteron measured eight by 17 columns, obeying the now canonical rule that the number of columns on the sides should be more than double those on the ends. The columns' height is 5.48 times their diameter, 10.4m (34.3ft) high. The stylobate, as usual, had three steps all round. Sited on the Acropolis' southern edge, the Parthenon remains strikingly visible from miles off. (It also remained essentially intact until its interior was wrecked in an explosion in 1683. That year the Venetians were besieging Athens, held by Turkish troops who were storing gunpowder in the temple. One direct hit gutted the Parthenon.)

In antiquity, worshippers who entered the Acropolis would at first have seen only the temple's carved pediment looming above a flanking wall. As they passed the Propylaea, their eyes would be caught by Pheidias' great outdoor bronze statue of Athena Promachos, 'the warrior', visible far out at sea. Turning a corner, worshippers could finally see the temple's east front ahead and enter the cella. Almost 30m (100ft) long by 10m (34ft) wide and divided in two, this was made of finely cut ashlar blocks. In its inner chamber stood the chryselephantine (gold-ivory over a wooden core) statue of the goddess, Pheidias' masterwork. A two-storeyed Doric colonnade framed the statue, while the outer chamber had internal Ionic columns, a radical innovation inside a Doric temple.

Unusually, all the metopes were sculpted in high relief, the pediments being filled with groups of figures, vividly painted. These include works by Pheidias depicting the city's legends. At each corner a lion's head was carved on the cornice, while above gilded winged victories mounted on *acroteria* seemed poised for flight.

TECHNICAL 'REFINEMENTS'

The Parthenon is renowned for its technical 'refinements', which make it the most accomplished of Doric temples. These include entasis and inward-tilting columns, so that those at the corners do not appear thinner, and the convexity in the stylobate and entablature. All were designed to make the temple look perfectly proportioned when seen from far off. (The columns' tilt means that theoretically they would meet in the sky 2.4km (1½ miles) above.)

Working in marble permitted such sophistication but inevitably required remarkable skills from the workforce. Their efforts produced the archetypal Greek temple.

Above: A view of the Parthenon from the north. It remained astonishingly intact until an explosion during a siege in 1683 blew it apart – it was being used to store gunpowder by the Turks.

Below: The Acropolis of Athens seen from afar, with its unsurpassable group of superb 5th-century BC temples.

ON THE ACROPOLIS
THE OTHER TEMPLES

Above: Jutting out high over the city, the tiny temple to Athena Nike, the first visible to worshippers approaching the Acropolis, was built in 428–425BC, probably by Mnesicles.

Below: The Erechtheum, completed in 405BC, rivals the Parthenon in elegance and surpasses it in ingenuity. It is named after Athens' legendary first king, Erechtheus. The close-spaced supporting caryatids emphasize the building's mass.

Around the Parthenon, smaller temples were subsequently built on the Acropolis, despite the war with the Peloponnesians that started in 431BC. Remarkably, even through the war's increasing disasters, work continued intermittently, bringing Greek classical architecture to its peak.

The Propylaea, the monumental Doric gateway at the west of the Acropolis, was the second building commissioned by Pericles. It was constructed in 437–432BC, work on it stopping before completion as war loomed. Little is known about its architect Mnesicles, but he probably also designed the Athena Nike temple opposite. The Propylaea was approached by a ramp about 25m (65ft) wide, the start of the Panathenaic Way leading down to the Agora (market place). It had two impressive temple-like façades of six Doric columns, one on each side.

IRON BARS AND CUNNING
Mnesicles solved the difficulty of erecting a symmetrical building on a sloping, irregular site by extending the architrave round the flanking buildings on the same level. However, the exterior junction of

the Propylaea's separate roofs must have looked awkward. The building is entered through a hexastyle (six-column) Doric porch, the two central columns being wider spaced to let sacrificial animals pass through. Beyond lay an imposing passage with Ionic columns supporting a rich marble ceiling. This, with its coffers (recessed panels) adorned with gold stars on a blue background, was a wonder of its age. It was also very expensive, the building costing 2,000 talents. The architraves over the colonnade were reinforced with iron bars, a remarkable innovation if superfluous structurally. Designing the Propylaea, the first complex building on different levels, required creating harmonious spatial relations between its varied parts. It inspired many later architects.

On the Propylaea's north side lay the *pinakotheke* (the picture gallery), where state banquets were held with platforms for dining couches round the walls. It also housed some of Athens' greatest pictures, depicting victories over the Persians at Marathon and Salamis, all long since lost.

On the other side of the Propylaea the tiny temple to Athena Nike was built, probably by Mnesicles, in c.428–425BC. It uses the Ionic order with four mono-lithic columns only 4m (13ft) high at each end, oddly thick for their size. The aim was probably to avoid too strong a contrast to the solid Propylaea. It had attachments for figures in its pediments and much fine carving, while its little cella is almost square. Jutting out high over the city, this exquisite temple is the first approaching visitors see.

THE ERECHTHEUM
Another Ionic temple on the Acropolis, the Erechtheum rivals the Parthenon in elegance if not size. Started in 421BC after the short-lasting Peace of Nicias and completed in 405BC, the year of Athens'

Above: The Propylaea, the monumental Doric gateway on the west of the Acropolis, was built in 437–432BC, work stopping before its completion as war loomed. Its architect was Mnesicles.

final catastrophic defeat, it was named after the legendary semi-divine first king of Athens. It is in fact a multiple temple, housing shrines to ten different gods and heroes, besides a pit of sacred serpents. Because the site is asymmetrical and on several levels, the Erechtheum is really two semi-detached temples with three porches facing in different directions. The asymmetry is minimized by the noble exterior, united by a harmonious Ionic order and frieze of low-relief figures in white marble on a dark background running around the temple like a belt. The whole Erechtheum, again built of marble, has carvings of an elaboration never repeated elsewhere in Greece.

The central larger temple, dedicated to Athena Polias (guardian), has a huge porch facing north over the city. It housed her ancient wooden statue, dating back to the Bronze Age, besides the supposed tomb of Erechtheus. Its smaller porch, on the south side facing the Parthenon, has famous caryatids (now copies) instead of supporting pillars. These draped female figures are close-spaced to create a massiveness echoing the Parthenon's.

The south porch, lower than the north, is raised on a wall to make it appear level. It was linked internally by a staircase.

The eastern temple was dedicated chiefly to Zeus, whose altar was in the porch. Inside were altars to Hephaestus, the fire god, Erechtheus and Poseidon. At the Erechtheum's west end stood the Pandroseum, an enclosure with the tomb of Cecrops, another Athenian mythical hero, and the sacred olive tree of Athena. Reputedly it sprouted fresh leaves after being burnt by the Persians in 480BC. The Erechtheum's interior suffered from being converted into the Turkish governor's harem under Ottoman rule (1455–1829).

Above: The hill of the Acropolis, towering above Athens, superbly displays the highest achievements of Greek classical architecture.

Below: The Erechtheum was a temple not to one deity but to ten, being in reality two semi-detached buildings with three porches, all on different levels. Its architect may also have been Mnesicles.

OTHER TEMPLES OF THE GOLDEN AGE

Above: The Temple of Poseidon the sea-god at Sunium was built by an unknown architect around 440BC. Superbly sited at Sunium on the point of Attica, it is made of local marble.

Below: The Hephaistion (Theseion) on the west side of the Agora was Athens' first all-marble temple. It was started in 449BC, being designed by the same unknown architect who built that at Sunium. It has survived better than any other Greek temple.

Although the temples on the Acropolis are Athens' most striking, many others were built in the city and across Greece in the 5th century BC. Oldest of the classical temples in central Athens itself was the Hephaistion (once called the Theseion) on the west of the Agora, the city's social and commercial heart.

Started in 449BC, it is the first all-marble Doric temple in Attica but lacks the Parthenon's subtleties. Its use of 'refinements' such as entasis is crudely obvious, so that the building only convinces when seen front-on. Happily, that is how most Athenians would have seen it, as trees or buildings on its sides probably prevented other views. Further, all its sculptured metopes are concentrated on its front or just around its corners. The relatively high entablature of 2m (6ft 6in), coupled with unduly slim columns of 5.7m (18ft 9in), would appear unimpressive if seen otherwise.

In plan the Hephaistion resembles the earlier temple of Zeus at Olympia in the Peloponnese, but is on half its scale,

ATHENS' LARGEST TEMPLE
The Pisistratids had started a gigantic temple to Olympian Zeus east of the Acropolis in c.520BC, its size reflecting both their dynastic pretensions and Zeus' status as supreme deity. They had got no further than its base before their expulsion in 510BC. For the next 350 years the site remained untouched until Antiochus IV, an energetic Seleucid king of Syria, paid for work to restart in 170BC. The architect was Cossutius, a Roman who had worked in the Greek east in opulent Hellenistic style. He continued with the basic plan but gave the temple gigantic columns of the Corinthian order. It was the first time this order had been used so grandly in Athens. But the temple was not completed as Antiochus' death in 164BC cut off funds. Sulla, the Roman general, removed some of the temple's capitals to Rome after sacking Athens in 86–85BC. Only when the philhellenic Emperor Hadrian visited Athens was the great temple finally completed in AD131. Hadrian's plan generally followed Cossutius' designs, but the standard of workmanship was not so fine. The columns are 16.7m (55ft) high and unusually proportioned, their height being equal to 8¾ of their lower diameter. The huge temple finally measured 108 by 41m (354 by 135ft).

measuring 31.7 by 13.7m (104 by 45ft). Possibly its carvings were influenced by those on the Parthenon, where work progressed more rapidly. The Hephaistion became a church in the 6th century AD, which explains why it is so well preserved. (Most temples were not converted to churches, chiefly because they were the wrong shape for Christian worship.)

THE TEMPLE OF POSEIDON

Very similar and probably built by the same unknown architect around 440BC is the Temple of Poseidon the sea-god. It is superbly sited at Sunium on the very tip of Attica. Though built of a less fine local marble, not pentelic, it shows the architect's skills developing. Its dimensions are similar to the Hephaistion's but the columns are 30cm (1ft) higher. Each column has only 16 shallow-carved flutes instead of the usual 20, removing the need for entasis. Whether seen by sailors rounding the cape or by worshippers approaching from land, the temple has always looked marvellous, gleaming hundreds of feet above the sea. It was built on the base of an earlier temple, which is thought to have beeen destroyed by the Persians in the invasion of 480BC.

BASSAE: A RADICAL INTERIOR

Equally impressive but very different is the Temple of Apollo Epikourius, Apollo the Helper, built by the small state of Phigaleia in Arcadia, the most rugged part of the Peloponnese. This was in thanks for divine deliverance from the plague, at least so wrote Pausanias 600 years later, who claimed that its architect was Ictinus who had just designed the Parthenon. But Apollo may have delivered the little state from foreign aggresion, not plague. *Epikouros* in ancient Greek can mean mercenary soldier.

The temple was probably started about 429BC and finished, after interruptions caused by Spartan occupation, in 400BC. Built of grey local limestone – at 1,127m (3,700ft) up amid mountainous ravines, Bassae is too remote to be supplied easily or cheaply with marble – the temple's proportions appear rather old-fashioned, with six by 15 columns. Externally it lacked most of the latest refinements such as entasis, which suggests that the builder was possibly a provincial.

However, its interior was remarkably radical, which suggests that Ictinus was indeed the real architect. Its cella is flanked by impressive Ionic half-columns

(sunk in the wall). Their bases are abnormally flared, echoing the flamboyant capitals. which have three-faced capitals with two volutes (scrolls) and curved tops. Most radical of all was a free-standing column with a Corinthian capital at the south end. (Originally there may have been two others. This column has since perished but is known from drawings.) Bassae is the first known use of the elaborate third order, which became so popular in the Hellenistic and Roman eras.

Above: The Temple of Olympian Zeus is the largest temple in Athens. Started in the 6th century BC, it was only completed in Hadrian's reign (AD117–138).

Below: The Temple of Apollo at Bassae in remote Arcadia was possibly designed by Ictinus, the Parthenon's architect, in 429BC.

THE WORLD'S FIRST
THEATRES

The Greeks built the world's first permanent theatres to stage their great plays. Athens, which pioneered drama and comedy in the 5th century BC, also pioneered the structural development of the Greek theatre. Its form then spread around the expanding Greek world and was finally taken over and adapted by the Romans. Greek theatres were always open to the sky, although March, the month of the Greater Dionysia and the annual drama contests, can be cold even in Greece.

Theatre in Athens began simply, using a natural hollow on the south slope of the Acropolis in the 6th century BC as its venue. This site was transformed over the next two centuries into the great Theatre of Dionysus, seating up to 17,000 spectators, and was embellished over the succeeding centuries into the Roman era. Classical plays are still performed in it, making it probably the world's oldest theatre still in current use.

Above: The vast theatre at Pergamum, capital of the wealthy Attalid kingdom in north-western Asia Minor, was carved from the steep acropolis side in the 2nd century BC.

Below: The theatre at Priene was small, suiting this tiny polis in Asia Minor. Built c.300BC, it is typical of many Greek theatres.

THE FIRST THEATRE

The auditorium of the first theatre was a simple semicircle of wooden benches perched on the steep 1 in 8 slope. Below was a round dancing area, the *orchestra*, about 25m (82ft) across. Here the chorus danced and sang and actors, first one, then two and finally more, stepped out to declaim. A plain stone wall acted as a backdrop. After the Persian defeat in 479BC, Xerxes' resplendent royal tent, 60m (200ft) wide, was used as a backcloth for plays, according to tradition. (*Skene*, later meaning background building or scenery, originally meant tent.) Outside the theatre stood a small temple to Dionysus, the god of drama.

As the city grew, the semicircle of tiered seating was expanded further up and round the Acropolis' slopes. Pericles is credited with building the first stone theatre in the 430s BC, along with the smaller covered *odeion* but many archaeologists date the oldest stone remains discovered to after 400BC However, there definitely was a wooden skene to which scenery could be attached in the 5th century. By the mid-4th century AD the theatre had achieved the form we associate with a Greek theatre: a hemisphere of stone benches rising above the semicircular orchestra, with a long stoa behind the stone skene, on which stage 'machinery' could create sometimes elaborate special effects.

EPIDAURUS, THE PERFECT THEATRE

The most beautiful and best-preserved of Greek theatres is that of Epidaurus in the north-western Peloponnese. Although Epidaurus was not a polis of much importance, it constructed the archetypal Greek theatre on a clear, uncluttered slope. (In Athens, buildings and a cliff hemmed in the theatre.) Probably built by the

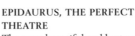

architect Polyclitus the Younger about 350BC, Epidaurus' perfectly symmetrical auditorium is 118m (387ft) in diameter and very nearly semicircular in plan. It boasts superb acoustics and also allows a good view from every seat – at least of the orchestra if not of the skene. The skene probably originally rose quite high. Later a proscenium, a structure jutting out from the skene, as the name suggests, was added on which actors performed. This suited the needs of the New Comedy, which depended more on individual characters interacting, less on grand choruses.

The stone seats are 76cm (2ft 6in) wide and 43cm (17in) tall. Like many ancient theatre seats, they are surprisingly comfortable. The best seats are in the centre low down. Two tall elegant doorways allowed easy entry and exit. The theatre seated about 12,000 people, a surprisingly large number for such a small city. It was probably seldom filled.

In the Hellenistic and Roman ages, theatres became steadily grander and more elaborate. That at Pergamum, capital of the wealthy Attalid kingdom, was carved dramatically from the steep acropolis side beneath the royal palace in the 2nd century BC. More typical was the theatre of Priene, which lay further south, a city rebuilt c.300BC, which resembles Epidaurus on a smaller scale. Here the skene had two storeys and a proscenium in front.

ODEIONS

All theatres were open-aired, seating many, sometimes all, the citizens, but covered buildings were erected for musical and literary events. Around 440BC, Pericles built the first odeion (from which comes our word 'odeum'), an immense covered building next to the theatre. Its wooden roof, topped by an open-sided lantern for light and ventilation but chiefly designed with acoustics in mind, was supported on 81 columns in nine rows. Reputedly, it too was modelled on Xerxes' tent, that paradigm of oriental luxury. The odeion hosted the musical and poetry contests at the four-yearly Panathenaic Games. Originally it had wooden benches but in the 4th century BC these were replaced by stone. Many cities later copied Athens' example.

Above: Epidaurus has the best-preserved and most beautiful theatre in the Greek world. Probably built by the architect Polyclitus the Younger c.350BC, its perfectly symmetrical auditorium has superb acoustics.

Below: Begun in the 6th century BC, the Theatre of Dionysus in Athens assumed its final form by the mid-4th century BC, when its tiers of seats and skene were completed in stone. Seating 17,000 spectators, it saw the premières of works by Aeschylus, Sophocles, Euripides and Aristophanes.

STOAS AND COUNCIL HALLS

Above: The Agora of Athens, the ancient heart of the city, showing the Stoa of Attalus, the only building of its kind fully restored, with the Acropolis in the distance.

Below: The Agora at Athens under the Roman empire, when it had become almost crowded with monuments. The oldest stoas from the 5th century BC are on the right (the Stoa Poikile housing with paintings) with the 'Royal Stoa'on the left. The bulky buildings, like the Stoa of Attalus at the top, are Hellenistic or Roman.

While temples and theatres are the Greeks' most famous public buildings, they developed many other buildings for urban life. From the 6th century BC on, increasing numbers of Greek cities built stoas: long, open-sided, pillared porticos, usually sited around the Agora. Giving shelter against winter rains or summer sun, and often carefully angled to admit warming winter sunlight, stoas sheltered many aspects of city life, from shopping or dining to philosophy. One important school of philosophy even took its name from a stoa: the Stoics.

THE FIRST STOAS

An early small stoa designed solely for shelter was at the Sanctuary of Hera in Samos from the 7th century BC. However, the first significant stoa that we know of was the Stoa Poikile (painted stoa), erected on the north side of the Athenian Agora soon after the Persian defeat in 479BC.

It took its name from the paintings on its north wall depicting heroic episodes in Athenian history. Ranging from

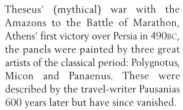

Theseus' (mythical) war with the Amazons to the Battle of Marathon, Athens' first victory over Persia in 490BC, the panels were painted by three great artists of the classical period: Polygnotus, Micon and Panaenus. These were described by the travel-writer Pausanias 600 years later but have since vanished.

Stoas were subsequently built all round Athens' Agora. Just south-west of the Stoa Poikile was the Royal Stoa, called after the 'King Archon', by then a purely ceremonial official. Beyond that another grander stoa to Zeus Eleutherios (Zeus the Deliverer) was built in the late 5th century BC. This had Doric columns externally but used the Ionic order inside. It was divided into compartments for different activities, which possibly included law courts.

THE STOA OF ATTALUS

Further stoas were built around the other sides of the Agora, the grandest being the Stoa of Attalus, the wealthy king of Pergamum. He endowed Athens with his superb two-storeyed stoa in the 150s BC. This has been totally reconstructed in recent years, to give a good impression of how the stoa must have looked when brand new. The lower floor has Doric columns, the upper floor and the interior Ionic. This arrangement soon became very common, even canonical, not only for stoas but also for other buildings. Even the Colosseum in Rome follows this pattern.

Many cities in Greece and across Asia, such as Miletus, Ephesus, Antioch and Pergamum, built extensive stoas lining their agoras and sometimes running down their streets. An unusually long stoa was the 'South Stoa' at Corinth, built around 300BC. It was 160m (525ft) long with 71 Doric columns along its straight façade. On the gutter was a row of water-spouts in the form of lions' heads, each separated by an acanthus scroll, a common decorative device. Water gushed up from wells inside the stoa, coming from the springs of Peirene at the Agora's east end. When the Romans sacked Corinth in 146BC, they found and burnt in the stoa shops containing paint, clay, lime, along with much elaborate pottery. This suggests that workshops were located there, making stoas truly multifunctional.

BOULETERIA: COUNCIL HALLS

Although the Assembly (*ecclesia*), the sovereign body in democratic Athens, met in the open – with a quorum of 6,000 it had to – the far smaller Council did not. The Council (*boule*), of 400 or 500 councillors chosen annually by lot, discussed and shaped new proposals before they went before the often unpredictable full Assembly. But unlike the Roman Senate, the boule had little real power, at least when Athens was a full democracy.

In Athens the older Council Hall (*bouleterion*) was a simple rectangular building on the west of the Agora, with a temple and document store attached. In the late 5th century BC a new bouleterion was cut into the hillside behind it, with tiers of seats in a semicircle like a theatre, the old building now housing the state archives. A ceremonial porch was added 100 years later. Other cities copied Athens' example. The small island of Thasos had an almost square bouleterion, and Miletus a grand semicircular building for up to 1,500 people. This looked out on to a colonnaded courtyard in the Doric order, with a gateway with Corinthian columns beyond.

Among the largest bouleteria was the Thersilion, built at Megalopolis in Arcadia. This new federal capital was founded late in 371BC after Sparta's long dominance of Arcadia had been ended by its crushing defeat at the battle of Leuctra. A rectangle measuring 86 by 67.7m (218 by 172ft), the Thersilion seated 6,000 people from all cities in the new confederate democracy. This meant a far bigger building than the Athenian

prototype. The centre of its front consisted of a series of doorways, but inside pillars were arranged to minimize obstruction between the speaker in the centre and his audience. The internal columns were unfluted Doric, and there was probably a lantern-type roof to admit light.

At Priene in Asia Minor a new bouleterion was built in *c.*200BC. Sunk into the slope like a theatre and seating 600 people – a high proportion of the tiny population – it was almost square, being 20.25 by 21m (64 by 66ft 6in).

Above: The bouleterion (council chamber) of Priene, that model Ionian polis, was rectangular in shape, but many such chambers were semicircular.

Below: Attalus II, King of Pergamum, gave Athens a grand stoa in the 150s BC. Now totally reconstructed, it shows how such a stoa must have looked when new.

THE PRIVATE HOUSE

In classical Greece, public magnificence was seldom matched by private affluence. Most houses in Periclean Athens remained modest. Citizens, who lived mainly in the open, happily spent their taxes (or their empire's tribute) on adorning their city, not their homes. But by the time Rome conquered Greece in the 2nd century BC, luxurious houses were being built in many places. These influenced Roman houses at Pompeii, that time-capsule buried by Vesuvius' eruption to give us vivid glimpses of antiquity.

Almost all Greek houses were built around courtyards with slits for external windows. Most in 5th-century BC Athens were built of mud-brick on a stone base and the windows had no glass. At first only the better houses had terracotta-tiled roofs, poorer ones using mud-tiles. Houses in Athens were crammed together without decent drainage or water supplies. For all its public splendours, classical Athens was not a salubrious city. Mud and filth clogged its narrow, mostly unpaved streets. However, some citizens always lived in markedly more lavish houses than others.

Above: In Delos, a thriving port in the 2nd century BC, rich merchants built fine houses with large courtyards that have survived remarkably well.

Below: The house of Diadomenus in Delos had a fine mosaic floor, a form of expensive but long-lasting decoration that would recur in many later houses in Italy.

HIPPODAMUS OF MILETUS

Hippodamus (*c.* 500–420BC) is considered the first town planner and the inventor of the grid-iron plan. Although Smyrna had been rebuilt on a regular plan after an earthquake in the 7th century BC, Hippodamus produced the first coherent urban theories. He planned the Piraeus in the 460s BC, when it was growing fast, laying out regular-sized blocks for housing. An agora, approached by a wide avenue, was named after him. He then toured the Greek world, advising poleis from Rhodes to Thurii in Italy how to plan their cities. Others later copied his ideas. Sometimes, as at Priene, rebuilt around 330BC, Hippodamus' ideas were applied irrespective of the actual topography, which is steeply hilly at Priene.

ON THE ACROPOLIS' SLOPES

Demosthenes, the great orator (384–322BC), declared that luxurious houses were unknown before his time, but he exaggerated. Very comfortable houses from earlier decades have been found behind the South Stoa. All had courtyards and upper floors, with walls of mud-brick on a stone base and roofs of terracotta tiles. Halfway up the slope to the Acropolis, three houses built after 400BC have been discovered. The largest, measuring 25 by 19m (82 by 62ft) overall, had 10 ground-floor rooms and a large courtyard with a colonnade supporting a balcony. One room had a fine mosaic floor, which was clearly important because mosaics were rare. Opposite it was the *andron* ('men's room'), where men, reclining on couches, dined, drank and talked or were entertained by flute girls and dancers. Upstairs was the *gynaekeion*, the women's quarters –

women in classical Athens led segregated lives. The walls were painted with bands of colour. Similar houses have been found at the Piraeus and Megara.

FROM OLYNTHUS TO POMPEII

Olynthus, a city in northern Greece, laid out a new quarter on a rectilinear plan after 430BC. (Olynthus was destroyed by Philip II of Macedonia in 348BC.) Most houses, measuring 15.2m (c.50ft) square, had two floors, with cobbled courtyards at their centre and verandas on the north side to catch the winter sun. Their timber columns supported stone capitals on burnt-brick bases. Some houses had mosaic floors in the main rooms. The 'House of Good Fortune' has a superb mosaic made of 50,000 pebbles showing Dionysus driving a leopard-drawn chariot. Houses still had sun-dried brick walls on burnt-brick foundations, however.

Far grander houses were built after Alexander the Great's conquests, which enriched at least some people. At Pella, Macedonia's capital, houses 45m (150ft) square had larger rooms with peristyles (colonnades around a building) with stone columns. They also had bathrooms with terracotta bath tubs but had the same overall layout as at Olynthos.

The island of Delos, which boomed after Rome made it a free port in 166BC, saw Greek houses growing positively luxurious, but they still centred on an inner courtyard. Such courts now had peristyles all around and boasted elaborate mosaics, made no longer of pebbles but of finely cut stones. The roofs of these houses drained into the court and so into an underground cistern – Delos was chronically short of water. Comparable houses of the period have been found across the Greek world, from Dura in Mesopotamia to Saint Rémy in southern France.

Right: Most Athenian houses of the Classical period were relatively simple. On two floors, they centred around a courtyard, with colonnades supporting balconies on the upper floor and blank exterior walls.

Many of Delos' richest inhabitants were Italian businessmen. Through them, and through Greek artists or slaves imported into Italy, the 'peristyle house' spread to Italy. The best surviving examples come from Pompeii, where the peristyled courtyard of the House of the Gilded Cupids, built c.150BC, is so large that it is almost a colonnaded garden.

Above: The finest surviving examples of later Greek houses come from Pompeii, a city in Italy much influenced by Greek culture and preserved by Vesuvius' eruption. This is the House of the Vettii, dating from the 1st century BC.

CHAPTER XIV

BUILDING STYLES AND TECHNIQUES

The Greeks invented a classical language for architecture that has proved uniquely influential. The Romans later adopted and adapted the Greek style, exporting it across their own empire. The results of this artistic union, deliberately revived after 1400 in the Renaissance, shaped Western architecture into the mid-20th century. Greek architecture was trabeated, meaning it relied mainly on the column and lintel for its effect. This made the proportions of their columns, and of the entablature (the horizontal mass the pillars supported) all-important. The Greeks worked out canons (rules) for their different orders, or styles, of columns, which appear almost magically perfect. All were mathematically based, their proportions deriving ultimately from idealized versions of the human body. Classical architecture has retained its appeal because it appears supremely harmonious. It really is 'architecture with a human face'.

While Greek architectural theories and craftsmanship became sophisticated, building techniques generally remained simple. The Greeks seldom used cement, relying instead on metal clamps and precise fitting of stone, and had little machinery. But they were brilliant craftsmen in both stone and marble, working with supreme precision to create monuments of unageing intellect.

Left: The perfect proportions of the Temple of Poseidon above Cape Sunium exemplify Greek architectural skill.

BUILDING MATERIALS

Above: The Temple of Aphaea in Aegina is built of gleaming local limestone but was originally colourfully painted.

Below: The massive Temple of Athena at Poseidonia (Paestum) of the 5th century BC in southern Italy was once covered in stucco and brightly painted, creating an effect that is hard to imagine today.

While the Parthenon appears to float with effortless perfection above Athens, such excellence had taken the Greeks centuries to achieve. They started building not in marble or stone but in perishable timber and mud-brick. To create perfectly proportioned buildings, however, they needed to quarry, and work in, one of the finest if hardest of materials ever used: Greek marble.

The Minoans built their elaborate rambling palaces out of a mixture of adobe (sunbaked mud-brick), timber and rubble, usually stuccoed both inside and out. They had bases of stone or burnt brick needed to keep structures dry, and palaces built after 1600BC boasted walls of ashlar (cut stone). However, the Minoans' pillars were of wood and so combustible, as events catastrophically showed.

The Mycenaeans on mainland Greece used massive stones, often weighing 6 or more tons, to build their citadels at Tiryns and Mycenae. For these they hacked polygonal limestone megaliths ('big stones') from local hills. These were laid without plaster or cement on top of each other. This seemingly crude way of building was done so skilfully that it created the large tholos of the 'Treasury of Atreus'. Like Mycenae's cyclopean walls, it has lasted more than 3,000 years, But the knowledge and ability to build on such a scale vanished during the 12th century BC.

TERRACOTTA AND WOOD

In the Dark Ages (1100–800BC) the Greeks, when they built at all, did so in wood, making tiny temples with thatched roofs. Occasional early buildings, such as the first Temple of Hera, encouraged the use of terracotta (fired unglazed clay) roofing tiles (with wooden beams). At first these were very heavy, weighing up to 20kg (66lb). This led to the walls of the temple cella being made of stone and mud-brick, and finally also to stone columns. Well into the 6th century BC pillars were still often timber. (Later, wooden columns were widely replaced by stone ones.) Entablatures were also made of terracotta in the 7th century, before stone replaced it as a building material.

BUILDING IN LIMESTONE

The Greeks of the mainland and of Ionia were fortunate in having abundant limestone to hand when they began learning again how to build in masonry around 650BC. Comparatively easy to quarry and work, limestone can also be precisely chiselled, as the fine columns of the Temple of Aphaea on Aegina of c.500BC show.

In Sicily and southern Italy, where builders often had only much coarser materials, such as sandstone, to hand, temples were usually covered in stucco

and painted, as the entablatures of almost all Greek temples across the Mediterranean always were.

The first masonry was curvilinear. Blocks fitted together like a jigsaw puzzle in the 'Lesbian style' (named after some rustic-looking fortifications on Lesbos island). By 550BC Greek temples and public buildings were being constructed of polygonal megaliths of well-cut masonry. Private houses, in contrast, were long made of mud-brick on a stone base, but increasingly had fired-clay roof tiles. These were, of course, far more weather-proof than unfired clay.

MARBLE PERFECTION

Fine though limestone was, marble was manifestly finer, requiring more skill but giving crisper outlines. In the 6th century marble was increasingly used for adorning buildings – and by the century's end also for statues – but it was expensive to build completely in it. The main sources of good marble were Cycladic islands such as Naxos and Paros. Hauling slabs over the mountains to Delphi must have made even small marble temples such as the Treasury of the Athenians expensive, although it must have been cheaper in cities like Ephesus, near the sea.

But the great source of Athenian marble was local: Mt Pentelicum, 13km (8 miles) from Athens – a fact that helped make all the Athenian architectural achievements possible. About 25 ancient marble quarries have been identified on the slopes of the mountain. The first workings had begun by 550BC, but systematic exploitation took off only early in the 5th century. It peaked under Pericles' grandiose works programme after 460BC.

The crystalline rocks of Pentelicum produced the fine white marble used for most great public buildings in Athens, including those on the Acropolis. It superseded all other marble except that from Paros, which is easier for sculpting. The marble of the pediments was often painted or even gilded, so the effect would have been less blindingly white.

Although the rich golden tint that age alone gives to Pentelic marble could not often have been appreciated in antiquity, it was considered the world's finest building material by Greeks and Romans alike. Pentelic marble long remained one of Athens' principal exports. By the 2nd century AD it was being shipped not just to Rome but also to rich African cities like Lepcis Magna. In this way too, Greek architecture spread across the world.

Above: The brilliant white columns of the Erechtheum on the Athenian Acropolis were built of marble quarried from Mt Pentelicum nearby.

Below: The quarries of Mt Pentelicum, whose crystalline rocks produced the fine white marble used for Athens' great public buildings.

THE THREE ORDERS
DORIC, IONIC, CORINTHIAN

Above: Columns of the Doric order, first and simplest of the three Greek orders, or types, of column.

Above: An Ionic column, the second order, with its distinctive scrolled capital.

Below: A Corinthian capital, the last and most luxurious of the three orders.

Greek architecture is defined by its columns. Every Greek temple was enveloped in them, every stoa composed of them, every major public building flanked by them. Today the columns' descendants adorn so many nondescript banks and government offices that we may see them as mere decoration or just ignore them. But they had vital functional roles in Greek architecture. Even when not supporting roofs and entablatures, they expressed Greek beliefs in mathematical harmony and proportion.

Harmony and proportion, of course, are central to most architecture. Unusually, Greek architecture derived these, at least in theory, from the idealized human form. (Many Greek architects wrote books on architectural theory but none has survived. Only those by Vitruvius, a Roman architect of the 1st century BC, have, incorporating earlier Greek ideas.)

The Greeks used three orders, or types, of columns, distinguished chiefly by their capitals (heads). These are, in order of emergence: Doric, Ionic and Corinthian. The names supposedly reflect the orders'

origins. But while Ionic columns certainly first appeared in Ionian cities, Athens, also an Ionian city, employed the Doric order to wonderful effect on its Acropolis. Doric became seen as suitable for masculine or official buildings, Ionic as graceful and matronly or scholarly and Corinthian as charming and feminine. (The Romans added a fourth order, the luxurious Composite, and perhaps a fifth, Tuscan, a stubby form of Doric.)

THE DORIC ORDER
First, stockiest and seemingly simplest of the orders, Doric columns had no base. Like the wooden pillars they replaced, they rose directly from the ground. Doric columns, like all Greek columns, were 'fluted', having shallow concave grooves. At the shaft's top was the capital, with

Below: The British Museum in London was built in 1823–46. Its noble Ionic columns were inspired by the Temple of Athena at Priene. They show the perennial, highly flexible appeal of the Greek orders, with their mathematically based proportions.

an *abacus* on an *echinus*, or moulding (literally 'hedgehog'). On this stood the entablature, the whole horizontal stone mass, about a quarter the height of the column. Its lowest element was the architrave, a stone beam.

Above the architrave ran the frieze, composed of triglyphs and metopes. These may derive from carpentry: triglyphs, protruding blocks scored with three grooves, originated as ends of the crossbeams of a wooden roof. (Another view suggests that the Doric order was inspired by Egypt's all-stone temples.) The metopes, the slabs between the triglyphs, were often decorated with sculptures. Above ran the cornice, the topmost ledge of stone, and above that the pediment, the low-pitched triangular gable at the end of every temple and stoa.

Triglyphs were theoretically set over the centre of every column and over the centre line of every *intercolumniation* – the space between columns measured in *modules* (column diameters). Intercolumn-iation was crucially important in Doric temples. Architects normally allowed for five modules, but this caused problems with thicker columns. About 20ft (6m) proved the maximum span possible for an architrave, so at times extra columns were inserted.

THE IONIC ORDER
In the mid-6th century BC, the Ionic order originated in Ionia and the Cyclades. (It is probably not linked to the earlier Aeolic order, whose volutes, scroll-like adornments, grow from the shaft of the column, enclosing a palmette.) The Ionic order was distinguished from the Doric in several ways: its shaft was more slen-der; the column was often taller; it always had a base; and its capitals ended in volutes that resembled either rams' horns or papyrus plants, according to the observer. The Ionian order was sub-divided between 'Asian' in Ionia proper and the islands, and 'Attic', the order of the mainland, which had a more elaborate base. (The Romans favoured the latter,

which consequently become common across the Mediterranean.) The Ionic frieze has no metopes or triglyphs, so there were no problems with intercolumn-iation. Ionic columns were used from the late 5th century BC on, when elegance rather than power was desired, as in the Erechtheum (421–405BC) on the Athenian Acropolis.

THE CORINTHIAN ORDER
The last of the three Greek orders to emerge was the Corinthian order. Vitruvius attributed its invention to Callicrates, a 4th-century BC architect, but the order was used internally on the Temple of Apollo at Bassae in Arcadia before 400BC. A Corinthian capital is richly decorated with two rows of acanthus leaves and other pieces of vegetation. This is its chief distinction from the Ionic order, whose measurements it otherwise generally shares. One of the finest surviving examples of a Corinthian building is the Choragic Monument of Lysicrates in Athens. Dating from 334BC, this is a beautiful circular memorial.

Above, l to r: The three great orders of columns, Doric, Ionic and Corinthian, which adorned every Greek public building.

Below: The Monument of Lysicrates of 334BC. Its circular form and Corinthian columns inspired the British architect 'Athenian' Stuart.

BUILDING PROCEDURES AND TECHNIQUES

Above: To construct the Parthenon and the other temples high on the Acropolis, builders had to haul heavy cuboids of marble from the quarries of Pentelicum on rollers or in ox-carts.

The Greeks had no powered machinery of any sort and relatively few mechanisms employing human or animal muscle power. Nor did they have huge armies of slaves, as the Egyptian pharaohs had done. However, slaves certainly worked on the construction sites in small groups alongside free citizens, who might well be their masters. Records have survived detailing the payments made to the small building companies – almost all family-type businesses – who built the temples of the 5th century BC. This small scale makes the Greek, especially Athenian, architectural achievement all the more remarkable.

Instead, the Greeks relied on their intellectual powers and remarkably skilled craftsmanship to erect their buildings. Few details survive of their actual building techniques, however.

The builders of the temples on the Acropolis and other parts of Athens first had to transport their heavy cuboids of marble up to the site high above the city. The requisite blocks were cut to size at the Pentelicum quarries, but

ancones, small protruding handles, were left on their sides to allow them to be lifted by ropes. (Ancones were usually chipped off after building work was finished but some can still be seen on the Propylaea, where the outbreak of the Peloponnesian War in 431 BC prevented the work's completion.)

The blocks were then transported by unpaved roads 13km (8 miles) to Athens. Transport was presumably by ox-cart – the Greeks never used horses for haulage because they had no suitable harnesses. Alternatively, wooden discs may have been fitted to the slabs on which they rolled. Most blocks were dragged up the steep slopes of the Acropolis like this.

CRANES AND MACHINERY

Cranes were almost certainly used to help raise the masonry up to the temples during construction, although no traces of such machinery have been found. Aristotle, the encyclopaedically knowledgeable philosopher of the 4th century BC, describes complex pulley systems, with two upright timbers joined at the top with a brace and spread at the bottom. (Vitruvius wrote of very similar devices being used in Rome in the 1st century BC. Technology advanced with painful slowness, if at all, in the ancient world, so the machinery was probably much the same.) Lifting power came from a windlass attached to the back of the frame.

The 46 Doric columns of the Parthenon's pteron (outer colonnade) were made of 11 drums of marble. These were lifted into place by cranes using the ancones on each side. The column's top section, which included the Doric capital with its abacus and echinus, had its 20 flutes cut into it before being heaved into place and secured by metal clamps. Probably the fluting was cut around the base of the bottom drum to

Below: Complex pulley systems, with two upright timbers joined at the top with a brace and spread at the bottom, as described by Aristotle, were used to help build the temples.

avoid harming the stylobate's paving. The rest of the fluting was carved after the column had been assembled on site.

'REFINEMENTS'

In building the Parthenon (447–437BC), Greek architectural 'refinements' – techniques designed to make temples appear perfectly proportioned from a distance – reached their climax. Foremost among these was entasis, the thickening of columns at the centre by 2.5cm (1in) one-third of the way up their 10.4m (34ft 4in) height. Corner columns, fully visible silhouetted against the sky, were 2.5 per cent wider than the other columns and leaned inwards. Similarly, the stylobate rises by 11cm (c.4⅓in) at the centre on each side, giving a marginally domed effect. The west end of the Parthenon was 44cm (17in) higher than its east end.

THE LACK OF CEMENT

One of the most remarkable aspects about the Greeks' construction techniques is that they never used mortar or cement until the Romans introduced it. Instead, they fitted their blocks with such precision on top of each other that their weight alone held them in place. In this way, Greek masonry resembles that of the Incas in Peru nearly 2,000 years later, who also created majestic and enduring buildings without mortar. The Greeks did use metal ties of iron or bronze to hold their massed masonry in place. Later generations pillaged many of these ties for their metals, particularly bronze ties, which were more valuable and less perishable than iron, so weakening the buildings. One technique that the Greeks employed instead of cement was *anathyrosis*, which probably originated in Egypt. This involves leaving the centre of the surface of each block rough and gently concave, while ensuring the edges were perfectly smooth, so creating a near-vacuum to hold the stones together.

LABOUR FORCE

All these refinements meant that there are almost no true straight lines of any length in the Parthenon, Hephaistion or many other Greek temples. As impressive as the mathematical knowledge needed for such calculations is the high level of craftsmanship involved. Compared with the pyramids or even some Greek temples in Asia Minor or the west, the Parthenon is not immense – its stylobate measures only 69.5 by 30.8m (228 by 101ft), but architecturally it is supremely accomplished.

How the Athenians assembled these temples, and indeed housed and fed the large, highly skilled workforce required to build them, so efficiently is unknown. They must have needed almost every skilled mason in Greece, which may have caused resentment among other Greeks. Certainly the use of taxes from the other poleis in their empire – which were originally intended for military purposes – to build temples for Athens' benefit alone was unpopular.

Above: For the Parthenon, heavy cuboids of marble were hauled from quarries on rollers or in ox-carts.

Below: Entasis makes columns look regularly spaced when seen from afar.

GATES, WALLS, WATER SUPPLIES AND SHIPYARDS

Above: The well-made but simple walls of the fort of Eleutherai, built c.400BC to defend Attica's western frontier, were typical of Greek defences for centuries.

Below: The walls built around newly liberated Messene in c.350BC were far more complex, having double gateways with enclosed courts in which enemy attackers could be trapped.

The Mycenaeans had built impressively massive and effective, if crude, walls. There was little further development in Greek city defences before 400BC, because there was no need. The Long Walls connecting Athens with the Piraeus, built in the 450s BC, baffled every Spartan attempt to take the city in the Peloponnesian Wars. The Peloponnesians had no success even when besieging tiny Plataea, having to starve the city out.

Similarly, when the Athenians attacked Syracuse in 414–13BC, they relied on building a wall to blockade the Syracusans. (Failure to complete this doomed the expedition.) Athens' own city walls, hastily rebuilt after the Persian wars, were c.2.5m (8ft) wide. A stone base of c.1m (3ft) supported upper walls of plastered mud-brick rising to c.8m (25ft). Towers c.5m (16ft) square reinforced the walls at key points.

In the 4th century BC, Dionysius I, tyrant of Syracuse, revolutionized siege warfare with his successful capture of Motya, a Carthaginian city off the coast off western Sicily, by using siege towers, causeways and catapults. Philip II of Macedonia and Alexander carried this revolution further. Alexander's capture in 332BC of supposedly impregnable Tyre, another massively walled island-city, signalled that cities must look anew to their defences. Over the next decades walls grew higher and thicker, to protect against missiles and to support catapults.

Towers, too, became larger and more frequent, with postern gates to allow sorties against besiegers. Semicircular towers, more costly to build but harder to attack, appeared in cities like Smyrna (Izmir) in the 3rd century BC. The towers of the small Ionian city of Perge were vaulted and had gabled roofs, presumably to keep torsion catapults dry.

The most famous defence of a city came in 305BC when Demetrius I, one of Alexander's flamboyant successors, failed to capture Rhodes after a year-long siege, despite assembling massive siege towers and catapults.

GATES

Athens' city walls had 15 gates. The most important, the Diplyon Gate, was elaborate, being of the 'courtyard' type. It was set back from the walls so that enemies exposed their flanks to javelins and arrows thrown by defenders on the towers and walls on either side. But the reasons for building such a grand gate like this were as much ceremonial as military. The great Panathenaic Procession entered the city by the Diplyon Gate, so it had to look impressive.

During the 4th century BC, gateways became more sophisticated. Double gateways with separated enclosed courts in which an enemy could be trapped were built at Messene c.350BC and Miletus c.300BC. The grandest such gate was at Pergamum, built c.200BC, which trapped attackers in successive enclosed courts.

WATER SUPPLIES AND SHIPYARDS

Adequate water supplies were clearly vital for any city. The Pisistratids about 530BC first brought water into Athens through rock-cut conduits piped from Mt Lycabettus north of the city. These supplied a fountain in the Agora, which was later roofed over. It had basins about 6 by 3m (20 by 10ft) at either end of a 18m (60ft) long building. The western basin was a reservoir into which vases

Below: A water conduit in Corinth, typical of many in which Greek cities channelled water through their cities.

could be dipped, the eastern end had spouts. This served as a prototype for other spring houses known from vases.

At Corinth, another important trading city, the 'Triglyph Wall', so-called because of its decoration, was built *c.*500BC above a spring chamber with steps leading down through an opening in the wall. More typical was the simple fountain niche such as that built into the walls at Priene *c.*330BC. Wherever possible, a large fountain was placed near the agora of each city. These gave women, who fetched the household water in amphorae balanced delicately upon their heads, a rare opportunity to meet and socialize.

Among Athens' grandest buildings were the naval shipyards at the Piraeus, essential to maintaining the fleet, for long the strongest in the Aegean. This had 372 shipyards in its final and grandest form. The huge fleet kept under cover could theoretically be launched very quickly. In practice, the Athenians lacked the crews to man all their ships when war finally came in 323BC. Athens' grandest naval building was the military arsenal built by the architect Philon in the 330s BC. It was a huge hall under a single-ridged roof. The interior measured 15 by 120m (50 by 400ft) and was 8.2m (27ft) high. It had a Doric frieze around the exterior and Doric columns, unusual for the time but meant to emphasize military strength.

Above: The defences of the small city of Perge in Asia Minor in the 3rd century BC boasted semicircular gable-roofed towers in which catapults could be mounted.

Below: The massive, if crude, walls of Mycenae, dating from the 13th century BC, were not surpassed as defences until the 4th century BC.

Above: A Corinthian capital, the most ornate of the three Greek orders, has a slender column similar to the Ionian order's but its capital has two ranks of acanthus leaves over the astragal, with caules rising over the acanthus leaves and sprouting volutes.

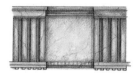

Above: Section of a Doric frieze showing how it is separately into blocks. The metope is the square space between the triglyphs, which have two vertical grooves (glyphs) in the centre and a half-groove at each end.

ELEMENTS OF ARCHITECTURE
GLOSSARY OF TERMS

Our architectural language remains predominantly Greek in origin. Some words have passed into common usage but many others may seem obscure today, so a glossary of terms used in the book follows. They should prove useful for understanding not just ancient architecture but also many more recent buildings.

ABACUS Slab on top of a capital supporting the architrave

ACANTHUS Plant with scalloped leaves used as a design on Corinthian capitals

ACROPOLIS Upper or higher city, often reserved for temples and shrines in the Classical Age

ACROTERIA Plinths for statues or ornaments at the end and top of pediments

AGORA Market, forum or meeting place at the centre of every Greek polis, often with ceremonial colonnades around it

ARCHITRAVE Beam or lintel, usually in stone or marble, forming the lowest section of an entablature

BOULETERION Council hall

CAPITAL Head or crowning feature of a column

CARYATID Sculpted, clothed standing female figure used in the same way as a column to support an entablature

Above: A volute spiral is a decorative device used on Ionic columns.

CELLA Main body of a temple containing the cult image of the deity

CORINTHIAN ORDER Third of the Greek orders, with base, slender column and capital with two ranks of acanthus leaves

CORNICE Topmost horizontal, usually projecting part of entablature

DENTIL Small square block used decoratively in cornices

DORIC ORDER First of the Greek orders, without base (Greek Doric)

ECHINUS Moulding beneath the abacus on a Doric capital

ENTABLATURE Whole horizontal upper part of a building carried on columns above the abacus

ENTASIS Slight convex curve used on columns to correct the optical illusion of concavity when seen from afar

FLUTING Shallow, concave grooves running vertically on a column

FRIEZE Middle division of an entablature between architrave and cornice

GUTTAE Small projecting pieces under each triglyph of a Doric capital

Left and far left: Caryatids are draped female figures, supporting an entablature on their heads. The photo shows caryatids on the south porch of the Erechtheum in Athens.

Left: A pediment, such as this from the Temple of Artemis on Corcyra (Corfu) of 580BC, is the triangular space created by the sloping eaves and horizontal cornice of a gabled temple or other building or ceremonial gateway.

INTERCOLUMNIATION Space between columns, normally measured in their diameters

IONIC ORDER Second of the Greek orders, with voluted capital and base

MEGARON Large rectangular hall in Mycenaean palaces, and a possible influence on early Greek temples

METOPE Square space between two triglyphs in a Doric order, often sculpted

MODULE Unit of measurement, often diameter or radius of column at its base

NAOS Innermost chamber of a Greek temple. See CELLA

ODEION Covered hall, smaller than the main city theatre, used for performances of music and poetry

ORCHESTRA Dancing floor for the chorus in Greek theatres

ORDER All the parts comprising a column and its entablature. See Corinthian, Doric, Ionic

PEDESTAL Substructure under a column

PEDIMENT Triangular space created by sloping eaves and horizontal cornice of gabled temple or other building or ceremonial gateway

PERIPTERAL Of a building surrounded by a single row of columns

Left: The slight convex curve on a column is known as entasis and makes the column appear to be straight.

PERISTYLE Continuous colonnade surrounding a temple or court

PLINTH Low plain block under the base of a column or pedestal

PODIUM Continuous pedestal with base supporting columns

PORCH/PORTICO Roofed space forming the entrance to a building, normally with columns and pediment

PROCELLA Vestibule

PROPYLAEUM Entrance gateway to an enclosure, usually of a temple

PTERON External colonnade

SHAFT Trunk or body of column

STOA Shallow long portico with colonnade on one side, wall on other

STYLOBATE Continuous base or plinth on which a row of columns is set

THOLOS Domed circular building, often a tomb in the Mycenaean Age

TORUS Convex semicircular moulding

TRIGLYPH Blocks separating the metopes in a Doric frieze, with two vertical grooves (glyphs) in the centre and a half-groove at each end

VOLUTE Spiral scroll at each end of an Ionic column

Above: The entablature is the upper part of an order showing, top to bottom, the cornice, frieze and architrave.

Above: The lower part of a column showing, top to bottom, the base and pedestal.

Left: Acroteria are plinths for statues or ornaments at the end or top of pediments (seen here on the Temple of Olympian Zeus). They were often highly decorated.

CHAPTER XV

CITIES OF THE GREEKS

Greek cities developed from high Mycenaean citadels, beneath which small townships huddled, to cities on the plain or coast. As Aristotle noted, aristocrats and kings preferred high places, but democracies chose lower ground, reserving the acropolis ('high city') for the gods. Nowhere illustrates this transition better than Athens, the archetypal Greek *polis*, or city-state. Above, on the Acropolis, stood the temples of Athena and other tutelary deities. Down below were all the other temples, public and private buildings, theatres, stadia, altars, gymnasia, stoas, houses, prisons, tombs and monuments. The Agora (market place) was the focus of social, intellectual and political life; around it hummed the city's turbulent life.

By 500BC Greek colonization had spread Greek *poleis* around the Mediterranean, from Egypt to southern France. After Alexander's conquests (336–323BC), there was an even greater expansion of Greek *poleis* east to the borders of India. These, too, were (for a time) self-governing cities, with theatres, agoras and gymnasia. West of the Euphrates, Roman rule ultimately saved and furthered Greek urban life, as impressive ruins attest, but some very important cities – Sparta, Thebes and Alexandria – have left few visible ruins. Ancient Thebes is mostly under modern Thebes; Alexandria's ruins are practically all under water; Sparta built relatively little. So attention turns to the sites and cities that do survive.

Left: The buildings on the Acropolis, created in the 40 years after 446BC, help to make Athens the supreme Greek polis.

THE ACROPOLIS TEMPLES

Above: The small Temple of Athena Nike, the first temple seen by visitors approaching the Acropolis, was built c.428–425BC, very probably by Mnesicles.

Below: Pericles and other Athenians admiring Pheidias at work on the frieze that decorated the Parthenon, as envisaged by the Victorian painter Alma-Tadema in 1868. In reality, women would not have accompanied the men.

In the Bronze Age, Athens was of secondary importance compared to great centres such as Pylos and Mycenae. However its Acropolis, the rock dominating central Attica, is superbly defensible. Remnants of a Mycenaean palace have been detected on its north side. The citadel was enclosed in Cyclopean walls 6m (20ft) thick, fragments of which are still visible. The palace occupied part of the Acropolis, the lower town spilling out beyond the gates to the west, protected by an outer wall.

The legendary Erechtheus, one of Athens' first kings, established the worship of Athena in the city. His descendant Theseus killed the Cretan Minotaur, uniting Attica for the first time. Athens was renowned as the 'unsacked city', the one Mycenaean stronghold to survive 12th-century BC cataclysms. This may have been due to a secret well down eight flights of stairs inside the rock, which helped the city to survive long sieges. The last king, Codrus, traditionally sacrificed himself to save Athens from invaders.

The myth cloaks the facts. By c.950BC Athens had expelled its kings, and aristocrats ruled the city, but not from the Acropolis. They did so from the nearby Areopagus (Hill of Mars), which gave its name to their council. Athens in the Dark Ages and Archaic period (at least down to c.560BC) built no more temples in stone than any other Greek city. Only with growing prosperity in the early 6th century BC did the Athenians start to build again in stone. A wave of competitive construction soon led nobles to erect splendid monuments where all could admire them: on the Acropolis.

THE FIRST STONE TEMPLES

In 566BC the massive ramp leading up to the Acropolis was constructed by Lycurgus, a leading nobleman for the Great Panathenaea, the city's main festival. Other nobles, very probably the Alcmaeonids, sponsored the building of the first proper temple to Athena Polias. Decorated with painted snakes, bulls, lions and tritons, it was built of limestone and at c.30m (100ft) was twice as long as it was wide. Inside stood an ancient statue of the goddess, the city's most sacred object, evacuated to Salamis when the Persians invaded in 480BC. (The dating – even siting – of the Acropolis' early temples remains debatable.)

The Pisistratids, in power from 546 to 510BC, gave Athens a huge boost economically and architecturally. They moved the Agora to north of the Acropolis, giving it more space, and built nine marble drinking fountains; they embellished the Temple of Athena Polias with marble and began the vast Temple of Olympian Zeus. This was left only knee-high when Hipparchus, last of the dynasty, was driven out in 510BC. (The Pisistratids seemingly lived on the Acropolis in their last years in power.)

BUILDING FOR DEMOCRACY

The democratic revolution that followed halted the building programme only briefly. Victory over the Persians at Marathon in 490BC boosted the new democracy's self-confidence. A grand gateway to the Acropolis with Doric marble columns, the Propylaea, was started and perhaps finished. Even grander but unfinished was the large temple on the south side of the Acropolis, also in marble. The Persians burnt all these temples in 480–479BC and they remained unrestored for 30 years, although the Propylaea was patched up. Themistocles, leader during the Persian wars, oversaw the city's hasty refortification and the building of the Piraeus on Hippodamus' orthogonal (grid-iron) plans, but such buildings were purely utilitarian.

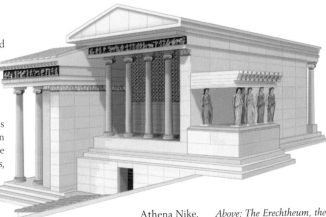

PERICLES' MASTERPLAN

Pericles had the very highest conception of his city, calling it the "school of Hellas", the exemplar of democracy at its noblest if not broadest. (It was a view shared even by some of Athens' traditional enemies. "O shining city, violet-crowned... Bastion of Hellas, glorious Athens, city of godlike men," wrote the Theban poet Pindar.)

More controversially, Pericles also thought that Athens was justified in using tribute money from the Confederacy of Delos, which had originally been intended solely for fighting the Persians, to rebuild its temples, themselves destroyed by Persia. The project that he persuaded the Athenian Assembly in 449BC to approve – after a long and stormy debate – would produce the grandest, most dramatic group of buildings Greece had yet seen.

Pericles chaired the committee overseeing the project, taking a keen interest in the work. Pheidias, the sculptor in overall charge, was his friend. Beneath Pheidias worked a team of architects. Ictinus was responsible for the Parthenon, Mnesicles for the Propylaea and probably the Erechtheum and the Temple of Athena Nike.

When completed (the Erechtheum, in some ways the most ingenious of all Athens' temples, was not finished until 405BC, the year of Athens' final defeat by Sparta at Aegospotomai), the grouped buildings, with their superb carved and painted friezes, astonished and awed contemporaries. Their feelings have been shared by most later generations.

Only in the Hellenistic and Roman periods, when absolute monarchs or emperors had far greater resources, would other architectural ensembles rival – and sometimes surpass – the Acropolis in size. None would ever surpass democratic Athens aesthetically.

Above: The Erechtheum, the last of the Acropolis temples to be completed, is really a multiple temple, housing 10 different shrines on two separate levels. It is named after Erechtheus, a legendary king of Athens.

Below: A reconstruction model of the Acropolis seen from the west, with its great staircase leading up to the Propylaea. Pheidias' statue of Athena rose just beyond this.

ATHENS' OTHER BUILDINGS

Above: The octagonal Tower of the Winds was designed c.454BC by the astronomer Andronicus of Cyrrhus. On its roof stood a large triton-shaped weathervane.

The splendours of democratic Athens were not restricted to its Acropolis. Down below, the Agora was surrounded from the 5th century BC on with increasingly fine official buildings. The old Bouleterion (Council Hall), a rectangular building about 23m (75ft) wide on the west side, was patched up after the Persian sack. It was replaced by a semicircular building better suited for meetings of the Council of 500, the advisory body, later in the century. The tholos, a domed circular building nearby c.18.3m (60ft) in diameter, was probably a clubhouse where councillors on duty ate their free dinners.

AROUND THE AGORA

On the north of the Agora the Stoa Poikile – Painted Stoa, called after paintings celebrating Athenian victories – was built c.470BC. It was the first such multi-functional structure. In the shelter of these extended porticos, citizens gathered to talk, listen and trade. Forty years later, the Stoa to Zeus Eleutherios (the deliverer) was built on the west side of the Agora. There was an altar to the 12 Olympian gods before it and the smaller Royal Stoa beside it. All had imposing Doric colonnades but were dwarfed by the huge, two-storeyed Stoa of Attalus, donated by the rich Hellenistic king Attalus II of Pergamum in the mid-2nd century BC.

Set back from the Agora, the temple of Hephaistus embodies all the principles of 5th-century BC Doric classicism, if lacking the 'refinements' of the Acropolis temples. More impressive due to its site but less well preserved, the Temple of Poseidon at Sunium is by the same unknown architect. So perhaps was the Temple of Ares, moved from Acharnae 24km (15 miles) away by the Romans. The huge Temple to Olympian Zeus, started under the Pisistratids, was half-completed thanks to Antiochus IV, the extravagant Seleucid king, with Corinthian rather than Doric capitals. Antiochus' death in 164BC abruptly ended work. Then Sulla, the Roman general who sacked Athens in 86BC for supporting Mithridates of Pontus, removed its capitals to Rome.

MONUMENTS

Athens was also a city of monuments. Most were erected not by the state but by rich individuals or families. Dozens of such monuments lined the Street of Tripods, one of the principal avenues.

Left: Famous partly due to its spectacular site, the Temple of Poseidon at Sunium is probably by the same unknown architect who built the Hephaistion in the Athenian Agora. Both temples embody the principles of Doric classicism in the mid-5th century BC.

Right: Athens grew around the Acropolis, where the city's finest temples stood, and the Agora below, the centre of social and political life. Walls enclosed the city, and Pericles' double Long Walls later linked it to Piraeus, the port.

The most famous and elegant of these is the Choregic Monument of Lysicrates, built in 335–334BC. As a *choregos* (producer), Lysicrates had put on dozens of plays at his own expense – one of the duties expected of a rich citizen. This circular structure, with its slender Corinthian columns, proclaimed both his generosity and a victory in a theatrical contest. Its roof carried a three-branched acanthus on which stood a victory tripod. Its elegance has an almost Hellenistic air.

Yet the classical tradition remained strong in Athens, as another much later edifice demonstrates. The octagonal Tower of the Winds was designed *c*.45BC by Andronicus of Cyrrhus in Mesopotamia, a noted astronomer. Julius Caesar may have paid for it, for Athens as a city was almost destitute at the time. On its roof stood a large weathervane in the form of a triton, which pointed at the relevant wind, as personified in one of the eight wind zones. Inside was an elaborate water-powered mechanism that reputedly drove a sort of clock. Oriented due north, the tower carried sundials on each side so that passers-by could read the time on it. Like the Choregic Monument, it was made of marble and much admired by the British architect James 'Athenian' Stuart, who visited Greece in 1751.

ROMAN ATHENS

Roman rule, finally established after 31BC by Augustus, proved benevolent overall. A large new odeion was built and a new Agora, complete with Athens' first public lavatories. He commissioned a small temple to Rome and himself on the Acropolis. While admiring Greek classical culture, he stressed Rome's political authority. Nero refurbished the Theatre of Dionysus in AD61–4. But the real

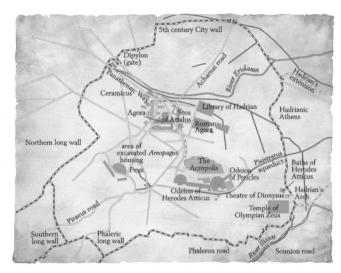

philhellene was Hadrian (reigned AD117–38). He became archon (ruler), made Athens head of a Panhellenic League and built a new quarter with aqueduct and library. Herodes Atticus then restored the stadium for the Panathenaic games and built a vast new odeion beneath the Acropolis. His was the last contribution to ancient Athens.

Below: The two-storeyed Stoa of Attalus, built by the wealthy Attalus II of Pergamum in the mid-2nd century BC, is Athens' largest stoa, now reconstructed.

OLYMPIA AND EPIDAURUS
RENOWNED SANCTUARIES

Above: The entrance and grassy banks of Olympia's main stadium, where 40,000 spectators gathered for the great Panhellenic festival, held quadrennially for 1,200 years.

Below: A model of the sanctuary at Olympia housing the enclosure of the Altis, at the centre of which was Olympia's great Temple of Zeus. So many votive statues were erected over the centuries that the precinct became crowded.

Not every place of importance was a major polis. Some sites became famous through being the centres of particular cults. Among the greatest was Olympia in Elis in the western Peloponnese. The Olympic Games were held there quadrennially for almost 1,200 years and its Temple of the Olympian Zeus contained one of the Seven Wonders of the World: the Athenian sculptor Pheidias' last masterpiece, the gold-and-ivory statue of the king of gods. This was reputedly so huge that, even though seated, Zeus' head brushed the roof.

OLYMPIA

According to Pindar in the 5th century BC, the games were founded by Hercules, the muscular superhero. Traces of Mycenaean settlement have indeed been discovered at Olympia, but traditionally the Olympic Games were founded in 776BC. They soon became a Panhellenic event, attracting competitors from all over Greece. The games were held around the time of the second full moon after the summer solstice – meaning in practice late August

or early September – the games imposed a rare truce on the otherwise constantly warring Greeks.

At the heart of the sanctuary lay the rectangular enclosure called the Altis. Three giant Doric columns of the 6th-century BC temple of Hera on its north side have been re-erected, but Olympia's main temple was that to Zeus, in the Altis' centre. One of the largest in mainland Greece, this had a stylobate made of huge stone blocks each c.2.75m (9ft) wide. About 63.9 by 27.7m (210 by 91ft), it was built by the local architect Libon between 470 and 456BC from soft limestone and was covered in stucco, with marble tiles, gutters and sculptures. It lacks the architectural 'refinements' of most contemporary Doric temples. This was possibly because Libon could not manage them.

The temple was destroyed by a huge earthquake in the 6th century AD. Only the drums of its columns remain *in situ*, but the well-preserved statues from its pediments rank among the finest of all Greek sculptures.

At the centre of the enclosure stood the great altar of Zeus. The area must have finally looked almost cluttered with 69 such altars. Just outside the south of the Altis lay the Bouleterion, with two wings united externally by a portico of 27 Ionic columns of the 3rd century BC. The east side of the Altis was lined with the Echo or Painted Stoa, rebuilt in the 4th century BC. Beyond that lay the Stadium, where the main Olympic events took place. It could accommodate 40,000 spectators, standing on raised banks. Its stone kerbs survive to give a vivid impression of this, the world's first great international stadium.

To the west of the Altis lay the Leonidaion, a large hostel for distinguished visitors built by Leonidas of Naxos in the 4th century BC, with an

open court 30m (100ft) square. North of that was Pheidias' workshop, a tall hanger-like building where his great statue of Zeus had been made, which itself became an object of wonder. (Its ruins were later quarried for a Byzantine church.) Just north of that stood the Palaestra, a colonnaded wrestling ground, and beyond that the Gymnasium.

Olympia thrived throughout the Hellenistic period and, despite Sulla's inevitable sack in 86BC, flourished under the Romans too. Augustus favoured it and Nero took part in the games, uniquely winning every single one – as the judges prudently decided. Hadrian later restored some buildings. The games were finally banned by the devoutly Christian emperor Theodosius I in AD393.

EPIDAURUS

Sited on the Argolid plain, Epidaurus emerged as an important sanctuary only in the 5th century BC. It was the shrine of the demigod Asclepius, son of Apollo. Asclepius had many attributes, the most famous being his medical powers. He could even raise people from the dead, but was killed by a jealous Zeus for his impiety. Asclepius' symbol of a staff with a serpent coiled around it has become the symbol of medicine. Of his temple, built *c*.420BC at the centre of the sanctuary, almost nothing visible remains.

To the south stood the great altar of Asclepius. Nearby was a tholos built *c*.370–340 BC by the architect Polyclitus of local limestone with marble ornaments. (Outside the shrine, of about the same date and wonderfully preserved, is the famous theatre.) Sick pilgrims would make visits to Epidaurus as if to a Hellenic Lourdes, sleeping the night in the *enkoimeterion* (sacred enclosure).

Right: The tholos built c.*370–340BC by the architect Polyclitus at Epidaurus is the best-preserved of the site's temples.*

Healing dreams sent by the god might come to them there. Such psychosomatic cures could be very effective.

The Ptolemies of Egypt honoured the site, enriching it with offerings. Even the then-distant Romans sent to Epidaurus in 293BC asking for advice on a plague that was afflicting them. Despite the disapproval of the newly Christian imperial establishment after Constantine came to control all the empire in AD326, pilgrims in search of the god's help still visited the shrine well into the 5th century AD.

Above: The Temple of Zeus at Olympia, one of the largest in Greece, was built by the architect Libon of Elis between 470 and 456BC. It housed one of the Seven Wonders of the Ancient World: the huge chryselephantine (gold-ivory) statue of Zeus by the Athenian master-sculptor Pheidias.

THE SANCTUARY OF DELPHI

Above: The all-marble Treasury of the Athenians, built c.500BC by newly democratic Athens, was re-erected in 1906.

Nowhere was more sacred to the Greeks than Delphi. Apollo, the archetypal Greek god of poetry, reason and prophecy, had there slain (or tamed) the chthonic serpent Pytho, making the site his. To this *omphalos* ('navel', i.e. holy stone), centre of the Greek world, worshippers came for more than 1,300 years to consult the oracular priestess Pythonia.

From *c.*580BC on, Delphi was administered by the Amphictyonic Council, with representatives of several Greek states, including Athens and Sparta – the closest Greece got to a UN. However there were at least three Sacred Wars over the control of the sanctuary, the last war (356–346BC) leading to Macedonian hegemony under Philip II.

AN INTERNATIONAL REPUTATION

By the 6th century BC the Delphic oracle had gained an international reputation. Croesus, King of Lydia (560–546BC), sent to inquire if he should attack Persia. The reply, typically ambiguous – "If you cross the river Halys you will destroy a mighty kingdom" – led to his kingdom's downfall. The oracle's fame remained undimmed, however, the pharaoh Amasis also consulting it. Many Greek cities and individuals began building 'treasuries', in effect mini-temples, around the shrine.

During the Persian invasion (480–479BC), Delphi played an ambiguous role. When Xerxes sent troops to plunder the temples, the Persians reportedly were crushed by boulders hurled down by the goddess Athena Pronaia (guardian) from the surrounding crags. Probably this was a landslide, Delphi being a seismically active region.

The sanctuary is dramatically sited *c.*600m (2,000ft) up the slopes of Mt Parnassus. Approaching from the east up the Sacred Way, an Athenian would have come first to the sanctuary of Athena Pronaia, a Doric temple built *c.*500BC and damaged by the 480BC rockfall. Further up, a ravine separated the two *Phaedriades* (Shining Rocks) that reflected the light.

Here the Castalian Springs bubbled up, where Apollo had once planted his laurel tree, and here pilgrims purified themselves. Emerging, they would see the tholos gleaming above them, a round temple built *c.*375BC, with Doric columns outside and Corinthian ones within. This temple lay inside the *temenos*.

Left: The theatre at Delphi is one of the best preserved in Greece. Built in the 4th century BC, it was restored by Eumenes II of Pergamum in 159BC and again by the Romans. Its 35 tiers of seats are of white marble from Mt Parnassus.

The temenos (sacred precinct) of Apollo contained many buildings arranged to great effect against the landscape beyond. Among the treasuries was that of the Siphnians, dating from c.525BC, with caryatids instead of pillars. Beyond is the marble Doric Treasury of the Athenians, built c.500BC by the new democracy in gratitude for defeating its Greek enemies. The Treasury was re-erected in 1906. Its walls are covered with ancient inscriptions, some of which record Athenian athletes' victories in the quadrennial Pythian Games.

THE TEMPLE OF APOLLO
The largest building in the temenos was the Temple of Apollo, c.60m (200ft) long. The first temple, of the 7th century BC, burnt down in 548BC. It was replaced by a larger Doric temple with marble facings – then a luxury – financed by the Alcmaeonids, in exile from Athens. Wrecked in 373BC, it was rebuilt, sacked by Sulla in 86BC, and restored under the Roman Empire. The temple had six stuccoed limestone columns at the end and 15 on its sides, with an omphalos at its centre. Almost nothing remains.

The theatre above, by contrast, is one of the best preserved in Greece. Built originally in the 4th century BC, it was

restored by Eumenes II, King of Pergamum in 159BC, and again by the Romans. The 35 tiers of seats were of white marble from Mt Parnassus. The orchestra measured 18m (60ft) across, being paved with polygonal slabs. The front of the stage had a frieze depicting the labours of Hercules.

Above: The tholos, the round temple built c.375BC by Theodorus of Phocaea, has Doric columns outside and Corinthian ones inside, some of which were re-erected in 1938. It offers superb views.

Below: The stadium at Delphi of the 5th century BC. Here the Pythian Games, second only to the Olympic Games, were held every four years.

ENIGMATIC ORACLE

The oracle at Delphi retained its reputation for infallibility impressively long, partly through its excellent intelligence. Croesus tested the oracle by asking what he would be doing on a particular day. "Boiling turtles in cauldrons on a beach", came the reply, fed by inside sources.

But Delphi's real forte was its enigmatic prophecies. Pronounced in baffling verse 'interpreted' by priests, they often merely said, "Apollo thinks it better to…" This meant that, no matter how bad the outcome, the alternative would have been worse. It could pay to persevere. When the Athenians, facing Persian attack in

480BC, asked the oracle's advice, the first reply was chilling: "Fly far, far away; Leave home, town and castle, do not stay." Athens' envoys, returning for a better prophecy, were told to trust in the "wooden walls" but warned: "Divine Salamis will destroy the children of women." Themistocles spun this to mean that Athens should rely on its fleet – correctly as events proved. Julian, Rome's last non-Christian emperor (reigned AD361–3), received a depressing reply when he consulted the oracle, perhaps because it had been bribed by the Christians. Delphi was finally suppressed in AD384.

CORINTH
COMMERCE AND LUXURY

Above: The Fountain of Peirene, once a natural spring, was so built up over the centuries that it now looks like an ornamental fountain. The present façade was built under the emperor Claudius (AD41–54).

Below: The lofty citadel of Acrocorinth has been a key fortress in Greece for millennia. The present walls are mostly medieval but have Hellenic and Bronze Age foundations.

Superbly sited controlling the Isthmus, with access to sea routes east and west, Corinth was inhabited from earliest times. It took the lead in founding western colonies such as Corcyra (Corfu) and Syracuse in 734BC. Corcyra proved a disobedient daughter and the first recorded naval battle occurred in 664BC between it and Corinth. Under Periander (reigned *c.*629–585BC), Corinth boomed, exporting fine pottery around the Mediterranean. By the 6th century BC the city was already noted for its luxury, a reputation it never lost. The Corinthian order, most ornate of the three Greek orders, traditionally originated there, while Corinth's 1,000 sacred prostitutes, servants of the goddess Aphrodite, were renowned for their beauty and skills.

The Greeks' headquarters during the Persian invasion, Corinth was an often unhappy ally of Sparta's alliance. Later, Corinth was the site of Philip II's Congress in 338–337BC, where he proclaimed his planned crusade against Persia. It was also the last home of the philosopher Diogenes, whose world-renouncing eccentricities were the very antitheses of Macedonian megalomania.

Acrocorinth, the citadel rising 548m (1,800ft) above the city, then became one of the 'chains of Greece', garrisoned by Macedonian troops. Joining the Achaean League, which had liberated it in 243BC, Corinth was razed to the ground by the Roman general Lucius Mummius in 146BC. In 44BC Julius Caesar refounded the city as capital of the province of Achaea and it boomed again, its population reputedly reaching 300,000. St Paul preached in Corinth, appalled by its depravity but finding a readier audience among its merchants than among Athens' intellectuals. Despite recurrent earthquakes, Corinth retained its importance until the end of the Roman Empire.

Ancient Corinth lay on a rocky plateau 60m (200ft) high between Acrocorinth and its port Lechaion, connected by long walls. The ruins we see today are more Roman than Greek, however. The Lechaion Road, 12m (40ft) wide and paved under Augustus, led up past a colonnade of shops and the Peribolus (courtyard) of Apollo, toward the Fountain of Peirene. Originally a natural spring, this was so built up over the centuries that it resembled a large ornamental fountain. Water for it was stored in four reservoirs fed by a tunnel and hidden by a six-arched façade "with chambers made like grottoes, from which the water flows into a basin in the open air", according to Pausanias, writing *c.*AD170. This basin is 9 by 6m (*c.*30 by 20ft).

The present two-storied façade, built under Claudius (AD41–54), replaced a row of Ionic columns of the 3rd century BC. Herodes Atticus, a munificent multi-millionaire, remodelled the fountain into its present imposing vaulted and marble-lined form around AD150.

Above: The Temple of Apollo, north of the Agora in Corinth, is one of the oldest Doric temples. Dating from c.550BC, it has seven massive columns still standing.

A HUGE AGORA

Entered through the Propylaea, which the Romans turned into a triumphal arch, the huge Agora is itself really a Roman forum measuring 210 by 90m (230 by 100 yards). West of the Propylaea stood the Captives' Façade, an ornate two-storeyed marble structure. With Corinthian columns on the lower floor and Atlantes (giant figures) of barbarian captives on the upper, it dates from c.AD100. Nearby is the Triglyph Wall of stucco-faced limestone, reputedly built by the great sculptor Lysippus in the 4th century BC. This guards the Sacred Spring, which was originally in the open but is now underground.

Stoas and temples line the Agora, with the Julian Basilica to the east and the South Basilica on the south – both Roman buildings. Also Roman are many of the small temples on the west side – including a Temple to Tyche (Fortune) and a little square Pantheon – the public baths and latrines. The Romans remodelled the theatre, originally a 5th-century BC building, and carved the Odeion from the rock. But the Temple of Apollo on a hillock north of the Agora is wholly Greek, one of the oldest Doric temples from c.550BC, with seven austerely massive columns still standing.

ISTHMUS: CANAL AND GAMES

On the Saronic (east) side of the isthmus lies Isthmia, with the ruins of a 5th-century BC Temple of Poseidon. Here the Isthmian Games, traditionally founded by Theseus, King of Athens, and ranking just behind the Olympic and Pythian Games in prestige, were held every two years. Here also Alexander the Great was nominated leader of the Greeks against Persia in 336BC.

Just north lie the remnants of the Isthmian Wall, built against the Persians in 480BC, and beyond lies the Corinth Canal. This dates from only 1882, but the idea of a canal goes back to the 6th century BC, when Corinthians used to drag small ships across the Isthmus on rollers. At Nero's orders, work began in earnest on a canal in AD67, his engineers getting as far as the bedrock before stopping, defeated.

Below: The emperor Nero ordered the cutting of a canal through the Isthmus in AD67, a project the Greeks had long dreamed of, but his engineers stopped when they hit bedrock. Today's canal dates from the 19th century.

PERGAMUM AND PRIENE
CONTRASTING CITIES

Above: The theatre of Priene, dating from the later 2nd century BC, is a perfect example of a Greek theatre. It has a two-storeyed skene building, providing fixed architectural scenery at ground level.

Below: Pergamum developed around its Acropolis, once a citadel, whose height emphasized its architectural drama. The theatre is in the foreground.

Pergamum, once a small hilltop citadel, became under its Attalid kings (241–133BC) a marvel of Hellenistic town-planning. Its theatre, temples, palace, altars and library were dramatically arranged along the summit and sides of its Acropolis to rival Athens'. Yet Pergamum was no free polis but an absolute monarch's grand capital. In it the king's word was law, although the Attalids, who prided themselves on their philhellenism, shrewdly allowed Ionian cities under their rule autonomy. Their last monarch bequeathed his kingdom to Rome in 133BC. If smaller than the greatest Hellenistic capitals Alexandria or Antioch, Pergamum, unlike them, largely survives, although its major monuments have been mostly removed.

The first kings built only modestly, but after 200BC close alliance with the rising power of Rome meant a vast growth in Pergamene power and wealth. The upper city, broadly crescent-shaped, was spread over the southern slopes of a hill that, contracting as it rises, ends in a ridge a few hundred feet wide. Here was sited the Acropolis, necessarily irregular in shape, facing west.

Above: The Temple of Athena Polias at Priene was a sublime Ionic temple. Designed by Pytheos, it was dedicated in 334BC by Alexander the Great.

AT THE ACROPOLIS' FOOT
Beneath the Acropolis lay the lower Agora, a large enclosed court. Beyond it, running north, was a huge Stoa 213m (c.700ft) long, supported by a retaining wall. At the Stoa's north end, a small temple was rebuilt by the emperor Caracalla in AD214. Scooped out of the hill above it was a vast theatre, partly rebuilt by the Romans. Above to the east was the imposing temple of the emperor Trajan of the early 2nd century AD – Pergamum remained important under the Romans. Behind Trajan's temple lay barracks and the relatively small royal palaces.

The small Temple of Athena, built in an old-fashioned Doric style, stood in a large colonnaded courtyard. On the court's north side was Pergamum's famous library, second only to Alexandria's in repute, housing 200,000 scrolls. Parchment, the tough writing material made from hides, was traditionally invented in, and named after, Pergamum. Parchment was intended to counter Egypt's monopoly of papyrus, then the commonest writing material. Ultimately it replaced it.

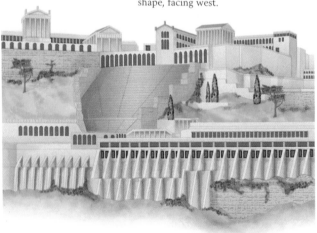

THE ALTAR OF ZEUS

Between the Temple of Athena and the lower Agora rose the melodramatic Altar of Zeus. Built by Eumenes II *c.*165BC, it was one of the grandest, most resplendent structures of its age, although large altars had been built earlier at Samothrace and Syracuse. From the front the building appeared as a U-shaped Ionic colonnade on a podium with a huge sculptured relief. A vast flight of steps led up to the altar itself, which was architecturally insignificant compared to its surrounds. Most notable was the sculpted gigantomachia (battle of giants) on the podium, symbolizing Pergamene victories over barbarous Celtic invaders. (This flamboyant altar later struck the Christian author of Revelations [II, 13] as "Satan's Throne".) The whole upper city was enclosed by stone ramparts. In the lower city, ordinary people lived in simple mudbrick houses, as they did in many other Greek cities.

PRIENE: AN IDEAL POLIS

A total contrast to opulent Pergamum was Priene in southern Ionia. A tiny polis with a population of *c.*4,000, it was slowly but completely rebuilt from 334BC on. Aristotle and Plato, those so often differing philosophers, would have agreed that Priene had the ideal size and form for a true polis. Occupying a terraced sloping site south of its almost inaccessible Acropolis 300m (1,000ft) above, Priene was laid out on the orthogonal principles of Hippodamus. This ignored the mountainous actuality of its site. Six main streets 4m (13ft) wide ran east–west on level ground, crossed at right-angles by 15 streets climbing sometimes very steep gradients.

Near the city's centre, its Agora was entered via an arched gateway of *c.*150BC. This is the first Greek ornamental arch.

Right: Pergamum's upper city, broadly crescent-shaped, was spread over the southern slopes of a hill that, contracting as it rises, ends in a ridge a few hundred feet wide.

It is far less pompous than Roman triumphal arches, which almost invariably celebrate military triumphs. Around the Agora, public buildings included a fine *dipteral* (two-rowed) stoa with Doric columns outside and Ionic columns inside. South of the Agora lay the Stadium and Palaestra (wrestling school), to the north was the theatre. The first theatre, dating from 300BC, was replaced in the later 2nd century BC with a two-storeyed scena building. This provided fixed architectural scenery at ground level with upper wooden scenery.

The Temple of Athena Polias lay northwest of the Agora. A sublime Ionic temple designed by Pytheos, it was very possibly dedicated in 334BC by Alexander the Great himself, then liberating Ionia from Persian rule. Its six by 11 columns stood on square plinths with 24 deep flutes. Capitals have the classic egg-and-dart decoration on their echinus.

The temple was designed in the proportions of a Greek human foot (which is somewhat shorter than a modern foot), on a width/length ratio of 1:2. Such perfect proportions suit so perfect a polis, creating a perfectly balanced building.

Above: The theatre at Pergamum, dramatically carved from the steep hillside beneath the Acropolis, reflected the general flamboyance of the Attalid dynasty.

SYRACUSE AND ACRAGAS
SICILIAN CITIES

Above: The grand theatre at Syracuse, dating back to the 5th century BC. It could seat 15,000 people, revealing the city's size and wealth under its democracy.

Below: Part of the impressive fortifications around Syracuse that were brought to their peak by Archimedes, the city's most famous son, and that for long successfully defied the besieging Roman army under Marcellus in 212BC.

Ancient Sicily has been called the Greek America, for its fertile land was potentially very rich. Such wealth let the western Greeks build cities with unprecented splendour and distinction, if not always with great aesthetic subtlety. Sicilian cities' ruins are among the best-preserved in the Greek world but their politics were often ruinously unstable.

SYRACUSE

Founded in 734BC on the superbly defensible Ortygia island, Syracuse was already wealthy in the 6th century BC, as the massive if simple columns of its Temple of Apollo show. It rose to power under the tyrants Gelon and Hieron I (485–467BC). Gelon routed Carthage in 480BC and Hieron transplanted other Greek cities' populations to Syracuse. Both tyrants built lavishly. A superb Doric temple to Athena (Minerva) from their era survives, with 14 columns embedded in the walls of the current baroque cathedral. Its doors were covered in gold and ivory and on its roof a golden statue of Athena acted as a beacon to sailors. It is notable for sophisticated intercolumniation. The city's first theatre, trapezoidal in shape, was built beneath the present one. A fountain to the nymph Arethusa helped supply the city with drinking water and provided almost the only source of papyrus, the Greek paper, outside Egypt.

The city became a democracy after Hieron's death and as such repelled the Athenians' great siege in 415–413BC. But when attack by Carthage in 405BC threatened the city, a soldier called Dionysius made himself tyrant. Under his tyranny – which was truly despotic but lasted until 367BC – Syracuse attained new splendour, gaining extensive walls on the heights of Epipolae, that made it almost impregnable. But it lost not only its liberties but also part of its essential Greekness, many non-Greek mercenaries being settled there. The subsequent reign of Dionysius II (367–344BC) led to endless civil wars that wrecked Sicily.

HIERON'S GOLDEN AGE

In the 3rd century BC Syracuse regained its wealth under the steady rule of Hieron II (269–215BC). Its superb theatre was constructed then, as was its immense altar, which at 198m (650ft) was the longest ever built. Hundreds of animals were sacrificed on it at a time – Greek religion could be gory. Hieron patronized the poet Theocritus and the scientist Archimedes, who further strengthened the city's fortifications. But these did not prevent the Romans capturing the city after a long siege in 212BC when it had rashly supported Hannibal in the Second Punic War. Archimedes' accidental killing by a Roman soldier in its sack symbolized the end of Syracusan glory. Despite this, Cicero could still praise it in the 1st century BC as the elegantly Greek capital of the Roman province of Sicily.

ACRAGAS

Founded in 582BC in western Sicily from Gelon, another Sicilian city, Acragas (modern Agrigento) soon became one of the richest cities in the Mediterranean, thanks to its fertile territory and trade. In 488BC Theron became its tyrant. He continued work on the vast Temple of Olympian Zeus, one of the largest and most unusual of Greek temples, with its Atlantes, giant figures half-buried in the walls. After Theron had provoked Carthage by seizing Himera in 483BC, his alliance with Syracuse helped defeat the resulting Carthaginian attack. Victory led to an influx of slaves, allowing Acragas to expand work on the magnificent 'Valley of the Temples'.

This parade of Doric temples is now a UNESCO World Heritage site. Best-preserved of its temples is the Temple of Concord, built c.430BC of a local limestone so rough that it precluded many 'refinements'. With 13 by six columns, whose height equals 4.61 times their lowest diameter, it measures 39.4 by 16.9m (122ft by 18ft 6in).

After Theron died in 472BC, Acragas became a democracy, led in the 440s BC by the aristocrat, philosopher and radical democrat Empedocles. At its zenith, Acragas' population reputedly reached 200,000, rivalling Athens. Its inhabitants had luxuriously soft beds, elaborate fishponds and even pet swans. The poet Pindar praised it as the "most beautiful of cities inhabited by mortals".

But Acragas' good times did not last. When Carthage's war of revenge began in 406BC, the Acragantines, despite help from Syracuse, proved incapable of effective resistance. They had become so soft that even soldiers on sentry duty at night reputedly demanded two pillows, a mattress and quilt. In 405BC the city was

abandoned to the Carthaginians, who sacked but did not destroy it. Later it was repeopled by Timoleon, the saviour of Syracuse, in the 330s BC.

Acragas suffered badly again in the First Punic War (264–241BC). The Romans, capturing the city after a long siege, enslaved the whole population. Under the Roman Empire, Acragas finally regained a modest prosperity, but as a minor provincial town, not a great city.

Above: The great Doric Temple of Concord at Acragas dates from the 5th century BC, the city's golden age when it was reputedly the richest city in the Greek world, home of the mystical philosopher and statesman Empedocles.

Right: A fountain to the nymph Arethusa supplied Ortygia, Syracuse's inner city, with drinking water and provided almost the only source of papyrus, the Greek paper, outside Egypt.

DELOS AND EPHESUS
DIFFERING FATES

Two Aegean sites, both very closely connected with Greek life, sacred and commercial, had very different fates.

DELOS

A tiny island in the central Cyclades, Delos was the mythical birthplace of the god Apollo and his sister Artemis, among Greece's holiest shrines. 'Long-robed Ionians' with their wives and children gathered to honour Apollo at the annual *Delia* festival. At first, nearby Naxos dominated the island, donating the fine if much-weathered marble lions from *c.*630BC. Athens, the mother Ionian city, played a major role at Delos from the 6th century BC on and Pisistratus 'purified' the island in 543BC. Persia respected Delos' sacred neutrality during the Marathon campaign in 490BC, but in 478BC the Ionians, under Athens' leadership, based their anti-Persian League at Delos. In 426BC Athens ordered another purification, forbidding births or deaths on its sacred soil, banishing all Delians. From then on,

Above: The Library of Celsus at Ephesus, noted for its projecting pavilions, dates from c.AD110, when the city was thriving in the long Roman peace.

Athenian officials governed the island shrine. Delos became independent in 315BC after Athens' defeat by Macedonia.

Soon it was thriving as a trading centre, building a new theatre and temples. Among these the little Temple of Isis of *c.*170BC reveals both the persistence of the Doric style and the presence of Graeco-Egyptians resident in Delos.

THE SLAVE EMPORIUM

But Delos could not escape Roman power. In 166BC, Rome, to curb Rhodes, made Delos a free port. Soon the island filled with Italian merchants who made it the centre of the booming slave trade and built their own agora. Ever larger houses and monuments were erected. The boom ended with the sack by Mithridates' forces in 88BC, killing thousands of Italian merchants. The island then sank into obscurity. Pausanias in the 2nd century AD noted that the shrines' guards were almost the only people on the island.

The religious centre of the island was the Hieron of Apollo, the sacred precinct enclosing temples and altars. A vast 7th-century BC statue of Apollo stood on the north side, but only its base survives. The Great Temple of Apollo, begun in 477BC and completed 200 years later, had a high granite base with 13 marble columns down its sides. A Doric temple, it measured 19.5 by 13.4m (97 by 44ft). To the north lay the Sacred Lake, now dry, where Apollo and Letis were born. (Delos, now treeless, once had poplar groves.) To the south lay the theatre and around it luxurious peristyle houses with mosaics and

Left: In AD118 Publius Quintillius erected the monument known today as the Temple of Hadrian, dedicating it to Hadrian, Artemis and the people of Ephesus. It shows how Greek classical architecture could be adventurously enlivened with Roman arches.

fine columns, such as the 'Maison des Masques'. Similar houses have been well preserved at Pompeii.

EPHESUS

Traditionally founded by Ionian colonists on the coast of Asia Minor in *c.*1000BC, Ephesus was actually even older, having been a Mycenaean settlement. It went on to become one of the greatest of all Greek cities, a home of the Ionian Enlightenment (the enigmatic philosopher Heraclitus was born there) and a wealthy port.

Above all, it became famed for its great Temple of Artemis (Diana), one of the Seven Wonders of the Ancient World. The first temple, paid for by Croesus, King of Lydia *c.*560BC and designed by Theodorus of Samos, measured 109.2 by 55m (358 by 171ft). Originally made of limestone covered in marble, it had giant Ionic columns 20m (65ft) high. (The other Seven Wonders were the Pyramids, Alexandria's *pharos* (lighthouse), Babylon's hanging gardens, the Mausoleum of Halicarnassus, Pheidias' statue of Zeus at Olympia and the Colossus of Rhodes.)

Within its cella stood a statue of Artemis shown not as the usual chaste huntress of Greek mythology but as a many-breasted fertility goddess, suggesting possible Asian origins. The devotees of this Artemis were enraged when St

Paul, visiting the city in the 40s AD, tried to attack their profitable cult. The sellers of religious trinkets rioted, crying: "Great is Diana (Artemis) of the Ephesians."

Ephesus suffered from the depression that hit all Ionian cities after the Persian wars, but recovered in the 4th century BC. Alexander's conquests made it a terminus for traders coming down the Meander from Asia. Resited in the early 3rd century BC (the old harbour was by then silting up) it continued to flourish, whether as a fully independent polis or under Seleucid or Attalid suzerainty. A new theatre at the foot of Mount Pion seating 25,000 was built *c.*200BC. But unwilling involvement in the wars of the Roman Empire after 130BC damaged the city.

However, in the *pax Romana*, the long Roman peace following Augustus' victory in 31BC, Ephesus flourished again as the capital of the wealthy Roman province of Asia (western Turkey). From this period, when Ephesus' population reached 250,000, date many grand buildings: the colonnaded street the Arkadiane, running through the city like a huge double stoa; the Temple of Hadrian; the Library of Celsus, noted for its projecting pavilions, and the opulent marble baths by the harbour. These show cosmopolitan Ephesians happily adopting the Roman arch and vault. Ephesus remained important into the early Byzantine era.

Above: The fine theatre at Delos dates from the 3rd century BC, when the island was enjoying a prosperous independence as the centre of an island confederacy.

Below: The 'Agora of the Italians' at Delos dates from the 2nd century BC. The island, by then effectively under Roman rule, became the greatest slave emporium ever known, reputedly handling up to 10,000 slaves a day.

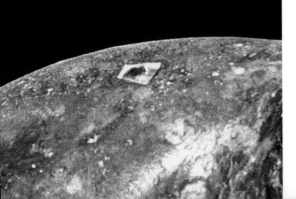

CHAPTER XVI

SCULPTURE

In the two centuries after 500BC, Greek sculptors created an art in which gods came to look like perfect human beings and humanity like incarnate gods. This art, simultaneously naturalistic and idealized, became the paradigm to which Western artists have recurrently turned. It also influenced non-Western art as far away as India. Greek sculptors focused on depicting the human form, often nude. Until after 400BC this meant exclusively nude males. While Greek men exercised naked in public, Greek women were cloistered away fully clothed. (Only in Sparta, nearly as devoid of art as it was of freedom, could female nudity sometimes be glimpsed.) Even when artists discovered the female nude in the 4th century BC, the heroic male nude still dominated Greek art.

A common misconception is that Greek sculpture was of lifeless white marble. In fact, many materials were used: limestone, terracotta, marble, wood, sometimes *chryselephantine* (wood covered in gold and ivory) and above all bronze. All were painted in lifelike colours, with eyes, lips, teeth and hair picked out so realistically they must have looked startlingly alive. Bronze, a valuable metal, was often melted down in the Middle Ages. Few of the great bronzes mentioned by ancient writers survive, although some statues have been found underwater. Instead, we must turn to later marble copies made for Romans, or images on coins or fragmentary carvings. Only the Elgin Marbles, original sculptures taken from the Parthenon, convey fully the lithe splendour of Greek sculpture.

Left: This majestic bronze of Zeus was rescued from the sea. Idealized yet also naturalistic, it dates from c.465BC.

MINOAN AND MYCENAEAN SCULPTURES 1700–1100BC

Almost no large statues survive from the Aegean late Bronze Age, when the Minoan and Mycenaean civilizations flourished. Possibly no statues of any size were ever made in Crete and the islands. Greek-speaking Mycenaeans (Homer's Achaeans) ultimately conquered Crete politically, but Minoan Crete conquered Mycenae culturally.

BULLS WITH GILDED HORNS

Minoan influence is often so overpowering on Mycenaean art – though not its architecture – that some archaeologists once posited a Minoan mainland empire. However, we now know that the influence came from Minoan artists or artists trained in Minoan techniques. This is revealed in two carvings of bulls' heads. (The cult of the bull was clearly central to Bronze Age religion.) One, from Cnossus, dates from *c.*1500BC. Carved out of steatite with gilded horns, the bull's-head *rhyton* (ceremonial cup) has eyes of red jasper and white shell for the lines around its nostrils. It is a superb work by any standard but only 30cm (12in) high. Remarkably similar is the bull with golden horns and silver eyes found in a grave of Mycenae of about the same date.

The same style remained dominant on the mainland until the fall of Mycenaean civilization after 1200BC. How far Minoan and Mycenaean art survived or resurfaced to influence later Greek art is debatable. But the naturalism and humanism that distinguish it from grandiose contemporary art in Egypt or Babylon were also to be among the hallmarks of Hellenic art proper.

A distinctive Minoan sculpture emerged when the first palaces were built in Crete *c.*2000BC. Initially rather stiff, this had developed by *c.*1700BC into a lively and fluid art. It peaked around 1500BC just as Crete was devastated by the eruption of Thira, a blow from which it never fully recovered.

Sculptors made small figurines of bronze, clay or other materials (but seldom of marble) or in sculptured mouldings on murals and vases. Minoan artists never attempted the monumental.

ATHLETES AND GODDESSES

The Minoans and Mycenaeans anticipated later Greeks in the importance they attached to athletics, including – in Crete at least – the perilous sport of bull-leaping. A figurine from the palace at Cnossus of 1500BC of a young acrobat or bull-leaper caught in mid-air, carved in wood once covered with gold, reveals a classic naturalism. More of its time is the bronze votive figurine a mere 15cm (6in) high of *c.*1550BC. The slim young man, almost naked, has a markedly concave back, a Cretan ideal, and his right hand is raised to his forehead.

The deity he was worshipping may have been the Snake-Goddess, a frequent image in Minoan art. In a painted faience statue about 30cm (12in) high found in the temple depository of Cnossus, the goddess is shown dressed in the height of Minoan court fashion: long, flounced skirts, tight bodice with breasts exposed. The figure may, however, represent a priestess rather than an actual goddess.

Above: The Snake-Goddess, a typically colourful painted Minoan figurine, about 30cm (12in) high, of the 16th century BC. Some archaeologists now think this statue has been put together from disparate pieces.

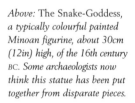

Right: A bronze figurine of a male worshipper, with hollowed back, from Tylissos in Crete, dating to c.1600BC.

Although few court ladies carried writhing snakes in each hand, as she does, sacred serpents were common in Minoan and later religion. (The goddess Athena was portrayed 1,000 years later in the Parthenon with a great snake coiling beside her. As there are references in the Linear B tablets at Cnossus to a goddess Athena, it is even possible that this image is of Athena.)

THE *LILY PRINCE*

An equally famous image of Minoan Crete is the *Lily Prince*, an unusually large-scale figure, about 2.1m (7ft) high on a relief fresco from Cnossus Palace. Heavily – and contentiously – restored, this graceful courtier or prince, almost naked apart from his kilt and feathered headdress, probably dates from *c*.1500BC. The figure embodies Cretan gracefulness, although he is unusually stiff.

By contrast, the *Harvester Vase* has vivid relief scenes of everyday rural life. It shows farmers laughing and chatting, presumably on the way back from harvest as they are carrying farming tools. The vase shows that Minoan artists were not interested only in courtiers.

A similarly vivid brilliant art in miniature appears in seals just 2.5cm (1in) in diameter from the mainland. One, probably dating to *c*.1300BC from a tomb near Sparta, shows a priest and a griffin, a mythical creature; another from the same tomb portrays two ducks with curved necks and is a triumph of Minoan or Mycenaean artistic naturalism.

THE LION GATE

Only one example of Mycenaean monumental sculpture survives: the great stone lions flanking the Lion Gate at Mycenae itself. Built *c*.1280BC, the Lion Gate consists of giant slabs of carved ashlar,

Right: The Lion Gate at Mycenae, dating from c.1280BC, displays Mycenaean sculpture at its most powerful. But it is the only large-scale carving to survive from the Aegean Bronze Age.

each weighing several tons. The now-lost heads of the two stone lions once snarled down in realistic fury. The sculpture's power may derive from Hattusa, the massively walled Hittite capital in Anatolia, but the lions flank a Minoan-style column. Sculptures would frequently be incorporated in temples by Classical Greeks, but the Lion Gate seems to have been a one-off in the Aegean Bronze Age.

Above: Tiny seals, often only 2.5cm (1in) long, reveal Mycenaean art at its vivid best. This seal, showing mythical beasts carrying offerings, dates from c.1300BC.

THE DARK AGES AND EARLY ARCHAIC PERIOD 1100–700BC

The collapse of Mycenaean civilization after 1200BC led to the Greek Dark Ages. Even less is known about this period than the Bronze Age, but artistically it certainly appears to deserve its name. The end of the elaborate palace-centred culture seemingly meant a nearly complete end to almost all artistic life for at least two centuries.

Only in Athens, safe thanks to its almost impregnably high rock and perhaps to its relative obscurity, did some form of civilized life in a sub-Mycenaean spirit continue without interruption. It was in Athens also that the first signs of a new art began to emerge. Such signs are, however, generally unimpressive before 800BC. During the 8th century BC the first truly Greek sculpture hesitantly takes shape, formed by the austere contemporary Geometric style that owed nothing to Bronze Age precedents.

STATUES FROM THE DIPLYON CEMETERY

Among the ivory figurines found in the Diplyon cemetery at Athens, one has a crown decorated with a meander pattern. This probably indicates that she is a goddess. Eastern influence underlies the choice of ivory as a raw material – there were never any elephants in Greece, so the material as well as the idea must have been imported – but there is a Greek solidity even in tiny figures only 24cm (9½in) tall. (Most items that have been recovered come from cemeteries or are votive offerings made to the gods.)

STATUES FROM OLYMPIA

From Olympia come several fine small bronzes of the mid-8th century BC. One shows a deer being attacked by dogs, another shows a man with a dog fighting a lion (this is a confused piece that takes some deciphering).

Above: This bronze figurine of a warrior in the Geometric style of the late 8th century BC heralds the revival of Greek sculpture after the Dark Ages. The naked human form was already the focus of interest.

Above: This head from the Diplyon cemetery at Athens reveals the highly stimulating impact of Asian art on Greek sculpture around 600BC.

Far more clearly depicted in action are the linked figurines of *The Hero and Centaur*, in which a man (or possibly a god, most probably Zeus) is shown with his arms locked around a centaur, a mythical beast shown as alternately wise and savage and long popular in Greek art. They are probably engaged in mortal combat.

Carved on a bronze tripod found at Olympia and dating from c.700BC, a vivid scene shows Apollo and Heracles fighting over a tripod. On a gentler note is a hind suckling her fawn.

More common than such bronze pieces as votive offerings – because they were far cheaper – are small terracotta figures

Above: Small, stiffly made bronze statues of animals dating from the late 8th century BC, *the very dawn of Greek art proper.*

such as that representing, rather than actually depicting, a horse of the late 8th century BC.

More realistic is the terracotta bird found in a cemetery south of the Eridanus in Athens. From such tiny, stiff, twig-like figurines, the whole grand tradition of Greek sculpture would develop.

BRONZE CASTING

Most of the greatest Greek statues were made in bronze, a material favoured because of its strength, durability and the way in which it can be easily worked.

Bronze is an alloy that typically consists of about 90 per cent copper, the rest being tin or other materials, including sometimes small amounts of lead or zinc. Bronze is easier to cast than copper because of its lower melting point. Its great tensile strength enables protruding parts – arms and legs – to be cast without supports, giving it an advantage over marble. Bronze statues' colour vary according to the amount of tin or other metals used, ranging from silverish to a rich red.

As it ages, bronze acquires a pleasing patina, although the Greeks painted all their bronze statues meticulously. Unfortunately, bronze has also always been highly valued as a metal, so most ancient statues were later melted down.

Initially, small bronze objects and tools were solid-cast in two-piece clay moulds. But by 1500BC larger statues were being cast across the ancient world using the *cire perdue* (French: 'lost wax') method. In this type of casting, a clay core was formed in the basic shape of the statue. A thin layer of wax following the shape of the sculpture was encased within two layers of heat-resistant clay or plaster. As the wax heated up, it poured away. Wax gates let the wax out of the mould and the molten metal into the space that the 'lost wax' had created. Wax vents allowed hot gases to rise while the liquid bronze was being poured. As this cooled, it formed the statue. The master-mould could be reused many times.

The Riace bronzes of two warriors of *c*.460BC found in the sea near Reggio, Calabria in southern Italy, have almost identical bodies, although their heads are different. This suggests that their torsos were cast using the same mould, if perhaps at different times. Large-scale bronze statues were often cast in pieces no more than *c*.1m (3ft) long, for two men could only handle with ease a crucible containing *c*.9 litres (2 gallons) of molten bronze weighing *c*.68kg (150lb). Bronze must be poured quite fast or it will start to cool and not pour uniformly. If bronze is not at the right temperature to be sufficiently fluid, the casting may fail, resulting in the bronze cracking and becoming deformed as it cools.

Right: One of the Riace bronzes, statues dating from c.460BC, *in the Classical period, are among the masterpieces of Greek sculpture made possible by bronze casting.*

THE IMPACT OF EGYPT
DAEDALIC SCULPTURE c.700–600BC

Above: This kouros from Attica, made c.620BC, still displays marked Egyptian-inspired stiffness.

Egypt's pharaohs had successfully repelled the invasions of the 'Sea Peoples' that wrecked Bronze Age civilizations further north. Hardly affected by a dark age, this ancient, wealthy land continued to produce superb stone sculptures in its almost unchanging millennial tradition. In the early 7th century BC, as trade revived, the Greeks began retracing Mycenaean trade routes south to Egypt and east to the Levant. Soon Greeks were settling in Egypt as traders and mercenaries, causing friction with the Egyptians at times. Naucratis in the Delta was finally established as the sole Greek city in c.570BC.

The impact of Egyptian statues, monumental in every sense, was overwhelming on the simple Greeks of the Archaic Age (700–490BC). Egyptian sculpture, carved from stone, was designed to overawe, being hieratically stiff and often massive. Such hieratic grandeur inspired Greek artists to produce the sculptures called Daedalic, after the mythical Athenian artist who

had designed the Labyrinth for Minos in Crete. (If Daedalus had existed, he would of course have been a Mycenaean, but this distinction was unknown to later Greeks.) But Egypt's grand solemnity was balanced by colourful 'orientalizing' influences from Asia that often featured beasts, mythical or real.

BLOSSOMING OF ART

This fertilization led to a blossoming of Greek art from the mid-7th century BC. Among the first examples is the more than life-size statue of Artemis dedicated by Nikandre of Naxos. The goddess stands solidly imposing on her two long legs with arms flat at her side. The upper part of her body is emphasized, despite the smallness of her head, framed by the triangle of hair falling on her shoulders. The whole statue, with its unified balance of static form and dynamic force, exudes a tender calm. Smaller but equally impressive is the wooden statue of Hera from the great temple to that goddess in Samos of 650BC.

Of about the same date but in far better shape is the limestone *Auxerre Statuette*. She stands realistically, the curves of her skirt and half-naked breasts vividly carved, her long hair and facial features endowing her with feminine humanity. This statue proved influential across Greece, with similar statuettes being found at Rhodes, Corinth, Mycenae and Taranto, a colony in southern Italy.

The grandest sculptural achievement of the 7th century BC was the Lion Avenue of Delos. Nine seated lions flank the Sacred Way, each c.1.5m (5ft) high. The idea of such 'avenues' was Egyptian and they show Greek sculptors attempting, if not always achieving, monumentality. Of the gigantic statues cut from Cycladic marble quarries, some

Below: The grandest sculptural achievement of the 7th century BC was the Lion Avenue of Delos. Nine seated lions flank the Sacred Way, each c.1.5m (5ft) high.

remained unfinished, clearly proving beyond their creators' powers. One such colossus that was abandoned half-hewn would have been 11m (36ft) high if it had been completed.

Lions were by then half-mythical creatures. They were probably extinct in Greece proper (though not in Macedonia), and so were treated fantastically, almost like sphinxes or chimaeras. From Corcyra (Corfu) in *c*.625BC comes a superb and quite realistic example. A mighty limestone lion, probably once part of a funerary monument, at 1.2m (4ft) long, lies menacingly on its plinth, its tail between its hind legs, forepaws extended, its fierce head expresses the dark menace of the wild.

KOUROS AND KOURE

But the focus of most Greek sculpture remained the human figure. Statues became increasingly impressive and large towards 620BC, as Greek sculptors gained confidence. The first great statues now emerge from Attica. The best-preserved is the *Kouros* by the 'Diplyon Master' of *c*.620BC. (Such naked archaic youths are called *kouros*, youth, and their female counterparts are called *koure*, maiden, the latter always portrayed fully clothed.)

Completely and proudly naked for the first time – unlike Egyptian statues – he stands more than lifesize at 1.84m (6ft 4in) tall, his long braided hair (an Archaic Greek fashion) well depicted. This kouros, imbued with Apollonian calm, probably stood on the grave of a young Athenian aristocrat, and embodies current ideals of beauty. Stylistic stiffness prevents complete realism, but anyway such statues were intended to represent, rather than depict accurately, human beings. The kouros remained a distinct type of statue down to 500BC, made according to specific rules.

A celebrated pair of kouroi are Cleobus and Biton by Polymedes of Argos of *c*.600 BC. They are bursting with muscular, youthful vigour. This is highly appropriate because, according to Herodotus the historian, these twin brothers pulled their mother in a heavy ox-cart to the Temple of Hera just in time for a ceremony, before sinking exhausted into a blessed oblivion granted to them by the gods as a reward.

Above: Found in Artemis' sanctuary on the island of Delos, with an inscription that it was dedicated to the goddess by Nikandre, this is the earliest extant all-marble statue. More than life-size, it dates to c.650BC.

Left: A celebrated pair of kouroi are Cleobus and Biton, probably made by Polymedes of Argos in c.600BC. They brim with muscular, youthful vigour.

THE 6TH-CENTURY AWAKENING c.600–490BC

Above: This statue of Croesus, an Athenian killed fighting, dates from c.535BC. His muscles and bones are clearly modelled and his arms hang freely from his body.

Right: This sublimely calm, massive kouros, c.525BC, from the shrine to Poseidon at Sunium, is over 3m (10ft) high. With a typically fixed, enigmatic Archaic smile, he was probably one of two colossal figures.

The whole tempo of Greek life – political, economic, intellectual and artistic – quickened in the 6th and early 5th centuries BC. In sculpture there was no sudden revolution or great leap forward comparable to that being made around the same time by philosophers in Ionia. Instead, there was a gradually accelerating discovery of naturalism that, with hindsight, paved the way for the titanic achievements in all the plastic arts of the next two centuries.

Slowly, the stiff geometry of an art inspired by Egypt, albeit less impressive, gave way to something more vivid and human and far more inspiring. What dominated Greek art at the time and for centuries afterwards was a persistent desire to express the ideal human form. Slow, unrecorded improvements in tools, running parallel with those in architecture, also gradually enabled sculptors to develop more expressive ways of carving.

THE ARCHAIC SMILE

Typical of statues of the beginning of the century is the sublimely calm, massive kouros from the shrine to Poseidon at Sunium. (The temple itself had not yet been built.) More than 3m (10ft) high, with a typically enigmatic, frozen Archaic smile, he was one of a pair of colossal figures visible from afar to seafarers. This recurrent Archaic smile was probably intended as a sign of a free citizen, for statues were still not intended actually to portray an individual. But names and inscriptions on the base begin to appear, making the kouroi more personal.

This is apparent in the koure (maiden) commemorating Phrasikleia, originally from Paros of c.550BC, which bears the rather cryptic dedication: "I could be called *koure* (maiden) for ever instead of wedded by the gods thus named, Ariston of Paros created me."

The so-called Apollo of Temea of around the same date was a funerary memorial statue, like many in the 6th century, almost life-size at 1.5m (5ft). He still has the fixed smile and elaborate long hair of the "young light-hearted masters of the waves" (Homer's phrase), but his body is treated more realistically

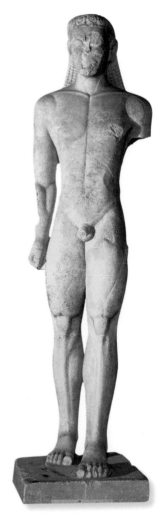

and smoothly. Slightly later, *c*.535BC, is the statue of Croesus, with the inscription: "Stand and grieve at the tomb of Croesus, killed in the front line by Ares (the war god)".

Croesus was a member of the powerful Alcmaeonid clan, enemies of Pisistratus who had become tyrant in 547BC. Croesus was presumably killed in internoble feuding. His muscles and bones are far more clearly modelled and his arms hang freely from his body. Even more realistic but badly damaged – giving it a probably unjustly brutish air – is the statue marked on its base 'Aristodicus.' He has short hair – a sign of dawning Classicism – and a natural rather than pinched-in waist, but he retains a stiff Archaic pose.

TEMPLE SCULPTURE

Equally important were the sculptures adorning temples, now being built in increasing numbers. At the Treasury of the Siphnians in Delphi, a radically new marble temple built *c*.525BC, were placed not only the famous marble caryatids but also a fine frieze showing the Council of the Gods. Like all sculptures, in bronze or marble, it was originally painted. From the Acropolis in Athens several votive kouroi still depict the maidens with enigmatic fixed smiles and stiffly elaborate robes, indicting their noble pedigree, but the shape of their bodies starts to emerge, hinting at a new realism. These date from the late 6th century BC and, like most sculptures then on the Acropolis, were damaged or sullied during the Persian invasions of 480–479BC, so that they were later jettisoned. On the metopes of the great new temple of Aphaea on Aegina some carvings are Archaic, such as the man hurrying to help a fallen comrade, and others Classical. Classicism arrived with a rush.

ON THE CUSP OF CLASSICISM

Classicism can be seen emerging in one of the rare surviving early bronzes, the *Apollo of Piombino*. Dating from *c*.490BC and found off the coast of Italy, this retains the long hair and formulaic pose of an Archaic figure but has the fully muscled torso of a Classical statue. Generally similar and thought to date from *c*.480BC – on the brink of the Persian invasion – is the *Standing Youth*, a gigantic 1.9m (6ft 3in) bronze figure. His long hair again looks Archaic but his flowing sculptural forms also show Greek art on the cusp of Classicism. He may have been a young Apollo, for his left hand may have held the god's bow.

Above: The still half-Archaic figure of a moscophoros *(calf-carrier) dating from* c.580BC *has increasingly realistic muscles.*

Left: The Apollo of Piombino, *found in the sea off Italy and dating from* c.490BC, *has the long hair and stiff pose of Archaic figures but the muscled torso is that of Classical statues.*

THE DAWN OF CLASSICISM
C.480–450BC

Right: The bronze originals of these Roman marble copies were made in 477BC by Critios and Nesiotes, honouring the Athenian tyrannicides Harmodius and Aristogeiton. Both show for the first time the 'hardness' of early Classicism, with muscles emphasized.

No earlier period in history matches the phenomenally rapid development of 5th-century BC Greece. After the Persians were defeated in 480–479BC, Athens became the pre-eminent Greek city, fully democratic. In high Classicism it realized its ideal style. In sculpture, the male nude was the focus of most attention, with female figures still being depicted fully clothed. Women were long considered of secondary interest in Greek art, as in Greek life.

REVOLUTIONARY REALISM

The *Critios Boy* of *c.*480BC (attributed to the sculptor Critios) is a standing youth wholly freed from the kouros conventions. He rests his weight realistically on his left leg, with his right leg slack, his right thigh pushed forward. His pelvis is correspondingly tilted, his right buttock slackened, his head and shoulders slightly inclined. This revolutionary realism comes closer to depicting a 'real' relaxed figure than any earlier artwork anywhere in the world. To create such a figure required genuine understanding of the human body. However the boy is also an idealized figure. For the first time the human body is depicted as perfectly beautiful and simultaneously symmetrical. Greek artists of the time were obsessed with mathematical symmetry. The statue is, however, atypical in one important way, for most Classical statues in the 5th century BC were in bronze, not marble. Sculptors now began to think in terms of 'moulding' – for bronze

Below: One of the two Riace bronzes, either athletes or warriors, depicted with unprecedented realism, made in c.470–460BC.

casting – rather than 'carving', even when they were actually working in marble, as in this instance.

THE RIACE BRONZES

This sculptural concern is evident in the magnificent Riace bronzes, fished from the sea near Riace in southern Italy in 1972. Dating from *c.*470–460BC, these two athletes or warriors have vigorous muscular bodies, depicted realistically. Their resting limbs convey the tension of recent exertions superbly. Each torso is nearly a mirror image of the other, conceivably cast from the same mould. Only their heads truly differ. They retain traces of copper on their lips and nipples, silver on their teeth and precious stones in their eyes. They were perhaps part of a group, among the many superb Greek artworks that the Romans looted. However, they are probably not by Pheidias, the great Athenian sculptor as was at one time thought, for they are not in his serenely idealizing style and are a little too early.

THE CHARIOTEER

A noble example of very early Classicism, in which traces of the Archaic style linger, is the *Delphi Charioteer*. Probably presented by Hieron, tyrant of Syracuse, as a votive offering after his victory at Cumae over the Etruscans and datable to *c*.473BC, the young charioteer has a solemnity suited to Greece's holiest shrine. He originally stood in the car of a four-horse bronze chariot with a groom standing beside him. Only this statue of the group has survived, thanks to an earthquake that dropped him down a

Below: The Delphi Charioteer *is a superb example of early Classicism, probably presented by Hieron, tyrant of Syracuse, as a votive offering after his victory at Cumae, so datable to* c.473BC.

ravine into an old drain. There he was somehow overlooked by subsequent pillagers of the shrine.

The extreme verticality of the statue would not have been so marked when he was riding inside his chariot. He wears the long robes suited to his windy profession, with a diadem band around his head. His eyes are marked in coloured stones and traces remain of the gilt once on his hair, eyes and lips. This must have given his face a richness and living warmth typical of Greek statues but hard to imagine today when looking at chilly marble copies.

THE TYRANNICIDES

In Athens itself two statues made at around this time commemorate what might be called Athens' first freedom fighters: Harmodius and Aristogeiton. These famed 'tyrannicides' were two (male) lovers who killed the tyrant Hipparchus in 514BC. They did so out of sexual jealousy but in so doing unwittingly paved the way for Athens' democratic revolution soon after – hence their statues prominently placed on the Acropolis. The first statues, possibly made by Antenor who had worked at Delphi, were carried off by King Xerxes to Persepolis when he sacked Athens in 480BC. Their replacements, the bronze originals of these Roman marble copies, were made in 477BC by Critios and Nesiotes. (Alexander the Great later returned the originals when he in turn burnt Persepolis in 330BC, but they have since vanished.)

These figures may be only Roman copies, but their heroic, masculine figures incarnate determined political action. The onlooker is effectively in the position of their victim. Slightly larger than life at 1.93m (6ft 4in), they reveal for almost the first time the notable 'hardness' of the Early Classical style, with their side muscles above their thighs emphasized unrealistically to increase the impression of male strength.

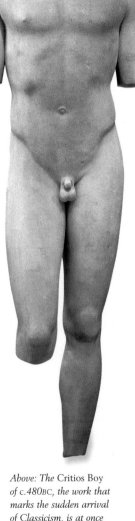

Above: The Critios Boy *of* c.480BC, *the work that marks the sudden arrival of Classicism, is at once naturalistic and idealized.*

IMAGES OF THE GODS

Above: Apollo, the archetypal Hellenic god of order, reason and light, carved on the western pediment of the Temple of Zeus at Olympia, 5th century BC. He is portrayed as a calm and pitiless deity, supremely confident in his inhuman beauty and power.

The portrayal of the gods as supremely perfect but utterly realistic human beings – the greatest achievement of Classicism – was perfected in the middle decades of the 5th century BC. From the sea off Artemisium on the island of Euboea comes one magnificent bronze. (Bronze does not rust in seawater, so shipwrecks have paradoxically proved excellent at preserving such works.) Once thought to be a statue of the sea-god Poseidon wielding a triton since lost, he is now considered to represent Zeus, king of the gods, hurtling his divine thunderbolt at an unseen adversary.

A NAMELESS MASTERPIECE

This Zeus is the work of an unknown master who clearly was a genius, not just a talented local carver. The figure probably originated in northern Greece and was being transported south, perhaps like many Greek artworks to a Roman customer,

when it was shipwrecked. (If it had been travelling north, it might have been the work of Onatas of Aegina.) While attempts to identify this masterpiece with a specific statue mentioned in literary sources have failed, it is securely dated on stylistic grounds to c.460BC, as Classicism was approaching its peak.

Certainly Zeus' features have the Homeric majesty expected of the king of Olympus and lord of thunder. Standing more than lifesize at 2.1m (6ft 10in), as befits a god, he is complete apart from his eyes, which were once inlaid with coloured stones. His hair is tied back by a braid, usual for the time, but otherwise he is shown sublimely naked, humanity raised to divine levels. His body is powerful but not absurdly muscular. His arms are unrealistically long, but presumably this was a deliberate styliza- tion. He is the noblest Classical bronze statue of a god to survive.

THE TEMPLE OF ZEUS AT OLYMPIA

But the chief centre of sculptural activity in Greece during the second quarter of the 5th century was at Olympia, site of the Olympic Games, a shrine second only to Delphi in Panhellenic importance. Here, in the sacred precinct around the great Temple to Zeus built in the 460s BC stood literally hundreds of statues of victors in the games. For competitors were taking part in a sacred rite, not just competing for a prize. Religion perme- ated athletics as it did almost every aspect of Greek life.

Unfortunately Christianity, a later religion, so detested such statues that only their bases remain. Some bronzes were

Left: One of the 12 metopes from the great Temple of Zeus at Olympia depicting the 11th labour of Hercules, carved by the anonymous 'Master of Olympia' in c.460BC.

destroyed on the orders of the emperor Theodosius I, a Christian zealot, when the Games were suppressed in *c*.AD393; others were looted or melted down for their valuable metal. The Temple to Zeus, only destroyed finally by an earthquake in the 6th century AD, was richly decorated with stone sculptures on its metopes. These have been pieced together to give a good idea of the work sometimes attributed to the 'Master of Olympia', an unknown sculptor (or sculptors) of undoubted genius, working in the severe style of early Classicism.

THE TWELVE LABOURS OF HERCULES

Hercules (Heracles) was the archetypal Greek mythical hero, semi-divine as a son of Zeus, and seen as the personification of physical strength and *areté* (excellence). Hercules was credited with founding the Olympic Games. To expiate the sin of killing his own family in a fit of madness, Hercules was ordered to carry out 12 almost impossible 'labours'. The 12 metopes of the Temple of Zeus at Olympia illustrate these in the 'severe' style, with figures about one and a half times life-size.

Among the best preserved is the 11th labour, Hercules' mission to fetch the golden apples of the Hesperides, the islands of the Blessed. Hercules passed on this particular labour to the giant Atlas, offering to carry the burden of the heavens on his own shoulders meanwhile. Atlas is shown returning with the apples in his hands to Hercules, who stands with every muscle in his body taut, upholding his titanic burden. Although the goddess

Right: The majestic face of Zeus, king of the gods, as portrayed by an unknown sculptor who was clearly a genius. Recovered from the sea off Artemisium, the Zeus is dated on stylistic grounds to c.460BC.

Athena, Hercules' helper in his trials, is putting a cushion on his shoulder to reduce the strain, the impression of tortured strength is overwhelming. Yet the hero's body is not that of some grotesquely over-muscled bodybuilder but harmoniously symmetrical.

APOLLONIAN SERENITY

One of the finest images of Apollo, the archetypal god of reason, comes from the west pediment of the Temple of Zeus. Apollo is shown, right arm raised in serene authority, quelling the bestial fury of the drunken centaurs. Calm, pitiless, supremely confident in his physical beauty, he is untroubled by any doubt or compassion.

Hercules' body is relatively flat and inexpressive compared to some contemporary works, but this only increases his divine yet dangerous power. Dating from *c*.450BC, this statue is the only original large-scale Apollo of the Early Classical Age that has survived intact.

Left: The Zeus of Sunium, c.460BC, fished from the sea, shown in awe-inspiring entirety. Originally the god is thought to have brandished a thunderbolt in his right hand.

PHEIDIAS, MAKER OF THE GODS ACTIVE C.460–430BC

Considered by many the greatest Classical sculptor, Pheidias (*c.490–c.428*BC) was an Athenian citizen and a close friend of Pericles, the supreme democratic states-man. Little is known of his life, although he reputedly studied under Hegias. By 447BC he had become effectively Athens' Minister for the Arts as he oversaw the building of the Parthenon, that pinnacle of Greek architecture and sculpture.

Pheidias created idealized forms so realistic yet sublime that he was called 'Maker of the gods'. Infuriatingly, not one freestanding work by him survives and Roman copies are even feebler than normal. However, we have many of the superb Parthenon carvings, including the Elgin Marbles now in the British Museum. This project, far too large for one man to execute, required scores of skilled sculp-tors, most working to Pheidias' designs and under his supervision. Carved in high relief, many figures are depicted almost in the round, leaping from their frames with remarkable vigour.

IMAGES OF ATHENA

Pheidias was most famous for his giant statues of gods. The first was *Athena Lemnia* (made for colonists of Lemnos) of 450BC, still partly in the 'severe' style. More typical was the huge statue *Athena Parthenos* (Virgin) that Pheidias made for the new Parthenon's interior, completed in 438BC. Standing *c.*12m (40ft) high, she was of chryselephantine: her skin was covered in ivory and her robes and armour in gold, fitted over a wooden core. She carried a winged Nike in her right hand. A shield rested on the ground

to her left, while a huge serpent coiled beside her. On her head was a triple-crested helmet. A pool of water in front reflected a dim sacred light on to this opulent cult image.

Outside on the Acropolis, Pheidias created another, more militant, image of the goddess *Athena Promachos* (Warrior) in bronze with shield, helmet and gilded spear, standing inside the Propylaea and immediately obvious to worshippers. The goddess was also visible far out to sea, proclaiming Athens' power and glory.

THE PARTHENON CARVINGS

The frieze running around the Parthenon, started in 447BC, is 60m (175 yards) long. More of it has survived in reasonable condition than any other sculpture of the age. However, it must have been hard to see many figures easily when *in situ*. Some may be by Pheidias himself: all reveal his spirit. The riders shown on the west frieze, young cavaliers naked apart from their cloaks, are taking part in the four-yearly Panathenaic Procession, the greatest event in Athens' civic and religious calendar. On the east frieze graceful, noble-looking gods and heroes process, also part of the festival. In thus worshipping its patron goddess, Athens also worshipped its idealized self.

Fine examples of *centauromachia* (centaur battles) from the temple's south side have been read as depicting Athenian civilization triumphing over savagery. But the centauromachia was always a popular theme, for it allowed sculptors to depict man and beast in combat. The west pediment showed Poseidon and Athena fighting for the city's loyalty – a contest Athena won by her gift of an olive tree. This central section has been lost but from the east pediment a masterly realistic study shows the wine-god Dionysus reclining wholly naked. Aphrodite,

Above: A model of the giant statue of Athena Parthenos, *made by Pheidias in* c.438BC *in chryselephantine for the interior of the new Parthenon.*

Left: The Apollo of the Tiber, *a Roman copy of a bronze original from Pheidias' workshop, perhaps by the master himself, suggests something of Pheidias' idealized but monumental style.*

goddess of love, is also reclining but with arched, quivering body. While she is fully clothed, her clinging dress reveals more than it conceals of her beauty.

WONDER OF THE WORLD

Pheidias, unjustly accused of embezzlement by Pericles' enemies, left Athens in 432BC for Olympia. Ancient writers considered the giant statue of Zeus he made there for the Temple of Zeus in *c.*430BC his masterpiece. It later ranked as one of the Seven Wonders of the World. Zeus was shown on a high throne, holding a Nike in his right hand and sceptre in his left. This was also a chryselephantine statue. Although portrayed seated, at seven times life size, 13m (42ft) high, Zeus almost touched the temple's ceiling. Only coins give us any idea of this work.

One statue survives to convey something of Pheidias' monumental style: the *Apollo of the Tiber*, a Roman copy of a bronze Apollo, perhaps by the master himself. The tall, graceful god looks down

with serene, dreamy detachment. This work and the Parthenon sculptures epitomize Pheidias' High Classicism. In it the human body, perfectly understood from within, is portrayed with an idealized yet wholly naturalistic harmony.

Above: A detail of the Elgin Marbles, from the west frieze of the Parthenon showing horsemen in the Panathenaic Procession, carved to Pheidias' designs in c.440BC.

Right: A Lapith and centaur fighting, from the Parthenon's south side, a contest at times read as depicting Athens' triumphing over barbarism, carved to Pheidias' designs.

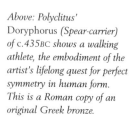

POLYCLITUS AND MYRON
ACTIVE 460–420BC

Polyclitus, a rival of Pheidias, pursued a very different approach to Classicism. Coming from Argos, he worked at times in Athens. One of the great intellectuals of Greek art, Polyclitus declared: "A well-made work results from numerous calculations, executed to within a hair's breadth." His statues did not aim to please but to incarnate the principles of mathematical beauty he had outlined in his book *The Canon*. This has not survived, nor have his original bronzes. He may have worked exclusively in bronze but we have only blockish marble copies that distort his genius. Only one marble copy, the *Theseus Diadoumenus*, is truly impressive.

SYMMETRICAL SOLIDITY
Polyclitus sought not to depict an idealized realism but to fulfil his quest for depicting symmetry in the human form. He succeeded triumphantly with the *Doryphorus* (Spear-carrier) of c.435BC. This shows a walking athlete/hero (he probably once held a spear). The weight of his body rests on one foot, his relaxed left leg bears no weight, his right hand hangs down freely. The sloping line of his hips resulting from his pose is carried through the torso into a correspondingly opposed shoulder line later called *con-trapposto*. All his body is drawn into this movement but his torso itself is stockily solid, with the typically heavily emphasized muscles.

Polyclitus' work was much admired and copied in antiquity. A true idea of his genius emerges in the *Torso of Doryphorus*, a copy in polished basalt that resembles bronze far more closely than marble. The *Prima Porta* statue of Augustus 400 years later repeated the *Doryphorus*'s stance, although the emperor is clothed. So did images of the body-builder Charles Atlas in the 20th century.

THESEUS DIADOUMENUS
This statue shows the legendary Athenian king as a victorious young athlete crowned with a diadem. The body is still solidly muscular but the youth's face reveals a softer side to Polyclitus' puritanical art, being delicately carved. Polyclitus also sculpted an Amazon, winning a competition at Ephesus with it. His wounded Amazon, shown bare-breasted, is leaning against a post, the first

Above: Polyclitus'
Doryphorus *(Spear-carrier) of c.435BC shows a walking athlete, the embodiment of the artist's lifelong quest for perfect symmetry in human form. This is a Roman copy of an original Greek bronze.*

Right: The symmetrical solidity typical of Polyclitus' work marks this statue, which once again is a Roman marble copy of an original Greek bronze.

AMAZONS: THE EXCEPTION

Amazons were, most exceptionally, portrayed half-naked even in the 5th century, when women were shown fully clothed from neck to ankle. There were good mythological reasons for this. Amazons were women-warriors who fought bare-breasted or, in some stories, after cutting off one breast to shoot better. Theseus carried off Antiope, an Amazon queen. Later the Amazons attacked Athens to revenge or regain their abducted queen but were repelled. This was often depicted as a triumph of civilization over barbarism and explains the prevalence of Amazons in Athenian art, even on the shield of Athena.

marble copies but not the bronze original. (Hitler so admired a copy of this work in Rome that he persuaded Mussolini to send it to Germany. It was returned to Italy after 1945.)

Myron was also famous for his bronze *Athena and Marsyas*. This does not survive as a group even in marble copies but has been reconstructed. According to Pausanias in the 2nd century AD, it showed "Athena striking Marsyas Silenus for taking up the flute that the goddess wished thrown away". Marsyas was a satyr, one of the licentious half-goats, over-proud of his flute-playing. Athena. who disdained such vulgar music-making because it distorted the face, clutches her spear, the model of Olympian calm, looking down at the satyr. Marsyas met a ghastly end: he competed on his pipe with Apollo, lost and was then flayed alive as a punishment.

Above: A Roman copy of a part of the bronze original of Athena and Marsyas by Myron.

time that a figure was shown supporting itself against another object. While still more athletic than feminine in form, she reveals the sculptor's versatility. Polyclitus is credited with making the great statue of the goddess Hera in Argos, which some writers preferred to Pheidias' statue of *Zeus* at Olympia.

MYRON ACTIVE 450–430BC

The third great sculptor of the 5th century, Myron, tended to an extreme realism. This was evident in his bronze cow on the Acropolis, said to be real enough to be mistaken for actual flesh and bones. (It was of course painted.) This statue has vanished, as has his renowned statue, the *Discobolus* (discus thrower). Lucian, a writer of the 2nd century AD, describes the original as "stooping in the pose of a man preparing to throw, turning towards the hand with the discus and gently bending the knee, as ready to rise and throw." Numerous marble copies of this work exist, showing the swing of the taut, muscular body. It looks so realistic some athletes have tried to emulate it – in vain, for this is no snapshot. The support behind the *Discobolus* was needed for

Left: The Discobolus *by Myron of c.440BC. Although a marble Roman copy, it still conveys the tension of the much-admired bronze original, which has not survived.*

Above: Paionius of Mende made this magnificent winged Nike (Victory), which was dedicated at Olympia by the Messenians in 421BC.

UNVEILING APHRODITE
C.420–390BC

While the male nude fascinated the greatest sculptors of the 5th century BC, the female nude was for long almost ignored. There was one exception: the *Esquiline Venus*, a marble copy of a bronze statue, showing a short but sensual figure, very realistic and completely naked, of c.450BC. But she was seemingly a one-off. This ignoring in part rose from the notoriously low status of women in Classical Athens. Their restricted appearance in art also reflected the tastes of a tough, heroic age, when sculptors found the muscular angularity of the male body, toned by constant exercise, more artistically challenging than the female body's curves.

By the last decades of the century, however, as the increasingly catastrophic Peloponnesian War ground on, tastes began to change. A less heroic, more sensually delighting art became appreciated

and the female form acquired – or regained – its fundamental appeal for sculptors, an appeal never since lost.

For a long time the female body was shown only under drapery. Increasingly, however, this consisted of thin clinging robes that gave almost a 'wet look'. This emphasized rather than concealed the body, until finally the female form emerged wholly naked.

THE WINGED GODDESS

The first half of the Peloponnesian War went relatively well for Athens and her allies, which included those Messenians not enslaved by Sparta. The Messenians, to commemorate their part in the victory over the Spartans at Sphacteria in 425BC, dedicated a statue of Nike at Olympia in c.421BC, with the inscription: "The Messenians and Naupactians dedicate her

Right: Nike Unlacing her Sandal, from the Temple of Athena Nike on the Acropolis of c.420BC.

GRAVE STONES

In sober contrast to such increasingly sensual statues are the tomb reliefs, particularly common in the later stages of the Peloponnesian War as Athenian casualties mounted. (Tombstones, while often found in the Archaic period, were for some reason rare in the early 5th century BC.) These usually took an architectural form with a pediment, as if the figures were outside the door of a home. Domesticity is the keynote, a reminder that even Athenians at their most public-spirited had their own families, which were the acknowledged foundation of society. The tomb of Hegeso and her servant commemorates the dead Hegeso, shown choosing a piece of jewellery from a box held by her maid. Even in this funereal carving of c.410BC, Hegeso's clothing reveals her body remarkably clearly.

restart in 415BC. Smallest and most exquisite of the temples overlooking the city was that of Athena Nike (Athena as Victory) built by Mnesicles about 428–423BC. Its frieze, which probably dates from after 420BC, shows a series of divine or mythical figures engaged in vigorous yet oddly elegant combat. One of them soon became justly famous and much copied in antiquity, that of *Nike Unlacing her Sandal*, which flanked a small staircase at the west of the temple.

For once we have the original, if without her head. Her clinging drapery, brilliantly carved, reveals a lithe but very feminine body as she bends in a marvellously fluid movement to lace up her sandal. With her breasts half-revealed, her thighs pushing against the soft fabric, this conveys as much sensuality as a nude.

APHRODITE IN THE AGORA

The true goddess of love, however, was Aphrodite (Venus), not chaste Athena or militant Nike. Aphrodite could more easily be found in the Agora, the buzzing commercial and social heart of Athens, than on the heights of the Acropolis.

One statue of Aphrodite – which suffered the indignity of being used as filling in a late Roman wall, erected in panic against renewed invasions in the 3rd century AD – reveals an almost baroque touch in her swirling robes that could slip off her at any moment. She could just be the work of Callimachus, who was one of the most famous sculptors of the late 5th century BC, although no works firmly attributed to him have survived. Callimachus was renowned for his free-flowing but fastidious grace, casting bronze 'like lace' – although some found his skills excessively ornate. He also reputedly pioneered the use of the drill in sculpture.

Above: The tomb of Hegeso and her servant, commemorating a citizen's dead wife. Even in this funereal carving of c.410BC, Hegeso's light clothing reveals her body clearly.

to the Olympian Zeus as a tithe of the enemy's booty. Paionius of Mende made her." Mende was in northern Greece but Paionius worked mostly in Olympia, where he made this statue, an original work in marble, one of the masterpieces of Greek art.

Nike, winged goddess of victory, is shown at the moment of alighting to crown success on the battlefield. The wind of her flight bares one breast and presses her clothing close against her wonderfully lithe body, some 2.2m (7ft) high. Paionius has managed to convey motion at the point of being arrested with brilliant vividness. There was originally an eagle, emblem of Zeus, at her feet, and she stood on a pillar about 10m (33ft) high. Unusually at the time, Paionius signed the work on the dedication block, a sign of his pride in his achievement.

NIKE UNLACING HER SANDAL
Work on the smaller temples of the Athenian Acropolis continued despite the wars that stopped in 421BC only to

Below: The Esquiline Venus, *a marble copy of a bronze of c.450BC by an unknown artist, may be the first female nude in Greek art. Although not typically idealized, she emanates a gentle sensuality.*

THE 4TH-CENTURY BC REVOLUTION

Above: A marble relief copy of Timotheus' lost bronze masterpiece, Leda and the Swan. *This illustrates the myth in which Zeus, assuming a swan's form, seduced Leda, depicted here with novel sympathy and tenderness.*

The Peloponnesian War ended in 404BC with Athens' total defeat. Sparta took over Athens' empire and proceeded to misgovern it, so causing resentment and further wars. These proved inconclusive, exhausting and disillusioning. Although Athenian democracy was restored after a short-lived fascist junta and democracy even spread to other cities such as Thebes later, the *polis* (the 'citizen-state') no longer commanded the same passionate undivided loyalty from its citizens that it had. Instead, private life – or life in the secluded grounds of an Academy like Plato's founded just outside the walls of Athens – proved increasingly attractive. This retreat from the public sphere, although by no means complete, gathered pace after Alexander the Great's conquests opened up a vast new world. They made life in the old polis seem less wholly satisfying to many people.

THE TOMBSTONE OF DEXILEUS

This mood was reflected in art, as the idealized, heroic but impersonal high Classicism of the previous century gave way to a new individualism. The new era's artists discovered people's real personalities, shown by their backgrounds and deeds. The art of truly individual portraiture emerged hesitantly.

An early example of this is the Tombstone of Dexileus of Thoricus, a young Athenian killed in the Battle of Corinth in 394BC. He is shown in the act of killing his crouching enemy. His pose on the rearing horse recalls the horsemen sculpted on the Parthenon 40 years before, but he seems oddly detached from the action, rather than heroically engaged. This is fitting for what was a private tombstone rather than a public monument.

Artists also began to discover women's personalities, just as they began to depict the female nude. Although in the male-dominated world of ancient Greece the female nude was never treated as frequently as the male (in contrast to the situation today), fully naked female statues now began to engage the greatest sculptors' attention. The finest sculptors were not concerned solely with depicting their bodies but developed new ways of portraying feminine emotions.

TIMOTHEUS AT EPIDAURUS

Timotheus (active 380–340BC) may have come from Epidaurus in north-eastern Peloponnese. He is recorded as being paid 500 drachmae for work on the sculptures of the pediment of its renowned Temple of Asclepius, the healer-god, in the early 4th century BC. However, he went on to work

Left: Timotheus made some of the carvings for the immense tomb of Mausolus, ruler of Halicarnassus, around 350BC – works of dynamic drama.

in several other cities, including Halicarnassus (now Bodrum in Turkey), where he made some of the dramatic carvings on the immense tomb for its dynast Mausolus.

From the acroteria of the Epidaurus temple a *Nike* by him survives. Although now only a battered fragment, it still reveals his remarkable talent in the way her right wing is raised to catch an invisible wind. Also from the temple is the almost intact figure of Hygeia, goddess of the hearth, another half-naked figure bending gracefully. (Other more complete figures such as Aura, a deity seemingly riding side-saddle, were probably executed by Theodotus, otherwise unknown, to Timotheus' designs.)

Timotheus was also responsible for the pediments of the temple. These have not survived but it is possible to reconstruct them. The west pediment depicted the Sack of Troy. This was hardly an original subject but one that Timotheus portrayed in a highly original manner by dwelling on the sufferings of the women in the captured city.

On the right side of the pediment a female figure, possibly Hecabe, King Priam's wife, turns to help her fatally wounded son, holding him in her arms as he collapses. The sorrows of other Trojan women such as Cassandra, about to be abducted, raped or killed by the victorious Achaeans, are also movingly depicted for almost the first time in Greek art.

LEDA AND THE SWAN

The masterpiece of Timotheus' maturity is his *Leda and the Swan*, a bronze that has since been lost. However, numerous marble copies survive, most of which are approximately life-size and give a good impression of the famous original. The work illustrates the myth in which Zeus, king of the gods, assumed a swan's shape to seduce Leda. She later gave birth to the divine twins Castor and Pollux. In the myth, Zeus also sent an eagle – not sculpted – which appeared to threaten the swan, a wily tactic that persuaded the

reluctant Leda to shelter the swan. Leda is shown holding her cloak up to hide the swan nestling against her, as she cranes her head anxiously upward. Her expression conveys mingled anxiety and innocence. No earlier Greek artist had ever managed to capture female emotions so convincingly.

In an *Athena* (another bronze, which is only known in marble copies), the imposing grandeur of the goddess as depicted by Pheidias has given way to a more girlish figure, which is far less exalted and godlike.

Above: The Tombstone of Dexileus, a young Athenian who died at the Battle of Corinth in 394 BC. Shown killing his cowering enemy, he lacks the aloof heroism of 5th-century horsemen, partly because this is a private memorial, partly because the exhausted post-war age felt differently about war.

PRAXITELES
ARTIST OF THE CENTURY

Praxiteles was ranked alongside Polyclitus, Pheidias and Lysippus by ancient writers as one of the supreme master sculptors. Working throughout the middle of the 4th century BC, he was renowned for the sensuous charm and grace of his art. This marked a further stage in the move away from the lofty idealism of high Classicism. Praxiteles was more concerned with portraying human emotions and creating gently beautiful objects, most famously his *Aphrodite of Cnidus*.

The master of sensual sweetness came from a family of sculptors. His father was the successful Athenian sculptor Cephisodotus, whose *Eirene* (peace) *Holding the Infant Ploutos* (wealth) was placed in the Athenian Agora in *c.*380BC. Such a prominent place for such a subject – inconceivable in earlier centuries – was a sign of the increasingly war-weary times. Praxiteles himself responded to the new mood by creating works of deliberate beauty, which may strike modern eyes as too smooth, bland and sugary. But if they fail to stir our emotions, they proved hugely influential then and long after. His son continued the family tradition after him in the same style.

Above: Praxiteles' Aphrodite of Cnidus *of c.350BC, "the finest statue in the world" according to Pliny.*

APOLLO AND THE LIZARD

One of Praxiteles' earliest works to show his distinctive genius is his *Satyr Pouring Wine* of *c.*375BC. Although we have only marble copies of this bronze, they show already the artist's hallmark of charm and beauty in this graceful youth – no trace of the bestial satyr here. (The jug and his left forearm have not survived.) Even more graceful is the later *Apollo Sauroctamus* (*Apollo Playing with a Lizard*). This shows the god as a

Left: A satyr, leaning against a tree trunk, displays to the full Praxiteles' typically languid sensuality.

Above: Despite the ravages of time that have broken her nose, this Aphrodite, carved in Praxiteles' workshop in c.325BC, has the soft beauty found in all his female figures.

smooth-limbed, beardless boy teasing a lizard crawling up a tree trunk. Instead of the sublime grandeur of earlier statues of the god, here we see the deity enjoying a languid, blissful sensuality – another key aspect of the divine from now on, but one seldom recognized earlier.

A SURVIVING MASTERPIECE

In 1877 archaeologists at Olympia discovered a marble statue of *Hermes and the Infant Dionysus* in the exact location noted by Pausanias 1,700 years earlier. This is almost certainly the famed original by Praxiteles, who often worked in marble. (His preference for doing so helped make the material fashionable again after long neglect.)

Despite being savagely over-cleaned by enthusiastic restorers, the statue still conveys an immediate sense of the splendour and glory Praxiteles could create in marble. Hermes, the messenger-god, props the tiny Dionysus, the wine god and his half-brother, on a tree-trunk to play with the child and offer him a bunch of grapes (missing from the original). Hermes was escorting the orphaned baby to Mt Nysa to be looked after by nymphs. The group shows a novel tenderness among the gods. They are still perfectly formed beings but they now exhibit less crushingly Olympian emotions.

The work was probably made around 330BC. At 2.15m (7ft 2in), it is rather larger than lifesize.

"THE FINEST STATUE IN THE WHOLE WORLD"

Praxiteles' most original and acclaimed statue was his *Aphrodite*, again made in marble. This, the first full-scale totally naked female nude of the goddess of love, was ordered in *c*.350BC by the island of Cos. The islanders were so shocked by the goddess's unprecedented nudity that they refused it. The people of nearby Cnidus happily took it instead and it became one of the most admired artworks in the ancient world. People made long journeys just to see her. One man reputedly fell in love with her. He embraced her so passionately that he could only be prised off with difficulty and left an indelible mark on her surface. Later, Pliny the Elder, the Roman writer of the 1st century AD, called her "the finest statue not just by Praxiteles but in the whole world".

Again, we have only semi-competent later copies, but they still reveal Praxiteles' great originality. *Aphrodite*, at 2m (6ft 7in) more than life-size, is depicted as a mature, shapely woman who has probably just emerged from her bath. A towel or robe is draped over a nearby vase. Her right hand covers her private parts but the rest of her body is fully exposed to the view for the first time in Greek art. She is realistically proportioned, with her hips larger than her breasts. (Ancient Greek artists were never fixated on outsized breasts.)

The copies we have, though imperfect, are often complete. They have helped create an archetype of female beauty that would later inspire Renaissance artists such as Botticelli, Raphael, Titian and Veronese, and so much of subsequent Western art. Such accepted ideals of female beauty are still apparent in almost every magazine, advertisement and film that we see today.

Above: Apollo Sauroctamus, one of Praxiteles' masterpieces, shows the god as a smooth-limbed, beardless adolescent teasing a lizard on a tree trunk. Instead of the divine sublimity conveyed by earlier statues, Apollo is shown as sensually relaxed.

Left: Discovered at Olympia in 1877, this original marble shows Praxiteles' genius at its height. Hermes, the messenger god, props the tiny Dionysus, the wine-god, and also his half-brother, on a tree-trunk to play with the child, offering him a bunch of grapes.

SCOPAS
SCULPTOR OF ECSTASY

Above: The head of a warrior, attributed to Scopas or his school, with all the master's characteristic passion still evident despite its much-battered state.

Not all art in the 4th century BC depicted the idyllic joys of gods or nymphs in Arcadia. Scopas, who worked in the middle of the century, specialized in depicting human or divine passions at their most intense. Born on the island of Paros, noted for its marble quarries, he had a famously fiery temperament. This comes through in his art, which differs radically from that of his contemporary Praxiteles, although both men preferred marble to bronze.

Scopas is recorded as working on the Mausoleum of Halicarnassus, the biggest project of the time; the great Temple of Artemis at Ephesus (then being again rebuilt); and at the Temple of Athena at Tegea in the Peloponnese. According to Pausanias, he designed this last temple.

FRENZIED BACCHANTES

The sculptures decorating the Mausoleum at Halicarnassus, later declared one of the Seven Wonders of the World, took many years of effort by some of Greece's greatest living sculptors, including Timotheus, Leochares and Scopas. Scopas, according to Pliny the Elder, the encyclopaedic Roman commentator writing 400 years later, carved the reliefs on the huge pyramidical structure's east face. Most notable were his depictions of ecstatic women, especially

Maenads or Bacchantes. (These were the female followers of the wine-god Dionysus, liberated from the normal constraints on Greek women by the ambiguously beautiful god.)

Although no originals survive of Scopas' *Maenads*, an unusually fine Roman copy in Parian marble powerfully conveys the divine madness and unleashed energy of Scopas' work. The orgiastic Maenad, with her long flowing hair and shapely body, is simultaneously a beautiful young woman and the terrifying embodiment of daemonic ecstasy. "Who carved this Bacchante?" asked an epigram of the time. "Scopas." "Who filled her with wild delirium – Dionysus or Scopas?" "Scopas." Almost naked – her short robe accentuates rather than hides her thrusting, twisting body – she is caught up in the drama of the god of wine and ecstasy.

Another less violent but equally ecstatic figure, this time totally naked, is Scopas' *Tritoness* (*Sea Goddess*), known in a copy found at Ostia. Her head is thrown back in ecstasy, her long thick hair cascades over her shoulders and toward her breasts, her flesh is modelled with remarkable vividness. Such art – "that has brought to its aid the impulse of growing life itself, so unbelievable is what you see, so invisible is what you believe", in the words of Callistratus, a near-contemporary writer – was unprecedented in Greece, probably the whole world.

AMAZONS AND HEROES
Scopas' talent for depicting emotional extremes was not restricted to Bacchantes, however. The *Amazonomachia* (*Amazon Battle*), a fragment from some part of the

Left: The Amazonomachia *(Amazon Battle), a fragment from the Mausoleum at Halicarnassus attributed to Scopas. Unarmoured in their short tunics, the Amazons show themselves equal adversaries of the male warriors. Here, Scopas ignores all Classical restraint while still working fluently in the Classical idiom.*

Mausoleum at Halicarnassus that is attributed to Scopas, shows his skills in a more military field. The fighting swirls between the helmeted warriors with their shields and helmets and the acrobatic, almost airborne Amazons. Although defenceless in their short tunics, the Amazons demonstrate that they are very much the warriors' equals. Their portrayer, Scopas, shows himself untrammelled by earlier Classical restraint but working wholly in the Classical mould.

From the middle group of figures on the west pediment of the Tegean Temple of Athena that Scopas carved, there survives a stupendous head of Achilles. Achilles was the archetypal warrior-hero of *The Iliad*, the prince with whose rising wrath the great epic poem opens and with whose sated wrath it ends. Although much battered, this surviving original stone head, with a lionskin helmet, still transmits Achilles' grimly murderous anger with chilling force. He is part of a group of warrior-heroes that originally included Hercules immediately to his left.

THE GOD OF LONGING
Less well known than his brother Eros, god of desire, Pothos was the god or personification of *pothos* (longing or yearning). Scopas made at least two statues of Pothos, one for Samothrace, mentioned by Pliny, and another for Megara. In depicting Pothos, Scopas adopted a gentler approach, suitable for an emotion less ravenous if perhaps less easily satisfied than Eros. This languid youth leans on one draped arm, with plump legs crossed and soulful eyes set in soft, effeminate features, all suggesting vague longing. In a broadly similar work, *Hypnos,* Scopas portrayed the god of sleep.

Above: Scopas did not solely depict women caught up in frenzy, as this beautifully calm, reflective head of Hygeia, attributed to him, shows. Hygeia was the goddess of health, daughter of the divine healer Asclepius.

Below: Hypnos, a bronze sculpted by Fernand Khnopff in the 1890s, was based on an original head of the god of sleep by Scopas.

LYSIPPUS
ALEXANDER'S COURT SCULPTOR

Above: Lysippus sculpted many bronze busts of Alexander, all since lost. This marble copy, made for the Roman Emperor Hadrian's collection at Tivoli outside Rome, captures the conqueror's ruthless determination and will mixed with his spark of romantic pothos (longing). Like most such portraits, it is probably very flattering.

Lysippus was the most prominent, prolific and longest-lived of the great 4th-century sculptors. He was active *c.*360–*c.*305BC, reputedly making 1,500 works, all of them in bronze. Considered the most accomplished artist of his age, Lysippus suitably became Alexander the Great's favourite – in fact, court – sculptor. The world-conqueror allowed almost no one else to sculpt him. Lysippus went on to make portrait busts of many of Alexander's warring Successors, such as Cassander and Seleucus I, who founded the Seleucid Empire in 312BC. A native of Sicyon in the Peloponnese,

Right: An ephebe (young man) from the sea off Marathon, of c.340BC. It is attributed to Lysippus or his school on stylistic grounds and dated to c.330BC. A rare bronze original, it has a graceful sweetness very different from the severity of 5th-century art.

THE *GETTY VICTOR*

An almost life-size bronze statue of a victorious young athlete, found in the Adriatic in 1964, has been associated with Lysippus or his workshop on stylistic grounds. It is very similar to the *Marathon Boy* also found in the sea off Marathon, another bronze original of *c.*330BC and now in Athens' National Museum. When sold to the Getty Museum in Malibu in 1977, the Adriatic bronze fetched $3,900,000, then a record sum for any sculpture. It has since become known as the *Getty Victor*. With their supple, relaxed, still half-boyish bodies and delicate features, both differ greatly from earlier tough super-masculine heroes.

Lysippus ran a workshop of almost industrial size that was continued after his death by his sons.

Ancient writers such as Pliny relate that Lysippus invented an entirely new canon, or mathematically calculated ideal of beauty, almost displacing that of Polyclitus. Lysippus' *Canon* postulated a smaller head, longer legs and a slender body, producing a generally more graceful, aristocratic air – exactly what his mostly royal or noble clients wanted.

Such new proportions also allowed Lysippus' statues to be viewed equally well from any angle, whereas Polyclitus' *Canon* only permitted a narrowly frontal approach. In this, as with his increasingly monarchical customers, Lysippus stands on the dividing line of the Classical and Hellenistic Ages.

THE *APOXYMENOS*

One of Lysippus' most famous and characteristic statues is the *Apoxymenos*, a young athlete scraping himself with a strigil after exercising, in the usual Greek manner. A surviving Roman copy in marble gives a good impression of this smooth-cheeked, long-limbed, young man. He is shown shifting his weight from one foot to another and stretching his right arm out, while his left hand holds the strigil. His slender body is supported by long, tensed thighs, his right leg set back with only his toes touching the ground; he hardly seems to have exerted himself at all. Such effortless elegance was novel when depicting an athlete. It was made *c.*340BC.

The statue was brought to Rome by Marcus Agrippa (63–12BC), the emperor Augustus' first minister, and set up outside the public baths he built. Later, when the emperor Tiberius removed it to his own palace, there was such an outcry from the Roman public suddenly robbed of one of its favourite artworks that even that most parsimonious of emperors had to return it.

THE *FARNESE HERCULES*
Very different but equally illustrative of Lysippus' versatile genius is the *Farnese Hercules*, which once belonged to the Farnese family in Rome. Again this is a marble copy of a bronze. It shows the semi-divine hero, a son of Zeus, wearily leaning on a tree trunk after his labours. Hercules became increasingly seen as a human role model, for he relied almost wholly on his own strength – admittedly huge – to achieve his ends, rather than divine assistance. Alexander regarded Hercules as one of his special heroes.

If weary, the hero is massively muscled, in a way inconceivable in earlier statues, the result of obsessive body-building in the gymnasium, and far from the ideal balance of earlier Classical art. In a few years his heroic muscles could easily turn to flab. Within decades such hulks would become common in Hellenistic art.

By contrast, Lysippus' *Hermes* of *c.*320BC shows the messenger god – adjusting his winged sandal on a support – as a model of easy relaxation, his stance free and elegant.

Left: The Farnese Hercules, *a marble copy of an original bronze, reveals another side of Lysippus' genius. Hercules is shown massively muscled, the result of manic body-building in the gymnasium. This is very different from the balance of earlier Classical art.*

Below: The Apoxymenos, *a young athlete scraping himself after exercise, a Roman marble copy of a bronze original. This elegant, long-limbed young man hardly seems to have exerted himself at all. It was made* C.340BC.

THE FACE OF ALEXANDER
Alexander was keenly aware of the value of his royal image, as the young, handsome and unconquered hero, divinely favoured and inspired – even possibly divinely fathered, a belief that Alexander himself may have held after his pilgrimage to the shrine of Amon-Zeus at Siwah in the Libyan desert.

Alexander commissioned many portrait busts by Lysippus. All were bronzes that have since been lost, but marble copies of several survive. Among the finest are the copy made for Hadrian's collection at his Villa at Tivoli outside Rome and one that is now in Istanbul. The former especially captures the mixture of the conqueror's ruthless determination and will with the spark of romantic *pothos* that was characteristic of Alexander. Such portraits almost certainly flattered the Macedonian king, giving him uplifted eyes, sweeping hair and a heroic air. They were widely copied after Alexander's death in 323BC.

THE HELLENISTIC GOLDEN AGE 320–200 BC

Right: The Winged Victory of Samothrace, *an original masterpiece in marble from the 3rd century* BC.

Below: The Apollo Belvedere, *a Roman copy of an original marble work of* c.320BC *attributed to Leochares. Its smooth beauty was once widely admired.*

The death of Alexander (323BC) conventionally marks the end of the Classical and the beginning of the Hellenistic ages, but there was no abrupt change in style. As the new Hellenistic kingdoms, often now of unprecedented size and wealth, established themselves as grand patrons, art began to explore new extremes, becoming more refined, more violent or more ecstatic.

THE *APOLLO BELVEDERE*

Typical of the new refinement was the *Apollo Belvedere*, carved *c.*320BC by Leochares. Leochares worked for Philip II of Macedonia and then Alexander and his Successors. He made gold and ivory statues of the older Macedonian monarch for a round temple, the Philippeion, in Olympia in a newly dramatic manner. But he was most noted for his representations of the gods, especially this *Apollo* (named after its present location). For centuries after its rediscovery in the Renaissance this marble was regarded as one of the supreme masterpieces of world art and the absolute summit of male beauty. It deeply impressed the German art critic Johann Winckelmann and the poet Goethe in the 18th century.

Tastes change. When the Elgin Marbles from the Parthenon revealed a new, less epicene and more dynamic canon of male beauty in the early 19th century, the *Apollo Belvedere* fell terminally out of fashion. But it remains, in its smooth, almost weightless way, a fine example of Hellenistic art at

its most exquisite. (It was, of course, originally painted.) Leochares also worked with Scopas, a very different artist, on the Mausoleum of Halicarnassus.

THE *WINGED VICTORY OF SAMOTHRACE*

The goddess Nike lands as if on the bow of a galley, her windswept drapery flying in the wind, her massive wings outstretched. An original marble work, she once stood on a marble carving of ship's prow in a sanctuary on the north Aegean island of Samothrace, where many Hellenistic kings commemorated successes. Probably she was set up to celebrate a great naval victory by one of Macedonia's kings, perhaps Antigonus II in the 250s BC. However, she could equally well date to about 50 years later and commemorate a Rhodian victory.

The sculptor's name remains unknown, but he was obviously inspired by Paionius' great *Nike* at Olympia of 200 years earlier.

THE *ALEXANDER SARCOPHAGUS*

The so-called *Alexander Sarcophagus* is the finest and most elaborate funerary monument to survive from the Hellenistic age. It has never, however, contained the body of Alexander the Great. This was interred in splendour in Alexandria by Ptolemy I but has long since vanished. This tomb was probably a commission made *c.*310BC for King Abdalonymus, a ruler whom Alexander had placed on the throne of Sidon in Phoenicia (Lebanon) in 333BC. The Phoenicians, although they rapidly became Hellenized, always preferred burial to cremation, then more common among the Greeks.

However, the Phoenicians employed sculptors from Greece to carve the friezes on the long sides. One shows Alexander fighting the Persians at the Battle of Issus in 333BC; the other depicts a hunt with both Macedonians and Sidonians together, so linking Abdalonymus' new regime firmly to Alexander. (Abdalonymus had been only the palace gardener originally. He ended up one of Alexander's Companions.) The reliefs have kept much of their colour, while the lid and chest are so richly adorned with finely carved metal mouldings that the sarcophagus resembles a giant jewel box.

He was also a genius, for this massive figure brims with tension and vigour. Originally 3m (9ft 9in) tall with her head, the *Nike*'s twisting axes and the contours of her wings and clothing are best viewed from below, as she was originally and now is once more in the Louvre. The statue shows Hellenistic art at its dynamic best.

THE *PHILOSOPHER'S HEAD*
Most statues were still made in bronze, however, and so have perished. One striking exception is the portrait bust found in the sea off Anticythera and probably dating from *c.*250BC. It has been called the *Philosopher's Head* because the face expresses such powerful intellectual energy and moral strength through the finely engraved beard, tousled locks and piercing gaze. Such qualities could only be fully conveyed in bronze, again emphasizing how much has been lost. The head was probably part of a group of

Right: The Alexander Sarcophagus *is the finest funerary monument of the Hellenistic age, packed with vigorous battle scenes, although it never contained the actual body of Alexander. It was probably a commission made* c.310BC *for King Abdalonymus, a ruler whom Alexander had placed on the throne of Sidon in Phoenicia.*

philosophers, for other fragments have been found nearby, mostly legs and feet that seem to have been torn off a plinth. They were probably *en route* to Rome, part of some victorious general's booty.

Above: A bust found in the sea from c.250BC. It is called the Philosopher's Head *because the face expresses such intellectual and moral energy.*

LATER HELLENISTIC ART
200–30BC

Right: Spinario, *or* Boy Pulling a Thorn from His Foot *may date from c.200BC, or may be a later Roman copy. It reveals the age's growing taste for sentimental genre subjects. This is a composite work, for the head and the body come from different statues.*

Below: A Crouching Aphrodite *of the later Hellenistic Age, c.150BC. This is typical of the works whose smooth bodies were for a long time much admired.*

After 200BC, the growing power of Rome began to affect the Greek art market. The Romans proved enthusiasts for the Baroque styles of later Hellenistic art, shipping off many artworks, frequently without paying. The influence of Greek art on Rome, for a time overwhelming, was all one way, however, for Roman art did not at this stage affect Greek artistic development. Greece's new masters simply wanted ever more copies of existing masterworks of the most blatantly dramatic or sentimental sort.

VENUS DE MILO

Typical of the age's more serene art, which today can seem bland, is the *Venus de Milo*, an original marble. The now armless statue of the goddess Aphrodite was found on the island of Melos in 1819 and taken to France, becoming world famous in the 19th century. Carved around 100BC, she has broad hips, a small head and primly arranged hair. The statue is signed by Hagesandros of Antioch, an otherwise unknown artist obviously influenced by the canonical beauty of his great predecessors Praxiteles and Lysippus. The statue was made in two parts, joined at the hips, with naturalistic drapery slipping off her finely carved naked upper body. Her missing arms may have held an Eros, often Aphrodite's companion.

A far more interesting earlier example of female beauty is *Crouching Aphrodite*, a copy of an original by Doidalsas of Bithynia. Although the goddess has lost both her

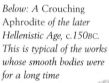

arms and the back of her head, the lovely sweep of her body as she bends, perhaps preparing to bathe, has all the naturalness of a nymph. Doidalsas' statue proved very popular and was much copied.

Among popular sculptures catering to the age's more sentimental side were small statues such as *Baby Playing with a Goose* or *Boy Pulling a Thorn from His Foot*, both of which date from *c.*200BC. Both these naked children, with their carefully brushed hair and almost Dickensian sweetness of manner, seem to be the offspring of good homes.

THE PERGAMUM ALTAR

But the age's real taste was for the melodramatic and exhibitionist. Nowhere was this better appreciated than in the newly rich kingdom of Pergamum in north-western Asia Minor. To commemorate his defeat of the invading Gauls in *c.*230BC, King Attalus I (241–197BC) erected a tremendous series of statues on

THE *LAOCOÖN'S* REDISCOVERY

In January 1506 Pope Julius I heard that some fine statues had been dug up in a vineyard near the ruins of Nero's palace in Rome. He ordered Sangallo, one of his architects, to inspect the statue. Sangallo invited Michelangelo, recently returned to Rome, along. Before they had even got off their horses, they agreed that the group must be the *Laocoön* praised by Pliny the Elder. Michelangelo later said that the discovery inspired him to portray spiritual anguish and physical torment through violent muscular movement. Many later artists, including El Greco, were influenced by the *Laocoön*. The statue is a copy of an original of *c.*180BC made probably in *c.*50BC by three sculptors: Agesander, Polydorus and Athenodorus of Rhodes, who created sensational works for the Roman market. The myth illustrated was retold in *The Aeneid* by Virgil. The priest Laocoön had warned the Trojans about the Greeks' wooden horse. His attempt to deflect the fated course of events angered the gods, who sent sea serpents to destroy him and his sons. The carving's amazing naturalism is typically late Hellenistic. (A recent theory that this is a fake made by Michelangelo himself has been generally discounted.)

Below: This Laocoön *group is a copy of an original of c.180BC made c.50BC by three sculptors of Rhodes, who created sensational works for the Roman market. The myth illustrated was later retold in* The Aeneid *by Virgil.*

Pergamum's citadel. Epigonus created the bronze *Dying Gaul*, a Gallic man propping himself up on his right arm to look at his fatal wound. Although we again have only a marble copy, it remains a brilliant study in anatomy and psychology, the wound most realistically sculpted. Epigonus also made the *Chieftain Killing Himself and His Wife*, an even more dramatic double piece showing a Gallic noble committing suicide rather than surrender.

The crowning achievement of the Attalid dynasty, and of Hellenistic baroque, was the vast Altar of Zeus, erected between 180 and 160BC, now in Berlin. Menecrates was among the named artists but many more were probably involved. The huge frieze, 121m (400ft) long, that encircles the base of the altar depicts a *gigantomachia*, a battle of the giants and gods. By casting this as the victory of Hellenism over barbarous Gauls, the Pergamene kings could justify their unpopular rule over the cities of Ionia.

The place of honour in the centre of the east frieze shows Zeus hurling a thunderbolt at Porphyrion, a serpent-footed giant. Elsewhere, Athena seizes a young winged giant by the hair, while below, sunk in the ground, Ge, mother of the giants, begs for mercy. The whole frieze surges with dynamic energy.

Below: The Altar of Zeus at Pergamum was the most spectacular work of the Hellenistic baroque, built between 180 and 160BC.

CHAPTER XVII

VASE PAINTING

While Greek pottery ranks among the finest in the world, vase painting was for the Greeks themselves a secondary form of art compared to painted panels and murals. These depicted events of grand historical or mythical importance. However, almost no Greek paintings before the 4th century BC have survived. By contrast, numerous vases survive from the Bronze Age on, giving fresh perspectives on the daily lives and beliefs of the Greeks.

Pottery has survived so well partly because its shards are nearly indestructible. Vases have been found in quantity over a wide area, for the Greeks seldom used glassware or other types of containers. Instead, they stored their wine, olive oil and water in vases and pots, and also exported their products, principally olive oil, around the Mediterranean in pottery of increasing splendour and magnificence. Often the container must have been more valuable than its contents, although Greek olive oil and wines were appreciated by the Etruscans, Gauls (in both France and northern Italy) and by the Romans.

At first, Corinth was the greatest exporter of vases, but during the mid-6th century BC, Athens replaced it as the chief producer of the best pottery. Athens continued to dominate the market for high-quality painted vases until the mid-4th century BC. By then, the golden age of vase-making was coming to an end, although opulent ware continued to be produced for long after.

Left: An Athenian red figure vase (on a black base) by the 'Niobid Painter' c.460BC, showing battling giants and gods.

BRONZE AGE VASES
1800–1100BC

Above: A Kamares-style cup. Pottery of almost china-like delicacy was produced in Crete at the time of the early palaces c.2000–1700BC.

The lively civilization of Minoan Crete produced colourful and vivid pottery throughout the 2nd millennium BC, the period of its great palaces. Minoan pottery styles – meticulously ranked by Arthur Evans (the archaeologist who rediscovered Cnossus Palace in 1900) into categories that not everyone, however, now accepts – show a culture reaching its peak around 1500BC. Soon after, Mycenaean Greeks from the mainland became dominant in Crete and across the whole Aegean. In their pottery, as in their other arts, the Mycenaeans essentially continued Minoan styles but in stiffer, more stylized and anthropocentric ways. But it can be hard to distinguish between the two civilizations' artefacts.

Left: An octopus design on the Dendra Vase, produced c.1500BC at the apex of Minoan civilization. It reflects both the Cretans' love of the sea and their brilliantly fluid art.

THE FIRST MINOAN STYLES
Pottery was the first art form in which the Minoan genius revealed its tremendous imaginative powers. The early style, called Kamares, probably originated in Phaestus, the main palace in southern Crete, but was discovered by archaeologists in the Kamares Cave, a burial site.

Kamares-style pottery is characterized by varied abstract spiral and curvilinear designs and dark mottled colours, combining drawings on the surface of the vase with varied relief patterns. These are mostly floral or zoomorphic (depicting animals). The human form is notably absent from this early art.

This style flourished at the time of the early palaces c.2000–1700BC, producing at its finest the so-called 'eggshell' ware. Thrown on the potter's wheel, such cups were designed to imitate the fine metal ware that has not generally survived. But they achieve a delicacy almost anticipating that of genuine china, which to many suggests a feminine influence typical of Minoan culture in general. What much Minoan art apparently lacks is the insistence on symmetry that would characterize later Greek art. Some time around 1700BC a major cataclysm, probably an earthquake, totally destroyed all the Cretan palaces. They were soon rebuilt on a grander, more systematic scale, and at the same time Cretan pottery entered its finest stage.

THE MINOAN ZENITH
Typical of Minoan vase painting at its liveliest and most naturalistic is the *Dendra Vase*, across whose curves an alarmingly lifelike octopus spreads

its tentacles. Similar vases are decorated with plants. They reflect both Cretan fascination with sea life – the Minoans were great sailors and fishermen – and their love of free-flowing forms. But the human image now figured also.

Three famous low reliefs, all of which would probably have been painted originally, come from Aghia Triada, a royal villa near Phaestus. They are the *Chieftain Cup*, the *Boxer Vase* and the *Harvester Vase*. All are decorated with typical serpentine patterns, giving vivid glimpses into life in Bronze Age Crete. The *Harvester Vase* in particular portrays cheerful peasants without the condescension that might be expected in an art normally geared to courtiers' tastes. A common decorative motif from Cnossus of this period is the lily, found on many vases, but the most frequent motifs feature spirals, animals, birds and fishes, depicted almost impressionistically.

All these are dated to the 'Late Minoan I' period of *c*.1550–1450BC, the seeming zenith of Minoan culture. It seems probable – although no consensus has been established – that the volcanic eruption of Thira cut short Minoan culture just as it was flowering.

THE ART OF THE MYCENAEANS

Despite their cultural debts to the Minoans, the Greek Mycenaeans favoured a markedly more militaristic art than the Cretans. This is immediately obvious in the *Chariot Krater* (mixing bowl) from Cnossus of *c*.1400BC. In the chariot, the 'tank of the Bronze Age', two tall, long-robed figures stand behind the pair of horses. The portrayal of the two horses follows Mycenaean customs in vase painting: the artist, trying to show the chariot seen head on in perspective, has painted only one horse's body, but this has two tails, two pairs of hind legs and forelegs and two heads. The whole scene has a stiffness about it

quite distinct from Minoan naturalness. So do the grandiose 'Palace-style' vases of the Mycenaean period at Cnossus.

From Mycenae itself in the 13th century BC comes the *Vase with Warriors*. This shows six helmeted soldiers with shields and helmets marching off, a woman in the background seeming to lament their parting. However, any intended pathos is undermined by the almost comically inept art.

Dating from *c*.1200BC, a terracotta vase shows an octopus, a creature loved by Minoan artists but that has here become heavily stylized. Similarly, a charging bull on a terracotta krater from Enkomi in Cyprus of *c*.1180BC retains nothing of the magnificent vitality of earlier bulls but is simply a schematic, nearly monochrome reminder of flesh-and-blood bulls. Some archaeologists think that only when Mycenaean vase painting is almost identical to Minoan does it really succeed as an art form. Others see in such simplified works the precursors of Geometric art.

Above: A Palace-style vase, made c.1400BC when Crete was under Mycenaean rule, is altogether stiffer in approach.

Below: This terracotta krater, showing a bull charging a bird, comes from Enkomi in Cyprus. It dates to the Late Mycenaean period c.1180BC.

PROTOGEOMETRIC AND GEOMETRIC ART c.1050–700 BC

After 1200 BC the elaborate palace-centred culture of Mycenae, with its bureaucracies, elegantly dressed courtiers, extensive trade routes and trading contacts with Egypt and the Levant, began to collapse. Traditionally this was due to Dorian invasions from the north, but other reasons, including civil wars and even climate change, have been suggested. By 1100 BC Mycenaean civilization had vanished almost completely. In its place came a simpler, more parochial way of life. Art soon reflected this change, abandoning the increasingly feeble Mycenaean attempts at realism in favour of an austere style that at times approached abstraction.

Most pottery in the early centuries after 1100 BC comes from Athens, the one major Mycenaean city that, according to legend, escaped total destruction. Within the shelter afforded by the walls of the Acropolis, Geometric art seems to have been born. The Diplyon Cemetery (named after the gate in the walls of classical Athens) has revealed many artefacts from this era.

PROTOGEOMETRIC: THE ART OF SURVIVORS

The first new style to emerge is called Protogeometric. Artists continued to use Mycenaean shapes, but with decorations restricted to circles, semicircles, rhombuses, crosses and hooks, arranged in bands. These designs were drawn using brushes fixed to compasses, marking a completely fresh approach to art. The ground (base colour) of the vases was generally light-coloured with decorations added in black gloss or glaze. Some Protogeometric vases may come from Cyprus, to which many Mycenaeans had fled. Such a limited range of decoration, devoid of human or animal figures, suited an age struggling for survival.

EARLY GEOMETRIC: THE FIRST AWAKENING

As Greek economic and cultural life began very tentatively to revive after 900BC, potters took to experimenting again. While they abandoned compass-controlled arcs in favour of grouped zigzags and obliques, they initially kept the mainly black base of the Protogeometric period. Decoration was increasingly organized into metopes (or panels), within which geometric patterns, especially the typically Greek shape of the *meander* (or Greek key design), were painted. Finally, artists began creating simple, silhouetted figures of animals.

An early example comes from a Cretan burial urn, which depicts some alarmingly feral creatures – possibly wild cats, but more probably creatures from some nightmarish myth. However, Athens remained the chief source of pottery. Horses, then very important in a Greek world that was strongly aristocratic, are among the first recognizable animals to appear on vases.

THE MIDDLE GEOMETRIC: THE HUMAN FORM RETURNS

By 800BC the tempo of Greek life was beginning to quicken. The century was to witness the real rebirth of Greece, with the writing of Homer's poetry, the invention of the Greek alphabet (derived from Phoenician examples), the beginnings of colonization and the establishment of great festivals such as the Olympic Games in 776BC.

This resurgence encouraged the reappearance of human forms, albeit still in rigidly geometrized form. Strange, stick-like figures gradually began to fill more and more of the vase areas. They also became freer and less rigid, although they long remained highly stylized.

Large burial urns containing the ashes of important people (cremation was then the normal form of burial, in contrast to the Mycenaean preference for inhumation) often carried scenes of mourning. One of

these, a terracotta krater about 1.5m (5ft) high dating from *c.*750BC, shows a funeral procession in the top band with a corpse lying on a bier, with identical stylized human forms on the other side. But the lower band rejoices in a multitude of figures, who seem to be wearing odd kilts or skirts. They are driving carts or more probably chariots. It is possible that they are meant to be competitors taking part in the deceased's funeral games. This typically Greek custom was by then widely established, at least according to Homer's poetry.

This grand vase is often attributed to the 'Hirschfeld Painter'. (Potters are often named after particular works, another example being the 'Diplyon Artist'). However, we know nothing at all definite about this putative potter. Even this particular vase may not have been the work of one individual.

THE LATE GEOMETRIC

By the Late Geometric period (750–700BC), decoration had spread to cover the entire surface of vases, with busy friezes of animals and humans. However, Geometric art, which had allowed the revival of decorative vase painting in a characteristically Greek form, strongly emphasizing symmetry, had by the century's end reached an artistic dead-end.

What had been necessary astringency after the collapse of Mycenaean art was in danger of becoming a straitjacket. Greek art needed a fresh direction and an injection of vitality. Both would come from Asia, then far more advanced.

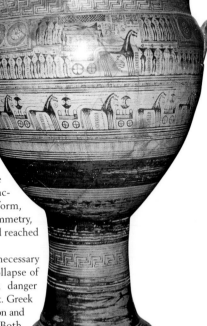

Below: Standing 1.2m (4ft) high, this terracotta Late Geometric krater by the Hirschfield painter from Attica is the finest burial urn from the 8th century BC. Such urns marked the burial pits in which cremated bodies were placed. The vase actually shows a grand funeral cortège with a long row of warriors in their chariots.

IDEAS FROM THE EAST
c.720–570 BC

The 7th century BC saw major changes in pottery painting. Although in some cities potters for a time retained Geometric motifs, elsewhere they began experimenting with new ways of depicting figures. They also discovered new, much more interesting subjects. (Possibly earlier artists were also illustrating myths and legends, but their starkly silhouetted forms make any narrative almost impossibly hard to discern.)

Greek artists began to borrow the flora and fauna motifs of Syria. The protypes of these may have first been introduced by the Phoenicians, then masters of the Mediterranean, and adapted by them for their own purposes.

Syrian polychromatic influence merged with the perennial Greek insistence on form to create the colourful 'orientalizing' art of the 7th century BC. The flourishing Isthmian port of Corinth, which was founding colonies across the Mediterranean, became for the next 100 years the leading centre of artistic innovation. Pottery styles are named after its innovatory use of clear-cut forms, although Athens always remained an important centre for ceramics.

Above: The Chigi Vase, *a very fine Corinthian-style vase with a triple tier of friezes, dates from* c.620BC. *It is made of terracotta with a dark and light glaze of paint, and covered in red and white figures of hoplite soldiers.*

Below: Corinth emerged as the greatest centre of vase-making c.700BC. *On this skyphos (drinking cup) of* c.670BC *from Kameiros in Rhodes, a black dog lollops with lithe energy across a white surface – an example of Corinthian art at its vivid best.*

Above: The Polyphemus Amphora *of* c.680BC, *fussily proto-Attic in style, illustrates the story of Odysseus blinding the drunken giant Polyphemus on its top frieze, while lower down animals run wild. Underneath them the Gorgons pursue Perseus, who has just killed their sister Medusa, in quite another myth.*

PROTOCORINTHIAN 720–640BC

A new interest in depicting myths and legends – which merged into religion and history – led to scenes filled with griffins, sphinxes and sirens. Homer's epics, *The Iliad* and *Odyssey*, quickly known all round the Greek world,

became one of the prime sources of myths for potters. The *Polyphemus Amphora* of *c.*680BC, found in a child's grave at Eleusis near Athens, illustrates the story of Odysseus blinding the drunken giant Polyphemus on its top frieze, while lower down animals run wild. Underneath them the Gorgons, the lethal sisters of decapitated Medusa, pursue Perseus, who has just killed the snake-headed horror, in quite another myth. Stylistically the vase is called proto-Attic. Despite its richness of detail, it lacks the purity of line of the best Corinthian work.

Much simpler in theme and artistically far more powerful is the *skyphos* (drinking cup) of *c.*670BC from Kameiros in Rhodes. The long black form of a dog lollops with superb energy across a white surface. This is a true Corinthian work, as is the *aryballos* (perfume flask) of *c.*650BC from Thebes. Its head is formed like a lion's mouth with savage fangs, while on its body hoplites are vividly depicted fighting with spears and shields. Such potent works typify the Protocorinthian style in its maturity.

THE *CHIGI VASE*

Perhaps the finest example of the Corinthian style is the *Chigi Vase*, with its triple tier of friezes. Dating from *c.*620BC, the vase, of a type called an *oinochoe* (wine-pourer), is made of terracotta with dark and light glaze paint covered in red and white figures. It comes from Formello near Veii, an important Etruscan city. The topmost frieze graphically depicts two armies approaching each other in battle formation. This vase also provides invaluable information about early hoplite warfare.

Below this scene a second frieze shows a procession of horsemen, chariots, a lion hunt and the Judgement of Paris. (The Trojan prince had had to make a perilous choice of deities: who was the most beautiful, Aphrodite, Athena or Hera? Choosing Aphrodite, the love goddess, he incurred the undying hatred of the other two, a fatal choice that

ultimately led to the fall of Troy. A sphinx meanwhile looks on impartially.) The bottom frieze shows a hare hunt. Figures are now no longer just bare silhouettes but are portrayed with a true muscular vigour.

THE 'NESSOS PAINTER'

A vase-painter known to us as the 'Nessos Painter' from his masterpiece, a huge amphora some 1.2m (4ft) tall depicting the legend of Hercules and Nessos, flourished in Attica in the late 7th century BC. Painted only on one side, this bears the names of Heracles (Hercules) and Netos (Nessos) above it for the first time. It illustrates a popular myth. Hercules, the archetypal hero, was escorting Deianeria, a princess, when Nessos, a centaur who worked as a ferryman, tried to rape her. Hercules is shown on the amphora's neck seizing the centaur by his neck and killing him. Deianeria later gave Hercules a shirt soaked in Nessos' poisoned blood, thinking it was a love potion. Maddened by the torment of the 'shirt of Nessos', the hero killed himself on a funeral pyre.

The story is painted with far more artistic verve and self-confidence than on earlier vases. So too is the lower story, again of the Gorgons chasing Perseus. Instead of the robotic figures shown on the *Polyphemus Amphora* of 70 years earlier, these monsters are depicted as horrific winged demons in hot pursuit of Perseus, who is not even present.

With masters like the 'Nessos Painter' working in Attica, Athens again displaced Corinth as the main manufacturer of vases, a position it retained until the end of the Classical Age. The potters' quarter in Athens was known as the Kerameikos, after its clay (ceramic) vase-makers.

Below: A vase-painter known as the 'Nessos Painter' produced this masterpiece, a huge amphora, 1.2m (4ft) tall, depicting the legend of Hercules and Nessos, in the late 7th century BC. Painted only on one side, this bears the names of Heracles (Hercules) and Netos (Nessos) above it for the first time.

CLASSICISM AND NATURALISM 570–480BC

As Athens emerged as the chief pottery centre *c.*570BC – just when Solon's economic and social reforms were starting to have beneficial effects – its individual artists developed the black figure style (on a red or pale ground) to its effective limits. Some artists then went on to pioneer red figure vases on a black ground. Although this was technically harder, it permitted the depiction of increasingly naturalistic and powerful scenes. With this style, Greek vase painting was to reach its zenith. Artists now often signed their vases, thus demonstrating a novel self-confidence.

Among the earlier notable works is the *François Vase* of *c.*560BC, a grand krater exported to Etruria. Signed by the potter Ergotimos and the painter Cleitias, its six friezes brim with mythological scenes, many relating the story of Achilles, the warrior-hero of *The Iliad*.

Cleitias signed many other works, as did Sophilos, who was both a painter and potter. This was now an increasingly common and effective combination.

Above: Among the grandest Attic vases of the 6th century is the François Vase *(named after its finder), a krater exported to Etruria. Signed by the potter Ergotimos and the painter Cleitias, its friezes brim with mythological scenes, many about Achilles, the warrior-hero.*

EXEKIAS THE MASTER

One of the age's greatest potter-cum-painters, some 30 pieces are attributed to Exekias. He worked between 550 and 520BC. Among his masterpieces are *Dionysus in a Ship*, a terracotta glazed *kylix* (cup) of *c.*540BC. The bearded wine god – only later was Dionysus shown as a beardless youth – lolls at ease in his ship, a drinking horn in his hands. The ship's mast is sprouting vines that bear luscious fruit above, while around cavort dolphins. The scene brims with joyful lyricism.

Different, but equally masterly, is *Ajax and Achilles*, showing the two heroes intent on a board game during a break in the Trojan Wars (not a scene mentioned by Homer). It demonstrates Exekias' skill in incised lines, which allowed greater realism in depicting armour and flesh. Also notable are his innovatory composition, with the strong diagonals formed by the spears, and the intimate subject-matter. Exekias was the first to paint such scenes from legend as complete pictures, and his work is often considered to make him the first great individual in Western art. But such black figure vases were inherently limited, for they lacked chromatic variety. To create this meant reversing the age-old formula of painting in the figures while leaving the background untouched.

Left: Ajax and Achilles, *showing the two heroes intent on a game during a break in the Trojan Wars, demonstrates Exekias' skill in incised lines, which allowed greater realism in depicting armour and flesh. Also notable are his innovatory composition, with the strong diagonals formed by the spears, and intimate subject-matter. As the first to paint such scenes as complete pictures, Exekias is sometimes considered the first great individual Western painter.*

THE RED FIGURE PIONEERS

In about 530BC Athenian painters pioneered the development of red figure vases, a truly revolutionary move. (Black figure works continued to be produced for a while as well, however.) The first such vase is attributed to Andocides, possibly a pupil of Exekias, who signed an amphora on which one side has red figures and the other has black figures, both showing Hercules reclining on a couch.

Among the best of the new painters-cum-potters, a group today called the Pioneers, was Euphronius. About 510BC he painted a kylix depicting Leagros, a beautiful youth riding a skittish horse with calm self-confidence. This shows a great advance in naturalism, as does his more elaborate vase showing the death of Sarpedon, a Trojan prince. Euphronius also depicted figures reclining at a *symposium* (party) with innovatory accuracy on a *psyketer* (wine cooler). The diners' half-naked bodies, even the pupils of their eyes, are remarkably lifelike.

There was keen competition among these painters, who must have known each other in the still small polis. Euthymides, a contemporary, inscribed a vase with his name and the boast: "As Euphronius could never have made it."

SOSIAS

One of the finest pieces of the period is a kylix by Sosias, a painter-cum-potter working in Athens around 500BC. It shows Achilles bandaging his comrade Patroclus' wounded arm (a scene inspired by, but not actually in, Homer's *The Iliad*). Sosios has painted Patroclus in such a way – his right leg bent, his left leg stretched out before him – that he fills the curve of the vase perfectly. Patroclus looks away in well-expressed pain as Achilles concentrates on his task. The faces and bodies of each warrior are shown in naturalistic perspective, marking a final break with Archaic art's frontalism.

The Dionysiac scenes painted on an amphora in *c.*490BC by the 'Cleophrades Painter' (also called Epictetus), a pupil of Euthymides, portrays the orgiastic rites of the wine god with great vigour. Dionysus, bearded and with his usual attributes of ivy and vine, is wearing long robes under which his legs move visibly, the first time that drapery was shown flowing realistically around a body. Around him, long-robed Maenads, the god's ecstatic followers, fend off impish satyrs.

The extensive use of a diluted glaze is also striking. Above, on the jar's neck, naked athletes compete. Attic potters' achievement of classical naturalism now matched that of contemporary sculptors and, presumably, panel painters.

Above: Dionysus in a Ship, *a terracotta glazed kylix of* c.540BC, one of Exekias's 30 known masterpieces. The wine god lolls at ease in his ship, a drinking horn in his hands, while the mast sprouts vines bearing fruit and dolphins cavort around.

Right: Achilles and Patroclus *by Sosias, a painter-cum-potter working in Athens around* 500BC. Among the finest early red figure vases, it shows Achilles bandaging his comrade Patroclus' wounded arm (a scene not actually in The Iliad).

Above: The Pan Painter *in c.450BC depicted a scene of heroic legend: Hercules killing the Egyptian king Busiris, who had intended to sacrifice him. The neat hairstyle and taut strength of the Greek hero contrast with the flabby ugliness of his opponents, perhaps reflecting Athens' aggressive new self-confidence at the time.*

ZENITH AND DECLINE
480–340BC

The Athenians emerged from the Persian wars (490–478BC) triumphant if battered. Rebuilding their wrecked city, they founded a new League against Persia, which soon became their empire, and completed their own progress to full democracy. This political upsurge was matched by artistic advances.

In painting, this was best exemplified by the large panel paintings of Polygnotus of Thasos. While all these have vanished, some fine vase paintings that survive are thought to be very similar in general design and approach.

Among these is a vase by an artist called the 'Niobe Painter' after another vase by him depicting the death of Niobe's children. His masterpiece of about 460BC shows Athena, goddess of the city, flanked by heroes, including Theseus, Athens' legendary king, and the muscular champion Hercules with his club. The vase probably commemorates

BURIAL VASES

One form of vase differed from the general run of black figure vases: the *lekythos*, literally an oil-flask with a white ground used for weddings or, more often, funerals. These cylindrical vases were made mostly from the 450s to the 420s BC. Among them is some of the finest Attic painted pottery. The 'Achilles Painter' is known also for his superb white-ground *lekythoi*. One shows a Muse on Mount Helicon (the rock is conveniently labelled) playing her lyre. The clear, simple lines of the young woman are timelessly classical. Other lekythoi could be more colourful but all remained relatively simple.

the Battle of Marathon, Athens' first victory over the Persians in 490BC. In that battle, Theseus and other long-dead heroes were rumoured to have returned to fight alongside living Athenians. The figures are not painted in perspective or as part of a whole narrative but are isolated around the vase, as was probably then the style in mural painting too.

HEROES AND AMAZONS

More dramatically interesting is the *Amazonomachia* (Battle of the Amazons) on a resplendent krater 75cm (2ft 6in) high. This popular legend – of the defeat of the attack on Athens by the Amazons, those warrior-women who so inverted Greek ideas about women's proper role – gave artists the licence to depict

Left: A detail from the large red figure vase opposite above, showing the goddess Demeter, the goddess of wheat and agriculture, in her chariot with Triptolemus, a prince. Red figure painting allowed much clearer lines against the black ground.

THE 'ACHILLES PAINTER'

During the period of Pericles' dominance of Athenian politics, in the high noon of Athenian democracy – around 450–430BC when the Parthenon with its superb sculptures was being built – an artist known as the 'Achilles Painter' also brought vase painting to its peak. He is so-called because of an amphora attributed to him showing *Achilles and Briseis*, the Homeric hero and the slave girl, another scene inspired by *The Iliad*. His compositions are simple, usually with just a couple of isolated but serene figures who radiate the same graceful nobility as Pheidias' great sculptures of the same period. Because of this, the 'Achilles Painter' is often considered the most deeply classical vase-painter of the High Classical period. About 200 surviving vases have, with varying degrees of certainty, been ascribed to him. Many lesser painters were reputedly his pupils. With him, Attic vase painting reached its peak.

DECLINE AND DECADENCE

Although fine vases continued to be made in the late 5th century BC in Athens, the 4th century BC saw a general decline in standards. In Athens artistic interest now increasingly focused on making vases in metals, including silver and even gold. But in Greek cities in southern Italy, lavish pottery vases such as the *Alcestis Vase* continued to be made.

Increasingly, these vases were floridly decorated with often flabby designs. Only when illustrating low-life scenes from theatrical comedy – as on a vase from Paestum, which shows actors with grotesque masks – can these painters be considered really successful.

half-naked women. It also served as a parable for the recent defeat of Persia, another non-Hellenic invader. The scene is crowded with violent action as armoured Athenians spear and hack at the Amazons, who are dressed as lightly as Scythian archers.

Above, on the vase's neck, in contrast, diners are shown peacefully drinking and listening to flute girls. *The Pan Painter* around 450BC depicted another scene of heroic massacre, Hercules killing the Ethiopian king Busiris, who had intended to sacrifice *him*.

A rather different scene of legendary violence on a *skyphos* or drinking cup shows Odysseus, home from his long wanderings, shooting his mighty bow at the suitors who had long been plaguing his wife Penelope. The Homeric hero is depicted on one side of the skyphos while the terrified suitors, one with an arrow sticking into him, cower from the returning king on the other. Dating from *c.*450BC, this piece achieves its impact with notably simple, uncluttered forms.

Left: A grand example of an Athenian red figure vase from the 5th century BC, the golden age of Athenian pottery, by the 'Niobe Painter', one of the master-potters. It shows the battle of the giants and gods above and Demeter and Triptolemus below.

Below: A lekythos, an oil-flask with figures on a white ground, was used for weddings and especially funerals. The clear, simple lines of the woman playing her lyre are very classical. Other lekythoi could be more colourful but all remained relatively simple.

CHAPTER XVIII

WALL PAINTINGS AND MOSAICS

The Greeks admired their painters as much as their sculptors. This may not now be apparent from artworks in museums, where statues predominate, but no real Greek painting before the mid-4th century BC survives. Instead, we must rely on descriptions by later writers such as Pliny, and what can be guessed from contemporary vases. We would have even less idea of Greek painting were it not for the eruption of Vesuvius in AD79, that preserved Pompeii and Herculaneum so well.

Pompeii is hugely important because, although never a Greek colony, it was very open to Greek cultural influences. Many of its houses were decorated with copies of Hellenistic masterpieces, often made by actual Greek artists. These works provide vivid examples of Greek painting in its illusionistic prime. Helped by recent discoveries from royal tombs in Macedonia and examples from houses in Rome, we can now see what master painters the Greeks were, even though they never fully grasped the principle of single unitary perspective that has underpinned realist Western art since the Renaissance. However painting in the Greek world starts far earlier with Minoan murals, some preserved by the volcanic eruption at Thira.

Left: Among the greatest of ancient paintings, The Finding of Telephus *at Herculaneum copies a work from Pergamum.*

MINOAN AND MYCENAEAN PAINTING 1700–1200BC

The art of the Bronze-Age Aegean Minoans and Mycenaeans forms a prelude to Greek art proper. While it is uncertain how much, if any, influence their paintings had on later Greek art, one convention certainly survived: that of depicting women as white-skinned and most men as tanned brown.

Minoan paintings have been found in Crete and southern Aegean islands. In the Second Palace period (c.1700–1400BC), the Minoans produced wonderfully vivid and free-flowing, if hardly naturalistic, art. (Their colouring was not realistic and they gracefully elongated the human form, while the whole eye is often visible on faces painted in profile, an anatomical impossibility.) Minoan art also showed a keen awareness of non-human nature.

In all this it differed radically from the monumental art of contemporary Egypt and the Near East, areas that the Minoans knew. Cretan artists, uninterested in attempting to overawe spectators, delighted in celebrating life's fleeting pleasures. They generally painted frescoes, that is they applied pigment directly onto wet plaster, as did many Greek and Renaissance artists later. This technique, feasible only in dry climates, is well suited to painting quickly.

PALACE FRESCOES

Among earlier frescoes is a mural called *The Saffron Gatherer* from the palace at Cnossus of c.1600BC. Restored originally by Arthur Evans to represent a human being, it is now thought to depict a monkey picking saffron in a field. Larger and livelier at 80cm (2ft 8in) high is the *Bull-leaping Fresco* from the east wing of the great palace of c.1500BC. With its border painted to imitate marble, this grand mural illustrates a rite at the heart of Cretan life, the bull game, played by girls as well as boys, both sexes wearing kilts.

THE PRINCE WITH THE LILIES

A courtly, even decadent, note is struck by the superb relief fresco *The Prince with the Lilies*, showing a young noble with a huge golden headdress in almost hieratic pose. More typically Minoan in its vivacity is the *Running Officer*, showing a man leading a row of African guards, all sprinting. Typical also is the woman with big eyes and elaborate hair called *La Parisienne (The Parisian Woman)* who was perhaps a priestess.

In the room Evans called the Queen's Bathroom, dolphins leap gracefully around the royal bathtub – the sea was always important to the Minoans. There are few signs of war or warriors until the palace's very last phase, when it was under Mycenaean rule. From that period date the griffins, noble if stylized beasts flanking the throne of Minos.

THE THIRA MURALS

The volcanic eruption at Thira around 1500BC (some geologists prefer an earlier date) has kept the murals in houses on that once wealthy island dazzlingly fresh. These provide different views of the Bronze-Age world from the Cretan palace murals, although painted in the same style: two boys (judging by their brown colouring) are boxing; blue monkeys (unmistakeable simians, this time) clamber up rocks, fleeing pursuing dogs; butterflies and swallows flit among tree-tops; a woman, elegant in Minoan dress with small waist and puffed sleeves, is gathering saffron; antelopes brush against each other's flanks – all are scenes pulsing with vitality. The inhabitants of Thira were presumably merchants, not kings, but many murals rivals those of Crete itself. There is nothing provincial here.

Nor were they always as peace-loving as the Cretans have been assumed to be. Other frescoes show the fleet – of Thira, or

Above: Typical of Minoan art, this c.1550BC mural of a woman with big eyes and hair is now called La Parisienne. *She was probably a courtier, possibly a priestess.*

Below: The Prince with the Lilies of c.1500BC, a superb relief fresco, shows a young noble in an elaborate gold headdress of great courtliness.

perhaps of all the Aegean islands – sailing off to visit and sometimes attack other cities. Some of these are thought to be in north Africa, revealing again the Minoans' links with Africa. The grand cycle of murals depicting the fleet's actions reveals a whole vanished Mediterranean world.

MYCENAEAN ART

The Mycenaeans, the Minoans' artistic as well as political heirs, continued the mural tradition. Unfortunately, many of their finest frescoes, such as those adorning the Palace of Nestor at Pylos in the south-western Peloponnese, were lost when that noblest of Achaean palaces was sacked. However, at Mycenae and Tiryns

enough remains to give some idea of their art. As might be expected, it was often concerned with war and hunting.

From the Mycenean fort of Tiryns comes a fine example of a boar hunt, showing long-bodied hounds leaping on their prey, a scene painted with almost Minoan vivacity. The dogs' elegant collars suggest a lighter side to Mycenaean life than is often apparent. Stiffer and more stylized, but still impressive, are frescoes from Mycenae itself portraying ladies of the court, all dressed in Minoan fashion. These murals are thought to date from the late 13th century BC, shortly before the sudden collapse of Mycenaean civilization.

Above: A fresco from Thira, the volcano-blasted island, showing the Aegean fleet at sea, perhaps approaching the coast of north Africa.

Below left: This colourful, lively fresco from a mural in a house on Thira was probably painted about 1600BC. It shows monkeys clambering up rocks.

Below right: A boar hunt from a mural in the Mycenaean fortress of Tiryns, painted in the 13th century BC.

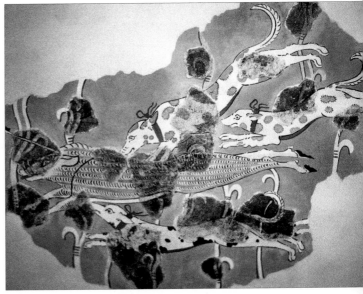

CLASSICAL PAINTING
480–320BC

Athens' pivotal role in the Greeks' grand victories over Persia from 490 to 479BC called for public commemoration. Polygnotus of Thasos, who worked c.470–440BC in Athens, was widely considered the first great Greek painter.

Polygnotus painted large pictures, mostly about semi-historical legends or religious myths, filled with numerous figures but little in the way of background landscape. Tentative reconstructions of his great *Sack of Troy*, which he painted for the Cnidians' Temple at Delphi, show a triple frieze of seemingly unconnected figures. As Polygnotus painted wholly on perishable wood panels, none of his work has survived.

Above: The Abduction of Persephone, *a mural from a tomb at Vergina (Edessa, the oldest Macedonian capital), dates from c.330BC. Only recently excavated, it is one of the very few Greek murals extant. Its light brush strokes convey the terror of Persephone as bearded Hades carries her off in his chariot to the underworld. Nicomachus, an artist praised by Pliny, probably painted this.*

MASTERS OF REALISM

Zeuxis of Heraclea in southern Italy, who worked c.435–390BC, was considered the supreme painter of his age and a master of verisimilitude. According to one story, when asked to paint a picture of Helen of Troy, whose dazzling beauty had caused the Trojan War, he assembled the city's five most beautiful women and combined their finest features into one ideal figure. This story, whether or not literally true, suggests that, like contemporary sculptors, Zeuxis aimed at depicting an idealized human form realistically, not at portraying actual individuals. Zeuxis, too, painted only on wooden panels, which have not survived.

Zeuxis' rival was Parrhasius of Ephesus, a master of realism so convincing that his work approached *trompe l'oeil*. According to Pliny, Zeuxis painted a picture of some grapes that were so lifelike that birds came to peck at them. But Parrhasius, when called to draw back the curtain concealing his rival's work, revealed that the curtain itself was a stunningly realistic painting. Again, nothing remains of his art, but he was reputedly also skilled at depicting facial expressions.

THE 4TH-CENTURY MASTERS

After 400BC, the heroic tendency to idealize in art began to slacken, although it always remained powerful. Nicias of Athens was a friend and pupil of the famous sculptor Praxiteles, some of whose statues he coloured. Renowned for his skill in *chiaroscuro* (dramatically juxtaposed shade and light), he painted many female figures in dramatic situations. Nothing by him survives either.

As power shifted north to Macedonia in the mid-4th century BC, Philip II and then Alexander the Great became the main artistic patrons in the Greek world.

Born c.380BC in Colophon in Ionia, Apelles was considered the age's greatest artist. He was court painter to both the kings, who realized the propaganda value of his work. Alexander reputedly so

Left: Lion Hunt, *dated c.320–300BC, is from Pella, the Macedonian capital. Signed by Gnosis, a renowned artist, it shows two naked youths, one Alexander the Great and the other perhaps his friend Craterus, attacking a lion. Such dramatic realism must have been common also in the wall paintings now lost.*

admired his painter that when Apelles fell in love with Pancapse, then the current royal mistress whose portrait he was painting, Alexander gave her to the artist. Or so the story goes. Apelles worked mostly in the eastern Aegean when he was not following Alexander's conquering path across Asia.

About 30 works by Apelles are mentioned by ancient writers, among them a *Calumny* (of which Botticelli made a Renaissance version) and an *Aphrodite Anadyomene* (*Aphrodite Rising from the Foam*) later taken to Rome by the emperor Augustus. Apelles was said to excel all other painters in grace and to be a master of chiaroscuro. The *Zeus Enthroned* in the House of the Vetti at Pompeii may be a copy of Apelles' work.

THE ROYAL TOMBS

Excavations at Vergina (Aegae, the ancient Macedonian capital in the hills above Pella) have recently produced remarkable murals. One, possibly from the tomb of Philip II himself and so dating to *c.*338BC, shows a dramatic and complex hunting scene in which for the first time landscape contributes to the picture's depth. The frieze, though much pitted, presents a panoramic view of the hunt, in which the young Alexander is shown on horseback.

Even more vivid is *The Abduction of Persephone*, a mural in a nearby tomb sketched with quick, light strokes that aptly capture the despair of the goddess Demeter. She is shown seated on the right as the shaggy-bearded god Hades carries off her terrified daughter Persephone in his chariot to the underworld. Nicomachus, an artist praised by Pliny, may have created this novel depiction of human emotion.

THE FIRST MOSAICS

Mosaics, that far more laborious and costly, if also far more enduring, form of art than murals or panels, were initially made in pebbles. *Lion Hunt*, dated *c.*320–300BC is from Pella, the

Macedonian capital, and is signed by Gnosis, a famous artist. It depicts two naked youths, one perhaps being Alexander and the other his friend Craterus, who with a hound are attacking a lion. It is a dynamically dramatic scene, the muscular bodies and flying cloaks of the naked hunters and the animals shown with convincing foreshortening and shadowing.

In the Hellenistic and Roman eras, mosaics became commoner and grander, but painted *tesserae* (glass or marble cubes) replaced pebbles. Tesserae were easier to work in than pebbles, which encouraged the spread of mosaics.

Above: The Birth of Venus *from the House of Venus, a mural from Pompeii that probably copies a lost Hellenistic original – a reminder that not all such paintings were masterpieces.*

Below: Botticelli's Calumny of Apelles, *painted in 1495, was a Renaissance attempt to recreate a lost masterpiece by Apelles. Often considered the greatest artist of antiquity, Apelles became Alexander's court painter in the 330s BC.*

THE EVIDENCE OF POMPEII
THE *ALEXANDER MOSAIC*

Above: A detail from the
Alexander Mosaic *showing
King Darius panic-stricken in
his chariot at Alexander's
sudden advance.*

Below: The Alexander
Mosaic, *the grandest copy of a
Greek masterpiece, was made
in Pompeii around* 100BC. *It
shows Alexander charging at
King Darius. Reproducing a
mural probably painted by
Apelles* c.328BC, *it keeps to
the original four-colour palette.*

Originally an Etruscan settlement, and so, like many other Etruscan cities, very receptive to Greek culture, Pompeii later became an Oscan town. It prospered on the fertile if, as it finally turned out, perilous lands beneath Mt Vesuvius. Only Romanized properly after Sulla had planted a military colony there in 80BC, Pompeii then expanded further, acquiring a permanent amphitheatre long before Rome did. But at its peak in AD79 its population reached only c.15,000, making it quite small even by the standards of the age.

But there was nothing pettily provincial about Pompeii culturally. It not only had all the trappings of a Graeco-Roman city – temples, baths, a forum, elected officials – it also had long been attracting fine artists from around the Greek world. They produced often excellent copies of renowned Hellenistic paintings that decorated royal palaces in Hellenistic

kingdoms such as Pergamum. The quality of the murals and mosaics uncovered at Pompeii and nearby Herculaneum are rivalled only by those excavated from Rome's largest houses and palaces.

THE *ALEXANDER MOSAIC*

Grandest of Pompeian paintings is the *Alexander Mosaic*, the most faithful full-size copy of a Greek masterpiece known. This intensely dramatic battle scene was made for a wealthy – and clearly philhellenic – Pompeian around 100BC and displayed in its own special *exedra* (recess) in his mansion, now called the 'House of the Faun'. The picture shows Alexander powering through the fighting towards his opponent, a terrified King Darius, who is about to flee in his chariot. (Whether the battle shown is the Issus in 333BC or Gaugamela two years later remains debated. The same dramatic incident occurred in both.) The mosaic

in Pompeii reproduces an earlier work that was almost certainly a mural due to the generally free style of its painting.

The mosaic meticulously follows the original work's restricted four-colour palette – red, yellow, black and white – employed by many of the greatest Classical artists from Polygnotus to Apelles. The picture uses highlights, deep-cast shadows and recession in depth to heighten its realism. More recent innovations are the three-dimensional modelling in black (of some of the horses) and the extreme foreshortening of a horse right in the centre, whose rear quarters are seen from behind. The reflected face of a fallen Persian in the burnished shield in the centre marks another advance in dramatic realism.

Very large at 2.7 by 5.1m (8ft 10in by 16ft 9in) and ringing with the tumult of battle, the picture rivals in its emotional impact the grandest works by later Renaissance and Baroque masters. Many archaeologists think that the original was painted by Apelles in *c*.328BC, soon after the battle depicted. Others attribute it to Philoxenos of Eretria, another famous artist of Alexander's age.

THE VILLA AT BOSCOREALE

Very different in tone is the cycle of fresco paintings made *c*.50BC for Publius Fannius Synistor, who owned a large villa at Boscoreale just outside Pompeii. These also copy Hellenistic royal pictures painted nearly 200 years earlier. There are five panels, each with one or two static, almost life-size figures. One shows a craggy philosopher leaning on a stick. In another, a woman personifying Asia is seated looking intensely at a pensive man with a shield opposite her, who has been identified as symbolizing a Macedonian king. Another panel shows a draped women in a gold headband playing a golden cithara, with a girl standing behind her high-backed chair, a contrasting scene of domestic tranquillity. The unknown creator of these pieces was clearly a highly adaptable artist.

Above: A mural from Pompeii of the 1st century BC *copying an older Hellenistic work. Depicting the hero Perseus, it shows remarkable illusionistic skills.*

THE FINDING OF TELEPHUS

From Herculaneum comes one of the finest paintings of antiquity, a copy of *The Finding of Telephus*. The original was made for Eumenes II of Pergamum in *c*.190BC. Telephus was the son of Hercules. Hercules, flanked by the royal lion and eagle, looks down at his son, being suckled by a doe in the foreground. The boy and deer are masterpieces of tenderly depicted realism. Behind the child sits a female figure personifying Arcadia. She is so majestic, massive and calm that she could have been painted by J.A.D. Ingres (1780–1867), the French Neoclassical master.

Below: This mural of c.50BC *from a villa at Pompeii copies a work of* c.240BC *for a Macedonian royal palace.*

IDYLLIC LANDSCAPES
THE GRAECO–ROMAN FUSION

Above: Dionysus riding a panther, a mosaic from a rich merchant's house on Delos made c.120BC.

Below: The great Nile Mosaic from Praeneste near Rome decorated a public building. It gives a bird's-eye view of the Nile in flood, with temples, boats and animals, copying a Ptolemaic original of c.100BC.

Landscape painting, seemingly unknown to Classical artists, emerged during the Hellenistic period as often idyllic illustrations of mythical scenes. The genre may have reflected a nostalgia for rural life among people in vast new cities such as Antioch, Alexandria and Rome itself. But it revealed, too, artists' growing skills in suggesting depth and recession, which were at times used to depict cityscapes too. One of the first such scenery painters, generally called *topographoi*, was Demetrius, who worked in Alexandria in the 2nd century BC.

At the Boscoreale Villa near Pompeii the murals of imaginary cities in the main *cubiculum* (bedroom) make superb examples of architectural *trompe l'oeil*. They copy stage scenery from Ephesus painted c.150BC and later described by Pliny. Like most original paintings described by writers, the Ephesus works have not survived.

THE ODYSSEY LANDSCAPES

The second more romantic Homeric epic about the wanderings of its homesick hero, *The Odyssey*, was a popular source of stories for painters in the Hellenistic and Roman worlds. (Educated Romans understood Greek.) Unearthed from a house on the Esquiline Hill in Rome in 1848–9, a cycle of eight magnificent murals, painted c.50BC but copying earlier Hellenistic work, depicts Odysseus' adventures done in sketches with an almost impressionistic lightness.

The landscapes gain a romantic, indeed menacing air from the huge boulders overshadowing the tiny figures, and from the great vistas of sea and islands opening up beyond them. Such backgrounds add to the drama of the stories. In the first panel Odysseus and his men have innocently arrive in the land of the Laestrygonians. They make inquiries of a graceful woman carrying an amphora descending a path. The tone is pastorally idyllic.

It changes abruptly in the next panels as the Laestrygonians attack Odysseus' men with rocks and trees. The Laestrygonians, who are really cannibals, then destroy many of the Greeks' boats, dragging off the slaughtered Greeks to eat them. Odysseus' ship alone escapes as he sails off with a few companions for Circe's island. Other scenes show Odysseus' descent to the Underworld. The unknown artist radically reduced the size of figures as they recede deeper into the landscape. To identify some of the men dwarfed by the landscape, he helpfully added labels.

THE 'HOUSE OF THE TRAGIC POET'

In the 'House of the Tragic Poet' at Pompeii an unknown painter created a masterpiece in *Achilles and Briseis*, illustrating a scene from *The Iliad*. Achilles smoulders with barely suppressed rage as

Left: From the Villa at Tivoli of the emperor Hadrian (reigned AD117–38) comes this mosaic of drinking doves, a copy of an original made by Sosus of Pergamum in about 150BC. Its realism approaches trompe l'oeil.

Briseis, his favourite slave girl, is forcibly carried off on King Agamemnon's orders. Behind the pitifully weeping figure of Briseis stand a line of threateningly armoured soldiers. The fresco copies a Hellenistic original of *c.*300BC.

In sober, dignified contrast the stucco panel from a villa in Herculaneum shows an exhausted actor resting in his dressing-room. His sceptre and sword indicate that he is playing a royal role. A woman crouches in front of a female tragic mask. (She is not an actress, because men played women's roles in Greek theatre and this painting copies a Greek original of *c.*300BC.) The work may portray the psychological tension between actors' grand roles and their low social status.

MOSAICS EAST AND WEST
The art of mosaic continued to develop, being carried west to Italy. In Delos, booming after Rome made it a tax-free port in 166BC, wealthy Roman or Italian merchants commissioned fine mosaics for their luxurious houses. One of the most striking comes from the 'House of Dionysus', named after its vibrantly coloured mosaic made *c.*120BC. It shows the wine-god on a panther, looking debauched and riding curiously side-saddle. His panther or leopard snarls with feral power, its claws painted with almost alarming realism.

Approximately contemporary is the great *Nile Mosaic* from Praeneste (Palestrina) near Rome made to decorate the apse of a public building. It shows a bird's-eye view of the Nile in flood, with temples, boats, soldiers and animals. Everything is teeming with life and colour. It probably copies a Ptolemaic royal original, but makes no attempt at using perspective.

From the Villa at Tivoli of Hadrian, that most philhellenic of Roman emperors (reigned AD117–38), comes a brilliant copy of a mosaic by Sosus of Pergamum, originally made *c.*150BC. It shows doves drinking from a burnished bowl, whose surface is disturbed by the beak of one sipping bird. This marvel of realism marks the climax of Graeco-Roman cultural fusion as the Roman empire itself passed through its zenith.

Below: From the 'House of the Tragic Poet' at Pompeii comes an anonymous masterpiece illustrating a scene from The Iliad. It copies a Hellenistic original of c.300BC.

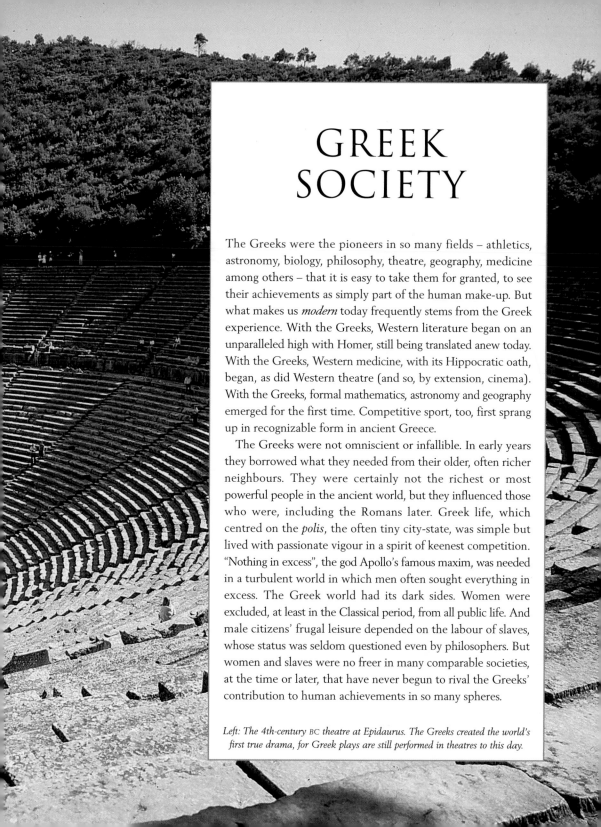

GREEK SOCIETY

The Greeks were the pioneers in so many fields – athletics, astronomy, biology, philosophy, theatre, geography, medicine among others – that it is easy to take them for granted, to see their achievements as simply part of the human make-up. But what makes us *modern* today frequently stems from the Greek experience. With the Greeks, Western literature began on an unparalleled high with Homer, still being translated anew today. With the Greeks, Western medicine, with its Hippocratic oath, began, as did Western theatre (and so, by extension, cinema). With the Greeks, formal mathematics, astronomy and geography emerged for the first time. Competitive sport, too, first sprang up in recognizable form in ancient Greece.

The Greeks were not omniscient or infallible. In early years they borrowed what they needed from their older, often richer neighbours. They were certainly not the richest or most powerful people in the ancient world, but they influenced those who were, including the Romans later. Greek life, which centred on the *polis*, the often tiny city-state, was simple but lived with passionate vigour in a spirit of keenest competition. "Nothing in excess", the god Apollo's famous maxim, was needed in a turbulent world in which men often sought everything in excess. The Greek world had its dark sides. Women were excluded, at least in the Classical period, from all public life. And male citizens' frugal leisure depended on the labour of slaves, whose status was seldom questioned even by philosophers. But women and slaves were no freer in many comparable societies, at the time or later, that have never begun to rival the Greeks' contribution to human achievements in so many spheres.

Left: The 4th-century BC theatre at Epidaurus. The Greeks created the world's first true drama, for Greek plays are still performed in theatres to this day.

CHAPTER XIX

RELIGION AND MYTHOLOGY

For the Greeks, the world was filled with gods and mythical beings. Greek religion underlay all society to a degree unimaginable today in the West, but it was very different from monotheistic faiths. As polytheists, the Greeks revered many different gods. To the Olympian deities worshipped by the polis, newer gods were often added. Greek gods were anthropomorphic – having human forms, faces, virtues and foibles – even when they personified natural forces such as the sun (*helios*).

If perfect in form, most gods were far from perfect in behaviour. Homer and Hesiod, whose poems shaped Greek views of the pantheon, recounted the gods' amorous, sometimes dishonest, exploits. This divine amorality later upset philosophers but hardly worried ordinary Greeks. Religion was not a matter of dogma or revealed truth, but of the correct rites performed in public. Gods had to be honoured and placated, usually by sacrifices, or the whole polis could suffer. The gap between gods and men was not wholly unbridgeable, as the cult of the heroes (semi-divine beings) reveals. Alexander the Great was worshipped as a god even in his lifetime. Greek religion flowed into myth, but *mythos* meant not 'falsehood' but 'story' or 'tale'. Greek mythology remains among the world's richest, open to many interpretations.

Left: Three of the principal Olympian deities – Poseidon, Apollo and Artemis – from the Parthenon in Athens.

THE TWELVE OLYMPIANS

Above: The wedding of Zeus, king of the gods, to Hera, queen of heaven, guardian of marriage and an often murderously jealous wife, 470BC.

Below: Zeus and Thetis, memorably painted by the 19th-century French artist Ingres. Zeus, always highly susceptible to female charms, is being urged by the sea-nymph Thetis to help her son Achilles in the Trojan War.

The cloud-capped peak of Mt Olympus, Greece's highest mountain, was the mythical home of the Twelve Olympians. Here the deities feasted, drank and slept with each other – or with mortals abducted from below – in palaces built by Hephaestus, the blacksmith god. Although Zeus, the thunder-wielding king of the gods, was their acknowledged lord, they were a querulous brood. In this they fittingly resembled the Greeks quarrelling and fighting on earth.

The Olympians, often called sky-gods, because they roamed through the skies (although Poseidon lived in the sea) were probably introduced by Indo-European invaders who over-ran the Aegean world *c.*2000BC. Tablets in early Mycenaean Greek of *c.*1200BC seem to show that some of the Olympians, including Zeus, Poseidon and Hera, were already being worshipped in the Late Bronze Age.

However these divine newcomers seldom displaced the older deities totally. Some of the latter were *chthonic* gods, living beneath the earth. As the myths vaguely indicate, the Olympian deities soon became the unchallenged rulers of the heavens but not always of the earth. Paganism's basic tendency anyway was to incorporate other gods into the pantheon, not to exclude them.

THE 'INHERITED CONGLOMERATE'

This inclusive tendency produced what has been called the 'inherited conglomerate', with cults superimposed on each other. Such an elastic pantheon suited popular and official needs remarkably well. Gods had different titles, depending partly on their locality but chiefly on their function.

Athena, patron goddess of Athens, was called Promachos (warrior) when depicted as a warrior outside on the

GREEK AND LATIN NAMES	
Greek gods today are often known by their Latin names in Western countries, for the Romans came to equate their deities with the Greek ones. Below on the right are the Roman names for the most common Greek gods.	
Aphrodite	Venus
Ares	Mars
Artemis	Diana
Athena	Minerva
Demeter	Ceres
Dionysus	Bacchus
Eros	Cupid
Hades	Pluto
Hephaestus	Vulcan
Helios	Sol
Hera	Juno
Hermes	Mercury
Pan	Faunus
Persephone	Proserpine
Poseidon	Neptune
Zeus	Jupiter

(Apollo and Orpheus had the same names in both Latin and Greek.)

Acropolis but Parthenos (virgin) inside the Parthenon. Hera, Zeus' wife, was similarly patron goddess of Argos. All Greeks revered Zeus, one of whose many titles was Panhellenios (god of all the Greeks). Another was Horkios (oath-keeper). For the king of the gods, who was a gentleman despite his repeated lechery, always insisted on the sanctity of oaths.

SACRIFICES AND ALTARS

In large cities such as Athens most important gods had their own temples, shrines and altars, but in a small city such as Priene in Ionia there might be only two or three shrines. Individuals chose a god for their particular purpose at the time,

OTHER GODS

If the Olympians were the city's official gods, honoured in great festivals, other gods or cults offered individuals personal consolations. Among these was salvation beyond the grave, for mainstream religion promised no afterlife worth the name. The Orphics and the Eleusinian Mysteries were the chief mystery religions, the details of which remain to this day mysterious. But Greek religion was generally concerned with this life, not the next. Typifying Greek this-worldly attitudes were the *herms* – phallic fertility figures that stood outside many people's homes.

A god of another type was the rustic Pan, originally the god of Arcadian shepherds who became increasingly popular in Athens and several other large cities. Dionysus, only a minor god in Homer, grew during the 6th century BC into a major deity. He was patron of the newly emerging theatre, and his cult offered ecstatic and rare release to women. Otherwise much repressed, they could run wild on the mountainside every spring.

Such bacchic ecstasy was exceptional. But religion was usually a cause for celebration, be it solemn for a great deity such as Athena or Zeus, or ribald for a minor rustic god such as Pan or Dionysus in his less awesome aspects as the god of wine.

Left: Aphrodite, the love-goddess, emerging from her bath attended by Eros, god of desire. According to Homer, she was the daughter of Zeus, but Hesiod gave a gory picture of her origins. This is a Roman copy of the bronze by the 3rd-century BC sculptor Doidalsas of Bithynia.

Below: A Roman copy of a statue of Artemis. The virginal hunter-goddess roaming the woods was associated with wild animals and girls' transition to womanhood.

but whole cities were involved in their collective public festivals. These were as much civic as religious rites.

Of these the Panathenaea, a religious festival honouring Athena, is the most famous and became the grandest. Religious rites centred on prayers – made standing up, not kneeling – libations (offerings of wine) and sacrifices. This involved domestic animals from cockerels to bulls, but only rarely fish or game and never human beings. (Even in myth, human sacrifice was always considered an abomination by the Greeks.) Bloodless offerings – the first fruits, grains, cakes and cheese – were acceptable from poorer citizens who could not afford even a cockerel. For them, public sacrifices meant a chance to eat meat, which was a luxury for most Greeks.

The altar was the focus of worship, assuming grandiose architectural forms in rich cities like Syracuse or Pergamum. The temple itself, which housed the god's statue in holy gloom, was less important if architecturally striking. Some country shrines never had a temple.

ZEUS, HERA AND ATHENA
THE OLYMPIAN ROYAL FAMILY

Three deities made up the 'royal family' of Olympus: Zeus, king of the gods; his consort Hera, goddess of marriage; and Athena, born directly from his head, goddess of the arts, wisdom and handicrafts.

ZEUS
The archetypal skyfather, whose name echoes that of Sanskrit Dyaus-Pita and Latin Jupiter, Zeus was the supreme ruler of gods and mortals, almost omnipotent. Embodying power, wisdom and majesty, he lived on Mt Olympus, from which his thunderbolts might blast his enemies. Zeus was also the father of justice and mercy, hailed as *Xenios*, protector of strangers and ultimate guarantor of law, human and divine. His own record was, however, no model of good behaviour.

The youngest son of Cronus (Saturn) who had devoured his older children fearing that they would usurp him, Zeus was hidden by his mother Rhea on Mt Ida

Above: A copy of Pheidias' giant chryselephantine statue of Athena that stood inside the Athenian Parthenon. Goddess of wisdom, the arts and crafts, she was the patron goddess of Athens but was worshipped in many other Greek cities.

Above: Hera, patron goddess of Samos, shaking hands with Athena, a carving made in 403BC to celebrate the loyalty of the island of Samos to Athens even in her defeat. At Samos, the Heraion, the goddess' temple, was one of the greatest in the Greek world.

in Crete. There he was brought up by nymphs. Later, Zeus made his father vomit up his siblings, then deposed him, crushed the giant Titans and established his own rule. He divided the world with his brothers, Poseidon taking the ocean and Hades the underworld. Zeus married Hera, who was his sister, but he constantly seduced women, both divine and mortal, fathering many children.

ZEUS' CONQUESTS
Among his conquests were Leto, mother of Apollo and Artemis; Europa, whom he seduced in the form of a bull, producing Minos of Crete; Danae, to whom he appeared as a shower of gold; Leda,

Left: Reconstruction of the massive statue of Zeus made by Pheidias that was once housed in the Temple of Zeus at Olympia.

At one stage Zeus, in exasperation, hung his wife upside down from Mt Olympus. But usually Hera held her own, intervening to great effect against the Trojans in war after Prince Paris had snubbed her.

Hera was the mother of Ares, the irascible war-god, and Hephaestus, the ingenious blacksmith of Olympus. Widely revered as the goddess of childbirth and marriage, Hera was particularly honoured in Argos and on the island of Samos, where one of the largest of all Greek temples was built in her honour.

ATHENA

Born fully formed from Zeus' forehead, Athena Parthenos, the Maiden, was Zeus' most brilliant child. She was often shown with shield and spear as a warrior-goddess (*Promachos*) in Athens, whose patron she became after winning a contest with Poseidon. He had offered a spring, while she produced an olive tree, symbol of peace and plenty. Athena was goddess of wisdom, learning and the arts, but she inherited her father's pride. She intervened actively on the Achaean side in the Trojan War after being spurned by Paris, who preferred the erotic Aphrodite to her own chilly beauty. Often shown with the chthonic earth snake coiled beside her and an owl symbolizing wisdom, she also sported the hideous snake-haired aegis of Medusa, whom her protégé Perseus had slain.

The Athenians celebrated Athena as the personification of their city at their great Panathenaic Festival, but she was also worshipped in many other places. At Syracuse in Sicily a particularly fine Doric temple to Athena survives inside the existing cathedral.

Left: Reconstruction of the huge statue of Athena that once stood in the Parthenon.

Below: A statue of Zeus made in Pergamum in the 2nd century AD during the Roman Empire, copying a presumed Greek original.

whom he seduced as a swan, fathering Helen, whose incomparable beauty started the Trojan War; Semele, who was burnt up by Zeus revealing himself in his full glory, but whose baby Dionysus was saved; and (with Zeus in the form of an eagle) Ganymede, a beautiful Trojan princeling, who became his catamite and was cup-bearer to the gods on Olympus.

Zeus was worshipped at sites throughout Greece, especially at Olympia in the Peloponnese, where the games were held in his honour. A giant chryselephantine (gold/ivory) image of Zeus by Pheidias filled Olympia's main temple. Dodona in Epirus in the north was another major sanctuary of Zeus, famed for its oracle, which Alexander and the future emperor Augustus consulted. Some poets and playwrights spoke of Zeus in tones of almost monotheistic awe, overlooking the god's more picaresque exploits.

HERA

The sister and unwilling wife of Zeus, Hera was portrayed as enthroned beside him, the queen of Olympus, majestic rather than beautiful. She often wore a triple crown, which reveals her links with the pre-Greek Great Goddess, and was accompanied by a peacock. Her temper was famously fiery – understandably so, considering Zeus' endless love affairs. Hera did not take these calmly, constantly threatening the lives of Zeus' mistresses.

APOLLO AND ARTEMIS
THE TWINS OF DELOS

Above: Apollo, god of medicine, prophecy, science and poetry, was often portrayed naked, like most male gods, as in this rare original bronze of c.490BC.

Right: The Apollo of the Tiber *showed the god as perfectly proportioned and almost dreamily aloof. This is a marble copy of the Greek original by the Athenian sculptor Pheidias.*

Apollo and Artemis were twins, born on Delos. Their father was Zeus, their mother Leto, a titaness driven by Hera's jealousy to hide on the island. The twins proved to be very different deities.

APOLLO
Apollo is the archetypal Greek god, epitomizing reason and civilization. Called Phoebus (bright/radiant), he was later identified with the sun-god Helios. But he had many titles and attributes, including Lysios, deliverer, for he was generally a beneficent deity. Typically he was portrayed as a noble, handsome, beardless young man. His cult, very strong in Sparta, spread across the Greek world and beyond, both the Etruscans and Romans welcoming him into their pantheons. Augustus built a temple to Apollo near his palace on the Palatine in Rome.

Fed with divine nectar, Apollo when only four days old strangled (or tamed) the serpent Pytho attacking his mother. He renamed the site of the attack Delphi. It became his principal shrine, its fame surpassing even that of Delos. The serpent itself became the Pythoness priestess, uttering prophecies. For Apollo was the god of prophecy, although the answers his oracle gave were famously obscure. His own motto was "Know thyself" (*gnosi seauton*), which Socrates took to heart. Apollo's other famous injunction was "Nothing in excess", a warning few Greeks heeded. Apollo promised another oracle, the Sibyl of Cumae in Italy, immortality if she loved him. When she rejected his advances, he damned her with eternal life but not youth, for she aged horribly through the centuries.

Apollo was the god of science, medicine, music and poetry. He is often shown with his lyre or bow, being called 'far-shooting'. Every winter Apollo went north to the land of the Hyperboreans, returning with spring in a gold chariot drawn by swans or griffins. Apollo's calm, remote yet sometimes perilous divinity is illustrated by his contest with Marsyas, a satyr proud of his flute-playing who rashly competed with the god of music. Judged the loser by the muses, Marsyas was tied to a tree and flayed alive.

APOLLO'S LOVE AFFAIRS
Apollo had many, sometimes unhappy love affairs, most notably with Daphne, a nymph and daughter of the river-god

Below: Apollo fell in love with Daphne, but she escaped him by turning into a laurel tree. This dramatic sculpture is by Bernini (1598–1680).

THE NINE MUSES

Apollo was at times called Apollo Musagetes (Apollo of the Muses). Seated on Mt Parnassus above Delphi by the Castalian spring of inspiration, he was shown flanked by the muses. Daughters of Zeus and Mnemosymene, these nine goddesses of poetic inspiration had, according to Hesiod, been begotten on nine successive nights. They are with their respective arts: Calliope (epic poetry); Clio (history); Erato (lyric and love poetry); Euterpe (music); Melpomene (tragedy); Polyhymnia (heroic hymns); Terpsichore (dancing); Thalia (comedy, pastoral poetry); and Urania (astronomy).

Peneus. Apollo pursued her passionately but in vain, for she prayed to her father who turned her into a laurel tree just as the god was grasping her. Another lover was the princess Coronis. When Apollo discovered she had left him, he killed her with an arrow, repenting of his anger too late. Their son Asclepius, saved by the centaur Chiron, grew up to be a divine healer. Apollo also loved Hyacinthus, a beautiful young Spartan prince, whom he taught to throw the discus. When Hyacinthus was killed by a flying discus, the hyacinth flower first sprang from the ground where his blood fell.

ARTEMIS

Apollo's twin sister, Artemis (Diana), was a paradoxical goddess. In one avatar she was the chaste hunting-goddess of the woods carrying a bow, attended by nymphs (ever-youthful and divine) whom she swore to celibacy. When a nymph Callisto, succumbing to Zeus' advances, became pregnant, Artemis changed Callisto into a bear and let the hunt dogs savage her. The hunter Actaeon, surprising Artemis and her nymphs bathing, was transformed into a stag and killed by his own hounds. As a hunting-goddess, Artemis is portrayed as tall and slim in a short skirt and carrying a bow. She had a chariot drawn by stags in this virginal woodland guise.

But Artemis was also revered as the many-breasted fertility goddess worshipped in her great temple at Ephesus, whose cult St Paul later attacked. Here she revealed a far older Asian ancestry, as the mother-goddess and Mistress of the Animals. In Classical times she presided over women's changes, most notably their transition from virgin (*parthenos*) to married woman (*gyne*). Artemis was later identified with the moon-goddess Selene, for a crescent moon was one of her symbols. The Spartans revered her as Artemis Orthia, connected with their *agoge*, their brutal education. Boys were ritually beaten at her altar in Sparta's savage initiation rites.

POSEIDON, HERMES AND ARES

The other major Olympian gods had less in common with each other but all were larger-than-life in their power, splendour and, very often, their anger.

POSEIDON

One of Zeus' older brothers, Poseidon was swallowed by his paranoid father Cronus and then regurgitated. He fought along-side Zeus against the Titans. Subsequently allotted the sea as his realm, he ruled it with his trident, riding through the waves in a chariot drawn by *hippocampi* (sea-horses) and dolphins. Poseidon had non-marine attributes too, as the god of horses, earthquakes and springs. Like his brother, he was normally portrayed as a powerfully built, bearded older man. Like the sea, he was given to unpredictable rages. Sailors and fishermen prayed to him for a safe voyage – hence the great temple to Poseidon on Cape Sunium, visible for miles – with rich sailors sacrificing a horse. In Mycenaean times he may have been more important than Zeus, judging by tablets from Pylos, but in Classical times he was inferior to his brother.

Homer calls him *enosichthon* (earth-shaker), a potent epithet in a land as seismically active as Greece. Poseidon, who hated Odysseus for blinding his son the Cyclops Polyphemus, sealed off the port of the Phaecians with massive rockfalls for helping the wanderer. Failing to win Athens' affections in a contest with Athena, he flooded half Attica in revenge, for he was a vengeful god.

His love life was happier than many gods'. He successfully courted the Nereid (sea nymph) Amphitrite. He had seen her dancing with her sisters on Naxos when she had run away from him in alarm, but he sent dolphins to persuade her to accept him. Amphitrite then became his aquatic consort, riding beside his chariot on a dolphin or in a cockle-shell drawn by dolphins, with a retinue of other Nereids and Tritons (mermen). He rescued Amymone, a Danaid, one of the 50 daughters of King Danaeus of Argos, from a satyr pursuing her. The Isthmian Games, one of the most important in the Greek calendar, were sacred to Poseidon.

HERMES

One of the Twelve Olympians, a son of Zeus, Hermes was the eloquent messenger-god, young, graceful and swift-footed, memorably depicted by Praxiteles. Born

Above: Poseidon was Zeus' brother and a formidable god, as this bronze of the 6th century BC suggests.

Below: Poseidon, god of the sea, rides through the waves in a chariot drawn by hippocampi (sea-horses) and dolphins. From a late 2nd-century AD Roman mosaic at La Chebba, Tunisia.

Above: Hermes was the ingenious messenger-god, ferrying messages from Mt Olympus to mortals. He was also the god of shepherds, here shown as a kriophoros (carrying a ram).

to the nymph Maia in a cave in Arcadia, he was only hours old when he stole some cattle belonging to his half-brother Apollo. He managed this thanks to his divine winged sandals. By his quick wit and the timely gift of the lyre that he had invented, Hermes then saved himself from Apollo's wrath. He normally wore a broad-rimmed winged hat and carried a magic wand with two snakes entwined round it that could send people to sleep.

His ingenuity led him to be regarded as the inventor of many things, among them the alphabet, numbers and weights and measures, while his eloquence made him the patron of merchants and of thieves. As *diactoros* (messenger-god), he was constantly ferrying messages from Olympus down to earth, and he went farther down still. As *psychopompos* he led the souls of the dead down to Charon, the boatman to Hades. As the patron god of travellers, herms were set up in his honour on doors and road posts, while as *agonios* he presided over games. The Roman god Mercury took on many of his attributes.

ARES

Even his parents, Hera and Zeus, disliked Ares, the irascible red-haired god of war. The other Olympians generally shunned him too. Attended by his sons Phobos (terror) and Deimos (fear), Ares roamed the battlefields in a chariot, killing for pleasure. He was seldom victorious on the battlefield, often being outwitted by Athena or by heroes like Hercules. Nor was Ares luckier in love, with one notable exception: Aphrodite, unwillingly married to the blacksmith god Hephaestus, fell for the dashing war-god and slept with him. But their affair proved brief, for Hephaestus forged a net, which he dropped over the sleeping lovers. Ares traditionally was of Thracian origin. Despite the fact that the Greeks were often at war, and that the Areopagus, the hill facing the Acropolis in Athens, was named after him, Ares' cult was insignificant outside Thebes. But he often received sacrifices on the battlefield.

APHRODITE, EROS AND HEPHAESTUS

No two deities have been less alike than Aphrodite, the beautiful goddess of love, and Hephaestus, the lame blacksmith, yet they married each other. It did not prove a match made in heaven, nor one blessed by Eros, the god of erotic love.

APHRODITE

The goddess Aphrodite, who embodied beauty, glamour and erotic allure, had disconcertingly foul origins, according to Hesiod. She was born from the foam (*aphros*) bubbling around the severed genitals of Uranus that Cronus had thrown into the sea after castrating his father. Emerging radiantly beautiful, Aphrodite was blown ashore on a seashell by zephyrs, landing at Paphos on Cyprus, which became a centre of her worship. There she was attended by three goddesses known as the Horae ('hours'), who adorned her divine nudity with jewellery and fine clothing. But Homer thought that she was simply – and more honorably – the daughter of Zeus and the minor goddess Dione.

Whatever her genesis, Aphrodite was the most desired deity on Olympus, a source of potential strife, as Zeus soon realized. He accordingly married her off to the sober Hephaestus, who made lavish jewels for her, including a magic gold girdle. But the pleasure-loving goddess, soon bored with being the wife of the industrious blacksmith god, had an affair with Ares and later with many others, both mortal and divine.

APHRODITE'S LOVE LIFE

Among her lovers was Adonis, in Greek myth the offspring of the incestuous union of King Cinyras of Paphos with his daughter Myrrha. Aphrodite fell in love with the handsome youth, but Adonis, a passionate hunter, was killed by a wild boar. Where his blood fell to earth, anemones sprouted.

Of greater legendary importance was her affair with the Trojan prince Anchises. Aeneas was their son, the Trojan who escaped from burning Troy and who, after many vicissitudes, landed in Latium to found the precursor of Rome. Julius Caesar and his imperial heirs claimed descent from Aeneas and so from the goddess.

Aphrodite won the fatal beauty contest of the Judgement of Paris. Hera, Athena and Aphrodite paraded before the dashing Trojan prince. The first two

Above: Aphrodite, the divine embodiment of beauty and desire, here kneeling with her long hair in her hands as if she has just been bathing.

Below: Aphrodite was, according to Hesiod, born from the foam (aphros). Emerging perfectly beautiful, she was blown to land on a seashell by zephyrs, and there attended by the Horae. The myth was sublimely painted by Botticelli in c.1486.

EROS, GOD OF DESIRE

The god of desire, Eros, was the son of Hermes (or Zeus) and Aphrodite, whom he often accompanied. Shown as a boy with a bow that shot arrows of desire at his victims, Eros was thought a dangerous deity, sexual passion being considered more a sickness than a joy. Homer did not regard Eros as a proper god, but later poets such as Sappho recognized his 'bitter-sweet' powers. In contrast, Plato saw erotic desire as potentially helping to power the soul in its ascent towards the impersonal Good.

offered him respectively glory and victory but Aphrodite offered love. Paris chose love and later eloped with Helen, queen of Sparta. So started the Trojan War, in which Aphrodite provided feeble support for the Trojans, unlike Hera and Athena who vigorously helped the Greeks.

Aphrodite in origin was related to Babylonian Ishtar and Syrian Astarte, fertility goddesses, but her worship spread around the Mediterranean in Hellenized form. Aphrodite's attributes are the dove, swan and pomegranate. Besides her shrine at Paphos, she was especially worshipped at Cythera, Eryx in Sicily and at Corinth, where her devotees reputedly prostituted themselves in her temple precincts.

HEPHAESTUS

The god of fire and metal-forging, Hephaestus, could be considered the odd god out among the Olympians, being lame and ugly. His lameness came from intervening in a quarrel between his parents

Zeus and Hera, who threw him from Olympus. Falling into the sea, he was rescued by Thetis, a sea-nymph. In revenge he devised a gold throne for Hera that trapped her. Only Dionysus could persuade him to leave the sea's depths and free his mother.

In return, Hephaestus demanded the hand of Aphrodite, loveliest of goddesses. When she fell in love with Ares, the dim war-god, Hephaestus was madly jealous. He secretly forged a net of gossamer-light iron that he draped over the sleeping adulterers. They awoke trapped in it as the other Olympians gathered to laugh at them.

More usually, however, Hephaestus was kept busy at his furnace, sited beneath Mt Etna in Sicily or on Stromboli island – both active volcanoes, his Latin name being Vulcan. He built palaces for the other gods and made Achilles a magnificent shield and some armour, so memorably described by Homer, at the request of Achilles' mother Thetis. Although Hephaestus was not the most popular Olympian, the best-surviving temple in Greece is the Hephaestion on the Athenian Agora.

Left: 5th-century BC *amphora showing the god of sexual desire. Eros was often shown shooting arrows of desire at his victims. He was thought to be a more dangerous than delightful deity.*

Above: Aphrodite emerging from the sea attended by the Horae in an Ionian carving from the early 5th century BC.

Below: Hephaestus, the stocky god of fire and metal-forging.

DIONYSUS
THE TRANSGRESSIVE OLYMPIAN

Above: Krater showing
Dionysus as an effeminate
youth holding a thyrsus, a
wand tipped with a pine cone.

Below: Dionysus rescuing
Ariadne, abandoned on the
island of Naxos, lavishly
painted by Titian in 1523.

Homer hardly mentioned Dionysus,
although the god's name appears on some
Mycenaean tablets. But in the 6th
century BC the god of wine, drama and
ecstasy became one of the most important
in the Greek pantheon, playing a major
role in public festivals. Dionysus also
offered a rare release for Greek women.
One of his epithets was *eleutherios*, the
liberator, for his great invention, wine,
dissolved social bonds.

Dionysus thus stood in marked contrast
to aristocratic Homeric gods. One of his
names, Bacchus (his Roman name) was
Lydian but he was no foreigner in Greece.
In legend, Dionysus was the son of Zeus
and Semele, a Theban princess. Urged by
ever-jealous Hera, Semele rashly asked
Zeus to reveal himself in his glory.
When Zeus did so, she was incinerated by
his intolerably manifest godhead. Zeus
rescued the child she was carrying and

BACCHAE AND MAENADS
One of the most distinctive aspects of
Dionysus' cult was the wild behaviour
of his (mostly) female followers. Freed
briefly from domestic drudgery,
Greek housewives left the city for the
mountains and woods to participate in
Dionysiac *orgia* (secret rites or mysteries). What exactly happened in these
orgies remains unclear. According to
Euripides, still our best source, women
known as Bacchantes got drunk and
roamed the hills. Attacking wild animals with their bare hands, they daubed
themselves with the blood, putting on
skins torn from the still-warm beasts. In
doing so they became like Maenads,
Dionysus' ecstatically intoxicated worshippers. Any man who met them in
their divine madness might suffer the
horrifying fate of Pentheus, who was
dismembered by his own raving mother.

Dionysus was brought up by nymphs on
Mt Nysa, taught by satyrs and Maenads
how to make wine. When he had recovered from a fit of madness sent by Hera,
he set off for India in a chariot drawn by
leopards, making laws, planting vineyards,
founding cities. Reurning, he married
Ariadne, abandoned by Theseus on the
island of Naxos. Dionysus could be a
benevolent, consoling god to those who
acknowledged him. To those who did not,
he could be lethal, as Euripides demonstrates in his last play, *The Bacchae*.

DIONYSUS IN THEBES
When Dionysus returned from India to his
native Thebes, he was welcomed by the
city's people but not by its puritanical
king Pentheus. The king locked up this
effeminate-looking youth whose orgiastic
rites affronted him. But the god mocked the

Right: Pompeii fresco of Dionysus' keenest followers, the Maenads, women intoxicated by his worship and wine who took part in secret orgia, *ecstatic rites held outside the city.*

uptight king, but sacred ivy burst through the prison walls to free him. Then Pentheus, demented by Dionysus, dressed up as a woman to spy on the Bacchantes, the god's drunk followers celebrating on the mountains. Among them was the king's mother Agave. Also maddened by the god, Agave saw in her son a wild animal and tore him to shreds.

The moral of *The Bacchae* was that Dionysus, incarnating the forces of nature, was as unstoppable as the rising sap or melting snows. His attributes were the *thyrsus* (wand), ivy, snakes, panthers, tigers and leopards, beautiful but dangerous creatures. Usually portrayed beardless and long-haired, he was a transgressive deity, dissolving boundaries – between male and female, animal and human, man and god, one individual and the next – in mass intoxication. On Olympus, Dionysus always remained an outsider.

GOD OF THE THEATRE

Dionysus became the god of Greek theatre in the 6th century BC. Theatre started as stylized re-enactments of the god's life and death on stage. It developed into wide-ranging but still (usually) legend-based dramas. Encouraged by the Pisistratid rulers of Athens, this led after 500BC to the world's first true tragedy. Athens' three greatest playwrights, Aeschylus, Sophocles and Euripides, raised tragedy to unsurpassed heights.

There were two festivals of Dionysus in Athens. The rural Dionysia was held annually in December, a jovial procession behind a giant phallus, followed by theatrical competitions. The main event was the Greater Dionysia held in the city late in March. On this grand public holiday, the god's statue was carried in a procession to his temple on the southern Acropolis where bulls were sacrificed. Four days of dramatic competition followed, with tragedies, comedies and satyr plays. Each playwright presented one new work in each genre, the winner receiving a crown of ivy. As patron of Athenian drama, Dionysus must rank among humanity's most beneficial deities.

Below: This mosaic from Delos shows Dionysus riding a leopard and dressed seemingly in drag, suggesting both his wildness and his sexual ambiguity.

MYSTERY CULTS
ORPHICS AND PYTHAGOREANS

Above: Orpheus Mourning
Eurydice, *a painting by
Gustave Moreau of 1875
showing the poet lamenting the
loss of his beloved wife.*

*Below: Orpheus charming
the wild beasts with the magic
of his lyre, from a mosaic at
Tarsus. Orpheus became and
remains the archetypal poet.*

Official Greek religion lacked two things
central to many religions: a belief in the
afterlife and a body of sacred writings. In
the 6th century BC two mystery cults, the
Orphics and Pythagoreans, emerged to
half-fill these gaps with private rituals and
beliefs. The latter derived from a real
man, the former from a mythical figure,
the archetypal poet. Both preached vegetarianism and personal immortality,
influencing Platonism, Neoplatonism and
finally Christianity.

ORPHEUS
Considered by Greeks as their first poet,
Orpheus   predates   even   Homer.
Mycenaean frescoes from Pylos of
*c.*1250BC depict an Orpheus-like figure;
Pindar around 480BC called Orpheus the
"father of song". Orpheus was credited
with inventing the lyre, inspired by
Apollo, his father. His mother was the
muse of poetry Calliope. Some
Theogonies (creation myths) attributed

to him show Hesiod's influence, but the
oldest extant full poems date only from
after 400BC.

In legend Orpheus was born in Thrace,
a land of wild mysteries to Greeks. Apollo
endowed the budding poet with magical
powers so that the music he played on his
seven-stringed lyre entranced wild animals,
who gathered around him to listen. His
music could even move rocks and trees
and divert rivers. Like other divine heroes,
Orpheus fostered the arts of civilization,
including agriculture, which he had learnt
in Egypt. Although he accompanied the
Argonauts on their quest for the Golden
Fleece, his music lulling the Sirens and
refloating their ship, he generally avoided
war, unlike most heroes.

Orpheus fell in love with the nymph
Eurydice, but their joy together was
short-lived. Eurydice, chased by Aristaeus
who had tried to rape her, was bitten by
a snake and died. Overwhelmed with
grief, Orpheus descended to the underworld. There his music so charmed Hades,
king of the dead, that he was allowed
to lead Eurydice back to the living –
provided he did not look back at her until
regaining the upper world. But Orpheus
turned to look at his beloved at the last
moment, and she was doomed.

After her final death, Orpheus lost all
interest in women, preferring boys or, in
most accounts, celibacy. This so outraged
the Maenads, Dionysus' followers, that
they tore him to pieces. His dismembered
head, thrown into the River Strymon,
floated, still singing, on the seas to Lesbos,
where it later became revered as an oracle.
Orpheus himself was then reincarnated
as a swan.

THE CULT OF ORPHISM
Orphism as a cult spread around the Greek
world, but it often had a dubious reputation, probably due to its secretiveness.

(Plato in *Republic* dismissed its contemporary peddlers as spiritual quacks.) Orphics believed that the soul existed separately from the body. Of divine origin, it could best return to the godhead through ascetic practices such as celibacy and vegetarianism. Some tablets recently unearthed give very detailed instructions on how to cope with trials in the afterlife.

PYTHAGOREANISM

Pythagoras was the first man actually to be termed a 'philosopher'. He was also the founder of an esoteric mystical cult of which very little is known. (None of his writings survive.) This second aspect was the more important during and after his lifetime, for adherents to his secretive cult wielded real political power in southern Italy. Pythagoras had fled there in *c.*532BC to escape Polycrates' tyranny in Samos.

Pythagoreans believed in the magic of numbers, which, manifested in music, governed the universe. Such a concept appealed to the Greeks. Pythagoreans also believed in reincarnation, even as animals. They were vegetarians, aiming to liberate the soul from the body in progressive re-embodiments. The religious community Pythagoras founded at Croton was open to men and women, then very unusual. Among its many odd taboos were prohibitions on eating beans.

Pythagoreanism died out or merged with Platonism after the rule of the Pythagorean Archytas at Taranto in the 4th century BC. Under the Romans the cult revived in a magical form as Neopythagoreanism. Apollonius of Tyana, born *c.*4BC, was a noted Neopythagorean who reputedly visited India. His life of miracle-working resembles that of Jesus.

Above: Pythagoreans hymning the rising sun from a 19th-century painting by Russian artist F.A. Bronnikov. Adherents of Pythagoras' mystical philosophy were vegetarians who believed in reincarnation. Pythagoreans wielded great political power in southern Italy in the early 4th century BC.

Left: Orpheus, the son of Apollo, was credited with inventing the lyre and being a wonder-working ascetic from the legendary past. His followers regarded his reputed poetry, much of which actually dates from the 5th century BC, as holding cosmic secrets. From a painting of 1618 by the Italian Marcello Provenzale.

HADES AND PERSEPHONE
GODS OF THE UNDERWORLD

Above: Demeter, Persephone and Triptolemus in a relief of the 5th century BC. Triptolemus was a prince of Eleusis to whom the goddess Demeter and her daughter Persephone, the unhappy queen of the underworld, revealed their mysteries.

Right: Hades, god of the underworld, violently abducting Persephone (Proserpine), the beautiful daughter of Demeter, goddess of corn, as passionately sculpted by Bernini in 1621.

In the three-part division of the universe that Zeus made with his brothers after they helped him to power, Hades seemingly came off worst. He got only the underworld. But what his infernal realm lacked in appeal, it made up for in horrific power. Hades, the underworld which took its ruler's name, was mentioned by the living only with huge reluctance. Hades himself was also known as Pluto, meaning wealthy, because he owned the earth's precious metals. He also grew rich on the misery of the dead, as Sophocles said. But Hades was a dim passive ruler, not an actively malevolent being.

Most Greeks anticipated a colourless, bloodless afterlife in Hades, as if in a particularly dismal retirement home. While only the notoriously wicked were actually punished by being imprisoned in Tartarus in one corner, very few even among the heroes were allowed into the delightful Elysian Fields in another area. When in *The Odyssey* Odysseus visits the underworld – making a most rare return trip – the ghosts who appear can only talk to him after he has made a blood sacrifice to give them physical substance. As Achilles' shade says, he would rather "be the most wretched slave alive on earth than a prince among the dead".

THE UNDERWORLD
Hades' realm was located underground and approached via deep caves or subterranean rivers. At its entrance lay a grove of gloomy poplars, the Grove of Persephone, and gates guarded by Cerberus. With 50 heads, each dribbling black venom, Cerberus made a formidable watchdog. Only

Orpheus managed to charm the beast with his music, although Hercules overcame him by force. Once past Cerberus, the souls of the dead faced the black waters of the River Styx (or Acheron). The boatman Charon demanded an *obol* as payment. Those buried without this small coin in their mouths were left wandering forever on the desolate shores.

The Greeks were unclear about the geography of Hades, but various figures were noted there. Minos, the legendary wise king of Crete, was thought to judge the dead, but this was no Last Judgement on Christian lines, more a reckoning of accounts. Around Hades flowed the River Lethe. All who drank from its icy waters forgot their former lives.

THE ABDUCTION OF PERSEPHONE
Hades seldom left his gloomy kingdom, although he had a helmet that made him invisible when he did. His most famous

Finally Zeus sent Hermes down to make Hades release Persephone. Hades grudgingly agreed, but before she went back he offered Persephone a magic pomegranate. Eating it, she became bound to Hades and had to stay underground for four months each year. The other months she spent with Demeter, alongside whom she was worshipped. This division explained the earth's barrenness during winter.

As goddess of the underworld, Persephone's attributes were the bat, narcissus and pomegranate. She fell in love with Adonis, competing with Aphrodite. Zeus decreed Adonis should spend four months of the year with her in Hades.

Above: Hades carrying off Persephone in his chariot to become his unhappy queen in the underworld, as depicted on a red figure vase of c.400BC.

Below: Hades enthroned with his reluctant queen Persephone. Around them swirl the bloodless shades of the dead, forever doomed to this gloomy realm. The monstrous hound Cerberus, who guarded the gates of Hades' kingdom, can be seen just below the royal couple. From an amphora found at Canosa.

excursion led to the abduction of Persephone. The daughter of Zeus and Demeter, who was goddess of the harvest and vegetation, Persephone was so beautiful that everyone loved her, even the under-sexed Hades. One day, when Persephone was picking narcissi on the fields of Enna, Hades burst up out of the earth to carry her off in his chariot. Unwillingly Persephone became his consort, queen of the underworld. No one but Zeus and the all-seeing sun, Helios, had noticed her disappearance.

Broken-hearted, Demeter wandered the earth looking for her daughter until Helios revealed what had happened. Demeter became so angry that she withdrew her cornucopic gifts, inflicting endless drought and sterility on the earth.

PAN, HELIOS AND HERCULES

The Greeks worshipped many gods besides the Olympians. Some were rural gods like Pan. Others such as Helios (the sun) flourished during the Hellenistic period (322–30BC). Closest to most people, however, was the cult of heroes, often worshipped in their own villages.

PAN

Originally an Arcadian shepherds' god, Pan always retained his rustic air. He had the legs, horns and cloven hooves of a goat but a man's head and body. Arcadia was considered a backward part of Greece (which it was), but it was also increasingly seen as a pastoral 'arcadia' of nymphs and centaurs. Pan, son of Hermes and a nymph, was worshipped by shepherds in caves. In return he made their flocks fertile. He cavorted with nymphs, who were often alarmed by his hairy appearance but usually won over by his persistence. One exception was the nymph Syrinx. Praying for help to her father the river-god Ladon, she was changed into a reed. Pan, left clutching a bunch of reeds, consoled himself by making a flute from them, the origin of pan pipes. He also joined the wild retinue of Dionysus, seducing every Maenad he could.

"GREAT PAN IS DEAD!"

The Athenian messenger Philippides, returning through Arcadia after begging the Spartans for aid against Persia in 490BC, had a vision of Pan. The god promised to help Athens. The panic that hit the Persian forces in the Battle of Marathon was therefore ascribed to Pan, whom the Athenians began worshipping. (However 'panic' was originally the terror that strikes flocks in the midday heat.) Pan's name, which can mean 'all' in Greek, later led to his being worshipped as a universal deity.

His cult produced the one reported death of a pagan god. A ship sailing from Greece to Italy in the reign of the emperor Tiberius (AD14–37) heard lamentations and a voice crying: "Great Pan is dead!" However, a century later Pausanias found Pan's worship still flourishing, so reports of his death were clearly much exaggerated. Pan, quite harmless despite his appearance with horns and hooves, became for Christians the very image of the devil.

HELIOS

Although the Greeks considered Apollo the god of light, the sun had its own deity: Helios (sun). Helios was the son of the Titans Hyperion and Theca and brother of the goddesses Selene (moon) and Eos (dawn). Every morning he emerged from the eastern ocean to drive his golden chariot, pulled by dazzlingly white winged horses, across the sky, giving light to gods and men alike. At noon Helios reached his zenith and began his descent towards the west, where he appeared to plunge into the encircling Ocean. There a barque waited to carry him back east again. Zeus gave Helios the island of Rhodes and the sun-god also owned herds of oxen on the island of Thrinacia. When Odysseus' men slaughtered the 'oxen of the sun', Zeus blasted them with lightning. The Rhodians, who worshipped Helios, in the 3rd century BC raised a huge statue 30m (100ft) high to him, the Colossus of Rhodes, one of the Seven Wonders of the World. Under the Romans, Helios became generally identified with Apollo.

Above: Pan and nymphs for once portrayed in an urban context at Pompeii, although the rustic god generally shunned cities.

Left: Pan crouching on a rock, an unusual statue of c.200BC. Pan was said to haunt the woods and hills, especially in the deep stillness of the noonday sun.

HERCULES, THE SUPERHERO

Midway between gods and men were the heroes. These were men, sometimes with divine parents (often Zeus and so in effect demigods), who had won undying fame. Sometimes their exploits were recounted in epic poetry and legends across the Greek world. More usually they were famous only locally, but there they were often worshipped for centuries. In Attica alone over 300 minor heroes had shrines. Only a very few, notably the muscular superman Hercules (Heracles in Greek) were Panhellenic gods.

Fathered by Zeus on the princess Alcmene, Hercules was harassed from birth by the ever-jealous Hera, who sent two snakes to kill him in his crib. The infant hero easily strangled both, however. Still madly jealous, Hera afflicted Hercules with a fit of madness, so that he killed his wife Meagre and his family. To atone for this fearful crime, Apollo ordered Hercules to perform his renowned Twelve Labours.

These tasks, regarded as utterly impossible for any normal human being, included killing the Nemaean lion, whose skin Hercules then wore, this making him almost invincible; slaying the huge Erymanthean boar and the Hydra of Lerna, a many-headed dragon; getting rid of the Stymphalian birds, which were iron-clawed man-eaters; cleaning the Augean stables fouled by 3,000 oxen; stealing golden apples from the Hesperides, the islands of the blessed; and, lastly, descending to Hades to seize Cerberus, its monstrous watchdog. All missions accomplished, Hercules became the archetypal conquering hero.

Hercules' end, however, was truly horrific. He was persuaded to wear a tunic soaked in the blood of Nessus, a centaur he had killed for trying to rape his second wife Denaira. Hercules became tormented by the poison it contained. He finally immolated himself on a pyre, but his soul ascended to Olympus. There he was deified as a constellation, like other demigods.

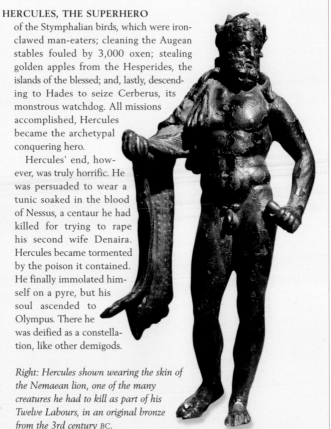

Right: Hercules shown wearing the skin of the Nemaean lion, one of the many creatures he had to kill as part of his Twelve Labours, in an original bronze from the 3rd century BC.

Left: The apotheosis (ascent to Olympus and deification) of the soul of Hercules the muscular superhero. From an 1813 engraving by Alexander de la Borde of an ancient Greek vase.

FESTIVALS, SACRIFICES, PRIESTHOOD AND ORACLES

Above: Consulting the oracle of Apollo at Delphi, the most revered of Greek oracles, from a vase of the 4th century BC.

Below: Sacrificial sheep being led up to the Acropolis for the Panathenaea, the great quadrennial festival, in part of a carving from the Parthenon.

Most Greek religion, closely connected with the political life of the polis, centred on festivals and sacrifices performed in public, except for mystery cults such as that at Eleusis. Public religion was generally a cheerful occasion. By celebrating their gods, citizens were celebrating their city and themselves, while public sacrifices gave poorer citizens a rare chance to eat meat. Gods were deemed content with sniffing the burnt skin and bones of sacrificed beasts.

THE PANATHENAIC FESTIVAL

Panhellenic festivals, such as the Isthmian or Olympian, were linked with their respective games attracting contestants from across Greece. More significantly,

ORACLES

Through oracles the gods spoke to men and through oracles men could ask the gods for advice and solace. The oldest known oracle in Greece was that to Zeus at Dodona in Epirus, mentioned by Homer and consulted 700 years later by the future emperor Augustus. The oracle of Zeus at Siwah in the Libyan desert later became famous, after being consulted by Alexander the Great. But Apollo was the chief oracular deity, with oracles at Didyma and Claros. All were eclipsed, however, by Apollo's oracle at Delphi, which emerged in the 8th century BC as the great Panhellenic oracle. After sacrificing a goat and paying a fee, the inquirer was admitted to the temple. There the Pythian priestess, crouched on a stool over a chasm, would enter a drugged trance. Her responses, transmitted by attendant priests, were usually in verse and always so ambiguous that they could never be proved wrong. Delphi's prestige lasted through the Roman era, the last pagan emperor Julian (AD361–3) consulting it with typically ambiguous results. It was suppressed in c.AD390.

each polis had its own special festivals. The Carnea was Sparta's greatest while Argos' was the Heraea, in honour of Hera, the city's tutelary goddess.

In Athens, the main festival was the Panathenaea in July. (Every four years a 'Greater Panathenea' was held.) Competitions – in music, poetry and sports – began five days before the main feast, with singing and dancing on the last night. At dawn, a sacrifice was offered to Athena and Eros, then a torch race with 40 runners carried the sacred flame to Athena's altar, high on the Acropolis.

Above: Athenians carrying vases in the great Panathenaic festival, from part of the Parthenon's renowned frieze.

At this the crowds, gathering since before dawn at the Diplyon Gate, set off in a grand procession. In front went the new *peplos* (tunic) to clothe the ancient statue of Athena Polias, the city's protector. It was carried by *arrephoroi*, four little girls chosen each year, and Athena's priestesses. More than 100 sacrificial oxen and sheep followed, with those leading them. Then came *metics* (resident foreigners), musicians, old men, military commanders and cavalry, marching in formation and carrying olive branches, and finally the rest of the city, *deme* by *deme*.

The procession moved on through the Agora and up the Acropolis, singing and chanting. In front of the little temple of Athena Nike, the best oxen were sacrificed. Only full Athenian citizens now entered the Acropolis, passing through the Propylaea to the great altar before the Erechtheum. There the little girls handed the *peplos* to the *ergastinai*, the women who had woven it, and the remaining animals were sacrificed to Athena. The ergastinai later entered the chamber of Athena Polias to change her peplos. The ceremony ended in a feast at which chosen members of each *demos* ate the sacrificed animals' meat.

This is the procession eternalized on the Parthenon carvings by Pheidias and his workshop. Here, god and heroes join idealized citizens, creating the archetypal

image of Athens at its zenith in *c.*430BC. (Many sculptures are now in the British Museum.) Every fourth year from 566BC the Greater Panathenaea was celebrated with pomp as a Panhellenic festival.

PRIESTHOOD

There was no priestly caste or profession in ancient Greece. Instead, priests and priestesses were appointed from full citizens of good repute – i.e. free from blood guilt but not usually celibate. Priesthood was generally unpaid and not full-time, except at Eleusis where the priestess lived in the sanctuary. Women played an important role, serving the goddesses. Many priesthoods were normally reserved for members of noble families. The hierophant at Eleusis was chosen from the Emoulpidaie family, for example. At Sparta, the two kings took the chief priestly roles. But for local cults, the head of a local household would officiate.

Below: The theatre at Dodona in northwestern Greece, dating from c.300BC. Here, Zeus' oracle, which claimed to be the oldest in Greece, spoke through a sacred oak tree.

Above: The Tholos, the circular sanctuary at Delphi dating from c.375BC. The Greeks regarded Delphi with awe as omphalos, the navel of the earth.

FUNERAL RITES AND BURIALS

Above: The Kerameikos, the main cemetery of Athens in the Classical Age, had superb funerary monuments. The city of the dead complemented the city of the living.

Below: An Athenian red figure vase depicting mourners. Dating from c.440BC and found in southern Italy, it was among Athens' many fine pottery exports.

The proper conduct of their funeral rites was always a matter of huge importance to the families concerned or, for those Greeks killed in battle, to comrades-in-arms or friends. Funeral rites determined what happened to the soul after death.

The souls of those left without the proper funeral rites were depicted by Homer in *The Iliad*, whose epics shaped all subsequent Greek religious beliefs, as forever roaming the desolate banks of the River Styx that flowed around Hades. Because of this, one way that a beaten Greek army conceded defeat was to ask permission from the victors to retrieve their dead for proper burial – a permission only rarely and most shockingly refused. (The Greeks also revered old age, and sons had by law to look after their ageing parents. But very old and infirm people were exceptional, although Sophocles lived to 90, Iscocrates to 94.)

In the Bronze Age, inhumation (burial) was apparently universal on both the islands and the mainland. The great grave-shafts of Mycenae were often superbly built structures, their many-corbelled chambers housing different members of a dynasty, the richer ones endowed with splendid grave goods. Such posthumous

affluence suggests that the Bronze Age Greeks' beliefs about the afterlife may have been influenced by Egypt, as their grave architecture was.

By Homer's time, cremation had replaced burial as the normal way to dispose of the dead. In Classical times this preference for cremation continued, although inhumation was common too. In later antiquity, perhaps partly due to the rise of Christianity, inhumation once more became the norm.

FUNERALS

Relatives of the dead, usually women, carried out the elaborate three-part burial rites: the *prothesis* (exhibiting or laying out of the body), anointing the corpse with oil and dressing it in clean garments. The body was then bound in waxed cloths and put in a coffin, leaving the face uncovered. A coin was placed in the corpse's mouth to pay Charon, the ferryman who transported the dead across the River Styx into the shadow-world of Hades. The body was then placed on a

Below: For long after the funeral, women mourners made regular visits to the grave with offerings of small cakes and libations.

bier in the entrance of the house for a day before the funeral. Mourning for the dead followed, being vividly depicted on vases as early as the Geometric period.

Before sunrise the next day the body was taken out of the city in the *ekphora* (burial procession), with male relatives carrying the bier. The procession normally was led by a woman holding a libation jar. Immediately behind her came the male mourners and then all the female relatives, all wearing black or dark colours.

At times professional mourners were hired to add grandeur to the procession, with flute-players following the mourners. Aristocratic funerals could become so ostentatiously opulent that sumptuary laws were passed in many democracies, including Athens, to restrict the amount of money spent on them.

After cremation, the ashes and bones were collected in a cloth and placed in an urn, or the body was placed in a grave. Very few objects were by Classical times interred with the body, unlike the burial rites of the Bronze Age. Libations of wine and oil were then poured on to the deceased and the procession returned home. Mourners had to undergo lengthy purification ceremonies, the house itself being cleansed with sea-water and hyssop, for the Greeks believed that corpses were spiritually polluting. Later, women in mourning used to make regular visits to the grave with offerings of small cakes and libations.

FUNERAL MONUMENTS

Lavish funerary monuments were erected from the sixth century BC on by richer Athenian families in private burial grounds along the roadsides near Athens, especially on the 'Street of Tombs' in the Kerameikos quarter. This area was used for such purposes for many centuries. Relief sculpture, statues and tall *stelai* crowned by capitals marked the numerous, often sculpturally impressive, graves.

Funerary monuments often had bases inscribed with epitaphs in verse commemorating the dead. A relief depicting the dead sometimes recalled aspects of the person's life, with a favourite slave or dog. Young men killed in action were often shown fighting, idealized as heroic nudes. Many of these stelai have survived to provide vivid pictures of ancient life.

Above: A fresco of a funerary banquet from the 'Tomb of the Diver' at Poseidonia (Paestum) of c.480BC. Funerals could be scenes of ostentatious consumption.

Below: Lavish funerary monuments were erected from the 6th century BC on by richer Athenians along the 'Street of Tombs' in the Kerameikos quarter. Relief sculpture, statues and tall stelai marked many graves. Funerary monuments had inscribed bases with epitaphs commemorating the dead. Young men killed in action were depicted as fighting.

CHAPTER XX

THEATRE

The Greeks produced the first tragedies and comedies still performed on stage today. Greek theatre had emerged in Athens shortly before 500BC, but its golden age lasted only 100 years. Although other dramatists wrote later, even the Greeks considered their plays relatively unimportant. Greek theatre originated in the rites of the god Dionysus, and long retained a religious aura. Highly stylized, with masked actors declaiming in verse, while a chorus chanted and danced, tragedy combined elements of opera and ballet and was normally set in a mythical past. Aristotle thought that true tragedy involved the downfall of a hero, humanly fallible, caught in a conflict with the laws of gods or men that reveal fatal character flaws. But such tragedy was never remotely mawkish. It showed adversity heroically endured or overcome, leading to resignation, even serenity. In contrast, Greek comedy offered a ribald view of the world.

Most works by the three great Athenian tragedians – Aeschylus, Sophocles and Euripides – and by Aristophanes, master of Old Comedy, are lost. Plautus and Terence, Rome's main comic playwrights, reworked Greek comedies for Roman audiences, but Roman tragedians wrote only for private readings. Roman theatre had mostly become a place of brutal thrills long before Christianity banned it. Only in the Renaissance did theatre regain its scope and humanity in the plays of Shakespeare and company. Greek theatre is the under-recognized ancestor of Western theatre, opera, musicals and even television.

Left: A red figure volute krater depicting actors preparing for a satyric drama about Dionysus and Ariadne.

PHRYNICUS AND AESCHYLUS
THE RISE OF TRAGEDY

Above: Actors on the Greek stage always wore masks, which were often very lifelike. This mask, unusual in being of gold, was perhaps made for a god's face.

Below: Tragedy was born in Athens in the 6th century BC. It reached its climax in the next 100 years with performances at the Theatre of Dionysus below the Acropolis.

Tragoidia (tragedy) originally meant 'goat-song'. It reveals Greek theatre's rustic origins in the ecstatic rites of Dionysus, who was, as god of dance, also the god of dramatic performances.

The first actors either wore goatskins or were given goats as prizes. In the mid-6th century BC, *tragoidia* came to town under the enlightened patronage of Pisistratus, Athens' tyrant or unconstitutional ruler. In 534BC Pisistratus established the Festival of the Greater Dionysia in late March, when the god's statue was carried to his temple beneath the Acropolis. There men dressed as satyrs, those mythical creatures who were half-goat half-man, danced and sang in *chorus* about the god's death and life. Soon rudimentary plays developed from these rites and drama was presented for the first time in Greece.

In 534BC the actor Thespis had made theatrical history by stepping out of the chorus and, by donning various different masks, taking different roles. Drama itself had been born. By *c.*500BC two actors were performing alongside the chorus, each one playing many parts.

PHRYNICUS c.540–c.470BC

The earliest known playwright – who also acted, like most playwrights – was Phrynicus. He won first prize for tragedy in 511BC and again for the last time in 476BC. He expanded drama by introducing female characters (played by men in masks) and by choosing serious legendary themes, not ribald subjects.

Only fragments of his plays survive. Among them are *Alcestis*, a mythical play, and two topical plays: *The Fall of Miletus* about the Persian sack of Miletus in 494BC, which proved such a painful subject for his audience (Athens had lent support to Miletus against Persia but only ineffectually) that he was fined; and his prize-winning *Phoenician Women* of 476BC. Phrynicus was most famed for his beautifully melodic verse.

AESCHYLUS c.525–456BC

Widely known as the father of Greek drama, Aeschylus was the first to write plays in trilogies, so making them suited for drama on the grandest scale. He is credited with introducing dramatic suspense, letting one character remain impressively silent, and with first employing special effects. Aeschylus himself, however, was proudest of having fought at Marathon in 490BC, according to the inscription on his tomb. (He probably also fought at Salamis.) He came from an aristocratic family, which explains this military pride, but he was no reactionary. *Eumenides*, one of his last plays, may contain radical democratic propaganda. He died in Sicily.

Aeschylus wrote 90 plays in all, winning 13 first prizes, but only seven works survive. (Some scholars doubt that

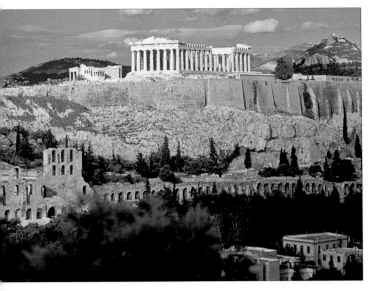

I wait for the beacon light to burn, to blaze the news that the city of Troy has fallen." Troy has indeed fallen, but King Agamemnon's final homecoming brings only disaster. Clytemnestra, his wife, has long been planning his murder. Agamemnon's murder occurs offstage – the iron rule in tragedy broken only once by Euripides. The chorus, horrified, emerges finally to cry for vengance over the royal corpse.

Revenge is the theme of the next play, *Suppliants*. Orestes, Agamemnon's son, helped by his sister Electra, revenges his father by killing his mother. For this, among the worst crimes imaginable, Orestes is pursued by the Furies (*erinnyes*), hideous supernatural hags, seeking sanctuary in Delphi. In the trilogy's last play *Eumenides* (*Kindly Ones*), Orestes finally flees to Athens. There Athena judges and acquits him. She founds a new court, the Areopagus, for homicide cases, turning the Furies into the Kindly Ones, benevolent guardian spirits. (This bit may be partly propaganda for Ephialtes' democratic reforms of 458BC.)

Aeschylus called his plays "mere crumbs from Homer's table". But deep, if unconventional, religious views underlay his bold imaginative attempt to give what were often gruesome myths a firm moral basis. With him, tragedy attained an eloquent richness and simple grandeur that rival the work of Homer.

he wrote *Prometheus Bound*.) *Persian Women*, his first surviving play of 472BC, deals with the recent Persian defeat at Salamis. The play is unusually topical, not mythological, although set in the far-off Persian capital of Susa. The theme is Xerxes' despondent return, but Aeschylus does not gloat. The viewpoint is Persian and mostly female. Xerxes is the tragic hero, belatedly realizing that his own *hubris* (excessive pride) has caused his defeat.

THE ORESTEIA TRILOGY

Aeschylus' one extant trilogy is *The Oresteia*, dealing with legends of the royal house of Atreus linked to the Trojan War. It starts with *Agamemnon*, whose majestic opening lines are spoken by a watchman: "I ask the gods for relief from these pains, as I watch from one year's end to another's, Hunched on the palace roof like a dog. I have come to know the crowds of the night stars, Bright kings glimmering in the upper regions, bringing winter and summer to the earth.

Left: Greek bust of Aeschylus. The 'father of Greek tragedy'. He was the first to write plays in trilogies, so making them suited for the highest drama.

Below: Orestes and Electra in a sculpture of the late 4th century BC. In Aeschylus' Suppliants, the central play of The Oresteia trilogy, Orestes, Agamemnon's son, helped by Electra, revenges his father by killing his mother.

SOPHOCLES
MASTER TRAGEDIAN c.496–406BC

To contemporaries, Sophocles' tragedies approached perfection, a view shared by many later commentators. Aristotle thought Sophocles' *Oedipus the Tyrant* the most sublime of tragedies, the summit of all Greek drama. Sophocles' language is clearer than Aeschylus' often heavy grandeur, lacking bombast or self-conscious grandeur but retaining an epic note. His characters are roundedly human but always noble. They certainly have their faults – there would be no tragedy otherwise – but generally they conform to Aristotle's formula that tragic characters should be "like us, only finer".

Dominating Athenian theatre for almost 50 years, Sophocles had just one real rival, Euripides. Only 11 years Sophocles' junior but very different in temperament and style, Euripides wrote romances and tragicomedies besides tragedies of shocking realism. Sophocles said: "I portray men as they ought to be, Euripides shows them as they are." Sophocles' long, productive life spanned the rise and fall of the Athenian Empire, to which he contributed in many ways.

SOPHOCLES THE MAN
Born to a wealthy family at Colonus near Athens, Sophocles was a handsome youth who led the boys' chorus in victory songs after Salamis in 480BC. Although not a politician, he had a successful public career as a Treasurer of the Athenian Empire in 442BC, and in 440BC served as *strategos* (general) with Pericles, his friend. Later in 412BC, he was one of the 400 Councillors charged with drawing up a new constitution. He was markedly pious, helping introduce the cult of the healer-god Asclepius to the city in 420BC – in effect founding a public hospital – for which he was honoured posthumously.

But Sophocles was no prig, being notorious for his love of both boys and girls. On campaign once, Pericles had to rebuke him for ogling a handsome young recruit, saying "a general must keep not only his hands clean but also his eyes". Later Sophocles joked about his declining sexual urges: "I thank old age for delivering me from a cruel master." His last public appearance in 406BC was leading the chorus on stage in mourning for Euripides, who had just died in Macedonia.

THE PROLIFIC PLAYWRIGHT
Sophocles wrote 128 plays, winning first prize in 468BC against Aeschylus, and on 23 later occasions. But only seven of his tragedies survive. His early style continued Aeschylus' grand manner; his middle style was more austere; his last richly expressive and dramatic. The cycle of legends connected with the Trojan War and the ill-starred royal house of Thebes supplies the material for much of his plays.

His *Ajax*, his first datable surviving play, was staged in 440BC. In *Antigone* the heroine ignores a ban by King Creon on burying her dead brother (who had attacked Thebes), claiming a higher moral authority than the city's. This clash of

Above: Sophocles, the most prolific and arguably greatest of the three classical tragedians, in a Roman copy of an original bust of the 4th century BC.

Below: A modern performance of Sophocles' Philoctetes in the theatre at Epidaurus. Most Greek plays were performed in such open auditoria – but never at night.

Left: Oedipus and the Sphinx
*painted by the French artist
J.A.D. Ingres (1780–1867).
The myth of Oedipus and
the Sphinx has recurrently
fascinated artists, writers and
psychoanalysts, from Sophocles
to Sigmund Freud.*

Below: Oedipus being
questioned by the man-eating
Sphinx near Thebes.
Answering the creature's
riddles correctly saved his life
but led to his doom later in
Thebes. Oedipus the Tyrant
is perhaps Sophocles' greatest
tragedy. From a vase of the
5th century BC.

principles leads finally to her death.
Electra treats the same myth as Aeschylus'
Libation Bearers but positively, for
Electra's recognition of her long-lost
brother Orestes brings her joy, not grief.
The play is more melodrama than tragedy.
In *Oedipus the Tyrant* Sophocles turned
to another Theban legend. Oedipus, king of
Thebes, married to Jocasta, vows to discover
which god's displeasure is behind the
plague ravaging the city. He consults
the Delphic oracle and finally discovers
that *he* is the cause. He has unwittingly
killed Laius, his father, the previous king,
and, married his mother. Jocasta, hearing
the news, kills herself. Oedipus, learning

the intolerable truth, stabs out his eyes
and leaves the city. "Call no man happy
until he is dead!" are the play's last lines.

A FINAL MASTERPIECE

Oedipus at Colonus, Sophocles' final masterpiece of 406BC, takes up the same
story. Oedipus, now a blind, tormented
vagrant, rejected by all for his horrendous
crimes, arrives at Colonus in Attica.
There he retells his fate to Theseus, king
of Athens. Theseus accompanies Oedipus
to his apotheosis, where, amid divine
thunder, the old king vanishes from earth.
This final play was first staged in 401BC
by his grandson, Sophocles the younger.

EURIPIDES
THE LAST TRAGEDIAN c.485–406BC

Above: Euripides, last and most controversial of the great Athenian tragedians, in a Roman copy of a Greek bust.

Below: 4th-century BC krater of Orestes with his sister Iphigenia in a scene from Iphigenia in Tauris, *a fantastical tragi-comedy written in c.412BC.*

Euripides was the last and most controversial of Athens' three dramatists. The least successful in his lifetime – he won only four first prizes – he became the most popular after his death. This is revealed by the high ratio of his plays to survive: 18 out of 90. Athenian captives, slaving in the mines at Syracuse after being defeated in 413BC, reputedly bought their freedom by reciting lines from Euripides' plays. With Euripides, Greek drama explored novel realms of tragi-comedy and romance before returning to the savage myth at its heart in *The Bacchae*. This, his final play, proved tragedy's stupendous epitaph. Aristotle called Euripides "the most tragic of poets" and he is still the most performed today.

THE DEATH OF TRAGEDY
Friedrich Nietzsche (1844–1900), the great iconoclastic philosopher and classicist, blamed "Socratic scepticism" for killing Greek drama. In his *Birth of Tragedy* of 1872, Nietzsche claimed rationalism had undermined the communal myths that alone made Greek drama possible, turning theatre from collective rite into mere entertainment. Socrates and Euripides were the villains. While Nietzsche was the first to reveal the importance of the irrational and Dionysiac in Greek life, this view is not widely held today. Euripides knew Socrates – many Athenians did – and his plays *are* more complex than his precursors'. But Athenian society was becoming more complex and Euripides' last play, *The Bacchae*, proclaims the triumph of the irrational and Dionysiac. Tragedy in fact died a natural death just before the brief eclipse of Athenian democracy. The two were intertwined.

EURIPIDES THE MAN
Born on the island of Salamis (part of the Athenian state) to a respectable family, Euripides had an excellent education. He attended the lectures of Anaxagoras, Prodicus and Protagoras, three leading Sophists (itinerant teachers). A fellow-student was Pericles, who became a friend. Euripides also came to know Socrates. Aspects of Socrates' unsettling heterodoxy perhaps colour some plays.

Euripides himself was a recluse, at least by the standards of his age, retiring to Salamis to write, allegedly in a cave. More certainly, he built up one of the first book collections worth calling a library. He took almost no part in public life, unlike other playwrights. Such behaviour, unusual at the time, was mocked by

Right: A mosaic from Pompeii of the princess Medea about to kill her children before flying off in a dragon-drawn chariot in Medea, *a tragedy that won Euripides second prize when it was premièred in 431BC.*

Aristophanes. So were his radical views that portrayed women and slaves sympathetically. He was married twice, each time unhappily, and had four children.

THE INNOVATORY PLAYWRIGHT
Euripides' earliest surviving play, *Alcestis*, won second prize in 438BC. Based on folk tale, not heroic myth, it is a piquant tragi-comedy, a form that the playwright made his own. *Medea*, a tragedy, also came second when staged in 431BC. It portrays the fiery barbarian princess Medea killing her rival and her own children before flying off in a dragon-drawn chariot.

His *Hippolytus* of 428BC innovates in depicting a tormented heroine. Queen Phaedra develops a disastrous passion for Hippolytus, her stepson sworn to celibacy (then most unusual). In beautiful verse, Hippolytus prays to Artemis: "Goddess, I bring you what I have created/A wreath picked from pure meadows/Where no shepherd ever pastures his flocks/Nor iron has touched, only the bees in spring..."

If reclusive, Euripides was not apolitical and *Trojan Women*, staged in 415BC after Athens had unprovokedly destroyed little Melos, highlights the fate of a captured city's women. It won him few friends in Athens at the time.

Electra in 413BC combined bitter pathos, romantic melodrama and farce in ways that still divide critical opinion, but Euripides' brilliant language captivated Athenian audiences. After the Syracusan disaster, he wrote fantastical semi-comedies such as *Helen* and *Iphigenia in Tauris*, plays with happy endings.

EXILE IN MACEDONIA
Euripides' last, and arguably greatest, play *The Bacchae* was written in Macedonia in 406BC, where he had gone at the invitation of its king, Archelaus. Returning to

the sources of Greek tragedy, the play is at once beautiful in its lyric power and horrifying in its revelation of the savagely irrational in human nature.

Dionysus, god of wine and often murderous ecstasy, returns to Thebes, whose uptight king Pentheus tries to arrest him – in vain, as he breaks free. Bewitched in turn by the god, Pentheus dresses in drag to spy on the Bacchantes, which include his own mother, Agave, who, seeing in her son only a wild animal, tears him to bits, brandishing his head in gory triumph. The chorus sings chillingly at the end: "Gods have many shapes/Gods bring many things to pass./What was most expected/Has not been accomplished./But the god has found his way/For what no one expected."

Below: A Roman mosaic showing Iphigenia, daughter of Agamemnon, about to be sacrificed to Artemis in a scene from Iphigenia in Tauris.

GREEK COMEDY
ARISTOPHANES AND MENANDER

Above: The Athenians' huge respect for Aristophanes, their greatest comic playwright, was shown by pairing his head with that of Sophocles, the master-tragedian, in a double bust of the 4th century BC.

Komoidia (comedy) – another Greek word for a Greek invention – emerged around the same time as tragedy. Officially introduced to Athens' Great Dionysia in 486BC, its rustic origins are far older, going back to the seasonal ribaldry of Dionysiac fertility cults. Greek comedy divides into two phases: the Old, the often savagely topical satire of the 5th century BC; and the New, the more romantic, relaxed comedy of manners that followed. Aristophanes was the greatest but not first exponent of Old Comedy, as Menander was of the New. One of the early comedians, Cratinus (*c.*484–420BC), was Aristophanes' greatest rival, winning first prize nine times, but none of his work survives.

ARISTOPHANES C.450–385BC

Little is known of Aristophanes' early life but, although born in Aegina, he was an Athenian citizen. He wrote about 40 plays of which 11 survive. His first play, *The Banqueters*, won second prize in 427BC; his last appeared in 388BC. Although winning first prize only four times, Aristophanes aimed primarily to

make his audiences laugh. This meant catering to its often conservative feelings, but his own views were probably more liberal. He appears in Plato's *Symposium* as a friend of Socrates, whom he ridiculed in his plays. Several of his plays show unusual sympathy for women.

Aristophanes' first extant play, *The Acharnanians*, won first prize in 425BC perhaps because it voiced general war-weariness. (The Peloponnesian war had lasted six years already.) *The Knights* next year also gained first prize. It attacked Cleon, a politician whom Aristophanes portrays as an unscrupulous demagogue outwitted by an even greater scoundrel, a sausage-seller. *The Clouds* of 423BC famously depicts Socrates as an intellectual charlatan running a school of spin where young men learn to make the bad cause appear good to escape their debts. The school is finally burnt down. Seemingly unperturbed by this attack, Socrates stood up to be identified among the first audience. In *The Wasps* of 422BC Aristophanes went on to lampoon the jury courts that were supposedly filled with buzzing old men.

Below: Terracotta figurines of Greek comic actors. As in tragedy, all actors in comedies wore masks and all roles were played by men.

Above: Grotesque comic figures from a 4th-century BC vase in southern Italy.

ARISTOPHANES THE PEACEMONGER

When war resumed after 415BC, Aristophanes produced *The Birds*, an escapist story about two Athenians who, disgusted by war, go off to find somewhere better. They join up with the birds to form 'Cloudcuckooland', a fantastic utopian state hung between heaven and earth. In 411BC, as the war turned catastrophically against Athens, Aristophanes wrote *Lysistrata*. Lysistrata persuades all Greek women to refuse their husbands sex until they make peace. This has a potent effect. Finally, the Spartan envoys, similarly frustrated, arrive with peace proposals. The humour, often obscene, scarcely hides the playwright's own longing for peace. It too was to be frustrated.

Women at the Themophoria contained attacks on two tragic playwrights, the effeminate Agathon and Euripides, who had reputedly offended the women of Athens. Aristophanes' last play, *Women in Parliament*, produced in 392BC, toys with ideas of feminism and communism but his satire now lacked topical bite. Much of his wit is lost in translation – the rest is often too obscene to quote – but certain passages of pure poetry are remarkably beautiful.

Right: A Greek vase painting of a scene from Lysistrata, *Aristophanes' most political comedy, where the women of Athens refuse their husbands sex unless they make peace.*

MENANDER C.342–290BC

An Athenian of good family and friend of the eccentric tyrant Demetrius of Phalerum, Menander founded the New Comedy. After Aristophanes' death, comedy had stagnated. By adding fantastical elements from Euripides, Menander developed a new escapist form. Politics was now too grim a business for laughter, so he turned to domestic sitcoms and romances. Of his 100 plays only one, from an Egyptian papyrus, survives complete: *Dyscolus* (*The Misanthrope*). Presented at the Lenaian festival in 317BC, it won Menander first prize. In the play, a bitter but wealthy recluse violently rejects the peasant girl his son wants to marry until he falls down a well and believes he is dying. The play ends with dancing and song. Such simple plots were what now appealed. Roman comedians copied Menander so closely that New Comedy survives chiefly through their works.

Above: A Pompeii fresco of Menander, chief playwright of the New Comedy, who had a huge influence on Roman comedians and modern sitcoms.

INSIDE THE GREEK THEATRE

Above: A bronze bust of
Sophocles from the 3rd
century BC. By that time,
the canon of the three great
Athenian dramatists –
Aeschylus, Sophocles and
Euripides – was already
firmly established.

Below: A mosaic of the 3rd
century AD from Antioch, the
great Hellenistic city in Syria,
showing an architecturally
imposing skene needed to
support the scenery.

In Athens, birthplace of Greek theatre, the main dramatic performances took place during the Great Dionysia festival of late March. For four days citizens flocked to see the latest plays, with ten judges, one from each Athenian tribe, allotting prizes. In the 5th century BC plays were always new productions. But judges in the 4th century BC, realizing that newer playwrights could not compete with the great trio of tragedians – Aeschylus, Sophocles, Euripides – permitted revivals and so a classical canon emerged. While entrance cost 2 obols, an unskilled worker's daily wage, a fund provided free entry for the poorest. In the 4th century BC, women citizens too were admitted to the theatre, very probably for the first time.

Performances lasted all day, spectators sitting motionless on unpadded benches in the open, even though March can be chilly in Greece. They brought refreshments

Above: A vase showing actors holding up their masks – the one prop vital for any Greek play.

with them, eating and drinking during plays – doing so especially, Aristotle noted, if the play was poor. But theatre generally was as popular as football is today, with 15,000 or more in the audience. It was also very expensive, being closer with its masks, costumes, dancers and musicians to opera or musicals than modern theatre. In classical Athens, richer citizens, *choregoi*, were chosen to fund and put on productions personally – an onerous but honourable duty.

THE THEATRE'S STRUCTURE

By 500BC the slope below the Acropolis by the Temple of Dionysus was the site of Athenian theatre, but at first there was no theatre building. The theatre's shape derived from the orchestra (circular dancing area) for the chorus, about 25m (82ft) across, with tiers of wooden benches rising in a semicircle.

At first there was little to distract the spectator's eye from the actors and chorus, but after Persia's defeat in 479BC,

the first *skene* (background building) appeared. Xerxes' luxurious tent, captured at Plataea that year, reputedly provided the first skene (the word can mean 'tent'). Some of Sophocles' plays needed scenery, but by his debut in 468BC Xerxes' tent may have been replaced by wooden structures.

Traditionally, Pericles built Athens' first stone theatre in the 430s BC, but the oldest parts excavated are now considered 4th century BC. By 330BC, Athens' theatre had a stoa 62m (200ft) long with a colonnade facing south, away from the theatre. It served to support the skene behind it on which scenery was raised and lowered. The semicircular auditorium was now built in stone and marble.

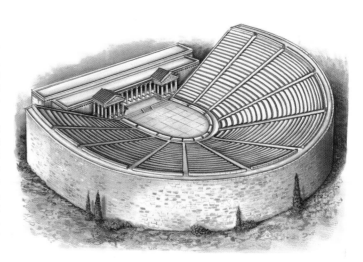

THE PERFORMERS

All actors wore masks and were male. Women were not allowed on the Greek stage. Masks were elaborate and often realistic, being made of strips of linen moulded on to the actors' faces. Some masks were horrific – one for Oedipus showed his gouged-out eyes bleeding. Aristophanes also insisted on realistic masks for the characters he was mocking, such as Socrates.

Most actors were men of good repute. A maximum of three actors played all speaking parts, making lightning-quick changes of mask and costume. Most costumes were simple, based on everyday dress. The most extravagantly dressed person on stage was the *aulos*, fluteplayer, who accompanied the chorus. This consisted of 12–15 actors who danced, recited and sang, but the importance of the chorus faded in the 5th century BC.

DEUS EX MACHINA

The Greeks used cranes to introduce gods from on high on to the stage and then to whisk them up again. Such cranes had

Right: Actors wearing comic masks representing a slave, a peasant and an idler respectively. In comedies, broad caricature was the norm.

to be strong. In Euripides' *Medea* the queen flies across stage in a chariot with the bodies of her dead children. Socrates in *The Clouds* goes up in a bucket to view the stars. The Greek phrase for this was, *theos ek mekhane* (Latin *deus ex machina*, god from the machine). A wheeled platform also displayed events that had occurred offstage, perhaps in a palace. It was moved into view bearing, for example, the corpse of the just murdered king Agamemnon. Greek theatre could be startlingly realistic – so much so that women in the audience were said to faint at times.

Above: An archetypal Greek theatre in the form that emerged after 400BC, with a stone-built auditorium exploiting any natural slope, and a solid skene or background with some grand architectural features.

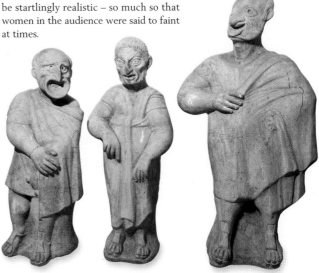

ΟΜΗΡΟΣ

ΑΝΔΡΩΝ ΗΡΩΩΝ

ΚΟΣΜΗΤΟΡΙ

ΙΛΙΑΣ   ΟΔΥΣΣΕ

ΕΙ ΘΕΟΣ ΕΣΤΙΝ ΟΜΗΡΟΣ, ΕΝ ΑΘΑΝΑΤΟΙΣΙ ΣΕΒΕΣΘΩ·

ΕΙ Δ ΑΥ ΜΗ ΘΕΟΣ ΕΣΤΙ, ΝΟΜΙΖΕΣΘΩ ΘΕΟΣ ΕΙΝΑΙ.

MODESTE TAMEN ET CIRCVMSPECTO IVDICIO DE TANTIS
VIRIS PRONVNCIANDVM, NE QVOD PLERISQVE ACCIDIT
DAMNENT QVAE NON INTELLIGVNT. AC SI NECESSE
EST IN ALTERAM ERRARE PARTEM OMNIA EORVM LEGENTIBVS
PLACERE QVAM MVLTA DISPLICERE MALVERIM.

CHAPTER XXI

LITERATURE

Greek literature begins on an unsurpassed high. Homer, the first and grandest of Greek poets, opened *The Iliad*, his epic about the Trojan War, with the "wrath of Achilles", the archetypal warrior-hero. The poem is mainly about war, heroism and killing, described with sometimes overwhelming vividness. But the violence is balanced by passages of tenderness and humour, especially on Mt Olympus, home to oddly human gods. His second great poem, *The Odyssey*, is very different, an account of Odysseus' picaresque adventures on his slow journey home from Troy. In contrast to Homer's life-affirming gusto, Hesiod, a grumbling farmer, gave the Greeks a detailed genealogy of their gods – portrayed much less glamorously – and some sound advice, mostly on farming.

Greek literature never regained Homer's epic poetic heights, but it had no need to. Instead, it branched out over the centuries into almost every other genre, from lyric poetry to travel writing. One of the finest lyric poets was a woman, Sappho, whose fragments burn with love's bitter-sweetness. Many lyric poets took a lighter note, writing most unheroic verse. Others praised the triumphs of aristocratic athletes and the deeds of tyrants. The Greeks also pioneered the development of libraries. The greatest, at Alexandria, held up to 600,000 volumes. The library's destruction symbolizes the loss of Greek literature, of which only a fraction has survived. Even this has inspired later writers from the Romans to the 20th century.

Left: The Apotheosis of Homer by J.A.D. Ingres, showing the poet honoured by other writers from Plutarch to Molière.

HOMER, THE MASTER OF EPIC
C.730BC

Above: A bust of Homer, made long after his death in c.700BC. No actual portraits exist of the first and greatest Greek poet.

Below: Phoenix, the tutor of Achilles, being served by Briseis, the slave girl – an apocryphal scene not in The Iliad. *Homer's great epic inspired many later Greek vase-painters.*

Homer's two great epics rank among the grandest tales, in prose or verse, ever written. Although he was the very first Greek poet – or at least the first we know anything about – he is astonishingly accomplished. There is nothing crude or unformed about his two great poems: *The Iliad*, about the siege of Troy (Ilium); and *The Odyssey*, about the wanderings of Odysseus on his long journey home.

Written in hexameters (lines of six metrical feet), they were learnt by heart by every Greek school boy and frequently quoted by every adult. Homer occupied the same authoritative role as the Bible and Shakespeare once did for all English-speakers. His poetic world – of gods, heroes, beautiful women and truly regal kings – had the larger-than-life glamour and danger that Hollywood has today.

Almost nothing is known of Homer himself. He probably lived in the mid-8th century BC. He may have been " a blind man living in Chios", as the poet Semonides suggested c.650BC, or he may have lived in Smyrna (modern Izmir), on the Ionian coast, for his poems are in Ionian Greek, mixed with some Aeolian phrases. At one time it was questioned whether the same man had written both poems, but today most scholars think that almost certainly one man compiled both epics. Both poems make recurrent use of Homeric epithets such as "wine-dark sea", "rosy-fingered dawn", "Mycenae rich in gold" and "grey-eyed Athena". Both are huge (15,689 and 12,110 lines respectively) and depict life as seen by the age's aristocracy.

The age was Homer's own and the generations just before him (c.900–750BC), but garbled memories of the Mycenaean world survive. Homer incorporated fragments from much earlier poems, but his genius alone created the majestic epics of compelling drive and power. He probably wrote down nothing himself, but the revival of literacy in Greece meant that others soon did. Homer's poetry was too good to be forgotten. A definitive 'Homer' was compiled in 6th-century BC Athens.

THE ILIAD

Paradoxically, *The Iliad*, the grandest war-exulting poem, brims with life, although it starts with a murderous quarrel and ends in a funeral. The "wrath of Achilles", the finest warrior in the Achaean army besieging Troy, is stirred when Agamemnon, High King of Mycenae, demands Briseis, Achilles' favourite slave girl. From their quarrel spring the events described in this, the siege's tenth year. Achilles, sulking in his tent, refuses to fight despite disastrous Greek defeats.

Finally, Achilles' friend Patroclus goes out in his place and wearing his armour, to be killed by Hector, the Trojan prince, King Priam's eldest son. Maddened by grief, Achilles takes to the field to kill Hector in turn. Triumphing, he drags the corpse behind his chariot until Priam comes to beg in person for it. Achilles, moved, gives way, knowing that he too is doomed to die soon. The poem ends: "And so the Trojans buried Hector, tamer of horses." Still to come, as Homer's audiences knew, were the death of Achilles and the bloody final sack of Troy.

Throughout, the gods frivolously intervene to help their favourites, adding to the massacres, but the poem's carnage is tempered by other scenes. Some are tender, such as that between Hector and

land of Phaecia. At one stage Odysseus descends to the underworld to question the ghosts who flit bat-like through it.

Odysseus survives his travails more by his wits than his strength – though that is immense, as he often shows. The book culminates in his return home to Ithaca after 20 years' absence, where understandably he is not recognized at first by some of his subjects. There follows his reunion with his wife Penelope, heroically faithful to him after 20 years' absence, and meeting his now grown-up son Telemachus. Then comes his bloody reckoning with the suitors. These have long been pestering Penelope to marry one of them, for the kingdom will go to whoever marries the seemingly widowed queen.

The Odyssey ends in connubial joy in the great bed that Odysseus long ago built for Penelope. Women, human and immortal, play prominent roles throughout *The Odyssey*, which is not, like *The Iliad*, so dominated by blood-mad heroes. But the fast-moving gusto and magnificence of the poem as a whole remain truly Homeric.

Left: Odysseus blinding the giant Polyphemus, a scene from Homer's second poem The Odyssey *on a 5th-century* BC *black-figure vase.*

Below: King Agamemnon's envoys arrive to demand the slave girl Briseis from Achilles, so firing the latter's implacable wrath, which forms the central theme of The Iliad. *From a 5th-century* BC *vase made by the potter Hieron.*

his wife Andromache, with their little boy screaming in fright at the sight of his tall father in armour; some are resplendent, such as the description of Helen, as breathtakingly beautiful as ever, or of Achilles' elaborate god-forged shield: "Here youths and girls...danced and danced, arm in arm...the girls wore light flowing robes, crowned with fresh garlands, the youths had golden knives swinging from silver belts." However, such peaceful interludes are rare.

THE ODYSSEY

The second great epic opens with Odysseus, the Greek leader "who excels all men in wisdom", held captive by Calypso, the "bewitching nymph", until Athena, his champion, intervenes to liberate him. Very different in theme, it relates Odysseus' wanderings around the limits of the then-known world, and his encounters with cannibalistic giants, lethal sirens, shipwrecking monsters and finally an enchanting princess in the delightful

HESIOD'S DARK GODS
C.700BC

Above: Athena's birth from the head of Zeus shown on a 6th-century BC vase. A story told in Hesiod's poem Theogony.

Below: Hesiod's Works and Days *includes the tale of Pandora, whose box released sorrow into the world. Painted by Jean Cousin, 1540.*

Hesiod is traditionally seen as Homer's opposite as a poet and man. He has been considered a hide-bound peasant who wrote gloomily about the gods' gory origins in his *Theogony*, and a farmer's almanac interspersed with moralizing in *Works and Days*. Certainly Hesiod could be pessimistic. He describes his home near Mt Helicon in Boeotia, central Greece as "a bad place in winter, sultry in summer, good at no season of the year".

Yet Hesiod was not just a parochial old grumbler. He seems to have ended life as a substantial farmer, while his father had migrated from Cyme in Ionia. However, Hesiod totally lacks Homer's aristocratic splendour and range. His gods are not all-too-human immortals living in palaces on Mt Olympus, but ominous, sometimes inchoate creatures of the night. But his view of the underside of creation, and detailed accounts of the gods' origins, exercised an influence on later Greek religion second only to Homer's. Hesiod's dark gods aptly complement Homer's sublime deities.

Hesiod claimed to have become a poet after an encounter on Mt Helicon with the Muses, who breathed divine inspiration into him. He then went on to win a tripod in a poetry competition on Euboea. Like Homer, Hesiod wrote in hexameters but his have been called "hobnailed" by comparison.

Hesiod probably lived around 700BC but scholars remain divided as to whether one man wrote both major poems. Stories that he met and competed with Homer can be discounted, but he too wrote in Ionian if with some Boeotian phrases.

EVA PRIMA PANDORA

THEOGONY

Hesiod's first poem, *Theogony*, on the genealogy of the gods, runs to 1,022 lines. After invoking the Muses, he starts by describing "Chaos" – meaning empty space, not disorder – from which sprang night and Gaia, earth. Uranus (Heaven) emerges next – there is no creator god – and his coupling with Gaia produces more gods, including Cronus and inchoate figures called simply Night and Dreams. Encouraged by his mother Gaia, Cronus castrates his father and devours his own children to avert a prophecy that they will overthrow him. But his wife Rhea tricks him by giving him a stone to swallow instead of Zeus, their youngest son. Zeus, after growing up in Crete, forces his father to disgorge his siblings. The divine brothers then join in war against the Titans and establish the Olympian hierarchy.

After listing at a length that soon becomes tedious the other gods and demigods – including Athena, born directly from Zeus' head, and Aphrodite, the love-goddess born from the foam of Uranus' severed genitals – Hesiod ends with another invocation of the Muses. Zeus is the real hero of the poem, whose omniscience, power and justice are repeatedly stressed. Babylonian and Akkadian creation myths possibly influenced Hesiod's cosmogony.

WORKS AND DAYS

The "works" of the title of this poem are the operations of the farmer's working year; the "days" are the astrologically lucky or unlucky days of the lunar month. The poem starts by berating his feckless and greedy brother Perses, who wants more than his due share of their inherited land. It continues by describing the descent of the world from the first Age of Gold under Cronus, when men lived peacefully, to the current Age of Iron, marked by endless strife. This explains why human life is now so cursedly hard. It must, however, be born with dignity. Above all, men must work hard all their lives.

AESOP

Aesop was a semi-legendary writer who probably lived around 600BC. Traditionally, he was originally a slave who was freed. He is credited with writing moralizing *Fables* often concerning animals. Among the best-known are *The Fox and the Grapes* (about sour grapes), *The Tortoise and the Hare* and *The Boy Who Cried Wolf*. None of his works survives in the original Greek. However, the Greek-born writer Phaedrus, writing in Rome in the early 1st century AD, reworked some into biting satires in Latin that incurred the emperor Tiberius' anger. Five of his books have survived. La Fontaine, the 17th-century French writer, was inspired by these to write *Aesop's Fables* as they are known today.

Below: Aesop's fable of the fox and grapes from a French 15th-century woodcut. Aesop's fables, once thought of minor merit, remain very popular.

Hesiod continues with farming advice that can be both sensible and poetic. "When the Pleiades, Atlas' daughters, start to rise/Begin your harvest; plough when they go down." He discourages Perses from trying to better his lot by trade, emphasizing the perils of the seas and the shortness of the sailing season – which amounts to only 50 days in his not very well informed view.

Among such brotherly admonitions come surprisingly beautiful versions of the tale of the Hawk and the Nightingale and Pandora's Box. The poem ends with a list of auspicious or lucky days.

OTHER POEMS

Some poems once attributed to Hesiod are now attributed to other writers, probably from the 6th century BC. *The Catalogue of Women* continues the *Theogony* in five books, with extensive genealogies with frequent notes, some of them on papyrus fragments recently found in Egypt. *The Shield* is a short narrative poem about Hercules' fight with Cycnus, so-called because of the detailed description of Hercules' shield with which the book starts.

Below: Cronos Devouring his Children, *one of Hesiod's darkest myths, painted by Francisco de Goya (1746–1828).*

DRINK, LOVE AND WAR
LYRIC POETS c.650–550 BC

Above: A girl with a writing tablet and stylus from a mural in Pompeii, once thought to be a portrait of Sappho.

Below: Sappho and Alcaeus, the two great poets of Lesbos, shown on a 5th-century vase.

Tiring of heroic epics, poets of later generations took a very different view of life as the Greek world revived culturally and economically. This led to new types of poetry in the Ionian or Aeolian cities and islands of the east Aegean, then probably the most developed parts of Greece. The poetry written about life in these cities was humorous, passionate and personal, very seldom heroic. Only a few of these lyric poems – intended to be sung to a lyre at *symposia* (dinner parties) – have survived, but these give us glimpses of an aristocratic, debonair yet passionate life.

ARCHILOCHUS (c.680–630 BC)

The illegitimate, penniless son of a noble-man of Paros and a slave girl, Archilochus had to leave home young. He became a mercenary, finally dying in battle against the Naxians. But his was hardly a tragic life, as his poems attest. "Some lucky Thracian has my fine shield./ I had to flee and dropped it in a wood./But I got right away, thank God!/Damn the shield, I'll find another just as good." Such insou-ciance, unthinkable for a Homeric hero (or a Spartan), typified the carefree aspect of the new age. Writing in a vernacular version of the Ionic dialect, he turned a keenly satirical eye on the aristocrat-ruled world. Unlike earlier poets, he freely expressed his own views, often using metaphors drawn from folklore. His sometimes savage but always original genius was recognized in antiquity.

SAPPHO (BORN c.630 BC)

The first – and only – Greek woman poet of note, Sappho was born into the aristo-cracy of Mytilene on the island of Lesbos. Exiled to Sicily as the result of a coup, she returned to establish not so much a school as a circle for young girls, which she dominated by her personality, antic-ipating Socrates' circle later in Athens. For some girls she wrote poems about the love that she may well have felt for them, giving rise to the (modern) term Lesbian.

All Sappho's poems, which survive only in the briefest fragments, concern erotic passion, although Sappho was married and had a daughter herself. Some of her poems celebrate her girls' forth-coming marriages. (The tale of Sappho leaping to her death from a cliff after being rejected by Phaeon, a male lover, is a later fiction.) Sappho wrote in the relatively obscure Aeolic dialect, not the canonical Ionic, which may explain her subsequent neglect by Hellenistic

and Byzantine scholars. (Some further fragments were discovered on papyrus scrolls in Egypt in the 1920s. Papyrus is well preserved in the desert sands.)

Whatever their subject, the intensity of Sappho's feelings fires her imagination to a white-hot passion never since surpassed. She wrote with deceptive simplicity, often in 4-line verses, couplets or even single lines. About one girl she wrote: "She outshines all the women of Lydia/As sometimes the rosy-fingered moon outshines all the stars, When its light spreads over the salt sea/ And over the many flowered fields, where the roses are blooming." Or, writing even more simply, perhaps about her own romantic loss: "The Pleiades are set/And here I Sappho lie alone."

Such poetry, despite so much being lost in translation, often has something of the heart-piercing beauty of Mozart's most lyrical arias. Catullus in the 1st century BC wrote poems that are almost exact Latin renderings of Sappho. Through his verse, which has mostly survived, Sappho came to influence the mainstream of European love poetry.

ALCAEUS (BORN C.620BC)

Another aristocratic poet of Mytilene who wrote in the Aeolic dialect was Alcaeus. A friend or acquaintance of Sappho, he fought as a young man for his city against Athens at Sigeum. He then became actively involved in factional politics, first as an ally and then as an enemy of Pittacus, the reforming "tyrant" who finally exiled Alcaeus and other nobles. Alcaeus visited Egypt and probably became a mercenary in the Lydian army. He was finally allowed home by 580BC, but was never reconciled to the new regime – for snobbish reasons as much as anything, it seems.

Alcaeus lived, fought and drank hard. He seems to have been better at hating than loving. This is reflected in his scathing political poetry. He wrote love poems – not just about his own affairs, which were mostly with boys, but also as the dramatic monologues of a lovesick girl – and cheerful drinking songs such as: "We should not abandon our hearts to despair/ For we gain nothing by groaning./ Bycchis, the best cure for us now/ Is to pour out the wine and start drinking".

Left: Sappho playing her lyre, theatrically imagined by the artist Léopold Burthe in 1849. Lyric poets are so-called because they accompanied their recitals on the lyre.

Below: Much lyric poetry celebrated symposia, here recalled on the funerary stele of Menelaus from Demetrias in Macedonia.

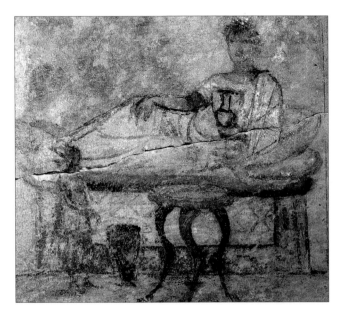

TYRANTS AND ATHLETES
THE LATER LYRIC POETS C.570–C.440BC

Above: Pindar of Thebes (518–438BC), the greatest poet of his age, in a Roman copy of a bronze Greek original.

Below: Anacreon (with Dionysus and Eros), as pictured by Jean-Léon Gérôme in the 19th century. A versatile poet, Anacreon wrote for Sicilian tyrants as well as Athenian democrats.

The advance of Persian power to the Aegean in the 540s BC meant the loss of Ionian liberty, but it did not harm lyric poets, who proved very adaptable. Most were happy to write for (Greek) tyrants and democracies. Some, like Pindar, preferred aristocratic oligarchies.

ANACREON C.570–485BC
Typical of the adaptable poet was Anacreon. Born on the small island of Teos, he followed other Teans who migrated to Abdera in the Hellespont (Dardanelles) rather than accept Persian rule. Soon much in demand as a poet and entertainer, Anacreon did accept an invitation from Polycrates, tyrant of Samos, in 532BC. Tyrant and poet became close friends and Anacreon wrote songs celebrating love and wine. After Polycrates' capture by the Persians in 522BC, the poet moved to the court of the Pisistratid tyrants in Athens. The fall of the Pisistratids in 510BC only briefly disconcerted Anacreon. He was soon back in

Athens praising the new democracy, which returned his regard. A statue to him was even erected on the Acropolis. His poetry is written in simple yet vigorous Ionic that conceals a detached ironic wit. It appealed to Romans like Horace.

SIMONIDES 556–468BC AND BACCHYLIDES 516–450BC
Poetry is seldom a family business, but Simonides managed to gain an entrée at court in Syracuse for his nephew Bacchylides. Born on Ceos, Simonides gained the patronage of Hipparchus the Pisistratid ruler of Athens. After the fall of the Pisistratids, he moved to Thessaly. He then returned to Athens to beat Aeschylus in the contest to write an epitaph on the dead after the Battle of Marathon in 490BC. A friend of Themistocles, the leading democratic politician, Simonides left Athens in 476BC as Themistocles' political power waned.

In Sicily he resolved the conflict between Hieron I, tyrant of Syracuse, and Theron, the ruler of Acragas, as a result becoming effectively Syracuse's court poet. Simonides was famed for his epigrams, especially his epitaphs, and also wrote hymns, elegies and drinking-songs. His style, always graceful, gained in power as he grew older.

Bacchylides, also a native of Ceos, first wrote poems in praise of local athletes but soon connections with Thessaly led to successes there and later on the wealthy island of Aegina. Gaining a post in Syracuse through his uncle, Bacchylides wrote odes praising Hieron's sporting victories at Olympia in 468BC.

After the death of Hieron in 467BC, Bacchylides found no other court post and had to return to Cos, where he praised his countrymen's athletic successes. His style was often compared to that of a nightingale.

PINDAR 518–438BC

Arguably the greatest poet of his age and the first notable Boeotian poet since Hesiod, Pindar came from an aristocratic family. Despite being educated in Athens and later travelling widely, Pindar remained essentially Boeotian – narrowly conservative – in outlook, devoted to his class and also to tyrants. Above all, he praised aristocrats' athletic victories, a field where they long remained supreme.

His first odes praised the Aleuad nobles of Thessaly. Soon commissions from Aegina and Sicily spread his fame, but, like many Boeotians, he faced an agonizing dilemma during the Persian invasion of 480–479BC about whether to "medize" i.e. support the Persians. How Pindar himself behaved is unclear. After the Persian defeat in 479BC, his Sicilian connections led to a welcome opening at Hieron's court in Syracuse and so to useful commissions from Syracuse and other tyrants. But Simonides and nephew were too well established at court to be dislodged, as Pindar sourly noted.

Back in Greece, Pindar's reputation as master of odes and hymns continued to grow, both in mainland cities such as Athens and Corinth and in the islands. Yet towards the end of his life, with the seemingly unstoppable rise of Athenian power and of democracy, Pindar felt increasingly out of tune with the age.

About 45 of Pindar's poems survive, nearly all odes about sporting victors. Four books of *Epinician Odes* (so-called because they were sung celebrating victories in the Games) are extant. Greatest of these is his Fourth Pythian Ode of 462BC. Very long (12 pages in translation), it contains some of his grandest poetry, full of mythical resonance and invocations, with complex, varied metres. His style has been called eagle-like, but he has also been called a scholars' poet.

Right: Many Greek poets celebrated athletes' victories in the Panhellenic games, of which the greatest were those held quadrennially at Olympia.

Whatever the judgement, Pindar had a high opinion of his calling: "Muse you have raised me up/To be your chosen messenger of fine words/To the fine dancing-places of Hellas."

Above: A fine dekadrachm *(ten-drachmae coin) of Syracuse, celebrating the defeat of Carthage in 480BC, which heralded a long peace.*

LATER POETS AND OTHER WRITERS C.310–80BC

Above: Roman fresco of Jason with the Golden Fleece and Medea, the subject of Apollonius' 6,000-line epic.

Below: Theocritus created the pastoral, poems about arcadian idylls in the country. His dreamy eroticism inspired Renaissance artists like Giorgione who painted Concert Champêtre *(Pastoral Concert). Titian probably completed this work after Giorgione died in 1510.*

The great literary achievements of Athens in the 5th century BC were in drama and history, with lyric poetry for a time becoming less popular. After Alexander the Great's conquests (334–323BC) overturned the Greek world, new audiences emerged for poetry in the new cities. Their increasingly urbane citizens enjoyed witty sophisticated poems, along with romantic pastoral verse tinged with nostalgia for country life. Poets were now often also scholars in royal libraries, sometimes feuding bitterly with one other. All now wrote in the *koine*, the common Greek dialect based on Attic (Ionian), the lingua franca of this wide new world.

THEOCRITUS C.310–250BC

Born in Syracuse, Theocritus' poetry was rooted in his early memories of Sicilian rustic life. The idyllic – in truth idealized – life of Sicilian shepherds figures so prominently in his verse that it is called 'pastoral'. Theocritus wrote poems to Hieron II, the new ruler of Syracuse, in 275BC but by 272BC he was writing a

panegyric praising Ptolemy II king of Egypt. For the next few years Theocritus lived at the glittering Ptolemaic court at Alexandria, but he finally settled on the island of Cos. There he wrote his famous pastoral poems. These are set in imaginary landscapes but contain accurate observations of plant life, especially that of the eastern Aegean. Theocritus' wit spices his nostalgia in a way that was very appealing at the time and proved hugely influential on later poets from Virgil in the 1st century BC to Shakespeare and Milton in more recent times.

APOLLONIUS RHODIUS C.300–247BC

Despite his name, Apollonius was a native of Alexandria, the booming metropolis. He became at one stage head of its famous Library. He had an (almost equally) famous blazing row with Callimachus, a rival poet who insisted that epic poetry was obsolete in the new era. To prove him wrong, Apollonius wrote a huge (6,000 line) epic, *Argonautica*, about Jason and the Argonauts. Seen in its totality, this is an over-detailed antiquarian failure, but it has fascinating and beautiful passages. Apollonius was especially good at portraying romantic love from a woman's viewpoint – a rarity among Greeks, which influenced the Latin poet Ovid's love poetry nearly 300 years later.

CALLIMACHUS C.305–240BC

Born in Cyrene (today in Libya, then part of the Ptolemaic Empire), Callimachus became a leading figure among the intellectual elite of Alexandria in its heyday. Like many other literary men, he was a polymath. Callimachus worked in the great Library – although he was twice passed over for the post of Head Librarian – and compiled its first huge catalogue in

120 books. His other prose works include a chronology of the great dramatists, a book on the Seven Wonders of the World and many books on topics ranging from the winds to nymphs, birds and rivers. He reputedly wrote 800 slim volumes of poetry, but only fragments survive. However, as he aimed at – and often achieved – perfection on a very small scale (hence his quarrel with Apollonius), this has not harmed his reputation. His elegant wit emerges in the fragment *The Lock of Berenice* praising the Ptolemaic queen Berenice. Judging by most of his love poems, though, Callimachus was mainly attracted to boys.

PAUSANIAS C.AD120–180

Living through the Roman Empire's peaceful zenith in the 2nd century AD, Pausanias was probably the first man who can be called a travel writer. But he was far more than a mere tourist guide, being encyclopaedically knowledgeable. Born in Lydia (western Turkey), he travelled around Asia Minor, Syria, Palestine, Egypt and Greece. His ten books about Greece have survived and kept him famous.

Pausanias wrote primarily for wealthy philhellenic Romans visiting what were already ancient cities. His books combine archaeology, history, art, religion, architecture and folklore. He not only wrote lengthily and intelligently about all the major sites – Delphi, Athens, Sparta, Olympia – but also sought out, and was genuinely interested in, the most obscure places and the rituals and legends connected with them.

Although he shows little interest in natural beauty, many sites give him an excuse for a historical digression. For example, in mentioning the statues of the

Ptolemies and Lysimachus in Athens, he launches into a detailed account of the wars of the Successors, the dynasts who carved out rival kingdoms at Alexander's death. His viewpoint is that of a patriotic Greek although he admired the emperor Hadrian. His books have proved invaluable for later historians and can be seen as forerunners of modern guide books.

Above: The palaestra *(wrestling-school) of Olympia, one of the many sites vividly described by Pausanias.*

Right: The statue of Zeus at Olympia, made by Pheidias in C.428BC, *was so huge that, even though he was seated, the god's head brushed the temple roof. Long destroyed, it is known to us chiefly through writers like Pausanias. This 18th-century engraving by J.A. Deisenbach is wildly imaginative.*

LITERACY, LIBRARIES, SCHOLARS AND SCROLLS

A	B	Γ	Δ
Alpha	Beta	Gamma	Delta

E	Z	H	Θ
Epsilon	Zeta	Eta	Theta

I	K	Λ	M
Iota	Kappa	Lambda	Mu

N	Ξ	O	Π
Nu	Xi	Omicron	Pi

P	Σ	T	Y
Rho	Sigma	Tau	Upsilon

Φ	X	Ψ	Ω
Phi	Chi	Psi	Omega

Above: The Greek alphabet from which our present Roman (Latin) alphabet derives. The Greek alphabet had fewer letters than ours.

Below: An ostrakon *(pottery fragment) with the name of Aristides, the Athenian statesman ostracized in 482BC. Pottery supplied a cheap writing material for such actions.*

Around 700BC the Greeks adopted the Phoenician alphabet, adding vowel symbols to the consonant signs adequate for Phoenician. In doing so they created a simple, flexible way of writing that was to help make mass literacy possible. Our own Roman (or Latin) alphabet derives from the Greeks'. Inscriptions in Greek are widespread on monuments – on tombs, temples, walls, gateways – and as graffiti, scratched even on the statues of Abu Simbel in Egypt by Greek mercenaries. By 500BC most Greeks, at least in the major cities, were half-literate i.e. they could read if not always write.

This limitation is revealed by the story about the Athenian politician Aristides. Facing ostracism (temporary exile) by popular vote in 482BC, he was stopped by a citizen and asked to inscribe his own name on an *ostrakon* (the pottery shard used for such votes). Aristides did, so meriting his nickname the Just but also indicating that citizens could generally read if not write names. The material used shows something else: the lack of a cheap and convenient writing material. Paper, today so common, was unknown.

PAPYRUS AND PARCHMENT
In antiquity the main writing material was papyrus, which comes from the papyrus plant – our word paper derives from it – grown almost exclusively along the Nile

Above: An imaginary painting of the great Library at Alexandria in one of the frequent fires that threatened it. It survived, however, until the end of the Graeco-Roman world.

in Egypt. A tiny amount was also grown in Syracuse. Papyrus, a royal monopoly in Egypt, was expensive, but provided a fine writing material when made into scrolls.

Text was written in vertical columns, which the reader slowly unwound from one roll and wound on to another. As many texts were 8m (25ft) long, this made reading a cumbersome business, requiring two hands. Also, papyrus was fragile. For daily use, other forms of writing material were used, from *ostraka* (discarded after use) to wooden boards rubbed clean of chalked messages.

In the 2nd century BC the kings of Pergamum, great rivals of the Ptolemies of Egypt, pioneered the development of parchment, made from treated animal hides. Parchment (vellum) was tougher than papyrus, though less easy to write on. When parchment sheets began being sewn together into a *codex* (bound book)

Right: A Ptolemaic schoolboy's workbook from Egypt, made of wood and showing Greek writing. Even in the land where papyrus grew, it was too expensive for schoolboys to use.

in the 3rd century AD, parchment slowly displaced papyrus. By the 6th century AD this process was almost complete.

LIBRARIES AND LIBRARIANS

Euripides, the Athenian dramatist, built up the first library in the 5th century BC. However Aristotle, the encyclopaedic philosopher, started the first proper library in the 4th century for his school, the Lyceum, in Athens. After his death in 322BC, scholarly studies moved to the richer city of Alexandria, where Ptolemy I founded the great Library in c.295BC. Attached to the Museum, which was more university than museum, the Library became the greatest in the ancient world, holding up to 600,000 scrolls. Scrolls were wrapped round sticks, identified with tags and stacked like loose rolls of wallpaper in numbered cupboards, boxes and barrels. The index alone came to 120 scrolls. Outside this "chicken coop of the muses", were cool, open colonnades beneath which scholars could work.

Many great literary or scientific men became head librarians: Apollonius of Rhodes, Eratosthenes and Aristarchus of Samothrace. The Library was concerned as much with science as the humanities.

Only slightly damaged in fighting between Julius Caesar's troops and the Alexandrians in 47BC, the Library thrived under the Romans. But the emperor Aurelian's brutal reconquest of Egypt in AD275 may have started its decline, which was accelerated by Christian attacks on Hellenic learning. By the time the Arabs captured the city in the 7th century AD, the Library had almost ceased to function.

Below: A terracotta figure found in Thebes dating from c.500BC of a man writing. By that time literacy was common among Greeks, at least in the major cities.

READING WITH MOVING LIPS?

It was once thought that the Greeks read only with their lips moving, suggesting they read with some difficulty. More recently, scholars, on re-examining ancient literary sources, have realized that many Greeks could indeed read silently. In Euripides' play *Hippolytus*, Theseus, confronted with his wife's corpse, silently reads the letter containing Phaedra's false accusation against his son Hippolytus. Then he bursts out saying that "the letter shrieks, its howls horror insufferable...

a voice speaks from the letter." Plutarch related that Alexander was silently reading a confidential letter from his mother when Hephaestion "quietly put his head beside Alexander's and read the letter with him. Alexander could not bear to stop him but took off his ring and placed the seal on Hephaestion's lips", reminding his closest friend that such letters are indeed confidential. All of which suggests that at least some of the Greeks could read without moving their lips.

CHAPTER XXII

PHILOSOPHY AND SCIENCE

Philosophy 'begins in wonder' – and it began with the Greeks. The Greeks were the first to think systematically, almost free of constraints, about the universe and humanity's place in it. Ethics, logic, metaphysics, philosophy itself – Greek words for concepts the Greeks originated. Western philosophy stands so firmly on Greek foundations that to call it "footnotes to Plato" (as the 20th-century philosopher A.N. Whitehead did) seems only an exaggeration. The freedom that Greek city-states gave their intellectually more daring citizens was not unlimited. There was the odd backlash against free thought, most famously in Athens with Socrates, but there was far more intellectual freedom in a polis than in any earlier (and most later) states. This freedom continued for almost 1,000 years even under Roman rule, although after 320BC many philosophers ignored politics, seeking instead inner happiness and freedom (*eudaimonia*).

Philosophical enlightenment affected the physical sciences. Early philosophers were often also scientists. Astronomy, biology, geography, maths and zoology are all Greek words. Although Socrates concentrated mostly on ethics, and Plato spurned the natural world, Aristotle was hugely knowledgeable about the natural world *and* human affairs. There were significant advances also in technology, too often under-rated. Medicine under the Greeks first became a field for rational inquiry, reaching levels unsurpassed for 1,500 years.

Left: Raphael's vision of The School of Athens *of 1510 shows Plato and Aristotle flanked by other philosophers.*

THE IONIANS: THE WORLD'S FIRST PHILOSOPHERS 600–500BC

Above: Thales (c.625–547BC), the first known philosopher and natural scientist, came from the great Ionian city of Miletus. He predicted the solar eclipse of 585BC.

Philosophy began in the small cities of Ionia on the west coast of Asia Minor around 600BC. There some men first had the freedom and audacity to ask fundamental questions about the universe. Their answers, if sometimes inaccurate, were never absurd. However most of our knowledge of them comes only through Aristotle, writing 200 years later.

THALES C.625–547BC

A native of Miletus, then the richest Greek city, Thales is considered the founder of natural philosophy. He foretold the solar eclipse of 28 May 585BC, which stopped a battle between the Lydians and Medes, both being superstitiously terrified. Such accuracy – about its exact place more than time – suggests that Thales knew of astronomy in Babylon, whose records went back centuries.

Traditionally Thales also visited Egypt to learn geometry from its priests, but his speculations about the nature of things owed nothing to priestly precedent. Observing that at low temperature water becomes like rock and at high temperature vaporizes, that land is surrounded by water and water falls from the sky, Thales deduced that water is the primary principle of everything.

He probably also regarded the Earth as spherical, a truly radical idea. Crucially, he reached his conclusions not through divine revelation or scripture but by observing and *thinking*. Although poor, Thales showed commercial acumen once by cornering the market in olive presses before a bumper harvest he had foreseen. He also urged the disparate Ionian cities to unite against the Asian empires rising in the east – in vain. He was later revered as one of the Seven Sages of Greece.

ANAXIMANDER C.610–C.540BC

A pupil of Thales, also from Miletus, Anaximander rejected his master's belief in the primacy of water. He thought instead that this world, and countless other worlds beyond our knowledge, came into being out of the *apeiron* – infinity, the basis of existence. From this have split off 'innumerable worlds'. He was the pioneer of geometrical (if mistaken) astronomy, suggesting the Earth was a huge cylinder, floating unsupported in space, equidistant from all else, and that the planets (counting the Sun and Moon as such) moved in orbits. Anaximander is also credited with making the first map and *gnomon* (sundial), of huge importance

Left: A Roman mosaic of Anaximander, the second Milesian philosopher, is credited with making the first gnomon (sundial). He also suggested theories about the evolution of animals from the sea after studying fossils.

in an age without clocks, and speculating about the evolution of living creatures from the sea after studying fossils.

His cosmological views were so radical that they were rejected by his own pupil Anaximenes, who thought the Earth was flat and the stars were fiery leaves. The cosmos consisted of air of differing densities. Anaximenes' views at the time proved more acceptable than his master's.

PYTHAGORAS C.570–C.497BC
The first man actually to be called a philosopher (lover of wisdom), Pythagoras was a philosopher/mathematician, conjuror and mystic. Born on the island of Samos, he left to escape the rule of its tyrant Polycrates. Settling at Croton in southern Italy in c.530BC, he founded a secretive community where his disciples long remained. Said to wear white robes and a gold coronet, Pythagoras declaimed (supposed) poems by Orpheus. Like the Orphics, he believed in an immortal soul that might be reincarnated as an animal. This made him a vegetarian.

Pythagoras' great mathematical discovery was that the sum of the squares on the two shorter sides of a right-angled triangle equals the sum of the square on the remaining side, the hypotenuse. He also discovered the harmony of octaves and had a mystical belief in Number, which he saw ruling the universe. Astronomy and harmony were, he said, sisters. Bertrand Russell considered him "one of the most important men that ever lived", for in him the perennial conflict in Greek thought between the rational and the mystical first surfaces. Although he left no writings, Pythagoras greatly inspired Plato.

XENOPHANES OF COLOPHON
C.570–C.480BC
Xenophanes quit his small native city after it fell to the Persians in 545BC to spend life in Sicily. He attacked Homer for his frivolous and immoral depictions of the Olympian gods, and poets for their anthropomorphic concepts of deities in general. "Thracians depict gods as

Left: Bust of Pythagoras of Samos, the first man to be called a 'philosopher', united mysticism and maths in an esoteric mixture. Reputedly he believed in reincarnation, but no writings by him survive. He and his followers settled in southern Italy.

Thracians, Africans as Africans. If horses or cattle had hands and could draw, they would create gods like horses or cattle," he claimed, a startlingly novel viewpoint that found few followers at the time. As a natural philosopher he oddly assumed that the earth was flat and the sky extended indefinitely upward. From this he concluded that each day a totally new sun rose in the east, expiring at sunset.

Below: Thales believed that the fundamental principle of the whole cosmos was water – a reasonable belief for a Greek living by the sea.

PRE-SOCRATIC PHILOSOPHERS OF THE 5TH CENTURY BC

After the defeat of the Ionian revolt against Persia in 494BC, intellectual life moved to Athens. The booming, usually liberal city for centuries attracted thinkers from around the Greek world. Those living before Socrates are called Pre-Socratic.

HERACLITUS
FLOURISHED C.500–490BC

A native of Ephesus, Heraclitus was renowned both for his personal arrogance and the obscurity of his philosophical aphorisms. About 120 of these survive. Heraclitus rejected earlier quests for a single imperishable entity beneath the constant flow of phenomena, proclaiming: *panta rei, ouden menei* (all is flux, nothing is stable). He saw the world as the unending conflict of opposites, governed by the unchanging Logos (principle, order, word). He believed that the world consisted of three cosmic

Above: Raphael's portrait of the enigmatic Heraclitus, another philosopher from Miletus, who proclaimed that "all is flux".

elements – earth, water and fire – forever changing into each other. The greatest was fire, linked to Logos: "Fire is the underlying element, the world is everlasting fire." Although he ridiculed Xenophanes, he too believed in relativism, pointing out that the way up a mountain is also the way down. Many of his more radical aphorisms shocked contemporaries. Dead bodies, he said, smell nastier than excrement.

PARMENIDES C.510–C.430BC AND ZENO C.490–C.430BC

Parmenides, said Plato, had "magnificent depths". He is increasingly seen as the most significant Pre-Socratic, for with his thinking consciousness becomes aware of itself. This led to the human mind first recognizing its unique cognitive powers, an intellectually vital step.

Parmenides was an aristocrat from Elea, a Greek city in Italy, who visited Athens in c.440BC. His work survives in a three-part poem in hexameters of 150 lines. The *Prologue* is a mystic revelation by a goddess who explains two ways. *The Way of Truth*, expounded with rigorous logic, concludes by showing that all that truly exists must be one, eternal, undifferentiated and changeless. Whatever is cannot come into being or cease to exist. Conversely, that which is *not* cannot come into being. Change, therefore, is impossible. As this is clearly not the phenomenal world our senses reveal, our senses are somehow wrong. In *The Way of Opinion* he restated conventional views but only to rebut them. By confining truth to the realm of an unchanging One, Parmenides' ideas deeply influenced Plato.

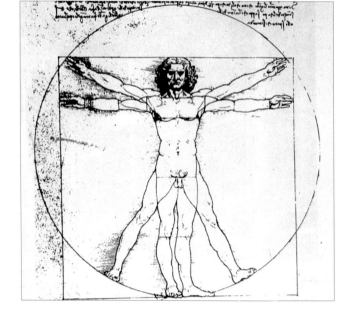

Left: Leonardo da Vinci's drawing of a perfectly symmetrical 'Vitruvian Man' illustrates Protagoras' belief that "Man is the measure of all things."

Zeno of Elea, Parmenides' main follower, defended his master's teachings against pluralist critics by extending their arguments *ad absurdum* in "Achilles' Paradox". Though Achilles runs much faster than a tortoise, if he gives the tortoise a head start in a race he will never *logically* catch up with it, because at each distinct stage the tortoise will still be an ever-reducing stage ahead.

ANAXAGORAS C.500–428BC
Born in the tiny Ionian city of Clazomenae, Anaxagoras moved to Athens in *c*.480BC. He lived there for nearly 50 years, becoming a teacher and friend of Pericles. He tried to refute Parmenides' logical monism by postulating a plurality of eternal, qualitatively different substances. His version of cosmic history began, rather like the Big Bang, when *Nous* (Mind) 'the finest and purest of all things', started a rotatory process that formed the stars and other bodies from air, separating dark from light, wet from dry. All creatures, not just humans, have minds but *Mind* is separate and infinite. Anaxagoras was nicknamed 'Mind' for stressing this but he was essentially a materialist. He was also a perceptive astronomer. He realized that the Moon shines with the Sun's reflected light and considered the Sun a "fiery rock larger than the Peloponnese." Such observations struck many Athenians as impious – the heavenly bodies were thought divine – and Anaxagoras had to retire to Lampsacus in 430BC when Pericles lost office. There he was honoured and died.

PROTAGORAS C.485–C.415BC
A native of Abdera on the Hellespont, Protagoras was probably the greatest Sophist. Sophists ('wise men') travelled around Greek cities teaching and charging fees. Protagoras taught *areté* (virtue, excellence, valour, goodness) not as an abstract virtue but as a form of life skill. Rhetoric (public eloquence) formed an important part of his training. Plato portrays him hostilely in the dialogue

Above: Athens became the centre of philosophy after the Ionian revolt was crushed by Persia in 494BC. Many Ionian thinkers found a welcome in its (usually) liberal democracy. It kept this reputation until the very end of the ancient world.

named after him, attacking his then novel concept of moral relativism, but Protagoras was widely admired. He was asked by Pericles to draw up a constitution for Thurii in Italy, and was Abdera's ambassador in Athens. In *On Truth*, one of his extant works, he famously proclaimed: "Man is the measure of all things!" Such exultant humanism led him to disregard theology. "Of the gods I know nothing, whether or not they exist nor what they are like. Many things prevent such knowledge: the obscurity of the subject, the shortness of human life." Instead, Protagoras concentrated on imparting areté in Athens at its Periclean noon.

Below: Black-figure amphora of runners. Zeno of Elea produced the argument ad absurdum *of "Achilles' Paradox". Although he runs faster, if Achilles gives the tortoise a start he can never logically* catch up with it.

SOCRATES: THE ARCHETYPAL PHILOSOPHER c.470–399 BC

Above: Greek bas-relief of Socrates talking to Diotima, the priestess sometimes called his muse, who revealed to him the potentially transcendent nature of eros (desire).

Below: The Death of Socrates, painted by J.L. David in 1787. Condemned to death for his unorthodox religious views, Socrates swallowed hemlock while debating with his disciples. He thus became a model martyr for free speech.

The first Athenian-born philosopher, Socrates changed the focus of philosophy from speculation about the physical world to ethical issues. In doing so, he also became the archetypal philosopher in his disdain for worldly riches, his intellectual curiosity and his bravery. Socrates likened himself to a gadfly, stinging people into thought. Like a fly, he was finally squashed. He has often been considered an intellectual martyr. Like Christ and the Buddha, he wrote nothing, so we must rely on others' conflicting accounts of his life and thought. But the bare facts of his life are clear.

SOCRATES THE MAN

The son of a stonemason of the hoplite middle-class, Socrates fought bravely in the army, notably at Delium in 424 BC. By then he was well-known enough to be ridiculed by Aristophanes in *The Clouds*, where he is portrayed as a charlatan teaching young Athenians to lie and study godless astronomy. If a travesty of the truth – although Socrates may have been interested in natural science for a time – this was an accurate enough portrait to amuse citizens.

Socrates was already attracting a circle of followers, mostly leisured young aristocrats, but anyone could listen to him debating in the Agora or street. Charging no fees, unlike the Sophists, Socrates became impoverished on abandoning his mason's trade, going around in rags. His wife Xanthippe objected to this neglect but Socrates had set his mind on higher things. This made him seem indifferent to wealth, sex and drink. The handsome young aristocrat Alcibiades tried to seduce Socrates – who was notably ugly if charming – but got nowhere, to his amazement. Equally amazing was Socrates' indifference to cold, shown on northern campaigns. He also was unaffected by alcohol, no matter how much he drank. However he was governed by his *daimon*, an inner guide that often forbade him to do things but never urged him on.

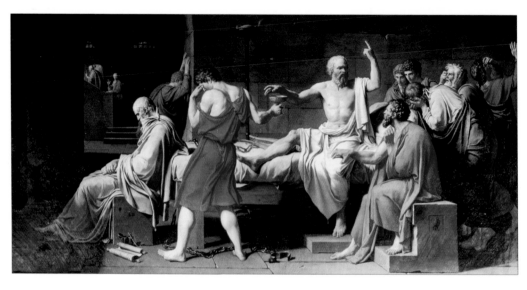

THE SOCRATIC METHOD

According to Plato's *Apology*, a prime biographical source, Socrates' intellectual quest began when the Delphic oracle declared that there was none wiser than him. Amazed, he declared himself ignorant but determined to find wise men by the Socratic method. (This is also called *elenctic*, refuting an argument by proving the contrary of its expected conclusion).

Such an approach led Socrates to question ordinary Athenians about fundamental, usually unchallenged concepts. "What is courage?" "What is justice?" "What is areté?" he asked, subjecting those who thought they knew the answers to probing inquiries that revealed their ignorance. This seldom made him loved, especially when he asked: "Who is truly fit to govern?" The answer appeared to be: no one.

But Socrates, despite a sharp-edged irony, was not playing word games. When he asked "What is justice?" he believed that, although laws might differ with different peoples, there was an underlying reality called 'justice'. Everyone could recognize it if they saw it clearly. Socrates wanted to demolish misconceptions to reveal the essence of justice, or of bravery or of areté. While he never claimed to have the final truth, he believed that no one knowingly does wrong. Wrong-doing stems from ignorance about man's real good. A man of true areté cannot be harmed by external factors such as imprisonment or death. Personal ruin comes from inner corruption.

TRIAL AND DEATH

Socrates did not seek public office but this was thrust on every Athenian at times by the city's direct democracy. In 406BC he was a member of the Council of 500 during the trial of the generals after the Battle of Arginusae, a pyrrhic victory with the generals blamed unfairly for the high losses after it. Amid demotic hysteria, the Council illegally tried and executed the generals collectively. Only Socrates protested against this injustice.

Two years later, with Athens under a fascistic junta, he showed equal courage by refusing its orders to arrest a prominent man whose wealth the junta wanted.

Democracy was restored in 403BC under a general amnesty, but memories persisted. Many recalled Socrates undermining old certainties, and that two of his ex-disciples had led the junta. Both reactionaries and democrats had reason to dislike him. In 399BC Anytus, a noted democrat, accused Socrates of "not recognizing the city's official gods and introducing new ones" and "corrupting the young" – strange charges superficially, for new gods were at times welcomed to Athens. In fact, both were ways of attacking Socrates for his views and associates. His self-defence was ironic and oddly jejune. The standard 501-strong jury found him guilty by a small majority.

He was not expected to remain for the death sentence but to go into exile. Instead, claiming he could not abandon his post, he stayed, discoursing on the immortality of the soul until his end. This came in a dose of hemlock – not a dignified death, involving convulsions and vomiting. "I owe a cock to Asclepius," were his last enigmatic words. Asclepius was the healer-god. Did Socrates mean he was freed at last from the disease of life?

Above: Socrates Snatching Alcibiades from Sexual Lures, *painted by J.-B. Regnault in 1791. In fact, Socrates failed to persuade the flamboyant aristocrat, once his star pupil, to devote himself properly to philosophy.*

Below: A Roman copy of a Greek bust of Socrates. The philosopher, although charming, was seen as shabby and ugly by contemporaries.

PLATO: THE GREATEST PHILOSOPHER? c.429–347BC

Plato, Socrates' most brilliant student, was arguably the greatest philosopher ever. Most of his work (c.500,000 words) survives, on subjects from cosmology to politics. Plato had a novelist's gift for portraying people vividly and wrote superb prose. His own views can be unclear because he usually wrote in dialogues, not verse as earlier thinkers had done, to stimulate discussion. His use of dialectic was to be very influential, in the 19th century G.F. Hegel and Karl Marx employed dialetic to great effect. Yet Plato considered all writing inferior to live debates.

Plato, although an aristocrat, rejected politics because of events early in his life: the junta of 'Thirty Tyrants' and the trial and execution under the restored democracy of his revered teacher in 399BC. Plato then left Athens, visiting Italy, where he stayed with the Pythagorean philosopher-ruler of Taranto and Sicily where he fell foul of the tyrant Dionysius I. Returning to Athens in c.387BC, he founded his Academy outside the city, for a select few to study philosophy.

Above: This bust from the 4th century BC is probably the most accurate portrait of Plato, suggesting his physical as well as intellectual strength. When young, he had been a noted wrestler.

Plato's 25 extant *dialogues*, along with several long letters, form the finest body of Greek prose ever written. Early dialogues, such as *Euthyphro* and *Crito*, and *Apology* (a rare monologue), give a vivid portrait of Socrates. They explore ethical, political and religious issues, with Socrates the genial, ironic, open-minded inquirer. In later dialogues Socrates the real person fades, as Plato's own ideas develop.

EROS HIGH AND LOW

In the *Symposium* (Banquet), the nature of eros (desire) is discussed. The comedian Aristophanes explains that, as once parts of a circular whole, we are forever seeking our divided selves. After the incursion of Alcibiades, very drunk, Socrates propounds what may be Plato's own view, relating a purported talk with Diotima, a priestess. She declared that physical sex of any type is the lowest form of eros. Higher is spiritual procreation, with souls uniting to create intellectual beauty. But eros at its highest transcends individuals, as the soul grasps the impersonal *idea* of beauty. Erotic desire is only the springboard for this ascent. (From *Symposium* comes our muddled concept of 'Platonic love'.)

THE MYTH OF THE CAVE

Central to Plato's philosophy is his Theory of Ideas (or Ideal Forms), propounded in the Myth of the Cave in *Republic*. (*Republic* also describes Plato's utopia, an austere society governed by an elite of Guardians, with poets and artists banned. While most people live lives of

Left: The myth of the prisoners chained in the cave, from which only philosophy can help them to escape. From a Flemish painting of the 16th century illustrating one of the crucial sections of Plato's Republic.

Right: Plato's Academy outside Athens, where the philosopher taught via dialectical debates. From a Roman mosaic.

unenlighted drudgery, women Guardians are men's equals – as revolutionary as the proposal to raise children communally.)

Imagine, says Plato, a row of prisoners in a cave, chained together facing inward, all unable to move. A great fire blazes behind them, separated by a parapet on which men walk carrying statues. Firelight casts the statues' shadows onto the inner wall. Prisoners, knowing only these shadows, take them for reality.

One day a prisoner, somehow escaping his shackles, turns round. He is at first blinded by the real fire. Even more overwhelming is the sunlight when he reaches the surface. Once over his shock, he is astonished by the beauty of reality. But, on returning to the cave, he cannot convince his fellow-prisoners of the real world above. *We* are those hide-bound prisoners, chained by our stupidity and desires to this world of shadows. Only through philosophy, grasping the eternal world of Ideas behind the transient sensual world, can we escape.

In *Phaedrus*, Plato related a complementary myth: that of the Charioteer with two horses, a savage black animal filled with base sensual desires, and a white one, its spiritual opposite. The charioteer must master the black horse or it will drag him to ruin. Plato believed that our souls must strive to control or transcend our carnal desires.

THE PHILOSOPHER-KING

In 367BC the 62-year-old Plato sailed to Syracuse to be adviser to its new ruler, Dionysius II. He had been invited by Dion, a former Academy student and Dionysius' cousin, who said that the young tyrant was interested in philosophy. Despite misgivings, Plato could not ignore this chance to turn Greece's most powerful ruler into a 'philosopher-king' guided by virtue. But Dionysius, although he had intellectual interests, proved more interested in wine and women than the tough

philosophical course grounded in maths that Plato proposed. Plato himself proved useless at court politics. Soon jealous courtiers turned the tyrant against Dion, who went into exile. Plato finally left Syracuse ignominiously. Yet he returned five years later at the pleading of Dionysius. He found that the tyrant now considered himself a philosopher. Plato was imprisoned and only managed to leave with great difficulty. Then Dion returned to Sicily and the island was engulfed in civil war. All seemed to show that politics and philosophy never mix.

Plato died in Athens working on *Laws*, his last, grimmest blueprint for an ideal society, based on Spartan models. This is truly authoritarian – even homosexuality is banned, although Plato himself was homosexual – and there is no religious or intellectual freedom at all. But Plato the man apparently could still laugh. After he died at a wedding-feast, Aristophanes' comedies were found by his bed.

Below: Plato disputing with Aristotle, his most brilliant pupil, who evolved a very different philosophy. Carved by Luca della Robbia in the 15th century.

ARISTOTLE: THE MASTER OF KNOWLEDGE 384–322BC

Aristotle and Plato, the twin giants of Greek philosophy, are often seen as polar opposites, the former systematically examining this world, the latter gazing mystically upward to the next world. In fact they complement almost as much as they contradict each other. Aristotle studied for decades at Plato's Academy and his work shows Plato's influence, which he only gradually rejected or modified. Aristotle himself said: "Plato is dear to me, but dearer still is truth."

Above: This bust, possibly based on an original by his contemporary Praxiteles, may portray Aristotle accurately rather than flatteringly.

Below: Aristotle contemplating a bust of Homer, from a painting by Rembrandt. Aristotle was as knowledgeable about literature as he was about the natural world.

THE COURTLY OUTSIDER

Aristotle was born at Stagira, a small Ionic city in northern Greece, so he was a foreigner in Athens. His father was court physician to the Macedonian king Amyntas II, and Aristotle grew up in a strange royal court, not as a citizen of a polis. All his life he was notably well-dressed but remained always an outsider.

After his father died in 367BC, Aristotle joined Plato's Academy in Athens, the "city hall of wisdom" in his words. He remained there for 20 years, his genius being recognized by Plato, but the Academy's increasing emphasis on maths did not suit its most brilliant student.

When, on Plato's death, his mediocre nephew Speusippus took over the Academy, Aristotle left to found a philosophical community near the Hellespont. There he fell in love with and married Phyllis (also called Pythias), niece of a local Greek ruler. In 342BC he returned to Macedonia, the rising superpower, as tutor to Alexander, Philip II's son. Alexander, headstrong and romantic, was very unlike his tutor. However Aristotle imparted to the prince a love of Greek culture – Alexander especially liked Euripides' tragedies, although Homer was his idol – if not, it appears, his contempt for 'barbarians' (non-Greeks).

THE LYCEUM

By 335BC Aristotle was back in Athens. There he founded his school: the Lyceum. Open to all, unlike the Academy, it had wide interests, becoming the world's first research institute, with library, museum, collections of natural objects and ultimately 2,000 students, then a huge number. Initially Aristotle taught while walking around its half-built colonnade, hence his school's traditional name: Peripatetic.

Aristotle systematically classified the natural world – botany and biology begin with his studies – from shellfish to stars. He dissected animal and human corpses, making notes and illustrations (since lost). Alexander sent his ex-tutor specimens during his world-conquest. When, after Alexander's death in 323BC, war broke out between Athens and Macedonia, Aristotle fled to Chalcis "to prevent Athens

repeating its mistake with Socrates", i.e. executing him. When he died in 322BC, he left 18 household slaves, indicating remarkable wealth for a philosopher.

THE GREAT CATEGORIZER

Aristotle was one of the most systematic thinkers known. He mapped out many still basic fields of inquiry, including biology, economics, logic, law, physics, metaphysics, politics, meteorology, ethics – probably no one else has ever *categorized* so many things as he did. Dante Alighieri, the medieval poet, called him *il maestro di color che sanno* (the master of those who know). However, Aristotle's writings survive only as dense, dry lecture notes, which restricts his wider appeal.

Unlike Plato, Aristotle accepted the material world, thinking it the only world we can investigate, but he was no crude materialist. While Plato believed that worldly objects are mere shadows of ideal forms, Aristotle asked: What *are* objects in this world? He thought that *form* is what give an object its purpose. A house is more than a jumble of building materials, necessary though they are. Similarly, Socrates was not just his physical constituents. An object's form exists within it, and could no more exist independently from it than a man's shape could exist apart from his body.

Aristotle's logically deduced views on form differed radically from Plato's mysticism. He posited four distinct but complementary Causes of form, which explains why a thing is what it is: the material, efficient, formal and final causes.

POETRY AND POLITICS

Aristotle's major works include *Poetics, Nicomachean Ethics, Politics, Rhetoric, Physics, Metaphysics* (so-called because it came *meta* [after] physics in the library).

Right: Aristotle (right) gestures toward the ground while Plato points to the heavens, indicating the former's less idealistic philosophy. From Raphael's School of Athens *in the Vatican, Rome.*

In *Poetics* Aristotle proclaimed poetry and tragedy superior to history because they portray noble actions that "rouse pity and fear, so achieving emotional cleansing (*catharsis*)." He posited a divine Unmoved Mover beyond the universe but was ambivalent about immortality.

In *Politics* (the last major Greek work on the topic), he wrote: "Man is by nature a political animal... Men come to the city to live, they stay to live the Good Life." Instead of the excellence/virtue (areté) sought earlier, he offered happiness (*eudaimonia*). Like Socrates, he saw virtue and happiness as connected. Happiness could be found through the Golden Mean. For example, bravery is the mean between cowardice and rashness. He was more realistic (or conservative) than Plato about his ideal society, accepting slavery and women's inferiority as natural, but still saw it as based on a medium-sized polis. While Alexander was overturning the political world, Aristotle was laying the groundwork of a logical philosophy that would dominate much of Western and Islamic thought in the Middle Ages.

Above: Aristotle being 'ridden' by his wife Phyllis. Aristotle, who had married for love, was reputedly later henpecked by Phyllis. From a drawing by Hans Baldung of c.1540.

IN SOCRATES' FOOTSTEPS
CYNICS AND SCEPTICS

Above: Diogenes, a bust of the 3rd century BC showing this most original philosopher in a sombre mood, unusual for someone normally so cheerful.

Below: Diogenes was noted for his ascetically minimalist life. Seeing a boy drinking without even a mug, he threw his away his own. From a painting by Etienne Jeurat of the 18th century.

Socrates' followers varied from the high-minded Plato to the hedonistic Aristippus of Cyrene (435–356BC). Aristippus thought undeferred pleasure the one worthwhile goal, preferably the "smooth motions of the flesh". He practised what he preached, but his school, perpetuated by his grandson, impressed few Greeks. In contrast, two other schools at odds with mainstream thinking flourished: Cynicism and Scepticism.

DIOGENES THE CYNIC c.404–325BC
Plato in irritation called Diogenes "Socrates gone mad". Certainly the great Athenian thinker inspired Diogenes, but for Diogenes life finally proved a comedy, not a tragedy.

Diogenes came from Sinope, a Greek city on the Black Sea, where his father was imprisoned for currency-forging. Diogenes, also implicated, was exiled, moving to Athens. There he became a follower of Antisthenes (*c.*445–360BC),

once a student of Socrates. Antisthenes dressed like a poor labourer, rejecting public affairs, private property, marriage and established religion. (That he could spurn religion publicly shows that Athens, after Socrates' trial, had regained its normal tolerance.) Antisthenes generally discouraged followers but Diogenes was his most persistent disciple, who would not be dissuaded even by a stick. With Diogenes the Cynics became a school – if dropouts can be said to form a school.

LIVING LIKE DOGS
Cynic (*cynicos*), meaning dog-like, was an insult happily accepted by Diogenes. He flouted social customs in an ultra-Socratic quest for truth and virtue, but was not remotely 'cynical' in today's negative sense. Once asked why he was carrying a lantern in daylight, he replied that he was looking for an "honest man".

Diogenes had no house but lived in a barrel. He had one ragged cloak for the day that was his blanket at night. He begged for his food, having one bowl and one mug. But when he saw a boy drinking from his cupped hands, he threw away even his mug as superfluous.

Diogenes satisfied all his bodily functions in public, even masturbating. When rebuked for this – the Greeks admired heroic nudity, not sexual exhibitionism – he simply said: "Ah, if only I could satisfy my hunger by rubbing my belly."

Effectively stateless, having no polis, he claimed to be a *cosmopolitan*, a "citizen of the universe". Captured by pirates and put up for sale as a slave, Diogenes was asked if he had any special skills. "Governing men," he replied, and pointed to a well-dressed man. "Sell me to him, he needs a master." He was freed by friends. Finally dying from eating raw octopus – to show that cooking is unnecessary – he ordered his corpse thrown in a ditch.

Ignoring these last wishes – which outraged the deepest religious beliefs – Athens erected a marble monument with a dog to this most original of thinkers.

Diogenes' aim was not to win fame by crude sensationalism but to show that almost all material wants can be discarded. Like many later philosophers, he sought not areté (virtue) but eudmamonia (happiness) and ataraxia (freedom from worry or care). His successor Crates of Thebes (*c*.365–285BC) renounced great wealth to live a similar wandering life. Crates' wife Hipparchia, who was famous for her beauty, was among the few noted female philosophers. Cynicism survived under the Roman Empire. It in some ways anticipated the Stoics, Christian ascetics and even, much later, the hippies.

PYRRHO THE SCEPTIC C.365–275BC

Among the Greeks who followed Alexander to India was Pyrrho of Elis. He was so impressed by the diversity of customs and beliefs that he saw, especially among Indian fakirs, that he became the founder of scepticism. He argued that the reasons for a belief are never better than those against, and that the only wise approach is to suspend judgement and accept the world as it seems. His goal was ataraxia, like Diogenes. Pyrrho often pointed to animals as living enviably undisturbed lifes. He retired to Elis, where he lived out a long and peaceful life amid admirers.

Pyrrho's chief pupil, Timon of Phlius, (*c*.320–230BC) took scepticism further, showing that every argument proceeds from premises not already established. To demonstrate those premises' truth by other arguments, they must be based on other undemonstrated premises, a potentially infinite and so absurd regression.

Timon's follower Arcesilaus (315–240BC) became head of Plato's Academy in 275BC, making it a bastion of scepticism for about 200 years. Timon's successor Carneades caused a stir when visiting Rome by arguing both sides of a cause on successive days. Cicero was later influenced by the Academy's scepticism. The best account of scepticism comes from Sextus Empiricus' summary of its arguments in the *Pyrrhoniarum* of *c*.AD200. David Hume, the great 18th-century Scottish philosopher, was inspired by Pyrrhonic scepticism.

Above: Bion of Olbia (c.325–255BC) was an eclectic philosopher, intellectually closest to the Cynics. He lived by wandering around the major cities teaching, but finally gained the patronage of Antigonus II, king of Macedonia.

Left: Alexander the Great and the barrel-dwelling Diogenes reputedly met in Corinth in 335BC. When Alexander asked what he could do for the thinker, Diogenes replied: "Get out of my sunlight."

RIVAL SCHOOLS
STOICS V. EPICUREANS

Above: A copy of an original statue of c.240BC of Chrysippus, the second great Stoic teacher, who emphasized ethics over logic and physics in a way that proved very appealing.

Two rival schools of thought, Stoicism and Epicureanism, emerged around 300BC in Athens to become the main forms of philosophy for centuries.

STOICISM

Stoicism was founded by Zeno of Citium (333–262BC). Zeno, reaching Athens in 311BC, attended the Academy, listened to Crates the Cynic and studied Aristotle before evolving his own philosophy. He taught in the Stoa Poikile (Painted Stoa) from which his school takes its name. His courses were tripartite: logic, physics and ethics. His teachings were refined by his successors Cleanthes and Chrysippus (c.280–207BC). Chrysippus downplayed logic and physics in favour of ethics, creating an appealing philosophical package.

The essence of Stoicism was that nothing happens by chance, all things being predetermined by the laws of the cosmos. There is nothing higher than the natural universe, of which we are part. We must live in harmony with it, accepting everything that happens. Stoics proclaimed a "brotherhood of man" that included slaves and non-Greeks. Although they raised a god (called Zeus) to quasi-pantheistic primacy, they did not believe in individual afterlife. Nor did they forbid suicide.

Left: The stern nobility of Epicurus is apparent in this bust. Far from advocating sensual indulgence, as his enemies said, Epicurus thought most pleasures were not worth the effort. He abjured politics, fame and – guardedly – any real belief in the gods, valuing friendship above everything.

Poseidonius (c.135–51BC), a polymathic Stoic, travelled widely before establishing his school at Rhodes, where important Romans, including Pompey and Cicero, visited him. Cicero later translated Greek philosophical ideas into Latin and Stoicism became the favoured philosophy of the Roman elite, who found its noble austerity appealing.

ROMAN STOICS

Seneca (2BC–AD65) was a playwright and courtier, the emperor Nero's tutor and then minister. Retiring from the increasingly paranoid emperor's court, Seneca turned again to philosophy until, implicated in a conspiracy against Nero in AD65, he committed suicide. He wrote (in Latin) essays, plays and 124 letters on varied subjects, especially the humane treatment of slaves. "Remember, the man you call your slave is of the same species and breathes, lives and dies under the same skies as you." His work, if unoriginal, inspired many later generations unable to read Greek.

Epictetus (AD55–135) also suffered from imperial paranoia, being among the philosophers exiled by the emperor Domitian in AD89. He accepted this as calmly as earlier maltreatment while a slave, settling in western Greece. There he taught an austere yet compassionate philosophy, attacking easy cures for human misery that ignored the "wisdom of God". Epictetus wrote in Greek.

So did the emperor Marcus Aurelius (reigned AD161–80). Antiquity's one philosopher-king. Marcus was brought up to rule as a sage but in practice had to spend much of his reign fighting invading barbarians on the Danube frontier. His *Meditations*, written on campaign, are the private records of an exhausted if great-souled man. Tinged with Platonism, they were the last true Stoic writings.

Right: An original – and very rare – bronze statue of Marcus Aurelius, the philosopher-emperor (reigned AD161–80). The last great Stoic, he wrote his Meditations *while campaigning on the Danube. They were not meant for publication.*

EPICUREANISM

Although Epicureanism was often damned by its enemies as encouraging gross sensuality, this was a travesty of the real aims of its founder Epicurus (341–270BC). The son of Athenian colonists on Samos, Epicurus settled in Athens in 307BC. He established his Garden – literally, it was a vegetable garden – near Plato's Academy, but with very different aims: to seek human happiness, not mystical truth.

Epicurus believed the chief causes of human misery were fear of what happens after death and frustrated desires for the superfluous while alive.

He set out to demolish fear of death by showing that the soul, like the rest of the universe, is composed of constituent atoms, which simply dissolve at death. Here he was echoing the thinking of Democritus (c.460–370BC), an earlier atomist. There is nothing to be feared or expected after death.

Contentment in this life is best achieved by intelligent frugality, Epicurus' extant maxims suggest. "Value frugality not for asceticism's sake but because it minimizes worries... It is better to sleep without fear on a straw mattress than trembling on a gold bed ... No pleasure is bad in itself but certain pleasures incur drawbacks far greater than the pleasure gained."

Epicurus shunned public life, seeing in the polis only a source of strife – an understandable reaction to the turmoil of his age, if one that marked the withdrawal of philosophers from society. Instead, he valued friendship above everything else. Never marrying, he made his Garden a refuge for the like-minded, be they citizens, slaves or women. Admitting slaves and women to his school – something Plato had only contemplated – caused a

scandal even greater than denying the afterlife. (Epicurus tactfully accepted the gods' existence but denied they were at all interested in humanity.) The Garden, emulating the Academy and Lyceum, had a communal life, with regular debates and monthly *symposia*. Often ill in later years, Epicurus lived mostly off bread and cheese and died in great pain with cheerful, indeed Stoical, fortitude.

Epicurus wrote more than 300 books on philosophy but none has survived. While his teaching proved popular in the Greek world, his greatest disciple was the Roman Lucretius (94–55BC). In *De Rerum Natura* (*About the Nature of Things*), Lucretius wrote a brilliant philosophical poem. Although Lucretius called his poetry just "honey round the edges" of his beliefs, Cicero was much impressed by this philosophy expounded so lyrically.

Below: Zeno of Citium, who settled in Athens in 311BC and founded the Stoic school of philosophy. This stresed acceptance of the universe as reflecting the divine will.

THE PLATONIST REVIVAL
PLOTINUS AND NEOPLATONISTS

*Above: The spiritual nobility
of Plotinus, the ancient world's
last great original thinker who
founded the Neoplatonist
school, shines through this
bust of the 3rd century AD.
This might well be a portrait
from life.*

The last great philosophical school of antiquity was Neoplatonism. Its founder was Plotinus (*c.*AD204–70), an Egyptian Greek. Plotinus saw himself not as founding a new school but as reviving true Platonism. However, he gave Plato's thinking a deeply mystical, overwhelmingly monistic turn by positing a superexistent *One* as the source of all being, far beyond sensory perception.

Plotinus first studied under Ammonius Saccas, an obscure figure who wrote nothing. He then joined the Persian expedition of the emperor Gordian III in AD243, apparently hoping to learn about eastern religions in India. After Gordian's murder by his troops, Plotinus moved to Rome. There he started his own school.

Among his aristocratic students was Gallienus, who became emperor in AD253. Gallienus so admired Plotinus that he offered to found Platonopolis, a city for philosophers in Campania, but court intrigues aborted this utopian project. After Gallienus' death in AD268, Plotinus withdrew from public life. He had never been a worldly man. Plato, while spurning Athenian democracy, had remained interested in politics. By contrast, Neoplatonists ignored the world falling into ruin about them. Instead, they turned to the mystical *Monos* (the One).

FLIGHT OF THE ONE TO THE ONE
Porphyry (AD232–305), Plotinus' biographer and most important follower, recorded the last words of his teacher as: "Strive to bring back the god within yourselves to the God in the Universe." This

*Left: Julian, the last significant non-Christian
Roman emperor (reigned AD361–3), was also
a Neoplatonist philosopher. His attempts to
revive Hellenism as an organized religion
died with him, but Greek philosophy itself
survived for a time.*

injunction lies at the heart of Plotinus' philosophy, simultaneously rational and mystical. His thinking incorporated Pre-Socratic, Aristotelian and Stoic ideas, creating a novel, moving philosophy.

Plotinus saw the One as the supernatural, ineffable basis of all being, resembling Plato's idea of the Good. Below this ineffable summit are tiers of being. The first is *Nous*, or Mind, the second *Psyche*, or Soul, a projection of Mind. Soul looks up to Mind but down to Nature (*Bios*), but the tiers are interdependent. Even at the lowest corporeal level, all things seek *epistrophe*, a return to the One. Plotinus' dynamic vision has been compared to an inexhaustible fountain of light whose waters constantly descend before returning to the source. He believed human beings can, via philosophy, attain ecstatic visions of the One as *fuge monou pros monon*, the "Flight of the One to the One". He claimed to have achieved this three times.

As a man, Plotinus was self-effacing and ascetic, so ashamed of bodily functions he did not even like to be seen eating. He never married, eschewing sex, but freely admitted women to his classes. These could be tortured sessions, the philosopher falling silent in his attempt to express the inexpressible. He wrote little and then only in his last years.

THE FOLLOWERS
Porphyry, born in Tyre, came to Rome in *c.*AD262 and joined Plotinus' classes. Soon the master's favourite, he recorded Plotinus' teaching in nine books, *Enneads* (*Ninths*). Like his master, Porphyry rejected Christianity because of its belief in a personal god and salvation by faith – the One is not a person, superficial resemblances to the Christian Trinity are accidental. Porphyry amended Plotinus' thought by positing the importance of

astrology. Plotinus, however, to whom the stars shone with the universe's divinity, always rejected astrology's basic premises.

Porphyry's successor Iamblichus (c.AD250–326) added *theurgy*, magical rites derived from Neopythagoreanism – more a religion than philosophy – to Neoplatonism. His synthesis shaped Neoplatonism as it spread around the Roman Empire. Schools sprang up at Alexandria, Pergamum and Athens. The last pagan emperor Julian studied this semi-magical philosophy at Athens and Pergamum. During his brief reign (AD361–3), Julian tried to revitalize paganism along Neoplatonist lines.

THE END OF GREEK PHILOSOPHY

In Alexandria one of the last Hellenic philosophers was a woman, Hypatia (c.AD370–420). A fine mathematician as well as a Neoplatonist, beautiful but celibate, Hypatia devoted her life to philosophy until one day she was dragged from her coach and murdered by a fanatical Christian mob. Despite her murder, Neoplatonism lingered on in Alexandria, but its last bastion was, appositely, Athens. There, Proclus (AD410–85) fused mathematics and mysticism to expound the interconnectedness of all things, arguing that time itself is a circular dance. Finally in AD529 the Byzantine emperor Justinian ordered the closure of the schools of Athens.

This marked the end of ancient Neoplatonism, but it had deeply influenced St Augustine (AD354–430), among the greatest Christian thinkers. Other early Christian writers, from the Roman patrician Boethius in the 6th century and Dionysus the Aeropagite (suposedly an Athenian converted by St Paul in the 1st century AD but actually a Greek

Right: Percy Bysshe Shelley (1792–1822) was one of many Romantic poets influenced by Neoplatonism, most notably in Adonais. *Here he sits writing amid the ruins of the Baths of Caracalla, Rome. From a posthumous painting by Joseph Severn.*

Right: Hypatia of Alexandria, one of the few women philosophers in Hellenic tradition, was traditionally very beautiful but celibate. A mathematician as well as a mystic, she was murdered by a mob of fanatical Christians in c.AD 420.

contemporary of Boethius) to Eriugena in the 9th century, were also profoundly affected by Neoplatonism. (How far the last two thinkers are really Christians, rather than mystical pantheists, remains debated.)

In Renaissance Italy, Neoplatonism re-emerged fully, first inspired by Greek thinkers fleeing the fall of Constantinople to the Turks. Marsilio Ficino translated the *Enneads* while Pico della Mirandola tried to reconcile Christianity, Platonism, Judaism and even Chaldean paganism in a mystical synthesis. His heroic efforts landed him briefly in a papal prison, but Neoplatonism spread north to England. Reviving again with the Romantics, its perennial philosophy underlies much of the poetry of S.T. Coleridge, P.B. Shelley, Ralph Waldo Emerson and W.B. Yeats.

THE FIRST MATHEMATICIANS
600BC–AD200

Above: Thales, visiting Egypt in the 6th century BC, was asked by the pharaoh to calculate the height of a pyramid. He waited for the time when his shadow equalled his own height and thus calculated the height of the pyramid itself.

Below: A monument built in Samos in 1989 to Pythagoras. The mystical mathematician, born in Samos, traditionally discovered the theorem that bears his name.

Mathematics as a proper discipline began with the Greeks in the 6th century BC. The Egyptians had long been brilliant at practical calculation and measuring and the Babylonians had first divided the circle into 360 degrees, but neither had developed a series of theories based on definitions with axioms and proofs. It took Greek intellectual passion and precision to do this. Maths became so central to Greek thinking that Plato stipulated that only the numerate should enter his Academy. But Greek maths had its limits. For example, it had no term for – or concept of – zero, unlike Indian maths.

EARLY MATHEMATICIANS

Thales is considered the first Greek mathematician. Visiting Egypt in the 6th century BC, Thales was reputedly asked by the pharaoh to calculate the height of a pyramid. He waited for a time when his shadow equalled his own height and then calculated the pyramid's height. He also worked out how to calculate a ship's distance from the shore. Around 520BC, Pythagoras traditionally discovered the theorem that bears his name: that in a right-angled triangle the square of the sum of the opposite side equals the squares of the other two sides. Pythagoreans also knew that the sum of all three angles of a triangle equals two right angles. They had a mystical belief in number, being the true (if secret) unity behind the universe, manifested in musical octaves. But their discovery of incommensurability – that some ratios could not be expressed as whole numbers, a seemingly insoluble problem already encountered in Babylon – led them to concentrate on geometry.

Eudoxus of Cnidus (*c.*408–347BC) studied with the Pythagoreans at Taranto and also in Egypt. In geometry he discovered the general theory of proportions

Above: Euclid (c.330–270BC), the greatest mathematician before the late 19th century. From a portrait by the Renaissance artist Girolamo Mocetto.

applicable to both incommensurable and commensurable magnitudes, later shown by Euclid in Book 5. He also showed by the "method of exhaustion" that the cone and pyramid are one third the volume respectively of the cylinder and prism with the same base and height.

EUCLID THE MATHEMATICAL MASTER

The greatest Greek mathematician was Euclid (*c.*330–270BC), who taught at the Museum/Library of Alexandria. His famous work is his *Elements* (*Stoichea*) in 13 books. The most influential book in mathematical history, it formed the basis of

Western maths until the late 19th century. Although not all the contents are original – Plato in *Timaeus* had anticipated the treatment of regular geometric solids – Euclid added a new logical structure of such elegant clarity that Bertrand Russell called *Elements* "the most perfect monument of Greek intellect". By deducing the geometrical objects' properties from a few axioms, Euclid in effect founded the axiomatic method of mathematics. Book 1 begins with definitions followed by the famous 5 postulates. Euclid then gives a list of common notions. The first definitions are:

1.1. *A point is that which has no part.*
1.2. *A line is a breadthless length.*
1.3. *The extremities of lines are points.*
1.4. *A straight line lies equally with respect to the points on itself.*

The common notions are axioms such as: "*Things equal to the same thing are also equal to one another.*"

LATER MATHS AND ARCHIMEDES

Archimedes (287–212BC) was a brilliant mathematician as well as famed inventor. His achievements in maths were prodigious, as a list of even his surviving works suggests: *On the Sphere and the Cylinder; On the Measurement of the Circle; On Conoids and Spheroids; On Spirals; On the Equilibrium of Surfaces* where the theory of the lever is propounded, enabling him to boast "Give me somewhere to stand and I will move the Earth!"; *On the Quadratura of the Parabola* and *The Sand Reckoner.* This last work deals with the problem of expressing huge numbers. It demonstrates that the number of grains of sand in the universe, far from being infinite, may on some asumptions be reckoned as 10^{63}.

Archimedes also calculated a far closer value for Pi. He designed his own tomb incorporating a sphere inside a cylinder, to record his discovery that the sphere occupies two-thirds of the space. His most famous discovery, 'Archimedes' principle', states that a body immersed in fluid loses weight equal to the weight of

Above: Reconstruction of the lighthouse at Alexandria. At c.115m (383ft) tall, its light both guided shipping and symbolized the city's intellectual brilliance.

the amount of fluid it displaces. Archimedes traditionally realized this on stepping into his bath, crying out "Eureka" (I have found it!).

Only two of 12 works attributed to Apollonius of Perge (*c.*260–190BC), the 'Great Geometer', survive. In *Conics*, he pioneered terms such as ellipse, parabola, and hyperbola describing various types of orbit. *Conics* distilled 200 years of earlier thinking. It remained canonical even for 17th-century revolutionaries such as Descartes, Fermat and Newton.

Later Greek maths continued to develop but less vigorously. Ptolemy summarized much of it in the 2nd century AD. Diophantus (*c.*AD200–80) was the one noted Greek contributor to algebra, although only six of his works survive. He influenced the Arabs, who later proved far more original at algebra.

Below: Archimedes, the great mathematician of the 3rd century BC, portrayed by José de Ribera (1591–1652).

ASTRONOMY
MAPPING THE COSMOS 600BC–AD150

Above: Ptolemy (Claudius Ptolemaeus), the last great Hellenic astronomer, who worked in Alexandria in the 2nd century AD. From a portrait by Pedro Berruguette and Justus of Ghent c.1475.

Below: The constellation of Hercules with Corona and Lycra, from Atlas Coelestis of 1729 by John Flamsteed, painted by James Thornhill. Viewing the cosmos scientifically and mythologically is one of the Greeks' lasting achievements.

The Greeks were not the world's first astronomers. Egyptians and Babylonians had compiled detailed star charts to predict eclipses, but their knowledge remained tied to their religions. Soon after 600BC, the Greeks began to observe and speculate boldly and rationally. Thales probably used Babylonian records to predict the solar eclipse of 585BC. But his other astronomical feat, suggesting Earth was spherical, was unprecedented. Inspired by him, Anaximander pioneered geometrical astronomy. He posited that the Sun, stars and Moon are rings of fire, respectively 27, 18 and 9 times the Earth's diameter, encased in tubes. Through holes in these tubes their light is seen. His concept of the Earth floating in space was too radical for his first successors, who reverted to cosier ideas.

CLASSICAL ASTRONOMY
In Periclean Athens (*c.*460–430BC), Anaxagoras daringly posited that the sun was a fiery stone "larger than the Peloponnese", the moon shining with its reflected light. (These were such novel ideas that Anaxagoras left Athens to escape impiety charges. These were really political, aimed at Pericles his patron.)

Pythagoreans living in Italy went much further. Restating Thales' idea of a spherical Earth, they suggested that the Earth itself is one of the planets, not the centre of the universe. All planets, including the Sun, move around the "central fire" whose light, in Pythagorean cosmogony, the Sun only reflects. The Pythagoreans also first realized that the morning and evening stars are the same planet: Venus.

Aristotle in the 4th century BC put the Earth solidly back at the centre of things, with the planets circling it. But he was an unoriginal astronomer, just restating the views of Eudoxus of Cnidus. Eudoxus had posited homocentric orbits for the planets to explain their *retrograde motions* (when seen from Earth, planets can appear to move backward). Around 330BC Callipus elaborated this system, adding further spheres for the lunar and solar orbits and calculating the year accurately at 365.25 days. Heraclides Ponticus (*c.*390–310BC) reputedly suggested that Mercury and Venus rotate around the Sun, which itself circles the Earth, pointing towards the heliocentric theory.

ARISTARCHUS' REVOLUTION
At Alexandria, whose new Library/ Mausoleum attracted Greece's brightest minds, Greek astronomy reached its climax. Its boldest thinker was Aristarchus of Samos (*c.*310–230BC). He posited the full heliocentric theory: that the Earth and other planets revolve around the Sun, the Earth itself turning every 24 hours on its own axis. To avoid the parallax (apparent movement) of the fixed stars, he placed them unimaginably far off. This solved all problems of retrograde motions. It proved too radical, however, for Aristarchus

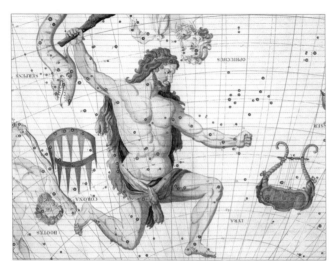

Right: The geocentric universe as envisaged by Ptolemy, with 27 concentric circles describing the orbits of the heavenly bodies from the Moon to Saturn, the farthest planet visible to the naked eye.

united other scientists against him, one trying to indict him for impiety in uprooting the Earth. Archimedes also rejected Aristarchus' ideas – without calling for his trial. Aristarchus had just one Greek follower, Seleucus, his ideas lying dormant until Copernicus in the 16th century.

THE ALEXANDRIAN ACHIEVEMENT

While sticking to the geocentric theory, Alexandria's astronomers made impressive contributions to science. Most were polymaths, such as Eratosthenes of Cyrene (275–194BC), who became Librarian in 235BC. He is renowned for calculating the Earth's diameter. Eratosthenes knew that on 21 June at noon in Syene on the Tropic of Cancer the Sun would be at its zenith. He also knew that in Alexandria the angle of the Sun's elevation would then be 7.2 degrees south of the zenith. He calculated the distance from Alexandria to Syene as 7.2/360 of the total circumference of the Earth. The distance between the cities was a known 800km (500 miles), so he worked out the Earth's circumference as 39,690km (24,663 miles), within 98% of the real figure. Like other Greek astronomers, he relied wholly on observations made by the naked eye, as they had no lenses.

Hipparchus of Nicaea (*c*.190–126BC) was probably the greatest Alexandrian astronomer. He discovered the precession of the equinoxes; estimated the length of the lunar month and catalogued 850 fixed stars, giving their longitude and latitude, and improved the theory of epicycles invented by Apollonius *c*.220BC. He based his theories both on observation and on tables going back to Babylonian records. He also noted a *nova* (new star).

Most of Hipparchus' work survives only in the *Almagest* of Ptolemy, the last Greek astronomer, living in Alexandria in the 2nd century AD. Ptolemy perfected the geocentric theory of the universe, providing detailed mathematical theories supported by observations. His belief that the same divine harmony resonated in the stars and the human soul passed to the medieval and Renaissance worlds.

Below: Syene (Aswan) in Egypt. Eratosthenes calculated the distance from Alexandria to Syene as 7.2/360 of the Earth's circumference, so giving him a remarkably accurate figure for it.

GEOGRAPHY
MAPPING THE EARTH c.550BC–AD170

Above: The Stoa at Miletus, the wealthy Ionian city where Hecataeus drew up the first known map of the world in the 6th century BC.

Below: Ptolemy of Alexandria's map of the Middle East, from Phoenicia (Lebanon) across to Babylonia (southern Iraq), drawn up in the 2nd century AD. His maps are both beautiful and functional.

The Greeks were the first geographers in the full meaning of the word. Their researches were linked to astronomers' theoretical findings – which led to the idea of the Earth as spherical – and to reports from navigators and other travellers. Greek geographical knowledge continued growing under the Romans.

THE FIRST GEOGRAPHERS
(c.550–420BC)

The first geographers were also historians – *historia* meant originally any inquiry or research. Hecataeus (*c*.560–490BC), born in Miletus, travelled widely around the Mediterranean, possibly venturing into the Atlantic. He was involved in the abortive Ionian Revolt against Persia of 499–494BC, despite initially opposing it because hostile to its leader Aristagoras.

Hecataeus' great work was a map of the whole world, possibly inspired by an earlier map by Anaximander. He saw the Earth as a disc surrounded by the all-encircling Ocean, divided into four

> ### PYTHEAS, THE
> ### GREAT EXPLORER
> The classical Greeks were seldom adventurous sailors, preferring to stick to known routes and landmarks. The Carthaginians, anyway, had long barred Greeks from the western Mediterranean and Atlantic. But Pytheas (*c*.380–310BC), a native of Marseilles, the largest Greek colony in southern France, managed somehow to break out to the Atlantic. He sailed up the west coast of Gaul (France) to Cornwall, then commercially very important due to its tin mines. He continued on up past the "Bretannic Isles" – as he is the first recorded person to call them – and reached a northern land called Thule. This could have been Iceland or Norway. It baffled Pytheas, who wrote of places where "land properly speaking no longer exists, nor sea nor air, but a mixture of these things, in which earth and water and all things are suspended… on which no one can walk nor sail." This sounds like pack ice and heavy fogs, both unknown to Greeks. Pytheas returned safely home but his account survives only through Strabo's summaries.

quadrants, east–west by the Mediterranean, and north–south by the rivers Ister (Danube) and Nile. Europe filled the northern half and Africa/Asia the southern half. If ridiculed for inaccuracies by Herodotus (*c*.484–420BC), his better-informed successor, Hecataeus' map was the first to state accurately the continents' relative positions.

In *Periegasis*, Hecataeus described many countries' customs, religions, fauna and flora. (In Egypt, he boasted to a priest that his ancestry went back 16 generations.

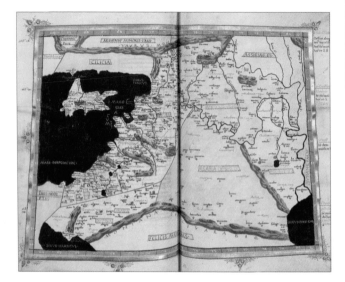

The priest replied that his own went back 345!) Hecataeus' map influenced many later generations' worldview. Herodotus, although fascinatingly informative about much of Asia and Europe, was not a cartographer.

Aristotle realized that the Earth was a globe, dividing it into zones, and his pupil Dicecarchus made a new map incorporating his changes. Otherwise geography had advanced little by the mid-4th century BC. Aristotle was uncertain whether the Caspian Sea opened on to the Ocean that Greeks thought encircled the Earth, and he confused the Caucasus with the Himalayan mountains. All changed radically with the philosopher's other pupil.

AFTER ALEXANDER
Alexander the Great's conquests (334–323BC) opened up a vast new world. Alexander himself reached the Punjab in northern India, and the voyage by his admiral Nearchus from the mouth of the Indus to the head of the Persian Gulf provided a flood of new information for geographers. This was collected and analysed at Alexandria's great Library/Museum. Eratosthenes in the 3rd century BC worked out not only the Earth's

Below: Herodotus the great historian was also an intrepid traveller.

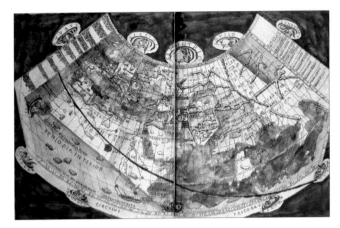

circumference but also longitudes and latitudes for many places – suggesting that he deserved more than his nickname of Beta, or second best. Hipparchus in the 2nd century BC and Posidonius in the 1st continued this work.

GRAECO-ROMAN GEOGRAPHY
Under the long *pax Romana* (Roman peace) after 30BC, geography remained primarily a Greek affair. Strabo (64BC–AD21), who came from the Greek city of Amasia on the Black Sea, travelled widely and wrote 17 books on geography. He held the view that the Earth was a sphere with all the continents, Europe, Asia and Africa, forming a single mass surrounded by the Ocean. Although Strabo claimed to have travelled as far as Ethiopia, his knowledge derives in fact mostly from Eratosthenes, whose works he thus helped to preserve.

The last great Hellenic geographer was Ptolemy of Alexandria. In the mid-2nd century AD he wrote his *Geography* in eight books. By then Rome's invasion of the British Isles, expeditions into the North Sea and trade links with India had vastly extended geographical knowledge. The map Ptolemy drew up reflected this, showing India and even, hazily, China. But he still imagined the three (known) continents as encircled by one ocean. His map remained canonical until 1492.

Above: The Earth as mapped by Ptolemy of Alexandria, who was a great cartographer as well as astronomer. Showing the three known continents, with even China hazily recognized, his ideas remained canonical until the discovery of America in 1492.

Below: Alexander's conquests led to a vast widening of Greek geographical knowledge. From an Indian Mughal painting of the 16th century.

TECHNOLOGY
THE FORGOTTEN ACHIEVEMENTS

Above: Archimedes, the most polymathic of Greek geniuses, inadvertently killed by a Roman soldier in the fall of Syracuse in 212BC. From a Roman mosaic.

Below: Found in the sea near Antikythera, dating to c.80BC, this complex bronze mechanism has 31 gear wheels. It was probably both an astronomical and a navigational device.

The Greeks were once thought to have neglected technology because they had no wish to dirty their hands with science's practical applications. Maintained by their myriad slaves, the argument ran, the Greeks saw science as a gentlemanly pursuit of no practical value. Plutarch, the 2nd-century AD historian, has been quoted to support this view: "Thinking mechanics and all utilitarian arts fit only for vulgar craftsmen, he [Archimedes] concentrated only on things where the beautiful and are not mixed with the necessary." No or little machinery meant little economic advance, and ultimately Graeco-Roman civilization's failure.

Plutarch's view is now seen as misleading, reflecting only the prejudices of his class. (Similar sentiments were frequently voiced by British aristocrats during Britain's Industrial Revolution.) If the Greeks could not match even medieval and early modern Europe's technological achievements, let alone

China's massive inventiveness, they made many useful inventions. Only the ancient world's political and economic limitations, and its general decline after c.AD200, precluded further technological advances by still creative polymaths. That the word *machine* comes from Greek *mekhane* is no coincidence.

One of the earliest known applications of machinery was in the theatre. Here large cranes lifted scenery and actors, usually representing gods (but once Socrates) on and off stage. These cranes, described by Aristotle, must have used a weight and pulley principle of some complexity but no remains have been found.

Similar machinery was probably used to build many of the great Greek temples, including the Parthenon in Athens, where massive blocks of marble had to be lifted high into place.

THE ANTIKYTHERA MECHANISM

A discovery from beneath the sea near the island of Antikythera has revealed Greek technological sophistication. Dating from *c.*80BC, this remarkable bronze mechanism has at least 31 gear wheels, making it a rival of any such mechanism, in Asia or Europe, before the 19th century. With orbits for the Sun, Venus and other planets, it was probably intended both as a clock and as an astronomical device, incorporating discoveries made in the Hellenistic period. It is the sophisticated ancestor of both computers and clocks, therefore. Although the only such device known today, it is unlikely to have been the only one made. Most bronze objects have been lost, however, melted down for their metal content in the Dark Ages, be they computers or clocks.

Above: The waterwheels of Bihiyat on the Orontes River. Known to the Greeks by the 4th century BC, *watermills spread in the Hellenistic and Roman periods. A watermill can grind 150kg (330lb) of grain per hour, compared to 7kg (15lb) ground by a slave.*

ARCHIMEDES' SCREW

A mathematician, astronomer and inventor of genius, Archimedes (287–212BC) was born in Syracuse. He worked in Alexandria before returning to become Hieron II's chief scientist. He devised for the powerful Syracusan king many military devices, including formidable walls, cranes that could pull ships from the sea and possibly solar mirrors to burn ships, besides a planetarium and star globe. Archimedes was killed accidentally by a Roman soldier in the capture of Syracuse, but the Romans took over his devices. He is deservedly best known for a utilitarian invention, his screw that helps irrigation.

Archimedes' Screw consists of a screw inside a hollow pipe. The lower end is put in water and the screw then turned, usually by manual labour. As the bottom of the tube turns, it scoops up water. This water slides up a spiral tube as the shaft is turned, until it finally pours out from the top of the tube to feed the irrigation systems. A cruder screw may have been used earlier by the Babylonians to water their Hanging Gardens, but Archimedes definitely developed the screw as used since.

An important labour-saving development that the Greeks adopted was the watermill. Known by the 4th century BC, watermills spread slowly across western Asia, under Roman rule becoming popular around the Mediterranean. A typical watermill could grind 150kg (330lb) of grain per hour, compared to only 7kg (15lb) by a slave.

HERON OF ALEXANDRIA

A mathematician and engineer, Heron, who lived in Alexandria in the mid-1st century AD, was another remarkable polymath. He listed more than 80 different devices in his numerous books, mainly about hydraulics, pneumatics and mechanics. Among them are drinking fountains, self-filling wine goblets, self-trimming lanterns and self-opening temple doors – all ingenious toys. But in his *Mechanics* he dealt with utilitarian devices such as cranes, hoists (lifts) and presses. Another book, *Stereometrica*, gave useful advice on measuring the contents of ships and *amphorae* (jars).

However, Heron perhaps remains best known for his prototype steam engine, a device that was probably of no use at all. In its developed form this was an *aelopile*, a sealed metal cauldron under a hollow metal sphere. Steam funnelled in tubes from the cauldron made the sphere spin, creating the world's first steam turbine Lack of accessible fossil fuels and crude metallurgy may have kept this steam engine a toy, despite legends that it carried fuel up Alexandria's giant *pharos* (lighthouse).

Above and below: Archimedes' most useful invention was his screw. Turned usually by manual labour, it lifted water for irrigation.

MEDICINE
FROM SUPERSTITION TO SCIENCE

Both the Hippocratic oath that doctors traditionally swear, and the snake-entwined staff of their profession, reveal medicine's Greek roots. The oath recalls Hippocrates, the 'first doctor', the latter Asclepius and medicine's religious origins. The Greeks pioneered the move from a religious to scientific approach in medical matters, the invention of rational medicine being among their finest deeds.

In Homer's time, Greek attitudes to sickness and medicine mirrored those of Egypt and Babylon. Treatment involved incantations, magical amulets, spells and prayers to Apollo, god of medicine, and his son Asclepius, the divine healer. These customs long persisted, as did *incubation*, sleeping in precincts at Cos sacred to the god, when healing dreams might come in the night. Such psychosomatic methods helped suggestible sufferers. From the 6th century BC, both attitudes and practice began to change, however.

Above: Galen, the great 2nd-century AD physician, believed that human health was governed by the balance of the 'Four Humours'. From a medieval drawing.

HIPPOCRATES, THE 'FATHER OF MEDICINE' (*c*.465–*c*.380BC)

Almost nothing is known of the first true physician, Hippocrates. Traditionally he was associated with the famous medical school on Cos, but surviving buildings there date from after his time and his very existence has been doubted. He probably lived about the same time as Socrates.

Hippocrates first made careful observation of the body the basis of medicine. Though he never practised dissection – which religion discouraged – prayers and sacrifices held no place in his theories. Instead, changes in diet, drugs, rest and keeping the body 'in balance' were key elements of his cure. This rational approach was his greatest single contribution to medicine. About 60 treatises, the *Hippocratic Corpus*, are attributed to him. In *Sacred Disease* he demolished the idea that epilepsy was a god-sent sickness; in *Airs, Waters, Places* he examined the effects of climate and locality on illnesses. Other treatises cover diagnosis, epidemics, paediatrics, nutrition and surgery.

Above: Hippocrates (C.460–380BC), the 'father of medicine', was the first to study medicine systematically and scientifically.

Below: Asclepius, the divine healer, treating a patient. Greek medicine never wholly lost its religious connections. From a relief of the 4th century BC.

In the 4th century BC Aristotle made a few significant discoveries. His pupil Diocles first practised dissection, so essential to discovering anatomy, and wrote a book on the subject. Dissection of animals was subsequently practised at the Lyceum, Aristotle's school.

ANATOMY IN ALEXANDRIA

In the rich new city of Alexandria, protected by a dynasty of powerful kings with scientific interests and freed from religious taboos, physicians could at last freely practise dissection and even, it is thought, vivisection. Foremost among the bold anatomists of the mid-3rd century BC were Herophilus from Chalcedon and Erasistratus, who had studied at Cos and Athens. Their discoveries about the importance of the heart, brain, vascular and nervous systems were carefully recorded and formed the basis for almost all subsequent medicine for 1,500 years in the Islamic and Christian worlds.

GALEN, THE GREAT SYNTHESIZER (AD129–200)

Galen was a native of Pergamum in Asia Minor. He studied philosophy and rhetoric before switching to study medicine at Pergamum, Smyrna and Alexandria. He began his career treating wounded gladiators at Pergamum. Going to Rome in AD162, he practised as a physician and a medical writer. As the former, he found himself in demand in the highest circles, treating Commodus, the emperor's son, the empress herself and later rulers. Despite fleeing the plague-stricken city in AD166, Galen remained very popular all his life.

As a writer, Galen was prolific. About 350 works are known to be by him. Galen sometimes lectured in public and even dissected pigs' corpses, but original research was not his chief interest. Instead, he tried to synthesize not only earlier findings but also his ideas on philosophy, derived from both Plato and Aristotle, with medicine. A revealing title of one work is *The Ideal Physician is also a Philosopher*.

Galen took a holistic view of health, stressing the importance of exercise, a balanced diet and general hygiene. Among his most vital ideas was the theory of the Four Humours, the four bodily fluids of blood, phlegm, yellow bile and black bile that must be kept in balance. Illness arose when they were out of balance, and might require bloodletting. The overall result was an integrated, comprehensive system summarizing all medical knowledge, canonical until the 17th century.

Above: The Asclepium at Pergamum, in whose sacred precincts patients slept, hoping for healing dreams from the healer-god Asclepius. Such incubation could be very effective with the right person.

Below: Galen's theory of the Four Humours was accepted in Europe and the Arab world for almost 1,500 years.

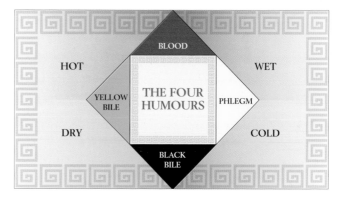

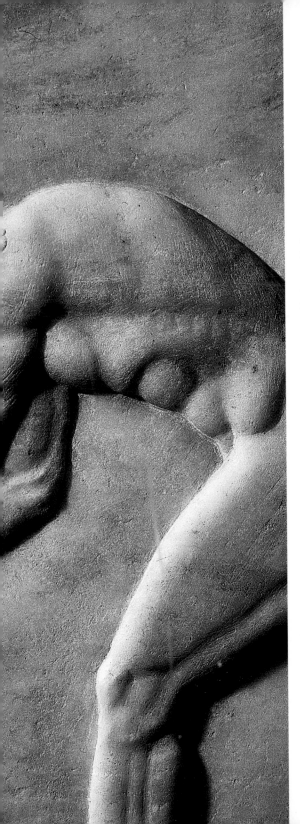

CHAPTER XXIII

ATHLETICS AND SPORT

Athletics, which culminated in the great sporting festivals, were central to Greek life. The *agon* (contest) was crucial to the Greek desire of 'striving always to be best'. Games were important in Homer in the 8th century BC and were still important 1,000 years later under the Romans. While Greek athletic contests are the ancestors of modern sporting events, the differences are as great as the similarities. Greek sports were long dominated by aristocrats, who alone could train properly. Only after 320BC did athletics become professionalized. Contests were between individuals, for there were no team sports. Each polis took intense pride in its victors, honouring them almost as demi-gods.

Excelling in athletics was an expected part of public life for an aspiring aristocrat, as was excelling in oratory or drama. Musical and poetry contests featured in many games, although professional musicians were not admired. Among aspects distinguishing Greek games from other cultures were the nudity of all contestants, which was extremely important – for the gods were shown naked — and the restriction on eligibility to freeborn Greeks from around the Greek world. (Romans were later admitted too, however.) As Greek culture spread around the Mediterranean and Black Sea coasts, and then thinly but widely across Asia after Alexander's conquests, the gymnasium, along with the theatre and agora, became a vital part of urban life.

Left: Two men in the palaestra (wrestling ground), naked like all Greek athletes. From an Athenian carving of c.500BC.

THE GREAT FESTIVALS
THE OLYMPICS AND OTHER GAMES

Above: The starting line of the stadium at Olympia, the site of the most important games in the Hellenic sporting calendar, for which all cities observed a rare truce.

Below: Spartan girls shocked and fascinated other Greeks by exercising only in skimpy tunics, like this girl from the 6th century BC. But they took no part in the main games.

Oldest and most important of Greek festivals, the Olympic Games in honour of Zeus traditionally date from 776BC. Significantly, this was the year at which most Greek cities later chose to start their calendars. According to myth, Hercules was the Games' founder. Olympia's location in the south-western Peloponnese meant that it was distant from major wars (although there were minor local ones) if vulnerable to earthquakes.

The Olympic Games were held quadrennially at the time of the second full moon after the summer solstice. This usually meant late August, not the coolest time of year. Over the centuries Olympia became filled with treasures and fine buildings, the greatest being the Temple of Olympian Zeus. This contained the sculptor Pheidias' last masterpiece, the gold-and-ivory statue of the king of gods, so huge that even seated Zeus' head brushed the roof, making it one of the Seven Wonders of the World. In AD393 Theodosius I banned the Games, whose paganism offended many Christians. (In 1896 the modern Olympics were founded by Pierre de Coubertin.)

THE OLYMPIC TRUCE
A distinctive feature of the Olympics was the proclamation of *Ekecheiria*, the Olympic Truce. Surprisingly, this was almost universally observed and the games were held regularly despite wars and invasions. For their duration, contestants, whether Athenian, Spartan, Theban or Syracusan, recalled they were *all* Greek. To stress this Panhellenism, the ten judges were called *Hellanodikai* (judges of the Greeks). An Olympic prize – a simple olive crown – was the supreme accolade for an athlete.

WOMEN ONLY GAMES
If women could not compete in the main Olympic Games, they had the consolation of holding their own games, the Heraea, honouring the goddess Hera. These too were quadrennial. According to Pausanias writing in the mid 2nd century AD: "The games are footraces for unmarried girls of varying ages. First the youngest run; then come the girls next in age, and the last contestants are the oldest. As they run, their hair falls free and their tunics do not even reach to the knee, while they bare their right shoulders as far as their breasts. The Olympic stadium is reserved for their games but shortened for them by about one-sixth. The winners receive crowns of olive leaves and part of the ox sacrificed to Hera. They may also dedicate statues with their names inscribed upon them." Men were not allowed to watch these games.

Competitors at the games were divided into three age groups: boys, adolescents and grown men. The games were only open to freeborn male Greeks, though from cities all over the Greek world. (Women were barred even from watching). However, there were exceptions. The kings of Macedonia, who claimed Hercules as their ancestor, could participate, but ordinary Macedonians, not classed as Greek, were excluded until after Alexander's conquests.

Later, Roman citizens were also permitted to enter. The most notorious Roman contestant was the emperor Nero, who won *all* the prizes in AD66. Nero introduced Hellenic games to Rome but with little success. The emperor Domitian also failed to interest the Romans in competitive athletics.

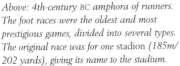

Above: 4th-century BC amphora of runners. The foot races were the oldest and most prestigious games, divided into several types. The original race was for one stadion *(185m/ 202 yards), giving its name to the stadium.*

FESTIVALS AND GAMES

Other Panhellenic games emulated the Olympics. The most important were the Pythian Games held in honour of Apollo at Delphi – originally every eight years and then, after a reorganization in 582BC, every four years. There were the usual athletic and equestrian events but poetry and music were also important contests. The prize was a wreath of bay leaves, a link to poetry.

The Isthmian Games near Corinth were founded – according to different legends – either by Sisyphus, king of Corinth or by Theseus, king of Athens. A less mythical founder was the Corinthian tyrant Periander in c.600BC. The games were held every two years. At the Isthmian Games in 336BC Alexander declared his plan to conquer Persia and there, in 196BC, the Roman general Flaminius proclaimed "liberty for the Greeks", to tumultuous applause. Unfortunately, Roman and Greek ideas of liberty proved very different, leading to prolonged wars.

The Nemean Games, again held every second year, were staged in honour of Zeus at Nemea in the Argolid. They became part of the Panhellenic circuit in 573BC and in the 4th century BC were moved to Argos. The games were similar to those at Olympia.

There were also many local festivals. The grandest were the Panathenaic Games, held every four years as part of the Panathenaic festival in Athena's honour. They included the usual contests but were solely for Athenians.

Above: Aerial view of part of Olympia showing the central Temple of Olympian Zeus and, in the top left corner, the Temple of Hera or Heraion.

Below: The ruins of the covered palaestra *(wrestling school) at Olympia date from the 3rd century BC. The site slowly filled with temples, monuments and other buildings donated by kings and cities.*

RACES ON FOOT AND BY CHARIOT

Above: An Olympic athlete sprinting for one stadion. From a vase painting of the 4th century BC.

The oldest and most prestigious of the games was the foot race. The word *stadion* (stadium), meaning race course, comes from *stade*, a Greek measurement of 185m (202 yards), the length of the first race on foot. The winner of this inaugural sprint at Olympia gave his name to the Olympiad.

Other foot races developed from this. The two-stade race was traditionally introduced at Olympia in 724BC. The *dolichos* (long race) was introduced in 720BC. Its actual length is uncertain but was probably about 20 stade or 4.8km (3 miles). As in a modern marathon, runners began and ended the race in the stadium, but ran through Olympia itself before returning.

THE HOPLITE RACE

Below: Chariot racing was the most glamorous, expensive and dangerous of the contests. It brought huge glory to the victor, although he often employed a driver who might be a slave. From a red figure vase of the 6th century BC.

The last running contest added to the Olympics was the *hoplitodromos* (hoplite race), in 520BC. Contestants ran around the stadium for 1.6km (1 mile), carrying a shield with greaves (leg guards) and helmet. As their armour weighed up to 24kg (60lb), runners often dropped their shields or tripped over fallen competitors,

making onlookers laugh. In vase paintings, runners are sometimes shown leaping over the fallen shields of their collapsing competitors as they pass them.

This race flaunted each polis' military strength. As in hoplite warfare, stamina counted for more than speed, the Spartans being particularly good at the hoplitodromos, as was to be expected from Greece's best hoplites. The link between sport and military training was always acknowledged by the Greeks.

CHARIOT RACING

The most expensive and dangerous Olympic contest was chariot racing, which only rich aristocrats or kings could afford. Chariots had long been used for racing – Homer describes chariot racing at Patroclus' funeral in *The Iliad*.

The sport was introduced to the Olympics in 680BC and soon eclipsed horse racing. Chariots were very light wooden two-wheeled vehicles, drawn by two or four horses. They were difficult to control but the glory and prize went not to the skilled and courageous charioteer, who might be a slave, but to the owner.

This was the one race in which the contestants were not nude but wore a long robe. Falling to the ankles, it fastened high at the waist with a plain belt. Two straps crossing high at the back prevented this from ballooning during the race. Like modern jockeys, charioteers were chosen for their light build.

Arcesilaus IV, king of Greek Cyrene (in Libya), won the chariot race at the Pythian Games at Delphi in 462BC. His slave driver was in fact the only one to complete the whole course. In 416BC the flamboyant Athenian aristocrat Alcibiades had seven chariots in one race at Olympia, which came in first, second and fourth. Philip II of Macedon entered and won an Olympic chariot race in 356BC, a victory that helped prove his true Hellenic credentials.

DANGEROUS GLAMOUR

Chariot races were notoriously dangerous, sometimes lethal. Each race began with a procession into the hippodrome, a herald proclaiming the drivers' and owners' names. About 550m (600 yards) long, the course at Olympia could take 60 chariots but normally fewer entered. The four-horse race – run anticlockwise – had 12 laps, with sharp turns around the posts at each end.

A vivid, perhaps eyewitness, description of the Pythian races comes in Sophocles' play *Electra*, in which the exiled Orestes takes part: "As the bronze trumpet sounded they were off, all shouting to their horses and urging them on… The clatter of rattling chariots filled the arena, the dust flew up as they raced along in a dense mass, each driver goading his team mercilessly trying to draw clear of rival axles and panting horses, whose steaming breath and sweat drenched the flying wheels with foam…

"Orestes kept his horse near the pillar at each end so skilfully that his hub just grazed the turning-post by a hair's breadth each time… But at the last bend he misjudged it, slackening his left rein before the horse was safely round, and so hit the post. The hub was smashed across and he was hurled over the chariot rail, entangled in the reins. As he fell, his horses ran madly on around the course… he was dragged along the ground, his legs pointing at the sky, until other charioteers stopped his horses and released him, so bloody that none of his friends could have recognized him."

Chariot racing, unlike most Greek sports, proved hugely popular in Rome The Circus Maximus, the largest building in Rome, reputedly held 250,000 people. Later, chariot racing was transplanted to Constantinople, capital of the Christian Byzantine Empire, somehow escaping Christian censure. The emperor's palace had a passage leading directly into the hippodrome, so central was chariot racing to Byzantine life. But the rioting mobs who supported the rival Green and Blue factions in Byzantium had long forgotten the ideals of the Classical agon.

Left: The hoplitodromos (hoplite race) was added to the Olympics in 520BC. Contestants ran around the stadium for 1,600m (1 mile) in full armour.

Below: The Charioteer of Delphi, a rare surviving bronze masterpiece of serene beauty, from c.473BC.

LIGHT AND HEAVY SPORTS

Above: Athletes wrestling, from a red figure vase attributed to the Euergides painter, an Attic artist of the 5th century BC. In wrestling, a contestant tried to immobilize his opponent, either by getting him in a hold or pinning him to the ground in a 'fall'. A victor won by getting three out of five falls.

Other sports included boxing and wrestling, both classed as 'heavy' sports, and the long jump and throwing the javelin or discus, considered 'light'. The pentathlon, which was considered by Aristotle the best of sports, combined all five. But all were individual contests. This was the one major difference between ancient and modern athletics: team sports of any sort, were quite unknown in Greece, that land of heroically ultra-competitive individuals.

BOXING AND WRESTLING

In wrestling (*pale*) the aim was to immobilize your opponent, either by getting him in a hold or pinning him to the ground in a 'fall'. The victor was the man who won three out of five falls. 'All-in' wrestling (*pankration*) was popular but could be brutal. Almost anything was allowed, including punching, kicking and strangleholds, only biting and eye-gouging being banned. A referee or judge stood by with a stick to enforce these minimal rules. In both sports the defeated person signalled submission by raising his hand with the index finger extended. Beforehand, contestants rubbed

themselves down with oil and sprinkled sand over their naked bodies. They also tried to soften the sun-baked earth by breaking it up or, in the case of the pankration, soaking it in water. This made the resulting bout a mud bath.

Boxing was even more dangerous. There were no 'Queensberry rules' to restrict where blows might land, and most were aimed at the head. Rabbit punches and blows with the butt of the hand were common. Boxers wore leather thongs around their hands, which later were iron-weighted.

Bouts were decided by a knockout, and often lasted hours. On rare occasions this could lead to the death of one contestant. In that case, however, the prize went to the dead man and his opponent was banned from contests for life. Boxers with their battered faces were notoriously ugly, and therefore not so widely admired as most other athletes.

'LIGHT' SPORTS

The long jump, which seems to have been the only Greek jumping contest, differed radically from the modern long jump. Contestants carried weights of up to 4.5kg (10lb), which they swung forward to increase their mid-air momentum. They reached lengths of 16.6m (54ft), possibly not in one single leap but in a series of rabbit-like jumps. Running remained one of the events at the Panhellenic games such as the Pythian, but the other 'light' sports were performed only as parts of the pentathlon.

The discus thrown by Greek athletes varied considerably in its weight, but as all competitors at a particular festival used

Left: A statue of Apollonius, a famous boxer. In the Hellenistic period (322–30BC) successful professional athletes could become celebrities.

FAMOUS ATHLETES

The cult of the victor was a striking aspect of the Panhellenic games. Winners were hailed as godlike heroes in their home towns. Statues were raised to them, poetry written in their honour – some of it, such as Pindar's, very fine – breaches were even made in the city walls to welcome them on their return. Down to *c.*400BC most victors were aristocrats because they alone could devote themselves to almost full-time training. From the 4th century BC athletes who were not nobly born began to rival these blue-blooded sportsmen. Later still, professional athletes in the modern sense became common.

Typical of an early victor was Milon of Croton in southern Italy. He won the Olympic wrestling prize several times in a career that began with winning the boys' contest in 540BC and lasted 26 years. When finally defeated by a younger man, he was carried shoulder-high around the stadium to cheers. Renowned for his strength, Milon was also known for his immense appetite. The boxer Melancomas of Caria became famous not only for his powerful body but also for his unusual technique. He preferred not to hit his opponents but instead to wear them out by dodging their blows.

Above: A youthful discobolus (disc-thrower). From a black figure vase attributed to the 'Epeleius Painter', c.480BC.

the same one, this did not matter. Surviving examples, made from marble, bronze or lead, weigh between 1.5 and 6.5kg (3 and 14lb), with diameters ranging from approximately 17 to 35cm (6 to 14 inches).

Javelins for athletes differed from the military javelins, being made of an extremely light elder-wood. They had throwing loops that made them spin in flight, keeping them on course. Throws of up to 92m (100 yards) were achievable, sources suggest.

THE PENTATHLON

The pentathlon combined all five sports: discus and javelin throwing, long jump, running and wrestling. It was considered the supreme test of an athlete, for it tested stamina, strength and speed. It was added in 708BC to the 18th Olympiad.

According to legend it was invented by Jason (who had earlier led the Argonauts on the Quest for the Golden Fleece). He combined the five contests, awarding the first prize to his friend Peleus, the father of Achilles, Homer's super-hero. The historical order of events is uncertain, as is how the prizes were awarded. Probably the winner of at least three parts of the overall contest won the pentathlon.

The Victorian British, with their ideals of fair play and the 'game being the thing', on looking at Greek athletics, fondly imagined they had found like-minded precursors. In reality most Greek athletes competed with the obsessive determination of modern professional athletes, although they seldom became rich by doing so.

Below: Athletes with a discus and a javelin. From a red figure vase of the 4th century BC. Both discus and javelin-throwing were considered 'light sports'.

THE GYMNASIUM AND PALAESTRA

Above: The 'Gladiators' Gymnasium' at Pompeii in Italy. The gymnasium, central to true Hellenic life, was adopted by many non-Greek cities too, if for different ends.

Below: Athletes being presented with victory tokens, from an Athenian red figure cup of the 5th century BC. Victorious athletes received only symbolic prizes but gained immense prestige.

The *gymnasion* (gymnasium) and the *palaestra* (wrestling ground) were as central to Greek life as the agora or temples. They were far more than modern gyms or fitness centres, serving as clubs and centres of social and cultural life.

In the gymnasia and palaestras of Athens, Socrates discoursed to Athens' brightest youth in the 5th century BC. Later, Plato and Aristotle founded their schools, the Academy and Lyceum, near gymnasia. These were built outside the city because they needed so much land. (Plato himself had been a wrestler in his youth). The ruins of the gymnasium at Ai Khanum in Afghanistan, a Greek city founded by Alexander the Great or his successors (perhaps originally an Alexandria), bear as quotations from Aristotle the maxims for the Five Ages of Man. Dating from *c.*200BC, these show that, even here, thousands of miles from Greece, the link between mental and physical exercise remained strong.

THE IMPORTANCE OF NUDITY

The word *gymnasion* comes from *gymnos*, naked, for all athletes exercised and competed nude. Athletes at the Olympics and other games always participated nude, the perfect state in which Greek artists depicted gods and heroes. This stress on nudity distinguishes Greek culture from all others. Even the Romans, in so many ways the Greeks' heirs, did not share this love of idealized nudity (although Romans at times exercised naked). Male nudity, openly admired, probably increased the general homoerotic aura of athletics.

THE PERFECT MALE BODY

The gymnasium was essentially a public sports ground open to all citizens. Usually stoas were built around the sanded area, originally a running track, where those not exercising could talk or ogle the athletes. In classical Athens there were private gymnasia, some socially exclusive. The politician Themistocles, mastermind of Persia's defeat in 480BC, had to join an un-smart gymnasium, but this suited his democratic instincts well.

Most cities established and maintained at least one public gymnasium. Citizens' physical fitness was seen as vital to the health of the city itself – unsurprisingly, as a polis relied for its existence on the fighting abilities of its citizen army. Socrates, in a dialogue written by Xenophon (a soldier), chided Epigenes, another disciple, for not keeping in good shape, for shirking his duty as a citizen: "You've got the body of someone who just doesn't care about public matters… You should care for your body like an Olympic athlete." In Athens, gymnasia were supervised by boards of ten *gymnasiarchs* (superintendents), one from

each tribe. In smaller poleis an honorary gymnasiarch hired professional trainers. Lucian, writing in the 2nd century AD, summed up the Greek ideal: "The young men have a tanned complexion from the sun ... they reveal spirit, fire and manliness. They are in fabulous condition, being neither lean and skinny nor excessively fat, but have perfectly symmetrical bodies." This perfectly describes the *Doryphorus* statue made by Polyclitus 650 years earlier, long a canon of male beauty.

PALAESTRA AND BATHS

Sometimes adjacent to the gymnasium but often separate, the palaestra or wrestling ground was similarly laid out as a rectangular court surrounded by stoas, often thicker on the north side to protect against winter winds. More compact than a gymnasium, a palaestra might be found inside the city, which increased its attraction as a social and intellectual centre. Before wrestling or boxing, athletes covered themselves with olive oil – a costly procedure, at times subsidized by public funds – and dusted themselves with fine sand. This gave some protection against the sun or wind. Younger men who could afford to spent much of the day toning up their bodies and, sometimes, their minds. Boys received most of their physical education in the paleastra's stoas, ogled by older men and watched over by their tutor (usually a slave), who was intended to deter would-be seducers.

After exercising, athletes scraped off their sweat, oil and dust with a strigal, a metal object, or a sponge. The Greeks had public baths that, if not luxurious like the Romans' opulent structures, had hip baths, a hot room and a communal plunge pool.

Above: The palaestra at Olympia, the most prestigious in the Greek world. Here contestants for the great quadrennial games did their final training.

Left: Polyclitus of Argos's Doryphorus (Spear-carrier), incarnating the perfectly honed, symmetrical Greek ideal. A Roman copy of the bronze original by the great 5th-century BC sculptor.

CHAPTER XXIV

WORK AND LEISURE

Greece's cultural brilliance rested on a very limited economic base. Greece has few fertile valleys. Much land is rough hill terrain, although Sicily and some other colonies were more fertile. Later, Alexander's conquests opened up wide new territories but widened the gap between rich and poor. Life for most Greeks, if frugal, was lived with passionate intensity. The Greeks celebrated marriages, funerals and other events with ceremony, almost always in the open. The idea of a private life was considered eccentrically antisocial – a charge levelled against the playwright Euripides when he retreated to Salamis Island. Women, however, remained at home most of the time, especially in Athens. Closeted in cramped houses, they enjoyed little freedom except in religious roles. Such seclusion may partly explain the prevalence of male homo-sexuality, which in Classical Greece enjoyed a status probably unique in history. But the monogamous family was the basis of society.

Not unique to ancient Greece, but hard for the modern world to accept, was the prevalence of slavery. Slavery in the Greek world lacked any racist element – one source of slaves was other Greeks – but it alone made possible the leisured life, whether devoted to athletics, politics, art, drama or philosophy. The Greeks' achievement in these fields distinguishes them from other, often richer, slave-owning societies such as Carthage, which is famed for little beyond its wealth.

Left: 6th-century BC cup of a man embracing a woman, probably a hetaera (courtesan). Greek artists celebrated all aspects of life.

FARMERS, SHEPHERDS AND FISHERMEN

Above: Two men threshing wheat by hand. Farming in Greece was traditionally small-scale, providing small surpluses even in good years.

Below: Despite most Greek cities' proximity to the sea, fish remained something of a rarity – if one much enjoyed, as this exuberant marine mosaic from Pompeii suggests.

Paradoxically, while Greek life was urban and focused on the polis, most citizens remained farmers, except in the rare trading city such as Corinth, which had little hinterland. Most farmer-citizens lived inside their polis for reasons of security and entertainment, commuting out to their fields. However, some built solid shelters in the countryside for the busy summer months. Land always retained its unique social, political and symbolic status as the basis of wealth.

SKILLED FARMERS

Greek farms were mostly very small, with a typical plot being only 6ha (15 acres). Technically, farming always remained simple, but within these limits Greek farmers exploited their land to the full. They multi-cropped their fields, mixing many different crops – vegetables including pulses, fruits, figs, vines and olives – and

FISH, A RARE DISH
Most Greek cities were near the sea, so fish might be thought to have been a staple food. But although authors mention fish-eating, and fishbones have often been unearthed, fish usually remained a relative luxury. The Mediterranean is not a particularly rich area for fishing. Without modern means of transport and storage, fish had to be eaten right away. This meant that the Greeks only ate fish occasionally and in small amounts, often only to add flavour to otherwise monotonous meals.

also letting fields lie fallow. They normally grew fruit and vegetables in plots close to town, while up on the hills shepherds tended flocks of sheep and goats. Transhumance was practised: moving animals up to mountain pastures in summer and back again in winter, so that their dung fertilized the land. Owners of such flocks were among the wealthier minority of farmers, however.

HARD TOIL

Greek rural life was far from idyllic. Described in *The Iliad* and more fully in Hesiod's *Works and Days*, it was for most people a daily grind. Better-off farmers had oxen, which could pull carts as well as ploughs but needed feeding and watering year round, plus a slave or two. Slaves provided more skilled muscle-power but needed feeding *and* clothing all year round. Both human and non-human live-stock represented major investments.

In the 6th century BC Greek farmers – except those in poor backwoods like Aetolia – were pulled into a 'market economy', a process speeded up by the introduction of coinage. Because early coins were high-value pieces, barter

Left: Greek sheep-farmers often practised transhumance, moving flocks up to the mountains in summer and back to the lowlands in winter, where they multi-cropped with olive groves. Sheep dung is a valuable fertilizer.

remained the norm for daily purposes, but wealth could now be measured and amassed. While the rich grew richer, the poor became ever more indebted, often being forced to make their own persons surety for debts, so losing their liberty along with their land.

To protect poorer farmers, in 594BC the Athenian reformer Solon banned enslavement for debt and the export of wheat from Attica. This led to an enduring enthusiasm for cultivating olive trees. It needed to endure, for olive trees take 15 years to start bearing fruit and about 40 to become fully productive. Attic olive oil was valued across the Mediterranean as a perfume as well as for cooking and lighting. The vases in which it was sold encouraged the phenomenal growth of Athenian pottery. Wheat was now imported to Attica from the Black Sea area or Egypt.

THE STAPLE CROPS

Barley and wheat were the main cereals grown in Greece. Olive groves allowed intercropping, i.e. land could be culti-vated beneath or between the trees, but olives cannot stand much frost. Vines, tougher and thriving on very rocky slopes, were even more widely planted. Wine was the main drink after water, a useful (if unrecognized) source of sugar and vitamins. Pulses formed a key part of the diet, and helped fix nitrogen in the soil. Cabbages, onions, garlic and lettuce were grown widely, but tomatoes, rice, peppers and potatoes were unknown. Figs, apples, grapes, plums and quinces were common

fruits, but meat was an expensive rarity for ordinary people. Cheese, from sheep, goats and cattle, was eaten more often.

PERENNIAL SHORTAGES

The Greek climate is hard for farmers. Rainfall, mostly concen-trated in the winter months, can vary dramatically from year to year and place to place. As Aristotle noted in his treatise on *Meteorology*: "At times drought or flood can affect large areas of the country simul-taneously, but sometimes it has only local effects. Often the country overall has the normal rainfall for the season or even more, but one part suffers drought. Occasionally the oppo-site happens, when the country all around has only light rainfall or even a drought, one particular part is deluged in rain." Farming pro-duced small surpluses in good years, and in bad years there were acute shortages.

Below: The olive harvest from a black figure vase. Olives were vital to Greek life, providing oil for cooking and lighting and serving also as a soap-substitute.

TRADERS AND TRADE ROUTES

Above: Most merchants ships remained small with one mast. Despite this, Greek traders criss-crossed the Mediterranean and the Black Sea. From a vase of c.500BC.

Mycenaean traders had crossed the Mediterranean from Sicily to Egypt, but they disappeared after 1200BC. By the 8th century BC, Greece's modest trade was dominated by Phoenician ships. Yet soon after, as growing populations pressed on limited land, Greek poleis began to found colonies around the Mediterranean and Black Sea. Trade was seldom the chief reason for this expansion – Naucratis in Egypt was one of the few colonies founded for trade – but good harbours were always sought. Even colonies founded as agricultural settlements initially needed goods from the homeland. Transport was always far cheaper by sea than land for heavy goods.

Pottery, at first mostly from Corinth but by the mid-6th century BC overwhelmingly from Athens, was Greece's main export. Black and red figure vases containing olive oil from Attica and fine wines – from Chios, Samos, Thasos and Lesbos, where the poet Sappho's brother was a wine merchant – went to Egypt, Italy and Gaul (France). But the Greeks also made other, even grander containers.

A PRINCESS'S TOMB

Herodotus in his *Histories* mentioned a *krater* (bronze jar) holding 300 amphorae of wine, made by Laconian smiths for Croesus of Lydia (560–546BC). He was thought to have exaggerated until the discovery in 1953 of a vessel at Vix in an Iron Age tomb in central France. The *Krater of Vix*, the largest known ancient bronze vessel, is 1.5m (5ft) high and could have held about 1,089 litres (240 gallons) of wine. Along with Athenian silver cups c.530 and 520BC, it was buried in the tomb of a Gallic princess around 500BC. It shows how Greek trade had already penetrated distant lands.

Massilia (Marseilles), founded c.600BC by settlers from Ionia, became the chief entrepôt for this trade. Gaul, on the overland routes north, was by 500BC very important to the Greeks as Carthage had closed the south-western Mediterranean to monopolize trade with northwest Europe.

THE GRAIN TRADE

During the course of the 6th century, Athens, growing fast, became critically dependent on grain imports from the Black Sea. The fertile Ukrainian and

Left: The Krater of Vix, the largest known ancient bronze vessel, which can hold c.1,089 litres (240 gallons), shows the extent of Greek exports. Unearthed in Burgundy, central France, it dates from c.520BC.

Left: Greek trade routes spread right across the Mediterranean and the Black Sea, exchanging Greek artefacts usually for wheat. After Alexander the Great, these routes extended far across central Asia and then down the Red Sea to India.

Russian steppes were then ruled by Scythian princes. Fortunately, they proved fond of the Greek wine, oil, pottery and other artefacts sold them in return for their exports of hides, timber, slaves and grain. Safeguarding the wheat route became a prime concern of Athenian politics from the time of the Pisistratids (545–510BC). Hence the importance of controlling the Hellespont and Bosphorus.

The Piraeus, rebuilt on the gridiron pattern after the Persian wars (490–478BC) by Hippodamus, became the greatest port in the eastern Mediterranean, secured to Athens by the Long Walls. An import-export tax of just 2 per cent made it an attractive place to do business, including banking, and many Greeks from ravaged Ionia settled there.

ROUTES ACROSS ASIA
After Alexander's conquest of the Persian Empire, new overland routes east opened up. In great Hellenistic cities such as Antioch or Alexandria, the rich demanded luxuries: perfumes, silks, drugs, spices and precious stones. Spices came from India and Arabia Felix (Yemen). Silk from China remained a great luxury even in the Roman Empire, as China jealously guarded its monopoly of sericulture. A rougher 'wild silk' came from the island of Cos. Caravan routes along the valleys of Asia Minor made coastal cities like Ephesus and Miletus wealthy.

The Ptolemaic rulers of Egypt encouraged exploration, sending expeditions up the Nile in search of gold and ivory and down the Red Sea looking for spices. This second route led to a lucky discovery in 116BC, when a sea captain in their service found the sea-route to India via the Red Sea port of Berenice. Utilizing the regular monsoon winds that blow across the Indian Ocean, he set sail in July, returning home blown by reverse winds in December. The routes east were outlined in the *Periplus Maris Erythrae*, a handbook for sailors of the 1st century AD.

Below: After 550BC Athens became increasingly dependent on grain imports from the Black Sea region. Safeguarding the wheat route through the Hellespont (Dardanelles), here shown at Gallipoli, became very important in Athenian politics.

TRADES AND PROFESSIONS
FROM POTTERS TO BANKERS

Above: Storage jars for olive oil from the Bronze Age. Oil was always one of the Greeks' main tradeable commodities.

Below right: Vase painting of a smith at work. Whether free or slave, all smiths worked in small forges, mass production being unknown.

Below: Marble stele (gravestone) of Sosinos of Gortyna, a bronze founder of the late 5th century BC. Classical Athens attracted many such specialized metal-workers.

Although Greek society always remained mostly agricultural, craftsmen had a recognized role by classical times in large cities such as Athens and Corinth. Even in the Bronze Age, Cretan potters and goldsmiths had produced fine artefacts exported around the Aegean and sometimes farther afield. A bronze tripod made in Crete is mentioned by the tablets in Linear B, an early form of Greek. One was found in the palace at Pylos, dating from c.1200BC. The ensuing Dark Ages ended such trade, which revived only after 700BC. Athens most notably then became, and long remained, noted for making goods of superb quality.

POTTERY
The most common Greek artefact is pottery. Pottery shards have the advantage (for archaeologists) of being almost indestructible. When reassembled, vases make a valuable guide to dating because styles changed fairly quickly and consistently. Olive oil and wine from Greece were almost always exported in pottery amphorae. The superb vases, often signed by their makers or found intact in Etruscan tombs, such as the *Chigi Vase* with its triple tier of friezes from c.620BC, were certainly regarded as artworks, not just as containers. However, with plastic unknown and glass rare and expensive, most storage vessels and domestic appliances, from cookers to hip-baths, were made of fired clay.

Corinth, which initially dominated the important carrying trade west, was home to the first great ceramicists. Then, in the mid-6th century BC, Athenian potters almost totally displaced them. From the late 5th century BC on they, in turn, faced rivalry from Boeotian and southern Italian potters. But booming demand kept all Greek potters busy. Other cities specialized in different products: Chalcis and Corinth in metalware, Miletus in textiles, Pergamum later in parchment. Potters in Athens originally worked in the Kerameikos, the potters' quarter (our word ceramic comes from Greek *keramikos*) south-west of the Agora. The hill on the west of the Agora, the Kolonos Agoraeus, was known for its concentration of blacksmiths and bronze-workers. The whole area must have rung with the sounds of hammered metal, with smoke from their charcoal forges forming a mini-smog. Appropriately, the temple on the low hill nearby was dedicated to Hephaestus, the blacksmith god.

CEPHALUS, SHIELD-MAKER EXTRAORDINARY
Later, the Piraeus, which became after 480BC the economic heart of Athens – indeed soon almost of the eastern Mediterranean – attracted numerous merchants and workshops. Many different types of craftsmen, free or slave, including bronze-, silver- and goldsmiths, cobblers, carpenters, and arms and armour makers, lived and worked there.

Left: The Temple of Hephaestus, the god of metal-workers, overlooked the Agora, the centre of Athens' social and economic life. Nearby was the smiths' quarter.

Below: A potter of the late 6th century BC, the period when Athenian ceramic products became pre-eminent around the Mediterranean.

One of the largest workshops known in the Piraeus belonged to Cephalus, a wealthy metic (resident foreigner) from Syracuse. He appears in the opening passages of Plato's great dialogue *Republic*. Cephalus was a historical figure, the owner of 120 slaves who specialized in making shields – an essential part of the Athenian war effort, the dialogue being set during the Peloponnesian War. However, these slaves were probably not all under one roof and certainly were not working on a production line. Instead, each would have made a whole shield himself. Cephalus was among the richest men in Athens. Socrates, Plato's protagonist in the dialogue, treats him with respect, so clearly tradesmen as such were not despised even by aristocrats such as Plato. Most workshops had a maximum of five or six workers.

BANKERS AND MONEY-LENDERS

Banking in Greece was originally a monopoly of the temples. People would deposit and borrow money on interest from priests, and temples remained important safe deposits for major sums until the end of paganism. But, when coins became common in the 5th century BC, money-lenders called *trapezitae* set up their 'tables' in public places such as the South Stoa in Athens, displacing most temples. (Greek *trapeza*, bank, comes from *trapeza* 'table', just as bank comes from Latin *bancus*, 'bench'.) This banking system operated primarily on letters of credit, not coinage. Pasion, an ex-slave, was one of the richest bankers of the 4th century BC. Another system was later developed by Ionian cities such as Miletus, where financial transactions became so complicated that they required professional managers. Often these worked with the city authorities to create an effective bank monopoly.

In Ptolemaic Egypt, where commerce on a grander scale required larger funds, a central state monopoly bank was established in Alexandria. It opened branches across the kingdom and continued in operation under Roman rule after 30BC.

DRINKING TOGETHER
SYMPOSIA AND BARS

Above: Diners at a symposium from a mural in the Tomb of the Diver, Poseidonia (Paestum), Italy, c.480BC. Symposia were among the highlights of Greek life, where conversation and entertainment, high or low, accompanied the wine.

Below: A scene from a symposium, where two diners, sharing a couch as was usual, seem drunk and mutually attracted. From a red figure Attic vase of c.500BC.

For Greek men, a symposium was the great occasion for socializing. *Symposion* means literally 'drinking together', and wine (the only alcohol the Greeks drank) flowed at these events. They could be celebrations – of an athletic or artistic victory – but many seemed to have just involved people dropping in uninvited. A true symposium was more than a mere booze-up. It offered, besides food, entertainment by dancers and flute girls, who were enjoyed as much for looks as their music. At the best type of symposium, wine-fired conversation was what finally counted.

A symposium took place in a house's *andron* ('men's room'), a special window-less room on the ground floor. Its floor was raised at the walls, against which couches were arranged. Greeks always dined reclining on couches, a custom copied by Etruscans and Romans. Guests on arrival had their sandals

Above: Pompeii fresco showing Ariadne seduced by Dionysus, the re-enactment of which myth in Xenophon's Symposium *fired onlookers with heterosexual lust.*

removed by slaves and might be garlanded with flowers and anointed before being shown to their couches. Two men shared one couch, reclining on their left sides. Finger bowls were placed on tables beside them – the Greeks ate chiefly with their fingers, throwing bones to the floor for the dogs.

THE SYMPOSIARCH

A crucial figure at a well-run symposium was the *symposiarch*, master of ceremonies, elected for the evening. He decided the proportion of wine to water. This varied, but about two parts of wine to five of water was usual. (Drinking wine undiluted was thought barbaric if not insane. Conversely Demosthenes, the great orator, was thought a prig for preferring plain water.) The two were mixed in a krater, a large elaborate bowl, snow sometimes first being used to cool the wine in a *psykter* (wine-cooler). Guests decided how many kraters of wine to prepare, as all drank the same amount. At most symposia, three kraters were thought enough. In the words of Eubulus, a playwright, "One krater is for health, one for love, one for sleep."

Wine circulated 'from left to right', i.e. anticlockwise, the symposiarch setting the pace. Libations – sprinkling wine on the floor – were made to Dionysus, the wine god, Zeus and to the special *agathon daimon*, the good spirit presiding. As wine flowed, diners might debate agreed topics, but there were other entertainments too.

FLUTE GIRLS AND PHILOSOPHY

In an atmosphere as enclosed as a modern nightclub's, with wine flowing ever more freely, diners played games such as *kottabos*, flicking wine at a target. Sex – with other guests, or more usually with dancing girls and serving boys (both often slaves) – might follow. Illustrations show some symposia degenerating into orgies.

But two famous dinner parties ended very differently. In Plato's novel-like *Symposium*, the guests – among them Aristophanes and the tragedian Agathon, the host – solemnly if not soberly discuss the nature of *eros*, sexual desire. Alcibiades bursts in drunk, takes over the symposiarch's role and falls asleep after wailing that Socrates seems as impervious to sex as he is to the effects of drink. The crux of the dialogue comes in Socrates' report of a talk with Diotima, a priestess, about the higher eros, ideally homoerotic, that engenders ideas, not bodies.

In *Symposium* by Xenophon, another of Socrates' disciples, an evening ends with an "imitation of the wedding-night of Dionysus and Ariadne… When the guests saw that 'Dionysus' was attractive and 'Ariadne' gorgeous, and the actors were not playing but really kissing, they

Right: Playing kottabos, a game in which wine was flicked across the room at small statuettes by diners. From a late 5th-century BC krater (drinking cup).

became fired up… When they finally saw the actors apparently going to bed together, the bachelors swore they must get married and the married men rode off on their horses to their wives with but one purpose in mind." The eroticism here is wholly heterosexual.

BARS AND TAVERNS

Poorer citizens could not afford such festivities and had to socialize elsewhere in a bar or tavern called *kapeleion*. If some *kapeleia* were only stalls, others were many-roomed buildings. Citizens could eat snacks and buy wine in flasks to take away along with torches to light their way home through Athens' unlit streets. Kapeleia were often condemned as sources of popular disturbance and riots, rather like pubs in modern Britain.

Above: A flute girl entertaining men at a symposium, a typical entertainment. From a red figure vase of c.450BC.

GREEK SEXUALITY
ACTS AND ATTITUDES

Ancient Greece was once seen as a sexual arcadia where happy pagans, free from Christian restraint, enjoyed sex in ways damned by the Bible or law. In particular, homosexuality, male and female, was openly celebrated. Such views of Greece as a homosexual paradise owe as much to

Left: 6th-century BC herm, a phallic good luck sign placed outside houses and at street-corners, originally dedicated to the god Hermes. Male nudity in all its forms was much celebrated by Greek art, encouraging or reflecting Greek homoeroticism.

Below: A man embracing a boy. Such paederastia (pederasty) was thought acceptable, even admirable, if the relationship was between social equals and suitably conducted. From a red figure cup by the 'Briseis Painter'.

fantasy as to reality. The Greeks had no words for, or concepts of, 'homosexual' or 'heterosexual' (terms coined in the late 19th century), nor for 'gay', which gained its current meaning even more recently. They would have thought people who so defined themselves as odd, bisexuality being the unspoken norm.

The Greeks did, however, have a word for *paederastia*, pederasty, the love of an adult man for boy – usually an adolescent. Far from regarding this as a crime, classical art and literature celebrated an idealized paederastia. This fact, which so embarrassed Victorian scholars, must be seen in the context of the Greeks' general attitudes to love and sex.

CONCEPTS OF 'LOVE'

For us 'love' means romantic love in the St Valentine's Day sense: couples – mainly if not always heterosexual – love each other physically and spiritually and aim to live 'happily ever after' together. Tragedy arises when requited love is blocked, as in *Romeo and Juliet*. Things were very different in antiquity.

Greek men were often fond of their wives. Certainly they felt a duty and responsibility to them. But they did not usually marry for love, marriages being arranged for social reasons. (Spouses presumably felt sexual desire for each other – the Greek birth-rate was certainly high enough.) Families were the acknowledged bedrock of any polis, essential to sustaining Greek society.

In contrast, eros, overwhelming sexual desire, was seen as a 'bitter-sweet' disruptive force, at times terrifyingly destructive, especially if it afflicted women. When eros strikes women in Greek myth and tragedy, the results are often catastrophic: the Trojan War was caused by the headstrong love of Helen for Prince Paris; Queen Clytemnestra, for the

Right: Red-figure painting of a man being served by a naked youth – perhaps a slave – at a symposium. Symposia could end with the diners having sex with the slaves, male or female.

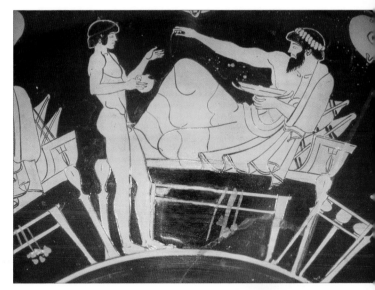

sake of her lover, murders her husband Agamemnon on his return from Troy, before being killed by her son Orestes; Phaedra, King Theseus' wife, conceives an unrequited passion for her stepson Hippolytus that leads to the deaths of both. No happy endings here.

Philosophers attempted self-control to gain *eudaimonia* (contentment) or *ataraxia* (stoical indifference) to escape sexual turmoil. Others, less high-minded, tried to possess the object of their desire, male or female, as swiftly as possible.

A HOMOEROTIC WORLD?

Every Greek city boasted a second marble and bronze population of athletes, heroes and gods. These statues portrayed idealized men with superb bodies, mostly naked. Balancing this Olympian idealism were statues of herms, phallic symbols topped by heads. While the city overflowed with male nudity, female statues, naked or clothed, were far less frequent, although beautiful nude goddesses were sculpted from the 4th century BC.

This possibly roused any latent homoerotic feelings. More crucially, unmarried Greek women were so secluded that young men hardly ever met them. Young girls, being uneducated, may have been uninspiring company. Nor were married women a better prospect. Adultery, according to an old Draconian law, was a capital offence. Unsurprisingly, many men turned to prostitutes, but some preferred other males, usually teenaged boys.

LOVER AND BELOVED

In the ideal homoerotic relationship, the *erastes*, a lover in his twenties, courted an *eromenos*, the beloved, a boy in his teens of similar social status. The gymnasium was a common meeting place, where each could admire the other working out naked. A boy received small gifts from his

admirer – a hare or cockerel – but was expected to behave with suitable modesty, rather as 'respectable' girls being courted in the West were once expected to behave. Any hint of effeminacy on either side was strongly deplored.

How much actual sex occurred remains debatable. Ancient authors tend to discretion, modern ones to speculation. But one thing is clear: such relationships were not viewed by either partner as degrading, for soon the eromenos would become a fellow citizen, fighting in the army and voting in the Assembly beside the older man. They would then no longer be lovers, because sex between grown men was thought a little absurd in Athens. In Sparta, predictably, pederasty was a rougher, compulsory affair. Only in Thebes was adult homosexuality fully accepted, being epitomized in the 'Sacred Band', the elite corps of 300 lovers.

However, affections could long persist, most notably in Sparta but also in Athens. The reformer Solon when young loved the teenaged Pisistratus. Years later, when Pisistratus had become tyrant, he ignored his aged ex-lover's loud criticisms of his regime for old time's sake.

Above: 2nd-century AD statue of Antinous, the youth loved by Hadrian, who was of reputed royal descent and so almost the emperor's social equal.

THE HETEROSEXUAL MAJORITY

Above: A stele commemorating marital affection. Monogamous marriage remained the bedrock of Greek society, whatever men did in their youth.

Below: A man and woman exchanging sexually significant glances. Heterosexual affairs between equals could be hard in classical Athens, as women were kept so secluded. From a red figure krater c.460BC.

Most men and women in ancient Greece were predominantly heterosexual, however. In Homer, *all* erotic passion is between men and women. *The Iliad* is the archetypal book of love and war – of love because, although war predominates, the Trojan War originates in Paris' love for Helen. The epic itself starts with Achilles and Agamemnon quarrelling over Briseis, a slave girl. In *The Odyssey* Odysseus on his wanderings has many affairs with women, divine and human – the shipwrecking sirens who lure him so strongly are prototypical *femmes fatales* – before returning to his ever-faithful wife Penelope. Connubial affection rather than erotic passion marks their reunion in the marriage bed, but then neither is young.

In classical Athens Pericles lived for years with Aspasia, his mistress. He enjoyed her company not just in the bedroom but also at symposia, where she entertained Athens' best minds. While Pericles and Aspasia were exceptional, the comic playwright Aristophanes often voiced the feelings – erotic and political – of the Athenian man-in-the-street.

LESBIANISM: A HIDDEN LOVE

While the male half of the population was amusing itself with hetaerae or each other, Greek women cloistered in small, dark houses sought what consolations they could. Sex with another man was so risky that they presumably turned at times to each other. Their love has remained unrecorded except for Sappho, whose incandescently lyrical poetry has immortalized her passions. In Sparta, where women paradoxically enjoyed considerably more freedom, often exercising half naked, lesbianism was almost openly accepted.

WIVES ON STRIKE

In *Lysistrata*, one of Aristophanes' typically outrageous plays, staged in 411BC, the women of Athens, tired of the endless Peloponnesian war, follow Lysistrata's advice. They organize a sex-strike, denying their husbands their beds until the men agree to make peace. The strike is exported to Sparta and Thebes, Athens' enemies. The women have to seize the Acropolis and treasury to make the strike effective, but Sparta's ambassadors arrive with tales of similar strike action by their wives – and their own similar frustration. If Greek husbands never enjoyed having sex with their wives, the comedy would have lacked all point. But heterosexuality also found many extramarital outlets.

COURTESANS AND PROSTITUTES

Aspasia was originally a *hetaera*, a word meaning (female) 'companion'. In a notoriously misogynistic speech *Against Neaera*, Apollodorus in *c*.340BC said: "We have *hetaerae* for pleasure, *pallakae* (concubines) for physical needs and *gynaekes* (wives) to bear us legitimate children and be faithful guardians of our households."

This neat division of womankind into three types owed more to Apollodorus' wish to pigeonhole women than to social reality. While married women were distinct from hetaerae, prostitutes ranged from glamorous courtesans to '2-obol' streetwalkers, 2 obols being a third of a workman's daily wage. Grand hetaerae, who might became great men's lovers, charged hundreds of drachmae not for specific sexual acts but for their 'company'– hence their name. They also retained the crucial right to refuse anyone, so retaining some independence.

For those at the bottom of the scale, things were starkly different. The Kerameikos quarter was a red-light district notorious for streetwalkers of both sexes. These could be brutally treated, for the streets of Athens at night, unlit and unpoliced, were dangerous. The fate of prostitutes locked up in brothels was little better, however, for they were often foreign slaves, perhaps speaking only a little or no Greek.

Above: A man caressing a woman playing a lyre, probably a professional entertainer who sold sexual favours with her music. From a red figure cup of c.510BC.

GRAND HETAERAE

Neaera was in fact an expensive hetaera from Corinth, a city famous for its prostitutes, but she was also originally a slave, bought by two former clients. She was not, therefore, exactly the independent, cultured lady that romantic historians once thought. But the orator Lysias had his hetaera initiated at Eleusis, obviously caring for his lover's (assumed) fate in the next world too.

Thais, an Athenian hetaera, accompanied Ptolemy, one of Alexander's generals, on the conquest of Persia. At a banquet after the capture of Persepolis, she demanded the Persian capital be torched in revenge for the Persians burning Athens 150 years earlier. Persepolis duly went up in flames. The episode reveals that when courtesans attended wild Macedonian symposia, their voices were at times heeded. Later Ptolemy, on becoming king of Egypt, settled Thais and their three children comfortably. Then he married someone dynastically suitable.

Left: A 19th-century statue by Claude Rame of Sappho, the supreme women poet who was reputedly 'Lesbian' in the modern sense. Lesbianism presumably flourished unrecorded.

FOOD AND WINE

Above: Ritual sacrifice of animals, such as this pig, followed by a democratic public banquet, gave poorer Greeks their best chance of eating meat. From a red figure vase of c.500BC.

Below: Seafood always supplemented meat across Greece, as this fresco from Thira of c.1550BC attests. Fish was seldom particularly cheap, however.

The ancient Greeks could never be accused of being gourmands or gluttons. Even among the rich, food usually remained simple to the point of repetitive frugality. The Greek diet, focusing on olive oil, bread, fish and vegetables, appears at first glance like the precursor of the Mediterranean diet so recommended today. In fact it was far plainer, being a product of general poverty, not health-consciousness.

However, the Greeks compensated for their gastronomic austerity by being enthusiastic, even excessive, drinkers. Greek wines were valued around the Mediterranean not only by the Greeks but by Etruscans and later the Romans of the imperial period. This has led some historians to the suspicion that either tastes or Greek wine-making must have changed considerably since then.

DIETARY STAPLES

Although Greeks ate more than "a sort of porridge followed by another sort of porridge", in the words of one unimpressed reseacher, their diet was based on cereals. Bread was made from wheat when they could get it or afford it, and from barley or millet when they could not. Olives and olive oil, along with cheese – from sheep and especially goats, far more often than cows – pulses, beans and vegetables such as cabbage, onions and garlic supplemented bread.

A thick soup made chiefly from beans and lentils was a standard Greek dish. The Spartans, as ever unique, lived mostly off a 'black broth' reputedly made partly from blood and so disgusting that other Greeks gagged on it. Before setting off on their military expeditions, large quantities of this repellent mixture would be mixed up and carried by helots, to give their masters the consolation of home cooking while in foreign parts.

Fruits, including apples, plums, figs and grapes, were eaten, fresh in season and dried out of season. Sugar was unknown, honey being the only sweetener. Also unknown in the ancient world were rice, potatoes, tomatoes, (bell) peppers, citrus fruits, bananas, chocolate and many other now common fruits and vegetables, since introduced from around the world.

THE LUXURY OF MEAT

Meat was a luxury enjoyed by most Greeks only following the public sacrifice of a chicken, sheep, pig or bull. The priest would, after killing the animal, butcher it, removing the thigh bones and covering them with a little fat that was burned on the altar as an offering to the god invoked. While gods were deemed content with the mere smell of the beast, their human worshippers tucked into a communal feast eaten in the open. The meat was grilled (broiled) or boiled in cauldrons, each portion being conspicuously fair.

Little meat found its way to the market except for pork. This was relatively inexpensive, a suckling pig costing about three drachmae or three days' average wages. Some pork was also made into sausages. (Homer's heroes ate meat daily, but then they were really super-humans and not to be judged by normal standards in any way.) Athletes, especially those taking part in 'heavy' sports such as the pentathlon, might occasionally be put on a high-protein diet, even eating meat on a daily basis.

Fish was a useful supplement to the Greek diet, some species being much prized. Exactly what types of fish ancient names refer to is not always known. But fish too was relatively expensive, and not part of most people's daily diets. Nor was game, which, like fish, was never sacrificed. Interestingly, the Pythagoreans, almost the only vegetarians in the ancient

world, especially avoided fish, while they occasionally would eat sacrificed meat to conform to a polis' religious customs.

In classical Athens most shopping for food was done by men. This might seem strange in a male-dominated society where cooking and food had such a low status, but it followed, logically enough, from women's seclusion. Cooking was a different matter, however. There were no celebrity chefs in the Greek world. Instead, anonymous slaves and/or women cooked in small dark kitchens. Over open fires, meat was boiled or grilled, cooking being generally very simple.

WINES FAMOUS AND ORDINARY

Wine was drunk by Greeks wherever they lived – indeed, it was a mark of a true Hellene that he drank wine rather than beer, a drink fit only for barbarians. Wherever Greeks settled, they planted vines, and in so doing spread viticulture from the Black Sea to Gaul. (Tea, coffee and other non-alcoholic drinks were unknown, as were spirits.) Wine was strong, probably around 15 per cent alcohol, but was universally diluted, so that it would be no stronger than beer is today.

The Greeks recognized three colours of wine: 'black', 'white' and 'amber' (*kirrhos*). White and amber wines could be sweet or dry, black wines could be dry or

'medium'. Most wines were drunk young and rough, with half-fermented pieces of grape floating in them. Such wines would have tasted strongly of wineskins or resinated barrels.

The best wines came from Chios, Lesbos, Thasos and Mende in the Chalcidice in the north. They were bottled in distinctive clay amphorae, sealed airtight, that have been found around the Greek world. Although classical Greeks did not date wines by vintage – unlike the Mycenaeans and Romans – they understood the need to age the best wine.

Above: Families did, if rarely, eat together for festivals such as weddings, as this relief from Cyzicus on the Sea of Marmara of the 3rd century BC shows.

Below: Grapes and wine were always vital parts of the sparse Greek diet. This sarcophagus from Alexandria shows a grape harvest.

CITIZENS AND FOREIGNERS

In 451BC Pericles introduced a law that restricted Athenian citizenship to those with two full Athenian parents. This measure, meant partly to encourage Athenian colonists to wed Athenian women, would have disenfranchised Themistocles, Athens' saviour in the Persian wars, who had a non-Athenian mother. The law reveals the high value placed on citizenship by the classical polis.

Although we translate polis as city-state, 'citizen-state' would be a closer description, for a polis consisted of its citizens. (The word 'politics' comes from this Greek root.) Citizenship could be restricted under oligarchies. In Sparta, only the Equals, who had helots to till their land for them, counted as full Spartiates. (Their number, originally set at around 8,000, had declined to only 1,500 in the 4th century BC.) More numerous were the *perioeci* ('dwellers-around'), who lacked a Spartiate's rights and obligations but provided much of the army and revenue.

In Athens after Solon's reforms in 594BC, all free men ranked as citizens, despite the poorest being excluded from important posts until the 5th century BC. By 432BC there were *c*.60,000 adult male citizens in Attica, although plague and war soon reduced their number. In 404BC the junta of the Thirty Tyrants restricted citizenship to the 3,000 richest citizens, but the revived democracy at once restored the full franchise.

DUTIES AND PRIVILEGES

The most demanding duty for an adult Athenian citizen was military service, which he had to undertake at any age between 18 and 61. Although Athens' hoplite army remained amateur and part-time compared to Sparta's – and later to Thebes' – military service was a recurrent, often dangerous burden. In contrast, the

Above: In 451BC Pericles introduced a law restricting Athenian citizenship to those with two full Athenian parents. This showed the value Athenians put on their citizenship but would have excluded Themistocles, the strategist behind victory at Salamis, whose mother was not Athenian.

Below: Ostraka (pot shards) with the name of Aristides, the politician ostracized in 482BC for opposing Themistocles' naval policy. Ostracism provided a useful safety valve.

Above: An Athenian citizen-soldier saying goodbye to his family, from an Attic vase of c.440BC. Military service was demanded of every citizen between the ages of 18 and 61.

Athenian fleet of *c*.300 triremes rowed by the *thetes*, free but poor citizens, rapidly became a semi-professional force after the Persian war. However triremes were usually laid up in winter.

Citizens also had to serve on the huge juries, typically 501 men strong, selected by lot from a roster of 6,000 men. At least once in their lives most also served on the Council of 500. Modest pay for these offices – as for fighting in the fleet or army – was introduced in the 5th century, but was no more an inducement for an able-bodied citizen than jury pay is today. Richer citizens also faced the extra burdens and honours of the *liturgies*, such as the choreogia (the financing and staging of plays).

Although the Athenian state had no real welfare system, it did provide modest support for the arts. By the 4th century BC, free tickets for the theatre, the greatest public entertainment and an occasion for the whole polis to manifest its collective identity, were available for poorer citizens. The orphans of citizens killed fighting for Athens also received state support as children.

METICS: TRADING PLACES

Foreign-born permanent residents of Athens were known as metics (*metoikoi*), meaning literally those who have changed their home. After the Persian wars (499–478BC), many Greeks from Ionia migrated to Athens to make their living. They had to pay a special poll tax (*metoikon*) of one drachma per month, as well as normal taxes. Failure to pay the metoikon promptly could mean enslavement.

While metics were liable for military service, they were not allowed to vote or hold office. Nor could they own land – a severe disadvantage in a society where land was still the safest form of wealth. They had, however, access to the courts, although they had to post bail, unlike citizens. Occasionally, citizenship, or citizen rights, were granted to exceptionally worthy metics such as Pasion. In 338BC, after Athens' defeat by Macedonia, it was proposed to enfranchise all metics to boost the citizen body, but the measure was not carried out.

Despite their disadvantages, the number of metics in Athens grew rapidly in the 5th century, reaching about 20,000 men by 431BC. These metics lived mainly in the Piraeus, where they played leading roles in commerce and banking. Many distinguished, wealthy men, including the shield-maker Cephalus, the philosopher Aristotle and the orator Lysias, were metics. Lysias had strongly supported the exiled democrats in 404BC. Granted citizenship at their triumph, he made cogent speeches before being disenfranchised again by the grudging Athenian demos.

The Roman emperor Claudius (reigned AD41–54) later compared Greek cities' parsimony in granting citizenship with Rome's generosity. This winning of conquered people's acquiescence and often their active support was seen as a secret of Rome's imperial success. But a Greek polis was inherently a small, autonomous unit in which citizens took active part. Roman citizens, by contrast, fought but seldom voted for their city, as Rome's empire grew. By AD212, when Caracalla gave all free men Roman citizenship, it had lost much of its value anyway.

Right: Marble bust of Lysias (c.455–380BC), a metic who was made a citizen for his services to democracy, only to be later demoted again.

Below: A cobbler, either a poorer citizen or a metic (a resident foreigner). From a black figure vase of the early 5th century BC.

SLAVERY
FACTS AND MYTHS

Above: A shaft in a silver mine at Laurium, where Greek slavery was at its worst. Tens of thousands of slaves worked and died there in appalling conditions that no free man would have accepted but which almost no one at the time condemned.

Greek civilization depended on slavery. This fact – which is indisputable but one that has made many Greek scholars uncomfortable – can mislead. To begin with, slavery in antiquity had no racial connotations. Although most slaves were foreign-born in the Classical period, Greeks themselves always risked being enslaved if they were captured. The Cynic sage Diogenes – and even Plato reputedly – suffered this philosophy-testing fate, although both were soon freed.

The Greeks did not pioneer what has been called 'chattel slavery', meaning buying and selling enslaved persons as objects. It was already common among other seafaring peoples like the Carthaginians and Phoenicians, while absolute monarchies such as Persia, Egypt and Babylon had long been accustomed to controlling vast armies of slaves.

Right: A man using a strigil (scraper) after exercising while his slave boy holds a jar of olive oil for him, c.400BC. Most slavery in classical Greece was small-scale. Many slaves came from the Black Sea area or Asia Minor, often being sold as children. War was another source of slaves, for captured cities' inhabitants were normally enslaved.

Nor did owning slaves make most Greeks rich, for slavery in the Greek world was normally small-scale. Slaves were, like cars today, generally thought of as useful, even essential, to everyday life.

Slaves worked in the house or workshop or on the farm alongside free labourers. Contrary to myth, slaves almost never rowed Athens' or other cities' galleys, a job done by poor citizens – who wanted the modest wages, and became highly professional oarsmen. (In the Hellenistic era, when fleets and ships grew massively larger, slaves were at times used.) Nor did slaves labour in great gangs on large estates. Most Greek farms were tiny.

An unskilled slave cost *c.*200 drachmae (a drachma was a skilled worker's daily wage) and the same to clothe and feed each year. Demosthenes, whose wealthy father had owned skilled metal-worker slaves, said each cost 500–600 drachmae. Neaera, the beautiful slave-prostitute, cost 3,000 drachmae, but she was exceptional. There was very seldom a quick profit to be made in owning a slave.

As most Greeks strongly disliked working for their fellow citizens, slave labour could be easier than employing free men. Slaves and free men worked side by side in small groups building the Acropolis temples, doing exactly the same work in the same conditions. The difference, of course, was that the free workers kept their modest pay while the slave workers saw it all go to their masters.

ASPECTS OF SLAVERY
The numbers of slaves in Athens, the best-documented as well as richest city, is estimated at *c.*80,000–100,000 in 431BC, about 25 per cent of the population. Most were in domestic service. The affluent Aristotle, who defended slavery, had 18 household slaves. More typical, however, is the disabled citizen for whom Lysias

made a speech claiming public support. He claimed his client was too ill to work himself but not yet able to buy a slave to work for him.

Female slaves worked in the house as servants and nurses, some becoming almost part of the family. However, they had no redress against their masters beating or sexually abusing them, although killing slaves was a crime. When slaves were witnesses in legal cases, they were routinely tortured first. Otherwise it was thought they would never dare testify against their masters.

Skilled male slaves were often set up in their own workshops. This was called 'living apart' and some earned enough extra money at their trade to buy their freedom. Freedmen had the same limited rights as metics. Pasion, a freedman probably born in Syria, became a rich banker and manufacturer – using slaves – in the 4th century BC. For donating armaments to Athens during a crisis, he was granted citizenship, a rare honour for anyone.

Pasion was exceptional, however. The real feelings of most Athenian slaves were shown by how many ran away to Deceleia, the fort occupied by the Spartans after 413BC: 20,000, according

to Thucydides. Although the nearest source of slaves was Greek war-captives, growing demand meant that slaves came from many areas. The Balkans, Asia Minor, Syria and the Black Sea were prime sources. These slaves often came through trade, not raids or conquest, i.e. other peoples sold the Greeks slaves, including often their own children.

HELOTS: SPARTA'S SERFS

Sparta, as always distinctive, had its own form of slaves in the helots, native Greeks of Messenia. Their forebears had been enslaved by Spartan conquest and they were tied to the land they cultivated, i.e. they could not be bought or sold, unlike slaves in Corinth or Athens. Although sometimes called serfs, helots were as unfree as any slaves. But, retaining their national identity, they were unusually prone to revolt. Spartans, Xenophon noted, always went around fully armed because of this threat. Every year Sparta formally declared war against the helots, allowing possible ringleaders to be murdered. Yet at times helots fought bravely for Sparta even abroad – for example under Brasidas in 424BC.

MINES: INFERNAL LABOUR

One form of slavery stands out for its sheer horror: the mines. Slave labour was the norm here, for few free men would work underground in poor conditions. About 20,000 slaves were employed at the peak of the silver mines at Laurium, revenues from which underpinned Athenian power. Nicias, the politician who led the Syracusan expedition to disaster, owned 1,000 slaves at Laurium, a fact not thought remotely shocking at the time. Slaves also laboured in the gold mines at Mt Pangaeus in Macedonia.

During the Hellenistic and Roman periods, slaves – including children who were small enough to crawl through very low tunnels – were employed in Egypt's gold mines on a massive scale. Many were literally worked to death underground, where tiny skeletons have been found.

Left: Bust of Aristotle, who defended slavery, saying some men were born so naturally brutish they were better off belonging to a master. He practised what he preached, finally owning 18 domestic slaves.

Below: Neaera, an exceptionally beautiful slave-prostitute from Corinth, as pictured by the Victorian artist H.J. Hudson. She cost 3,000 drachmae but most slaves were much cheaper.

WOMEN
A VARYING STATUS

The traditional picture of Greek women is bleak. Excluded from politics and culture, never owning property in their own right, always dependent on a male relative, they seem hardly freer than slaves.

Aristotle's generally misgoynistic views provided intellectual support for female subordination. Women were, he thought, too emotional and passionate to act rationally, even if they could *think* clearly. Even their role in child bearing was only as passive receptacles for male seed. If his views reveal women's oppressed status in classical Athens, the fate of women elsewhere in Greece possibly differed markedly over the centuries. It appears, though firm evidence is lacking, that other Greek women at times had far more freedom.

Above: Women, left on their own as their men went out into the city, turned to entertaining themselves, here making music. In Plato's Symposium *it was suggested that the auletris, the female flute-player, should go upstairs to entertain the house's women.*

MINOANS TO MACEDONIANS

In Minoan Crete women probably played a prominent role in religious and social life. Whether they had any political power is unknown, although the idea of a matriarchy is implausible. Mycenaean Greece was a militaristic society, but its women were probably not cloistered away. The prominent role of women in myth and tragedy may reflect memories of their Bronze Age importance.

In Homer, women have significant roles. In *The Iliad* Helen is less condemned for her adultery than admired for her imperilling beauty. In *The Odyssey* women are often active players: Calypso the nymph entraps Odysseus while the princess Nausicaa helps his final return. However, the patient cunning of Penelope, epitomized by her unravelling the tapestry she has woven every night to put off suitors wanting her hand and fortune, was probably far more typical of a woman's role.

In the Archaic Age (700–500BC) Sappho enjoyed enough freedom to write and love, traditionally setting up her own female academy in Lesbos. As she went into exile for a while, she presumably had an active interest in politics too. In Sparta, women always enjoyed unusual freedom. To help produce tough soldier-sons, they exercised half-naked, shocking if fascinating other Greeks. By the 4th century BC they could inherit land and choose husbands, with disastrous consequences, as wealth became concentrated in ever fewer hands. In Doric Crete, culturally half-Spartan, women in Gortyna could inherit half their brothers' share of land.

Left: A Maenad dancing to flute music. The orgiastic rites of Dionysus, celebrated outside the city, gave some women a rare break from their usual life of domestic drudgery. From a red figure kylix of c.510BC.

In Macedonia, still half-reminiscent of the Homeric world, women at times had crucial roles. Olympias, Alexander's tempestuous mother, had furious rows with her husband Philip, going into exile once. After Alexander's death, she became a major player in dynastic politics. In the Hellenistic age, queens at times ruled, the most famous monarch being Cleopatra VII of Egypt (69–30BC), who tried to revive Ptolemaic power through her affair with Mark Antony, the Roman general.

SECLUSION IN ATHENS

In Athens, women could hope for no such potential glory. Married off young, at best half-educated, women in theory had to content themselves with domestic duties in their houses. This included weaving, for most clothes were home-made – even Penelope, queen of Ithaca, wove. (Poorer women had to work in the fields or in shops as well.)

As men or slaves did most shopping, women's best chance to socialize was collecting water from the fountains, as private water supplies were almost unknown. Even this was denied rich women, whose slaves fetched the water.

Respectable women did not attend symposia. Only flute girls, dancers and prostitutes entered the andron, the men's room. Instead, women were restricted to the gynaeikon, their rooms upstairs. But they may at times have been entertained there. In Plato's *Symposium* it was suggested that the *auletris*, the (female) flute-player, should go upstairs and entertain the women. Women also seem to have attended the theatre after *c.*400BC; some are reported to have fainted at alarming performances. This exception to their seclusion emphasizes their high status as Athenian citizens, albeit unenfranchised female ones.

PRIESTESSES AND MAENADS

In one area women played a decisive role even in Athens: religion. The patron deity of the city was the goddess Athena, served by priestesses. In the great Panathenaea

Right: A vase from Apulia of 340BC showing Penelope, Odysseus' faithful wife, spinning wool.

every July, four nobly born maidens, the *arrephoroi*, led the procession. Other goddesses also had their own priestesses, especially Artemis, whose sanctuary at Brauron had female acolytes.

Some festivals were for women only. Men were excluded from the *Thesmophoria*, a major three-day festival throughout Greece. Celebrated in the autumn to honour Demeter, goddess of agriculture, the rites culminated in the sacrifice of a pig.

Another, far more thrilling, god offered women intoxicating release from their daily grind: Dionysus, god of wine and drama. His ecstatic rites took place in March outside the city, when women, drunk on wine and the god, went raving mad – the literal meaning of 'Maenad' – as they roamed the countryside. Men avoided these rites for their lives' sake.

Below: Preparations for a marriage, giving a relatively rare glimpse into domestic life. From a red figure vase of c.470BC.

FAMILY AND MARRIAGE

Above: A woman spinning with a distaff, spindle and whorl, typical activities expected of a housewife. From a lekythos (white background vase) of c.490BC.

Below: A wedding procession with the bride and groom in the chariot and Eros, god of desire, hovering overhead. From a red figure pyxis of the 5th century BC.

Women never legally came of age in classical Athens or in most other Greek cities. This meant that they always remained wards of their *kyrios* (master/lord), who might be their father, their uncle, brother or, of course, their husband. Woman could never control or own any property, nor could they choose their husband.

A girl, who would have spent her life inside her home, was betrothed, often as young as 5, and married around the age of 14 or 15 to a man, selected by her family, usually twice her age.

The overriding concern in Greece was the continuation of the family line, not a girl's happiness. Women's prime role in life was seen as producing children, as men's was fighting for the polis.

Xenophon, the historian and general, wrote: "My bride would have known nothing of how I lived, for until she entered my house she had had a very restricted life, trained from childhood ... to ask no unnecessary questions." A wife then saw her husband only in private, his social, political and intellectual life being barred to her – at least in theory. In practice, relations between the sexes were often happier, Greek fathers being

as fond of their children as any others. But Socrates was not that unusual in dismissing his family to debate with his friends before his death.

MARRIAGE AND WEDDINGS

In Athens wedding festivities lasted three days. At the betrothal (*egge*, pledge) the groom formally accepted his bride, who was given away by her kyrios with the words: "I give you this woman for the begetting of legitimate children."

The wedding itself was often set for the day of the full moon. Celebrations started on the day before, when sacrifices were made to varied gods, including Artemis, goddess of virginity, Hera, goddess of marriage and Aphrodite, the love-goddess. The bride then took a sad farewell of her childhood toys, offering them to the gods, while the women of her family fetched water in a torchlight procession from the Fountain of Callirhoe for her *loutron nymphikon*, ritual bath. She was then carefully dressed, with a special bridal veil. (This was, however, almost the only time Greek women wore veils.) The groom meanwhile had a similar bath. Olive and laurel branches adorned both houses as the groom, garlanded and anointed with myrrh, went with his relations and best man to the bride's house in the afternoon.

After sacrificing to the gods, they sat down to a banquet given by the bride's kyrios – one of the rare occasions women and men ate together in public, although they still sat separately. The traditional food included sesame seeds, symbolizing fertility, one of Persephone's attributes. Guests then gave the bride wedding presents and at night fall the kyrios formally presented the bride to the groom.

Bride and groom then went in a chariot amid a procession to her husband's house. An *amphithales*, a child with both parents

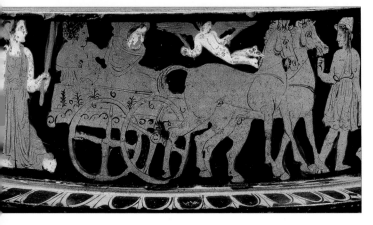

still alive, escorted the bride. He represented prosperity and good luck for the couple and their expected children. The bride carried a sieve and a grill, symbolizing her coming domestic duties. On arrival, the crowd threw nuts and dried figs at the happy couple, who then retired to their bedchamber. Outside, the groom's friends sang marriage hymns lustily. The next day, the bride's parents or other relatives brought their gifts and the dowry to the couple in their new home. Then the door closed on a wife's life of domestic drudgery.

SPARTAN CUSTOMS

In Sparta, they organized things differently. The bride had her hair hacked off, she was dressed in a boy's short tunic, and her husband pretended to rape her. Such sexual violence was thought to help beget warriors. For the first years of marriage a husband could only slip away from his barracks at night to visit his wife secretly. Only later could couples properly set up house together.

Despite this, and perhaps because of the consequent fall in birth rate, a Spartan woman may have led a freer life than her Athenian counterpart, who bore an estimated nine children during her life.

INFANTICIDE

As the Greeks had no contraception and abortion was dangerous, the chief form of birth control was infanticide. Killing one's child was illegal in Athens, but a father could reject a child because it was an unwanted daughter or because it was sickly. (In Sparta the state decided which children should live.) The child was then exposed on a hill outside the city. Sometimes such babies were rescued by childless women and brought up as their own, but most of them died. The classical polis would have been surrounded by the tiny skeletons of such abandoned infants. It was a hard world.

Above: Callicrate and her daughters, one playing with a tortoise. From a relief at Smyrna of the Hellenistic era.

Left: Mother and child, a fine funerary relief from classical Athens. Women's quiet efforts were perhaps sometimes appreciated only after their deaths, although many couples were presumably devoted to each other.

CHILDHOOD AND EDUCATION

Above: A baby crawling, on a vase painting from c.400BC. Such family scenes were pictured in classical Athens.

Below: A terracotta figurine of a schoolboy, from c.300BC from the Lebanon, by then a Hellenized region.

Greek education aimed to produce soldiers for the citizen-armies, and for a select minority, orators for public life. For most Greeks education was limited to the three Rs. Music mattered, but physical education in the gymnasium was what counted for most. For a fortunate few, however, education higher than anything known before developed during the later 5th century BC.

FIRST STEPS

About a week after a baby's birth it was formally accepted in a ritual cleansing, the *amphidromia*, followed by a banquet. Richer mothers had wet-nurses and nannies to look after their infants. Children learnt fairy tales from Aesop's fables, as Socrates recalled in his death cell.

Elementary education was not compulsory, being private and fee-paying if inexpensive. From the age of six, most boys attended three types of school: one for gymnastics, under a *paidotribes* (physical trainer); one for music and poetry under a *kitharistes* (lyre player), for poetry was often accompanied by music; and one for the three Rs under a *grammatistes* (school teacher). Homer was the great authority whose poems every boy learnt by heart. There were no desks, boys sitting on stools using wood-backed wax writing tablets and a stylus of bone or metal. Papyrus, paper's precursor, was very expensive.

Many boys had a *paidagogos*, a slave tutor to teach them good manners and punish them if they misbehaved. Meanwhile, girls from wealthier families were taught at home to read, write and play the lyre. Most teachers were slaves or underpaid freedmen. The exception was the paidotribes, a stern-looking figure with cloak and stick, who supervised boys' exercises in the gymnasium or palaestra (wrestling-ground), who was well paid. In the Hellenistic cities scattered across Asia, gymnasia were far more than just gyms, being social and cultural beacons of Hellenism. Libraries now also became important for scholars.

THE FIRST UNIVERSITIES

On his return to Athens around 387BC after years of travel, Plato founded what became the first university. He chose an olive grove sacred to the hero Academus. It stood nearly a mile (1.6km) from Athens, outside the city that had executed Socrates but would tolerate his own muted yet more radical criticisms of it. The curriculum included mathematics, dialectic and political theory. Despite his belief in an ideal world, Plato intended to train philosopher-rulers for this world. But only one graduate, Dion of Syracuse, ever had real power, and his career proved disastrous. Plato headed the Academy for 40 years, his nephew Speusippus succeeding him. After a period dominated by the Sceptics, the Academy returned to Platonism in the 1st century BC. It later became a beacon of Neoplatonism, surviving until AD529, when it was closed by imperial decree. Aristotle, the Academy's most brilliant student, founded his own school, the Lyceum, in 334BC. Modelled on the Academy, with similar common meals and symposia, it was less exclusive and less anti-democratic. Systematic large-scale scientific research began in the Lyceum's large library and collections. After Aristotle's death, this encyclopaedic approach was neglected in favour of narrower philosophical studies. Rhodes, Pergamum and Alexandria later offered places of similar higher education.

Left: A master and pupil at an Athenian school, where the central curriculum included music. Teaching was an underpaid profession, some teachers even being slaves. From a red figure kylix of c.480BC by the Athenian artist Duris.

RHETORIC: AN AMBIVALENT GIFT

At the age of 12, the sons of wealthier men went to secondary schools offering courses in law, rhetoric or medicine. Then for two years, from the age of 18, ephebes did military training, although this appears to have become institutionalized only in the 4th century BC. For the politically ambitious, being able to speak well, to sway the Assembly or lawcourts, was vital. Rhetoric, the art of speech-making, was the glamorous new way to attain the gift of the gab.

The main teachers of rhetoric in the 5th century BC were Sophists (literally, wise men). Some were unscrupulous spin-doctors, but the best, including Protagoras and Gorgias, were profound thinkers. Isocrates (436–338BC), a notably prolific writer – or windbag – embodied the worst excesses of rhetoric.

The finest rhetorician was Demosthenes of Athens (384–322BC). Reputedly afflicted with a bad stammer when young, he cured himself, later delivering some of the most impassioned if ineffectual speeches in democratic history. Rhetoric became a revered subject –

Aristotle wrote a whole book on it – being widely taught under Roman rule, despite democracy's demise. A chair in rhetoric was even established in the new university of Constantinople, the Byzantine capital, in AD425.

THE SPARTAN EXCEPTION

In education the Spartans had their own special *agoge*, or upbringing. Boys, taken from their mothers at the age of seven, were for ten years brought up in singularly brutal boarding schools run by older boys. Institutionalized pederasty was the norm there. Dancing and singing were taught but were subordinate to overall physical toughening and testing.

This training included survival techniques such as having to steal their daily food and being savagely whipped if caught. With it went the regimentation that made Spartans both feared and mocked. From the age of 20 to 30, men lived in barracks undergoing yet further military training.

Below: Among the vital skills aspiring young citizens learnt in a democracy was rhetoric – oratory that could sway the Assembly or the courts. Demosthenes overcame a stammer to become one of Athens' greatest orators.

CLOTHING AND HAIRSTYLES

Above: Minoan women curled their hair and wore colourful dresses, typical of their cheerful culture, which was so different to later Greek severity.

The Greeks were never the slaves of fashion. Indeed at first glance their clothing seems to have remained unchanged over centuries. But styles did alter slowly, becoming simpler at the beginning of the Classical period and a bit more luxurious – for those who could afford it – in the Hellenistic Age. But the chief character-istic of Greek dress was its simplicity.

Minoan and Mycenaean styles differed radically from later fashions. Women in Crete wore long, elaborately flounced dresses, nipped in at the waist with little jackets that often left their breasts bare. Men went naked to the waist, with tightly belted kilts. Mycenaean women copied Minoan styles, but men usually wore breeches or shorts and tunics. Both sexes wore jewellery. The collapse of these palace-based civilizations after 1200BC meant the end of luxurious styles. Clothes became far simpler as classical Greek clothing emerged over the centuries.

THE MALE ESSENTIALS
Free men wore a loose-fitting tunic (*chiton*) made of wool or sometimes linen, fastened at both shoulders and tied at the waist. A young man's chiton reached to his knees, an older man's to his ankles. Over the chiton they often wrapped a cloak (*himation*), a large rectangular piece of cloth draped over the left shoulder with the back brought round under the right arm. Surplus material hanging down over the body could be gathered up in cold weather. The *chlamys*, a short cloak or cape, was worn for hunting or riding and by soldiers. Draped around the shoulders, it was fastened at the throat with a clasp,

Left: Women's hairstyles and clothes became far simpler at the beginning of the Classical Age (c.480BC). From then on, fashion changed only marginally over a long period.

Above: A koure (girl) showing her hair elaborately braided and wearing an ornate multi-coloured dress in the Archaic style. An Athenian statue of c.530BC.

for the Greeks did not use buttons, a much later invention. Nor did they wear under-clothes of any sort. Men normally went bare-headed, but a wide felt or straw hat, the *petasos*, was worn at times by trav-ellers and hunters, and a skull cap, the *pilos*, by labourers. The Macedonians were especially noted for wearing the petasos.

Labourers and slaves wore a single garment fastened over the left shoulder, the *exomis*, or in hot weather simply a loin cloth (*zoma*). Athletes, of course, competed and exercised naked.

Footwear was simple for both sexes and all classes, consisting of sandals of varying types, often no more than a sole with two or three straps. In winter, sturdier laced-up boots were sometimes worn but socks were unknown.

WOMEN'S CLOTHES

Female fashions were also simple and changed very slowly. In the Archaic period, women at times wore elaborate multi-coloured dresses, but by 500BC these had given way to the Doric style of dress, far closer to men's clothing. It consisted of a plain long woollen or linen chiton held by two pins at the shoulder and falling to their ankles. Some variety was introduced by sleeves being gathered at different points, creating pleats. The himation was draped over the tunic in much the same way as men's but could be wrapped around the whole head and body so that only the eyes were visible.

Women are often shown with bare feet on vases, but this was probably a convention or depicted them at home.

Silk from China became known after Alexander's conquests but remained very expensive, worn only by great queens such as Cleopatra. Cheaper but coarser was 'wild silk' from the island of Cos.

HAIR AND BEARDS

Down to the late 6th century BC, Greek men usually wore their hair long. A sign of the advent of Classicism, typified by the *Critios Boy* of *c.*480BC, was the adoption of shorter hair by men, although the Spartans were as always slow to change. This trend was not universal. Some gods and priests were still shown with long hair in the 5th century, as were some heroes. By the 4th century BC almost all men wore their hair short, but Alexander wore his romantically long.

Minoan men seem to have been clean-shaven, but Mycenaeans always wore beards. So did all adult Greek men right down to about 350BC. Then a fashion, started by the sculptors Praxiteles and Lysippus for showing men clean-shaven, was adopted enthusiastically by Alexander and his successors. From then on, men were clean-shaven, apart from philosophers and seers. This style was emulated by the Romans until Hadrian.

Women always had long hair, often pulled back in a ponytail or a bun and fastened by ribbons, or tied in elaborate patterns. Sometimes hair was artificially curled, judging by vase paintings. Head scarves of various types and colours were popular, allowing flashes of decoration.

Above: On the frieze of the Parthenon, carved under the direction of the master-sculptor Pheidias, the calm, timeless simplicity of Classical clothing is apparent for both men's and women's clothes.

Below: In the Archaic period (c.700–480BC) men's hair and even beards were often tightly curled, as this Athenian statue shows.

THE END AND REBIRTH OF ANCIENT GREECE

Above: Athen's Temple of Olympian Zeus, finally completed after 600 years under the emperor Hadrian in c.130AD, epitomizes the Graeco-Roman synthesis.

Below: Greek cultural prestige was so strong across the Roman Empire that even Leptis Magna in Libya, a city with no Greek connections, began importing pentelic marble from Attica for its finest buildings.

In 146BC the Roman general Lucius Mummius sacked Corinth, totally destroying the city and enslaving its inhabitants. This act of exemplary brutality – one of many at the time, as Rome stamped its power across the Mediterranean world – marked the end of independence in Greece proper. Over the next 120 years the whole Hellenistic world west of the Euphrates passed under Roman sway, at times being dragged into Rome's ruinous civil wars. Mummius had taken great care, however, to have Corinth's finest artworks packed and shipped to Rome, where they were displayed to appreciative observers. His actions symbolize the dual-faced nature of Roman rule. This preserved, indeed even revived, Greek cultural life while crushing the Greeks' final hopes of regaining their political liberty.

ROME, GREECE'S CAPTIVE

The Romans by c.120BC had the greatest admiration for Greek culture but almost no regard at all for contemporary Greeks, whom they saw as frivolous, unworthy heirs of the great age of Pericles. One building epitomizes Rome's philhellenism at the time: the temple of Hercules

Victor in the heart of Rome. Built c.120BC as a perfect circle with slim marble columns, it is supremely Greek in form, owing very little to native Italian tradition. Equally Greek in form and spirit are the wall paintings of Pompeii, which were probably made by actual Greek artists copying Hellenistic masterworks. Horace, one of the greatest Latin poets, later wrote: "Greece made captive captured its conquerors and introduced the arts into backward Latium."

Greek culture transplanted remarkably well to Rome. It had shown it could thrive almost as much under monarchies as in democracies – from Pisistratus' enlightened tyranny in 6th-century BC Athens to the absolutism of Ptolemaic Egypt in the 3rd, when Alexandria's Museum/Library became the powerhouse of Hellenic culture. The Romans now showed a genius for absorbing, adapting and transmitting Greek culture across western Europe, albeit in vulgarized form. (The typical buildings of a Roman city were the amphitheatre, forum and public baths, not the theatre, library and gymnasium.)

PHILHELLENIC ROMANS

By the time of Cicero (106–43BC), almost every educated Roman spoke fluent Greek. Many, including Cicero, went to Greece to complete their education. (Few Greeks ever learnt much Latin, however.) Cicero, when he had a moment to spare from politics in the Republic's last years, translated and summarized Greek philosophy in books such as *De Finibus* (*Concerning Aims*) and *Republic*. In doing so he invented terms such as *moralis*, *qualitas*, *beatitudo* (moral, quality, happiness), still current today. Roman playwrights such as Plautus and Terence, poets such as Catullus, Virgil and Ovid and architects such as Vitruvius were all acutely aware of their debt to Greece.

Above: Roman statue of Cicero (106–43BC), who translated much Greek philosophy into Latin – a huge gain for a posterity in the medieval West after it had forgotten Greek.

Above: The well-preserved theatre of Sabratha in Roman Africa (Libya) reveals how Greek culture spread under the Pax Romana, *shaping life and art even in areas never previously Hellenized.*

Augustus, Rome's first emperor (reigned 30BC–AD14), was not as openly philhellenic as his defeated opponent Mark Antony, who had debated with philosophers in Athens and been hailed as Dionysus by Greeks in Alexandria. But, by establishing a lasting peace, Augustus allowed the Greek east to recover its wealth and, ultimately, its self-confidence. He ended being worshipped by Greeks as a saviour-god in gratitude.

The last of Augustus' dynasty, Nero (reigned AD54–68), went further, in effect trying to turn Rome into a Hellenistic kingdom. While Greeks might applaud acts of Neronian generosity such as granting Achaea (Greece proper) 'freedom' from taxes and starting the Corinth Canal, Romans, appalled by his extravagance, rebelled. Nero's reign ended in civil wars and was followed by a brief anti-Hellenic reaction.

THE ANTONINE SYNTHESIS
Under Hadrian (reigned AD117–38) and his Antonine successors, considered among Rome's finest emperors, the Greeks finally became Romans' social and political equals. Plutarch the biographer (AD46–125), whose grandfather as a boy had had to carry grain sacks across mountains to help feed Antony's troops, accepted imperial office as procurator of Achaea, although his heart remained in his native Chaeronea. More eloquently symbolic, the aristocratic Greek historian Arrian became a consul – the highest post in the empire after the emperor's – and then commanded a Roman army.

Hadrian himself became archon at Athens, ordering the completion of the vast Temple to Olympian Zeus begun 630 years earlier and being initiated into the Eleusinian Mysteries. He also had a very public affair with Antinous, a boy reputedly descended from Hellenized Bithynian kings, something which might be called truly Hellenic.

Right: The proudly imperial Prima Porta statue of Augustus, first Roman emperor, was based on Polyclitus' classical Diadomenus of 400 years earlier. The 'Classical Canon' was by then definitively established.

Above: The Neoplatonist philosopher-emperor Julian (reigned AD361–3), Rome's last non-Christian ruler, wanted to create an organized pagan religion to counter Christianity. But his reign ended in military disaster in Persia and he had no philhellenic successors.

Fifty years after Hadrian's reign, the philosopher-emperor Marcus Aurelius endowed four chairs of philosophy at Athens: the Platonist, Peripatetic (Aristotelian), Stoic and Epicurean. Marcus wrote his *Meditations* in Greek.

TWILIGHT OF THE GODS

A religion that satisfied people's varied needs as well as Graeco-Roman polytheism might have been expected to last indefinitely. Philosophical scepticism did not touch popular religion, which happily incorporated new gods such as Isis. Around AD250 the Olympic Games were still being held, sacrifices were still made to the Olympians and the Eleusinian Mysteries still promised initiates salvation in the afterworld. Urban decay did not harm a religion rooted in rural life.

Christianity could and did. After AD312 Christianity slowly became the officially favoured religion and then the only religion tolerated. Early Christians thought the pagan gods not charming myths but active malicious demons. Although at least 90 per cent of the population in AD312 was still pagan, Christians vehemently attacked the ancient cults, whose adherents lacked monotheists' fanaticism.

JULIAN, THE LAST PHILHELLENE

Rome's last non-Christian ruler, the philosopher-emperor Julian (reigned AD361–3), attempted to restore urban self-government, long decayed, and to create an organized pagan priesthood to counter Christianity. Although he refused actually to persecute Christians, he forbade them to teach Greek literature, the core of Graeco-Roman life. But Julian's reign ended in disaster in Persia and he had no philhellenic successors. In c.AD386 the fanatical Christian Theodosius I banned most pagan worship.

Even so, paganism was a long time dying. The cult of the healer-god Asclepius at Epidaurus thrived into the mid-5th century AD; a century later peasants in Asia Minor were still being converted en masse. In Athens the philosophy schools remained proudly Hellenic until closed in AD529. When the Byzantines reconquered the Peloponnese in c.AD830, they found peasants in remoter corners still worshipping Zeus.

HELLENISM REBORN

At the Councils of Ferrara and Florence in 1438, called to try to reunite the Catholic and Orthodox churches, the Greek philosopher Gemistus Plethon dazzled Westerners with his esoteric Neoplatonism. Bessarion, a more orthodox scholar, stayed on to rekindle knowledge of Greek in the West, where it had been forgotten. The fall of Constantinople in 1453 and the diaspora of Greek scholars fuelled Italian passion for things Greek. In 1462 the Academy was founded in Florence – its name deliberately recalling

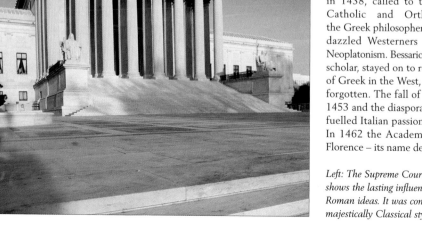

Left: The Supreme Court in Washington DC shows the lasting influence of Graeco-Roman ideas. It was constructed in majestically Classical style in 1935.

Above: The rediscovery of truly Greek architecture in the later 18th century led to much simpler styles, such as that of the British Museum, London, built by Robert Smirke in 1823–46.

Plato's school – to study Greek literature and philosophy. It proved vastly influential, begetting similar bodies across Italy and inspiring artists such as Botticelli – whose *Birth of Venus* hides a Neoplatonist allegory – and Michelangelo. Michelangelo was moved by the spiritual anguish he discerned in the newly unearthed Laocoön group to create works on a gigantic scale, from his hopeful *David* to his overwhelming *Last Judgement* in the Sistine Chapel. When even Pope Leo X (reigned 1513–21) could celebrate the birthday of 'Saint Socrates', Hellenism was clearly resurrected and walking the streets of Italy.

By 1500 the passion for Greek culture had crossed the Alps. A chair in Divinity was founded at Cambridge University in England, Erasmus (1466–1536), the Dutch humanist and scholar, being among its first occupants. Erasmus had learnt Greek primarily to translate the New Testament. His new version revealed so many faults in the old Latin Bible that it helped trigger the Reformation. Protestantism and Platonism formed a fruitful synthesis at Cambridge. In the 17th century the scholars known as the 'Cambridge Platonists' found in Platonism a way of rebutting both fanatical Calvinism and Hobbesian reductionism.

REVIVALS AND REVOLUTIONS

The late 18th century saw a revolution in the arts as in politics. West Europeans returned from seeing at first hand the ruins of Greece (then under Turkish rule) with news of heroic, austere architecture and art. Superseding the impact of discoveries at Pompeii, this led to radically simpler fashions in art, architecture and even clothing. Jane Austen's heroines wore free-flowing 'Grecian' gowns.

This Greek revival led to a new appreciation of Hellenism, especially in Britain and Germany. The poet John Keats was overwhelmed on seeing the Elgin Marbles – carvings removed from the Parthenon by Lord Elgin, a deeply controversial act – as his poetry reveals. Almost the whole work of Shelley, his contemporary and a superb classicist, breathes Greek fire.

Some of Germany's finest poets, such as Goethe and Friedrich Hölderlin, were similarly moved. In the mid-19th century Richard Wagner, arguably the greatest opera composer ever, tried to recreate the totality of Greek drama in his huge *Ring* cycle, with results still resounding to this day.

In the 20th century Greek ideas also proved potently inspiring, in art, literature and philosophy. Martin Heidegger (1889–1976), among the century's most fundamental philosophers, grounded his radical thinking on Greek foundations, looking back partly to the Presocratics. Heidegger was the godfather of Existentialism, the century's most influential – or fashionable – philosophy. Ideas first aired by the Greeks seldom stay dead for long.

Below: In 1504 Michelangelo completed his heroic David, the first truly gigantic nude statue since antiquity. It incarnates Hellenic ideals both of male beauty and democracy – that of the Florentine republic, which Michelangelo ardently supported.

INDEX

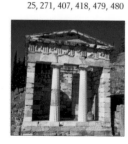

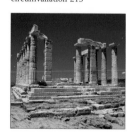

511

ACKNOWLEDGEMENTS

The Ancient Art & Architecture Collection Ltd: 4.1, 6.3, 8l&r, 12t, 13t, 20–1, 22tl, 23t, 24t&b, 26b, 27t, 28tr, 30b, 31tl, tr&b, 32b, 35, 36tl&tr, 37t&b, 38t&b, 39b, 40b, 41b, 42t&b, 43t&b, 44t, 45t&b, 46 t&b, 47t, 52t, m&br, 53b, 55b, 59tl, 62t, 64t&b, 65b, 66t&b, 68t, 69t, 70t, 71b, 72tl&tr, 73t, 74t, 75t, 76t&b, 77t&b, 80b, 81b, 85bl, 86br, 88l, 89r, 90t&b, 91l&r, 93t&b, 95b, 96b, 97t, 99, 100tl, 101l&r, 104t, 105t, 107b, 112t&b, 113t&b, 114b, 115, 118b, 119t&b, 120t, 125t&bl, 128b, 130t&b, 136t, 137b, 142tr&b, 143b, 144t, 145t, 147t, 150t, 151t, 154b, 155b, 156t, 157b, 161t, 162t&b, 163t&b, 165b, 166b, 168tl&b, 169b, 172t, 175t, 182tr, 186b, 187t, 188b, 189b, 193b, 194t, 197t, 198t&b, 199t, 200b, 202b, 208t&b, 209tl, 210b, 211t, 215b, 216t&b, 217l&r, 218b, 220b, 221t, 224t&b, 225t, 226t&b, 227b, 229tl, 230tl, 231t, 233t, 235b, 238tr, 240t, 241t, 242b, 243t, 244t, 251tr&b; /C.M. Dixon 4.4, 52tl, 78–9, 214b, 228br, 240b; /Prisma 5.4, 83b, 109t, 184–5; /R. Ashworth 57t; /G. Tortali 67b; /Ronald Sheridan 95t, 167b, 180t, 192t, 201t, 206t, 219b, 246t, 303b, 307t, 355tr, 363b, 395b, 485t; /A. Pronin 106b, 258b, 259t, 264–5, 268tl&br, 269t&b, 270t, 271t, 273t, 274tr, 275t&b, 276tl, 277b, 278t, 279b, 280t&b, 282b, 284t, 285t, 286t, 292t, 294b, 295t&b, 297b, 300t&b, 304–5, 308tl, 309b, 310b, 312t, 315b, 316b, 317b, 320b, 321, 323t, 326b, 328t, 336b, 338t, 341, 344l&r, 349b, 350t, 352br, 354t, 355b, 356, 357b, 362t, 364b, 374br, 385tl, 396t, 406t, 407b, 409, 414t&b, 415t, 419t, 420t, 421t, 437t, 441t, 454b, 470t&b, 478b, 479b, 483t, 484t, 488t, 489t&b, 491t, 494t, 495br, 499t&b; /C.M. Dixon 270b, 326t, 403b; /M. Williams 282t; /G.T. Garvey 283t, 296t, 352tl; /Interfoto 7.2, 288–9, 429t; /Prisma 350b, 498t; /D.R. Justice 366t; /C. Hellier 415b; /P. Syder 442b; /Mike Andrews 450b

The Art Archive: 373b, 423b, 438t, 439m, 456t; /JFB 3, 343b; /Acropolis Museum Athens/Gianni Dagli Orti 5.1, 134–5, 138t, 229b, 258t, 312b, 327t, 329b, 333t; /Agora Museum Athens/Dagli Orti 310t, 450t; /Alfredo Dagli Orti 50b; /Antalya Museum Turkey/ Gianni Dagli Orti 139b; /Antioch Museum Turkey/ Gianni Dagli Orti 148b; /Archaeological Museum Alexandria/Gianni Dagli Orti 237b; /Archaeological Museum Aquileia/ Alfredo Dagli Orti 153t; /Archaeological Museum Athens/ Dagli Orti 487b; /Archaeological Museum Bari/ Gianni Dagli Orti 231b; /Archaeological Museum Châtillon-sur-Seine/Dagli Orti 349t; /Archaeological Museum Cherchel Algeria/Gianni Dagli Orti 92b, 140b; /Archaeological Museum Chora Greece/Gianni Dagli Orti 27b; /Archaeological Museum Corinth/ Gianni Dagli Orti 34t; /Archaeological Museum Delphi/ Gianni Dagli Orti 233b; /Archaeological Museum Ferrara/Alfredo Dagli Orti 120b, 234b; /Archaeological Museum Florence/Gianni Dagli Orti 118tl, 244b; /Archaeological Museum Istanbul/ Dagli Orti 7.5, 237t, 402b, 418b, 448–9; Archaeological Museum Izmir/ Gianni Dagli Orti 245t, 346b; /Archaeological Museum Naples/ Dagli Orti 6br, 287, 331t, 378–9, 385b, 407tl, 412t, 416t, 424tr, 443tr, 453b, 478t, 490b; /Archaeological Museum Ostia/ Gianni Dagli Orti 200t; /Archaeological Museum Paestum/Gianni Dagli Orti 157t; /Archaeological Museum Salonica/ Dagli Orti 7.1, 380–1, 389t, 400t; /Dagli Orti (A) 271t, 328b, 320t, 358–9, 370b, 347t, 377t, 390b, 391b, 402, 428t, 471t; /Archaeological Museum Spina Ferrara/ Alfredo Dagli Orti 4.5, 110–11, 121t, 164b; /Archaeological Museum Syracuse 368t; /Archaeological Museum Teheran 405b; /Archaeological Museum Volos/Gianni Dagli Orti 177b; /Archeological Museum Piraeus

/Dagli Orti 6.4, 6.6, 266–7, 314, 318–19, 352; /Bibliothèque des Arts Décoratifs Paris/Gianni Dagli Orti 23bl, 151b, 153b, 420b; /Bibliothèque Municipale Reims/ Dagli Orti 439b; /Bibliothèque Nationale Paris 461b; /Bodleian Library Oxford 445b; /British Library 396b; /British Museum 468t; /British Museum/ Eileen Tweedy 145br, 209b, 290t, 317t, 462t; /Chiaramonti Museum Vatican/Dagli Orti (A) 374tr, 388t; /Collection Antonovich/ Dagli Orti 384t, 385tr, 475r; /Dagli Orti 6.1, 256b, 274b, 286b, 291b, 293b, 296t, 298t, 306b, 3163b, 325t, 333b, 339b, 351b, 362b, 366b, 368br, 372b, 374tl, 376b, 382b, 384b, 385tl, 387b, 388b, 395t, 400b, 404, 405t, 406b, 408t, 429b, 442t, 447t, 458t&b, 459t, 469b, 471b, 472t&b, 479t, 482b, 486b, 494b, 495t, 496b, 497t, 498b; /Eleusis Museum Greece/ Gianni Dagli Orti 116tr; /Ephesus Archaeological Museum Selcuk Turkey/ Dagli Orti 487t; /Galerie Berko Louvre des Antiquaires/ Gianni Dagli Orti 18–19; /Galleria Borghese Rome/Alfredo Dagli Orti 141, 149b, 150b; /Galleria degli Uffizi Florence/ Alfredo Dagli Orti 127b, 144b; /Gianni Dagli Orti 4.2, 9b, 12b, 13b, 25b, 26t, 28tl, 30t, 32t, 33t, 34b, 39tl, 40t, 48–9, 50t, 51t, 56b, 57bl&br, 70b, 71t, 132–3, 181t, 220t, 228t, 311b, 348t, 418t, 457t; /Harper Collins Publishers 140t; /Hellenic Institute Venice/Dagli Orti (A) 394t; /Heraklion Museum /Dagli Orti 248tl, 268tr; /House of the Poet Menander Pompeii /Alfredo Dagli Orti 167tr; /Jean Vinchon Numismatist Paris/ Gianni Dagli Orti 179t; /Kerameikos Museum, Athens/ Gianni Dagli Orti 245b; /Musée Archéologique Naples/ Alfredo Dagli Orti 94t, 131b, 143t, 147t, 152t, 176t, 191b, 221b, 239t; /Musée d'archéologie méditérranéenne, Marseilles/ Gianni Dagli Orti 121br; /Musée des Beaux Arts Antwerp/Dagli Orti 493t; /Musée des Beaux

Arts Grenoble/Dagli Orti 493b; /Musée du Louvre Paris/ Gianni Dagli Orti 5.6, 7.6, 106tr, 145bl, 146t, 172tr, 173t&b, 174b, 180b, 183b, 218t, 219t, 222–3, 230b, 232b, 235t, 259b, 290b, 292b, 399, 433, 437b, 455b, 463b, 464–5, 474t, 484b; /Musée Gustave Moreau Paris/Marc Charmet 148t; /Musée Jean Vinchon Numismatist Paris/ Dagli Orti 302t&m, 387t, 466t, 486t; /Musée Municipal Sémur en Auxois/Dagli Orti 461t; /Musée Thomas Dobrée Nantes/ Dagli Orti 346t; /Museo Capitolino Rome/ Dagli Orti (A) 374tl; /Museo Capitolino Rome/Alfredo Dagli Orti 97br, 131t, 164t, 369t; /Museo del Prado Madrid/ Dagli Orti (A) 397t; /Museo della Civita Romana Rome/Dagli Orti 496t/ Museo di Villa Giulia Rome/Dagli Orti 116tl, 278b; /Museo Naval Madrid/ Dagli Orti 456b; /Museo Nazionale Palazzo Altemps Rome/ Gianni Dagli Orti 137t, 247b; /Museo Nazionale Reggio Calabria /Gianni Dagli Orti 59bm, 107tr; /Agora Museum Athens/Gianni Dagli Orti 63b, 182b, 238b; /Museo Nazionale Romano Rome/Alfredo Dagli Orti 196t; /Museo Nazionale Taranto/Gianni Dagli Orti 100tr, 142tl, 154t, 167tl, 373t, 403t; /Museo Profano Gregoriano Vatican 408b; /Museo Tosio Martinengo Brescia/ Dagli Orti (A) 345t; /National Archaeological Museum Athens/ Gianni Dagli Orti 5.5, 81t, 82r, 83tl, 84tl, 85tr, 86tl, 92tl, 98t, 102tl, 103t, 104m,

117, 152b, 212–13, 236b, 271b, 273b, 361t, 444tl, 455t; /National Gallery London/Eileen Tweedy 146b; /National Museum Beirut/ Gianni Dagli Orti 246b, 394b; /Neil Setchfield 160b, 343t; /Olympia Museum Greece/Gianni Dagli Orti 82l, 96tl, 324bl; /Pella Museum Greece/ Dagli Orti (A) 7.2, 383b, 392–3, 398b, 440t, 446b; /Private Collection/Dagli Orti 446tr; /Royal Palace Caserta Italy/Dagli Orti 436b; /Stephanie Colasanti 29b; /University Library Istanbul/ Dagli Orti 389b; /Victoria & Albert Museum/Eileen Tweedy 207br. **The Bridgeman Art Library:** 126t; / Private Collection/© Whitford & Hughes, London 103; /© Ashmolean Museum, University of Oxford 183t, 239b, 324 tr, 453t; /© Birmingham Museums & Art Gallery 62b, 315t; /© Bradford Art Galleries & Museums, West Yorkshire 241b; /© Bristol City Museum & Art Gallery 477t; /© National Museums of Scotland 451t; /© Wakefield Museums & Galleries, West Yorkshire; 7mr, 413b; /All Rights Reserved 207t; /Biblioteca Estense, Modena 206b; /British Library, London; /Bibliotheque Nationale, Paris, France 490t, 491b; /Bibliothèque Nationale, Paris, France, Giraudon 390t; /British Museum, London 116b, 238tl, 371b; /Fitzwilliam Museum, University of Cambridge 409t; /Galleria degli Uffizi, Florence, Italy 462b; /Galleria degli Uffizi, Florence, Italy, Alinari 331b, 363t; /Hermitage, St. Petersburg, Russia 474t; /Iraq Museum, Baghdad 427tr; /Louvre, Paris, France 417b, 452; /Louvre, Paris, France, Giraudon 348b;

/Louvre, Paris, France, Lauros/ Giraudon 342t, 350t; /Louvre, Paris, France/Peter Willi 425t, 451b; /Musee de la Chartreuse, Douai, France /Giraudon 192b; /Musee de la Ville de Paris, Musee du Petit-Palais, France, Lauros/ Giraudon 426t; /Musee des Beaux-Arts, Dijon, France, Lauros/ Giraudon 426b; /Musee Gustave Moreau, Paris, France, Lauros /Giraudon 401t; /Museo Archeologico Nazionale, Naples 108b, 207bl, 285t; /Museo Archeologico, Florence, Italy, Lauros / Giraudon 397b; /Museo Capitolino, Rome, Italy, Giraudon 345b; /National Archaeological Museum, Athens/Lauros /Giraudon 232t; /National Gallery, London, UK 481; /National Museum of Iran, Tehran, Iran, Lauros/ Giraudon 428b; /Palazzo Ducale, Mantua 234t; /Palazzo Labia, Venice, Italy, Alinari 492b; /Palazzo Vecchio (Palazzo della Signoria) Florence, Italy 339t; /Private Collection 355tl, 377b, 442b; /Private Collection, © Look & Learn 450b; /Private Collection, © The Fine Art Society, London, UK 330b; /Private Collection, Archives Charmet 371t, 427tm; /Private Collection/The Stapleton Collection 181b, 204b; /Stapleton Collection, UK, 364t; /Tretyakov Gallery, Moscow 149b; /Louvre, Paris 166t, 174t; /Vatican Museums & Galleries, Vatican City 105br, 195b; /Vergina, Macedonia, Greece, 384b; **Corbis:** /© Wolfgang Kaehler 4.3, 60–7; © Araldo de Luca 94b; 432b, 435b; /© John Corbett/ Ecoscene 7.4, 430–1; /© Ric Ergenbright 436t, 440b; /© Olivier Matthys/epa 439t; /© Lloyd Cluff 441b; /© Paul Almasy 444tr; /© Michael Nicholson 444 bl; /© Roger Wood 459b; /© Christel Gerstenberg 463t; /© Araldo

de Luca 466b; /© James Marshall 482t. **Alan Hakim:** 250b, 251tl. **Sylvia Kapp:** 276tr, 303t, 327b, 357t, 368bl, 506, 507t, 509b, 510b. **Mary Evans Picture Library:** 360, 361b, 376t, 446tl, 485b. **Medioimages/Photodisc/Disco ver Greece/Getty Images:** 1, 268br, 281b, 294t, 306t, 313t, 364t, 476t&b, 488b, 500t&b, 501t, 502t&b, 503, 504t&b, 505, 507b, 508, 509t, 510t, 511. **Photo12.com:** 2, 39tr;/Albert Arnaud 51b, 73b, 256t, 272t, 352tr, 370t, 382t, 398t; /Ann Ronan Picture Library 5.3, 6.5, 125br, 126b, 138tl, 170–1, 190b, 194b, 204t, 210tl, 247t, 334–5; /ARJ 23br, 69b, 87tr&bl, 109b, 136b, 156bl, 175b, 177t, 178b, 190t, 191t, 195t, 196b, 202tr, 203b, 214t, 215tl, 228bl, 236t, 243b, 252t, 279t, 309t, 354b, 401b, 424b, 427b, 434t, 445t, 460t&b, 467b, 473t, 480t&b, 497b; /Bertelsmann Lexikon Verlag 186t, 205t, 210tr, 308tr; /Francis Latreille 435t /Jean Guichard 422b, 423t, 477b; /JTB Photo 41t, 127t, 187b, 189t, 205b, 253t, 308bl, 332t&b, 338b; /Oasis 160t, 257b, 276br; /Oronoz 4.6, 5.2, 7.3, 74b, 80t, 88tr, 89bl, 100bl, 102b, 108t, 114tr, 122–3, 124t&b, 128t, 129t&b, 155tl, 156br, 158–9, 161b, 165t, 168tr, 176b, 178t, 188t, 193t, 197b, 199b, 201b, 225b, 230tr, 248tr&b, 249t&b, 274tl, 283b, 299t, 307b, 320t, 322, 337t, 342b, 347b, 367t, 372t, 383t, 391t, 407tr, 410–11, 417t, 443tl, 454, 473b, 474b, 492t, 512; /Société Française de Photographie 75b, 369b; /World Religions Photo Library 432t. **Frances Reynolds:** 495bl. **Werner Forman Archive:** 56t; /British Museum, London 98b; /Christie's, London 340b; /Museo Ostia, Italy 340t.

This edition is published by Lorenz Books, an imprint of Anness Publishing Ltd, Blaby Road, Wigston, Leicestershire LE18 4SE; info@anness.com

www.lorenzbooks.com; www.annesspublishing.com

Anness Publishing has a new picture agency outlet for images for publishing, promotions or advertising. Please visit our website www.practicalpictures.com for more information.

Publisher: Joanna Lorenz
Editor: Joy Wotton
Designer: Nigel Partridge
Illustrations and maps: Vanessa Card, Anthony Duke, Peter Bull Art Studio
Production Controller: Bessie Bai

ETHICAL TRADING POLICY
Because of our ongoing ecological investment programme, you, as our customer, can have the pleasure and reassurance of knowing that a tree is being cultivated on your behalf to naturally replace the materials used to make the book you are holding. For further information about this scheme, go to www.annesspublishing.com/trees

© Anness Publishing Ltd 2012

Previously published in two separate volumes, *The Rise and Fall of Ancient Greece* and *The Ancient Greek World*

PUBLISHER'S NOTE
Although the advice and information in this book are believed to be accurate and true at the time of going to press, neither the authors nor the publisher can accept any legal responsibility or liability for any errors or omissions that may be made.